Intelligent Cyber-Physical Systems for Healthcare Solutions

Mamta Mittal · Jyotindra Narayan
Editors

Intelligent Cyber-Physical Systems for Healthcare Solutions

From Theory to Practice

Springer

Editors
Mamta Mittal
Delhi Skill and Entrepreneurship University
New Delhi, Delhi, India

Jyotindra Narayan
Department of Mechanical Engineering
Indian Institute of Technology Guwahati
Guwahati, Assam, India

ISBN 978-981-97-8982-5 ISBN 978-981-97-8983-2 (eBook)
https://doi.org/10.1007/978-981-97-8983-2

This Springer imprint is published by the registered company Springer Nature Singapore Pte Ltd.
The registered company address is: 152 Beach Road, #21-01/04 Gateway East, Singapore 189721, Singapore

To our family for unwavering love and support

Foreword

The integration of intelligent Cyber-Physical Systems (CPS) with healthcare holds transformative potential, enabling advanced monitoring, personalized treatments, and enhanced patient care. "Intelligent Cyber-Physical Systems for Healthcare Solutions: From Theory to Practice" explores this emerging field, detailing state-of-the-art CPS design and implementation, and addressing key challenges and opportunities. The book covers architecture, communication protocols, data processing, monitoring, diagnosis, rehabilitation, and assistive technologies, while also emphasizing critical issues such as security, privacy, and ethics to ensure the safety and reliability of healthcare CPS.

This book aims to bridge the gap between theory and practice, offering valuable insights for healthcare professionals, researchers, and students. It highlights the impact of CPS applications, from wearable devices and remote monitoring systems to robotics and medical imaging, all of which can revolutionize patient care by improving outcomes, reducing costs, and increasing efficiency. By focusing on healthcare-specific CPS, this book promotes interdisciplinary collaboration and ethical considerations, fostering innovation, and improving patient outcomes.

New Delhi, India — Mamta Mittal
Guwahati, India — Jyotindra Narayan

Preface

Intelligent Cyber-Physical Systems (CPS) has the potential to revolutionize healthcare by improving patient outcomes, reducing costs, and increasing efficiency. The impact of intelligent CPS for healthcare solutions can be seen in several ways such as improved patient outcomes by enabling personalized treatments, remote monitoring, and faster diagnosis, and optimizing healthcare delivery. From theory to practice, this can increase the efficiency of healthcare systems and enhance the overall patient experience. Moreover, there are also challenges that need to be addressed, such as ethical considerations, security and privacy concerns, and regulatory issues. Therefore, it is important to ensure that the design and implementation of intelligent CPS for healthcare solutions is done in a responsible and ethical manner, with a focus on patient safety and well-being. This book focuses on the transformative potential of intelligent CPS in healthcare—improving patient outcomes, reducing costs, and increasing efficiency.

The book has been organized into nineteen chapters that describe different case studies and topics on the impact of intelligent CPS for healthcare solutions.

Chapter "A Scoping Review of Intelligent Cyber-Physical Systems in Healthcare" explores the transformative role of Intelligent Cyber-Physical Systems (CPS) in healthcare, highlighting their potential to revolutionize patient care, enhance safety, and streamline operations. By integrating real-time monitoring, predictive analytics, automation, and remote connectivity, intelligent CPS enables early health issue detection, personalized treatment plans, and error reduction, thus improving patient outcomes. The chapter discusses how CPS optimizes workflow management, automates data processes, and strengthens supply chain efficiency. It also underscores the importance of CPS in expanding healthcare access, particularly through telehealth services, and its role in incorporating genetic data for precision medicine. Addressing cybersecurity and data privacy concerns, the chapter advocates for robust security measures and regulatory compliance. Through case studies and success stories, it demonstrates the tangible benefits of CPS, emphasizing the need for ongoing research and collaboration to fully realize its potential in healthcare.

Chapter "Importance and Potential Benefits of Intelligent CPS in Healthcare" discusses adoption of intelligent CPS is transforming the healthcare sector by enhancing operational performance and patient care. It explores the significance of intelligent CPS in improving remote monitoring, predictive analytics, and customized medications, which facilitate proactive interventions and early diagnoses to enhance patient outcomes. These technologies can minimize errors, optimize workflows, and increase productivity, ultimately reducing healthcare costs and enhancing organizational performance. They also aid in inventory management, workflow management, and resource allocation. However, implementing intelligent CPS in healthcare presents moral and practical challenges, including privacy, security, interoperability, and biases in decision-making algorithms. Addressing these issues through robust governance frameworks and legal constraints is essential for responsible and equitable deployment. By leveraging real-time data and artificial intelligence, intelligent CPS has the potential to transform healthcare systems into proactive, customized, and efficient entities, provided they are integrated harmoniously with existing infrastructures.

Chapter "Recent Trends in Medical Cyber-Physical System—A Brief Survey" provides recent trends in Medical Cyber-Physical Systems (MCPS) at dynamic intersection of healthcare, information technology, and engineering, poised to revolutionize healthcare delivery and enhance patient outcomes. This chapter focuses on technological advancements, applications, and associated challenges. By analyzing articles published between 2020 and 2023 on Scopus, the study examines the multifaceted roles of cyber-physical systems in healthcare, benefiting both patients and medical professionals. Key technologies such as artificial intelligence, machine learning, blockchain, and the Internet of Things are highlighted for their potential to enhance MCPS capabilities. The chapter addresses critical challenges and outlines future directions, offering valuable insights for researchers, practitioners, and policymakers aiming to advance MCPS for better healthcare delivery and patient outcomes.

Chapter "Role of Intelligent Techniques for Cyber-Physical Systems in Healthcare" explores how the integration of computer and physical elements through CPS is revolutionizing healthcare. Enhanced by machine learning, AI, and data analytics, CPS utilizes data from interconnected systems and medical equipment to analyze patient interactions. Through data analytics and predictive modeling, CPS can detect patterns and anomalies in patient data, accelerating diagnostics, predicting adverse events, and personalizing treatment plans. Advanced algorithms enable continuous real-time monitoring of vital signs, medication doses, and patient responses, enhancing safety and care. Secure data exchange, supported by anomaly detection and secure communication, is crucial for protecting patient information. Decision support systems within CPS optimize resource allocation and operational efficiency by analyzing historical data and predicting patient flow. The chapter emphasizes innovative approaches to managing the complexity of healthcare CPS, detailing the significant components and aspects, and discussing the benefits, drawbacks, and recent developments in decision support systems, predictive analytics, and real-time monitoring. It also addresses cybersecurity and patient data privacy concerns.

Chapter "Hypertension, Heart Rate Reserve, and Cognitive Impairment: Exploring Relationships, Implications, and Measurement Techniques" provides a comprehensive overview of the interplay between hypertension, lower heart rate reserve, and the risk of non-amnestic cognitive impairment, particularly in older adults. It delves into the prevalence of hypertension and dementia in this demographic, highlighting their significant impact. The association between hypertension and cognitive impairment is explored, alongside the increased risk of falls in older adults with cognitive decline. The discussion extends to functional impairments related to dual-tasking, elucidating theories surrounding dual-task costs. Furthermore, it examines the intricate relationship between executive function, the prefrontal cortex, and hypertension, offering insights into prefrontal cortex activation during dual-task testing. The chapter concludes by outlining the benefits of measuring heart rate reserve in at-risk individuals and the advantages of utilizing Functional Near-Infrared Spectroscopy (fNIRS) in this context.

Chapter "Concerns and Future Prospects of Medical Devices and Sensors for Intelligent Cyber-Physical Healthcare Systems" explores the significant role of Artificial Intelligence (AI) in revolutionizing healthcare through intelligent CPS. By integrating AI with medical devices and sensors, CPS facilitates precise diagnosis, personalized treatment regimens, and efficient patient monitoring, ultimately leading to improved medical outcomes. Remote patient monitoring enabled by intelligent CPS enhances patient comfort and convenience while allowing early detection of health deterioration, thereby reducing hospital readmissions. The utilization of wireless sensor networks (WSNs) is highlighted as crucial for robust CPS applications, owing to their strong sensing capabilities. Overall, the chapter emphasizes the transformative potential of AI-powered CPS in healthcare, showcasing recent advancements and highlighting opportunities for enhancing patient care and healthcare delivery.

Chapter "Reviewing the Evolution of Intelligent Cyber-Physical Systems in the Internet of Medical Things" delves into the pivotal role of the Internet of Medical Things (IoMT) in advancing intelligent CPS for healthcare solutions. It elucidates the fundamental components of IoMT, encompassing medical devices, sensors, connectivity, and data analytics, while tackling challenges such as privacy, security, interoperability, and regulatory compliance. The integration of real-time patient monitoring, smart medical devices, and data-driven decision-making is underscored, illustrating how IoMT augments CPS capabilities to deliver personalized and efficient healthcare. Through compelling real-world case studies, the chapter showcases successful IoMT-enabled CPS implementations and their tangible impact on patient outcomes, workflows, and cost-effectiveness. It culminates by envisioning future trajectories and emerging trends in the IoMT realm for intelligent CPS, underscoring the imperative of sustained research and innovation. In essence, this chapter serves as an indispensable resource for researchers, practitioners, and policymakers aiming to harness IoMT's potential to drive innovation and elevate healthcare delivery within the realm of intelligent CPS.

Chapter "Addressing Healthcare Challenges with IoMT in Intelligent Cyber–Physical Systems" discuss how the integration of Internet of Things (IoT) technologies into the medical field has led to the emergence of the Internet of Medical Things (IoMT), which is transforming healthcare through intelligent and interconnected cyber-physical systems. They highlight the role of IoMT devices, such as wearable sensors, medical implants, and smart healthcare equipment, in collecting real-time data and communicating with CPS platforms. This integration facilitates advanced monitoring, diagnosis, and treatment, leading to personalized and proactive healthcare services. The authors emphasize the benefits of improved healthcare access for remote communities through telemedicine and virtual consultations, as well as increased patient engagement. The chapter provides a comprehensive overview of IoMT and its revolutionary potential in healthcare.

Chapter "Towards Smarter, Interconnected Futures: The Crucial Role of Data in Cyber-Physical Systems" highlights the fundamental aspects of data collection, analysis, and management in CPS, emphasizing their crucial role in enhancing CPS efficiency and performance across various domains. It discusses the process of data collection, involving sensing, digitization, and transmission from physical and digital sources, facilitated by sensors and computational components. Data analysis techniques such as statistical analysis, machine learning, and data mining are employed to process collected data, identify patterns, and make predictions, while data management encompasses storage, maintenance, security, and governance to ensure data integrity and protection. The successful implementation of these processes not only enables intelligent decision-making and informed predictions within CPS but also paves the way for their widespread adoption in sectors like transportation, healthcare, energy, and smart cities. By addressing challenges and outlining future directions, this chapter serves as a valuable guide for researchers, engineers, and policymakers, fostering the integration and utilization of CPS across diverse applications.

Chapter "Restoring Human Grasp Functionality Through Soft Hand Exoskeletons" thoroughly examines existing soft hand exoskeleton models, identifying their limitations and challenges while proposing design enhancements centered on adaptability, comfort, and compactness. It emphasizes key areas like the tendon-driven mechanism, tendon routing, and dynamics analysis, crucial for selecting optimal design, materials, and functional features to enhance usability for individuals with hand impairments. The analysis involves determining maximum forces and tendon tensions for structural integrity, evaluating flexibility through tendon routing, and assessing responsiveness via dynamics studies. By addressing these critical aspects, the chapter provides insights into design considerations, material selection, and functional elements, paving the way for more effective and user-friendly soft hand exoskeleton designs tailored to improve functionality and usability for individuals with hand restrictions.

Chapter "Human-Robot Interaction in Lower Limb Rehabilitation: A Scoping Review" discusses the increasing disability rates worldwide due to chronic diseases and an aging population, highlighting stroke as a major cause of disability that requires effective rehabilitation for lower limb motor function recovery. It focuses on the potential of human-robot interaction (HRI) in lower limb rehabilitation, which offers personalized feedback and intensive training. However, the chapter notes a gap in the optimization of these elements through machine learning and advanced technologies. The review systematically examines the design criteria, modalities, and control strategies of HRI systems, aiming to enhance user outcomes. It underscores the importance of integrating advanced technologies with personalized approaches and emphasizes interdisciplinary collaboration to advance HRI systems for lower limb rehabilitation.

Chapter "LMI-Based Robust Control Strategy for a Knee Rehabilitation Exoskeleton: Addressing State Constraints, Parameter Uncertainties, and External Disturbances" delves into the development of a robust control strategy tailored for a 1-DoF knee rehabilitation exoskeleton robot, aimed at precise position control to aid individuals with limb disorders in regaining mobility. Employing an affine state-feedback controller, the study addresses challenges including state constraints, parameter uncertainties, and external disturbances. By formulating Linear Matrix Inequality (LMI) stability conditions on the feedback gains of the controller using mathematical tools such as the Schur complement and Young's inequality, robust stabilization of the exoskeleton robot is achieved. Two different design methods are compared, and simulation studies confirm the efficacy of the proposed stability conditions in achieving robust position control, offering valuable insights for the advancement of rehabilitation exoskeleton control strategies.

Chapter "Robust Position Control of an Exoskeleton Robot for Knee Rehabilitation Utilizing an LMI-Based Affine State-Feedback Controller" focuses on the development of a robust control strategy for rehabilitation exoskeleton robots, specifically targeting the regulation of knee joint position. The proposed methodology employs an LMI-based linear state-feedback controller, considering nonlinear dynamics that incorporate factors like frictions and uncertainties in system parameters. By formulating expanded dynamics to capture differences between nonlinear and linearized models, the chapter establishes LMI conditions for feedback gain selection via two design approaches, ensuring stabilization of desired position regulation. Robustness of the controller is validated against external disturbances, with a comparison of two control strategies. Simulation results and performance indexes demonstrate the controller's effectiveness in controlling knee exoskeleton position amidst uncertainties and external disturbances.

Chapter "LMI-Based Design of an Affine PD Controller for the Position Control of Robotic Systems with Application to Human Upper-Limb Rehabilitation via an Exoskeleton Robot" delves into the intricacies of controlling the motion dynamics of robotic systems, particularly exoskeleton robots aimed at rehabilitating upper/lower limb impairments in disabled individuals. Researchers explore controller design methodologies, emphasizing linearization of nonlinear dynamics around desired points. They propose leveraging the difference between the system's nonlinear dynamic model and an approximate linear model to meet specific Lipschitz constraints, facilitating stability. An affine PD controller is proposed, with three approaches ensuring closed-loop stability through Linear Matrix Inequality (LMI) conditions. By creating minimization problems based on LMI constraints, researchers determine the maximal Lipschitz constant and suggest new LMI conditions to limit feedback gains. The study culminates in numerical findings evaluating the feasibility of the LMI challenges, demonstrating the efficacy of the affine PD control law in stabilizing the robotic system, particularly a two-degree-of-freedom upper-limb exoskeleton robot, through simulation results.

Chapter "Smart Hospitals and Healthcare Facilities for CPS" explores the pivotal role of robust and intelligent healthcare systems, particularly in the context of technological advancements and the rise of smart hospitals. It highlights the emergence of CPS in Smart Healthcare, driven by innovations in IoT, AI, big data analytics, and automation. Smart healthcare leverages advanced CPS technology to monitor and manage patients' physical dynamics through intricate embedded systems with network connectivity. The chapter begins with an overview of CPS components—sensors, actuators, communication networks, and data analytics—and then delves into their application in healthcare facilities, focusing on the transformative potential of smart hospitals. It discusses the integration of pervasive technologies like wireless sensor networks, wearable sensors, and ambient systems with the IoT to enable data exchange and collection, facilitating the creation of interconnected intelligent healthcare environments. Finally, it emphasizes the integration of physical and cyber worlds in smart healthcare CPS for efficient treatment, enabling constant communication and transaction of physiological data.

Chapter "Advancing Patient-Centric Care: Harnessing CPS for Smart Hospitals and Healthcare Facilities" delves into the transformative impact of Cyber-Physical Systems (CPS) on patient-centric care within smart hospitals and healthcare facilities. It outlines the pivotal role of CPS in offering real-time monitoring, automation, and data analytics, thereby revolutionizing healthcare delivery. The chapter provides a comprehensive overview of smart hospitals, detailing their components and functionalities, and explores how smart technologies integrate physical infrastructure, medical devices, data systems, and decision-making processes. Various CPS applications are examined, including patient safety, workflow optimization, resource management, and personalized care. Challenges such as security, privacy, interoperability, and scalability are discussed, emphasizing the need for robust infrastructure, effective data governance, and stakeholder collaboration. The chapter also outlines prospects and emerging trends for CPS deployment in healthcare, serving as a valuable resource for researchers, healthcare professionals, and policymakers envisioning the future of healthcare integrated with smart computing technologies.

Chapter "Enhanced Cyber-Physical System in Healthcare Using LSTM and Bi-LSTM" provides an in-depth examination of cyber-physical systems (CPS) in healthcare, emphasizing their crucial role in integrating communication, computation, and control. With healthcare data being vulnerable to cyber threats, CPS becomes indispensable for safeguarding personal health information. The chapter presents an analysis of Enhanced Cyber-Physical Systems in healthcare (ECPS-HC), showcasing the utilization of machine learning models to analyze healthcare data acquired through IoT sensors, stored in the cloud, and processed using Machine Learning (ML) and Deep Learning (DL) techniques. Notably, machine learning models are employed to predict and mitigate cyber-attacks, aiding in decision-making processes. The focus lies on understanding the architecture of CPS in healthcare, particularly how it integrates LSTM, Bi-LSTM, and the Adam optimizer, offering insights into designing and modeling CPS for optimal performance in the healthcare sector.

Chapter "Harnessing Intelligent Cyber-Physical Systems for Advanced Healthcare Delivery: A Scoping Review and Future Directions" provides an in-depth exploration of the integration of medical equipment and devices in virtual and physical forms, facilitated by advanced technological techniques. These systems utilize machine intelligence algorithms to process health-related data, ultimately improving the quality of healthcare delivery. The chapter aims to highlight the key findings including enhanced accountability and coordination in healthcare services, support for remote patient monitoring, provision of comprehensive healthcare packages, continuity in care delivery, disease surveillance and outbreak prediction, efficiency improvements, vaccination program enhancements, patient-centered services, quality improvement initiatives, cybersecurity measures, and improved accessibility to care, even in remote areas. The chapter underscores the urgency for global healthcare reform, particularly emphasized by the challenges posed by the recent global pandemic, highlighting the pivotal role of intelligent cyber-physical systems in healthcare in addressing modern healthcare challenges and improving service delivery.

Chapter "Transformative Impact of Modern Technology on Healthcare: Advancements, Challenges, and Opportunities" explores the profound impact of technological advancement on healthcare delivery, highlighting how modern technologies have revolutionized diagnostics, treatment options, and patient care. It emphasizes the integration of technology in healthcare facilities, facilitating easier access to systems and more accurate diagnoses tailored to individual health challenges. Virtual consultations and the widespread use of smart mobile devices democratize access to quality healthcare services, transcending geographical and social barriers. The chapter reviews literature on the application of technology in healthcare, discussing challenges such as cybersecurity threats, data ownership and breaches, outdated equipment, and interoperability issues. Despite these challenges, the chapter advocates for the transformative potential of technology in overcoming healthcare obstacles, promoting better healthcare outcomes even in resource-limited settings. It underscores the role of ICT in modern healthcare, enabling remote monitoring systems that empower patients to track their medical conditions and facilitating disease surveillance, ultimately enhancing healthcare delivery in the twenty-first century.

Chapter "Unleashing the Power of Intelligent Cyber Physical Systems in Healthcare: A Paradigm Shift for the Workforce" discusses the transformative impact of Intelligent Cyber Physical Systems (ICPS) on the healthcare workforce, addressing concerns about job displacement and replacement. It examines the challenges and opportunities presented by ICPS and investigates the factors shaping the future of work in healthcare. Emphasizing the need for proactive measures, the chapter suggests strategic investments in workforce development and fostering a culture of continual learning to prepare healthcare organizations for the evolving landscape. While acknowledging the potential for job displacement, it also highlights the creation of new employment opportunities facilitated by ICPS, underscoring the importance of adapting to this paradigm shift in healthcare.

New Delhi, India | Mamta Mittal
Guwahati, India | Jyotindra Narayan

Contents

Editors and Contributors

About the Editors

Dr. Mamta Mittal is working as an Associate Professor and Programme Anchor for Data Analytics and Data Science at Delhi Skill and Entrepreneur University, New Delhi (under Government of NCT Delhi). She has received Ph.D. in Computer Science and Engineering from Thapar University, Patiala; M.Tech. (Honors) in Computer Science and Engineering from YMCA, Faridabad and B.Tech. in Computer Science and Engineering from Kurukshetra University Kurukshetra. She has been teaching for the last 18 years with emphasis on Data Mining, Machine Learning, DBMS, and Data Structure. Dr. Mittal is a Lifetime member of CSI and has published more than 80 research papers in SCI, SCIE, Scopus indexed Journals. She holds five patents and two copyrights in the area of Artificial Intelligence, IoT, and Deep Learning. Dr. Mittal has edited/authored many books with reputed publishers like Springer, IOS Press, Elsevier CRC Press, etc. and working on DST approved Project "Development of IoT based hybrid navigation module for midsized autonomous vehicles" with research grant of 25 Lakhs. Currently, she is guiding Ph.D. scholars in the field of Machine Learning and Deep Learning. She is the editor of book Series Edge AI in Future Computing with CRC Press, Taylor & Francis, USA. Dr. Mittal is member of Editorial Board with InderScience, Bentham Science, Springer, and Elsevier and Associate Editor with SCIE Indexed Journal of Springer. Email: mittalmamta79@gmail.com

Dr. Jyotindra Narayan is a Postdoctoral Research Associate in the domain of healthcare robotics and artificial intelligence at Brain and Behaviour Lab, Imperial College London (United Kingdom) and University of Bayreuth (Germany). He completed his Ph.D. in January 2023 from the Mechanical Engineering Department at the Indian Institute of Technology Guwahati (IIT Guwahati), India. His research work was dedicated to the design, development and control of passive-assist and active-assist control schemes for the lower-limb exoskeleton systems for pediatric gait training and assistance. Dr. Narayan had completed Master of Engineering (ME) from Thapar

University, India, in 2017 with a specialization in CAD/CAM and robotics, where he worked on the patient side medical manipulators. His journey in academia has been marked by a fervent dedication to advancing the fields of control theory and bioengineering. Over the years, he has delved deep into classical and modern control theory, focusing on robust and adaptive control methodologies. This has culminated in the publication of over 65 articles in reputed peer-reviewed journals and conferences, including more than 25 Science Citation/Scopus Indexed (Q1 and Q2) journals. He serves as an academic editor in PLOS ONE Journal in bioengineering, control theory, and artificial intelligence. Additionally, he serves as a guest editor in International Journal of Advanced Robotic Systems. He hosted and chaired special sessions on robust and adaptive control schemes for many reputed International conferences like CoDIT 2024 and IC ASET 2023. He is a lead reviewer in SCI indexed Journal of Springer, IEEE, Elsevier, MDPI, and international conferences. Email: n.jyotindra@gmail.com

Contributors

Jasleen Kaur Bains DCSA, Panjab University, Chandigarh, India

Santushti Santosh Betgeri Vishwakarma Institute of Technology, Pune, Maharashtra, India

Chirag Bhalodia Marwadi University, Rajkot, Gujarat, India

Rajesh Kumar Bhatia Department of Computer Science and Engineering, Punjab Engineering College (Deemed to Be University), Chandigarh, India

Urvi Bhatt Marwadi University, Rajkot, Gujarat, India

Alka Bishnoi Department of Physical Therapy, College of Health Professions and Human Services, Kean University, Union, NJ, USA

Ashok K. Chikaraddi KLE Technological University, Hubballi, India

Dheeraj Kumar Dhaked Indian Institute of Technology Guwahati Technology Innovation and Development Foundation, Guwahati, Assam, India

Obiora Reginald Ejinaka Office of the Deputy Provost, Federal College of Medical Laboratory Science and Technology, Jos, Nigeria;
Office of the Provost Academics, Federal College of Medical Laboratory Science and Technology, Jos, Nigeria

Nkereuwem Sunday Etukudoh Office of the Provost/CEO, Federal College of Medical Laboratory Science and Technology, Jos, Nigeria

S. Godfrey Winster Department of Computer Science and Engineering, School of Computing, SRM Institute of Science and Technology, Chengalpattu, India

Hassène Gritli Laboratory of Robotics, Informatics and Complex Systems (RISC Lab—LR16ES07), National Engineering School of Tunis, University of Tunis El Manar, Tunis, Tunisia;
Higher Institute of Information and Communication Technologies, University of Carthage, Ben Arous, Tunisia

Karuna C. Gull S.G. Balekundri Institute of Technology, Belagavi, India

Seema C. Gull Karnataka State Open University, Mysuru, India

Anshika Gupta Department of Biotechnology, Dr. Ambedkar Institute of Technology for Divyangjan, Kanpur, UP, India

Shyamanta M. Hazarika Indian Institute of Technology Guwahati, Guwahati, India

Kazuaki Ito Gifu University, Gifu, Japan

Sahar Jenhani Laboratory of Robotics, Informatics and Complex Systems (RISC Lab—LR16ES07), National Engineering School of Tunis, University of Tunis El Manar, Tunis, Tunisia

A. Kalaivani Department of Computer Science and Engineering, Sathyabama Institute of Science and Technology, Chennai, India

Iye Wariso Kalu Department of Information and Communication Technology (ICT), Federal College of Medical Laboratory Science and Technology, Jos, Nigeria

Suvarna G. Kanakaraddi KLE Technological University, Hubballi, India

Karima Karam Department of Anesthesiology, Aga Khan University Hospital, Karachi, Pakistan

Kalpana Katiyar Department of Biotechnology, Dr. Ambedkar Institute of Technology for Divyangjan, Kanpur, UP, India

Amandeep Kaur Department of Computer Science and Engineering, Punjab Engineering College (Deemed to Be University), Chandigarh, India

Twinkle Keshvani Marwadi University, Rajkot, Gujarat, India

Anwar Ahmed Khan Department of Computer Science, Millennium Institute of Technology and Entrepreneurship, Karachi, Pakistan

Ausaf Ahmed Khan Department of Anesthesiology, Aga Khan University Hospital, Karachi, Pakistan

Muazzam Ali Khan Khattak Department of Computer Science, Quaid-e-Azam University, Islamabad, Pakistan

Manish Kumar Department of Computer Science and Engineering, Punjab Engineering College (Deemed to Be University), Chandigarh, India

Neeru Mago DCSA, PUSSGRC, Hoshiarpur, Punjab, India

M. Maheswari Department of Computer Science and Engineering, Sathyabama Institute of Science and Technology, Chennai, India

G. Maria Jones Department of Computer Science and Engineering, Sathyabama Institute of Science and Technology, Chennai, India

D. Menaka Department of Computer Science and Engineering, Sathyabama Institute of Science and Technology, Chennai, India

Ankita Mishra Banasthali University, Tonk, Rajasthan, India

Mamta Mittal Data Analytics and Data Science at Delhi Skill and Entrepreneur University, New Delhi, India

Monisha Mohan Marwadi University, Rajkot, Gujarat, India

Megha Mudholkar Marwadi University, Rajkot, Gujarat, India

Pankaj Mudholkar Marwadi University, Rajkot, Gujarat, India

Valayapathy Lakshmi Narayanan Indian Institute of Technology Guwahati Technology Innovation and Development Foundation, Guwahati, Assam, India

Jyotindra Narayan Department of Computing, Imperial College London, London, UK;
Chair of Digital Health, Universität Bayreuth, Bayreuth, Germany

Uchejeso Mark Obeta Department of Medical Laboratory Management, Federal College of Medical Laboratory Science and Technology, Jos, Nigeria

Kathiravan Pannerselvam Department of Computer Science, Central University of Tamil Nadu, Thiruvarur, Tamil Nadu, India

Subhash Pratap Indian Institute of Technology Guwahati, Guwahati, India;
Gifu University, Gifu, Japan

Aswathy R. Nair Marwadi University, Rajkot, Gujarat, India

Saranya Rajiakodi Department of Computer Science, Central University of Tamil Nadu, Thiruvarur, Tamil Nadu, India

Sanjib Saikia Indian Institute of Technology Guwahati, Guwahati, India

Sathyaprasad Department of Computer Science and Engineering, Sathyabama Institute of Science and Technology, Chennai, India

Aaditya Sharma Department of Computer Science and Engineering, Punjab Engineering College (Deemed to Be University), Chandigarh, India

Shama Siddiqui Department of Computer Science, DHA Suffa University, Karachi, Pakistan

Shilpa Singhal Marwadi University, Rajkot, India

R. Sundar Department of Computer Science and Engineering, Sathyabama Institute of Science and Technology, Chennai, India

Om Prakash Suthar Marwadi University, Rajkot, India

Kajalben Tanchak Marwadi University, Rajkot, India

Pranav Tank Marwadi University, Rajkot, Gujarat, India

Akriti Verma Department of Biotechnology, Dr. Ambedkar Institute of Technology for Divyangjan, Kanpur, UP, India

Sadia Younis Department of Biomedical Engineering, Government College of Engineering and Technology Ganderbal, Ganderbal, India

A Scoping Review of Intelligent Cyber-Physical Systems in Healthcare

Karuna C. Gull, Suvarna G. Kanakaraddi, Ashok K. Chikaraddi, and Seema C. Gull

Abstract The chapter delves into the pivotal role of Intelligent Cyber-Physical Systems (CPS) within the healthcare domain, elucidating their transformative potential and myriad benefits. Amidst the burgeoning complexities confronting healthcare, CPS emerges as a beacon of innovation, promising to revolutionize patient care and safety, streamline operational workflows, enable remote healthcare services, and bolster diagnostics and treatment modalities. By amalgamating real-time monitoring, predictive analytics, automation, and remote connectivity, Intelligent CPS orchestrates a dynamic healthcare ecosystem poised for unparalleled advancements. The chapter meticulously examines how Intelligent CPS facilitates early health issue detection, tailors treatment plans, and mitigates medical errors, consequently elevating patient outcomes. Moreover, it probes into the operational enhancements brought forth by CPS, optimizing workflow management, automating data processes, and fortifying supply chain efficiency. Emphasizing its pivotal role in expanding healthcare access, particularly in underserved regions, and empowering patients through education and self-management, the chapter underscores the transformative impact of CPS-enabled telehealth services. Furthermore, it elucidates the integration of genetic data and precision medicine in CPS frameworks, auguring personalized and effective treatment paradigms. Addressing paramount concerns regarding cybersecurity and data privacy, the chapter advocates for robust security protocols and regulatory adherence in CPS implementations. While navigating through interoperability challenges, ethical considerations, and societal implications, the chapter emphasizes

K. C. Gull (✉)
S.G. Balekundri Institute of Technology, Belagavi, India
e-mail: karunagull74@gmail.com

S. G. Kanakaraddi · A. K. Chikaraddi
KLE Technological University, Hubballi, India
e-mail: suvarna_gk@kletech.ac.in

A. K. Chikaraddi
e-mail: chikaraddi@kletech.ac.in

S. C. Gull
Karnataka State Open University, Mysuru, India

M. Mittal and J. Narayan (eds.), *Intelligent Cyber-Physical Systems for Healthcare Solutions*, https://doi.org/10.1007/978-981-97-8983-2_1

the imperative of continued research and collaborative efforts to unlock the full potential of Intelligent CPS in reshaping the healthcare landscape. Through compelling case studies and success narratives, it elucidates the tangible benefits of CPS, paving the way for future innovations and opportunities in healthcare transformation.

Keywords Cyber-physical systems · Machine learning · Internet of medical things · Artificial intelligence · Sensors · Big data · Cloud computing

1 Introduction

In the dynamic and rapidly evolving landscape of technological innovation, Intelligent Cyber-Physical Systems (CPS) have emerged as a transformative force, seamlessly integrating networking, computation, and physical processes. This chapter delves into the profound implications of CPS within the intricate domain of healthcare, exploring its historical evolution, diverse applications, challenges confronting the healthcare industry, and the imperative rationale guiding the adoption of a scoping review methodology. The integration of wireless technologies [1, 2] and the inherent adaptability of CPS are, emphasized, illustrating their pivotal role in shaping modern, intelligent systems [3].

1.1 Background on Intelligent Cyber-Physical Systems

Historical Context: Conventional control systems and industrial automation can be linked to the origins of CPS. These systems have developed into complex, networked systems that describe the core of contemporary CPS over time [4]. The growth from basic control mechanisms to the complexities of modern cyber-physical integration is highlighted by this historical journey, which offers a contextual backdrop [3].

Features: The ability to interpret data in real time, integrate computational and physical components seamlessly, and make adaptive decisions are the hallmarks of intelligent CPS. These features highlight the dynamic and adaptable nature of CPS and define its core, setting it apart from traditional systems. The foundation for comprehending the many uses of CPS is a clear definition [3].

Applications in a Range of sectors: The adaptability of CPS is applicable to a variety of sectors, including the complex healthcare system as well as manufacturing and transportation. The wide range of applications is highlighted in this part, which also demonstrates how CPS has evolved into a crucial element in the transformation of several sectors' processes [3]. As an illustration: The range of services offered has greatly increased with the incorporation of CPS in healthcare. Applications include claims and payment administration, transparency, access, and control over patient records, medical information verification and transaction for financial auditing, and medical IoT security monitoring [5, 6]. By using real-time updates to an encrypted Global Network Record (GNR), these technologies give healthcare organizations more control over private medical data [5].

Machine Learning in CPS: Machine Learning (ML) [7] has emerged as a vital technology enhancing the security control of CPS. By addressing the limitations of model-based techniques, ML models capture complex and nonlinear interactions in data. This enables the discovery of subtle patterns and correlations that may be imperceptible with traditional methods. The continuous learning and adaptation of ML models contribute to the creation of extremely safe and dependable cyber-physical systems, meeting the stringent requirements of modern applications [8]. Example: ML applications in CPS security are explored through a survey by Fei [9], providing insights into correlations between inputs and outputs established by learning from vast volumes of data.

Figure 1 elucidates the dynamics of the CPS domain, featuring mobile nodes engaged in wireless communication [3]. This visual representation emphasizes the versatility and applications of CPS in diverse scenarios, including connected robots, autonomous cars, Vehicular Ad hoc Networks (VANETs), smart grids, and more.

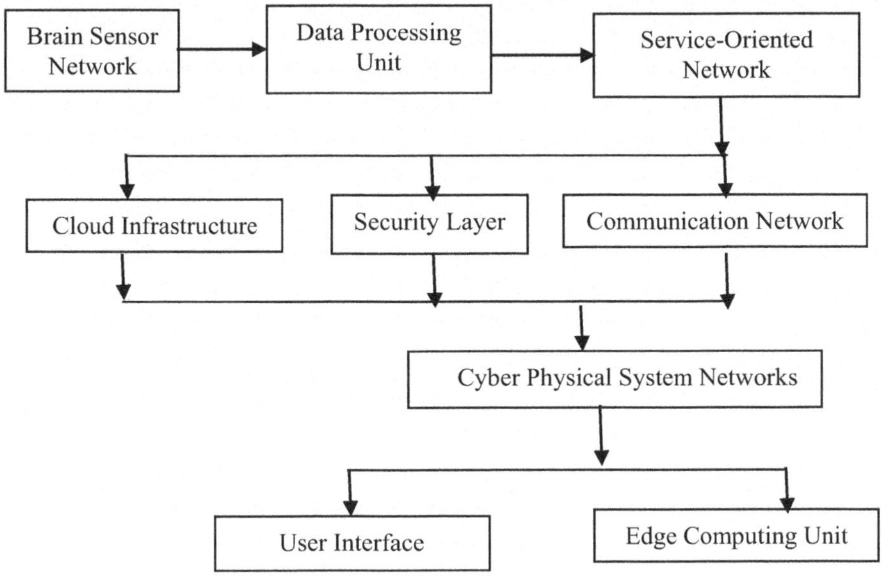

Fig. 1 Cyber physical system overview [3]

1.2 Overview of Healthcare Industry and Its Challenges

Current Landscape: The healthcare industry represents a complex ecosystem with diverse settings, including hospitals, clinics, and remote care facilities [10]. This section offers an in-depth overview of the current state of the healthcare industry, emphasizing its multifaceted nature and the increasing demand for high-quality and accessible healthcare services. The integration of recent technologies [11], such as Big Data, Cloud computing, the Internet of Things, and Artificial Intelligence, further shapes the contemporary healthcare landscape [1]. Example: Recent years have witnessed the broad adoption of emerging technologies in healthcare, leading to new application scenarios like mobile ward rounds, remote diagnosis and treatment, and medical record sharing. The digital medical big data information management system, serving as the principal IT system in hospitals, exemplifies the role of technology in data processing, registration, diagnosis, and treatment [12].

Healthcare Industry Challenges: There are several obstacles facing the healthcare sector, such as rising prices, disjointed healthcare systems, unequal access to treatment, and the urgent need for creative, patient-centered solutions. These difficulties are explained in this part, which also provides insight into the intricate dynamics of the healthcare system [1]. For instance: Technological gaps—like data silos and interoperability restrictions—are highlighted, highlighting the necessity of creative ways to deal with these issues. In order to close these gaps and transform healthcare procedures, the use of technologies such as CPS becomes essential.

The integration of modern technologies in healthcare is demonstrated in Fig. 2, which offers a graphic depiction of the AI-powered smart digital medical Big Data Analytics Platform or information management system [13]. Hospital data procedures, such as registration, diagnosis, and treatment, are supported by this system [12].

1.3 Rationale for a Scoping Review on CPS in Healthcare

A thorough explanation of the rationale behind selecting a scoping review technique as the best means of investigating CPS applications in the healthcare industry is given in this section. It highlights the distinctive qualities of CPS applications in the field of healthcare and draws attention to the necessity of using an expansive and exploratory research methodology in order to fully capture the variety of studies and applications. The inclusiveness of scoping reviews—which permit the inclusion of different research designs and sources, including both academic and non-academic literature—is also emphasized. Mapping the landscape of CPS applications in healthcare in a thorough way and finding important topics, trends, and gaps in the literature is the main objective of the scoping review [3].

Detailed Description of the Scoping Review Process: The choice to utilize a scoping review approach for the study of Intelligent Cyber-Physical Systems (CPS)

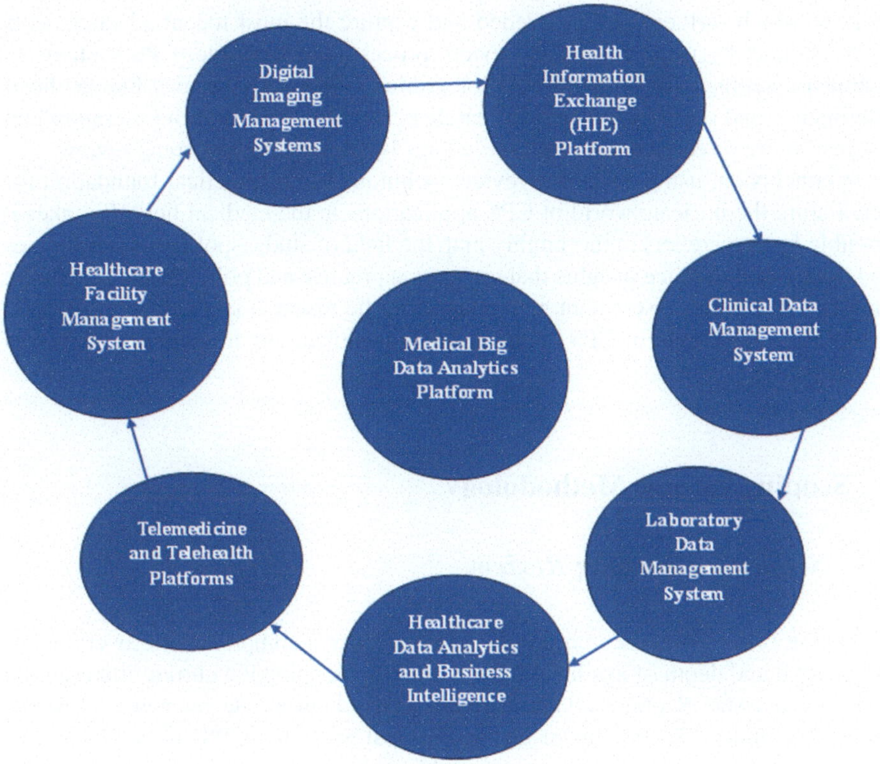

Fig. 2 Medical big data analytics platform/digital health data management system [12]

in the healthcare industry is based on the understanding that CPS applications are intricate and dynamic. In contrast to conventional systematic reviews, which concentrate on combining data to address certain research issues, a scoping review provides a more adaptable and exploratory methodology. It makes it possible to do a thorough analysis of the volume and breadth of literature on CPS in healthcare, which helps to clarify the state of the field.

A scoping review's inclusion is one of its main benefits. A scoping review facilitates a more comprehensive understanding of the issue being investigated by including a range of study types and sources, such as scholarly papers, grey literature, and expert opinions. In the case of CPS applications in healthcare, where innovation frequently outpaces conventional research approaches, this inclusion is especially crucial. For instance, company reports and conference proceedings may give insightful case studies and real-world implementations, whereas academic publications may offer insights into theoretical frameworks and experimental investigations.

Furthermore, because CPS applications are dynamic and always changing, a flexible approach to new trends and technologies is required. Researchers can identify areas in which further study is needed and capture the most recent advancements in the subject by using a scoping review process. For example, CPS systems in healthcare settings are progressively integrating future technologies like artificial intelligence and edge computing. Researchers might find gaps in the literature and suggest future research areas to fill these gaps by performing a scoping review.

In conclusion, using a scoping review technique offers a tactical foundation for negotiating the intricate world of CPS applications in the medical field. It makes it possible for researchers to thoroughly map the field of study, spot important themes and trends, and produce insights that may guide practice and policy in the healthcare industry. A scoping assessment guarantees that the research strategy stays relevant to the changing nature of CPS applications in healthcare by highlighting inclusion and flexibility.

2 Scoping Review Methodology

2.1 Scope of a Scoping Review

A scoping review is a research process that provides a comprehensive overview of the breadth and depth of available information by mapping the current literature on a particular issue. Scoping reviews are especially appropriate for new and developing disciplines like Intelligent Cyber-Physical Systems (CPS) in healthcare, as they give a thorough examination of a subject, in contrast to systematic reviews, which concentrate on certain research questions [14].

Scoping reviews' exploratory character permits the inclusion of a variety of study designs, sources, and evidence kinds. Because of its inclusion, the landscape of research on CPS applications in healthcare is thoroughly examined, capturing a wide range of viewpoints, approaches, and conclusions.

Identifying important themes, patterns, and gaps in the literature about CPS applications in healthcare is one of the main goals of this scoping study. By taking a thorough approach, the review hopes to shed light on the state of knowledge at the moment and promote a greater comprehension of the subtleties and difficulties associated with the integration of CPS in healthcare settings.

2.2 Search Strategy and Inclusion/Exclusion Criteria

Comprehensive search strategy will be implemented to provide a methodical approach to the literature evaluation. This approach will involve certain databases, pertinent keywords, and search phrases associated with healthcare and Intelligent Cyber-Physical Systems (CPS). The terms "cyber-physical systems," "healthcare applications," "intelligent systems," and "medical IoT" will be combined to search databases including PubMed, IEEE Xplore, Scopus, and Google Scholar. To ensure the retrieval of a wide range of academic works that are both pertinent and precise, the search strategy will be carefully designed.

Inclusion Criteria: Predetermined inclusion criteria must be met by studies, publications, or reports that are included in the scoping review in order to ensure their relevance to the goals of the study. The following is an explanation of the inclusion criteria:

a. **Relevance to CPS in Healthcare**: Studies that are chosen for inclusion must specifically address the use or integration of intelligent cyber-physical systems (CPS) in healthcare environments. This includes but is not limited to, applications of CPS in medical monitoring, diagnosis, treatment, healthcare infrastructure management, and patient care delivery.
b. **Technological Components**: Included studies should discuss the technological components or features of CPS relevant to healthcare, such as sensor networks, data analytics, machine learning algorithms, real-time monitoring systems, and interoperability standards.
c. **Healthcare Domains**: The scope of included studies should encompass various domains within the healthcare sector, including hospitals, clinics, primary care facilities, remote care settings, and public health initiatives.
d. **Outcome Measures**: Studies reporting on the outcomes, impacts, benefits, or challenges associated with the integration of CPS in healthcare will be considered for inclusion. This includes evaluations of system performance, patient outcomes, cost-effectiveness, and user experiences.

Exclusion Criteria: To maintain the coherence and relevance of the scoping review, a set of exclusion criteria will be defined to filter out sources that do not align with the research objectives. The exclusion criteria will be as follows:

a. **Irrelevant Topics**: Studies that do not focus on the integration or application of CPS in healthcare settings will be excluded. This includes studies on CPS applications in non-healthcare domains such as manufacturing, transportation, and smart cities.
b. **Publication Type**: Grey literature, conference abstracts, editorials, opinion pieces, and non-peer-reviewed sources will be excluded from the review to ensure the quality and reliability of the included studies.
c. **Language**: Only studies published in English will be included to facilitate comprehension and analysis by the research team.

Justification: The defined inclusion and exclusion criteria aim to ensure the systematic selection of relevant studies while minimizing the risk of bias or subjectivity in the review process. By clearly outlining the criteria for study selection, transparency and reproducibility in the research methodology are ensured, enhancing the credibility and validity of the scoping review findings.

2.3 Data Extraction and Synthesis Methods

Data Extraction: A structured approach will be utilized to extract data, with an emphasis on particular data points including the kinds of CPS applications, the technology elements involved, the healthcare sectors that are covered, and the most important discoveries. Information from chosen studies will be easier to organize and analyze due to this uniform procedure.

Methods of Synthesis: The process of synthesising data will entail a thorough examination of the material that has been retrieved, utilizing thematic analysis to identify recurring themes, patterns, and trends in the literature. The goal of this synthesis process is to provide readers a comprehensive understanding of the subject and insightful knowledge of the many aspects of CPS applications in the medical area.

This part ensures willingness and reproducibility in the research approach by giving a clear description and outline of a scoping review, describing the search strategy and inclusion/exclusion criteria, and outlining the data extraction and synthesis procedures. It prepares the reader for a thorough analysis of the literature on intelligent CPS in the medical field.

3 Current Landscape of Intelligent Cyber-Physical Systems (CPS) in Healthcare

3.1 Overview of Existing Literature and Research

Literature Sources: A wide variety of literature sources, such as scholarly databases, journals, conference proceedings, and pertinent reports, will be consulted for the scoping review. This wide-ranging strategy assurances a thorough review of the body of knowledge about CPS uses in healthcare.

Scope of Literature: By highlighting the range of research, papers, and publications that add to our knowledge of CPS applications in healthcare, the literature review will determine the breadth and depth of already available material. This comprises research on the application of CPS in various healthcare contexts and domains.

Research Methodologies: The various research approaches used in previous studies will be highlighted in the scoping review. This might include case studies, experiments, qualitative analysis, and other types of research methods. Understanding the variety of methodologies will contribute to a nuanced assessment of the current state of research [15, 16].

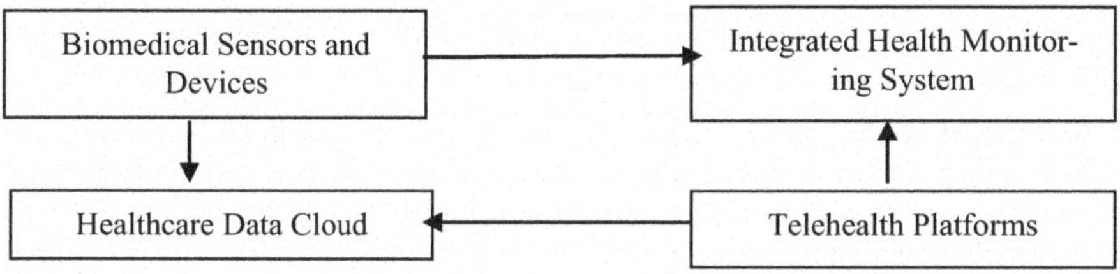

Fig. 3 Cyber-physical system (CPS) framework for IoT healthcare [5]

3.2 Key Themes and Trends in CPS Applications in Healthcare

Patient Care Innovations: Exploring themes related to patient care, the scoping review will analyze how CPS contributes to real-time monitoring for early detection of health issues, personalized treatment plans, and enhanced patient engagement. Examples from the literature will be used to illustrate innovations in patient care facilitated by CPS.

Operational Efficiency: Trends in operational efficiency, such as workflow optimization, automated data collection and analysis, and improved inventory management, will be analyzed. The scoping review will showcase how CPS applications contribute to streamlining healthcare processes and improving overall operational efficiency.

Technological Advancements: Highlighting trends in technological advancements, the review will explore the integration of predictive analytics, automation, and artificial intelligence in CPS applications within healthcare settings. Examples from relevant studies will be discussed to illustrate these advancements.

Figure 3 presents an example of an IoT-health CPS [5, 17], demonstrating how clinicians can remotely monitor patients via the internet [18]. The intelligent computational components and network in cyberspace contribute to the operations of the CPS. The figure serves as a visual representation of the integration of CPS in healthcare, emphasizing the role of intelligent components in facilitating remote healthcare services.

3.3 Identification of Gaps and Areas Requiring Further Exploration

Underexplored Healthcare Domains: The scoping review will identify specific healthcare domains that may be underexplored in the literature, signaling opportunities for further research. For instance, if certain areas like mental health or preventive care lack sufficient coverage, they will be highlighted as potential areas for future exploration.

Technological Gaps: Gaps in technological applications within CPS will be identified, emphasizing areas where innovation is needed to address specific healthcare challenges. Gaps in technology applications within CPS will be discovered. This research will help identify areas in which more technology development is required as well as the limits of present CPS implementations.

Implementation Challenges: This section will cover implementation challenges pertaining to the use of CPS in healthcare settings, including as interoperability problems, ethical dilemmas, and social effects. The scoping assessment will guide future research on the practical elements of integrating CPS into hospital facilities by identifying these issues.

This section adds to a comprehensive knowledge of the present state of Intelligent CPS in healthcare by offering a thorough survey of the body of literature, examining major themes and trends, and bringing out areas that require more research. It provides as a basis for the CPS applications' further classification and categorization in the chapter's future parts.

4 Categorization and Classification of CPS Applications in Healthcare

4.1 Grouping CPS Applications Based on Healthcare Domains

The Intelligent Cyber-Physical Systems (CPS) applications are systematically categorized in this section of the chapter according to different healthcare disciplines. This classification enables a thorough comprehension of the ways in which CPS tackles certain difficulties in various healthcare domains [14]. Among the notable domains are:

Patient Care: Real-time monitoring systems that track vital signs, anticipate health problems, and offer immediate assistance are the main focus of CPS applications in patient care. By guaranteeing proactive and ongoing health management, these technologies improve the standard of treatment provided to patients.

Operations: Within the operations domain, CPS optimizes workflow management, automates data collection and analysis, and enhances inventory management and supply chain efficiency in healthcare settings. These applications contribute to operational excellence and resource optimization.

Diagnostics: CPS applications in diagnostics involve the integration of real-time data, predictive analytics, and machine learning algorithms [7] to support accurate

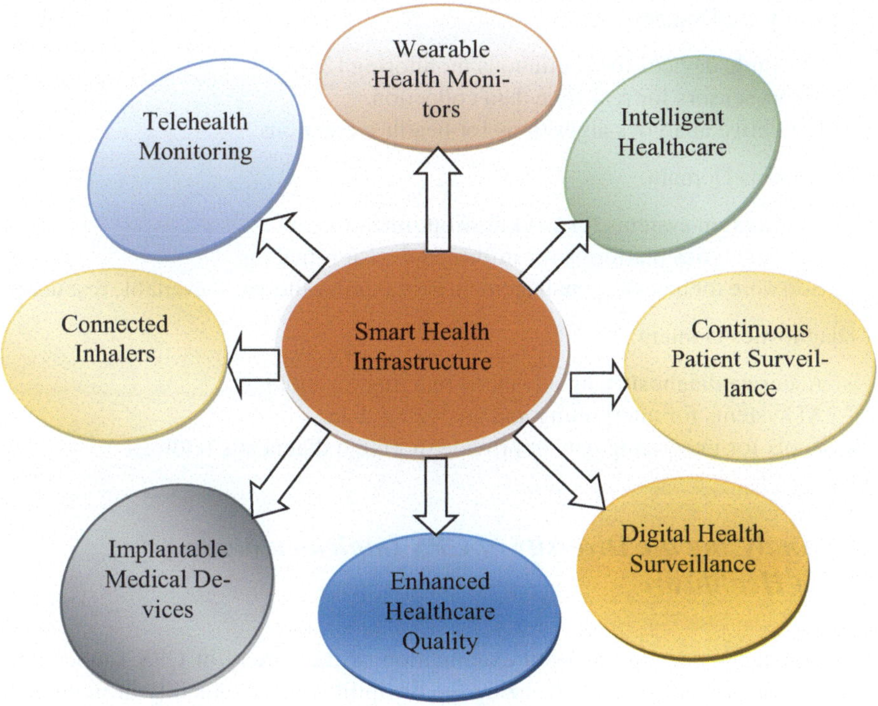

Fig. 4 Smart health infrastructure [8]

and timely medical diagnostics. This domain emphasizes technological solutions that aid healthcare professionals in making informed diagnostic decisions.

Figure 4 showcases the application of Smart Health Infrastructure, which may constitute the Internet of Medical Things (IoMT) [8, 19], transforming traditional clinics into smart healthcare systems [3, 20]. IoMT sensors use intelligent gadgets to collect and transmit patient data, facilitating remote patient diagnosis, assessment, and treatment [13]. The digitization of physician services has streamlined patient data transfer and documentation, reducing time requirements and halting the spread of illnesses.

4.2 Identifying Technological Components and Features in Each Category

Within each healthcare domain, the chapter systematically identifies the technological components and features that characterize Intelligent CPS applications. This detailed examination enhances readers' understanding of the intricate technologies underpinning CPS applications in various healthcare contexts [21].

- Patient Care Domain:
  - Wearable devices for continuous monitoring [22].
  - Smart sensors for real-time data collection.
  - Predictive analytics algorithms for health predictions.
- Operations Domain:
  - Automation systems for workflow optimization.
  - Data analytics platforms for informed decision-making.
  - Software for inventory management to maximize the use of available resources.
- Diagnostics Domain:
  - Accurate diagnosis with advanced imaging technology.
  - AI systems for interpreting and analyzing data.
  - Tools for integrating data to provide thorough diagnostic findings.

4.3 Analyzing the Diversity of CPS Implementations in Healthcare

This section provides an in-depth examination of the variety of CPS applications in the healthcare industry, emphasizing the flexibility and adaptability of Intelligent CPS [23]. Here are some instances of this diversity:

Variations in Healthcare Settings: There are differences in the problems and possibilities that CPS applications bring in telemedicine, clinic, and hospital settings [24]. Comprehending these variances is essential to customizing CPS interventions to particular healthcare environments.

Adaptation to Particular Patient Needs: CPS implementations may be customized to meet the special requirements of various patient groups, including the elderly and those with chronic illnesses. The efficacy and applicability of CPS applications are improved in a variety of healthcare contexts by this customization.

Integration with Current Systems: Another area of diversity is the seamless integration that CPS applications provide with current electronic health records, medical devices, and healthcare information systems. An integrated and interoperable healthcare environment is ensured by this integration.

This chapter's part on applications of CPS offers readers a comprehensive understanding of the many healthcare fields where Intelligent Cyber-Physical Systems are used by classifying applications, identifying technology components, and analyzing variety. It emphasizes how different technologies may be used to solve certain problems, improving patient care and operational effectiveness in the process.

5 Case Studies and Examples in the Literature

5.1 Review of Specific Case Studies and Success Stories

A thorough analysis of particular case studies and success stories pertaining to the application of intelligent cyber-physical systems (CPS) in healthcare is provided in this subsection. The goal is to give readers detailed insights into real-world instances of successful CPS implementations. Some examples may be:

Remote Patient Monitoring: The case studies that are provided show how CPS applications for this type of monitoring have helped with early health issue detection, decreased readmissions to hospitals, and eventually led to better patient outcomes. These examples demonstrate how CPS can be used to improve patient care outside of traditional hospital settings. For instance, wearable technology with CPS functionality was used in an ABC Hospital trial to provide ongoing patient monitoring. This device reduced hospital readmissions among the patient group under observation by 20% by enabling healthcare practitioners to remotely monitor vital signs, identify abnormalities in real-time, and take timely action.

Workflow Optimization: To show how CPS implementations have increased workflow efficiency, simplified healthcare operations, and improved the patient experience overall, success stories will be studied. These examples underscore the transformative potential of CPS in optimizing administrative and clinical processes within healthcare organizations. For example, a case study from ABC Health System details the implementation of CPS-enabled workflow automation software in their emergency department. This system reduced patient wait times by 30%, optimized staff allocation based on real-time demand, and improved patient satisfaction scores by 15%.

Telehealth Services: Case studies are analyzed to examine how CPS technologies facilitated the delivery of telehealth services, thereby providing healthcare access to remote or under-served populations. This exploration underscores the role of CPS in expanding healthcare reach and addressing disparities in access to medical services. One notable example is the TeleMed initiative implemented in rural communities by DEF Healthcare Network. Through the utilization of CPS-enabled telehealth platforms, DEF Healthcare Network managed to provide specialist consultations to remote patients, leading to a 40% reduction in travel time for patients seeking specialized care, along with a significant increase in patient engagement and satisfaction.

5.2 *Analysis of the Impact of CPS on Patient Outcomes and Healthcare Efficiency*

Building upon the case studies, this part involves a rigorous analysis of the impact of CPS on patient outcomes and healthcare efficiency. Examples of the analysis may include:

Improved Diagnosis and Treatment: Diagnostic Accuracy Improvement: Conduct a comparative analysis of diagnostic accuracy rates before and after the implementation of CPS-enabled diagnostic tools. Quantify the increase in accurate diagnoses and highlight specific conditions or diseases where CPS has shown the most significant improvement.

Treatment Personalization: Evaluate the extent to which CPS facilitates personalized treatment plans by analyzing patient data collected through CPS systems. Discuss how CPS enables healthcare providers to tailor treatments based on individual patient characteristics, leading to better health outcomes and reduced treatment side effects.

Clinical Outcome Measures: Measure clinical outcomes such as mortality rates, disease progression, and patient recovery times for individuals receiving CPS-supported treatments compared to traditional care. Provide statistical data to demonstrate the superior outcomes associated with CPS interventions.

Reduction in Medical Errors: Error Detection and Prevention: Detail specific instances where CPS technologies have detected and prevented medical errors in real-time. Provide case studies illustrating scenarios such as medication administration errors, patient identification mistakes, or surgical errors that were mitigated by CPS systems.

Adverse Event Reduction: Quantify the reduction in adverse events, including hospital-acquired infections, medication-related complications, and surgical errors, attributable to CPS interventions. Present statistical data comparing adverse event rates before and after CPS implementation to highlight the effectiveness of these technologies.

Cost Savings Analysis: Conduct a cost–benefit analysis to estimate the financial impact of avoided medical errors facilitated by CPS. Calculate potential cost savings related to reduced malpractice claims, shorter hospital stays, and decreased healthcare expenditures resulting from fewer adverse events.

Enhanced Operational Efficiency: Resource Allocation Optimization: Analyze data on staff utilization rates, equipment availability, and patient flow patterns to demonstrate how CPS optimizes resource allocation in healthcare facilities. CPS enables more efficient use of personnel and equipment, which leads to cost effective and enhanced patient throughput.

Workflow Streamlining: Process mapping exercises and time motion studies are conducted to identify the domains where CPS reduces the inefficiencies and streamlines the workflows. Through CPS implementation processes or tasks are automated and optimized which results in minimized waiting time and smoother operations for patients.

Data Management Improvements: Assessment parameters like data accuracy, accessibility, and security are evaluated to know the impact of CPS on data management. Real time data collection, interoperability between systems and analysis of data leads to improved patient care outcomes and well-versed decision making for CPS systems.

5.3 *Intuitions Gained and Best Practices from Current Implementations*

This subsection shares valuable lessons and best practices from existing healthcare CPS implementations. Examples of lessons and maneuvers may include:

User Engagement and Training: To maximize the effectiveness of CPS applications, the importance of user involvement and a comprehensive training program for health professionals is emphasized. Successful implementations often require extensive training and ongoing staffing to ensure smooth implementation and use of CPS technologies. In contrast, cases lacking user involvement and training experienced resistance to change and suboptimal use of CPS systems, highlighting the critical role of user acceptance in successful implementation.

Scalability and Adaptability: Best practices for designing CPS systems that are scalable and adaptable to changing healthcare needs and technological advancements are identified. Successful implementations demonstrated a modular and flexible design that allowed for seamless integration with existing infrastructure and future expansion. In contrast, in cases where CPS systems lacked scalability, there were difficulties in adapting to growth and challenges in keeping pace with changing health services, underscoring the importance of scalability for long-term sustainability.

Data Governance and Privacy: The lessons learned entail the implementation of effective data management strategies and data protection measures to safeguard patient data. Successful implementations have prioritized data encryption, access control and regulatory compliance to protect patient confidentiality and trust. In contrast, cases where privacy and data protection measures were ignored or not implemented properly resulted in a backlash from patients and regulators, leading to reputational and legal consequences.

Through the analysis, discussion and distillation of case studies, the chapter aims to offer readers tangible illustrations of successful implementation of CPS in healthcare. The technique facilitates a more comprehensive comprehension of the actual impacts and outcomes of these technologies. In addition, by drawing lessons and best practices, the chapter contributes to the knowledge base for future applications and ensures a more informed and strategic approach to the implementation of intelligent CPS in healthcare settings.

6 Findings and Interpretations

6.1 Synthesis of Findings from the Scoping Review

In this subsection, the chapter summarizes the main results of the field review to ensure a systematic and comprehensive overview of literature. This synthesis explores common themes, patterns, and trends in the integration of intelligent cyber-physical systems (CPS) in healthcare.

Emerging Domains of CPS Application: Announces novel and innovative healthcare domains that will benefit from CPS' influence, such as personalized medicine, mental health applications, and community-based health monitoring. In this synthesis, the changing healthcare landscape is being captured and synthesized through the use of CPS technologies.

Technological Advancements: Identify data concerning technological breakthroughs like the utilization of artificial intelligence, blockchain for safe information transmission or real-time monitoring. Innovative technologies are identified as a key factor in the transformative role of CPS in healthcare by this analysis.

Critical Challenges: A summary of the critical issues identified in literature such as interoperability problems, security challenges, barriers to widespread adoption. This summary demonstrates the difficulties that must be resolved to incorporate CPS into healthcare.

6.2 Critical Analysis of the Current State of CPS in Healthcare

In this section, a critical analysis of the current status of CPS in health care is presented by summarizing findings.

Effectiveness of CPS Applications: The effectiveness of CPS implementations is evaluated through critical analysis of patient outcomes, operational efficiency measures, and quality of healthcare. This analysis offers a more detailed depiction of the actual outcomes of CPS implementations.

Addressing Limitations and Challenges: The literature's strategies and innovations are examined in order to address the limitations and difficulties encountered in the implementation of CPS in healthcare. This critical review offers practical insights into how healthcare organizations can overcome barriers to implementing CPS.

Societal and Ethical Implications: We examine the social and ethical aspects of the widespread use of CPS in healthcare, as well as issues related to data protection, consent, and equity. This study enables an efficient process for carrying out CPS and addresses issues beyond the technical level.

6.3 Implications for Policy, Proactive, and Future Research

In this subsection, the review results are examined in detail to determine the implications of these findings for policy, practice, and future research in healthcare regarding intelligent CPS.

Policy Recommendations: Policy recommendations based on proposed opportunities and challenges, such as the creation of standard protocols, information security guidelines, and incentives for healthcare organizations to adopt CPS. These recommendations aim to shape a loyal policy environment for CPS integration.

Practice Guidelines: Provides healthcare professionals with practical advice on integrating CPS technologies into their daily workflow, while also providing guidance on user education and engagement. These guidelines help to make the integration process as smooth as possible and give maximum benefit to CPS applications.

Future Research Directions: Elucidates the deficiencies in the literature and suggests potential avenues for further investigation. The proposal may entail conducting further research on the long-term effects of CPS on patient outcomes, exploring new applications, or investigating the social impact of these technologies. The focus of this section is on mapping the future research directions towards intelligent CPS in healthcare.

The chapter provides a comprehensive and critical examination that will help readers comprehend the current state of intelligent CPS in healthcare and its potential implications for healthcare policy, practice, and future research. It serves as an important link between the outcomes of coverage evaluation and some practical knowledge to inform decision-making within the health sector.

7 Challenges and Opportunities in Implementing CPS in Healthcare

7.1 Barriers and Limitations in Current CPS Adoption

In this section, we examine the barriers and challenges that exist in the present utilization of intelligent cyber-physical systems (CPS) for healthcare. Identifying these challenges will help us understand the difficulties and limitations involved in implementing CPS technologies in healthcare.

Interoperability Issue: The implementation of CPS in existing healthcare systems can pose challenges due to interoperability issues. Different systems and devices may not be able to communicate effectively, which prevents the smooth exchange of information. These challenges must be addressed to create a cohesive and interdependent healthcare system.

Data Security Concerns: Concerns about patient data security and privacy arise from the increased connectivity of CPS. The implementation of robust cybersecurity measures is crucial for minimizing risks and maintaining the confidentiality of sensitive health information.

Cost and Resource Constraints: The initial expenses incurred during the adoption of CPS technologies, along with maintenance costs, can be considerable. Resource constraints, both in terms of budget and skilled personnel, may pose challenges to widespread CPS adoption in healthcare settings.

7.2 Opportunities for Improvement and Innovation

This section of the chapter looks at ways to improve the implementation of CPS in health care and promote innovation. Identifying and exploiting these opportunities is essential for improving the effectiveness and efficiency of CPS implementations. Examples of opportunities include:

Standardization Initiatives: Industry standards for CPS technologies can be established to improve interoperability, and the implementation of these systems may be made easier in various healthcare settings. These standards are used in their development and implementation as a common framework for the delivery of CPS solutions.

Advancement in Cybersecurity: Research and development of cyber security technologies can solve information security problems related to CPS implementation. Advances in encryption, authentication and data protection measures ensure the security and privacy of patient data.

Collaboration and Knowledge Sharing: Fostering collaboration between healthcare providers, technology developers and researchers will facilitate the sharing of best practices and innovative solutions. The collaboration contributes to a mutual understanding of the challenges and opportunities of implementing CPS in health care.

7.3 Implications for Future Research and Development

The section focuses on the implications for future research and development in healthcare with intelligent CPS. These implications must be addressed to enable the revolutionary use of CPS technologies in healthcare. Examples of implications include:

Research on Ethical Considerations: Future research should examine the ethical implications of CPS for health care and address issues such as patient consent, data ownership, and the responsible use of AI algorithms. Ethical considerations play a central role in shaping the responsible implementation of CPS technologies.

Enhancing System Integration: Further research may focus on developing strategies to enhance the seamless integration of CPS into existing health information systems, thereby reducing interoperability issues. Better integration promotes a more cohesive and efficient health system.

Investigating Patient Outcome: Research studies can investigate the long-term impact of CPS applications on patient outcomes, satisfaction, and overall healthcare quality. Understanding the impact of CPS on patient care is essential to evaluating its effectiveness and identifying areas for improvement.

The chapter aims to provide an overview of how healthcare organizations can handle the challenges associated with implementing a smart CPS, by providing solutions that overcome these issues. Furthermore, the chapter highlights its implications for future research and development to advance the progress of this groundbreaking technology in healthcare.

8 Conclusion

8.1 The Scoping Review's Key Findings

This part provides an overview of the insights learned throughout the chapter by offering a succinct and thorough explanation of the major conclusions drawn from the scoping review. Key results might include, for example:

Dominant Themes and Trends: Outlining the most common themes and patterns seen in CPS applications in a range of healthcare areas, including patient care, operations, and diagnostics. This synopsis demonstrates the widespread influence of CPS on several facets of healthcare provision.

Technological Developments: Outlining the technological developments that have arisen from the scoping review and demonstrating the evolution and integration of CPS with other state-of-the-art technologies. This synopsis provides an overview of the rapidly changing world of technology-driven healthcare innovations.

Opportunities and Difficulties: highlighting the significant obstacles and openings found and highlighting how they affect the application of CPS in healthcare environments. This synopsis provides a framework for comprehending the intricate interactions between barriers and opportunities for CPS adoption advancement.

8.2 Recommendations for the Future Direction of Research and Implementation

This section ensures a useful and forward-looking conclusion by offering specific recommendations to direct future research and implementation efforts. Examples of suggested reading may be:

Consider Interoperability First: urging a concentrated effort to resolve interoperability issues in order to guarantee the smooth integration of CPS with current healthcare systems. The significance of an integrated and interconnected healthcare environment is emphasized by this proposal.

Spending on Cybersecurity Tools: Promoting greater funding for cybersecurity measures in order to protect patient information and foster confidence in the application of CPS technology. This suggestion recognizes that data security in healthcare CPS applications is extremely important.

Research on Patient Outcomes via Longitudinal Studies: Suggested that studies be conducted to evaluate the long-term effects of CPS applications on patient outcomes, overall quality of care, and healthcare efficiency. This suggestion encourages evidence-based understanding of the long-term impacts of CPS initiatives.

8.3 Further Exploration and Collaboration in This Area

The paper concludes with a strong call to action that advocates for more research and cooperation in the area of Intelligent Cyber-Physical Systems (CPS) in healthcare. A call to action may look something like this:

Promoting Collaborative Research: To promote interdisciplinary research in this developing sector, there is a call for greater collaboration between scholars, healthcare professionals, and technology developers. This call to action emphasizes the collective effort needed for comprehensive advancements.

Advocating for Industry Standards: Urging stakeholders to advocate for and contribute to the development of industry standards that can enhance interoperability and facilitate the widespread adoption of CPS in healthcare. This call to action seeks to establish a common framework for CPS integration.

Promoting Continued Investment: Emphasizing the need for continued investment, both financial and intellectual, to drive innovation, overcome challenges, and unlock the full potential of CPS in transforming healthcare. This call to action underscores the ongoing commitment required for sustained progress.

By concluding with a summary, recommendations, and a compelling call to action, the chapter aims to leave readers with a clear understanding of the current state of Intelligent CPS in healthcare and inspire them to contribute to the ongoing advancement of this transformative technology in the healthcare domain.

References

1. Vyron Kampourakis, Vasileios Gkioulos, Sokratis Katsikas, A systematic literature review on wireless security testbeds in the cyber-physical realm, Computers & Security, Volume 133, 2023, 103383, ISSN 0167-4048.
2. Shah Zeb, Aamir Mahmood, Sunder Ali Khowaja, Kapal Dev, Syed Ali Hassan, Mikael Gidlund, Paolo Bellavista, Towards defining industry 5.0 vision with intelligent and softwarized wireless network architectures and services: A survey, Journal of Network and Computer Applications (2023), https://doi.org/10.1016/j.jnca.2023.103796.
3. A. Razaque et al., "A Mobility-Aware Human-Centric Cyber–Physical System for Efficient and Secure Smart Healthcare," in IEEE Internet of Things Journal, vol. 9, no. 22, pp. 22434–22452, 15 Nov. 15, 2022, https://doi.org/10.1109/JIOT.2021.3140090.
4. Abdul Ahad, Zahra Ali, Abdul Mateen, Mohammad Tahir, Abdul Hannan, Nuno M. Garcia, Ivan Miguel Pires, A Comprehensive review on 5G-based Smart Healthcare Network Security: Taxonomy, Issues, Solutions and Future research directions, Array, Volume 18, 2023, 100290, ISSN 2590-0056, https://doi.org/10.1016/j.array.2023.100290.
5. T. Hemalatha, A. Bhuvaneswari, N. Poornima, B. Shubha, K. Santhi, M. Lawanyashri, Geeta C. Mara, Secure and private data sharing in CPS e-health systems based on CB-SMO techniques, Measurement: Sensors, Volume 27, 2023, 100787, ISSN 2665-9174, https://doi.org/10.1016/j.measen.2023.100787.
6. Prabhat Kumar, Randhir Kumar, Govind P. Gupta, Rakesh Tripathi, Alireza Jolfaei, A.K.M. Najmul Islam, A blockchain-orchestrate deep learning approach for secure data transmission in IoT-enabled healthcare system, Journal of Parallel and Distributed Computing, Volume 172, 2023, Pages 69–83, ISSN 0743-7315.
7. Fengzheng Wang, Remote Data Security Monitoring Technology for Computer Networks Based on Machine Learning Algorithms Fengzheng Wang. Procedia Computer Science 228 (2023) 325–332.
8. Shrabani Sutradhar, Sunil Karforma, Rajesh Bose, Sandip Roy, A Dynamic Step-wise Tiny Encryption Algorithm with Fruit Fly Optimization for Quality of Service improvement in

healthcare, Healthcare Analytics, Volume 3, 2023, 100177, ISSN 2772-4425, https://doi.org/10.1016/j.health.2023.100177.
9. Cheng Fei, Jun Shen, Machine learning for securing Cyber–Physical Systems under cyber attacks: A survey, Franklin Open, Volume 4, 2023, 100041, ISSN 2773-1f863.
10. Mohd Javaid, Abid Haleem, Ravi Pratap Singh, Rajiv Suman, An integrated outlook of Cyber–Physical Systems for Industry 4.0: Topical practices, architecture, and applications, Green Technologies and Sustainability, Volume 1, Issue 1, 2023, 100001, ISSN 2949-7361.
11. Giuseppe Cascavilla, Damian A. Tamburri, Francesco Leotta, Massimo Mecella, WillemJan Van Den Heuvel, Counter-terrorism in cyber–physical spaces: Best practices and technologies from the state of the art, Information and Software Technology, Volume 161, 2023, 107260, ISSN 0950-5849.
12. B. Ji, Y. Wang, L. Xing, C. Li, Y. Wang and H. Wen, "IRS-Driven Cybersecurity of Healthcare Cyber Physical Systems," in IEEE Transactions on Network Science and Engineering, vol. 10, no. 5, pp. 2564–2573, 1 Sept.–Oct. 2023, https://doi.org/10.1109/TNSE.2022.3213082.
13. M. Adil, M. K. Khan, M. M. Jadoon, M. Attique, H. Song and A. Farouk, "An AI-Enabled Hybrid Lightweight Authentication Scheme for Intelligent IoMT Based Cyber-Physical Systems," in IEEE Transactions on Network Science and Engineering, vol. 10, no. 5, pp. 2719–2730, 1 Sept.–Oct. 2023, https://doi.org/10.1109/TNSE.2022.3159526.
14. Mohammed A.M. Yassin, Ashish Shrestha, Suhaila Rabie, Digital twin in power system research and development: Principle, scope, and challenges, Energy Reviews, Volume 2, Issue 3, 2023,100039, ISSN 2772-9702, https://doi.org/10.1016/j.enrev.2023.100039.
15. Fredrik Heiding, Sotirios Katsikeas, Robert Lagerström, Research communities in cyber security vulnerability assessments: A comprehensive literature review, Computer Science Review, Volume 48, 2023, 100551, ISSN 1574-0137, https://doi.org/10.1016/j.cosrev.2023.100551.
16. Shrabani Sutradhar, Sunil Karforma, Rajesh Bose, Sandip Roy, A Dynamic Step-wise Tiny Encryption Algorithm with Fruit Fly Optimization for Quality-of-Service improvement in healthcare, Healthcare Analytics, Volume 3, 2023, 100177, ISSN 2772-4425, https://doi.org/10.1016/j.health.2023.100177.
17. Abderahman Rejeb, Karim Rejeb, Horst Treiblmaier, Andrea Appolloni, Salem Alghamdi, Yaser Alhasawi, Mohammad Iranmanesh, The Internet of Things (IoT) in healthcare: Taking stock and moving forward, Internet of Things, Volume 22, 2023, 100721, ISSN 2542-6605, https://doi.org/10.1016/j.iot.2023.100721.
18. H. Abie, "Cognitive Cybersecurity for CPS-IoT Enabled Healthcare Ecosystems," 2019 13th International Symposium on Medical Information and Communication Technology (ISMICT), Oslo, Norway, 2019, pp. 1–6, https://doi.org/10.1109/ISMICT.2019.8743670.
19. A. Irshad, G. A. Mallah, M. Bilal, S. A. Chaudhry, M. Shafiq and H. Song, "SUSIC: A Secure User Access Control Mechanism for SDN-Enabled IIoT and Cyber–Physical Systems," in IEEE Internet of Things Journal, vol. 10, no. 18, pp. 16504–16515, 15 Sept. 15, 2023, https://doi.org/10.1109/JIOT.2023.3268474.
20. S. Amin, T. Salahuddin and A. Bouras, "Cyber Physical Systems and Smart Homes in Healthcare: Current State and Challenges," 2020 IEEE International Conference on Informatics, IoT, and Enabling Technologies (ICIoT), Doha, Qatar, 2020, pp. 302–309, https://doi.org/10.1109/ICIoT48696.2020.9089638.
21. K. Baranitharan, Dineshbabu V., Robert Concepción-Lázaro, Balamanigandan R., K. Selvakumarasamy, Mahaveer Kannan R., Mohammed Wasim Bhatt, A collaborative and adaptive cyber defense strategic assessment for healthcare networks using edge computing, Healthcare Analytics, Volume 3, 2023, 100184, ISSN 2772-4425, https://doi.org/10.1016/j.health.2023.100184.
22. M. A. Jan et al., "Lightweight Mutual Authentication and Privacy-Preservation Scheme for Intelligent Wearable Devices in Industrial-CPS," in IEEE Transactions on Industrial Informatics, vol. 17, no. 8, pp. 5829–5839, Aug. 2021, https://doi.org/10.1109/TII.2020.3043802.

23. Alessandro Simeonea, Rebecca Grantb, Weilin Yec, Alessandra Caggiano. Operator 4.0 intelligent health monitoring: a Cyber-Physical approach, Procedia CIRP 118 (2023) 1033–103.
24. Vonteru Srikanth Reddy, Kumar Debasis, DLSDHMS: Design of a deep learning-based analysis model for secure and distributed hospital management using context-aware sidechains, Heliyon https://doi.org/10.1016/j.heliyon.2023.e22283.

Importance and Potential Benefits of Intelligent CPS in Healthcare

Jasleen Kaur Bains and Neeru Mago

Abstract The adoption of the latest technologies is causing a rapid shift in the healthcare sector, and the rise of intelligent cyber-physical systems (CPS) holds great potential for enhancing operational performance and patient care. In this study, the significance of intelligent CPS in healthcare is investigated, with a focus on how it might potentially alter patient care through improved remote monitoring, predictive analytics, and customised medications. The potential for these technologies to enable proactive interventions, provide healthcare professionals with relevant data access, and help early diagnosis to enhance patient outcomes is discussed. By minimising errors, optimising workflows, and increasing productivity, intelligent CPS can also optimise healthcare operations. As a result, healthcare costs will be reduced and organisational performance will be enhanced. They can assist with inventory management, workflow management, and resource allocation. Implementing intelligent CPS in healthcare, however, is fraught with moral dilemmas and practical challenges. In order to achieve responsible and equitable deployment, it is essential to address privacy, security, interoperability, and any biases in decision-making algorithms through robust governance frameworks and legal constraints. Through the use of real-time data, advanced analytics, and artificial intelligence, intelligent CPS have the ability to transform healthcare systems into proactive, customised, and efficient entities. To fully realise their potential, it is crucial to address moral concerns and make sure that they work in harmony with existing healthcare infrastructures.

Keywords Intelligent CPS in healthcare · Importance of intelligent CPS · Stakeholders in healthcare · Potential benefits of intelligent CPS

J. K. Bains (✉)
DCSA, Panjab University, Chandigarh, India
e-mail: jasleen@pu.ac.in

N. Mago
DCSA, PUSSGRC, Hoshiarpur, Punjab, India
e-mail: neerumago@pu.ac.in

M. Mittal and J. Narayan (eds.), *Intelligent Cyber-Physical Systems for Healthcare Solutions*, https://doi.org/10.1007/978-981-97-8983-2_2

1 Introduction

The emergence of cutting-edge technologies such as Artificial intelligence (AI), Deep learning, Machine learning, Big data analytics, Block chain, Cloud computing, Internet-of-things (IoT) and Robotics has led to the discovery of novel approaches for addressing core issues and delivering services across various fields like the manufacturing industry, governance, healthcare, businesses and academia. These have significantly impacted the way humans interact, access information and conduct business nowadays compared to a few decades ago. The separation between the physical world and cyberspace is diminishing nowadays, applications such as smart homes, smart cities, telemedicine and autonomous vehicles, use well-devised systems that integrate both the physical world and cyberspace. These systems are referred to as Intelligent Cyber-Physical Systems (CPS). They combine physical, networking, and computer processes to create networked frameworks that can perceive, analyze, and react to events in the real world. They are transformative because they can make intelligent decisions and take autonomous actions by analyzing the data they get from the physical environment.

These systems use sensors, computational processes, communication devices, controls and actuators as shown in Fig. 1. The sensors collect data from the physical systems such as temperature, humidity, pulse rate, glucose level and many more depending on the physical system. This data is sent via the wired or wireless computer networks to the cyber space where this data is analyzed using computational processes designed using technologies like big data analytics, machine learning or artificial intelligence. After analysis of data, the underlying control mechanism decides what actions need to be taken to bring the physical state to normal. Actuators enable accurate and dynamic control of the related processes or devices by converting the control signals from a system's controller into physical actions. The particular action taken varies depending on the application's needs and the system's desired functionality. These actions could be such as activating or deactivating heating elements or cooling systems, moving a robotic arm and many more. The sensors are inbuilt in the physical devices which are used to gather data from the physical environment or the subject such as the person. They are customized to capture one or more types of data at regular intervals and this data is sent via the communication network for further analysis and decision making by the cyber components. Based on the decision taken by cyber components, action is performed by actuators to bring the physical environment or the subject under control for example moving the robotic arm, adjusting the temperature, controlling the speed of the motor or fan and many more.

Intelligent CPS frameworks and applications have played a significant role in Industry 4.0 [1]. Automation of several production processes envisioned by Industry 4.0 has been made possible by CPS, which increases productivity and decreases the need for manual intervention. Utilizing CPS, smart manufacturing systems monitor and manage production in real-time, maximizing resource efficiency and reducing downtime. By analyzing the large volume of real-time data gathered from sensors

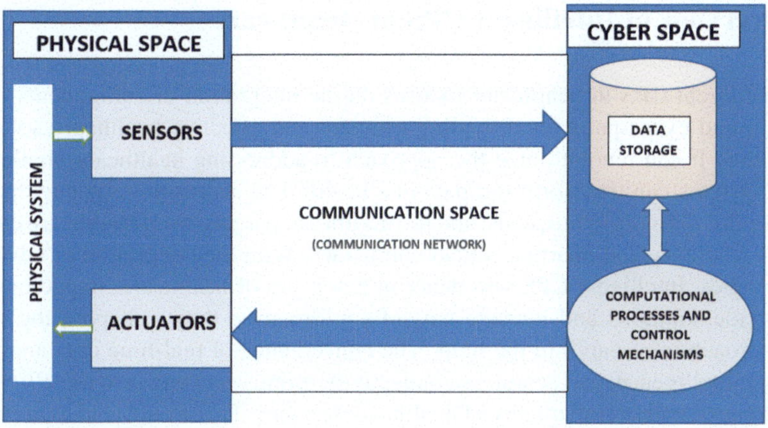

Fig. 1 A general cyber physical system

integrated into production equipment, industries can anticipate maintenance requirements, make well-informed decisions and better streamline ongoing manufacturing processes. Industry 4.0 enabled by CPS helps in predictive maintenance, increases equipment lifespan, optimizes supply chain management and better collaboration between operators and machines [1].

Society 5.0 is a Japanese visionary approach towards creating a human centric technologically advanced society [2]. It envisions addressing the human challenges related to healthcare, education, sustainable living environment, workforce transformation, cybersecurity, digital privacy and global collaboration. This would require designing and implementing robust, intelligent and efficient technological systems which can cater to these challenges and create a sustainable and inclusive society. Intelligent CPS is critical for implementing Industry 4.0 and Society 5.0 compliant solutions by integrating physical processes with advanced technologies. It offers human-centered solutions, real-time data analysis, and effective automation to tackle intricate industrial and societal issues.

The applications of Intelligent CPS are in diverse areas such as manufacturing, logistics, production, business, agriculture, healthcare, smart cities, energy conservation, transportation and many more. Due to its massive applicability in diverse fields many researchers have shown interest in this area and few of them have carried on an extensive review of CPS in healthcare [3–6]. In this paper, the primary focus is on discussing the benefits and potential of CPS in healthcare for its various stakeholders like patient, doctors, insurance companies, hospitals and government.

The next section will delve into the discussion of Intelligent CPS in healthcare, where we will explore various technologies and components specifically tailored to the healthcare domain. Section 3 emphasizes the importance of Intelligent CPS in healthcare. Section 4 focuses on the potential benefits of Intelligent CPS in healthcare and Sect. 5 provides Conclusion.

2 Overview of Intelligent CPS in Healthcare

The Intelligent CPS in healthcare focuses on the integration of components of the physical and cyberspace for providing efficient and effective healthcare solutions to patients. It can revolutionize the approach to addressing healthcare challenges. These systems can transform the patient's health data acquisition, manage patient data, service delivery in hospitals, and the traditional paradigms of healthcare entities such as insurance and pharmaceutical companies. With the integration of advanced technologies, Intelligent CPS will usher in a new era of healthcare, impacting how we provide solutions and manage patient's information thus reshaping the scientific approach to research in the field. The convergence of real-time data analytics, artificial intelligence, and seamless connectivity promises to enhance the efficiency, effectiveness, and overall quality of healthcare services. This would lead to improved patient outcomes and a more responsive and adaptive healthcare ecosystem. Figure 2 shows the basic components of an Intelligent CPS in healthcare.

The basic components comprise of the following:

1. **Sensor devices**: They capture the real-time physical data of the patients or their environment. These devices could be wearable such as patient monitoring systems for blood sugar, blood pressure and other parameters [7]. They can include special devices to monitor the movement of the patient in case of a fall detection system [8]. The various types of smart devices are smart watches built

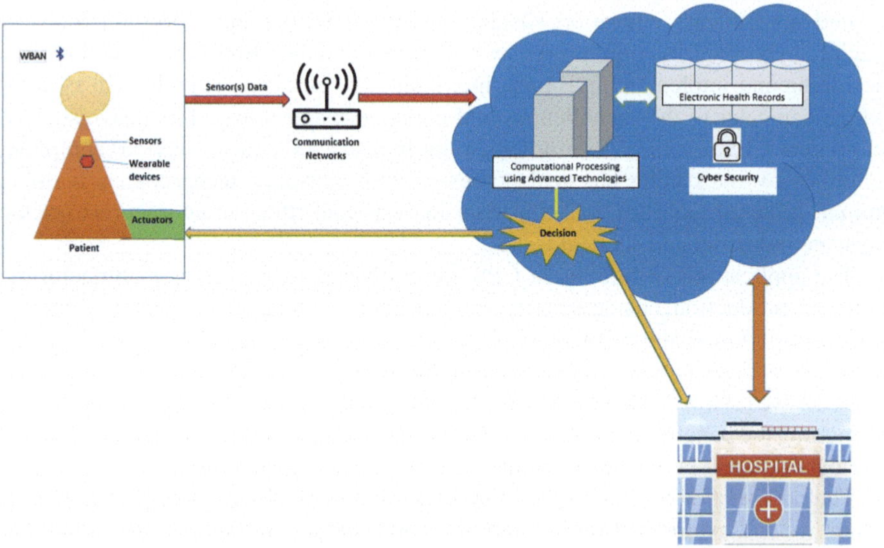

Fig. 2 A general intelligent CPS in healthcare

with activity trackers, sleep trackers, smart thermometers for tracking temperature, smart inhalers, pulse oximeters, wearable ECG (Electro CardioGram) Monitors, smart glucose monitors and many more [9].

2. **Communication network**: It facilitates the seamless exchange of data between different components of the Intelligent CPS. This can include wired and wireless communication technologies. The Wireless Body Area Network (WBAN) comprises various sensors and actuators that can be attached to the clothing, worn as a wearable device or implanted in the body of the patient. It helps to provide real-time health monitoring of the patient, communication among various devices, and also exchange of information via wired or wireless network to the cloud environment for further analysis. Some WBAN technologies used are Bluetooth, Zigbee, IEEE 802.15.6, ANT (Adaptive Network Topology), WiFi (Wireless Fidelity), NFC (Near Field Communication) and many more [10].
3. **Data storage and analysis**: The physiological or environmental data is sent via the wired or wireless communication network to the cloud storage preferably for data analysis. Cloud platforms help to handle large amounts of data received from the sensor devices used by patients [11]. As the sensor data can grow enormously over some time therefore cloud storage provide cost effective solutions for data storage as they do not require significant infrastructure changes. The organizations take up the cloud storage and analysis services depending on their requirement. They do not need to invest much in the infrastructure and computing facilities at their end. Additionally, it provides ease of accessibility as it can be accessed virtually from any location by authorized users. It provides the flexibility for multiple stakeholders from different organizations to work collectively on the same data simultaneously. It enhances the Intelligent CPS as better informed decisions can be taken to ensure better health for the patients. The cloud platforms are secure, compliant with industry specific standards for handling sensitive data, provide proper encryption and access controls for the dataset. They also provide data analysis services, tools and technologies for performing computation on the dataset. Some popular cloud platforms are Amazon Web Services (AWS), Google Cloud Platform (GCP), Microsoft Azure and Salesforce Health Cloud. The Electronic Health Records (EHR) which contains the medical history of the patients is also stored in the cloud storage. They may contain data such as patient medical history, diagnosis, medication details, immunization history, allergies, surgery details, lab results, family history of the disease, doctor notes, diagnostic images and treatment plans by a doctor.

   The machine learning based data analytical tools can use the data from EHR and sensor data to predict an apt decision on the action to be taken. This action is sent in the form of control signals to the actuators present at the patients end for example raising an alarm to alert the patient or sending a message to the hospital in case of an emergency to send an ambulance to the patient. It can further inform the patient support group so that they can reach the spot and help the patient like in the case of falls in elderly people [8].
4. **Actuators**: These are the specialized devices that perform a physical action based on the control signal received after analysis of the sensor data. Some of the

actuators are linear actuators used to control the syringe movement for infusing fluids or medication, peristaltic pumps, Pneumatic actuators used with ventilators or surgical robots, actuators used in prosthetic devices to control their movement, hydraulic actuators used in patients beds for lifting and piezoelectric actuators for controlled drug delivery or to optimize the sound of speakers or microphones.

The above components can vary as per the healthcare organization providing the Intelligent CPS services to its patients. The Intelligent CPS solutions are not limited to just patient monitoring systems they can cater to multiple other tasks such as automated inventory management, scheduling resource allocation, remote consultation, telemedicine, smart facility management and enhanced patient engagement [5]. All of these solutions collectively enhance overall healthcare and can help in strategic planning.

3 Importance of Intelligent CPS in Healthcare

The Intelligent CPS in Healthcare can be beneficial to various stakeholders such as healthcare providers, patients, hospital staff, insurance agencies, health regulatory bodies, health policy makers, vendors, industry, research institutions, academia, caregivers and community (Fig. 3). For each of them the importance of Intelligent CPS in Healthcare differs.

- **Patient:** The patient is the key stakeholder in an Intelligent CPS in Healthcare. The primary motive of such a system is to provide better healthcare to its patient in following ways:
  - It helps in continued monitoring of the crucial physiological patient data via the sensors. This ensures early intervention thus ensuring timely treatment of the health condition. It can help to reduce the mortality rate and ensures patients safety. For example, in the case of a fall detection system the patients can be helped via the care group by informing them immediately about the fall, the doors can be opened via the actuators and additionally an alert message can be sent to hospital to send the ambulance [8].
  - The continuous monitoring can also help to identify any abnormalities in the physiological data, thus helping in the early detection of the health problem.
  - Personalized and targeted care can be provided to the patient by analyzing the sensor data using data analytics and machine learning algorithms. Treatment plans can be modified based on the analysis of the current data from sensors and past data from EHR. This ensures better care for the patient.
  - The sensor data can help to track the physical activity of the patient and the physiological data like blood sugar levels, oxygen levels and blood pressure help to give a fair idea about food intake of the patients. This can help to know the adherence of the patient to the recommended treatment plan. Further, it may also help the health providers to make any changes for increasing effectiveness

Fig. 3 Various stakeholders in intelligent CPS in healthcare

of the treatment plan. For example, the prescribed dosage of medicine can be increased or decreased based on the physical activity of the patient.

- The patients can be provided additional educational material in the form of audio, video or text for creating awareness about their underlying health problem. Regular communication can be kept with the patients that can help them to resolve queries and engage them in self-care practices. These practices can enhance the overall health and quality of life of the patient.
- Virtual consultation can be arranged for the patients who cannot come frequently to hospitals or are specially-abled. This can help them to provide frequent consultation and avoid stress related to waiting in long queues at hospital or commuting to the hospital.
- The patient's data such as ailment detail, doctor's medical prescription, hospital medicines, lab tests and surgery bills are all available to the insurance companies thus it is easier to get the insurance claims processed quickly with ease.

Overall the Intelligent CPS in healthcare can enhance the patient health and engagement independent of their geographical location.

- **Healthcare providers**: The healthcare providers in Intelligent CPS in healthcare are the physicians, nurses and technicians for operating medical equipment. Their centric approach is to provide better treatment and care to the patient. The Intelligent CPS in healthcare can benefit them in the following ways:
  - The Intelligent CPS helps to analyze the vast amount of data present in the EHR and the real-time data from patient's monitoring devices. All this data is available in the cloud storage and is accessible to the authorized healthcare provider from anywhere. The Intelligent CPS uses state of the art data analysis tools and techniques to analyze the patient's complete data. Based on the outcome of these tools the healthcare providers can make effective decisions regarding the patient's health diagnosis, treatment plan and medication.
  - The sensor data from wearable and other sensor devices like activity tracker, sleep tracker, oximeter, blood pressure monitor, glucose monitor and many others can help the healthcare provider to track the patient's vital, adherence to the prescribed treatment plan and progression of the disease. This data can help healthcare providers to intervene and proactively manage the disease.
  - The Intelligence CPS system can use devices that can aid health providers during surgery, patient safety is ensured as the usage of such can reduce human error.
  - Technology like dual twin, in which a digital twin is created for the patient and the physical twin is the patient itself. This helps to analyze the effect of the medical procedures before they are actually done on the real patient. This reduces the human error and also increases the effectiveness of the overall treatment.
  - The patients at high risk can be easily identified by analyzing the real-time patient data. The data like number of re-admissions and their causes can also be understood by analyzing the physiological data of the patient. This way the patient can be informed and educated about the underlying health condition and the triggers which need to be avoided to prevent further complications. This system helps to keep the patient and health care providers in close communication which enables better patient care and reduces healthcare costs.
  - The Intelligent CPS helps to automate many tasks like patient appointments, admissions, transfers, and discharges, workflow related tasks such as patient admission, billing, order entry and management, clinical documentation and many more. As these tasks are mostly automated thus healthcare providers can concentrate more on patient care rather than the routine tasks.
  - Optimized resource allocation can be performed using Intelligent CPS in healthcare. It helps to manage the allocation of resources like patient beds, rooms and other medical equipment depending on the patient inflow. This helps to effectively manage and avoid any challenges in the allocation of resources at hand.

  - The use of Intelligent CPS promotes the seamless sharing of data among various healthcare providers and hospital staff as majority of routine tasks is automated. This helps to increase collaboration and communication among the doctors, nurses, hospital staff and technicians thus creating a healthy environment in the hospital.

- **Insurance companies**: The Intelligent CPS can help the insurance companies in number of ways as follows:
  - As explained before the claim process can become simpler in an Intelligent CPS as patient's details regarding ailments, various tests, medication and surgery are all available to the insurance company. Further, the claim process is also automated which helps the insurers to get the claims quickly.
  - Intelligent CPS helps to detect the claim pattern of the insurer from its past and current data. This analysis helps to detect and prevent any fraud related to false claims, scams or thefts. The insurance company can take necessary steps to combat such suspicious activity and discourage the insurer.
  - The analysis of the patient's data done by the Intelligent CPS can help the insurance company to identify the patients at high risk of developing disease in the future. They can identify such patients and can intervene in their healthcare process to enable them to take preventive measures to avoid potential health risks in the near future. This will help to bring down the healthcare costs and improve the health of the insurer too.
  - The insurance companies can look for cost-effective treatment plans and alternatives for their insurers. The Intelligent CPS can also help insurance companies identify best health providers based on their treatment and cost effectiveness. They can measure metrics such as patient satisfaction scores, ratings, reviews and health outcomes. They can facilitate such high performing health providers. They may additionally promote such health providers who provide high quality services and treatment to their patients.
  - Intelligent CPS in healthcare can help to take measures on a community or mass level by addressing health issues prominent in the masses. For example, diseases like diabetes, obesity and neural disorders are more prevalent in a particular section of society due to unhealthy lifestyle practices. Such insights can help insurance companies design preventive care programs, campaigns for the masses in close collaboration with the healthcare providers. This can help to bring awareness among the masses regarding health challenges. Timely action can help many people avoid the disease in the future.
  - Using data from Intelligent CPS the insurance companies can increase personal engagement with their insurers by educating them regarding how to minimize the potential risks. They can motivate them to take preventive measures, thus reducing potential health risks and related costs as well.
  - Intelligent CPS helps insurance companies to introduce new plans as per the latest health trends and treatment costs. This way they can be abreast with the competition in the healthcare industry.

- **Health regulatory bodies and policy makers**: The Intelligent CPS can benefit the health regulatory bodies and policy makers in following ways:
  - The data from various devices that are part of the Intelligent CPS in healthcare can be analyzed comprehensively. This helps health regulatory bodies to identify potential safety issues. They may as a result implement preventive measures, regulatory interventions, and quality improvement initiatives to protect patient safety.
  - Intelligent CPS gives a deep insight into the healthcare system to the regulatory bodies. This enables them to ensure complete compliance of the healthcare providers with the underlying regulations and policies. In case of any noncompliance, the reasons for the same can be understood by analyzing the healthcare data. This would help them to design more effective regulations and policies to improve overall healthcare for their region.
  - The changing trends in healthcare can help to recognize the upcoming healthcare challenges and prompt them to make evidence-based policy changes.
- **Industry**: The Intelligent CPS can benefit the various industry stakeholders like medical device manufacturers, technology vendors, and service providers in the following ways:
  - Technologies such as AI and machine learning can help the vendors to innovate new software and hardware products which can help to provide better healthcare experience for the various stakeholders.
  - The vendors can capture the opportunities provided by the Intelligent CPS to capture the product market which ensures better healthcare. By analyzing the trends in healthcare from Intelligent CPS, the vendors can launch products that can cater to changing trends, give better performance and client satisfaction.
  - The Intelligent CPS helps the vendors to keep compliance with the security standards and regulations laid by health care regulatory bodies such as FDA's (Food and Drug Administrations) Quality System Regulation (QSR) and European Medical Device Regulation (MDR).
  - It also helps the vendors to come up with cost-effective solutions in minimal time by optimizing the development processes.
- **Research institutions and academia**: Intelligent CPS in healthcare offers numerous benefits for research institutions and academia, such as:
  - It motivates the researchers to conduct research in areas of medical diagnostic and personalized medication using cutting edge technology. Innovative solutions can be developed using the IoT, AI and machine learning algorithms [12]. This can boost scientific knowledge and discovery.
  - The Intelligent CPS can boost interdisciplinary research among researchers, engineers, healthcare professionals and clinicians. This can lead to innovative solutions.

  - The researchers can collaborate with industry partners, startups, and investors to commercialize Intelligent CPS technologies, spin off new ventures, and create economic value. This would lead to job creation and industry growth.
  - Academic Institutions can teach Intelligent CPS related technologies and processes in their academic curriculum to prepare students for careers in the healthcare, data science and biomedical fields.

- **Caregivers**: The Intelligent CPS can help caregivers to provide timely and effective care to their patients. The patient monitoring system used by the patient can alert them regarding any untoward or major fluctuation in the physiological data of the patient.
- **Community**: Intelligent CPS in healthcare offers numerous benefits for the community. By analyzing the enormous amount of data from the environmental sensors, hospital databases and public healthcare platforms the Intelligent CPS can predict health hazards and epidemics. The government can make timely interventions to help healthcare providers combat such a situation. Additionally, immunization drives can be conducted to increase the immunity of the community against the potential threats. The Government can plan campaigns for educating the communities for taking better healthcare measures to enhance their overall healthcare experience.

4 Potential Benefits of Intelligent CPS in Healthcare

- As discussed in Sect. 3, the main focus of Intelligent CPS in Healthcare is on improving overall healthcare. At the core of the system is providing the best care and treatment to the patient by regular monitoring and intervention. The potential benefits of such a system are diverse as it is beneficial for all its stakeholders. Intelligent CPS helps to provide tailored treatment plans for the patients based on the predictive analysis done on continuously monitored data stored in EHR and received from sensors. This would improve the patient's health. Continuous monitoring via wearables and other sensor devices would help to ensure patient's compliance with the treatment plan and medication. In case of deviation, the health giver may intervene. Overall timely interventions can effectively reduce hospital readmissions as an approach to healthcare would be preventive. Extensive usage of wearables and other sensor devices would generate real-time data with high accuracy. The analysis of such real-time accurate data can help researchers and healthcare providers expand their knowledge base and look beyond the traditional approach of catering to a problem. The massive amount of critical data also demands more secure data standards, privacy policies, encryptions and access controls to be used to protect data from unauthorized users. Intelligent CPS helps in automating routine tasks such as patient appointment scheduling, registration, medication details and billing. This reduces administrative burden and allows healthcare providers to focus more on patient care. Intelligent CPS anticipates patient needs, allocates resources efficiently, and improves decision-making. This is possible due to extensive predictive analysis done on the comprehensive data from patients and health providers, Intelligent CPS helps to minimize the cost of healthcare for patients by providing a preventive approach thus avoiding unnecessary health complications and hospitalizations. It enhances patient satisfaction and faith in the healthcare system by increasing patient engagement via telemedicine, remote consultations, and mobile health apps. These solutions give convenience and accessibility to healthcare services while sitting in their comfort zone.

It holds potential opportunities for the pharmaceutical and equipment manufacturing industries to come up with innovative solutions that can integrate seamlessly into the Intelligent CPS in healthcare. This would boost the industry and create more revenue. It improves supply chain management by automating tasks such as inventory management systems in healthcare organizations. It provides an opportunity for the research and academia to conduct extensive research that aids the functioning of Intelligent CPS in healthcare and improves the overall health experience for its major stakeholders. Researchers can come up with innovative solutions, and explore new treatment approaches, and therapies for improving healthcare. The implementation of Intelligent CPS in healthcare would open up multiple job avenues for people specialized in building solutions for CPS and operating and managing these systems. The Government can benefit from cost savings in the healthcare budget by implementing of such a robust system. This ensures timely ordering of medicines, devices, and other office supplies before they are out of stock. It helps to build up a resilient system by minimizing human error. It helps to give equal healthcare opportunities for all citizens irrespective of their place as it has the potential to serve people living in remote areas as well.

5 Conclusion

Intelligent CPS in healthcare has revolutionized healthcare delivery, improved patient outcomes, and driven innovation in the healthcare industry. By using advanced technologies such as artificial intelligence, machine learning, and the Internet of Things it has created software solutions that have boosted the health services provided by the healthcare providers. It has transformed the way healthcare is delivered, managed, and experienced. Remote patient monitoring via the use of wearables has led to personalized treatment plans for patients, helped health providers to check the adherence of the same, and early interventions in case of potential risk or non-adherence by the patient. Patient safety is ensured by taking measures well in time to avoid any extremities. The benefits of this system are varied such as improved clinical workflows, better resource management, inventory management, streamlined administrative processes and many more. These increase the overall operational efficiency of the healthcare system. This system weighs high on patient engagement via telemedicine and usage of mobile health apps. It also helps to educate patients regarding health management practices which can aid in better quality of health for them. These experiences increase overall satisfaction and build faith in the healthcare system.

The future scope of Intelligent CPS in healthcare is promising and expansive. With evolving technologies like blockchain technology, 5G, virtual reality, and generative AI healthcare will have very accurate diagnoses, targeted treatments, and remote care delivery. Collaborative research needs to be carried out by computer scientists and medical professionals to implement a robust Intelligent CPS in healthcare. There is a lot of scope for the manufacturing industry to develop more precise and accurate diagnostic machines, computationally fast and reliable machines. The health-related policymakers need to come up with newer laws and security norms to ensure the complete safety of vital patient data. Robust network protocols and algorithms need to be used to ensure data security. A strong collaboration among all the stakeholders is required for the effective implementation of this system. Intelligent CPS has the potential to bring a paradigm shift in the healthcare industry as never seen before. It will immensely improve the quality of life for all communities around the world.

References

1. Yang, F., Gu, S.: Industry 4.0, a revolution that requires technology and national strategies. Complex Intell. Syst. (7), 1311–1325 (2021).
2. Deguchi, A. et al: What Is Society 5.0? In: Society 5.0. Springer, Singapore (2020).
3. Kavitha, A., Manicka Chezian, R.: A review on smart healthcare in cyber physical system, European Chemical Bulletin, 12 (2023).
4. Chen, F. et al: Medical Cyber-Physical Systems: A Solution to Smart Health and the State of the Art. IEEE Transactions on Computational Social Systems, 9, 1–28 (2021).
5. Verma, R. Smart City Healthcare Cyber Physical System: Characteristics, Technologies and Challenges. Wireless Pers Commun 122, 1413–1433 (2022).
6. Maki K. Habib, Chukwuemeka Chimsom I: CPS: Role, Characteristics, Architectures and Future Potentials, Procedia Computer Science, 200, Pages 1347–1358 (2022).
7. Ramasamy, L.K.; Khan, F.; Shah, M.; Prasad, B.V.V.S.; Iwendi, C.; Biamba, C. Secure Smart Wearable Computing through Artificial Intelligence-Enabled Internet of Things and Cyber-Physical Systems for Health Monitoring. *Sensors, 22* (2022).
8. Taleb, Tarik & Bottazzi, Dario & Guizani, Mohsen & Nait-Charif, Hammadi. (2009). ANGELAH: a framework for assisting elders at home. Selected Areas in Communications, IEEE Journal on. 27. 480–494. https://doi.org/10.1109/JSAC.2009.090511.
9. Yilmaz, T.; Foster, R.; Hao, Y.: Detecting Vital Signs with Wearable Wireless Sensors. Sensors 2010, 10, 10837–10862 (2010).
10. Dey, N., Ashour, A.S., Shi, F. et al. Medical cyber-physical systems: A survey. J Med Syst 42, 74 (2018).
11. Zhang, Y., Qiu, M., Tsai, C., Hassan, M.M., & Alamri, A.: Health-CPS: Healthcare Cyber-Physical System Assisted by Cloud and Big Data. *IEEE Systems Journal, 11*, 88–95 (2017).
12. Haque SA, Aziz SM, Rahman M.: Review of Cyber-Physical System in Healthcare. International Journal of Distributed Sensor Networks. 10(4) (2014).

Recent Trends in Medical Cyber-Physical System—A Brief Survey

Dheeraj Kumar Dhaked and Valayapathy Lakshmi Narayanan

Abstract Medical cyber-physical systems (MCPS) have arisen as a dynamic field intersecting healthcare, information technology, and engineering to revolutionize healthcare delivery and enhance patient outcomes. This paper presents a concise overview of recent trends in MCPS, emphasizing technological advancements, applications, and associated challenges. Through an analysis of articles published between 2020 and 2023 on Scopus, the study explores the multifaceted roles of cyber-physical systems in healthcare, catering to the needs of both patients and medical professionals. Furthermore, developing knowledge such as artificial intelligence, machine learning, blockchain, and the Internet of Things are highlighted for their potential to augment MCPS capabilities. By addressing critical challenges and outlining future directions, this study offers valuable insights for researchers, practitioners, and policymakers striving to advance MCPS for improved healthcare delivery and patient outcomes.

Keywords Architecture · Medical cyber-physical systems · Smart health · Machine learning · Internet of things

1 Introduction

In the modern medical landscape, the fusion of advanced technologies with healthcare has led to the advent of Medical Cyber-Physical Systems (MCPS), which play a key part in the prevention, detection, and management of healthcare challenges, including the ongoing COVID-19 pandemic [1]. MCPS, as a subset of Cyber-Physical Systems (CPS), are equipped with implanted control systems and independent network infrastructure, facilitating seamless interaction between the physical and cyber realms [2].

D. K. Dhaked (✉) · V. L. Narayanan
Indian Institute of Technology Guwahati Technology Innovation and Development Foundation, Guwahati 781039, Assam, India
e-mail: ddhakar9@gmail.com

M. Mittal and J. Narayan (eds.), *Intelligent Cyber-Physical Systems for Healthcare Solutions*, https://doi.org/10.1007/978-981-97-8983-2_3

This interaction forms the backbone of MCPS, enabling real-time monitoring, analysis, and control of medical processes [3], thereby revolutionizing patient care and healthcare delivery systems.

The fundamental framework of MCPS consists of two essential components [4]: cyberspace and physical space, as shown in Fig. 1. The physical space encompasses the tangible infrastructure of MCPS, comprising numerous health sensing and diagnostic devices that collect real-time data from patients [5]. Simultaneously, the user space, consisting of diverse stakeholders such as patients and healthcare providers, interacts with the physical space to transmit sensory information to cyberspace and receive control instructions in return [6]. On the other hand, cyberspace acts as the nerve center of MCPS [7], responsible for processing, storing, and securing sensitive health data, as well as generating feedback control signals to regulate physical devices [8].

In contrast to the Internet of Things (IoT), CPS emphasizes the integration of virtual applications into the physical world, creating a closed-loop ecosystem that enables real-time analysis, decision-making, and exact implementation between the cyber and physical domains [9]. MCPS leverages this closed-loop architecture to address the complexities and uncertainties inherent in healthcare processes, thereby enhancing resource allocation efficiency and optimizing healthcare services [10].

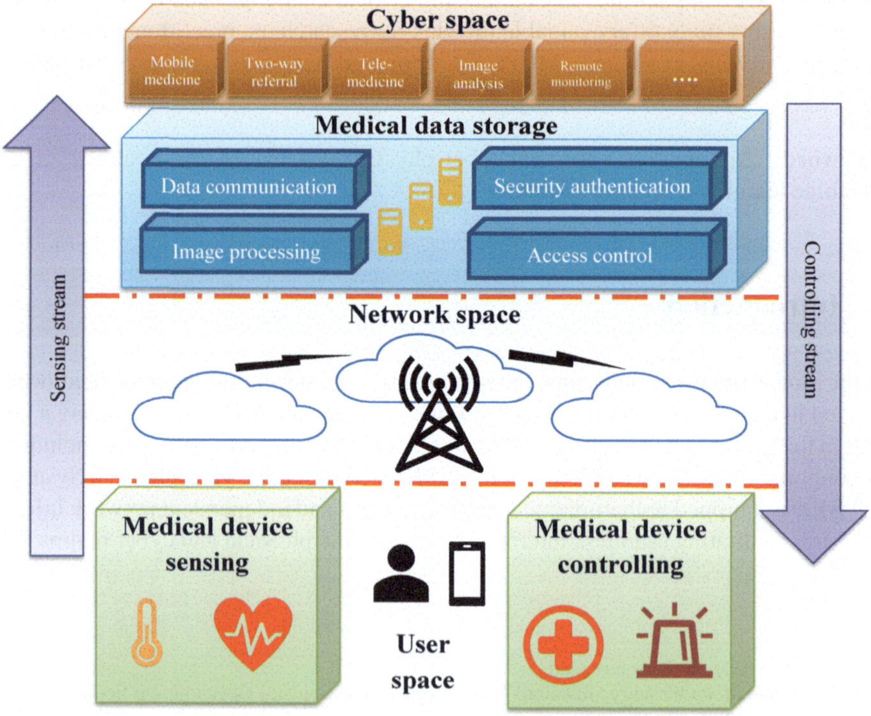

Fig. 1 Overview of medical CPS

Moreover, intelligent [11, 12] and Machine Learning (ML) methods [13, 14] have been preferred in various applications due to their significant advantage. The MCPS represents a pivotal technological precursor to the development of intelligent healthcare systems, offering significant potential for improving medical practices and enhancing patient outcomes [15].

Traditionally, MCPS architectures have focused primarily on patient monitoring and data feedback mechanisms. However, recent research endeavors have expanded the scope of MCPS to encompass broader interactions between the cyber and physical spaces [16]. Some researchers have adopted a CPS-based architectural approach, leveraging big data and Cloud Computing (CC) technologies to establish medical consortia capable of collaborative data analysis and decision-making [17]. Advancements in IoT-based architectures have facilitated the integration of wearable medical devices and remote monitoring systems, enabling seamless communication between patients, healthcare professionals, and medical facilities [18].

Against the backdrop of the increasing adoption of CPS in healthcare, MCPS offers a flexible framework for facilitating comprehensive, three-dimensional medical treatment [19]. By harnessing dynamic data generated by sensor networks and monitoring systems, MCPS shifts computational and monitoring tasks from isolated systems to centralized monitoring centers, effectively transforming the medical system into a unified cyber-physical entity [20, 21]. Moreover, MCPS exhibits characteristics such as high integrity, limited physical resources, cross-domain transmission, and dynamic reorganization, underscoring its suitability for addressing the complex challenges of modern healthcare [22].

As MCPS continues to evolve, several key research areas warrant attention, including control and fusion systems, sensor, security, mobile networks, reliability, and model development [23]. Additionally, issues related to data security [24, 25], privacy protection [26], and regulatory compliance must be addressed to ensure the safe and effective deployment of MCPS in clinical settings [27, 28]. By advancing research in these domains, stakeholders can unlock the full potential of MCPS [29] in revolutionizing healthcare and improving patient outcomes [30].

Moreover, given that MCPS represents a relatively new application domain with limited scholarly discourse, there is a noticeable absence of comprehensive literature reviews covering the layered architecture of CPS and previous studies exploring various aspects of novel technology utilization within diverse healthcare frameworks, including discussions on challenges and emerging opportunities. Considering these the objectives of this article are framed and they are: Investigate the architectural framework of MCPS and assess their diverse applications within the healthcare sector. Analyzing the technological landscape of MCPS through a comprehensive review of published articles from the Scopus database spanning the years 2020–2023. To anticipate future advancements and enhancements in healthcare delivery systems.

2 Taxonomies of MCPS

A comprehensive taxonomy is essential for characterizing and classifying CPS approaches in healthcare. Based on an extensive literature review, we have compiled a taxonomy for CPS in healthcare, as illustrated in Fig. 2. In this section, we delve into the classifications within each of these elements.

The exploration of the potential medical applications of MCPS is still in its nascent stage. Combining active patient data, such as feedback systems and electronic health records, with passive patient data from biosensors and smart devices could facilitate the gaining information crucial for efficient decisions in MCPS. However, there has been limited examination on how this amalgamation of data collection and decision-making could enhance healthcare. Given the diverse sources of information required, the price of studying the possible applications of MCPS in medical services and addressing associated healthcare tasks is significant. The interoperability of autonomous and adaptable devices presents a chance for deploying MCPS in healthcare. Calculation and control, miniaturized fixed smart devices, body area networks, programmable devices, and innovative manufacturing techniques hold potential for overseeing and operating therapeutic physical systems.

Architecture: MCPS design requires special attention due to its criticality to system quality and performance. The architecture should be tailored to the application

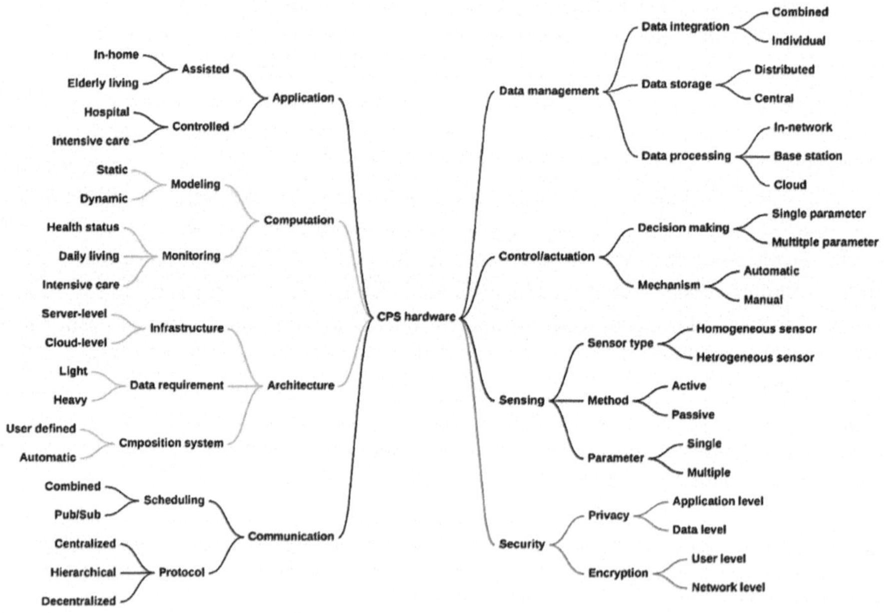

Fig. 2 Taxonomy of medical CPS

domain, client data requirements, and system integration to preserve functionality. The three pillars of MCPS system architecture are cloud-based, mobile-first, user-defined, and automatic.

Sensing: Biomedical sensors play a crucial role in gathering vital physiological data, which is then transmitted to the communication system for more application. Sensing is vital in healthcare as discovered attributes serve as information parameters for the system. For instance, a radio-based, sensor-based, non-invasive method for blood glucose level monitoring has been employed for diabetic patients.

Data Management: MCPS's data management system facilitates controlling sensor data according to user needs. Data preparation enhances information gathering and transmission by converting sensed data into usable formats, thereby addressing high bandwidth requirements and inefficient processing.

Computation: Computation is utilized for modeling and monitoring purposes in MCPS. The CC enables healthcare professionals to monitor and screen patients remotely, ensuring quick access to necessary data. It is crucial to employ techniques for data bottleneck reduction and data size determination to ensure system efficiency.

Application: MCPS finds applications in various healthcare domains, including medical centers, assisted living, and elderly care. The complexity of the system majorly depends on the precise application at hand.

Security: Given the sensitivity of patient information, security is integral to MCPS. Patient data confidentiality must be meticulously addressed throughout the architectural design phase to comply with legal, ethical, and moral standards.

Communication: Collecting patient data and interfacing with the cloud system constitute the main communication methods in MCPS. Successful communication hinges on meticulous planning and adherence to established protocols. Recent progress in visual communications through wireless multimedia sensor networks holds promise for improving tolerance monitoring and perception within MCPS.

In conclusion, while MCPS holds promise for revolutionizing healthcare, it also presents significant challenges that must be addressed, particularly concerning data and communication scheduling. Various communication protocols and security mechanisms are employed to ensure data transmission security and privacy.

3 Technologies in MCPS

The current pandemic has exerted unprecedented pressure on healthcare systems in cities, leading to extended work hours for medical professionals and staff. Future healthcare systems will require the integration of Smart City Healthcare CPS, with expertise playing a pivotal role in their effective deployment [31]. The CPS represent a convergence of various technologies aimed at enabling the smart and competent functioning of interconnected devices. The internet assists as the spine for communication in these systems, acting as a critical enabler for skills like the IoT, blockchain and cloud computing [32]. Various technologies role in MCPS are given below.

Digital twin [33] is a virtual replica of a practical product or method. In healthcare, organizations are increasingly embracing digital twins to enhance resource planning, regulation, and coordination. These digital twins aid in researching, analyzing, and predicting patient health by simulating medical devices, equipment, and treatment processes. The ML techniques are employed to categorize patients' health conditions based on data represented in graphs.

The IoT [34] enables Machine-to-Machine (M2M) communication through wireless networks, Bluetooth, and other technologies. In MCPS, IoT facilitates the transfer of data generated by sensor networks to remote servers for analysis and management. Lightweight authentication and cryptographic algorithms ensure data security in medical IoT devices. Wearable devices like smartwatches and smart bands monitor patients remotely, transmitting vital signs to the cloud for health analytics.

Big data analytics [35] involves continuous data capture by heterogeneous nodes and sensors in MCPS results in large datasets that require storage, processing, and analysis. Cloud-based models and Fog Computing (FC) enable real-time communication and control, addressing challenges in handling unstructured data and ensuring data veracity.

Dew computing [36] enhances the efficiency of CPS by reducing latency through distributed service architectures. By deploying smart systems closer to IoT devices, dew computing reduces latency and improves energy efficacy. The FC benefits healthcare services by enabling effective patient monitoring and analytical services.

Blockchain technology [37] ensures the reliability and trustworthiness of electronic health records by creating a tamper-proof distributed ledger system. It securely records medical device transactions, vaccine sales, and patient-level occurrences, enhancing transparency and traceability in healthcare processes.

The AI and ML [4], have applications in various healthcare domains, including patient classification, automated illness identification, and drug development. These technologies analyze massive patient records to identify patterns and insights, aiding medical professionals in patient management and treatment. AI algorithms predict mortality rates and patient symptoms, enabling personalized healthcare interventions.

Robots [38] play a crucial role in healthcare from diagnostic testing to repetitive tasks like drug and food carriage. AI-based cognitive models enable robots to function in complex environments, enhancing efficiency and reliability in healthcare operations. Robots like MOXI and MITRA assist healthcare workers by performing tasks such as patient care and temperature monitoring. Industrial robots contribute to rapid and precise production, supporting the manufacturing of essential medical supplies during crises.

In summary, the integration of these technologies into MCPS holds immense potential for enhancing patient care, optimizing resource utilization, and improving overall healthcare delivery.

4 Application of CPS in Healthcare Research

This section will present a survey of recent MCPS architectural frameworks developed specifically for healthcare. The survey encompasses the latest papers in MCPS from 2020 to 2023, covering various aspects such as security and incorporating the latest CPS technologies like FC, CC, ML, Health Cloud (HC), Prediction Systems (PS), Internet of Medical Things (IoMT), Real-time Alert Generation (AG), and Security System (SS), particularly in healthcare contexts. Table 1 provides a summary of recent work in MCPS as the primary component. Further subsections offer categorization of different CPS.

Table 1 Existing work review in medical realm

References	Year	IoMT	ML	MCPS	HC	FC	CC	AG	PS	SS
[39]	2023	✓	✓	✓	✓	✗	✗	✗	✗	✓
[40]	2023	✓	✓	✓	✓	✗	✓	✗	✓	✓
[4]	2022	✓	✓	✓	✓	✗	✗	✗	✗	✓
[6]	2022	✓	✓	✓	✗	✗	✗	✗	✗	✓
[34]	2022	✓	✓	✓	✓	✗	✗	✗	✓	✓
[8]	2022	✗	✓	✓	✗	✗	✗	✗	✗	✓
[41]	2022	✗	✓	✓	✓	✗	✗	✗	✓	✓
[42]	2022	✓	✗	✓	✓	✗	✓	✗	✗	✓
[16]	2022	✓	✓	✓	✓	✗	✓	✓	✓	✓
[33]	2022	✓	✓	✓	✓	✓	✓	✗	✓	✓
[31]	2022	✓	✓	✓	✗	✗	✓	✗	✓	✓
[37]	2022	✓	✓	✓	✗	✗	✓	✗	✓	✓
[1]	2021	✗	✓	✓	✓	✗	✗	✗	✗	✓
[7]	2021	✓	✓	✓	✓	✗	✓	✗	✗	✓
[23]	2021	✓	✗	✓	✓	✗	✗	✗	✗	✓
[43]	2021	✗	✓	✗	✓	✗	✗	✗	✓	✓
[44]	2021	✓	✓	✓	✓	✓	✓	✗	✓	✓
[21]	2021	✗	✓	✗	✓	✗	✓	✗	✓	✓
[28]	2021	✓	✓	✓	✓	✗	✓	✗	✓	✓
[45]	2020	✓	✓	✓	✗	✗	✗	✗	✗	✓
[46]	2020	✓	✓	✓	✓	✓	✓	✗	✓	✓
[47]	2020	✓	✓	✓	✓	✓	✓	✗	✓	✓
[48]	2020	✓	✓	✓	✓	✓	✓	✗	✓	✓
[17]	2020	✓	✓	✓	✓	✗	✓	✓	✗	✓
[29]	2020	✓	✓	✓	✓	✗	✓	✗	✗	✓
[35]	2020	✗	✗	✓	✓	✗	✓	✓	✗	✓

4.1 MCPS for Patients

The knowledge and quality improvement of healthcare services for patients is vital for the efficiency of MCPS, given that patients are their primary beneficiaries. MCPS applications [41] aimed at serving patients exhibit diverse functionalities tailored to specific objectives, yet they often interconnect and complement one another.

Patient Management: Numerous applications currently exist to assist patients in locating suitable healthcare providers, scheduling appointments, completing medical forms, managing insurance profits, ordering medications, and accessing self-care and wellness information [49]. In the realm of MCPS, these applications, along with others offering similar functionalities, can be seamlessly integrated into a unified system. Patients would access this system, specify their requirements, and the system would automatically guide them through necessary steps while efficiently transferring relevant data from their medical records to various stakeholders, including doctors, nurses, laboratories, and pharmacies. Furthermore, integration with additional systems and components could enhance these functionalities. For instance, granting the system access to a patient's smart devices would enable tracking of health metrics and activities, scheduling appointments based on availability, sending reminders for appointments or medication doses, delivering updates and reports to the patient's devices, and alerting healthcare providers to any recurring anomalies or issues affecting the patient.

Public Healthcare: Ensuring the well-being of individuals and mitigating the risks associated with illness, disease transmission, and chronic conditions is a multifaceted endeavor involving various elements such as individuals, facilities, equipment, materials, and information. Within the scope of Health 4.0, applications aimed at preventive care, wellness initiatives, public health surveillance, and health advocacy can play a pivotal role [45].

Risk-Stratified Care: Care for patients includes three primary stages: (1) primary deterrence targeting healthy individuals at danger of emerging chronic conditions; (2) secondary deterrence focusing on patients managing existing chronic conditions; and (3) third deterrence addressing patients with progressive chronic diseases or important difficulties. MCPS applications offer solutions for real-time data collection to monitor fluctuations in risk levels and provide comprehensive historical insights based on collected data. Healthcare providers can tailor individualized tactics for patients according to their risk profile, life routine, nutrition, and medication regimen [31]. Additionally, these applications can be enhanced to predict the progression of chronic diseases for individual patients, communities, or entire populations.

Health Exposure Risk: Health 4.0 can implement context-aware services to monitor an individual's mobility, activities, and environmental exposure risks in real-time. By continuously collecting bio-measures and contextual data, correlations between various factors and an individual's health status can be identified. For instance, deviations in air quality may affect asthma patients, prompting timely interventions such as avoidance measures or treatment adjustments [4]. Integrating MCPS data gathering and study with existing medical systems and private nursing devices can enable such actions, thereby enhancing patient care.

Health Behavior: MCPS structure and tenders leverage smart devices and sensors to monitor daily routine and activities continuously [19]. This enables the identification of trends to offer personalized advice for adopting healthier lifestyles, increasing individuals' engagement in decision-making processes, promoting responsibility and devotion to healthcare protocols, and monitoring overall health conditions across diverse demographics.

In-patient Care: Patient who is availing the Medicare, numerous submissions can support the requisite procedures. Presently, most hospitals utilize digitized data of health, programmed medical nursing and cure handling devices and other related uses to facilitate these procedures. In the context of Health 4.0, the aim is to seamlessly integrate all relevant services for in-patient care, ensuring optimal accessibility for all stakeholders. For instance, an integrated application could streamline the admission process by promptly accessing all available patient records, potentially connecting with other healthcare services for added data. Subsequently, it could allocate essential resources such as rooms or beds, doctors, nursing, and service staff. Additionally, the application could interface with eating facilities to accommodate nutritional limitations, thereby customizing daily food according to the patient's illness [22]. Moreover, it could manage nursing devices, incident alerts, and suppository schedule. Further functionalities may include scheduling tasks like sample collection, initiating surgery preparations, and updating visit limits. Lastly, such applications can facilitate release processes by sending automatic remedies to pharmacies, printing home care advices, alerting caregivers with updated instructions, and seamlessly connecting to the patient's smart devices for continued nursing and guidance post-discharge.

Home Care: In addition to outdated patients requiring provisional home care (post-surgery or wound), there is a growing population of elder grownups in need of home care due to age-linked problems. Based on the World Health Organization (WHO), chronic non-communicable illnesses predominantly distressing older individuals impose significant burdens on healthcare systems. Consequently, there is a burgeoning demand for capabilities aimed at enabling older adults to prolong their independence, mobility, and self-care at home. Health 4.0 offers the potential to integrate various services to support this objective. An application could be developed to monitor patients at home, manage medication reminders, alert healthcare providers during emergencies, and facilitate connections with necessary healthcare services. Additionally, bio-measurement devices could be united to provide a constant view of the patient's state [50]. This approach offers greater flexibility for healthcare providers and optimizes resource utilization based on individual patient needs. Furthermore, MCPS applications can join with community caregivers to monitor patients within their area and ensure prompt responses when necessary. This proactive approach may delay the need for devoted in-home caregivers, as medical wants are promptly addressed. By aggregating and making patient data accessible to healthcare providers, these applications can reduce the need for follow-up visits and routine check-ups.

Personal Medicare: The pinnacle achievement of Health 4.0 applications lies in personalized healthcare. The applications outlined in the preceding categories serve as the foundation for achieving this goal by providing tailored prevention and treatment plans for individual patients [34]. By integrating data collected across various domains and leveraging advanced analysis and imagining methods, healthcare specialists can make more precise valuations and offer highly specific solutions for each case. For instance, consider two patients both woe from heart illness, but each with distinct medical backgrounds, lifestyles, and genetic predispositions to other conditions. While both may require similar treatment for their heart condition, their overall treatment plans are likely to differ significantly to accommodate these variations. Furthermore, this comprehensive understanding can lead to better insights into which medications or treatments are most effective for each patient, mitigate potential adverse effects of treatments, and enable dynamic adjustments based on evolving circumstances.

4.2 MCPS for Medical Professionals

Healthcare professionals, aside from patients, stand to gain significantly from the integration of Health 4.0 applications into their work environments. These applications offer opportunities to enhance working situations, systematize routine tasks, and incorporate innovative smart services to augment their capabilities [51]. Given the vast amounts of data collected, stored, and analyzed by MCPS applications, valuable insights can be gleaned regarding personnel performance and task execution, leading to the development of applications aimed at streamlining and optimizing personnel management.

Personnel Management: Managing healthcare personnel is notoriously complex, given the diverse array of roles, varying skill levels, round-the-clock schedules, and extensive resources involved. MCPS applications utilize data analytics to backing managers in assessing working events, scheduling staff, allocating resources, and addressing patient treatment needs [30]. These applications can provide decision-making support tools, enabling administrators to review current operations, forecast future requirements, and explore potential changes. Moreover, healthcare professionals can benefit from analytics models that identify disease patterns, health trends, and personalized treatment plans for patients. By alleviating healthcare professionals of mundane tasks, Health 4.0 applications empower them to focus more on delivering quality care.

Arrangement: Arranging the schedules of health experts such as doctors, surgeons, nurses, and therapists involves numerous complexities, including factors like specialization, experience level, shifts, mandate fluctuations, and resource availability.

MCPS applications can leverage data on personnel, resources, demand levels, and historical data to develop optimized schedules using advanced algorithms [41]. These applications can also create contingency plans and accommodate emergencies, providing professionals with better schedules, predictable necessities, and an better work atmosphere.

Vindicating Fatigue: Health workers face immense pressure to perform their duties effectively amidst high demand and limited resources. Engaging in routine, repetitive tasks, such as data entry during patient visits, can exacerbate this pressure and lead to burnout. Health 4.0 applications can alleviate this burden by facilitating better scheduling, providing access to necessary resources, streamlining work processes, and automating tasks. For instance, implementing dictation tools for doctors to record patient notes during consultations can minimize time spent on administrative tasks [38]. Advanced technologies like natural language processing and smart medical interpretation algorithms can ensure accuracy in transcribing dictated data. Additionally, personalized wellness features integrated into Health 4.0 applications can guide healthcare professionals toward adopting healthier practices, enhancing efficiency, and effectively managing personal and professional challenges.

Resource Accessibility: Health workers need entree to many resources, including conference rooms, analytic devices, operating rooms, and things like caring gear and analytic gears. Allocating and managing these resources efficiently can be challenging, particularly when certain clearances or scheduling are required [22]. MCPS works combined with innovative controllers can deliver a comprehensive view of existing funds, improve scheduling of common properties, warrant nonstop accessibility of goods, and track usage, waste, and shortages. By analyzing this data over time, healthcare facilities can identify overutilized resources, underutilized resources, and abnormal usage patterns, allowing for process optimization and increased resource accessibility.

Collaboration: Effective collaboration among healthcare personnel within and across facilities is crucial for patient care. Healthcare professionals often need to consult with colleagues, experts, and administrators, as well as collaborate with external entities such as equipment suppliers, transportation companies, and insurance providers. MCPS adoption facilitates connectivity across all system components, enabling seamless communication, data exchange, virtual meetings, and online collaboration both within and between healthcare systems [29].

Remote Access: Many healthcare facilities lack access to advanced equipment and expertise, necessitating remote access to specialized resources. Health 4.0 connectivity enables secure and convenient remote access to equipment and expertise unique to specific facilities. For instance, facilities with advanced MRI analysis tools can offer their services to other facilities remotely, with defined terms, costs, and policies managed through MCPS platforms [30]. Advanced skills like blockchain can more improve distant access by facilitating secure data exchange, creating usage contracts, and tracking dealings.

5 Key Challenges and Future Perspectives

Adopting MCPS to enhance healthcare efficiency and quality offers opportunities to improve various aspects of healthcare and introduce value-added functionalities that current systems may lack. However, several challenges must be addressed for the successful implementation and adoption of MCPS. These challenges also present opportunities for enhancement through MCPS integration. Some examples of these issues include:

Fragmented and incompatible health records: Addressing the fragmentation and lack of compatibility among medical records and health data across different divisions within healthcare providers and multiple providers.

Standardized data representation: Overcoming the absence of standardized data representation models and interfaces across various applications within healthcare systems.

Enhanced data collection: Implementing improved methods for continuous and fine-grain data collection in healthcare areas to enable advanced analytics, decision-making, and the integration of smart features.

Data privacy and protection: Developing effective models to ensure data privacy and protection for patients, staff, healthcare organizations, and all entities involved in the healthcare value chain.

Secure data sharing: Providing secure methods for managing the sharing and exchange of medical records, health data, and organizational information across multiple healthcare providers while addressing access policies and privacy concerns.

Automation and monitoring: Introducing efficient automation tools and monitoring services for healthcare records, procedures, and operations.

Process optimization: Assisting healthcare systems managers in designing leaner processes with increased reliance on technology to achieve optimized operations and reduced costs.

Resource utilization analysis: Analyzing resource usage and operational expenditure in detail to identify optimization methods that enhance resource utilization and sharing.

Intelligent techniques and algorithms: Integrating intelligent techniques and algorithms for smart operations, improved forecasting [52], and improved picturing tools.

Flexibility for technological changes: Creating mechanisms to accommodate and adopt emerging technologies seamlessly, including the mixing of new policies, apparatus and services.

Secure collaboration: Implementing secure cooperative methods to ease cooperation among diverse health workers and linked industries [41], streamlining workflows, enhancing the supply chain, identifying faults, identifying trends [53], and predicting future needs.

6 Conclusion

This paper scrutinizes the structure and uses of Medical Cyber-Physical Systems (MCPS), analyzing technologies showcased in articles published on Scopus between 2020 and 2023. It investigates CPS systems and their role in healthcare, catering to both patients and medical practitioners. Key challenges and forthcoming outlooks regarding MCPS and healthcare are discussed, emphasizing the transformative influence of medical CPS approaches on the healthcare sector. Special attention is given to data security concerns, particularly in managing the vast datasets associated with individual patients.

References

1. Tyagi AK, Aswathy SU, Aghila G, Sreenath N (2021) AARIN: Affordable, accurate, reliable and innovative mechanism to protect a medical cyber-physical system using blockchain technology. Int J Intell Networks 2:175–183. https://doi.org/10.1016/j.ijin.2021.09.007
2. Alruwaili FF, Alabduallah B, Alqahtani H, Salama AS, Mohammed GP, Alneil AA (2023) Blockchain Enabled Smart Healthcare System Using Jellyfish Search Optimization With Dual-Pathway Deep Convolutional Neural Network. IEEE Access 11:87583–87591. https://doi.org/10.1109/ACCESS.2023.3304269
3. Shen Z, Ding F, Jolfaei A, Yadav K, Vashisht S, Yu K (2023) DeformableGAN: Generating Medical Images With Improved Integrity for Healthcare Cyber Physical Systems. IEEE Trans Netw Sci Eng 10:2584–2596. https://doi.org/10.1109/TNSE.2022.3190765
4. Ramasamy LK, Khan F, Shah M, Prasad BVVS, Iwendi C, Biamba C (2022) Secure Smart Wearable Computing through Artificial Intelligence-Enabled Internet of Things and Cyber-Physical Systems for Health Monitoring. Sensors 22:1076. https://doi.org/10.3390/s22031076
5. Gan W, Hu K, Huang G, Chien W-C, Chao H-C, Meng W (2023) Data Analytic for Healthcare Cyber Physical System. IEEE Trans Netw Sci Eng 10:2490–2502. https://doi.org/10.1109/TNSE.2023.3278674
6. Lian Z, Yang Q, Wang W, Zeng Q, Alazab M, Zhao H, Su C (2022) DEEP-FEL: Decentralized, Efficient and Privacy-Enhanced Federated Edge Learning for Healthcare Cyber Physical Systems. IEEE Trans Netw Sci Eng 9:3558–3569. https://doi.org/10.1109/TNSE.2022.3175945
7. Ravichandran D, Praveenkumar P, Rajagopalan S, Rayappan JBB, Amirtharajan R (2021) ROI-based medical image watermarking for accurate tamper detection, localisation and recovery. Med Biol Eng Comput 59:1355–1372. https://doi.org/10.1007/s11517-021-02374-2
8. Cui Z, Zhang Z, Hu Z, Geng S, Chen J (2022) A Many-Objective Optimization Based Intelligent High Performance Data Processing Model for Cyber-Physical-Social Systems. IEEE Trans Netw Sci Eng 9:3825–3834. https://doi.org/10.1109/TNSE.2021.3073911

9. Yi X, Wu J, Li G, Bashir AK, Li J, AlZubi AA (2023) Recurrent Semantic Learning-Driven Fast Binary Vulnerability Detection in Healthcare Cyber Physical Systems. IEEE Trans Netw Sci Eng 10:2537–2550. https://doi.org/10.1109/TNSE.2022.3199990
10. Choudhary G, Astillo PV, You I, Yim K, Chen I-R, Cho J-H (2020) Lightweight Misbehavior Detection Management of Embedded IoT Devices in Medical Cyber Physical Systems. IEEE Trans Netw Serv Manag 17:2496–2510. https://doi.org/10.1109/TNSM.2020.3007535
11. Narayanan VL (2023) Reinforcement learning in wind energy - a review. Int J Green Energy 1–24. https://doi.org/10.1080/15435075.2023.2281329
12. V. L. Narayanan and R. Ramakrishnan (2021) Pitch Control of a Digital Hydraulics Pitch System for Wind Turbine Based on Neuro-Fuzzy Digital Pitch Controller. Int J Renew Energy Res. https://doi.org/10.20508/ijrer.v11i1.11626.g8153
13. Narayanan VL, Mathew AT (2022) Experimental investigation on load mitigation of a 5 MW wind turbine in digital fluid power pitch system test rig based on predictive load mitigation controller. Energy Sources, Part A Recover Util Environ Eff 44:7194–7216. https://doi.org/10.1080/15567036.2022.2107120
14. Narayanan VL, Ramakrishnan R, Rengaswamy R (2022) Real-Time testing of novel robust digital pitch controller for digital hydraulic pitch system in wind turbine. Energy Sources, Part A Recover Util Environ Eff 44:3477–3496. https://doi.org/10.1080/15567036.2022.2064944
15. Al-Ghuraybi HA, AlZain MA, Soh B (2023) Ensuring authentication in Medical Cyber-Physical Systems: A comprehensive literature review of blockchain technology integration with machine learning. Multimed Tools Appl. https://doi.org/10.1007/s11042-023-17065-3
16. Verma R (2022) Smart City Healthcare Cyber Physical System: Characteristics, Technologies and Challenges. Wirel Pers Commun 122:1413–1433. https://doi.org/10.1007/s11277-021-08955-6
17. Qiu H, Qiu M, Liu M, Memmi G (2020) Secure Health Data Sharing for Medical Cyber-Physical Systems for the Healthcare 4.0. IEEE J Biomed Heal Informatics 24:2499–2505. https://doi.org/10.1109/JBHI.2020.2973467
18. Roy PK, Singh A, Desai JV, Singh SK (2023) Healthcare Data Security Using Lightweight Protocol for Cyber Physical System. IEEE Trans Netw Sci Eng 10:2597–2606. https://doi.org/10.1109/TNSE.2022.3186437
19. Ganesan A, Paul A, Nagabushnam G, Gul MJJ (2021) Human-in-the-Loop Predictive Analytics Using Statistical Learning. J Healthc Eng 2021:1–14. https://doi.org/10.1155/2021/9955635
20. Lakhan A, Mohammed MA, Nedoma J, Martinek R, Tiwari P, Kumar N (2023) Blockchain-Enabled Cybersecurity Efficient IIOHT Cyber-Physical System for Medical Applications. IEEE Trans Netw Sci Eng 10:2466–2479. https://doi.org/10.1109/TNSE.2022.3213651
21. Ding D, Han Q-L, Ge X, Wang J (2021) Secure State Estimation and Control of Cyber-Physical Systems: A Survey. IEEE Trans Syst Man, Cybern Syst 51:176–190. https://doi.org/10.1109/TSMC.2020.3041121
22. Bao Y, Qiu W, Cheng X (2023) Privacy-preserving and fine-grained data sharing for resource-constrained healthcare <scp>CPS</scp> devices. Expert Syst 40. https://doi.org/10.1111/exsy.13220
23. Zhuang Q, Xiao M, Ding J, Yang Q, Cao J, Zheng WX (2023) Spatiotemporal Evolution Control of Malicious Virus Propagation in Cyber Physical Systems Via PD Feedback Control. IEEE Trans Control Netw Syst 1–12. https://doi.org/10.1109/TCNS.2023.3340288
24. Hossain MS, Shorfuzzaman M (2023) MetaParkinson: A Cyber-Physical Deep Meta-Learning Framework for n-Shot Diagnosis and Monitoring of Parkinson's Patients. IEEE Syst J 17:5251–5260. https://doi.org/10.1109/JSYST.2023.3308333
25. Qianmin S, Wei P, Xiaoqiong C, Hongxing L, Jihan H (2023) COVID-19 clinical medical relationship extraction based on MPNet. IET Cyber-Physical Syst Theory Appl 8:119–129. https://doi.org/10.1049/cps2.12049
26. Kumar M, Chand S (2022) A Provable Secure and Lightweight Smart Healthcare Cyber-Physical System With Public Verifiability. IEEE Syst J 16:5501–5508. https://doi.org/10.1109/JSYST.2021.3120553

27. Singh D, Kaur M, Kumar V, Jabarulla MY, Lee H-N (2022) Artificial Intelligence-Based Cyber-Physical System for Severity Classification of Chikungunya Disease. IEEE J Transl Eng Heal Med 10:1–9. https://doi.org/10.1109/JTEHM.2022.3171078
28. Condry M, Quan XI (2021) Digital Health Innovation, Informatics Opportunity, and Challenges. IEEE Eng Manag Rev 49:81–88. https://doi.org/10.1109/EMR.2021.3054330
29. Shu H, Qi P, Huang Y, Chen F, Xie D, Sun L (2020) An Efficient Certificateless Aggregate Signature Scheme for Blockchain-Based Medical Cyber Physical Systems. Sensors 20:1521. https://doi.org/10.3390/s20051521
30. Condry MW, Quan XI (2023) Remote Patient Monitoring Technologies and Markets. IEEE Eng Manag Rev 51:59–64. https://doi.org/10.1109/EMR.2023.3285688
31. Bharathi. V, Vinoth Kumar CNS (2022) A real time health care cyber attack detection using ensemble classifier. Comput Electr Eng 101:108043. https://doi.org/10.1016/j.compeleceng.2022.108043
32. Liu W, Zhao F, Shankar A, Maple C, Peter JD, Kim B-G, Slowik A, Parameshachari BD, Lv J (2024) Explainable AI for Medical Image Analysis in Medical Cyber-Physical Systems: Enhancing Transparency and Trustworthiness of IoMT. IEEE J Biomed Heal Informatics 1–12. https://doi.org/10.1109/JBHI.2023.3336721
33. Almaiah MA, Hajjej F, Ali A, Pasha MF, Almomani O (2022) A Novel Hybrid Trustworthy Decentralized Authentication and Data Preservation Model for Digital Healthcare IoT Based CPS. Sensors 22:1448. https://doi.org/10.3390/s22041448
34. Premalatha G, Bai VT (2022) Wireless IoT and Cyber-Physical System for Health Monitoring Using Honey Badger Optimized Least-Squares Support-Vector Machine. Wirel Pers Commun 124:3013–3034. https://doi.org/10.1007/s11277-022-09500-9
35. Karatas M, Eriskin L, Deveci M, Pamucar D, Garg H (2022) Big Data for Healthcare Industry 4.0: Applications, challenges and future perspectives. Expert Syst Appl 200:116912. https://doi.org/10.1016/j.eswa.2022.116912
36. Lv Z, Singh AK (2024) Edge-Cloud-Based Wearable Computing for Automation Empowered Virtual Rehabilitation. IEEE Trans Autom Sci Eng 1–14. https://doi.org/10.1109/TASE.2023.3289908
37. Egala BS, Pradhan AK, Badarla V, Mohanty SP (2022) iBlock: An Intelligent Decentralised Blockchain-based Pandemic Detection and Assisting System. J Signal Process Syst 94:595–608. https://doi.org/10.1007/s11265-021-01704-9
38. Ragno L, Borboni A, Vannetti F, Amici C, Cusano N (2023) Application of Social Robots in Healthcare: Review on Characteristics, Requirements, Technical Solutions. Sensors 23:6820. https://doi.org/10.3390/s23156820
39. Adil M, Khan MK, Jadoon MM, Attique M, Song H, Farouk A (2023) An AI-Enabled Hybrid Lightweight Authentication Scheme for Intelligent IoMT Based Cyber-Physical Systems. IEEE Trans Netw Sci Eng 10:2719–2730. https://doi.org/10.1109/TNSE.2022.3159526
40. Wazid M, Thapliyal S, Singh DP, Das AK, Shetty S (2023) Design and Testbed Experiments of User Authentication and Key Establishment Mechanism for Smart Healthcare Cyber Physical Systems. IEEE Trans Netw Sci Eng 10:2697–2709. https://doi.org/10.1109/TNSE.2022.3163201
41. Ch R, Srivastava G, Nagasree YLV, Ponugumati A, Ramachandran S (2022) Robust Cyber-Physical System Enabled Smart Healthcare Unit Using Blockchain Technology. Electronics 11:3070. https://doi.org/10.3390/electronics11193070
42. Ahmed CM, Palleti VR, Mishra VK (2022) A practical physical watermarking approach to detect replay attacks in a CPS. J Process Control 116:136–146. https://doi.org/10.1016/j.jprocont.2022.06.002
43. Khan HA, Sehatbakhsh N, Nguyen LN, Callan RL, Yeredor A, Prvulovic M, Zajic A (2019) IDEA: Intrusion Detection through Electromagnetic-Signal Analysis for Critical Embedded and Cyber-Physical Systems. IEEE Trans Dependable Secur Comput 1–1. https://doi.org/10.1109/TDSC.2019.2932736
44. Sodhro AH, Zahid N (2021) AI-Enabled Framework for Fog Computing Driven E-Healthcare Applications. Sensors 21:8039. https://doi.org/10.3390/s21238039

45. Al-Jaroodi J, Mohamed N, Abukhousa E (2020) Health 4.0: On the Way to Realizing the Healthcare of the Future. IEEE Access 8:211189–211210. https://doi.org/10.1109/ACCESS.2020.3038858
46. Hassan MU, Rehmani MH, Chen J (2020) Differential Privacy Techniques for Cyber Physical Systems: A Survey. IEEE Commun Surv Tutorials 22:746–789. https://doi.org/10.1109/COMST.2019.2944748
47. Guo J, Tian S, Xian H, Gao L, Xiang J, Yang Y, Yan Z, Ning Y, Liu K, Guo J (2021) Cyber–Physical Healthcare System With Blood Test Module on Broadcast Television Network for Remote Cardiovascular Disease (CVD) Management. IEEE Trans Ind Informatics 17:3663–3670. https://doi.org/10.1109/TII.2020.3010280
48. Yohanandhan RV, Elavarasan RM, Manoharan P, Mihet-Popa L (2020) Cyber-Physical Power System (CPPS): A Review on Modeling, Simulation, and Analysis With Cyber Security Applications. IEEE Access 8:151019–151064. https://doi.org/10.1109/ACCESS.2020.3016826
49. Kadhum Idrees A, Saieed Khlief M (2023) A new lossless electroencephalogram compression technique for fog computing-based IoHT networks. Int J Commun Syst 36. https://doi.org/10.1002/dac.5572
50. Do Q, Martini B, Choo K-KR (2018) Cyber-physical systems information gathering: A smart home case study. Comput Networks 138:1–12. https://doi.org/10.1016/j.comnet.2018.03.024
51. Seiger R, Huber S, Schlegel T (2018) Toward an execution system for self-healing workflows in cyber-physical systems. Softw Syst Model 17:551–572. https://doi.org/10.1007/s10270-016-0551-z
52. Dhaked DK, Dadhich S, Birla D (2023) Power output forecasting of solar photovoltaic plant using LSTM. Green Energy Intell Transp 2:100113. https://doi.org/10.1016/j.geits.2023.100113
53. Dhaked DK, Kumar P, Ganguly S (2024) Development of Data Driven Model for Proton Exchange Membrane Fuel Cell Using Machine Learning Approaches. In: 2024 IEEE 3rd International Conference on Control, Instrumentation, Energy & Communication (CIEC). pp 67–72

Role of Intelligent Techniques for Cyber-Physical Systems in Healthcare

Kajalben Tanchak, Shilpa Singhal, Ankita Mishra, and Om Prakash Suthar

Abstract The merging of computer and physical aspects is revolutionizing healthcare via Cyber-Physical Systems (CPS). The capabilities and security of CPS are enhanced by machine learning, AI, and data analytics. The data collected and analyzed by these systems comes from interconnected systems, medical equipment, and interactions with patients. Data analytics and predictive modeling allow CPS to find patterns and outliers in patient data, which speeds up disease diagnostics, predicts adverse occurrences, and develops personalized treatment programmes. Advanced algorithms in CPS enhance patient safety and care by continuously monitoring vital signs, medication doses, and responses in real time. Secure data exchange, backed by anomaly detection tools and secure communication mechanisms, is crucial for networked CPS to protect patient information. By analyzing past data, predicting future patient flow, and allocating resources efficiently, decision support systems within CPS optimize healthcare resources, leading to improved operational efficiency and cost savings. The chapter highlights the necessity for inventive techniques to overcome the inherent complexity of healthcare CPS while covering the most significant components and aspects. Next, it delves into the ways in which intelligent methods, such as decision support systems, predictive analytics, and real-time monitoring, could enhance healthcare CPS. It looks at the benefits and drawbacks of each use, as well as recent developments and market trends. Cybersecurity and the preservation of patient data are two of the healthcare CPS privacy and safety concerns covered in this chapter.

Keywords Cyber-physical systems (CPS) · Cybersecurity · Healthcare cyber-physical systems (HCPS) · Predictive modeling · Healthcare system

K. Tanchak (✉) · S. Singhal · O. P. Suthar
Marwadi University, Rajkot, India
e-mail: tanchakkajal123@gmail.com

A. Mishra
Banasthali University, Tonk, Rajasthan, India

M. Mittal and J. Narayan (eds.), *Intelligent Cyber-Physical Systems for Healthcare Solutions*, https://doi.org/10.1007/978-981-97-8983-2_4

1 Introduction

The integration of intelligent methods with Cyber-Physical Systems (CPS) has become a guiding light of progress and change in the dynamic field of contemporary healthcare [1–3]. This merging represents a significant change in the way healthcare is thought of, provided, and perceived. At its core, the Role of Intelligent Techniques for Cyber-Physical Systems in Healthcare is a strategy that unites the worlds of physical equipment and processes with the capabilities of cutting-edge tools like Artificial Intelligence, Machine learning, and real-time data analytics [4, 5] as shown in Fig. 1.

"Intelligent techniques" encompass a wide range of cutting-edge tools that can understand, process, and understand data in order to draw conclusions and make choices based on that knowledge. Cyber-physical systems, on the other hand, integrate digital processing and communication with the real world [6, 7]. This integration, when applied to healthcare, means coordinating technology that combines digital and physical aspects in a way that improves patient care, streamlines healthcare operations, and changes clinical procedures.

The goal of incorporating smart methods into healthcare CPS is to use technology to solve complicated problems in the healthcare system. Its goals include improving diagnostic accuracy, providing individualized treatment options, enabling real-time patient monitoring, and empowering healthcare personnel with data-driven insights. Furthermore, this approach seeks to streamline administrative trials and optimize the utilization of existing resources in order to allow the transfer of more operations and PCHS (Patient-Centric Healthcare Services). Various circumstances can benefit from the intelligent strategies used in healthcare CPS. There is a vast range of applications for these methods, from improving surgical precision with robotic aid

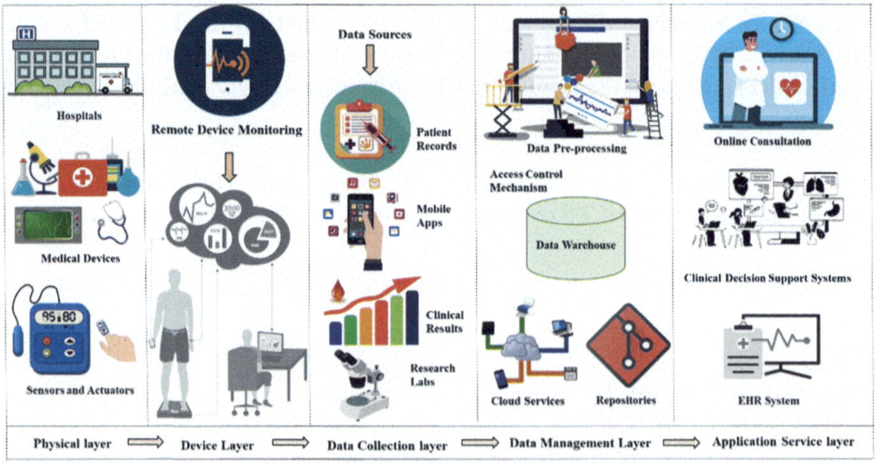

Fig. 1 A basic component diagram of intelligent CPS in healthcare

to giving doctors evidence-based clinical decision support [8]. Among their many uses, the power telemedicine services, allow for constant patient monitoring via networked devices, and propel predictive analytics for preventative healthcare interventions. Disease detection, treatment planning, and medical research are all expected to undergo revolutionary changes because of the application of AI and ML, which enables the identification of significant patterns from comprehensive datasets.

Improvements in efficiency, accuracy, and patient-centeredness in healthcare delivery are the key motivations for integrating intelligent approaches into healthcare CPS. The goals of this strategy are to boost the precision of diagnoses, the efficacy of treatments, the decrease of medical mistakes, and the quality of life for patients. At the same time, it hopes to free up medical staff from paperwork so they can devote more time to providing direct care to patients and making important medical decisions. Our ultimate goal is to revolutionize healthcare by making it more accessible and efficient through the use of technology.

Intelligent Techniques for Cyber-Physical Systems in Healthcare, in essence, represents a technological revolution in healthcare that goes beyond traditional methods. In it, the goals of improving healthcare services generally, providing prompt and accurate care, and using data to make educated decisions are embodied. In the future, a more connected, responsive, and efficient healthcare ecosystem will be possible thanks to this mutually beneficial relationship between technology and healthcare, namely intelligence driven CPS.

Integration of the digital and physical domains is achieved through a cyber-physical system (CPS). Interactions between individuals can become smarter as a result. An analytical system that can intelligently adapt to rapidly shifting real-world settings by combining data from physical devices like sensors and cameras with data from digital ones. CPS has several potential uses, including in intelligent healthcare systems, assisted living facilities, environmental management systems, and transportation systems.

Intelligent CPS approaches have the potential to revolutionize healthcare, but there are still obstacles to be overcome, such as protecting patients' personal information, overcoming barriers to interoperability, and integrating with existing systems without disrupting patient care. These obstacles are, however, being overcome as technology develops, opening the path for a future in which CPS-driven intelligent solutions are fundamental to the healthcare ecosystem.

The target of this chapter is to inspect recent developments in the application of intelligent approaches for CPS in the medical field. Insights into the innovative opportunities for improving patient care and safety in the years ahead can be gained by assessing the benefits, challenges, and prospective uses of these technologies, providing a holistic picture of how intelligent CPS is redefining healthcare.

2 Healthcare Cyber-Physical Systems Levels

The hierarchy of healthcare CPS consists of the following (Fig. 2):

- Unit-Level HCPS
- Integration-Level HCPS
- System-Level HCPS
- Acceptance-Level HCPS
- Evolutionary-Level HCPS

(A) Unit-Level HCPS

Unit Level systems, which serve as the foundational level of healthcare cyber physical systems, are responsible for monitoring and controlling patients in critical care units and other hospital settings. Currently, it collects data from the health actuators connected to the patient and transmits it to the intelligent systems responsible for evaluating and regulating various parameters, including as heat rate, pressure, temperature and so on. The medical personnel is also linked to the HCPS network, enabling them to promptly get updates and guidance from healthcare experts.

(B) Integration-Level HCPS

During the second phase of HCPS, hospitals collaborate with interconnected residences to provide patients with remote monitoring and healthcare services. Hospitals can collaborate with intelligent ambulances to monitor the real-time condition of critically ill patients during transportation and proactively prepare for emergencies by assuring the availability of essential resources such as beds and ventilators.

(C) System-Level HCPS

The third stage of a Healthcare Cyber Physical System (HCPS) entails the integration of multiple independent systems that collaborate to build a Smart City Healthcare Cyber Physical System. Patients receive high-quality healthcare through an interconnected system where the smart grid serves as the primary energy source and the

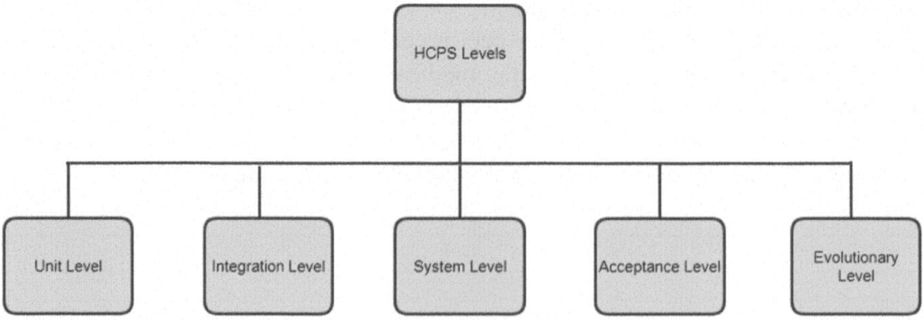

Fig. 2 HCPS system levels

foundation for various cyber physical systems, including smart ambulances, smart homes, smart hospitals and smart hospital manufacturing units.

(D) Acceptance-Level HCPS

Researchers, technicians, engineers, health professionals, and academics collaborate at the acceptance stage of the healthcare delivery process to establish norms and standards that will streamline the implementation of the healthcare ecosystem, ensuring its efficiency and effectiveness.

(E) Evolutionary-Level HCPS

HCPS systems at an advanced evolutionary stage are optimal for the future due to their inherent ability to autonomously adapt and operate. Cyber physical systems with self-adaptation capabilities utilize historical data to guide their current activities. The dynamic nature of cyber-physical systems necessitates the vital and substantial role of evolutionary behavior.

Actuators, sensors, and physical machines that are controlled by external inputs, such as mobile devices, at the dew layer and systems at the cyber level, are just a few examples of the various sorts of devices found in CPS. Data formats may be organized or unstructured, and the I/O of various devices use different forms, calling for format translation via interfaces. When it comes to the efficacy and dependability of Healthcare Cyber Physical Systems, Time is of the essence. Seconds or microseconds of delay in dosing patients can compromise the system's efficacy and dependability. For optimal performance, CPS require constant control and monitoring, giving rise to the concept of a Health-monitoring system (HMS) for CPS. Health Monitoring System (HMS) has a dual function: it assesses the condition of each physical component of the Cyber-Physical System (CPS) and employs a preventive approach to determine the likelihood of the CPS being in a state of good health. A passive monitoring technique would be to examine behavioral models of physical components, while an active technique involves identifying anomalies by responding to stimuli.

2.1 Advancements in Healthcare CPS

Feeling the effects of the recent epidemic, the global healthcare system has experienced unprecedented strain, compelling medical professionals and healthcare workers to endure extended working hours and demanding conditions. Smart-City-Healthcare-Cyber-Physical-Systems integration is crucial for the future of healthcare systems, and technology is emerging as a key catalyst in this endeavor. Cyber Physical Systems (CPS) represent a dynamic application realm where an array of technologies coalesce to facilitate intelligent and efficient interactions among interconnected devices [9]. Notably, We rely on the internet as our foundation for CPS's communication infrastructure, contributing significantly to the development of other important technologies such Cloud Computing [10], the IoT [11], and blockchain [12]. Within the context of healthcare cyber physical systems, this section explores the significant

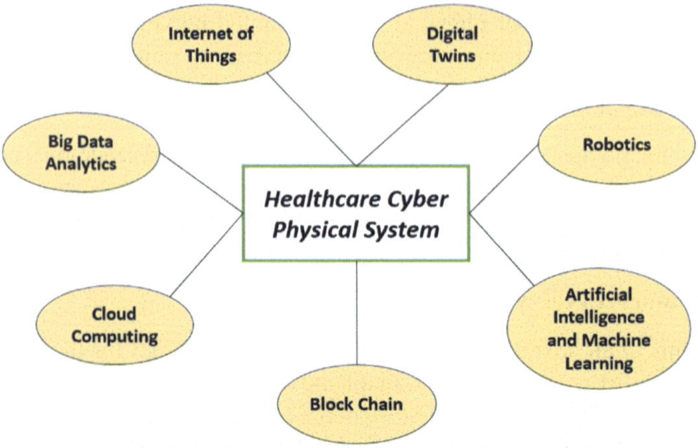

Fig. 3 Technologies in healthcare CPS

contributions made by a variety of technological tools, having digital twins and IoT, as well as big data, cloud computing, blockchain, AI, ML, and robots as shown in Fig. 3.

In this context, the recent global pandemic has underscored the pressing need for transformative healthcare solutions. The demands placed upon healthcare professionals and the healthcare system as a whole have spurred the urgency for innovative approaches that streamline patient care, optimize operational efficiency, and foster real-time insights. It is within this context that the concept of Smart-City-Healthcare-Cyber-Physical-Systems emerges as a beacon of hope. At the heart of these systems lies the convergence of diverse technologies that collectively empower a dynamic and interconnected healthcare landscape. The pivotal role of the internet, serving as the connective tissue that binds together disparate technologies, becomes immediately apparent. This interconnectedness serves as a foundation upon which technologies like the Internet-of-Things (IoT) flourish, facilitating seamless message and data exchange among a plethora of medical devices and sensors.

Moreover, the realm of Healthcare CPS draws strength as of advancements like Cloud computing, enabling the storage and retrieval of voluminous patient data with unprecedented ease and scalability. The potency of big data analytics, underpinned by Artificial-Intelligence [13] and Machine learning [14], empowers health care professionals to extract meaningful insights from data, facilitating proactive diagnosis, personalized treatment plans, and predictive analytics to forecast healthcare trends. Blockchain technology, renowned for its data security and transparency attributes, makes a distinctive appearance in this landscape, confirming the integrity and patient information's privacy. Additionally, the advent of robotics [15] and digital twin technology [16] redefines surgical precision, simulation, and diagnostics, elevating healthcare services to new heights of efficiency and accuracy.

As the world navigates the uncharted waters of modern healthcare challenges, the fusion of these groundbreaking technologies unveils a horizon brimming with potential. The Smart-City Healthcare-Cyber-Physical-Systems offer a glimpse into a future where technology becomes an indispensable ally, revolutionizing patient care, augmenting medical expertise, and ushering healthcare into an era of unprecedented efficiency and precision.

3 Lifecycle of Cyber-Physical-Systems in Healthcare

Lifecycle outline depicting the stages involved in the role of intelligent techniques for Cyber-Physical Systems (CPS) in health-care (Fig. 4).

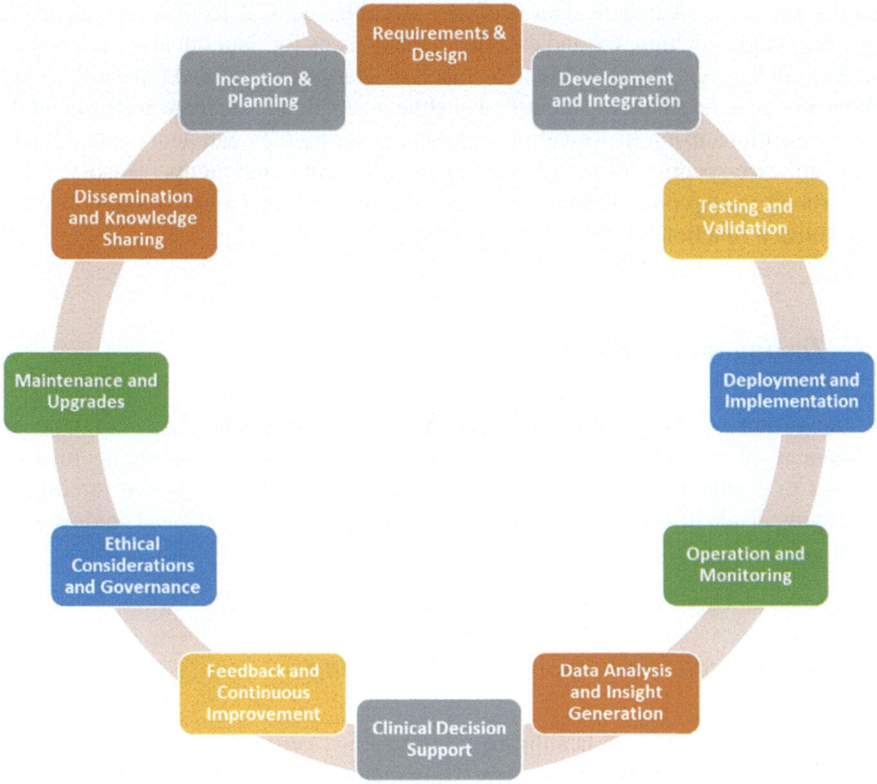

Fig. 4 Lifecycle of cyber-physical systems

3.1 Inception and Planning

Recognize healthcare problems that can benefit from intelligent techniques and CPS integration, such as remote patient monitoring, personalized treatment, or surgical assistance. Clearly outline the goals of integrating intelligent techniques, whether it's improving diagnosis accuracy, enhancing patient care, or optimizing healthcare operations.

3.2 Design and Development

Identify the types of patient data needed, including medical records, sensor readings, and diagnostic images, and establish mechanisms for data integration. Choose suitable intelligent techniques, such as machine learning models, AI algorithms, or robotic systems, based on the identified healthcare challenges. Create and train intelligent algorithms using historical patient data, ensuring they can analyze and interpret healthcare-specific information. Integrate physical components (sensors, actuators, robots) with computational elements (AI systems, communication networks) to establish a functional CPS.

3.3 Testing and Validation

For the purpose of testing the interaction between the physical and computational components of the CPS in a controlled environment, simulations should be utilised. In order to evaluate the efficacy, precision, and safety of the integrated intelligent procedures inside healthcare settings, it is necessary to conduct clinical studies with actual patients [16].

3.4 Deployment and Operation Monitoring

Deploy the CPS in various healthcare environments, verifying that it is functional with the current systems and processes. Train medical staff, patients, and caregivers on how to utilize and communicate with the CPS in an efficient manner. Continuously collect patient data through sensors, wearables, and medical devices to monitor health conditions and gather real-world evidence. Regularly evaluate the performance of intelligent algorithms and CPS components to ensure accurate diagnoses and reliable operations.

3.5 *Data Analysis*

Apply AI and machine learning algorithms to analyze the collected data, extract meaningful patterns, and generate actionable insights. Use historical and real-time data to predict patient conditions, potential complications, and healthcare trends. This provides clinical diagnoses, treatment strategies, and actions based on solid proofs. Encourage the use of both combining the expertise of healthcare professionals with AI-driven insights to generate optimal results.

3.6 *Feedback and Ethical Considerations*

Make it possible for the system to analyze its own performance, make algorithmic adjustments, and gradually increase its accuracy. To pinpoint problem areas and make necessary adjustments, collect input from healthcare providers, patients, and administrators. Applying rigorous security measures will safeguard patient information and guarantee adherence to data protection regulations. Create moral standards for the appropriate application of AI in healthcare, taking into account concerns of equity, transparency, and prejudice.

3.7 *Maintenance and Upgrades*

It is essential to have a constant awareness of the most recent developments in algorithms, software, and hardware components in order to guarantee the highest possible level of performance and to address any problems that may crop up. Check that the physical components of the CPS, such as sensors and robots, are in good working order and that they are being maintained in the appropriate manner.

3.8 *Dissemination and Knowledge Sharing*

Contribute to the healthcare CPS body of knowledge by publishing and presenting research papers, essays, and presentations outlining your results, accomplishments, and problems. Get involved with other healthcare organizations, universities, and IT companies to share knowledge and experiences. Intelligent techniques for Cyber-Physical Systems (CPS) play an important part in healthcare, and this lifecycle lays out the steps required, from creation and planning to monitoring and ethical issues, as well as continual improvement.

4 Role of Intelligent Techniques in Healthcare Cyber-Physical Systems

Intelligent methods play a major role in Healthcare Cyber-Physical Systems (HCPS), which incorporate systems that connect technology for communication and information with healthcare services. These technologies aim to improve the efficiency, precision, and caliber of healthcare delivery while preserving the privacy and security of patient data.

Intelligent techniques like artificial intelligence (AI) and machine learning are transforming many facets of the medical industry. These systems sort through enormous volumes of healthcare data, including sensor readings, medical imaging, and patient information, to find patterns, trends, and possible threats. This could help in the early detection and prevention of illness, which could improve patient outcomes. Personalized medicine is also gaining attention as doctors use cognitive skills to tailor patient therapies based on specific patient characteristics, genetic profiles, and medical records. This approach increases medicinal effectiveness while reducing the possibility of side effects.

In addition, the combination of smart technologies has resulted in the development of virtual health assistants and patient assistance. Telemedicine and remote patient monitoring provide fast access to medical treatment and interventions for people who live in remote regions or have limited mobility. When it comes to medical imaging and diagnostics, intelligent technologies act as decision support tools for medical practitioners, helping them make well-informed decisions about diagnosis, treatment strategies, and prescription medicine recommendations. These systems can review relevant scientific literature and patient information to suggest the best methods of action.

With the health care sector moving toward more digitization, security and privacy issues are more important than ever. Sensitive medical data must be protected from unauthorized access and internet threats using intelligent ways that offer effective cybersecurity solutions [17].

Real-time monitoring is another area where intelligent techniques have brought about change. Healthcare professionals can now quickly identify abnormalities or emergencies by continually monitoring a patient's vital signs. In an emergency, swift alerts allow medical personnel to react immediately, possibly saving lives. Creative approaches also benefit the process of discovering and creating new drugs. Through the analysis of massive datasets, prediction of drug interactions, and identification of viable treatment alternatives, AI-driven solutions reduce the time required to develop novel drugs [18]. Essentially, the possibility of a future defined by enhanced patient care, greater precision, and faster medical advancements is presented by the integration of intelligent approaches across the healthcare spectrum.

When all factors are taken into account, the application of smart techniques in Healthcare Cyber-Physical Systems has the potential to transform the healthcare industry by providing personalized and efficient care while resolving problems with data management, security, and decision-making. Ensuring the ethical application of these technologies and resolving issues related to algorithmic bias and data privacy are crucial.

4.1 Artificial Intelligence in Healthcare CPS

Artificial intelligence (AI) integration in healthcare cyber-physical systems (CPS) has the potential to transform patient outcomes and transform healthcare delivery. CPS are at the forefront of advancing intelligent and networked healthcare systems because they combine computing and networking skills with physical components like sensors and medical equipment [13]. The use of AI in many CPS scenarios in healthcare is essential because it makes breakthroughs in patient monitoring, diagnosis, therapy, and overall healthcare management possible. AI algorithms are essential to medical imaging and diagnosis because they allow pathology slides, X-rays, and MRIs to be analyzed for more precise detection of diseases like cancer and tumors. Additionally, wearables and sensors are used by AI-powered CPS systems to offer real-time analysis of health data, which enables predictive analytics and patient monitoring, fast assistance and customized treatment [19, 20].

In addition, artificial intelligence expedites the identification of promising drug candidates, predicts drug interactions, and analyzes large amounts of biomedical data to speed up the drug research and development process. Another field that AI has a big impact on is precise medicine, where data on a patient's genetics and lifestyle may be analyzed to improve treatment outcomes and customize treatment plans [21]. AI-powered surgical robots and robotics in general are assisting surgeons perform intricate surgeries with greater accuracy and efficiency.

Also, unstructured data from medical literature and electronic health records (EHRs) is being mined by AI-based natural language processing (NLP) tools, which help healthcare professionals in their research and decision-making. Artificial intelligence (AI)-driven chatbots and virtual health assistants are improving patient engagement and access to care by optimizing procedures, making appointments, addressing inquiries from patients, and providing preliminary diagnosis. AI additionally improves patient flow, operational performance, and cost-effectiveness in hospitals and resource management. Conversely, machine learning (ML) approaches in CPS aim to improve real-time monitoring and diagnosis procedures by observing the behavior of interrelated computer and physical components [22].

When it comes to anomaly detection, cybersecurity, fault diagnosis, predictive maintenance, analysis of time-series data, control and optimization, handling resources, self-healing and adaptability, prognostics, and enabling human–machine interaction, machine learning algorithms are excellent. Human operators are able to track and identify CPS behavior with efficiency thanks to ML-powered interfaces and NLP technology [23], which facilitates smooth human-intelligent system collaboration [24].

4.2 *Data Analytics for Predictive Analytics and Decision Support*

Cyber-Physical Systems (CPS) integrate computer-based and physical components to provide data that is evaluated and comprehended using data-driven approaches for decision support and predictive analytics [25]. CPS refers to systems where physical entities, such as sensors, actuators, and machines, are closely coupled with computational and communication aspects in order to monitor, regulate, and optimize complex processes. In this context, data analytics is critical to making sense of the massive volumes of data generated by CPS, facilitating predictive maintenance, optimizing workflows, and supporting decision-making. Below is an in-depth description of data analytics in CPS (Fig. 5).

4.2.1 Data Collection

Data collection is a crucial task in a cyber physical system, data can be collected from a variety of sensors and actuators installed in physical systems. These sensors collect real-time information about the equipment's performance, environmental conditions, physical processes, and other relevant aspects. In order to offer context, CPS may also obtain data from outside sources, such as weather forecasts or market moves.

4.2.2 Preprocessing of the Data

Sensor-collected raw data may contain outliers, noise or missing data. Data cleaning and preparation techniques are used to prepare data for analysis. To ensure accuracy and consistency, this stage involves reducing noise, resolving missing data, and normalizing or scaling the data.

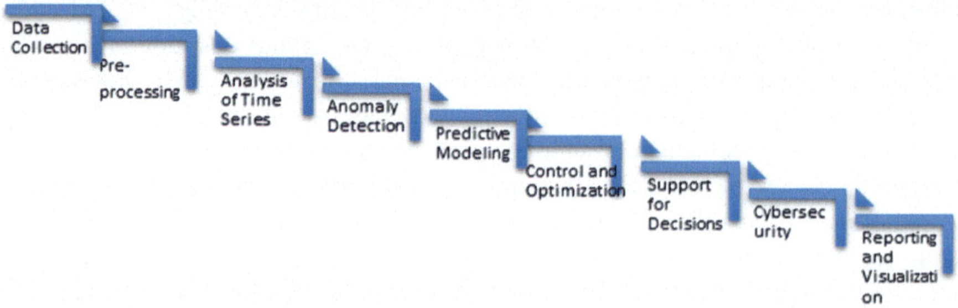

Fig. 5 Illustration for data analytics prediction

4.2.3 Analysis of Time-Series

Time-series presentations of CPS data, which are made up of data points collected at certain points in time, are widely utilized. Time-series analysis is used to identify temporal trends, patterns, and seasonality in data. Techniques for analyzing time series data include autoregressive models, Fourier analysis, and moving averages.

4.2.4 Anomaly Detection

Finding anomalies in CPS data is crucial to identifying possible problems, malfunctions, or unusual activity in the system. Anomaly detection techniques, such as statistical methodology, machine learning algorithms, or pattern recognition, are utilized for recognizing abnormalities from the usual pattern. Combining these methods allows CPS to proactively identify and handle anomalies, reducing risks and guaranteeing the system's dependability and security. Furthermore, in order to keep robust anomaly detection capabilities in CPS and adjust to changing threats, continuous monitoring and improvement of anomaly detection methodologies are essential.

4.2.5 Predictive Modeling

The use of predictive modeling in the CPS is the process of creating models that can predict future conditions or events based on past data. Machine learning methods such as regression, time-series forecasting, and predictive classification models are used to make predictions. For example, predictive maintenance models can predict when equipment may go down, allowing for proactive maintenance.

4.2.6 Control and Optimization

CPS also uses data analytics for optimization and control. Real-time data processing and feedback loops enable adaptive control approaches, allowing physical systems to dynamically alter their behavior in response to external stimuli or changing circumstances. Adaptive control strategies employ data analytics to dynamically change a system's behavior in response to external interruptions, operational needs, or changing environmental conditions. CPS can increase efficiency, robustness, and flexibility by iteratively optimizing operations using data analytics insights and using feedback loops.

4.2.7 Support for Decisions

In CPS, data analytics assists stakeholders in making choices by giving information on system performance, energy efficiency, cost reduction, safety, and other topics. These insights can help decision-makers make informed decisions about risk management, process optimization, and resource allocation.

4.2.8 Cyber Security

Data analytics is essential to CPS cybersecurity because it tracks network activity, finds irregularities, and employs modern techniques like machine learning and anomaly detection to avert cyberattacks before they happen. Through the analysis of data from different CPS sources, including communication networks and sensors, it improves threat detection, even for complex attacks that target both digital and physical components. Furthermore, anticipatory defense tactics based on historical data are made possible by prediction models created through data analytics. All things considered, data analytics improves CPSs resilience, reduces risks, and guarantees system integrity and security.

4.2.9 Reporting and Visualization

The outcomes of data analytics are presented in reports and visualizations to aid decision-making. The functioning of the system is clearly outlined through interactive dashboards and real-time monitoring tools, which also allow stakeholders to react swiftly to shifting circumstances.

In order to provide predictive analytics, control, optimization, and decision support, data analytics in Cyber-Physical Systems entails gathering, preparing, and analyzing data from sensors and other sources. Data analytics insights improve the productivity, dependability, and security of CPS applications across a variety of sectors, including manufacturing, transportation, energy, healthcare, and smart cities.

4.3 Advances and Trends in Intelligent Techniques for Healthcare Cyber-Physical Systems (CPS)

Intelligent approaches have enabled transformative healthcare Cyber-Physical Systems (CPS). This chapter discusses Deep Learning and Neural Networks, IoMT, and AR/VR in Surgical Applications. These cutting-edge technologies could revolutionize patient care, diagnostic accuracy, and surgical outcomes. Healthcare practitioners and researchers who want to use technology to improve treatment must understand these sophisticated methods.

4.3.1 Deep Learning and Neural Networks

(A) Image and Speech Recognition

Deep learning algorithms, especially Convolutional Neural Networks (CNNs), have made great strides in the field of image recognition. For example, they can use X-rays, MRI scans, and pathology slides to identify medical conditions. In the context of speech recognition, Recurrent Neural Networks (RNNs) are employed to achieve precise transcription of medical dictations [26].

(B) Disease Diagnosis and Prognosis

Deep learning models possess the capability to analyze extensive quantities of patient data, encompassing medical records, genetic information, and lifestyle factors, with the aim of aiding in the identification and prediction of diseases. These models provide significant insights into individual optimization treatment plans and preventative strategies.

(C) Drug Discovery

Drug discovery is expedited through the utilization of deep learning techniques, which facilitate the prediction of molecular interactions, the identification of potential drug candidates, and the optimization of drug development procedures. The implementation of this approach has the potential to substantially decrease the duration and expenses associated with the introduction of novel pharmaceutical products into the market.

(D) Predictive Analytics

Predictive Analytics: Neural networks possess the capability to analyze real-time patient data, encompassing vital signs, with the purpose of forecasting unfavorable occurrences and facilitating timely interventions (Fig. 6). This, in turn, leads to enhanced patient outcomes and a decrease in hospital readmissions.

4.3.2 Internet of Medical Things (IoMT)

The "Internet of Medical Things" (IoMT) is a system of medical devices, wearables, and sensors that work together to collect and send patient data, allowing for remote tracking and better healthcare [27].

(A) Remote Patient Monitoring

Remote Patient Monitoring (RPM) is made possible through the Internet of Medical Things (IoMT), which allows for the ongoing monitoring of patients in non-traditional healthcare environments. This technology enables healthcare providers to remotely monitor vital signs, medication adherence, and the progression of diseases. The implementation of a proactive healthcare approach has the potential to mitigate complications and lower rates of hospitalization.

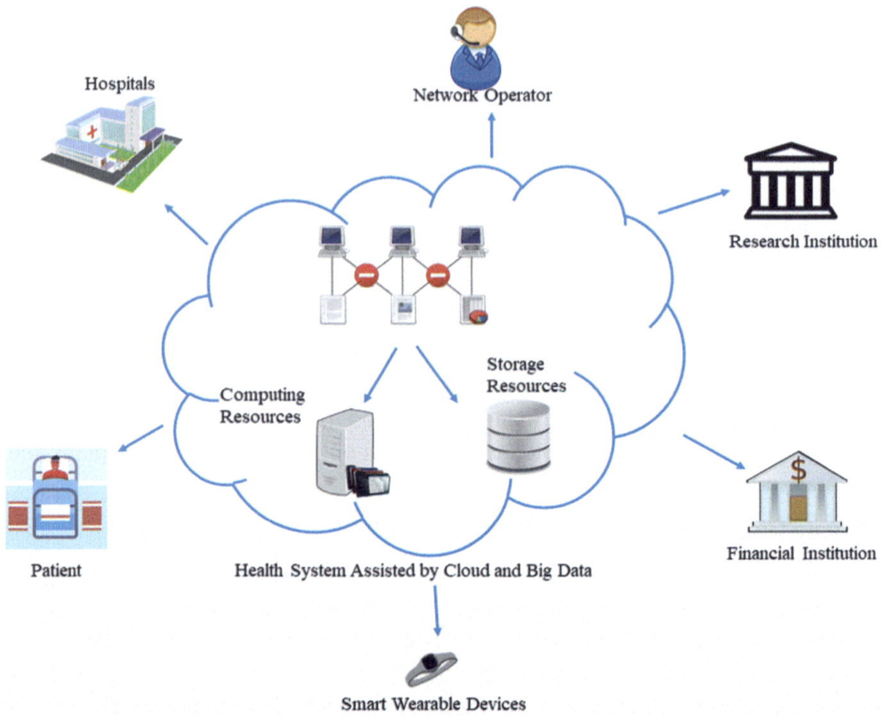

Fig. 6 Illustration for the extended healthcare ecosystem

(B) Real-Time Data Analytics

Health patterns in patients and population health management can be better understood with the use of real-time data analytics made possible by the massive amounts of data collected by IoMT (Internet of Medical Things) devices. It makes it easier to improve care coordination through the use of evidence-based decision-making.

(C) Personalized Healthcare

Patients are given more control over their health care by the personalized health data provided by the Internet of Medical Things (IoMT) devices. On top of that, by considering each patient's distinct health profile, this technology allows doctors to craft individualized treatment plans.

(D) Efficient Resource Utilization

With the use of the Internet of Medical Things (IoMT), healthcare practitioners can access accurate and up-to-date patient condition data, which improves resource allocation. Enhanced resource allocation, shorter wait times, and happier patients are the outcomes of this effort.

4.3.3 Augmented Reality and Virtual Reality in Surgical Applications

Both AR (Augmented Reality) and VR (Virtual Reality) have begun to find widespread use in the field of surgery, where they are transforming surgical education, preparation, and practice.

(A) Surgical Training and Simulation

By combining AR and VR, we can build very lifelike surgical simulators that will help train the next generation of surgeons to perform complex surgeries in a risk-free setting. Improving surgical proficiency, reducing medical errors, and improving patient welfare are all goals of this intervention [28].

(B) Preoperative Planning

While a surgeon is performing surgery, intraoperative guiding uses augmented reality (AR) technology to superimpose crucial information, such as patient records, images, and surgical plans, into their visual field. The accuracy of surgical treatments is enhanced by this technology, which provides real-time guidance.

(C) Intraoperative Guidance

A surgeon can build a three-dimensional model of their patient's anatomy with the use of AR and VR technology. Both the decision-making process and pre-operative planning benefit from this. The level of precision obtained allows for more effective surgical processes and better results for patients.

(D) Telemedicine and Remote Consultations

Technology advancements in augmented and virtual reality have opened up new avenues for remote medical care and counseling. Technological developments have allowed highly trained surgeons to assist in operations and provide remote advice, irrespective of their geographical location. This technique ensures that specialized knowledge is readily available and helps get the word out.

5 Applications of Intelligent Techniques in Healthcare CPS

Intelligent techniques have caused a paradigm shift in healthcare cyber-physical systems (CPS), which has changed the way therapy is given and how it is administered. These methods incorporate several different technologies, including machine learning and artificial intelligence, each having specific uses (Fig. 7).

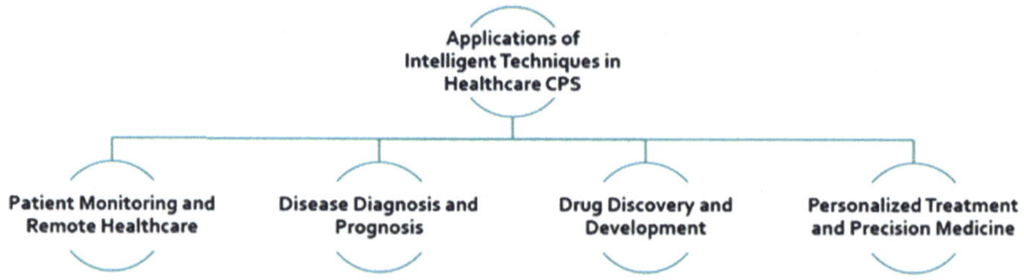

Fig. 7 Applications of HCPS

5.1 Patient Monitoring and Remote Healthcare

Intelligent technologies are used to track patient's health and deliver medical care remotely as part of patient monitoring and remote healthcare [29]. With this strategy shown in Fig. 8, healthcare professionals may continuously monitor patients, even from a distance, and deliver necessary interventions in a timely manner.

Vital signs, activity levels, and other health-related information are monitored by wearable technology, including smartwatches, fitness trackers, and medical sensors. These tools have sensors that can measure a variety of parameters, such as oxygen saturation, body temperature, heart rate, and blood pressure [30].

Connected medical sensors and other wearable devices are an integral part of the IoT ecosystem. They send up-to-the-minute health information to a central hub [30]. The patient data that has been gathered is safely kept in the cloud. Large amounts of patient data can be stored on the cloud in a scalable and convenient manner [31]. To evaluate the incoming data, intelligent algorithms powered by AI and machine

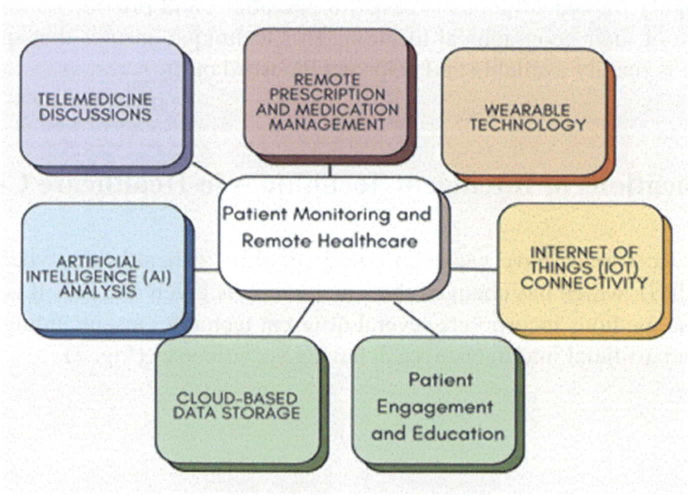

Fig. 8 Patient monitoring and remote healthcare

learning are used. Based on previous patient data, these algorithms can recognize patterns, find abnormalities, and forecast trends.

Using the data being tracked, medical professionals can have online discussions with patients. They can talk about the patient's health, offer medical guidance, and modify treatment plans as appropriate using video conference or chat [32]. Electronic prescriptions and drug management might become much easier with these solutions. Healthcare providers now have the option to remotely prescribe medications and even track patients' adherence to their prescribed pharmaceutical regimens. It is possible for patients to receive customized health records, reminders for upcoming appointments or medication due dates, and disease management tools through the use of element patient engagement in remote healthcare systems.

5.2 Disease Diagnosis and Prognosis

Advanced data analytics, machine learning, and artificial intelligence (AI) algorithms can greatly simplify the diagnosis and prediction of diseases in Cyber-Physical Systems (CPS) [33]. Here are a few instances when sophisticated CPS tactics can be applied.

Utilizing intelligent techniques such as advanced data analytics, machine learning, and artificial intelligence (AI) algorithms in Cyber-Physical Systems (CPS) can greatly simplify the process of diagnosing and forecasting the progression of a disease [3, 4]. Here are a few instances when sophisticated CPS tactics can be applied. The integration of intelligent techniques has led to the emergence of several applications in the field of healthcare cyber-physical systems (CPS), revolutionizing conventional practices. These programmes utilize data collected from diverse sources, including wearable sensors, medical devices, electronic health records, and patient-provided information. The many data streams are merged and examined using sophisticated intelligent data fusion algorithms to provide a comprehensive assessment of a patient's health. The interconnected data environment enables rapid and precise illness diagnosis by leveraging insights derived from the amalgamation of data.

Machine learning algorithms play a crucial role in identifying trends and aiding in the process of making diagnoses. These algorithms analyze patient data to identify subtle trends that can serve as indicators for specific diseases or conditions. Deep learning models excel at detecting abnormalities in images such as X-rays or MRI scans in the domain of medical imaging, hence enhancing diagnosis accuracy [34]. Healthcare professionals can enhance the accuracy of their diagnoses by utilizing these pattern recognition abilities. Early warning systems, which are part of intelligent cyber-physical systems (CPS), continuously monitor and track various health indices of patients. These systems generate alerts when particular parameters deviate from established standards, enabling timely interventions and early detection of illnesses. This real-time monitoring has the potential to significantly improve patient outcomes by facilitating prompt therapy actions.

Intelligent CPS enhances the decision-making process employed by healthcare providers. To offer effective decision assistance, these systems analyze patient data, compare it with pertinent medical literature, and propose suitable therapy. These systems utilize knowledge gained from empirical research to offer appropriate diagnostic procedures, therapy options, and prognosis predictions. Moreover, intelligent cyber-physical systems (CPS) utilize artificial intelligence (AI) to analyze patient data and generate prognostic prediction models. These models evaluate the factors that impact patient outcomes while forecasting the probability of recovery or disease progression. Prognostic models facilitate the selection of suitable treatments and allocation of resources by medical practitioners [35].

An intelligent cyber-physical system (CPS) enables the feasibility of remote patient monitoring, which is especially crucial for managing chronic illnesses. Remote patient data is evaluated using intelligent algorithms, providing instant feedback to both patients and healthcare providers. This seamless data flow enhances the early detection of worsening conditions, hence facilitating the enhanced management of chronic disorders. Personalized medicine has made major advancements thanks to machine learning algorithms that assess genetic data, lifestyle factors, and medical histories. This methodology provides valuable insights and enables the creation of personalized treatment programmes that consider the unique characteristics of each patient.

Furthermore, the expansion of medical ontologies and knowledge graphs exemplifies the extensive scope of intelligent cyber-physical systems [36]. These frameworks classify medical knowledge and establish connections between diseases, symptoms, and therapies. This knowledge arrangement assists in clinical decision-making, differential diagnosis, and the systematic classification of diseases [37]. Ultimately, the integration of intelligent techniques into the Healthcare CPS signifies a fundamental shift towards achieving more precision, customization, and proactive management of healthcare. Integrating sophisticated Cyber-Physical Systems (CPS) techniques into disease diagnosis and prognosis can provide healthcare staff with data-driven insights, more accurate predictions, and personalized treatment plans. This will improve patient outcomes and lead to more efficient healthcare delivery. In order to safeguard patient data and maintain patient trust in the healthcare system, it is imperative to ensure that new technologies are implemented in an ethical manner and with the necessary privacy and security measures in place [38].

5.3 Drug Discovery and Development

Cyber-physical systems (CPS) facilitate the application of state-of-the-art tools, data-driven tactics, and computational approaches to accelerate and improve the quality of drug discovery and development. CPS, or Cyber-Physical Systems, is a field that combines physical elements with computing, communication, and control systems in an interdisciplinary manner. When utilized in the context of drug research and development, the implementation of CPS can expedite the procedure, diminish expenses, and bolster precision medicine endeavors. Here are some ways in which CPS technologies are employed in the process of drug discovery and development.

5.3.1 High-Throughput Screening (HTS)

CPS technologies facilitate the mechanization and fusion of high-capacity screening procedures, allowing for the swift evaluation of numerous chemicals against particular biological targets or disease models. This process of automation enables a more comprehensive and methodical evaluation of possible medication candidates.

5.3.2 Computational Drug Design (CPS)

CPS employs computational modeling, artificial intelligence, and machine learning techniques to forecast and enhance the interactions between drug candidates and their targets. This approach obviates the necessity for costly empirical screening and facilitates the identification of potential lead compounds with enhanced rates of success.

5.3.3 Personalized Medicine

The integration of clinical trial data, genomic data, electronic health records, and other extensive patient data can be achieved through the utilization of CPS technology in the field of personalized medicine. This data-driven methodology facilitates the discovery of patient subgroups that may exhibit enhanced response to specific drugs, leading to the development of personalized medicine approaches [39].

5.3.4 Virtual Clinical Trials

Clinical trial simulations can be created using virtual patient models thanks to CPS. Before investing in costly and time-consuming real-world studies, these virtual trials can assist researchers in evaluating the efficacy and safety of drug candidates.

5.3.5 Drug Repurposing

CPS technologies employ data integration and analysis to identify pre existing drugs that have the potential to be utilized in the treatment of different ailments. Implementing this drug repurposing technique can significantly reduce the time and cost associated with traditional drug research endeavors [40].

5.3.6 Predictive Toxicology

CPS technologies employ in vitro testing and computer models to forecast the probable toxicity of medication candidates. This obviates the necessity of doing experiments on animals and expedites the quest for more secure pharmaceuticals.

5.3.7 Continuous Manufacturing

Incorporating CPS technology into continuous manufacturing processes can enhance the scalability and efficacy of medicine production. Continuous manufacturing enables real-time process monitoring and control, ensuring consistent product quality.

5.3.8 Real-Time Patient Monitoring

Clinical studies can utilize CPS technologies to collect data on side effects, treatment reactions, and other relevant characteristics. This data can provide valuable insights about the efficacy of the medication in real-world scenarios.

In summary, the utilization of CPS technology in drug discovery and development will bring about a significant transformation in the pharmaceutical industry. Utilizing current computing, data analytics, and automation, CPS approaches can accelerate procedures, enhance success rates, and ultimately lead to the creation of more efficient and personalized medications for various ailments.

5.4 Personalized Treatment and Precision Medicine

Systems that integrate physical parts with computational and communication skills are known as cyber-physical systems (CPS) and can be used for precision medicine and individualized treatment as shown in Fig. 10. Advanced data analytics platforms, remote patient monitoring systems, and smart, connected medical equipment can all be developed in the healthcare industry using CPS [41]. Including concepts from customized care and precision medicine in CPS can provide the following advantages.

5.4.1 Real-Time Monitoring and Personalized Alerts

Real-time monitoring and customized alerts are possible with CPS, which can also continuously track patients' physiological metrics and overall health. The system may identify anomalies or deviations from typical patterns by using individualized treatment algorithms, and it can then provide targeted alerts to healthcare professionals or patients. The prompt detection and treatment of medical disorders can benefit from the use of this early warning system.

5.4.2 Therapies That Are Adaptable and Individualized

CPS is capable of gathering and analyzing a sizable quantity of patient data, including genomic details, lifestyle variables, and treatment outcomes. CPS can help healthcare professionals choose the most suitable and efficient treatments for specific patients by incorporating this data. This adaptability may improve patient outcomes and minimize negative effects.

5.4.3 Predictive Modeling

CPS can use machine learning and artificial intelligence approaches to forecast the development of diseases and determine a person's risk of contracting particular illnesses. Healthcare professionals can adopt preventive measures and individualized interventions before a condition worsens by employing this predictive skill.

5.4.4 Remote Patient Management

It is made possible by CPS, particularly for managing chronic diseases. Patients can wear linked gadgets that send data on their health indicators to medical specialists on a continuous basis. Because of the timely therapies and improved illness management made possible by this real-time monitoring, fewer frequent hospital visits are required.

5.4.5 Integration of Multiple Data Sources

CPS is capable of integrating data from a variety of sources, including wearable technology, genetic databases, electronic health records, and environmental sensors. This connection makes it possible to fully comprehend a person's health profile, improving the accuracy and customization of medical therapies [42].

5.4.6 Optimal Resource Allocation

CPS can optimize the distribution of healthcare resources by analyzing vast quantities of data from multiple patients, hence enhancing the efficiency and efficacy of delivering personalized therapies.

Integrating personalized care and precision medicine into CPS presents several challenges, such as concerns over data privacy and security, system compatibility, and the need for robust data analytics and machine learning algorithms. The integration of personalized therapy and precision medicine principles is expected to have a substantial impact on the delivery of healthcare services as technology advances and the use of Cyber-Physical Systems (CPS) becomes more prevalent in healthcare settings. This will ultimately enhance patient outcomes and establish a more efficient and enduring healthcare system.

6 Intelligent Techniques in Healthcare Cyber-Physical Systems (CPS): Benefits and Challenges

The implementation of intelligent techniques in Healthcare Cyber-Physical Systems (CPS) has brought about substantial transformations in the healthcare sector. Contemporary healthcare systems have a promising prospect to enhance operational efficiency, accuracy, and patient results by utilizing advanced technologies such as artificial intelligence, machine learning, and information analytics. However, the incorporation of these technologies also brings about a range of difficulties, including ethical deliberations, privacy worries, and compatibility problems. This section explores the benefits and challenges of intelligent approaches for healthcare cyber physical systems (CPS), offering an understanding of their potential impact on the healthcare field. Figure 9 shows the representation for above CPH System using WSN cloud integrated Framework.

6.1 Benefits in Healthcare Cyber Physical System

The application of intelligent techniques in healthcare cyber-physical systems (CPS) offers numerous advantages that span the whole healthcare field, including patient care, diagnostics, operational efficiency, and resource optimisation. These advantages not only boost healthcare systems' capabilities, but also have the potential to revolutionize healthcare delivery and the patient experience. Here are some of the key benefits.

6.1.1 Enhanced Efficiency and Accuracy

Intelligent techniques optimize healthcare processes by automating routine tasks, reducing manual errors, and expediting decision-making. Healthcare providers are able to devote more time to direct patient care through CPS-enabled technologies that streamline the management of patient information, scheduling, and paperwork.

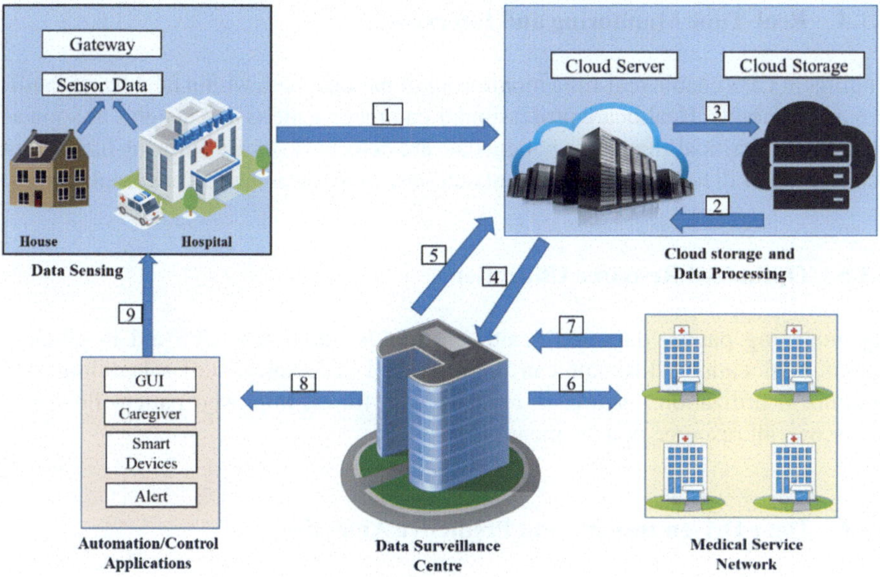

Fig. 9 Secured CPS architecture for healthcare, utilizes WSN-cloud integrated framework

AI-powered algorithms analyze complex medical data with a level of precision and speed unattainable through manual efforts, leading to more accurate diagnoses and personalized treatment plans [43].

6.1.2 Early Diagnosis and Proactive Interventions

Intelligent techniques in CPS empower healthcare professionals to detect potential health issues at their earliest stages. By continuously monitoring patient data, deviations from baseline health indicators can be swiftly identified, enabling timely interventions [44]. Detecting health problems before they worsen has multiple benefits, including better patient outcomes and less strain on healthcare systems.

6.1.3 Personalized Treatment Plans

Using a patient's specific medical history, genetic makeup, and lifestyle choices, healthcare CPS equipped with smart procedures can personalize treatment plans. This personalized approach enhances treatment efficacy, minimizes adverse reactions to medications, and improves patient adherence to prescribed regimens.

6.1.4 Real-Time Monitoring and Intervention

Intelligent CPS enable real-time monitoring of patients both within healthcare facilities and remotely. Healthcare professionals can receive alerts and insights as soon as anomalies or critical changes in patient data are detected [18]. By allowing for prompt actions, this skill helps improve patient outcomes and lower the risk of complications.

6.1.5 Optimized Resource Utilization

By analyzing patient data and healthcare trends, intelligent CPS aid in efficient resource allocation. Hospitals can optimize bed occupancy, staff scheduling, and equipment utilization, leading to reduced wait times, improved patient flow, and better overall resource management [45].

6.1.6 Data-Driven Insights and Predictive Analytics

Intelligent techniques analyze large datasets to extract valuable insights and predict healthcare trends. These insights aid in evidence-based decision-making, enabling healthcare professionals to anticipate patient needs, allocate resources effectively, and proactively address potential challenges.

6.1.7 Telemedicine and Remote Care

Healthcare CPS with intelligent techniques facilitate telemedicine, allowing remote consultations, diagnoses, and treatment monitoring [32]. This remote care approach extends healthcare services to underserved areas, reduces travel-related stress for patients, and promotes timely access to medical expertise.

6.1.8 Surgical Precision and Innovation

Intelligent CPS enhance surgical procedures through robotic assistance, augmented reality visualization, and predictive modeling. Surgeons can perform complex operations with higher precision, reducing invasiveness and recovery times.

6.1.9 Continuous Learning and Improvement

Intelligent CPS have the ability to learn from past data and experiences. They adapt over time, improving their accuracy, diagnostic capabilities, and decision-making as they accumulate more data and insights.

In summary, intelligent techniques in Healthcare Cyber-Physical Systems revolutionize patient care, diagnostics, and healthcare operations by harnessing the power of AI, machine learning, and automation. These benefits not only lead to improved clinical outcomes but also contribute to a more patient-centric and efficient healthcare ecosystem.

6.2 Challenges in Healthcare Cyber Physical System

6.2.1 Difficulties in Effectively Implementing HCPS

Energy-flow, integrating diverse devices at different HCPS layers, achieving the least tolerable latency for time-critical processes, and mitigating security concerns are only some of the challenges that are standing in the way of a fully realized HCPS.

Cyber Physical System Energy Flow: A constant energy source, either by a direct power source or powerful batteries, which is necessary for cyber physical systems to function autonomously and for their use in critical markets like healthcare. To keep the healthcare cyber physical system running efficiently, it is crucial to estimate the energy consumption of each component throughout the system design and modeling phases of HCPS. There are numerous energy-saving techniques available for efficient energy management; however, this has a knock-on impact on the trade-off between energy quality and quantity, since smart sensors within these devices respond to environmental demands and adjust the operating mode appropriately. To ensure cyber physical system (CPS) operation and integration into smart city healthcare CPS, the Smart Grid—the energy backbone of CPS—must be in place. As the need for energy in cyber physical systems continues to grow at an exponential rate, the Smart grid can benefit from the installation of solar panels in homes, hospitals, and factories.

Heterogeneous Device and HCPS Level Integration: In order to facilitate communication and secure data storage that can be accessed by researchers, patients, insurance companies, and medical professionals, the smart city healthcare ecosystem must incorporate cyber physical systems that depend on third party service providers. Integrated and encapsulated devices are necessary for an efficient and successful environment in cyber physical systems due to the diverse nature of the devices involved. In a heterogeneous setting, the necessity for interfaces to communicative devices at various stages of technological development from the standpoint of available software and hardware would be the primary difficulty. Integration and higher HCPS levels require system-level planning, design, and prototype testing for collaborative functioning and data sharing.

Delay/Latency: For time-sensitive uses, such as healthcare, a low latency is essential. Telemonitoring cycles in cyber-physical systems are disrupted, which can delay patients' medicine and care if transmission delays exceed a certain threshold value. Furthermore, having a short fault latency—the time it takes to detect and handle a fault—is essential in real-time applications like healthcare because it improves system reliability.

Security: Denial of service, replay, fake data injection, and deception attacks are only some of the threats to healthcare cyber physical systems that must be mitigated. A Cyber-Physical system attack model in the form of a tree, with each branch representing a different type of attack (e.g., Injection of faulty signals, manipulation of sensor hardware, packet replay attack, theft of data in closed loop communication channels among sensors, controllers, and actuators, malfunctioning software in computing resources, and equipment failure). Critical infrastructures, such as smart healthcare systems, cannot function without cyber security technologies. As they keep a constant vigil for any injected faults that could cause malfunctions or inaccurate data.

Future digital systems, such as Smart-healthcare-cyber-physical-systems, will need to be forensically prepared to cope with and counter cyber security breaches. Autonomous systems rely heavily on artificial intelligence and machine intelligence to carry out activities like fault and cyber-attack detection. Identifying malicious software is crucial to ensuring the reliable operation of cyber physical systems. Malwares are identified using a variety of machine learning techniques that take into account system calls, operation codes, and energy consumption trends. Smart waste management is a major physical challenge for healthcare systems that must be met alongside digital world challenges. For the sake of the city's ecosystem, efficient trash management, comprising its gathering at generating locations, transference, and management techniques, is essential given the alarming rate at which hospitals are producing garbage. Because of the recent epidemic, more people are using personal protective equipment (PPE) kits and disposable masks, necessitating a more efficient system for discarding these items. With the advancement of technology, healthcare CPS will advance from its current unit or integration level and into a higher CPS in the near future. Advanced level CPS, such as those used to produce vaccines or medical equipment, feature subsystems with self-aware and self-managing features that can be switched into self-configuration mode in order to maximize the different real-time manufacturing procedures.

6.2.2 Ethical Considerations and Privacy Concerns

With the growing dependence of healthcare cyber-physical systems (CPS) on intelligent methodologies, it becomes imperative to acknowledge and tackle the ethical implications and privacy issues that arise from the acquisition and examination of confidential patient information [46].

Informed Consent: The process of gathering patient data for the purpose of intelligent analysis necessitates obtaining explicit and informed consent in the individuals involved. It is imperative for patients to possess knowledge regarding the utilization and dissemination of their data in order to uphold principles of transparency and foster a sense of trust.

Data Security and Privacy: The implementation of robust data security measures is imperative in order to protect patient information from unauthorized access or breaches. Compliance with law that is pertinent, including HIPAA (Health Insurance Portability and Accountability Act), necessitates that healthcare CPS comply with stringent data protection measures.

Bias and Fairness: Intelligent methodologies may exhibit vulnerability to bias, thereby resulting in disparate treatment or erroneous diagnostic outcomes influenced by variables such as race or gender. The implementation of measures that reduce bias and ensure fairness in the provision of healthcare is of utmost importance.

Human Oversight: Although intelligent systems hold significant potential, it is imperative that they do not completely supplant human judgment. It is imperative for healthcare professionals to uphold supervision and assume ultimate accountability for decisions derived from intelligent system recommendations.

6.2.3 Integration and Interoperability Challenges

To integrate intelligent approaches into healthcare CPS, numerous problems must be addressed.

Data Standardization: Healthcare data often originates from a wide range of sources, which can result in variations in formats and structures. The implementation of uniform data standardization plays a pivotal role in facilitating streamlined data interchange and fostering compatibility among heterogeneous systems.

Technical Compatibility: The integration of intelligent systems with pre-existing healthcare Cyber-Physical Systems (CPS) may necessitate substantial technical modifications and enhancements to guarantee seamless communication and collaboration.

Training and Education: It is imperative that healthcare professionals undergo comprehensive training in order to proficiently utilize and interpret the valuable insights offered by intelligent systems. A sound education guarantees precise comprehension and suitable implementation in accordance with the system's suggestions.

Cost and Resource Allocation: The incorporation of intelligent techniques may necessitate substantial initial expenditures and allocation of resources. Healthcare organizations must conduct thorough evaluations of the long-term benefits and return on investment (ROI) in order to substantiate these investments.

7 Security and Privacy in Healthcare CPS

Healthcare Cyber-Physical Systems (CPS) integrate technology, medical equipment, and data to enhance healthcare results. Nevertheless, these systems also pose distinct difficulties in guaranteeing security and privacy. Now, let's explore in more detail the precise cybersecurity strategies and techniques that may be used for Healthcare CPS in order to safeguard patient data and privacy.

7.1 Cybersecurity Measures for Healthcare CPS

Robust cybersecurity is crucial in the rapidly changing field of Healthcare Cyber-Physical Systems (CPS). Comprehensive security measures are necessary due to the integration of medical devices, networked networks, and sensitive patient data. Now, let's examine the essential cybersecurity measures that healthcare organizations should adopt to protect the security and privacy of Healthcare CPS (Fig. 10).

7.1.1 Risk Assessment and Management

A risk assessment entails the identification of potential shortcomings, risks, and deficiencies in the Healthcare CPS [47]. This process helps healthcare organizations understand the likelihood and potential impact of security breaches [48]. The next step in risk management is to design methods to either eliminate or significantly reduce the impact of identified risks. Protecting sensitive patient information and keeping the system running smoothly are top priorities, and this feature guarantees both. Figure 11 shows the general framework of ISO 31000 risk assessment model that can be integrated into CPS framework. This model enables the establishment of a structured risk assessment process, encompassing risk identification, analysis, evaluation, treatment, and continuous monitoring and ensures that both the digital and physical aspects of the healthcare CPS ecosystem are safeguarded against a wide spectrum of potential threats.

7.1.2 Network Segmentation

To segment the Healthcare CPS network means to divide it up into separate, smaller networks. Each segment has specific functions and levels of sensitivity. By doing so, the impact of a security breach is limited to the affected segment, preventing unauthorized access to critical patient information and sensitive systems.

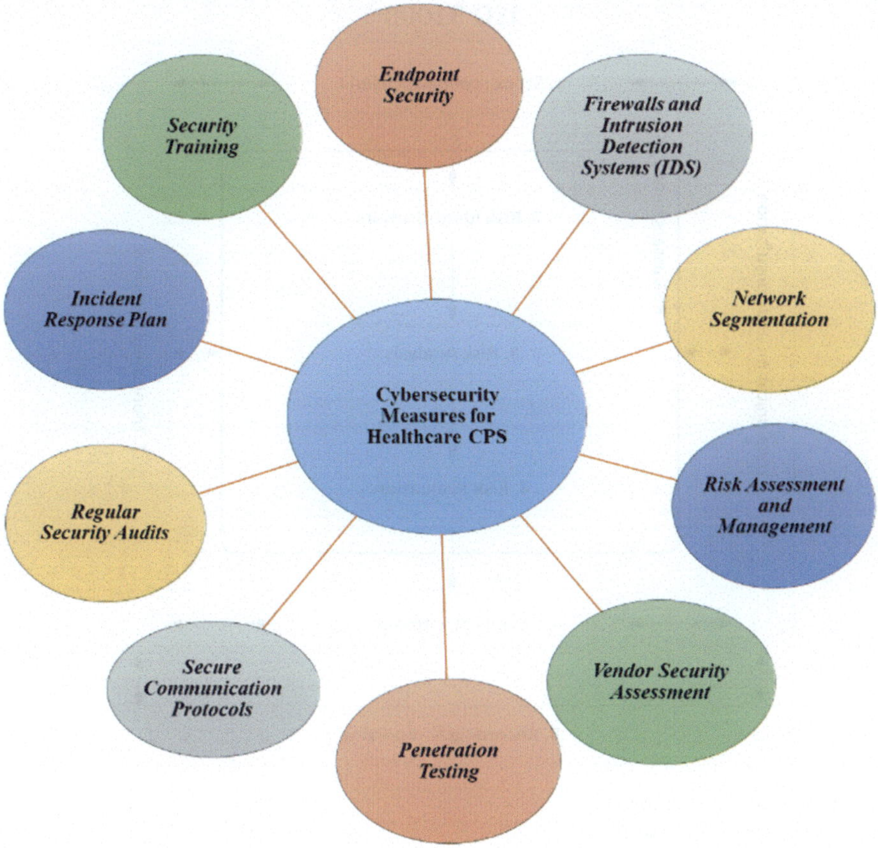

Fig. 10 Cyber-security measures for healthcare CPS

7.1.3 Firewalls and Intrusion Detection Systems (IDS)

Firewalls are responsible for preserving the internal network of the Healthcare CPS against unauthorized access by intruders on the internet and other networks. They monitor and control all incoming and outgoing data, enforcing security regulations. The purpose of intrusion detection systems (IDS) is to constantly monitor network activity for any strange trends or behaviors. IDS can be either software or hardware. When possible security vulnerabilities are recognised, they issue alerts, enabling prompt response and mitigation [49].

7.1.4 Endpoint Security

Endpoint security encompasses the process of safeguarding all endpoints inside the Healthcare CPS, which includes medical devices, laptops, and cellphones. This is

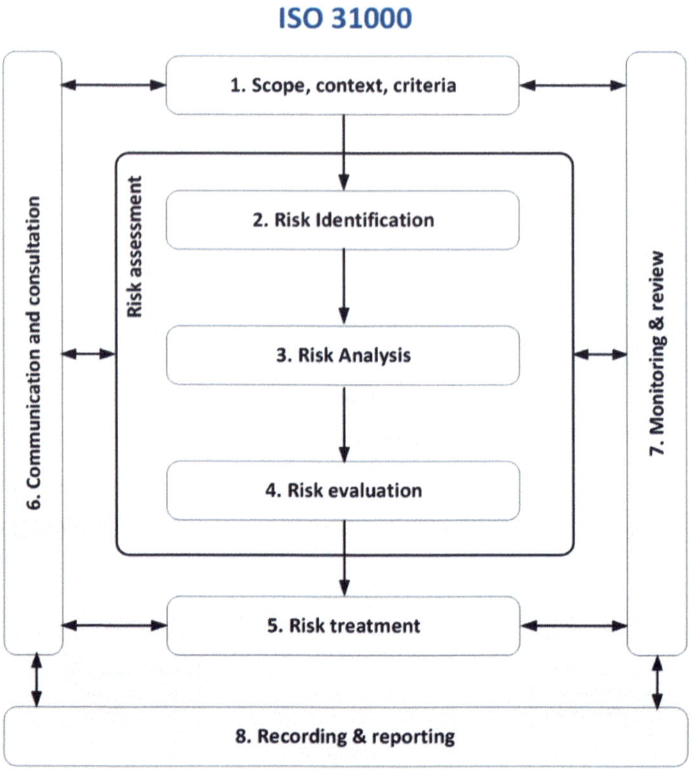

Fig. 11 Risk assessment model

accomplished by employing measures such as installing and regularly updating antivirus software, enabling encryption, and setting access controls to prevent unauthorized access.

7.1.5 Security Training

Providing healthcare personnel with cybersecurity training is essential to enhance their comprehension and promote the adoption of optimal security practices. The security awareness training covers several topics such as identifying phishing emails, creating strong passwords, avoiding risky behaviors, and promptly reporting incidents.

7.1.6 Incident Response Plan

An organization should have an incident response strategy in place in case of an information breach or other risk related to cybersecurity. The strategy offers a systematic method to manage and minimize the consequences of the incident, restore compromised systems, and prevent future incidents of the same nature.

7.1.7 Regular Security Audits

Regular security audits entail assessing the efficacy of cybersecurity measures and pinpointing any vulnerabilities or flaws in the Healthcare CPS. These audits are conducted to verify that security controls are regularly updated and in line with the changing threat landscape.

7.1.8 Secure Communication Protocols

Employing robust communication protocols such as HTTPS (for websites) and VPN (Virtual Private Network) guarantees that data exchanged between devices and systems is encoded, rendering it arduous for assailants to intercept or manipulate the data.

7.1.9 Penetration Testing

Ethical hacking, also referred to as penetration testing, involves systematically searching for vulnerabilities in the Healthcare CPS by simulating an attack. Conducting controlled testing assists in assessing the system's ability to withstand and enhances its security position.

7.1.10 Vendor Security Assessments

Performing vendor security evaluations when utilizing third-party software or medical equipment guarantees that these suppliers conform to security protocols, fulfill industry benchmarks, and abide by data protection rules. It aids in reducing the risks linked to external suppliers.

7.2 Protecting Patient Data and Privacy

Cyber-Physical Systems (CPS) in Healthcare must adhere to the utmost standards to ensure the confidentiality, integrity, and availability of patient information. Data secrecy and patient privacy are paramount in these systems because of the sensitive nature of the personal information and medical records they process [50]. Now, we will take a look at the main ways that Healthcare CPS protects patient data. In order to keep patient information private and secure within the Healthcare CPS, the following are some key considerations.

7.2.1 Data Encryption

Data encryption is one of the cybersecurity technique that is used in data security by converting the plain text to cipher text using cryptography It ensures that the unauthorized parties are not allowed to decrypt the data without decryption key. It is a useful technique in protecting sensitive data such as healthcare records, patient data or any financial data.

7.2.2 Role-Based Access Control (RBAC)

Role-Based Access Control (RBAC) restricts personnel's ability to access patient records according to their assigned roles and responsibilities. This guarantees the confidentiality of data and stops unauthorized parties from obtaining critical patient details.

7.2.3 Anonymization and De-identification

Removal or alteration of personal identifiers from data makes it difficult to relate the data again to a particular individual; this process is known as anonymization or de-identification. This method protects patients' privacy while facilitating data sharing and research.

7.2.4 Consent Management

To ensure patient privacy and autonomy, it is vital to get patients' express and informed consent before acquiring and employing their data. People who get medical care should be able to decide what happens with their information and not let it be used for certain things.

7.2.5 Data Minimization

Obtaining and retaining just the bare minimum of patient data required for clinical purposes is what data minimization is all about. Reducing the quantity of information gathered can better protect patients' privacy and lessen the probability of a data breach.

7.2.6 Audit Logs

It is important to keep complete audit logs that document all activities and access to patient data. These records are helpful for monitoring user actions and can be utilized to identify and examine potential instances of privacy breaches or unauthorized access.

7.2.7 Patient Education

Providing education to the patients about their rights and protection techniques will help in better decision making and building trust in the healthcare system. As a result, a stronger relationship can be established between the patient and healthcare providers.

7.2.8 Secure Data Sharing

To ensure patient privacy and compliance with data protection requirements, it is important to employ safe data exchange techniques and systems when transferring information about patients with other medical professionals or researchers.

7.2.9 Physical Security

Physical security measures are crucial for protecting any physical access points to medical devices and patient data storage. This category encompasses facilities such as installing surveillance cameras to data centers, server rooms, and hospitals. It also includes the system such as biometric scanners, PIN based systems that prevent the access from unauthorized users.

7.2.10 Regular Data Backup

To minimize the risk of hardware failure or cyber-attacks such as ransomware it is necessary to create a backup of the patient data regularly. Creating a backup assures that the data will continue to be accessible and recoverable in the event. It also helps in maintaining the patient trust and integrity of patient data.

By implementing these cybersecurity measures and privacy protection strategies, healthcare organizations can significantly enhance the security and privacy of

Healthcare CPS, safeguard patient data, and maintain patient trust in the healthcare system.

8 Conclusion

In conclusion, a new age of revolutionary patient care and safety is on the horizon when intelligent techniques are integrated with CPS (Cyber-Physical Systems) in healthcare. By combining digital capabilities with physical infrastructure, health care organizations may leverage data-driven decision-making, real-time monitoring, customized treatment plans, and advanced diagnostics. Despite ongoing challenges over privacy and interoperability, recent advancements in technology are significantly addressing these issues. This chapter delves into the advantages, disadvantages, and possible uses of intelligent CPS, highlighting its significant influence on healthcare. To build a healthcare system that is more personal, effective, and patient-centered, it is essential to leverage technology. This means that clever CPS techniques are leading the healthcare business to new heights of efficiency, accuracy, and accessibility.

References

1. S. A. Haque, S. M. Aziz, and M. Rahman, "Review of Cyber-Physical System in Healthcare," *Int. J. Distrib. Sens. Networks*, vol. 10, no. 4, p. 217415, Apr. 2014, https://doi.org/10.1155/2014/217415.
2. O. Rahaman, A. Shuvo, and Ma. Kashem, "CYBER PHYSICAL SYSTEMS FOR HEALTHCARE," *Int. J. Adv. Res.*, vol. 6, no. 11, pp. 36–46, Oct. 2018, https://doi.org/10.21474/IJAR01/7968.
3. N. Dey, A. S. Ashour, F. Shi, S. J. Fong, and J. M. R. S. Tavares, "Medical cyber-physical systems: A survey," *J. Med. Syst.*, vol. 42, no. 4, p. 74, Apr. 2018, https://doi.org/10.1007/s10916-018-0921-x.
4. F. Chen *et al.*, "Medical Cyber–Physical Systems: A Solution to Smart Health and the State of the Art," *IEEE Trans. Comput. Soc. Syst.*, vol. 9, no. 5, pp. 1359–1386, Oct. 2022, https://doi.org/10.1109/TCSS.2021.3122807.
5. J. Shi, J. Wan, H. Yan, and H. Suo, "A survey of Cyber-Physical Systems," in *2011 International Conference on Wireless Communications and Signal Processing (WCSP)*, Nov. 2011, pp. 1–6. https://doi.org/10.1109/WCSP.2011.6096958.
6. M. Groshev, C. Guimaraes, J. Martin-Perez, and A. de la Oliva, "Toward Intelligent Cyber-Physical Systems: Digital Twin Meets Artificial Intelligence," *IEEE Commun. Mag.*, vol. 59, no. 8, pp. 14–20, Aug. 2021, https://doi.org/10.1109/MCOM.001.2001237.
7. D. Cogliati, M. Falchetto, D. Pau, M. Roveri, and G. Viscardi, "Intelligent Cyber-Physical Systems for Industry 4.0," in *2018 First International Conference on Artificial Intelligence for Industries (AI4I)*, Sep. 2018, pp. 19–22. https://doi.org/10.1109/AI4I.2018.8665681.
8. M. A. Musen, B. Middleton, and R. A. Greenes, "Clinical Decision-Support Systems," in *Biomedical Informatics*, Cham: Springer International Publishing, 2021, pp. 795–840. https://doi.org/10.1007/978-3-030-58721-5_24.
9. Y. Lu and X. Xu, "Resource virtualization: A core technology for developing cyber-physical production systems," *J. Manuf. Syst.*, vol. 47, pp. 128–140, Apr. 2018, https://doi.org/10.1016/j.jmsy.2018.05.003.

10. M. J. Kaur, S. Riaz, and A. Mushtaq, "Cyber-Physical Cloud Computing Systems and Internet of Everything," 2020, pp. 201–227. https://doi.org/10.1007/978-3-030-33596-0_8.
11. K. T. Chui *et al.*, "A Survey of Internet of Things and Cyber-Physical Systems: Standards, Algorithms, Applications, Security, Challenges, and Future Directions," *Information*, vol. 14, no. 7, p. 388, Jul. 2023, https://doi.org/10.3390/info14070388.
12. F. E. Tanha, A. Hasani, S. Hakak, and T. R. Gadekallu, "Blockchain-based cyber physical systems: Comprehensive model for challenge assessment," *Comput. Electr. Eng.*, vol. 103, p. 108347, Oct. 2022, https://doi.org/10.1016/j.compeleceng.2022.108347.
13. P. Radanliev, D. De Roure, M. Van Kleek, O. Santos, and U. Ani, "Artificial intelligence in cyber physical systems," *AI Soc.*, vol. 36, no. 3, pp. 783–796, Sep. 2021, https://doi.org/10.1007/s00146-020-01049-0.
14. N. V. Sharma, N. S. Yadav, and S. Sharma, "Machine learning and security in Cyber Physical Systems," in *Cyber-Physical Systems*, Elsevier, 2022, pp. 171–187. https://doi.org/10.1016/B978-0-12-824557-6.00015-7.
15. N. Deo and A. Anjankar, "Artificial Intelligence With Robotics in Healthcare: A Narrative Review of Its Viability in India," *Cureus*, May 2023, https://doi.org/10.7759/cureus.39416.
16. R. J. Somers, J. A. Douthwaite, D. J. Wagg, N. Walkinshaw, and R. M. Hierons, "Digital-twin-based testing for cyber–physical systems: A systematic literature review," *Inf. Softw. Technol.*, vol. 156, p. 107145, Apr. 2023, https://doi.org/10.1016/j.infsof.2022.107145.
17. G. A. Fink, T. W. Edgar, T. R. Rice, D. G. MacDonald, and C. E. Crawford, "Security and Privacy in Cyber-Physical Systems," in *Cyber-Physical Systems*, Elsevier, 2017, pp. 129–141. https://doi.org/10.1016/B978-0-12-803801-7.00009-2.
18. M. Barrere *et al.*, "CPS-MT: A Real-Time Cyber-Physical System Monitoring Tool for Security Research," in *2018 IEEE 24th International Conference on Embedded and Real-Time Computing Systems and Applications (RTCSA)*, Aug. 2018, pp. 240–241. https://doi.org/10.1109/RTCSA.2018.00040.
19. T. Davenport and R. Kalakota, "The potential for artificial intelligence in healthcare," *Futur. Healthc. J.*, vol. 6, no. 2, pp. 94–98, Jun. 2019, https://doi.org/10.7861/futurehosp.6-2-94.
20. S. Secinaro, D. Calandra, A. Secinaro, V. Muthurangu, and P. Biancone, "The role of artificial intelligence in healthcare: a structured literature review," *BMC Med. Inform. Decis. Mak.*, vol. 21, no. 1, p. 125, Dec. 2021, https://doi.org/10.1186/s12911-021-01488-9.
21. F. Pesapane, M. Codari, and F. Sardanelli, "Artificial intelligence in medical imaging: threat or opportunity? Radiologists again at the forefront of innovation in medicine," *Eur. Radiol. Exp.*, vol. 2, no. 1, p. 35, Dec. 2018, https://doi.org/10.1186/s41747-018-0061-6.
22. C. de Cock, M. Milne-Ives, M. H. van Velthoven, A. Alturkistani, C. Lam, and E. Meinert, "Effectiveness of Conversational Agents (Virtual Assistants) in Health Care: Protocol for a Systematic Review," *JMIR Res. Protoc.*, vol. 9, no. 3, p. e16934, Mar. 2020, https://doi.org/10.2196/16934.
23. R. Kumar Attar and Komal, "The Emergence of Natural Language Processing (NLP) Techniques in Healthcare AI," in *Artificial Intelligence for Innovative Healthcare Informatics*, Cham: Springer International Publishing, 2022, pp. 285–307. https://doi.org/10.1007/978-3-030-96569-3_14.
24. H. Mohammadi Rouzbahani, H. Karimipour, A. Rahimnejad, A. Dehghantanha, and G. Srivastava, "Anomaly Detection in Cyber-Physical Systems Using Machine Learning," in *Handbook of Big Data Privacy*, Cham: Springer International Publishing, 2020, pp. 219–235. https://doi.org/10.1007/978-3-030-38557-6_10.
25. A. J. Jara, D. Genoud, and Y. Bocchi, "Big Data for Cyber Physical Systems: An Analysis of Challenges, Solutions and Opportunities," in *2014 Eighth International Conference on Innovative Mobile and Internet Services in Ubiquitous Computing*, Jul. 2014, pp. 376–380. https://doi.org/10.1109/IMIS.2014.139.
26. V. S. Padilla, R. A. Ponguillo, A. A. Abad, and L. E. Salas, "Cyber-physical system based on image recognition to improve traffic flow: A case study," *Int. J. Electr. Comput. Eng.*, vol. 10, no. 5, p. 5217, Oct. 2020, https://doi.org/10.11591/ijece.v10i5.pp5217-5226.

27. A. Gatouillat, Y. Badr, B. Massot, and E. Sejdic, "Internet of Medical Things: A Review of Recent Contributions Dealing With Cyber-Physical Systems in Medicine," *IEEE Internet Things J.*, vol. 5, no. 5, pp. 3810–3822, Oct. 2018, https://doi.org/10.1109/JIOT.2018.2849014.
28. A. Gupta, J. Cecil, and M. Pirela-Cruz, "A Virtual Reality enhanced Cyber Physical Framework to support Simulation based Training of Orthopedic Surgical Procedures," in *2018 IEEE 14th International Conference on Automation Science and Engineering (CASE)*, Aug. 2018, pp. 433–438. https://doi.org/10.1109/COASE.2018.8560602.
29. T. Shah *et al.*, "Remote health care cyber-physical system: quality of service (QoS) challenges and opportunities," *IET Cyber-Physical Syst. Theory Appl.*, vol. 1, no. 1, pp. 40–48, Dec. 2016, https://doi.org/10.1049/iet-cps.2016.0023.
30. L. K. Ramasamy, F. Khan, M. Shah, B. V. V. S. Prasad, C. Iwendi, and C. Biamba, "Secure Smart Wearable Computing through Artificial Intelligence-Enabled Internet of Things and Cyber-Physical Systems for Health Monitoring," *Sensors*, vol. 22, no. 3, p. 1076, Jan. 2022, https://doi.org/10.3390/s22031076.
31. E. Kajati, P. Papcun, C. Liu, R. Y. Zhong, J. Koziorek, and I. Zolotova, "Cloud based cyber-physical systems: Network evaluation study," *Adv. Eng. Informatics*, vol. 42, p. 100988, Oct. 2019, https://doi.org/10.1016/j.aei.2019.100988.
32. Bokolo Anthony Jnr., "Use of Telemedicine and Virtual Care for Remote Treatment in Response to COVID-19 Pandemic," *J. Med. Syst.*, vol. 44, no. 7, p. 132, Jul. 2020, https://doi.org/10.1007/s10916-020-01596-5.
33. B. Beatrix-May, S. I. Stefan, P.-N. Alina-Claudia, P. Florin, and U. Andreea, "A Cyber-Physical Systems Approach for Health Care Prediction," in *2021 International Conference on e-Health and Bioengineering (EHB)*, Nov. 2021, pp. 1–4. https://doi.org/10.1109/EHB52898.2021.9657667.
34. C. S. Wickramasinghe, D. L. Marino, K. Amarasinghe, and M. Manic, "Generalization of Deep Learning for Cyber-Physical System Security: A Survey," in *IECON 2018 - 44th Annual Conference of the IEEE Industrial Electronics Society*, Oct. 2018, pp. 745–751. https://doi.org/10.1109/IECON.2018.8591773.
35. M. M. Hossain, M. A. Kashem, N. M. Nayan, and M. A. Chowdhury, "A Medical Cyber-physical system for predicting maternal health in developing countries using machine learning," *Healthc. Anal.*, vol. 5, p. 100285, Jun. 2024, https://doi.org/10.1016/j.health.2023.100285.
36. F.-Z. Hannou, F. Atigui, N. Lammari, and S. S. Cherfi, "SafecareOnto: A Cyber-Physical Security Ontology for Healthcare Systems," 2021, pp. 22–34. https://doi.org/10.1007/978-3-030-86475-0_3.
37. K. Liu, F. Wang, Z. Ding, S. Liang, Z. Yu, and Y. Zhou, "Recent Progress of Using Knowledge Graph for Cybersecurity," *Electronics*, vol. 11, no. 15, p. 2287, Jul. 2022, https://doi.org/10.3390/electronics11152287.
38. A. Calhan and M. Cicioglu, "Remote Health Monitoring System Modeling for Cyber-Physical Systems," in *2022 30th Signal Processing and Communications Applications Conference (SIU)*, May 2022, pp. 1–4. https://doi.org/10.1109/SIU55565.2022.9864788.
39. P. Bogdan and Y. Xue, "Cyber-physical systems for personalized and precise medicine," in *2015 IEEE 58th International Midwest Symposium on Circuits and Systems (MWSCAS)*, Aug. 2015, pp. 1–4. https://doi.org/10.1109/MWSCAS.2015.7282205.
40. A. Kusiak, "Smart Manufacturing," 2023, pp. 973–985. https://doi.org/10.1007/978-3-030-96729-1_45.
41. P. Bogdan, "A Cyber-Physical Systems Approach to Personalized Medicine: Challenges and Opportunities for NoC-based Multicore Platforms," in *Design, Automation & Test in Europe Conference & Exhibition (DATE), 2015*, 2015, pp. 253–258. https://doi.org/10.7873/DATE.2015.1127.
42. A. Bagozi, D. Bianchini, and A. Rula, "Multi-perspective Data Modelling in Cyber Physical Production Networks: Data, Services and Actors," *Data Sci. Eng.*, vol. 7, no. 3, pp. 193–212, Sep. 2022, https://doi.org/10.1007/s41019-022-00194-4.
43. F. Jamil, T. Y. Pang, and C.-T. Cheng, "Developing an I4.0 Cyber-Physical System to Enhance Efficiency and Competitiveness in Manufacturing," *Appl. Sci.*, vol. 13, no. 16, p. 9333, Aug. 2023, https://doi.org/10.3390/app13169333.

44. Z. P. Ori, "Integrated Cyber-Physical System to Support Early Diagnosis and Prevention of Prediabetes and Complications of Type 2 Diabetes," in *Type 2 Diabetes - From Pathophysiology to Cyber Systems*, IntechOpen, 2021. https://doi.org/10.5772/intechopen.94232.
45. Z. Li, C. Huang, X. Dong, and C. Ren, "Resource-efficient cyber-physical systems design: A survey," *Microprocess. Microsyst.*, vol. 77, p. 103183, Sep. 2020, https://doi.org/10.1016/j.micpro.2020.103183.
46. A. Thekkilakattil and G. Dodig-Crnkovic, "Ethics Aspects of Embedded and Cyber-Physical Systems," in *2015 IEEE 39th Annual Computer Software and Applications Conference*, Jul. 2015, pp. 39–44. https://doi.org/10.1109/COMPSAC.2015.41.
47. W. Wu, R. Kang, and Z. Li, "Risk assessment method for cyber security of cyber physical systems," in *2015 First International Conference on Reliability Systems Engineering (ICRSE)*, Oct. 2015, pp. 1–5. https://doi.org/10.1109/ICRSE.2015.7366430.
48. X. Lyu, Y. Ding, and S. Yang, "Safety and security risk assessment in cyber-physical systems," *IET Cyber-Physical Syst. Theory Appl.*, vol. 4, no. 3, pp. 221–232, Sep. 2019, https://doi.org/10.1049/iet-cps.2018.5068.
49. R. Panigrahi *et al.*, "Intrusion detection in cyber–physical environment using hybrid Naïve Bayes—Decision table and multi-objective evolutionary feature selection," *Comput. Commun.*, vol. 188, pp. 133–144, Apr. 2022, https://doi.org/10.1016/j.comcom.2022.03.009.
50. G. A. Fink, T. W. Edgar, T. R. Rice, D. G. MacDonald, and C. E. Crawford, "Overview of Security and Privacy in Cyber-Physical Systems," in *Security and Privacy in Cyber-Physical Systems*, Wiley, 2017, pp. 1–23. https://doi.org/10.1002/9781119226079.ch1.

Hypertension, Heart Rate Reserve, and Cognitive Impairment: Exploring Relationships, Implications, and Measurement Techniques

Alka Bishnoi

Abstract The chapter offers an in-depth summary of the connection between hypertension, heart rate reserve (HRR), and the risk of non-amnestic cognitive impairment. It starts by addressing the prevalence of hypertension and dementia among older adults. It then delves into the association between hypertension and cognitive impairment and how cognitive impairment increases the risk of falls in this population. The review also emphasizes functional impairments related to dual tasking and presents theories explaining the costs of dual task performance. Additionally, the chapter explores the relationship between executive function and the prefrontal cortex, along with the connection between HRR and hypertension. It provides insight into the biological mechanisms underlying HRR. The chapter further discusses various findings on prefrontal cortex activation during dual task testing and their implications. Finally, it outlines the benefits of measuring HRR in at-risk individuals and highlights the advantages of using Functional Near-Infrared Spectroscopy (fNIRS) over other neuroimaging techniques, such as functional magnetic resonance imaging (fMRI) and electroencephalography (EEG).

Keywords Hypertension · HRR · FNIRS · Dual-task · Walking · Prefrontal cortex · Dementia

A. Bishnoi (✉)
Department of Physical Therapy, College of Health Professions and Human Services, Kean University, Union, NJ, USA
e-mail: abishn2@gmail.com

M. Mittal and J. Narayan (eds.), *Intelligent Cyber-Physical Systems for Healthcare Solutions*, https://doi.org/10.1007/978-981-97-8983-2_5

1 Introduction

1.1 Prevalence of Hypertension and Dementia in Older Adults

The population of adults aged 65 and older is projected to reach 83.7 million by 2050. This demographic shift is contributing to a global rise in age-associated dementia, with one in ten people over 65 currently living with the condition. The number of people with dementia is expected to increase from 50 to 152 million by 2050 [1]. This growing prevalence of dementia is closely intertwined with the widespread occurrence of hypertension, a condition that affects one in three adults today [2]. Hypertension, or high blood pressure, is a significant risk factor for the development of dementia. As the population ages and the prevalence of hypertension continues to rise, addressing this issue becomes increasingly critical in mitigating the impact of dementia on public health.

Hypertension is not only a significant risk factor for cardiovascular diseases but also for cognitive decline. Research by Reitz et al. has shown a clear link between hypertension and non-amnestic cognitive impairment [3]. This cognitive impairment can begin early in hypertensive adults and, if left untreated, can progressively worse, leading to severe consequences in later stages. The transition from the prevalence of hypertension to its impact on cognitive health is marked by several key factors.

Chronic Hypertension can lead to damage in the blood vessels of the brain, reducing cerebral blood flow, contributing to brain damage over time. This damage manifests as cognitive decline, which is often observed as difficulties in memory, executive function, and processing speed. Such impairments are not only challenging for individuals but also significantly affect their daily lives. For instance, cognitive decline associated with hypertension can lead to gait impairments, making it difficult for individuals to maintain balance and coordination. This, in turn, negatively impacts instrumental activities of daily living, such as cooking and gardening, which require both physical and cognitive effort. As a result, hypertensive individuals with cognitive decline are at a higher risk of falls and subsequent hospitalization. Addressing hypertension effectively can therefore play a crucial role in mitigating the risk of cognitive decline and its associated complications, highlighting the importance of early intervention and continuous management of blood pressure to maintain cognitive health and overall quality of life in older adults.

Both fall injuries and hospitalizations significantly diminish the quality of life and are associated with substantial medical costs. In 2010, the cost of unintentional fall-related injuries—including fatalities, hospitalizations, and treatments—was approximately $111 billion [4]. These financial burdens reflect not only direct medical expenses but also the long-term care and rehabilitation required for many fall-related injuries.

Falls can lead to a range of severe outcomes, including fractures, head injuries, and increased dependency, which in turn affect an individual's ability to perform daily activities and maintain independence. The psychological impact is also profound, as fear of falling can lead to decreased mobility and physical fitness, further increasing the risk of future falls.

Given these severe consequences, it is essential to assess and address the causes of falls early in at-risk populations, particularly older adults. Early assessment allows for the implementation of preventive measures, such as balance training, home modifications, and management of underlying health conditions like hypertension and cognitive impairments. These interventions can significantly reduce the incidence of falls, thereby improving the quality of life and reducing the overall healthcare costs associated with fall-related injuries.

Furthermore, understanding the multifactorial nature of falls is crucial. Falls are often the result of a combination of factors, including poor vision, muscle weakness, medication side effects, and environmental hazards. Comprehensive fall prevention strategies should therefore be multidisciplinary, involving healthcare providers, caregivers, and the individuals themselves. By addressing both the medical and environmental factors contributing to falls, we can better safeguard the health and well-being of older adults.

1.2 Cognitive and Physical Function in Older Adults

As people age, physical function diminishes, which in turn affects cognitive abilities. Motor slowing or reduced walking speed often precedes cognitive decline in healthy older adults [5] (Fig. 1). This relationship between decreased gait function and the development of dementia has been well-documented. Since walking is a complex task that engages various cognitive processes, it can serve as an early marker of cognitive decline, making early diagnosis crucial.

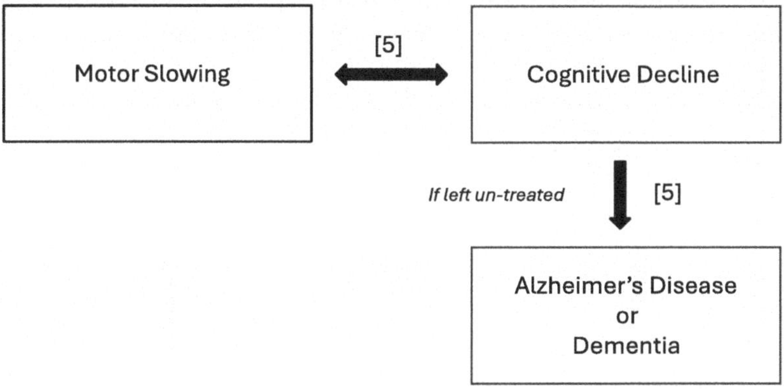

Fig. 1 Relationship between motor slowing or reduced walking speed, cognitive decline and dementia

Walking involves a widespread network of brain areas responsible for attention, execution, and visuospatial functions. These brain regions work together to coordinate the intricate task of walking, and impairments in any of these areas can lead to noticeable changes in gait. Therefore, monitoring gait function can provide valuable insights into the cognitive health of older adults and help identify those at risk for dementia early on (Fig. 1).

1.3 Cardiovascular and Cognitive Dysfunction

Cardiovascular dysfunction in older adults has been associated with varying degrees of cognitive dysfunction, ranging from mild cognitive impairment to dementia. This association unfortunately goes above and beyond the normal aging process. Impaired cognitive function is seen in people with cardiovascular disease (CVD) such as hypertension, even in the absence of major cardiac events (Fig. 2). Older adults with CVD have reported this cognitive dysfunction at an early stage in life [3].

Heart rate reserve (HRR), which is one of the major risk factors of cardiovascular dysfunction is also linked with cognitive impairment in older adults [6]. Also, heart rate variability, heart rate recovery, and blood pressure variability have also shown to be associated with cognitive dysfunction in older adults [7]. However, these associations have been shown with global cognitive function, it is still unknown which areas of the brain are strongly associated with cardiovascular dysfunction and if this dysfunction is associated with executive dysfunction and dual task walking performance.

A previous study by Bishnoi et al. showed that dual task walking cost is associated with executive function in healthy older adults with impaired HRR [6]. They found a strong association of lower HRR with executive dysfunction in older adults. If there is an association found in this study with dual task walking, it seems important to examine this association in adults with impaired HRR in further studies with

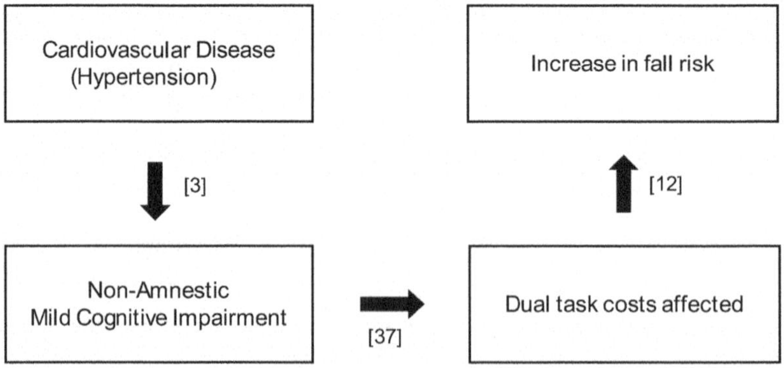

Fig. 2 Relationship between hypertension, mild cognitive impairment (MCI) and fall risk

different dual task paradigms to provide a stronger conclusion of the association of cardiovascular dysfunction and cognitive impairment (Fig. 2).

2 Executive Function and Prefrontal Cortex

Executive function is a higher level of cognitive function that involves having the ability to effectively plan, monitor, adjust, inhibit, and update working memory [8]. It has been established that executive function is essential for dual tasking. Research on neuroimaging methods such as fNIRS, has shown that the prefrontal cortex (PFC) controls executive function and is responsible for overseeing and coordinating the attentional resources while dual tasking [9]. There is a relationship between PFC activity and dual tasking, due to which examining the function of the frontal lobe seems important. In addition, it has been found that the PFC is also responsible for standing balance control [10]. Thus, because it is known that the PFC control's executive function and the attention allocated towards dual tasking, it is important to examine how to improve executive function.

2.1 Dual Task Walking

Walking is complex and is usually performed while doing some secondary tasks, due to which it has connections among falls risk, performance, and cognition in older adults; those who reported more falls would stop walking when doing a secondary task. Walking has been typically thought to be an automatic process controlled by subcortical regions of the spine [11]. More recent thinking is that walking is no longer an automatic process. The ability to do a dual task (e.g., walking and talking) has challenged the idea of walking as an automatic process due to its effects on gait. Walking performance is altered (e.g., slower gait speeds and longer stride and step times, wider step widths, shorter stride lengths and single support time, longer double support time, decreases in stride velocity, and increase in gait variability) during a dual task when compared to a single task in older adults [12]. Furthermore, these dual tasking gait impairments have been linked with increased risk of falls [12].

2.2 Dual Task Cost

A dual task (DT) paradigm is a behavioral procedure in which individuals are required to perform two tasks simultaneously. Dual tasks can involve a wide range of concurrent sensory, motor, or cognitive tasks, and may be analogous to activities in daily life such as cooking, shopping, or walking while talking. Despite such variety, dual tasking often results in a decline in performance in one component or both components of the dual task as compared to the single task, which is called ***dual task interference or dual task cost***. The concept of capacity limitation in cognitive resource and performance limitation have been used to explain this dual task interference [13].

DT paradigms have received a lot of attention among researchers because it provides a gold standard for evaluation of the "central executive system" [14]. Moreover, in the context of gait, the use of DT paradigms allows researchers to assess the causal effect attentional resources have on walking performance under circumstances that better approximate real-life conditions. In comparison to a single task condition, DT conditions have shown activation in the dorsolateral prefrontal cortex of the brain. This pattern of increased cortical activation in the prefrontal cortex has also been demonstrated through functional near infrared spectroscopy (fNIRS) studies of dual task walking.

3 Heart Rate Reserve

3.1 Biological Mechanism of Heart Rate Reserve

The chronotropic response is described as the heart's ability to adequately respond to increased activity and is tied with cardiac output. Chronotropic response (CR) considers **heart rate reserve** and metabolic reserve and is measured by the graded exercise stress test. Increased CR is associated with better cognitive performance because of its association with increased HRR [15] (Fig. 3).

As HRR affects executive function by causing vascular changes induced by autonomic nervous system dysregulation and abnormal CR [7], measuring it at an early age seems important. This dysregulation and abnormal response are due to failure to achieve target HR during exercise or unable to decrease resting HR, putting them at risk of CVD [7] (Fig. 3).

HRR and HR recovery have been used frequently in measuring the CVD and cognitive impairment risk in older adults. Although, these variables have been measured with a treadmill stress test (an index of autonomic nervous system function) and are related to multiple cognitive domains, including global cognitive functioning, speeded executive function, and language abilities [7], but they can also be measured through Karvonen's formula (maximum HR minus age) for quick assessment of CVD risk [16]. However, it is crucial to tailor measurements to an individual's fitness level. Tanaka et al. argued against using Karvonen's formula for non-fit adults and instead recommended using an age-predicted maximum heart rate for sedentary individuals [16]. Studies have demonstrated that an increase in HRR and HR recovery corresponds with the cognitive improvements found in CVD patients following cardiac rehabilitation [17], measuring them at a regular basis can help clinicians designing better physical and cognitive rehabilitation.

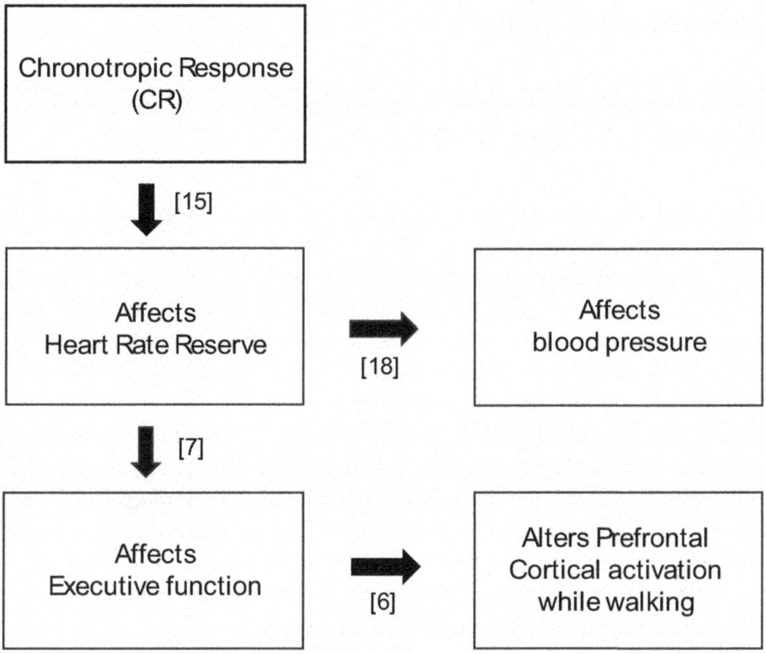

Fig. 3 Relationship between heart rate reserve (HRR), chronotropic response (CR), and executive function

3.2 *Prefrontal Cortex and Heart Rate Reserve*

As executive function is affected due to impaired HRR, and is controlled by the PFC, and can be associated with falls' risk, new research has started to examine the PFC activation patterns related to HRR levels. Using fMRI, research has established a positive relationship between activation patterns, cardiovascular function and cognitive performance in older adults; adults with better HR recovery and HRR exhibit better cognitive performance and less activation [15]. Interestingly, in our preliminary study, we found high HRR older individuals can cope with dual tasking better and exhibit decreases in PFC activation [6]. Till date, there has been only few studies examining the effect of HRR on cognitive function but not on dual task walking in at-risk older adults [18] (Fig. 3).

4 Neuroimaging Techniques

4.1 *Advantages and Disadvantages of Functional Magnetic Resonance Imaging (fMRI)*

While the use of fMRI has been considered the gold standard for assessing metabolic activity of the brain, research has outlined various limitations associated with it. fMRI is expensive, requires participants to be fully immobilized [19], and only measures HbO_2. Functional near infrared spectroscopy (fNIRS) has also been used and overcomes some of the limitations associated with fMRI. fNIRS is a non-invasive and portable device with good temporal sampling resolution (e.g., 0.01 s) and better signal-to-noise ratio when compared to fMRI [19].

In addition, it is the only device that can accurately measure the levels and changes of both oxyhemoglobin (HbO_2) and deoxyhemoglobin (Hb) [20] during movement. It is important to be able to get both values while assessing hemodynamic behavior because they can be used to separate the two signals that are due to the increases in flow or oxygen consumption. Lastly, fNIRS has been found to produce similar results as fMRI [21]. It is important to note that fNIRS has its own limitations in that it can only be used for more superficial tissue recording.

4.2 *Functional Near Infrared Spectroscopy (fNIRS)*

Brain activity or cortical activity can be measured by various neuroimaging methods such as functional magnetic resonance imaging (fMRI), magnetoencephalography (MEG), positron emission tomography (PET), electroencephalography (EEG), and functional near-infrared spectroscopy (fNIRS). Although fMRI is considered the gold standard for the assessment of activity in cortical areas, it suffers from the susceptibility of motion artifacts and restrictions in doing walking activities [22].

Similarly, MEG exhibits high vulnerability towards motion artifacts [22]; while PET doesn't allow repeated measurement due to the injection of radioactive tracers [23]. On the other hand, EEG has a weak spatial resolution, takes time to prepare, is vulnerable to artifacts and signal processing is difficult for non-experts in the field [24]. Due to these restrictions among neuroimaging techniques, Functional Near Infrared Spectroscopy (fNIRS) has been used to record cortical activity while walking. fNIRS is an optical neuroimaging technique for assessing cortical activity through the hemodynamic response of the brain while the participant walks freely, especially while dual task walking.

An fNIRS apparatus is composed of a light source that is placed over a tissue source head via light-emitting diodes (LEDs) with a detector that receives the light after it has been scattered through the tissue. This imaging device is based on near-infrared (650–1000 nm) light that is propagated into the tissue and is absorbed by oxyhemoglobin (HbO_2) and deoxyhemoglobin (Hb), which have been established as being markers of oxygen utilization and delivery [25]. HbO_2 has been established as a being a direct reflection of cortical activation and the most reliable for measuring movement changes in cerebral blood flow. Moreover, PFC HbO_2 levels have been validated after being correlated with levels measured by the more commonly used method of functional magnetic resonance imaging (fMRI).

5 PFC Activation Theories

An increase in neural activity showed through an increase in cerebral blood flow to regions of interest which ultimately leads to higher blood oxygenation in those areas. As such, higher blood oxygenation denoted by higher HbO_2 levels indicate higher PFC activation patterns. This is referred to as ***neurovascular coupling*** [26]. With increasing age, there are mixed findings with cortical activation behavior. As measured with fMRI and Positron Emission Tomography (PET), older adults exhibit more activation in the frontal cortices compared to younger adults [27, 28]. Also, the pattern of PFC activation observed in older adults is more diffused in comparison to young adults [29]. Various models have been proposed to help explain these PFC activation behaviors:

- The increase in PFC activation observed in older adults versus young adults has been explained by an *age-related cognitive decline* and the increased effort needed to perform better. De-differentiation has been used to explain how older adults inefficiently recruit additional regions of the brain when compared to younger adults. The ***compensation theory*** states that due to age-related structural declines, there is compensation by recruiting more areas as task performance increases [27].
- With increasing age, lateralized PFC activation is also ineffective and leads to activation increases in bilateral areas of the brain. This additional recruitment of brain areas seen only in the elderly has been referred to as the ***hemispheric asymmetry reduction in older adults (HAROLD)*** [30].
- Another phenomenon is known as the ***posterior-anterior shift in aging (PASA)***, in which older adults exhibit a decrease in activation of the occipitotemporal region of the brain while increasing activation in frontal areas, has also been discussed in the literature [31].
- ***Compensation-Related Utilization of Neural Circuits Hypothesis (CRUNCH)*** theory [32] explains that at low loads of cognitive demand, older adults recruit more regions of the brain/cognitive resources due to less efficient processing while younger adults demonstrate more focal activation.
- The ***scaffolding theory of aging and cognition (STAC)*** [33] refers to the ability of the aging brain to adapt and compensate by using both the declining and compensatory brain networks to maintain task performance.
- The ***neural compensation theory*** refers to recruiting a new brain network to compensate for the current brain network that is no longer capable of functioning the same due to age-related declines [34]. This is also detailed in a meta-analysis

by Spreng et al., they concluded that older adults do recruit more of the frontal areas of the brain than younger adults which reflects a compensatory action due to the less efficient or effective use of these regions.

In contrast to these increases in PFC activation theories, research has also found lower activation in older adults compared to younger adults. This negative correlation between increasing age and PFC activation was found in some studies which demonstrated smaller increases in PFC activation compared to younger adults while doing the task [35]. Another study by Schroeter et al. found that older adults showed lower activation in comparison to younger adults while doing Stroop conditions. Hermann et al. found that older adults exhibited less PFC activation and no lateralization during a verbal fluency task in comparison to young adults.

Using fMRI and PET techniques, older adults exhibit under-activation of brain areas. This leads to less metabolic demand being placed on the brain and thus reflect the smaller increases in blood flow. Reuter-Lorenz et al. stated that older adults should demonstrate activation of the cortical regions in parallel with performance; under-activation would lead to declines in cognitive performance [33]. The dedifferentiation hypothesis helps explain the re-organization of the functional brain that leads to a reduction in activation in some areas of the brain while others are activated. Reuter-Lorenz and Lustig [32] stated that as task demand increases, older adults reach a resource ceiling, which results in under-activation relative to young adults [32].

- The ***cognitive reserve theory*** [36] was introduced to explain why young adults demonstrate greater increases in brain activation in response to increased cognitive task demands. An individual who has brain networks that are more efficient, flexible, or have greater capacity, will have a higher coping capability even with any brain pathology disruptions present. This can be explained by younger adults with a higher working memory span (e.g., higher score on the reading span test) exhibited increased PFC activation during a dual task.

It is important to note that because these models were developed from fMRI and PET studies, they cannot be automatically applied to fNIRS studies explaining PFC activation behavior. Thus, Bishnoi et al. (2020) concluded in her systematic review that fNIRS should be used as a suitable technique for examining hypotheses on superficial cortical areas such as the PFC while dual task walking [37]. Furthermore, when examining neurodegenerative disorders such as Alzheimer's disease or Mild cognitive impairment in older adults, the meta-analysis found that individuals with neurodegenerative disorder exhibited PFC activation deficits in comparison to a healthy control group especially during dual task [37]. Thus, research examining the PFC activation patterns of older adults with affected cardiovascular dysfunction during a dual task walking is needed.

6 PFC Activation While Dual Tasking

Research examining PFC activations while dual tasking has shown conflicting and mixed results. While dual tasking, increases in PFC activation have been observed in older adults when compared to both performing a single task and to younger adults [38]. This increase in activation has been explained by the compensatory theory discussed above, older adults compensate and exhibit bilateral activation of the PFC during demanding tasks to enhance cognitive performance when compared to young adults. In contrast, research has also found a decrease in PFC activation while dual tasking in older adults versus young adults. This type of behavior can be explained by a possible shift of processing from the PFC to other regions of the brain to manage the dual tasking demands. This opposes the cognitive resource theories which state that with increasing age, as task demands increase, there are greater increases in brain activity or additional utilization of contralateral brain areas.

The ***neural inefficiency model*** states that due to age-related changes in structure and function, the brain is inefficient in its ability to allocate resources [39]. In addition, it can be partially explained by neural plasticity and the cognitive network strategies utilized in dual tasking [32]; with increasing age, there is a decrease in plasticity in sedentary individuals and fewer strategies to use while doing complex tasks leading to decrease in the activation. Therefore, among these contrasting results regarding PFC activation patterns in older adults while dual tasking, it is uncertain what to expect in older adults while doing a certain dual task. When examining older adults only, research has found that PFC activation increased during dual task walking when compared to normal walking [40]. Surprisingly, a study by Mirelman et al. found that both young and older adults increased PFC activation during dual task. Research has made links between PFC activation, behavior, and cognition. A study by Holtzer et al. found that older adults with better cognitive performance exhibited higher PFC activation during dual task walking.

In addition, research has examined relationships between PFC activation and motor performance while dual tasking in older adults. Holtzer [38] found that older adults with neurological gait abnormalities and cognitive performance deficiencies exhibited higher levels of PFC activation while dual tasking [38]. Similarly, while examining post-stroke individuals, Al-Yahya (2016) found a link between the increases in PFC activation from single to dual task and motor performance decrements [40]. Together, these studies indicate that the increases in PFC may be compensatory for individuals with gait abnormalities or post-stroke individuals.

7 Potential Limitations of the Study

The potential study might have several key limitations. Firstly, obtaining a large sample size of older adults with similar age and physical function may be challenging. Studies need to focus on cohorts that are matched in age, gender, and physical performance, which is difficult to achieve. Secondly, the cohort might display varying levels of cognitive impairment, making it challenging to find adults with comparable cognitive deficits. Thirdly, as fNIRS data is limited to the prefrontal cortex (PFC), there may be additional cortical and sub-cortical areas involved in dual task walking in adults with cardiovascular disease (CVD) that are not captured. This would help clarify the cognitive and motor regions contributing to dual-task walking. Finally, while the study suggests that individuals with age-predicted heart rate reserve (HRR) exhibit greater cognitive-motor interference during more challenging dual tasks, the cross-sectional design prevents establishing causal relationships between HRR and cognitive-motor interference in middle-aged to older adults. Therefore, future research should examine the effects of intervention programs on cognitive-motor interference in older adults with impaired age-predicted HRR.

8 Conclusion

In conclusion, this chapter underscores the significance of dual task walking paradigms in approximating the locomotion demands encountered in natural settings, where individuals must navigate visual and auditory stimuli that challenge the maintenance of safe gait. The ecological validity of these paradigms enhances their predictive utility, making them valuable tools for assessing cognitive and motor functions.

The chapter highlights the importance of examining the impact of various cardiovascular dysfunction variables on executive function during dual tasking in older adults. This approach can help identify early cognitive decline in individuals at risk for cardiovascular disease (CVD), who are prone to developing cognitive impairments.

Despite extensive research on the effects of hypertension and cardiovascular dysfunction on cognitive function and brain activation, a significant gap remains. To date, no studies have investigated how hypertension and heart rate reserve levels, a major risk factor for cardiovascular diseases, influence neural performance during dual task walking, as measured by functional near-infrared spectroscopy (fNIRS), or behavioral performance, as measured by dual task cost in older adults. Addressing this gap is crucial for establishing the link between CVD, cognitive decline, and mobility impairment in older adults. Such research could ultimately contribute to reducing fall risk and hospitalization rates in this vulnerable population.

References

1. K.B. Rajan, J. Weuve, L.L. Barnes, E.A. McAninch, R.S. Wilson, D.A. Evans, Population estimate of people with clinical Alzheimer's disease and mild cognitive impairment in the United States (2020–2060), Alzheimer's & Dementia 17 (2021) 1966–1975. https://doi.org/10.1002/alz.12362.
2. C.W. Tsao, A.W. Aday, Z.I. Almarzooq, C.A.M. Anderson, P. Arora, C.L. Avery, C.M. Baker-Smith, A.Z. Beaton, A.K. Boehme, A.E. Buxton, Y. Commodore-Mensah, M.S.V. Elkind, K.R. Evenson, C. Eze-Nliam, S. Fugar, G. Generoso, D.G. Heard, S. Hiremath, J.E. Ho, R. Kalani, D.S. Kazi, D. Ko, D.A. Levine, J. Liu, J. Ma, J.W. Magnani, E.D. Michos, M.E. Mussolino, S.D. Navaneethan, N.I. Parikh, R. Poudel, M. Rezk-Hanna, G.A. Roth, N.S. Shah, M.P. St-Onge, E.L. Thacker, S.S. Virani, J.H. Voeks, N.Y. Wang, N.D. Wong, S.S. Wong, K. Yaffe, S.S. Martin, Heart Disease and Stroke Statistics - 2023 Update: A Report from the American Heart Association, Circulation 147 (2023) E93–E621. https://doi.org/10.1161/CIR.0000000000001123.
3. C. Reitz, M.-X. Tang, J. Manly, R. Mayeux, J.A. Luchsinger, Hypertension and the Risk of Mild Cognitive Impairment, Arch Neurol 64 (2007) 1734. https://doi.org/10.1001/archneur.64.12.1734.
4. S.K. Verma, J.L. Willetts, H.L. Corns, H.R. Marucci-Wellman, D.A. Lombardi, T.K. Courtney, Falls and fall-related injuries among community-dwelling adults in the United States, PLoS One (2016). https://doi.org/10.1371/journal.pone.0150939.
5. R. Holtzer, C. Wang, J. Verghese, The relationship between attention and gait in aging: Facts and fallacies, Motor Control 16 (2012) 64–80. https://doi.org/10.1123/mcj.16.1.64.
6. A. Bishnoi, G.N.; Chaparro, M. Hernandez, Effect of heart rate reserve on prefrontal cortical activation in healthy older adults while dual task walking, in: Society of Neuroscience, Chicago, United states, 2019. https://doi.org/10.13140/RG.2.2.28693.76005.
7. T.A. Keary, R. Galioto, J. Hughes, D. Waechter, M.B. Spitznagel, J. Rosneck, R. Josephson, J. Gunstad, Reduced heart rate recovery is associated with poorer cognitive function in older adults with cardiovascular disease, Cardiovasc Psychiatry Neurol 2012 (2012). https://doi.org/10.1155/2012/392490.
8. V. Anderson, R. Jacobs, P.J. Anderson, Executive functions and the frontal lobes: A lifespan perspective, 2011. https://doi.org/10.4324/9780203837863.
9. G.R. Turner, R.N. Spreng, Executive functions and neurocognitive aging: Dissociable patterns of brain activity, Neurobiol Aging (2012). https://doi.org/10.1016/j.neurobiolaging.2011.06.005.
10. M. Mihara, I. Miyai, M. Hatakenaka, K. Kubota, S. Sakoda, Role of the prefrontal cortex in human balance control, Neuroimage (2008). https://doi.org/10.1016/j.neuroimage.2008.07.029.
11. O. Beauchet, G. Berrut, [Gait and dual-task: definition, interest, and perspectives in the elderly]. Psychol Neuropsychiatr Vieil (2006).
12. E. Al-Yahya, H. Dawes, L. Smith, A. Dennis, K. Howells, J. Cockburn, Cognitive motor interference while walking: A systematic review and meta-analysis, Neurosci Biobehav Rev 35 (2011) 715–728. https://doi.org/10.1016/j.neubiorev.2010.08.008.
13. K. Watanabe, S. Funahashi, Toward an understanding of the neural mechanisms underlying dual-task performance: Contribution of comparative approaches using animal models, Neurosci Biobehav Rev 84 (2018) 12–28. https://doi.org/10.1016/j.neubiorev.2017.08.008.
14. A. Baddeley, Exploring the Central Executive, Quarterly Journal of Experimental Psychology Section A: Human Experimental Psychology (1996). https://doi.org/10.1080/713755608.
15. L.L. Law, S.A. Schultz, E.A. Boots, J.A. Einerson, R.J. Dougherty, J.M. Oh, C.E. Korcarz, D.F. Edwards, R.L. Koscik, N.M. Dowling, C.L. Gallagher, B.B. Bendlin, C.M. Carlsson, S. Asthana, B.P. Hermann, M.A. Sager, S.C. Johnson, D.B. Cook, J.H. Stein, O.C. Okonkwo, Chronotropic Response and Cognitive Function in a Cohort at Risk for Alzheimer's Disease, Journal of Alzheimer's Disease 56 (2017) 351–359. https://doi.org/10.3233/JAD-160642.

16. H. Tanaka, K.D. Monahan, D.R. Seals, Age-predicted maximal heart rate revisited, J Am Coll Cardiol 37 (2001) 153–156. https://doi.org/10.1016/S0735-1097(00)01054-8.
17. S. Dimopoulos, M. Anastasiou-Nana, D. Sakellariou, S. Drakos, S. Kapsimalakou, G. Maroulidis, P. Roditis, O. Papazachou, I. Vogiatzis, C. Roussos, S. Nanas, Effects of exercise rehabilitation program on heart rate recovery in patients with chronic heart failure, European Journal of Cardiovascular Prevention & Rehabilitation 13 (2006) 67–73. https://doi.org/10.1097/01.hjr.0000198449.20775.7c.
18. Y.J. Cheng, C.A. Macera, T.S. Church, S.N. Blair, Heart rate reserve as a predictor of cardiovascular and all-cause mortality in men, Med Sci Sports Exerc 34 (2002) 1873–1878. https://doi.org/10.1097/00005768-200212000-00003.
19. S. Lloyd-Fox, A. Blasi, C.E. Elwell, Illuminating the developing brain: The past, present and future of functional near infrared spectroscopy, Neurosci Biobehav Rev 34 (2010) 269–284. https://doi.org/10.1016/j.neubiorev.2009.07.008.
20. D.R. Leff, F. Orihuela-Espina, C.E. Elwell, T. Athanasiou, D.T. Delpy, A.W. Darzi, G.Z. Yang, Assessment of the cerebral cortex during motor task behaviours in adults: A systematic review of functional near infrared spectroscopy (fNIRS) studies, Neuroimage (2011). https://doi.org/10.1016/j.neuroimage.2010.10.058.
21. G. Strangman, D.A. Boas, J.P. Sutton, Non-invasive neuroimaging using near-infrared light, Biol Psychiatry (2002). https://doi.org/10.1016/S0006-3223(02)01550-0.
22. S. Cutini, S. Brigadoi, Unleashing the future potential of functional near-infrared spectroscopy in brain sciences, J Neurosci Methods 232 (2014) 152–156. https://doi.org/10.1016/j.jneumeth.2014.05.024.
23. J. Saliba, H. Bortfeld, D.J. Levitin, J.S. Oghalai, Functional near-infrared spectroscopy for neuroimaging in cochlear implant recipients, Hear Res 338 (2016) 64–75. https://doi.org/10.1016/j.heares.2016.02.005.
24. M. Smith, Shedding light on the adult brain: a review of the clinical applications of near-infrared spectroscopy, Philosophical Transactions of the Royal Society A: Mathematical, Physical and Engineering Sciences 369 (2011) 4452–4469. https://doi.org/10.1098/rsta.2011.0242.
25. S.C. Bunce, M. Izzetoglu, K. Izzetoglu, B. Onaral, K. Pourrezaei, Functional near-infrared spectroscopy, IEEE Engineering in Medicine and Biology Magazine 25 (2006) 54–62. https://doi.org/10.1109/MEMB.2006.1657788.
26. M. Fabiani, B.A. Gordon, E.L. Maclin, M.A. Pearson, C.R. Brumback-Peltz, K.A. Low, E. McAuley, B.P. Sutton, A.F. Kramer, G. Gratton, Neurovascular coupling in normal aging: A combined optical, ERP and fMRI study, Neuroimage (2014). https://doi.org/10.1016/j.neuroimage.2013.04.113.
27. R. Cabeza, Cognitive neuroscience of aging: Contributions of functional neuroimaging, Scand J Psychol (2001). https://doi.org/10.1111/1467-9450.00237.
28. P.A. Reuter-Lorenz, J. Jonides, E.E. Smith, A. Hartley, A. Miller, C. Marshuetz, R.A. Koeppe, Age differences in the frontal lateralization of verbal and spatial working memory revealed by PET, J Cogn Neurosci (2000). https://doi.org/10.1162/089892900561814.
29. K. Hagen, A.C. Ehlis, F.B. Haeussinger, S. Heinzel, T. Dresler, L.D. Mueller, M.J. Herrmann, A.J. Fallgatter, F.G. Metzger, Activation during the Trail Making Test measured with functional near-infrared spectroscopy in healthy elderly subjects, Neuroimage (2014). https://doi.org/10.1016/j.neuroimage.2013.09.014.
30. R. Cabeza, Hemispheric asymmetry reduction in older adults: The HAROLD model, Psychol Aging (2002). https://doi.org/10.1037/0882-7974.17.1.85.
31. S.W. Davis, N.A. Dennis, S.M. Daselaar, M.S. Fleck, R. Cabeza, Qué PASA? the posterior-anterior shift in aging, Cerebral Cortex (2008). https://doi.org/10.1093/cercor/bhm155.
32. P.A. Reuter-Lorenz, K.A. Cappell, Neurocognitive aging and the compensation hypothesis, Curr Dir Psychol Sci (2008). https://doi.org/10.1111/j.1467-8721.2008.00570.x.
33. P.A. Reuter-Lorenz, D.C. Park, Human neuroscience and the aging mind: A new look at old problems, Journals of Gerontology - Series B Psychological Sciences and Social Sciences (2010). https://doi.org/10.1093/geronb/gbq035.

34. Y. Stern, C. Habeck, J. Moeller, N. Scarmeas, K.E. Anderson, H.J. Hilton, J. Flynn, H. Sackeim, R. Van Heertum, Brain networks associated with cognitive reserve in healthy young and old adults, Cerebral Cortex (2005). https://doi.org/10.1093/cercor/bhh142.
35. I.L. Kwee, T. Nakada, Dorsolateral prefrontal lobe activation declines significantly with age: Functional NIRS study, J Neurol (2003). https://doi.org/10.1007/s00415-003-1028-x.
36. Y. Stern, Cognitive reserve, Neuropsychologia (2009). https://doi.org/10.1016/j.neuropsychologia.2009.03.004.
37. A. Bishnoi, M.E. Hernandez, Dual task walking costs in older adults with mild cognitive impairment: a systematic review and meta-analysis, Aging Ment Health (2020) 1–12. https://doi.org/10.1080/13607863.2020.1802576.
38. R. Holtzer, M. Izzetoglu, M. Chen, C. Wang, Distinct fNIRS-Derived HbO2 Trajectories during the Course and over Repeated Walking Trials under Single-and Dual-Task Conditions: Implications for Within Session Learning and Prefrontal Cortex Efficiency in Older Adults, Journals of Gerontology - Series A Biological Sciences and Medical Sciences 74 (2019) 1076–1083. https://doi.org/10.1093/gerona/gly181.
39. E. Zarahn, B. Rakitin, D. Abela, J. Flynn, Y. Stern, Age-related changes in brain activation during a delayed item recognition task, Neurobiol Aging (2007). https://doi.org/10.1016/j.neurobiolaging.2006.03.002.
40. E. Al-Yahya, H. Johansen-Berg, U. Kischka, M. Zarei, J. Cockburn, H. Dawes, Prefrontal Cortex Activation While Walking Under Dual-Task Conditions in Stroke: A Multimodal Imaging Study., Neurorehabil Neural Repair 30 (2016) 591–599. https://doi.org/10.1177/1545968315613864.

Concerns and Future Prospects of Medical Devices and Sensors for Intelligent Cyber-Physical Healthcare Systems

Akriti Verma, Anshika Gupta, and Kalpana Katiyar

Abstract Artificial intelligence (AI) has emerged as a crucial component in altering various aspects of our lives in the modern day. Particularly in the medical field, AI is especially pertinent in the medical area for leveraging Medical Devices and sensors within intelligent Cyber-Physical Systems (CPS). CPS blends computational and physical-world communication abilities. They also can improve operational efficiency and lower production prices. These intelligent systems, empowered by AI, enable transformative advancements in healthcare. They provide precise diagnosis, personalized treatment regimens, and efficient patient monitoring, resulting in precise medical results. Furthermore, intelligent CPS enables remote patient monitoring, allowing healthcare personnel to remotely check patient's health states. This not only increases patient comfort and convenience, but it also allows for early identification of deteriorating health and lowers hospital readmissions. The inclusion of wireless sensor networks (WSNs) is essential for the robust application of CPS, as their strong sensing capabilities serve as a crucial driving force for various CPS applications. This manuscript provides a glimpse of the recent achievements in this domain and emphasizes the potential for improving patient outcomes and healthcare delivery.

Keywords Medical devices · Artificial intelligence (AI) · Cyber-physical systems (CPS) · Wireless sensor networks (WSNs)

A. Verma · A. Gupta · K. Katiyar (✉)
Department of Biotechnology, Dr. Ambedkar Institute of Technology for Divyangjan, Kanpur 208024, UP, India
e-mail: kalpna@aith.ac.in

M. Mittal and J. Narayan (eds.), *Intelligent Cyber-Physical Systems for Healthcare Solutions*, https://doi.org/10.1007/978-981-97-8983-2_6

1 Introduction

1.1 Introduction

CPS (Cyber-physical systems) is characterized as the convergence of computing and physical processes, with embedded computers and networks playing a critical role in monitoring and regulating these processes. This integration generates feedback loops in which changes in physical processes affect estimations and vice versa. Rather than just combining the physical and cyber worlds, CPS poses an intellectual task at the junction of these two regions, emphasizing their connectivity and reciprocal effect [1].

CPS entails the gathering of several data kinds from the physical environment via sensors. These data are then sent to the cyber world for analysis and processing. The major idea of CPS is to incorporate intelligence into daily items and services, allowing them to execute crucial tasks independently or with least human participation. This intelligence integration has enormous promise for many social service models based on information technology (IT). One obvious area where CPS can have a substantial influence is in the medical and healthcare areas. Healthcare systems may benefit from increased monitoring, diagnostic, and treatment capabilities by utilizing CPS. For example, can enable the creation of sophisticated medical equipment that continually monitors the vital signs of patients, automatically recognize irregularities, and send timely alarms to medical personnel. Furthermore, CPS can promote the smooth interchange of medical data between various healthcare providers, enhancing cooperation and continuity of treatment. CPS can improve efficiency and effectiveness in social services more widely. For example, be used to optimize transportation networks, allowing for current–time traffic monitoring and dynamic traffic control. This can result in less congestion, more safety, and a better overall transit experience for passengers [2].

1.2 Overview of Intelligent Cyber-Physical Systems (CPS) in Healthcare

The integration of actual physical operations with virtual computing processes is the notion of cyber-physical systems (CPS). According to Cyber-Physical Systems Week, CPS is a term that refers to sophisticated engineering systems that rely largely on the seamless integration of physical, computational, and communication processes. A major amount of the equipment we use in our daily lives in today's world may be categorized as cyber-physical systems. It's critical to understand that cyber-physical systems that interact with the real world don't work in a controlled setting [3]. They must be prepared to deal with unexpected circumstances and be adaptable in the case of system or subsystem failures. This chapter introduces cyber-physical systems by diving into their history and providing an overview of their major components and characteristics. Readers may acquire insight into the integration of both physical and computer processes, as well as realize the complexity involved in their construction and operation, by comprehending the fundamental elements of cyber-physical systems.

(A) The Evolution of Embedded to Cyber-Physical Systems

The ever-increasing need for diverse organizing information systems has prompted the optimization of computing tool design methodologies. Embedded systems and networks now make up a sizable component of the world's data management systems [4]. These systems are critical in controlling and managing a wide variety of elements and operations. Embedded systems are classified according to their respective application areas, which is included in Table 1.

Since its introduction in the 1950s, the idea of embedded systems has travelled a great distance. With their broad use and integration, these technologies have developed into a crucial aspect of contemporary life. A linked future is made possible by the growing integration, safety, and networking abilities of embedded systems, which are driving innovation [5].

Embedded systems are primarily concerned with computer aspects, whereas cyber-physical systems are concerned with the relationship between computation and physical components. Applications for cyber-physical systems include medical,

Table 1 Classification of embedded systems

Embedded systems	Description
Automatic control systems	These systems are meant to independently regulate and control processes or equipment
Measuring systems and sensor-based information retrieval systems	These systems collect data from sensors and extract useful information or measurements
Real-time "question–answer" information systems	These systems respond to inquiries or requests for information in real-time
Digital data transmission systems	These systems enable the quick and safe transfer of digital data between multiple devices or locations
Complex real-time systems	These systems are designed to manage complex tasks in real time, requiring several processes and interactions that must be completed under stringent time limitations
Moving object management systems	These systems are concerned with successfully managing and controlling moving items, such as automobiles or robots
General-purpose computer system subsystems	These embedded systems are essential elements or subsystems of large computer systems designed to perform general-purpose computing operations
Multimedia systems	These systems make it easier to process, store, and display many types of multimedia content, such as video, audio, and graphics

traffic enforcement, industrial control, environmental monitoring, robotics, and system security. Cyber-physical systems must be flexible, scalable, cost-effective, and provide security, safety, and efficiency in all operations to be widely used in medical facilities.

(B) M2M Systems

CPS is enabled by machine-to-machine (M2M) applications and modernization [6]. M2M incorporates a computer, sensors, and device communications with little human intervention, making it essential for modern cyber-physical systems [7]:

- **Multitude**—M2M applications and upgrades enable cyber-physical systems. M2M incorporates a computer, sensors, and device communications with little human intervention, making it. The number of linked devices has surpassed those directly utilized by people as a result of M2M technology, which has had a huge impact. As a result of the explosion in device connection, application designs and network loads are under tremendous strain, which results in scalability problems. Due to their initial inability to handle the massive flood of M2M devices with unusual usage patterns, mobile networks in particular encounter difficulties. To facilitate the integration of a large number of M2M devices, modifications are being made to alleviate these early instances of issues.
- **Invisibility**—One of the major advantages of M2M devices is to operate independently of human control, which reduces workplace mistakes, is one of its key advantages. They can supply services without disturbing people thanks to their ability to blend in.
- **Criticality**—Blood captors and voltage detectors, respectively, are crucial components of the eHealth and Smart Grid systems. The maintenance of vital infrastructure and the preservation of life depend on these gadgets. However, their operational requirements, such as low latency and high dependability, frequently exceed what conventional networks can offer. Cyber-physical systems, in which electrical equipment communicates with one another, are not complete without M2M systems.

(C) Concept of Cyber-Physical Systems

In comparison to embedded systems, cyber-physical systems (CPS) have more physical components. CPS places more emphasis on the interplay between computational and physical factors than embedded systems, which are primarily concerned with computer components. Between the components of the CPS system, which are managed by computer algorithms, information is transmitted. Due to its integration of these three elements, CPS is represented by the letters C3 (Computation, Communication, and Control) (see Fig. 1). The range of possible CPS applications is increased by strengthening the connection between computational and physical aspects.

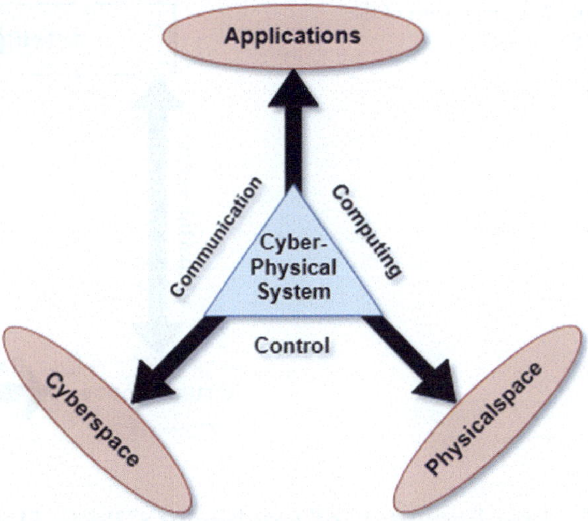

Fig. 1 Main three component of cyber-physical system

1.3 CPS Foundation

The seamless integration of computing, communication, and control is the cornerstone of Cyber-Physical Systems (CPS). CPS blends physical elements with computational platforms to provide real-time observation, evaluation, and management of physical processes. CPS makes it possible to coordinate and automate complex systems by combining sensors, actuators, networks, and algorithms. This foundation gives CPS the ability to improve safety, increase performance, allow cutting-edge features, and open up new opportunities across a range of industries, including manufacturing, transportation, and healthcare, among others.

A method for modeling and constructing cyber-physical systems is known as "cyberizing the physical" (CtP). This method comprises encapsulating physical components in software abstractions. An early use of CtP is the use of database inferences to describe physical dimensions acquired from sensor networks. CtP improves the administration and modification of physical data inside cyber-physical systems by using software representations. Aside from "cyberizing the physical" (CtP), another technique for modeling and creating cyber-physical systems is to "physicalize the cyber" (PtC). This method entails providing abstractions suitable for communicating with physical subsystems to software and networking components. One significant problem in PtC is to offer clear time semantics to this software along with network components. This includes in-depth knowledge and representation of time-associated features such as timing restrictions and synchronization to allow efficient communication and coordination between the system's cyber and physical parts [1].

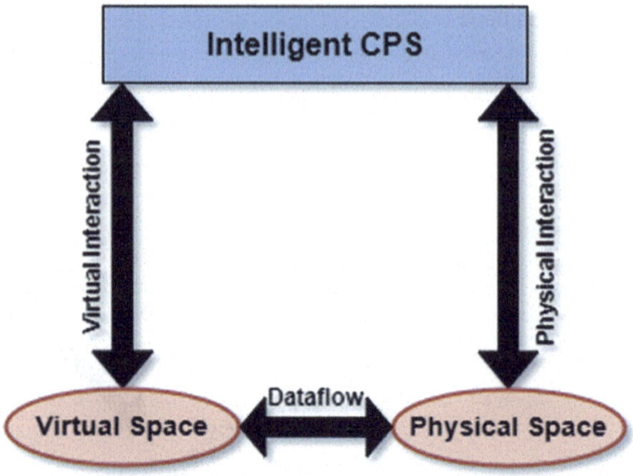

Fig. 2 Components of the CPS system

2 Fundamentals of Intelligent CPS in Healthcare

2.1 Definition and Components of Intelligent CPS

A cyber-physical system (CPS) connects the virtual and physical worlds, allowing for the integration of more intelligence into our day-to-day activities. CPS develops an analytical system capable of intelligent *feedbacks* to changing real-world events by fusing physical devices like imaging equipment and sensors with cyber components. This technology has a wide range of uses in many different industries, such as smart medical innovations, assisted living options, environmental control, and effective traffic management, see Fig. 2.

2.2 Architecture Development of Cyber-Physical Systems

There has been a considerable movement in architectural evolution toward systems integration during the previous decade, with a special emphasis on the role of Service-Oriented Architecture (SOA) in numerous technical areas [8]. By using reusable services supplied by these systems, SOA enables the quick and cost-effective construction of interoperable and scalable systems.

In one research, the authors developed "WebMed," a simpler middleware Cyber-Physical Systems (CPS) architecture that connected with online services. This approach sought to make the interaction between physical devices and compute services as simple as contacting a web service. By following service-oriented ideas, the authors created a loosely connected architecture that exposes physical device functions to the web, allowing for application development.

Sanislav et al. [9] on the other hand, saw the necessity to handle CPS architecture more completely to obtain cohesive handling of both cyber and physical parts. While the software architecture provided a strong base, they emphasized the importance of expanding the notion to CPS by establishing a new lexicon that includes both physical and cyber-physical features. This enhancement would allow for a more in-depth examination of the system's behavior and attributes.

Tan et al. [10] provided a prototype architecture that illustrates the notion of Cyber-Physical Systems (CPS) in their study. They emphasized the cyber world, which consists of events and information, as a physical world abstraction regulated by semantic rules. This method adapted the traditional architecture of embedded systems to meet modern technological demands.

Another research looked at Machine-to-Machine (M2M) communication, Wireless Sensor Networks (WSNs), CPS, and the Internet of Things (IoT). They emphasized the fields' linkages and links. The authors also analyzed residential M2M networks and developed the HCPS CPS scenario. The HCPS scenario illustrated how to upgrade M2M systems with decision-making and autonomous control capabilities to CPS. In addition, the writers discussed crucial research.

To summarise, Tan et al. suggested a CPS prototype design that emphasizes the cyber realm as an abstraction of the physical world. In a second research, the authors examined the characteristics of M2M, WSNs, CPS, and IoT, and demonstrated the transition of M2M systems to CPS via the HCPS scenario. They also highlighted key research suggestions and CPS design issues [11].

3 Taxonomy of CPS in Healthcare

A comprehensive set of taxonomies have been developed properly to characterize and categorize diverse Cyber-Physical Systems (CPS) techniques of Cyber-Physical Systems (CPS) in the healthcare sector [12]. The taxonomy for characterizing and categorizing CPS methods in healthcare includes the following eight fundamental elements that are discussed below.

3.1 Application

CPS has a wide range of applications in healthcare, including hospitals, assisted living institutions, and senior care. The complexity of these systems varies greatly depending on the application. Depending on the application, the architectural parts may necessitate customized organization [13]. The architecture may include regulated aspects in a controlled setting, such as an intensive care unit. In contrast, higher integration of automated features in the construction of an assisted living home may be required. CPS healthcare applications are roughly classified into two categories:

a. Assisted

The aided use of CPS in healthcare emphasizes health monitoring while maintaining persons' independence in their daily lives. Patients can now receive personalized medical advice using biosensors to collect real-time physiological data. This strategy allows for the support and care of an increasing number of old persons in both elderly living facilities and private homes while considering their special medical needs. As elderly people lose motor, sensory, and/or cognitive abilities, their capacity to live independently deteriorates, frequently leading to hospitalization. This not only has major emotional implications, but it also has financial consequences. Solutions like ANGELAH [14], which leverages computer technology, can provide great prospects for improving in-house safety and increasing autonomy in the workplace.

b. Regulated environments

The use of CPS in a controlled setting is most common in hospitals and intensive care units, where quick medical assistance is readily available. The amount of monitoring in these environments is strong and concentrated. To guide medical operations, hospitals rely on combining data from numerous sources, such as bedside monitors, biosensors, and clinician observations. Networked closed-loop systems with active human participation have the potential to improve medical processes and patient safety. With the advent of remote patient care technology, healthcare practitioners may now obtain crucial information on how everyday activities affect an individual's health, allowing them to make better-educated intervention decisions. Merging these formerly distinct parts of healthcare would convert the healthcare system into a big and complex cyber-physical system.

3.2 Architecture

The architecture is critical to ensuring the quality and performance of CPS in healthcare. It is critical to create an architecture that matches the unique application domain, user data needs, and system integration [15]. Three fundamental features characterize the architecture of CPS in healthcare.

3.2.1 Infrastructure

One key issue to consider while creating the CPS architecture for healthcare is the infrastructure viewpoint, which may be classified as server-based or cloud-based. Smaller architectures benefit from server-based infrastructure, which requires individual upkeep. In contrast, because of its scalability, cost-effectiveness, and accessibility benefits, cloud-based infrastructure has recently been adopted in healthcare CPS [10]. The complexity and resource constraints inherent with CPS, on the other hand, offer hurdles, rendering both cyber and physical components susceptible. As a result, building CPS for healthcare applications necessitates extra work to overcome these difficulties while still ensuring the system's security and stability.

3.2.2 Data Requirement

To effectively manage CPS architecture in healthcare, many sorts of data must be handled, including input data, historical data, and output data. Depending on the type of biosensor being utilised, the data size in healthcare applications may change. Although smaller datasets, like magnetic resonance imaging (MRI) scans, can be collected, processing is also necessary for larger datasets, such temperature observations. Measures like blood pressure and temperature are examples of low data rate applications, whereas measurements that require more data, such high-density surface electromyograms (EMGs), are indicators of high data rates [16]. It is also possible that certain functions will need the retrieval of old data from storage. As a result, the data requirements for the architecture can be split into two groups: light data requirements for datasets that are simpler and heavy data requirements for datasets that are larger.

3.2.3 Composition

Parallel computation and communication processes are ubiquitous in the design of CPS in healthcare. The system architecture must be capable of recognizing and organizing system composition depending on usage requirements. Depending on the system setup or the demands of the user, application creation can be accomplished dynamically or manually. Interaction with gadgets and software applications is also facilitated by the system. Dynamic composition, on the other hand, entails conducting computation and communication operations automatically, without the need for human participation. This allows for the smooth integration and operation of the CPS components, encouraging efficient system functionality and interaction.

3.3 Sensing

Sensing facilitates the physical part of CPS for healthcare. Biomedical sensors are critical in gathering vital physiological data, which is subsequently communicated to the processing and communication system for further analysis and utilization. Sensing is critical in healthcare applications because the detected quantities serve as system input parameters. It is crucial to note, however, that sensing treatments can occasionally cause discomfort or agony to individuals. Detecting blood glucose levels in diabetic patients, for example, has typically included pricking the finger and taking a sample [17]. To solve this issue, noninvasive blood glucose level monitoring systems based on radio-based sensors have been developed. From a sensory standpoint, the components are as follows.

3.3.1 Sensor Type

The quantity and kind of sensors used in healthcare applications might vary greatly. These sensors might be homogeneous (many sensors of the same type) or heterogeneous (a combination of different types of sensors). The sensing system can range from monitoring a single metric for a group of individuals to monitoring an individual's health state using several sensors. The chosen sensing approach has a significant impact on the system's complexity. This refers to the type of sensor used, which might be biosensors, wearable sensors, or radio-based sensors.

3.3.2 Method

Biosensors nowadays are capable of effectively collecting crucial patient information. These sensors can gather data from patients in the hospital or at home and send it to a sink (or controller) that can use it locally or transfer it to other networks (e.g., the cloud network) through a gateway. The sensors might be connected to a wireless sensor network. Data can be gathered either actively or passively as part of the sensing process. ECG data, for example, can be collected by active sensing, whereas heart rate can be retrieved passively from ECG data. As a result, it is critical to identify the sensing mechanism for improved CPS efficiency in healthcare.

3.3.3 Parameter

The parameter definition is critical for a better computation and communication approach. For a personal health application, a basic single-parameter system may suffice; however, a complete status monitoring system may necessitate many parameters [18]. Wearable and wireless sensors continuously monitor critical data such as heart rate, oxygen level, blood flow, respiratory rate, muscle activity, movement patterns, body inclination, and oxygen absorption and feed it into a multi-parameter system. The large diversity of sensor characteristics in metrics, schemes, and methodologies can make monitoring health status difficult.

3.4 Data Management

Data management is critical in developing methods to successfully handle acquired data and satisfy user expectations in CPS for healthcare. It entails integrating and storing data from many sensors for future use, while data processing allows for increased information collection and transmission. However, raw sensed data may be difficult to use due to high bandwidth needs and inefficient processing. Kang et al. [19] presented an innovative information-centric method that makes use of network-enabled real-time embedded databases (nRTEDBs) to enable secure and timely connection with wireless sensors. These databases are remarkable in their capacity to handle raw data. They also provide real-time data processing and routing, dependable event detection, security, and resilience. This information-centric strategy improves the efficiency and efficacy of healthcare data administration in CPS.

The data management process consists of three major components.

3.4.1 Data Integration

It entails merging and consolidating data from several sensors to generate a single and complete dataset.

3.4.2 Data Storage

This is the process of storing and organizing collected data to allow for efficient retrieval and future usability.

3.4.3 Data Processing

It entails using suitable methods and techniques to process and analyze gathered data, converting it into useful information for decision-making and communication.

3.5 Computation

Computations in CPS for healthcare are used for two purposes: (a) modeling and (b) monitoring. The computation involved in the model specification is critical in healthcare CPS applications because it dictates which methods should be implemented. Doctors and clinicians must be able to remotely monitor and watch patients, as well as obtain correct patient data from anywhere and at any time. Cloud computing comes into play here.

Cloud computing offers large-scale and complicated processing and connectivity, allowing clinicians to readily collect patient data via biosensors from hospitals and remote observation centers. To maintain system efficiency, algorithms that solve issues such as data bottlenecks and data size computations must be executed. Cloud computing systems provide the computational services required to accomplish these processes [20].

Furthermore, cloud computing offers extra benefits to CPS in healthcare. It supports high-performance computing, mobile device integration, and a variety of operating system platforms. Cloud computing's flexibility and scalability improve the overall efficiency and effectiveness of CPS in healthcare systems by allowing for smooth data management, efficient calculations, and effective communication between healthcare professionals and their patients.

By leveraging cloud computing services, CPS can overcome data processing and storage limitations and provide doctors and clinicians with real-time access to critical patient data, thereby improving care quality and facilitating better healthcare decision-making.

3.6 Communication

Communication is crucial in two components of the CPS architecture for healthcare: detecting patient data and transferring it to the cloud. Minor communication contacts, such as those between observation centers and healthcare services, do occur throughout the system.

Wireless multimedia sensor networks (WMSN) advancements have opened up opportunities for picture transmission inside CPS architecture. This advancement enables the effective transmission of extracted or compressed images, hence assisting in patient monitoring, observation, and study of image data about certain physiological factors. CPS in healthcare can improve its capabilities while using less energy by utilizing picture transmission through WMSNs.

Scheduling and communication protocols are essential for effective communication in CPS architecture. Data collection, transmission, and processing are all coordinated through scheduling to eliminate conflicts and maximize system performance. Communication protocols, on the other hand, give standards and rules for data interchange and interaction across architectural components [21]. The efficient use of network resources and the smooth integration of sensor data are made possible by these protocols, which provide dependable and timely communication. By creating efficient scheduling systems and communication protocols, CPS in the healthcare industry may enhance information flow, facilitate real-time monitoring, and help transfer vital patient data to the cloud for additional analysis and decision-making. This leads to better patient care and outcomes by enhancing the overall functioning and performance of the healthcare system.

3.7 Security

Data security is critical in CPS design for healthcare applications, given the sensitive nature of patient data from a legal and ethical standpoint. As a result, when building such architecture, extra consideration must be paid to data protection through rigorous security mechanisms. Security in CPS for healthcare has two main domains.

3.7.1 Privacy

Security measures are put in place to safeguard sensitive patient information from unauthorized access and to guarantee that privacy rules are followed. To protect patient privacy, authentication procedures, strict access restrictions, and data anonymization techniques must be implemented. CPS design may limit the risks associated with data breaches and unauthorized disclosures by integrating privacy controls and ensuring the confidentiality of patient data.

3.7.2 Encryption

Encryption is a critical security technique used to protect the integrity and confidentiality of patient data while it is being transmitted and stored. CPS design can guarantee that patient data stays secured by utilizing encryption methods and protocols, making it impossible for unauthorized parties to intercept or understand the information. Encryption adds another layer of protection against data breaches and unauthorized access, improving overall system security. CPS in Healthcare applications may provide a safe environment for managing patient data by including strong privacy features and encryption techniques in the CPS architecture. This fosters appropriate and ethical handling of sensitive information among patients, healthcare professionals, and regulatory agencies.

3.8 Control/Actuation

Present healthcare systems are ineffective at recognizing emergency patient data and informing authorized medical carers. The vast majority of alert systems in use today are threshold alarms that activate when a vital sign passes a specified threshold value. These threshold alarms, however, may not always offer fast and accurate notifications, possibly leading to delays in emergency action. Two major elements must be addressed to improve the control and actuation capabilities of healthcare CPS.

3.8.1 Decision Making

Timely and suitable responses to emergency circumstances need effective decision-making procedures. This entails creating cognitive algorithms and decision support systems capable of analyzing patient data in real-time, identifying key trends or abnormalities, and sending useful warnings to healthcare personnel. Decision-making capacities may be improved by employing modern analytics and machine-learning approaches, allowing for the early identification of crises and rapid medical treatments.

3.8.2 Mechanism

The infrastructure and processes in place to support control and actuation inside the CPS architecture are referred to as the mechanism. This involves the smooth transfer of emergency data and the timely delivery of alerts to authorized medical carers through the integration of medical devices, communication systems, and alert mechanisms. The system should be set up to prioritize emergency notification (Fig. 3).

4 Applications of Medical Devices and Sensors in Intelligent CPS

The fields of medicine and healthcare cover a wide variety of issues that touch on many physiologic characteristics of patients. Due to the various research opportunities that medical applications provide, there is a noticeable concentration on them within the subject of Cyber-Physical Systems (CPS) study. These possibilities include a wide range of industries, including home healthcare, assisted living, smart operating rooms, intelligent medical equipment (including pacemakers, medical ventilators, and infusion pumps), and high-tech prescription management systems [4, 22].

- **Home Healthcare**: By providing remote monitoring and individualized treatment for patients in the comfort of their own homes, CPMS technologies have the potential to revolutionize home healthcare. This includes tracking medication adherence, remote vital sign monitoring, and virtual consultations, which enhance patient outcomes and cut down on hospital visits.
- **Assisted Living**: By combining smart gadgets and systems, CPMS can improve the quality of life for people who reside in assisted living services. Remote resident monitoring, sophisticated fall detection devices, ambient assisted living technology, and individualized healthcare management are some examples of this.
- **Smart Operating Rooms**: By using smart technology, CPMS can increase the effectiveness and security of operating rooms. Real-time monitoring of patient vital statistics, intelligent surgical equipment, automated medicine administration systems, and sophisticated imaging and visualization tools for surgeons can all be examples of this.
- **Intelligent Medical Equipment**: Such as pacemakers (heart rate monitors), medical ventilators, and infusion pumps, may perform more effectively and be connected to other medical tools due to CPMS. These gadgets can provide better

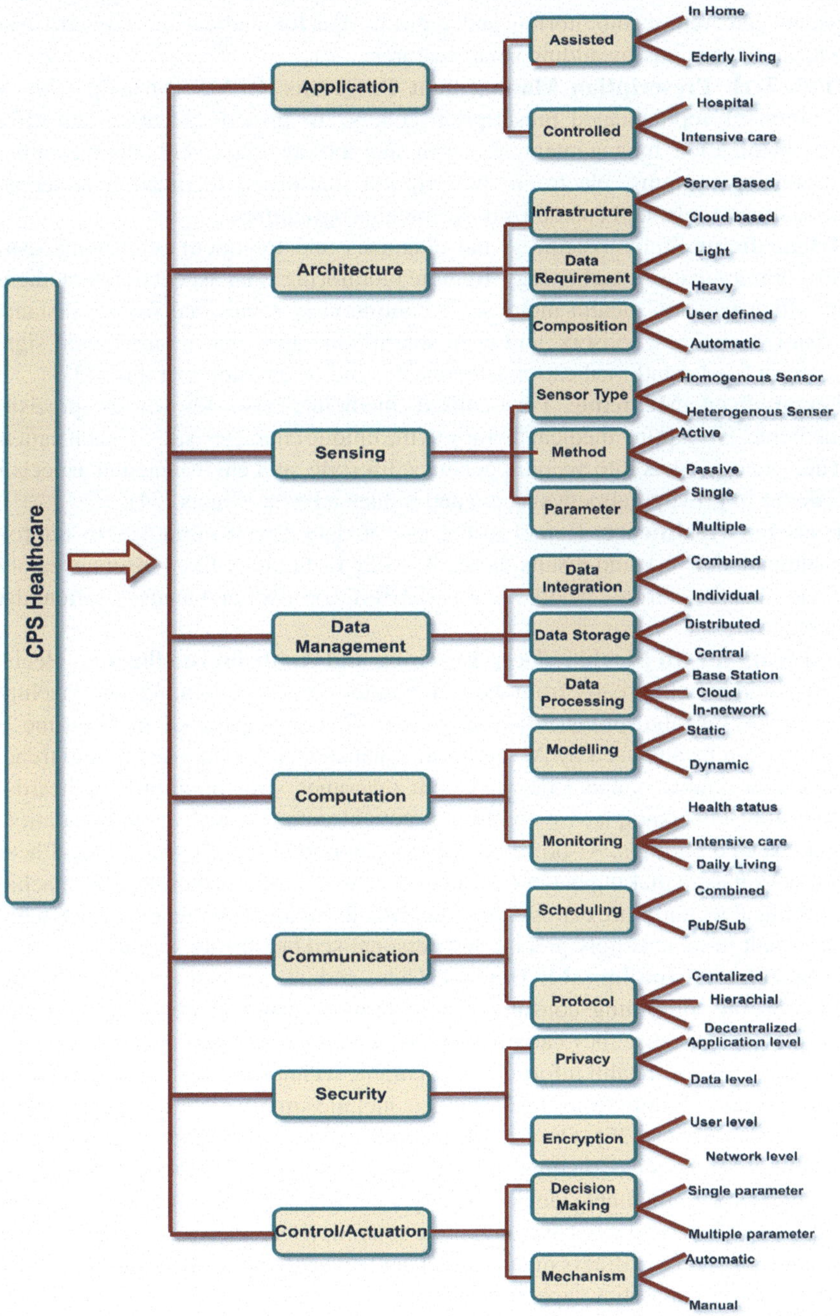

Fig. 3 Overview of taxonomy in CPS healthcare (from [12], licensed under CC-BY 3.0)

patient care, remote monitoring, and real-time data for medical specialists to make educated decisions by adding smart features.

- **High-Tech Prescription Management Programs**: CPMS can help with the creation of sophisticated prescription coders. To provide accurate and effective medication management, this can incorporate intelligent pharmaceutical dispensing systems, electronic prescription platforms, medication adherence assessment tools, and customized treatment programmes.
- **Telemedicine**: Telemedicine is the diagnosis and treatment of patients using telecommunications technology. Remote monitoring is an aspect of telemedicine in which patients' health metrics are continuously monitored from a distance. Wearable devices, sensors, and even smartphone apps that monitor vital signs, exercise levels, and medication adherence could be examples of this [23].
- **Personalised Medicine**: Personalised medicine, also known as precision medicine, is adapting medical therapy to the unique characteristics of each patient. This strategy takes into account genetics, lifestyle, and environmental aspects in order to improve treatment success and reduce adverse effects [24].
- **Precision Healthcare**: Refers to the use of data-driven initiatives to improve healthcare delivery and results. It entails using technology like sensors, wearable devices, and electronic health records (EHRs) to collect and analyse patient data in real time.
- **Integration with Machine/Deep Learning and Artificial Intelligence**: Healthcare could benefit greatly from the combination of sensor data, AI, and machine/deep learning algorithms. Massive patient data sets gathered in real-time by sensors can be analysed by AI algorithms, which can then be used to find trends, spot abnormalities, and forecast health outcomes with previously unheard-of precision. For example, by combining patient data, clinical recommendations, and research findings, AI-powered decision support systems can assist healthcare professionals in making better treatment decisions [25]. Furthermore, as machine learning algorithms are exposed to more data, they can get better over time, which can result in increasingly precise and personalised healthcare solutions.
- **Wearable and Implantable Devices**: These gadgets are getting more advanced all the time, providing consumers with individualised feedback and ongoing monitoring. Because they can track physical activity, monitor sleep patterns, and provide real-time health information, wearable technology has become more and more popular. Examples of these gadgets include smartwatches, fitness trackers, and smart clothes [26]. On the other hand, patients with chronic diseases can benefit from targeted therapy delivery and ongoing physiological monitoring provided by implantable devices like pacemakers, insulin pumps, and neural implants. These gadgets have the power to completely transform remote patient monitoring, chronic illness management, and preventive healthcare as their sensor and AI-driven analytics capabilities grow.

There are various significant elements to the present landscape of technological advancements in healthcare. There is a growing need for continuous patient monitoring in a variety of settings, such as home healthcare, assisted living, telemedicine,

Personalised Medicine, Wearable and Implantable Devices, and sport-activity monitoring. These include the development of reliable software solutions to enable the delivery of new functionalities. Future development of CPMS is projected to heavily rely on modeling and model-driven engineering. These methods will facilitate the design and construction of complex models that capture the intricate connections between the physical and digital elements of healthcare systems, supporting the creation of cutting-edge CPMS solutions [27]. The achievement of system-level interoperability is critical in the development of CPMS. Recognizing this need, collaborative projects have been launched to meet it, such as the development of the Medical Device Plug-and-Play (MD PnP) Interoperability program in 2004. This platform has been a driving force in the creation of open platforms as well as guidelines for medical device interoperability [28].

These developments enable diverse systems to smoothly integrate and work in a plug-and-play manner by encouraging interoperability. This, in turn, has important consequences for patient safety since it enables the interchange of crucial information and the acceptance of innovative treatment options. Furthermore, these advancements pave the path for greater adoption of digital technologies in healthcare settings, encouraging invention and enhancing patient outcomes [29].

The current medical technology has limits in data availability, and integration, especially manual device integration. The future of CPMS intends to provide broad data integration, detailed analysis, closed-loop control, energy conservation, real-time visualization, and plug-and-play interoperability with medical equipment.

5 Wireless Sensor Networks Toward the CP

A body area network (BAN), also known as a body sensor network (BSN) or wireless body area network (WBAN), is a network of wirelessly communicating wearable computing devices. These networks, which incorporate various types of implanted, tiny, or wearable sensors, implantable devices are mostly utilized for health monitoring. These biosensors may measure vital physiological factors including blood pressure, respiratory rate, heart rate, body and skin temperature, and electrocardiogram (ECG) measurements.

The acquired data from these sensors can be linked to a central node, such as a microcontroller board or a Personal Digital Assistant (PDA), via wireless connections [2]. The information acquired by this central node can subsequently be displayed on a user interface or transmitted to a healthcare center. Wireless sensor networks (WSN) and mobile ad hoc networks (MANET) researchers are actively investigating BAN-related technologies.

Cyber-Physical Systems (CPS) are distinguished by the flow of heterogeneous information, intelligent decision-making, and sensor collaboration across domains. As a result, CPS systems may be used efficiently in a variety of applications.

Human–machine interaction in Medical Cyber-Physical Systems (MCPS) is an intriguing subject within CPS. The connection between people and medical devices/

systems might take two forms: subjects or operators/users of the systems. Patient-specific modeling and simulation are required to provide patient-specific and adaptable therapy. It is critical to design interfaces that allow for natural interaction [18]. These interfaces should provide shared understanding between cyber and human components, including various system states (both normal and failure), accepting actions, and sharing authority between humans and medical equipment. In conclusion, MCPS emphasizes the need for seamless interaction between humans and medical systems via interfaces that enable shared knowledge, action acceptability, and shared authority, ultimately leading to patient-specific and adaptive treatments.

6 IoT-Based CPS for Digital Healthcare

Cyber-Physical Systems (CPS) based on the Internet of Medical Things (IoMT), as well as necessary parts like base stations, service providers, and associated organizations, are included in the expansive network of interconnected elements that make up digital healthcare. The demand for this developing technology has increased significantly over the last decade, owing mostly to its capacity to produce cost-effective results. Through the use of Cyber-Physical Systems (CPS), the integration of Internet of Things (IoT) technology into healthcare facilities and services has considerably improved human life. However, as technology advances, new cyber-attacks arise, posing a tremendous challenge to cybersecurity professionals. It is becoming increasingly difficult to keep up with the ever-changing and sophisticated assault strategies. As a result, there is an urgent need for breakthrough cognitive cyber security strategies to protect the CPS-IoT-enabled healthcare environment [30].

Cyber-Physical Systems (CPS) and Internet of Things (IoT) technology application in the healthcare sector has resulted in substantial vulnerabilities to a variety of new cyber-attacks. Healthcare facilities and infrastructures that are CPS-IoT enabled are categorized as safety and security essential systems and are characterized by heterogeneity, fragmentation, interconnectivity, and a cross-organizational aspect. As a result, prospective threats have a far larger attack surface. Cybersecurity attacks on CPS-IoT systems in healthcare can have far-reaching effects, including invasions of user privacy, bodily harm, monetary losses, and even putting human life in peril. Recent studies highlight the worrying rise in assaults, which includes the pervasive practice of medical identity theft that results in millions of medical information being taken globally. The avoidance of such assaults becomes of the highest importance given the seriousness of these hazards. The growing frequency of cyber-physical assaults brings to light the shortcomings of present security solutions in successfully tackling the dynamic, complex, unpredictable, and highly linked character of CPS-IoT-enabled healthcare services and vital infrastructures. To address these issues, the combination of cognitive architecture and artificial intelligence has enormous promise for improving automated intelligent cybersecurity decision-making processes and endowing them with expert-level skills. The cybersecurity

Table 2 Components of CPS-IoT-enabled healthcare systems

Components	Description
Cognitive architecture	To predict and respond to new security and privacy concerns, a cognitive architecture modeling human cognitive behavior will be created
Trade-offs in decision making	By accounting for uncertainty and maximizing temporal feedback loops, cyber-security systems seek to keep ahead of the cognitive decision cycles of attackers
Innovative methods	To improve threat avoidance, identification, incident response, and impact reduction, innovative methods will be incorporated. This entails implementing metrics, a dynamic security-related knowledge base, security and privacy, and security
Privacy-aware collaboration	To protect privacy while enabling efficient cyber-security measures, computational methods, adaptive data collecting, and actuation will be highlighted
Cross-cutting methods	Cross-cutting methods including run-time verification, evidence gathering, predictive analytics, and tracing will be incorporated. These methods provide dynamic forensics, evidence-based risk management, and overall system security

defenses may respond intelligently to changing threats by utilizing these technologies, greatly enhancing the safety posture of CPS-IoT-connected healthcare systems. The suggested strategy's primary goal is to offer a mechanism for thwarting dynamic and adaptable attacks on the healthcare ecosystem that is enabled by CPS and IoT. The paramount CPS-Io_T healthcare syetem components to acheive improved cybersecurity are given above (Table 2) [15].

7 Challenges and Issues in CPS

There are several challenges in designing, developing, and deploying CPS in healthcare and other sectors. Because of concerns like software stability, system interoperability, computational intelligence, security, privacy, and context-awareness, healthcare CPS design is extremely difficult. In CPS enabled devices, the software works in tandem with hardware to provide flawless performance [12] (Fig. 4). The definitions and characteristics of certain significant CPS challenges:

- ***Reliability***—Physical system (CPS) reliability is the system's capacity to carry out its intended function effectively. System capabilities are not necessarily flawlessly performed just because they have been certified. A highly trustworthy CPS guarantees that activities are completed appropriately. As open, dynamic, and uncertain settings are those in which CPSs function, it is crucial to measure uncertainties throughout the design phase to accurately describe CPS dependability. The accuracy of physical and cyber components, possible design/control flow mistakes, and ad-hoc network connections across domains are some examples of factors that

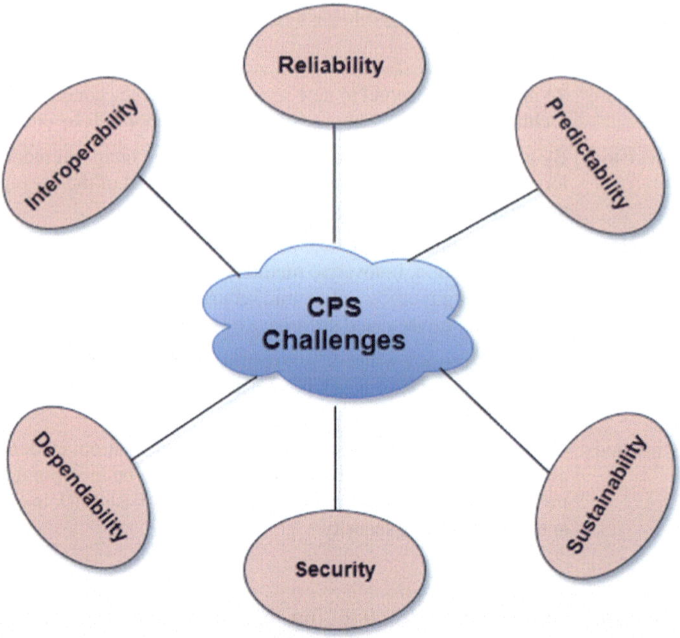

Fig. 4 CPS challenges

may restrict the CPS's dependability. Other factors include uncertainty in knowledge, qualities (such as time), process outcomes, and correctness of physical and cyber components [31].

- ***Predictability***—In a system relates to its ability to predict and foresee its state, behavior, and functioning, either qualitatively or quantitatively. A highly predictable device delivers consistent and defined results in its activities while fulfilling all criteria. In the framework of Cyber-Physical Medical Systems (CPMS), intelligent medical equipment and advanced control technologies are meant to adapt to patient situations, forecast motions, and modify their features depending on context awareness in the surrounding environment.
- ***Security and Privacy***—It is critical to ensure the security and privacy of gathered patient data. Unauthorized access or misuse of this information can lead to reputational injury, loss of personal privacy, emotional anguish, and possibly bodily harm.
- ***Interoperability***—The capacity of systems or components to interact, communicate information, and use that information to perform specified services is referred to as interoperability. A highly interoperable system allows for effective communication and smooth collaboration across its components. In the event of Unmanned

Aerial Vehicles (UAVs) involved in lengthy military operations, effective communication between UAVs and diverse ground vehicles is critical. The lack of interoperability standards frequently impedes the efficacy of complicated and critical operations [8].
- ***Accuracy***—The amount of conformity between a system's observed or perceived output and its real or calculated value is referred to as accuracy. A highly precise system aims to be as near to the real result as possible. Accuracy is especially important in CPS applications, where even little errors can cause system failures. In a motion-based object tracking device with faulty sensor conditions, for example, erroneous estimation of object location may result in untimely control actions, eventually resulting in system failure [32].
- ***Integrity***—The capacity of a system to protect itself or the information it carries from unauthorized tampering or change ensures the accuracy and veracity of the data. A high-integrity system includes rigorous authorization and consistency checks. A Cyber-Physical System (CPS) must have a high level of integrity [33].

- **Issues in CPS**

To improve the performance of future healthcare cyber-physical systems, it is critical to solve the following issues:

- **Variability of Parameters**: Current suggestions for healthcare CPS focus on restricted parameters, limiting system possibilities. Incorporating numerous criteria will improve system trustworthiness and context awareness.
- **Data Workflow**: The complexity of healthcare CPS necessitates well-designed data processes to increase system quality and efficiency.
- **Implementation**: The majority of suggested healthcare CPS systems are currently in the planning and simulation stages. Exploring actual implementation will provide research possibilities as well as real-world implementation obstacles.

8 Conclusion

The internet and computing revolutions have created tremendous opportunities in control systems, affecting many sectors of human existence such as transportation, healthcare, energy management, and services. These cyber-physical systems are distinguished by their networked, hybrid, and integrated nature, incorporating several subsystems with human interactions at their center. This study gives an in-depth examination of cyber-physical systems (CPS) in healthcare. It begins by providing a broad overview of CPS. The authors then propose a characterization of CPS for healthcare applications, based on a taxonomy that includes eight different perspectives: application, architecture, sensing, data management, computing, communication, security, and control/actuation [28]. The goal of this characterization is to portray existing trends, methodologies, and possible CPS solutions in certain healthcare applications. The authors also apply this classification to current CPS initiatives in healthcare, such as those that just use wireless sensor networks (WSN) or cloud computing. They find gaps between WSN/cloud-based healthcare solutions and CPS-based solutions in this way. Although CPS has the potential to improve event prediction in healthcare, little research has been conducted in this area.

References

1. E. A. Lee, "CPS foundations," *Proc. - Des. Autom. Conf.*, pp. 737–742, 2010, https://doi.org/10.1145/1837274.1837462.
2. N. Dey, A. S. Ashour, and S. J. Fong, "Medical cyber-physical systems: A survey," pp. 1–13, 2018.
3. E. A. Lee, "Cyber physical systems: Design challenges," *Proc. - 11th IEEE Symp. Object/Component/Service-Oriented Real-Time Distrib. Comput. ISORC 2008*, pp. 363–369, 2008, https://doi.org/10.1109/ISORC.2008.25.
4. B. K. Kim and P. R. Kumar, "06176187," vol. 100, pp. 1287–1308, 2012.
5. E. Sultanovs, A. Skorobogatjko, and A. Romanovs, "Centralized healthcare cyber-physical system's architecture development," *2016 57th Int. Sci. Conf. Power Electr. Eng. Riga Tech. Univ. RTUCON 2016*, 2016, https://doi.org/10.1109/RTUCON.2016.7763155.
6. J. Wan, M. Chen, F. Xia, D. Li, and K. Zhou, "From machine-to-machine communications towards cyber-physical systems," *Comput. Sci. Inf. Syst.*, vol. 10, no. 3, pp. 1105–1128, 2013, https://doi.org/10.2298/CSIS120326018W.
7. E. Darmois and O. Elloumi, "Introduction to M2M," *M2M Commun. A Syst. Approach*, pp. 1–20, 2011, https://doi.org/10.1002/9781119974031.ch1.
8. S. H. Ahmed, G. Kim, and D. Kim, "Cyber Physical System: Architecture , Applications and Research Challenges," pp. 0–4, 2013.
9. T. Sanislav and L. Miclea, "Cyber-physical systems - Concept, challenges and research areas," *Control Eng. Appl. Informatics*, vol. 14, no. 2, pp. 28–33, 2012.
10. Y. Tan, S. Goddard, and L. C. Pérez, "A prototype architecture for cyber-physical systems," *ACM SIGBED Rev.*, vol. 5, no. 1, pp. 1–2, 2008, https://doi.org/10.1145/1366283.1366309.
11. J. Wang, H. Abid, S. Lee, L. Shu, and F. Xia, "A secured health care application architecture for cyber-physical systems," *arXiv Prepr. ArXiv1201.0213*, 2011.
12. S. A. Haque, S. M. Aziz, and M. Rahman, "Review of cyber-physical system in healthcare," *Int. J. Distrib. Sens. Networks*, vol. 2014, 2014, https://doi.org/10.1155/2014/217415.
13. N. Ho, P. M. Wong, N. S. Hoang, D. K. Koh, M. C. H. Chua, and C. K. Chui, "CPS-based manufacturing workcell for the production of hybrid medical devices," *J. Ambient Intell. Humaniz. Comput.*, vol. 12, no. 12, pp. 10865–10879, 2021, https://doi.org/10.1007/s12652-020-02798-y.
14. T. Taleb, D. Bottazzi, M. Guizani, and H. Nait-Charif, "Angelah: A framework for assisting elders at home," *IEEE J. Sel. Areas Commun.*, vol. 27, no. 4, pp. 480–494, 2009, https://doi.org/10.1109/JSAC.2009.090511.
15. H. Abie, "Cognitive Cybersecurity for CPS-IoT Enabled Healthcare Ecosystems," *Int. Symp. Med. Inf. Commun. Technol. ISMICT*, vol. 2019-May, pp. 1–6, 2019, https://doi.org/10.1109/ISMICT.2019.8743670.
16. H. Kailanto, E. Hyvärinen, and J. Hyttinen, "Mobile ECG measurement and analysis system using mobile phone as the base station," *Proc. 2nd Int. Conf. Pervasive Comput. Technol. Healthc. 2008, PervasiveHealth*, pp. 12–14, 2008, https://doi.org/10.1109/PCTHEALTH.2008.4571014.

17. Q. Mary, M. E. Road, and M. End, "Wearable Wireless Sensors Research for Healthcare Applications," *Int. Work. Antenna Technol. Wearable*, pp. 376–379, 2014.
18. T. K. Lepasepp and W. Hurst, "A systematic literature review of industry 4.0 technologies within medical device manufacturing," *Futur. Internet*, vol. 13, no. 10, 2021, https://doi.org/10.3390/fi13100264.
19. K. D. Kang, S. H. Son, and J. A. Stankovic, "Managing deadline miss ratio and sensor data freshness in real-time databases," *IEEE Trans. Knowl. Data Eng.*, vol. 16, no. 10, pp. 1200–1216, 2004, https://doi.org/10.1109/TKDE.2004.61.
20. L. A. Tang *et al.*, "Multidimensional sensor data analysis in cyber-physical system: An atypical cube approach," *Int. J. Distrib. Sens. Networks*, vol. 2012, no. 2, 2012, https://doi.org/10.1155/2012/724846.
21. J. Hatcliff *et al.*, "Challenges and Research Directions in Medical Cyber – Physical Systems," *Proc. IEEE*, 2011.
22. A. A. Letichevsky, O. O. Letychevskyi, V. G. Skobelev, and V. A. Volkov, "Cyber-Physical Systems," *Cybern. Syst. Anal.*, vol. 53, no. 6, pp. 821–834, 2017, https://doi.org/10.1007/s10559-017-9984-9.
23. N. M. Hjelm, "Benefits and drawbacks of telemedicine," *Introd. to Telemedicine, Second Ed.*, pp. 134–149, 2017.
24. A. M. Vicente, W. Ballensiefen, and J.-I. Jönsson, "How personalised medicine will transform healthcare by 2030: the ICPerMed vision," *J. Transl. Med.*, vol. 18, pp. 1–4, 2020.
25. J. S. Banerjee, S. Bhattacharyya, A. J. Obaid, and W.-C. Yeh, *Intelligent Cyber-Physical Systems Security for Industry 4.0: Applications, Challenges and Management*. CRC Press, 2022.
26. S. Amin, T. Salahuddin, and A. Bouras, "Cyber physical systems and smart homes in healthcare: Current state and challenges," in *2020 IEEE International Conference on Informatics, IoT, and Enabling Technologies (ICIoT)*, 2020, pp. 302–309.
27. I. Lee and O. Sokolsky, "Medical cyber physical systems," *Proc. - Des. Autom. Conf.*, pp. 743–748, 2010, https://doi.org/10.1145/1837274.1837463.
28. V. Gunes, S. Peter, T. Givargis, and F. Vahid, "A survey on concepts, applications, and challenges in cyber-physical systems," *KSII Trans. Internet Inf. Syst.*, vol. 8, no. 12, pp. 4242–4268, 2014, https://doi.org/10.3837/tiis.2014.12.001.
29. D. Arney, S. Fischmeister, J. M. Goldman, I. Lee, and R. Trausmuth, "Plug-and-play for medical devices: Experiences from a case study," *Biomed. Instrum. Technol.*, vol. 43, no. 4, pp. 313–317, 2009, https://doi.org/10.2345/0899-8205-43.4.313.
30. M. A. Almaiah, F. Hajjej, A. Ali, M. F. Pasha, and O. Almomani, "An AI-Enabled Hybrid Lightweight Authentication Model for Digital Healthcare Using Industrial Internet of Things Cyber-Physical Systems," *Sensors*, vol. 22, no. 4, 2022, https://doi.org/10.3390/s22041448.
31. L. Monostori, "Cyber-physical production systems: Roots, expectations and R&D challenges," *Procedia CIRP*, vol. 17, pp. 9–13, 2014, https://doi.org/10.1016/j.procir.2014.03.115.
32. V. Gunes, S. Peter, and T. Givargis, "Modeling and mitigation of faults in cyber-physical systems with binary sensors," *Proc. - 16th IEEE Int. Conf. Comput. Sci. Eng. CSE 2013*, pp. 515–522, 2013, https://doi.org/10.1109/CSE.2013.83.
33. Y. Mo and B. Sinopoli, "Integrity attacks on cyber-physical systems," *HiCoNS'12 - Proc. 1st ACM Int. Conf. High Confid. Networked Syst.*, pp. 47–54, 2012, https://doi.org/10.1145/2185505.2185514.

Reviewing the Evolution of Intelligent Cyber-Physical Systems in the Internet of Medical Things

Shama Siddiqui, Anwar Ahmed Khan, and Muazzam Ali Khan Khattak

Abstract This chapter explores the role of the Internet of Medical Things (IoMT) in enabling intelligent Cyber-Physical Systems (CPS) for healthcare solutions. It highlights the core components of IoMT, including medical devices, sensors, connectivity, and data analytics. The chapter addresses challenges and opportunities in IoMT implementation, such as privacy, security, interoperability, and regulations. It emphasizes the integration of real-time patient monitoring, smart medical devices, and data-driven decision-making, showcasing how IoMT enhances CPS capabilities in providing personalized and efficient healthcare. Real-world case studies demonstrate successful IoMT-enabled CPS deployments and their impact on patient outcomes, workflows, and cost-effectiveness. The chapter concludes by discussing future prospects and emerging trends in the IoMT landscape for intelligent CPS, emphasizing the need for ongoing research and innovation. Overall, this chapter serves as a comprehensive guide for researchers, practitioners, and policymakers interested in leveraging IoMT to drive innovation and improve healthcare delivery in the era of intelligent CPS.

Keywords Internet of medical things (IoMT) · Intelligent CPS · Healthcare solutions · Real-time patient monitoring · Data-driven decision-making

S. Siddiqui (✉)
Department of Computer Science, DHA Suffa University, Karachi, Pakistan
e-mail: shamasid@hotmail.com

A. A. Khan
Department of Computer Science, Millennium Institute of Technology and Entrepreneurship, Karachi, Pakistan
e-mail: anwar.ahmed@mite.edu.pk

M. A. K. Khattak
Department of Computer Science, Quaid-e-Azam University, Islamabad, Pakistan
e-mail: muazzam.khattak@qau.edu.pk

M. Mittal and J. Narayan (eds.), *Intelligent Cyber-Physical Systems for Healthcare Solutions*, https://doi.org/10.1007/978-981-97-8983-2_7

1 Introduction

Internet of Medical Things (IoMT) refers to the interconnected network of medical and handheld devices used for collecting, transmitting, reporting, and analyzing health data. It has been designed as a type of Internet of Things (IoT), with a specific focus on improving patient outcomes and enhancing healthcare service delivery [1]. IoMT could integrate a large variety of sensors, actuators, and controllers as per the application requirements. IoMT works with a diverse set of applications; for example, on one hand, an IoMT solution may be used for simplest applications of fitness tracking, but on the other hand, it could be used for remote monitoring of patients suffering from life-threatening diseases.

Conventionally, the goal of IoMT was to continuously monitor patient's state by collecting and reporting real-time data [2]. Today, due to the advancements in supporting technologies such as artificial intelligence and big data, novel applications are introduced every day. Typical architecture of IoMT has been shown in Fig. 1.

At the starting point/input side, IoMT architecture relies on medical devices and sensors to collect data. The sensors could be wearable or implantable [3]. Moreover, the handheld devices may collect data from these sensors, or may require users to input their data manually. Again, it depends on the application; for example, smart watches or mobile health applications keep track of the exercise routine of the users, manage trends on the handheld devices as well as on the cloud. Here, the available networking technologies such as Bluetooth, Wi-Fi, 4G/5G is used for transmitting the data, first from sensor to the handheld device and subsequently from handheld device to the cloud. It is also to be noted that it may not be required to always send

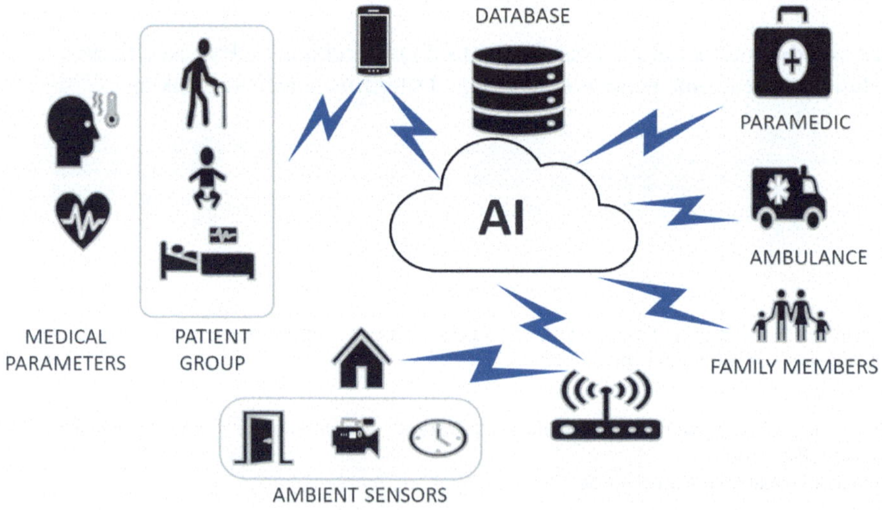

Fig. 1 Conventional architecture of internet of medical things (IoMT)

data from the sensors or wearable device to the handheld device; in some cases, these devices may directly send the data via gateway.

Once the data reaches the cloud, the technologies deployed on the server, such as big data analytics or artificial intelligence may be utilized. Finally, the data reaches the final destinations of medical databases, routine physicians, emergency care providers or family caregivers [4]. Today, we see lots of emerging technologies being integrated with the IoMT such as big data analytics, Artificial intelligence, blockchain, computer vision etc. Hence, there have been several survey studies focusing on each of these integrations. For example, a review of Big Data and IoMT solutions as deployed for COVID-19 detection and prevention has been presented in [5]. The role of responsible Artificial Intelligence for enhancing the potential of IoMT has been discussed in [6], and integration of IoMT with blockchain has been described in [7].

The present chapter focuses on providing a detailed review of IoMT components and its integration with Cyber physical systems. We discuss various applications supported by this fusion, such as integration of sensors with physical systems, enhanced decision making and predictive maintenance. It is crucial to note that although IoMT promises to revolutionize the healthcare, there are various implementation challenges due to the unique nature of healthcare data and systems. In this context, we present a review of challenges such as standardization, data protection, legal and regulatory compliance, etc. We also present some use cases such as smart homes, explainable AI and medical resources management. Since the focus of this chapter is to provide a foundation to the readers, we also present a list of recent development in the area such as advancements in the wearable devices, integration with AI and blockchain, genomic sequencing and precision medicine and interactions with Natural Language Processing (NLP) and Speech Recognition technologies.

Next, we discuss each component of IoMT, including medical devices, sensors, connectivity, and data analytics in detail.

2 Core Components of IoMT

2.1 Medical Devices

A large array of medical devices has been integrated with the IoMT solutions. The functionalities of connectivity and ease of use have been embedded into these cutting-edge devices, to ensure the use of technology for enhanced patient care. The major design goal of these devices is to continuously monitor various health conditions in order to timely diagnose and trigger proactive care. Some examples from the devices we see connected to the IoMT ecosystem are discussed below:

Wearable Devices mark one of the major aspects of revolution in the healthcare sector today. The application areas of these devices are diverse, ranging from preventive health measures to chronic disease management. Figure 2 presents a glimpse of wearable devices' applications in healthcare.

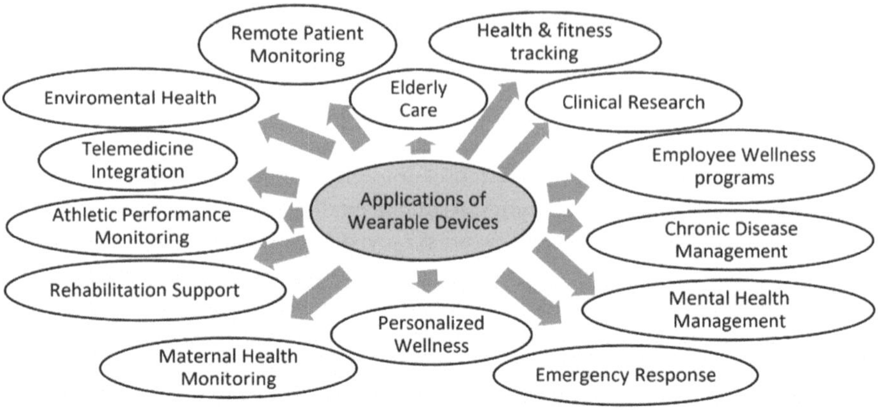

Fig. 2 Common applications of wearable devices

We now discuss each application briefly:

Physical Health and Fitness Tracking. Wearable devices are commonly used for tracking physical activity levels, exercise effectiveness, sleep patterns and dietary statistics. Today, these devices do not only monitor conventional health parameters such as heart rate and activity level, but advanced health metrics have been included in the scope of IoMT solutions. In this regard, the features of Electrocardiogram (ECG), blood oxygen saturation levels (SpO2) and even stress monitoring have been practiced.

Chronic Disease Management. This dimension has gained rapid popularity and interest of researchers and practitioners. Continuous monitoring and reporting of vitals offer a valuable opportunity of keeping all the data stored, which is then used for trend analysis and customized diagnosis, discussed later in the chapter. The chronic disease management such as for hypertension, diabetes or heart diseases has become easier and cost-effective with the help of wearable devices.

Elderly Care. Elderly living independently often face the challenges of disease management. Moreover, they also have to face high risk of falls and sudden health emergencies such as heart attack. Using a wearable device ensures proactive solutions for the patients and caregivers. First, the continuous monitoring of vital signs guarantees early detection of health pattern changes, which leads to preemptive interventions and enhanced well-being. Similarly, in the scenarios of health emergency or fall, the sensors deployed within the wearable device detect the abrupt changes in vital signs or movement/activity and generate alerts. The alerts are not only generated for notifying the patients, but these may also be sent to the caregivers or emergency services.

Remote Monitoring. The patients with chronic conditions are heavily facilitated through wearable devices which generate real-time data and alerts in a non-invasive manner. Patients can remain aware of their vitals all the time, while they engage in routine activities. The physicians may access patient data on their handheld devices and can offer remote diagnosis/consultation whenever required. Moreover, the remote monitoring technique is not only useful for the patients at home, but also those who are actually admitted. For example, during COVID-19, when social distancing was a crucial requirement, various healthcare facilities made use of wearable devices to monitor the vitals of critical patients continuously without risking the health of staff.

Telemedicine Integration. The use of IoMT devices has revolutionized the method of virtual consultations. Earlier, telemedicine was restricted to video conferencing during the patient-doctor interaction. The physicians had to rely on the information provided by the patient only; however, now, the landscape of telemedicine has been significantly changed. The smart wearable and portable sensing devices transmit real-time patient data as they communicate with the remote physician. Various companies have installed digital health pods all around the world, enabling accurate delivery of patient data, such as temperature, pulse rate, blood pressure, weight, etc. An example digital pod along with its uses has been illustrated in Fig. 3. Clearly, when the physicians get accurate information from the digital monitors, the probability of accurate and timely diagnosis increases considerably.

Rehabilitation Support. Wearable devices can offer crucial support during the rehabilitation journey of patients. It often becomes a challenge for the patients and their caregivers to optimize the benefit of physical therapy and other recommended treatment strategies once the patients are discharged. Since there is no available expertise on hand, in the absence of wearables, it used to increase the cost and recovery time for rehabilitation patients. However, due to the wearable and remote consultation option, it has become convenient for the patients as well as physicians to maintain

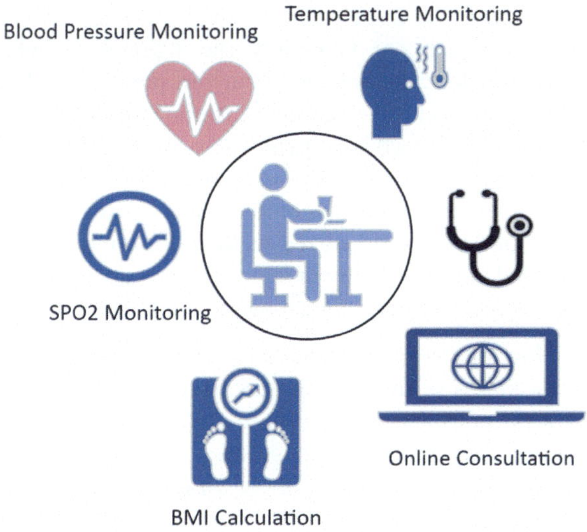

Fig. 3 Example of a digital health pod

the posture, track movement and gauge rehabilitation progress. For example, a system based on low cost hardware and interoperability standards has been developed in [8], that detects the shoulder movement to identify whether the patient's posture during the exercise is in accordance with the physician's recommendations.

Maternal Health Monitoring. Monitoring the health and wellbeing of pregnant women and their fetuses is a mandatory requirement for ensuring safe and healthy pregnancy. Conventionally, the vitals and other crucial physical/physiological parameters of both the pregnant women and their babies were observed only on the routine visits, which could be once a month. This significantly increases the risks of pregnancy such as lack of fetal growth, movement, or raise/decline in mother's crucial vitals. Due to the continuous use of wearable devices (such as wristbands), it becomes possible to monitor the health of mothers and babies in the real-time and generate alerts immediately in case any abnormality is detected [9]. Wearables may measure mothers' heart rate, uterine contractions, blood pressure, fetal heart rate, number of kicks and movement rate. This data may be stored on patients' devices and may also be transmitted to the physicians, allowing them to intervene timely and develop customized treatment plans. Moreover, AI/ML is also being integrated with the IoMT infrastructure for ensuring even better prenatal care [10].

Emergency Response. Wearable devices promise to be invaluable tools for patients with risks of fall/accident or sudden health deteriorations. The wearable devices embedded with sensors alert the patient and their caregivers in the real-time about the critical situations; for example, a helmet has been proposed in to identify the worsening of neurological symptoms early to identify stroke-in-evolution [11]. Similarly, the emergency situations for chronic diseases can be dealt by IoMT wearable devices in an efficient manner, as these devices generate immediate alerts on detecting abrupt changes in the heartbeat, blood pressure or other health emergency indicators.

Personalized Wellness. One of the most interesting features of wearable devices is personalized care. Generally, the digital knowledge and emerging mobile apps provide generic guidelines about the population data and health risks. With the help of wearable devices and customized dashboards, it has become possible to develop customized treatment plans as a response to customized risk assessment. For example, there are various mobile apps, which in integration with the wearable devices, provide guidance on the dietary plans, meditation and breathing exercises [12]. Similarly, personalized wellness also encompasses techniques such as precision medicine development which focuses on developing the medicines based on the customized response of each patient.

Employee Wellness Programs. The organizations interested in prioritizing the health and wellness of their employees have started to invest in wearable devices. These devices contribute to fostering a culture of fitness among employees as well as to prevent occupational health issues. Using wearables, the employees and their bosses may gather real-time data about vital parameters, sleep patterns, stress levels and physical activity; this leads to employees making informed lifestyle choices, while employers may improve their work-life balance and workload management strategies in accordance with the customized health requirements of employees. Moreover, the employers may also offer incentives to the employees who achieve their fitness goals, to nurture an overall healthy workplace culture. In addition to offering health benefits and higher motivation for the employees, the use of wearable tracking devices will also result in the cost-effectiveness for the organizations by assuring higher employee productivity and retention.

Athletic Performance. Wearable devices have also been used for monitoring, analyzing, and optimizing the performance of professional athletes. First, these devices are used for monitoring performance by tracking parameters such as heart rate variability, speed, acceleration, and biomechanical movements. Based on the collected data, a detailed insight into the athletes' physiological responses can be established, both during training sessions and actual competitions. Second, the collected data also informs the coaches about the patterns that could lead to injuries. The sensors can provide timely alerts about situations such as improper posture/form, excessive strain, or overexertion; hence, timely intervention can be made to reduce the risk of injuries during sports. Thirdly, the data can also be used to optimize the performance of athletes during the training sessions; the data can be analyzed using emerging AI algorithms for improving the performance strategies and training regimens. Therefore, the training programs can be made customized and effective through having details about the strengths and weaknesses of each athlete, rather than relying on general statistics.

Mental Health Management. Wearable devices today, in addition to physical health, also play a crucial role to monitor and manage mental health of populations. For example, a large number of mobile applications are available in the market which take data of vitals from individuals and assess the states of anxiety and depression. These applications deploy sophisticated algorithms and machine learning models for analyzing various parameters such as activity levels, sleep patterns and heart rate variability to identify mental health. Such applications of wearables lead to offering personalized insights into patients' health, based on which physicians/psychologists may plan timely interventions. Furthermore, these applications also assist the users in taking control of their mental health as they may track relevant trends on their smart phone applications, avail themselves of online consultations and even get community support.

Environmental Health Monitoring. The wearable devices also inform the users about environmental health, if equipped with relevant software applications. For example, considering the global degradation in the environmental quality, the users might be alerted about the environmental quality right on their smart wearable, while they take a hike. These devices, integrated with sensors capable of detecting air quality, temperature and humidity, UV radiation levels, or pollution indexes, offer users valuable insights into their immediate surroundings. Additionally, the users may also get alerts about the possible presence of allergens on the routes they have chosen. Users may also get alerts/early warning about natural disasters, further enhancing their personal safety. Thus, the wearable devices aid the users to plan their outdoor activities while remaining aware about their surroundings.

Clinical Research. Wearable devices have also revolutionized the medical research domain through providing opportunities for real-time data collection and analytics. Conventionally, the data collection from the trial participants was much less frequent as compared to the regular monitoring of physiological markers offered by IoMT. The continuous data streams obtained from the participants significantly enhance the quality of medical research as the practitioners develop a deeper understanding about health patterns of study participants. Also, due to the facility of remote monitoring, the wearable devices provide data of study participants from anywhere anytime, reducing their need to physically come to the location of clinical trials. Moreover, in the past, medical research studies mostly focused on collecting patient-reported data, which was often subjective and was also difficult to verify. On the contrary, wearable devices provide quantifiable data which improves accuracy and reliability and reduces bias. Finally, the wearables also provide an insight into the participants' responses to any medication or treatment strategy which leads to customized diagnostics and intervention planning.

2.2 Sensors

Some of the most commonly used sensors which enable IoMT to serve for the applications mentioned in the previous section, are listed below:

Temperature Sensors are used for monitoring body temperature and are often integrated with smart patches or smart thermometers. Temperature sensors offer an opportunity to monitor the variations in health conditions or fever in real-time. Moreover, these sensors enable healthcare practitioners to remain protected. During the era of Covid-19, various healthcare facilities such as Shanghai Public Health Clinical Centre (SPHCC) made use of Bluetooth enabled smart thermometers to collect temperature from COVID affected patients [13]. Hence, the nurses and other healthcare staff were able to maintain social distancing while still getting patients' data at their nursing counters.

Blood Pressure Sensors are often integrated with smart wrist band monitors and are used to measure systolic and diastolic blood pressure. Smart blood pressure monitors transmit data to the smart phone applications, and subsequently to the remote dashboards. Hence, the trends are not only available to the patients for managing their lifestyle choices, but also visible to the physicians. These sensors offer critical support for chronic patients for whom it is vital to maintain and monitor the trends for enhancing the treatment plans.

Heart Rate Monitors. Optical sensors or electrodes measure heart rate variations by detecting pulse signals. Wearable devices such as smart watches, patches or chest straps integrate these sensors. These wearables are often used for hospitalized patients where the nurses may remotely maintain the heart rate information of the patients. Similarly, the heart rate data may be collected from patients anywhere anytime to monitor their heart health regularly.

Glucometers integrate glucose sensors which measure the glucose levels in interstitial fluid or blood. These glucometers then transmit data to the handheld devices via Bluetooth or similar connectivity protocol; subsequently, the data is transmitted to the healthcare providers. Therefore, smart glucometers significantly help in diabetes management.

Pulse Oximeters. For some critical diseases where patients suffer from respiratory issues chronic obstructive pulmonary disease (COPD), pneumonia, or asthma, measuring pulse oximetry becomes crucial. These meters use non-invasive methods to measure the oxygen saturation levels in the blood. Smart pulse oximeters transmit data of oxygen saturation in real-time. This could help in detecting various medical conditions like hypoxemia; based on the customized risks of each patient, the physicians may set threshold values of oxygen saturation and may request alerts to detect severe risks. Moreover, these oximeters offered imperative support during the COVID-19 outbreak as they could early diagnose the probability of respiratory distress in the patients. Innovative applications such as automated music therapy [14] was also introduced with the help of remote pulse oximetry data to ensure that patients may get alternative care to maintain social distancing.

Accelerometers and Gyroscopes. These sensors play a diverse role for monitoring movement, steps, posture, and orientation changes. As previously discussed, athlete performance optimization is one of the core applications of IoMT, accelerometers and gyroscopes make it possible to track the fitness levels of athletes. Moreover, these sensors also significantly enhance the clinical research and rehabilitation journeys of individuals as they offer a chance to continuously monitor the posture, balance, and gesture. Innovative applications of enhancing ergonomics design for the workplaces and healthcare facilities are also facilitated by these sensors.

Electrocardiogram (ECG/EKG) Sensors have always been used for capturing electrical activity which is subsequently used for analyzing the heart rhythms for detecting irregularities and cardiac conditions. Today with the advent of IoMT, these sensors enable seamless monitoring of cardiac health in remote settings. ECG sensors provided with Bluetooth or other connectivity modules may offer real-time insight into the heart health for patients during their hospital stay, at the remote clinics (like one shown in Fig. 3), or while at home. Compared to only collecting ECG data while at the hospital, remote wearable provides an opportunity of continuous tracking, especially for those suffering from chronic cardiac conditions.

Biochemical Sensors are used for detecting concentrations of various biomarkers in the body fluids such as saliva or blood. Specific biomarkers that are associated with certain diseases can easily be identified using these sensors; for example, glucose levels in human sweat may be monitored for diabetes management or the concentration of lactate can be measured in the sweat of athletes to measure the exertion and optimize their performance accordingly. Also, these sensors are often used for detecting anxiety by measuring cortisol hormone in human saliva. While integrated with IoMT, these sensors could offer an insight into the real-time insights into the health conditions of individuals [15]. Particularly, the non-invasive biochemical sensors can offer help in remote health monitoring, early detection of diseases and fitness issues, proactive disease management. Thus, these sensors contribute to the domains of developing personalized treatment plans/medicines, clinical research, and fitness tracking.

Environmental Sensors are often used with IoMT for monitoring outdoor and/or indoor environmental conditions. This category includes temperature, air quality, vibration/motion, UV radiation, allergen, humidity, noise, gas, and chemical sensors as well as cameras. The ambient sensors often used in the IoMT applications for assisting elderly may track their health, fitness, movement patterns in the indoor environment [16]; these sensors are often configured to work in conjunction with the wearables to ensure real-time detection of risky events such as fall or a heart attack.

2.3 Connectivity Infrastructure for IoMT

The goal of connectivity infrastructure for IoMT is to transmit data from the sensors/wearables to the remote locations, to enable reliable and efficient management and analysis of the collected data. The transmission of data is made seamless as much as possible for ensuring real-time decision making, which in turn holds the power to revolutionize the healthcare systems of today. End-to-end transmission mechanism of health data has already been illustrated in Fig. 4. In this section, we briefly describe the core elements required by the IoMT infrastructure.

A large array of wireless communication technologies is utilized by IoMT, where the choice is governed by factors such as range, compatibility, power consumption, and data transfer rate. Some of the core technologies used in this context include Bluetooth, Wi-Fi, and cellular networks as briefly defined below:

Bluetooth has still been the most commonly used protocol for short-range connectivity between the wearable devices/ambient sensors and the handheld devices. To further reduce the power consumption and ensure long-term operation, Bluetooth Low Energy (BLE) variants are often used. Moreover, *Wi-Fi* is used for IoMT data transmission where high-bandwidth and longer range (as compared to that supported by BLE) are required. Most commonly, Wi-Fi is used at healthcare facilities where a large number of wearable devices transmit continuous data to the nursing stations, etc.

Subsequently, for communication beyond the conventional indoor environment, *cellular networks* come into play. Using these networks, the data is carried from handheld devices or wearables to remote locations. Thus, these networks play a vital

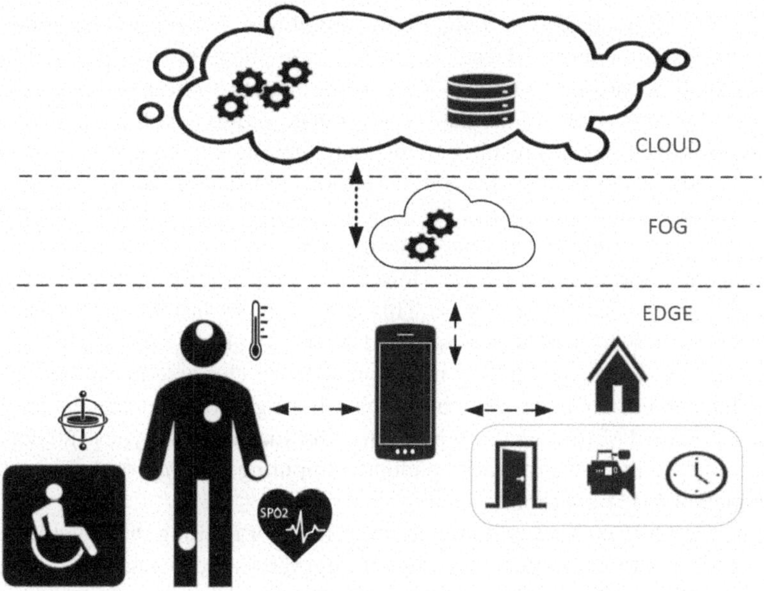

Fig. 4 Distributed communication architecture illustrating edge, fog, and cloud

role when developing applications that require monitoring of patients from anywhere at any time. Various communication standards 3G, 4G and 5G have been employed for providing connectivity. In fact, 5G even has standards such as Ultra-Reliable Low Latency Communication (URLLC) for ensuring enough resource provision for IoMT solutions. This standard guarantees high reliability, minimal latency, and consistent connectivity, which are essential for mission-critical healthcare scenarios such as real-time patient monitoring, emergency response systems or remote surgeries.

Today, the distributed computing approach has been adopted for ensuring efficient data processing and storage, considering the resource constraints of devices operating at various levels. Thus, the processing of medical data is split between three levels of *edge, fog, and computing.* The interaction between these levels has been illustrated in Fig. 4, and discussed next.

Edge Computing refers to the device where the data is to be processed near the point of generation. For the IoMT scenarios, the edge device could be wearable, ambient sensor or the handheld device. It depends on the processing capability embedded within each device; if the wearable device is configured for performing some type of processing, then it will be regarded as an edge device. For example, if a wearable watch is configured to send data to the handheld device only when a certain threshold is reached, it would be categorized as edge device; on the other hand, if the wearable device just sends all the data to the smart phone application, then only smart phone would be considered as an edge device.

There are numerous benefits associated with the approach of edge computing in IoMT. First, the latency reduces and the chances of conducting real-time analytics improve [17]. All the data is no longer transmitted to the cloud, so data transit and response time significantly reduce. Therefore, the applications which require quick responses such as those of vital sign monitoring benefit from the edge computing technology. Second, when all the data is not transferred to the cloud, patient confidentiality improves and as a result, patients may feel more confident in using IoMT solutions for their routine fitness/health monitoring. In such scenarios where all the data is not transmitted to a central location, emerging data analytics and machine learning techniques such as federated learning are used.

Subsequently, the second tier in the IoMT communication architecture is the fog computing layer, as shown in Fig. 4. This level acts as an intermediary between the devices and cloud, and it is positioned at the local network level. Fog layer thus enables local data processing and storage. Fog can essentially be regarded as an enhancement to edge computing by offering more extensive computing resources. The goal of fog layer in IoMT is to offer localized analytics and decision-making, which reduces the reliance on cloud computing and improves the real-time performance of IoMT solutions.

Finally, fog layer interacts with the remote cloud for availing the scalable remote storage and computing resources. This layer offers various advantages to the patients, healthcare facilities, physicians, and other stakeholders through performing centralized data aggregation and analytics. Cloud can be considered as a large-scale and remote repository of the massive data collected from the edge and fog layers. However, it depends on the application requirements/user preferences and other factors that what data is transmitted to the cloud; for example, some application may only allow data indicating health risk to be transmitted to the cloud, whereas some other application may require transmitting all the data to the cloud layer. Cloud computing offers advantages of the most comprehensive analytics (since it has access to large scale population data), long-term storage possibilities, personalized patient care and access to historical data. Historical population data is often used for trend analytics and developing innovative diagnostics and treatment strategies.

Challenges and Opportunities: Although the distributed approach offers numerous opportunities to the IoMT, there also exist several challenges for deploying the approach that uses edge, fog, and cloud. Firstly, when utilizing the distributed approach, lesser data is transmitted to the cloud which reduces the bandwidth requirement and latency. However, at the same time, it takes away from the users the benefits of anytime, anywhere access as some data might never be stored centrally. Secondly, although the confidentiality improves with the distributed approach as all the data is not sent to the centralized location, security issues may actually increase; this happens because with the increase in number of edge and fog devices, the chances of attacks such as man-in-the-middle and IP spoofing increase. Third, the security may improve for all the data and the bandwidth is also reduced for the edge and fog architecture, but the equipment cost may go up significantly.

2.4 Data Analytics

The ultimate objective of developing IoMT architecture is to be able to analyze health data trends. Data analytics technology is used to investigate the vast amounts of data collected from individuals through IoMT devices. The focus of data analytics within the domain of IoMT is to derive meaningful patterns and trends which could enhance healthcare service delivery and patient outcomes. The steps involved in the process of data analytics within the sphere of IoMT are detailed below:

Data Collection/Aggregation. As discussed in the previous sections, most of the IoMT devices are designed to collect a continuous stream of data which might indicate various physical/physiological parameters. The data is then aggregated from various sensors and devices and is often sent to smart phone applications for recordkeeping and trend identification.

Preprocessing and Cleaning. In this step, the data is cleaned to manage inconsistencies, any outliers, and missing values. This step is mandatory for the data analytics process in order to maintain the quality of data.

Descriptive Analytics. One of the most preliminary applications of IoMT data analytics involves describing and summarizing the trends obtained from the patient data. The patterns, correlations and trends between various variables are explained, which could shed light on the historical trends.

Predictive Analytics. Based on the identified trends in the population health data, predictions are made using machine learning algorithms and advanced statistical models. It deals with predicting the future health risks or outcomes. Using this technique, timely intervention strategies may be developed with the help of massive historical data.

Prescriptive Analytics. Predictive models are subsequently used for recommending optimal treatment strategies or medication. Customized treatment plans based on the patient's medical history and trends identified by machine learning are developed for improving patient outcomes.

Population Health Management. Since the focus of IoMT is to collect massive population data and store/manage them centrally, Assessment of massive population data helps to identify the health trends, diseases prevalence and other concepts within specific demographic unit. This domain deals with offering customized programs for public health interventions.

3 Integration of IoMT and Cyber Physical Systems

The fusion of IoMT and CPS systems presents a great opportunity to enable efficient health outcomes through offering automation and greater control to the users. Some of the aspects achieved through this integration are described in this section.

3.1 Integration of Sensors with Physical Systems

The IoMT solutions focus on collecting real-time health data, whereas CPS focus on merging this data with the physical systems. For example, one of the scenarios of integrating IoMT and CPS could be the movement of hospital bed in accordance with the patients' needs as identified by the sensor data (by detecting posture).

3.2 Enhanced Decision-Making

The decisions needed for improved health outcomes are efficiently implemented in real-time through integration of IoMT and CPS. In this regard, we may consider the emerging application of invasive/non-invasive IoMT applications of drug delivery. Although in the development stage at present, it has been proposed to deliver the drug within the body upon detection of vitals above thresholds. Again, this is realized by integrating the capabilities of sensors and actuators, which trigger the release of medicine fluid within the stomach. A common example is diabetic management system where insulin is injected into the skin through a patch, upon detection of high glucose values [18].

3.3 Predictive Maintenance

The integration of CPS and IoMT also offers the opportunity of predictive maintenance for medical equipment. The CPS algorithms may efficiently be used at large healthcare facilities to identify the chances of equipment failure and subsequently engage in the proactive maintenance activities, which not only improves the continuous provision of care to the patients, but also reduces the downtime for services and cost associated for major repair or replacement of the equipment.

4 Challenges for Integration of IoMT and CPS

4.1 Standardization

As is the case with general IoMT solutions, it is also crucial to ensure standardization and compatibility between the CPS and IoMT protocols and systems. There will be significant complexities involved with the heterogenous data and protocol requirements of diverse set of platforms and devices. The IoMT devices generally generate various forms of data, which may not fit the requirements of CPS systems. Hence, there might be a need to develop more generic protocols/frameworks for efficient integration of IoMT and CPS.

4.2 Data Protection

Although fusion of IoMT and CPS systems significantly enhance the opportunities of improving healthcare service delivery, at the same time, introduction of more devices and network links would also add to the complexity and security threats. Therefore, there is a crucial need to ensure efficient security mechanisms both in terms of software and hardware.

4.3 Legal and Regulatory Compliance

In addition to ensuring the data security and privacy of users, it will also be a major challenge to obtain regulatory and legal compliance certificates for the integrated solutions based on IoMT and CPS. A detailed assessment of all the possible threats and associated licensing requirements need to be conducted by the healthcare service providers to assure that privacy, security, and ethical use of data is guaranteed. Similarly, legal compliance would also encompass the aspects of fair data use, ownership, liability, and relevant penalties.

5 Use Cases for Integration of IoMT and CPS

Novel use cases for deploying the fusion of IoMT and CPS have been developed. Some of these are detailed in this section.

5.1 Smart Home

For supporting independent living of elderly or physically challenged people, IoMT and CPS solutions are fused together to build smart homes. As per the conventional architecture of IoMT, the data is collected from the wearable or ambient sensors, taken to the fog/cloud and the decision is communicated back to the actuators (CPS) to take appropriate actions. The integration between IoMT and CPS in the context of smart home has been illustrated in Fig. 5.

There could be various applications of smart homes to provide emergency/routine care to the residents. For example, the sensors detect the temperature and lightning values in the home, and the ambient/wearable sensors detect the patients' state (such as sleep, falling body temperature, etc.); in accordance with these values, the thermostat settings may be adjusted, lights may be turned on/off, or other home appliances may be managed.

In addition to controlling the home appliances, the integration shall also facilitate the management of medical equipment that may be installed at home. Thus, the IoMT shall be continuously monitoring the health conditions of residents (heart rate, temperature, blood pressure, glucose levels etc.). As the IoMT transmits this data to the cloud and remote locations, the CPS may adjust the functionality of medical equipment, such as injecting/dispensing medicine.

The CPS and IoMT can improve the quality of life significantly for the physically challenged residents. For example, if a visually impaired person uses wearable devices and lives in a smart home, the alerts in the form of announcements may be generated to caution them to prevent collision with some obstacle. Similarly, if installed, barriers may be automatically activated if a baby or visually impaired person unintentionally goes into an unsafe area. Hence, there could be endless opportunities of improving the safety and well-being of residents though integrating CPS and IoMT.

Fig. 5 Interplay between IoMT and CPS in a smart home environment

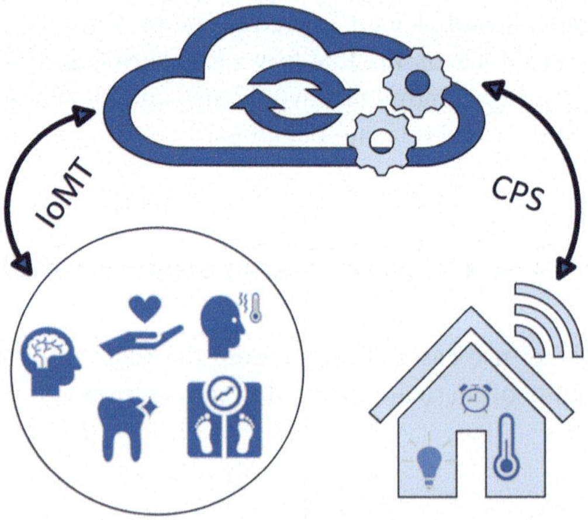

5.2 Explainable AI (XAI) for IoMT and CPS

Explainable AI enhances the performance of AI solutions as they describe decisions made by AI in a form which is understandable by humans. For the crucial domain of healthcare, it might not only be sufficient for the practitioners to rely on the decisions of complex AI models without developing the full understanding behind them. Therefore, XAI has been heavily recommended to be used in healthcare settings so the doctors may be informed about the decisions of diagnosis and recommendations for treatment that are suggested by AI algorithms. This emerging AI concept promises to play a pivotal role for supporting integration of IoMT and CPS.

XAI can be used for enhancing the trust and transparency of the medical image analysis conducted by AI systems [19]. Knowledge reasoning and machine learning come together to provide explanation about the diagnosis reached after analysis of images obtained through Medical CPS. Although there is a great opportunity of using XAI for the purpose of medical image analysis, there are also challenges associated with the technique, such as ensuring the privacy and security of patient, and possibility of attacks on the connected sensors and medical imaging systems.

5.3 Medical Resources Management

Without connectivity, medical facilities can be regarded as islands of huge information. Through integration of sensors and CPS, valuable information may be conveyed to the healthcare stakeholders in a timely manner. The medical data generated at the healthcare facilities may revolutionize the operations of insurance companies, pharmacies, state health departments, scientific research organizations, and other relevant stakeholders. Each of these stakeholders may use the medical data for diverse reasons; for example, the state department may track the number of patients to identify the outbreak of viruses/epidemics; the pharmaceutical companies may identify the consumption of drugs; the insurance providers may track the history of patients and so on.

In addition to supporting the patients, the IoMT and CPS also help to monitor the condition of medical staff and equipment. The doctor's past health history may easily be tracked through these systems and CPS may provide them with guidelines to maintain their safety [20]. Similarly, as previously discussed, the CPS may generate timely alerts about any possible malfunction in the medical/diagnostic equipment.

6 Recent Developments

In addition to wireless communications and networking, there has been a rapid evolution in other technological fronts such as AI, ML, Blockchain, smart fabrics integration of which are leading towards a revolution of healthcare. We discuss some of these in the following.

6.1 Advancements in Wearable Devices

In addition to routine applications of wearable devices, novel integration with home monitoring systems have been developed. For example, sleep monitoring has been proposed by capturing the brain activity data and categorizing sleep disorders and quality [21]. Such solutions aim at improving the sleep quality for populations, which holds potential for improving health and productivity. Similarly, athletes have increasingly been advised to use wearables for improving their sports performance [22]. Particularly, the wearable imaging devices can provide detailed insights about performance and health not only for the usual players, but also those going through rehabilitation programs.

Due to the advancement in wireless networking such as introduction of 6G, the concept of Internet of Wearable Things (IoWT) has also been introduced [23]. For 6G enabled wearables, the major benefit would be due to long-range low-power communications, in-network intelligent computing services and ultra-reliable low-latency communications. Multiple levels of topologies are expected in this direction, such as wearable-to-wearable, wearable-to-hub and wearable-to-infrastructure. Moreover, the communication will also take place at various levels, the communication within implantable networks (molecular or THz communication), implantable and on-body (THz) and on-body nodes to conventional wireless infrastructure (Bluetooth/6G or like).

6.2 Integration with Artificial Intelligence (AI) and Machine Learning (ML)

The performance of conventional IoMT can improve a lot with the help of AI techniques including machine learning, deep learning, fuzzy logic and neural networks [15]. With the help of these systems, the clinical diagnostics system becomes more sophisticated, with a lesser need for human intervention. Critical healthcare sectors such as cancer diagnostics, cardiac care and diabetes management can potentially benefit through the integration of AI and ML with flexible wearables [24]. Similarly, AI can also facilitate customized drug management by using molecular modeling.

The use of AI with the clinical systems and IoMT solutions, enables a more effective decision-making process. The diagnosis, prognosis and therapies all are improved, as the decisions are no longer taken by a single person, but by efficient AI techniques [25]. With the wearable and other IoMT devices, the prediction of disease, and even the risk level for each disease likely to be faced by a certain patient has become possible. For example, personalize heart health risk assessment can be performed through using AI algorithms of TabNet and catBoost [26], where TabNet is known for its efficient feature selection in the tabular data, and catBoost is a powerful gradient boosting algorithm which can significantly improve the model's accuracy.

6.3 Integration with Blockchain

Blockchain serves the fundamental requirements of IoMT, such as medical secrecy and patient confidentiality as it can resist the unauthorized access through data transmission. Various approaches for integrating blockchains with IoMT have been found in literature. It has been proposed to use a three-tier blockchain-integrated communication architecture where IoMT data is collected over edge devices and forwarded to the cloud gateway [27]. Smart contracts are integrated to ensure data protection and health information is broadcasted and stored in a centralized health blockchain. Once the central decision-making is performed at the cloud, the decision is communicated to all the peer nodes, to make information secured yet accessible for the healthcare professionals.

Moreover, intrusions can easily be detected for the IoMT edge networks, using blockchain. A collaborative IDS (CIDS) can be formed, where the nodes have trust due to blockchain by ensuring accountability and consensus [28]. The CIDS nodes engage in the monitoring or analysis of monitoring operations and transactions are stored at all the nodes. Subsequently, any new record is stored in the blockchain only after a consensus protocol is run. This approach ensures both authorization and authentication of the nodes injecting any data into the patient/hospital records.

6.4 Genomic Sequencing and Precision Medicine

Genomic sequencing involves analyzing the sequence of base pairs in a DNA molecule, which typically consists of billions of nucleotides. This process can reveal the genetic code of an organism, including variations, mutations, and other genetic markers that may influence traits, susceptibility to diseases, and responses to treatments. Today, the process of genomic sequencing has become much more common, with the goal of developing personalized treatment and medication plans. The data sent through wearables and other smart hospital-based CPS play an essential role for developing genomic datasets. These datasets then provide an insight into the genetic basis of diseases, identifying genetic variations associated with traits or conditions, tracing evolutionary relationships, and developing personalized approaches to healthcare, such as precision medicine; here, precision medicine is the approach of incorporating personal factors such as medical history, genes, environment and lifestyle while developing the medication plans. Moreover, due to the facility of continuous monitoring, precision medicine also refers to customize the plan or medication based on the reactions/feedback received from the patient's data.

Several works have been proposed to identify the role of genes on health conditions. For example, Mitochondrial and Multifactorial genetic inheritance disorder is predicted using IoMT and ML algorithms in [29]. Support vector machine (SVM) and K-Nearest Neighbor (KNN) algorithms have been used in this work, with the novel contribution of using patients' medical history. Similarly, deep learning and big data analytics techniques are often combined with data collected through CPS for developing the personalized and preventive medication plans [30]. Thus, the extensive data available about each patient, including their genomic profiles provide an immense opportunity for personalizing the healthcare.

6.5 Natural Language Processing (NLP) and Speech Recognition

Natural Language Processing (NLP) is a modern technique aiming at facilitating interactions between computers and humans by using artificial intelligence (AI) and computational linguistics. NLP emphasizes on enabling computers to understand, interpret, and generate human language in a way that is both meaningful and contextually relevant. Some of the major tasks that NLP performs include: text analysis, speech recognition, language translation, language understanding and language generation. IoMT devices, such as wearables and home monitoring systems, can capture patients' spoken language and convert it into text using Speech Recognition technology [31]. NLP algorithms can then analyze the text to extract relevant information about patients' symptoms, medication adherence, and overall health status.

CPS in the settings of smart hospital can integrate with NLP and speech recognition for a wide array of applications. IoMT devices, such as smart medical implants and home healthcare appliances, can be equipped with Speech Recognition capabilities to enable hands-free operation and voice-controlled interactions. Patients with limited mobility or dexterity can easily control these devices using voice commands, improving accessibility and user experience [32]. Moreover, using the NLP enabled IoMT architecture, Healthcare providers can remotely monitor patients' conditions and communicate with them in real-time, providing timely interventions and support. Similarly, NLP also integrates with the massive data available with the hospitals' documentation and decision support systems; NLP algorithms can automatically transcribe spoken medical notes, dictations, and conversations between healthcare providers and patients into structured text. This streamlines clinical documentation processes and reduces the burden on healthcare professionals, allowing them to focus more on patient care. Subsequently, the transcribed text can also be integrated directly into Electronic Health Records (EHRs), which is expected to ensure accurate records.

Moreover, as AI and robotics continue to evolve for smart health settings, IoMT platforms can incorporate virtual health assistants and chatbots equipped with NLP capabilities. The bots can talk to the patients in the real time and answer their questions, and provide personalized health advice [33]. The AI-powered assistants can assist with appointment scheduling, medication reminders, symptom triage, and health education, improving patient engagement and adherence to treatment plans.

7 Summary

Integrating IoMT and CPS has the potential of revolutionizing healthcare practices by integrating sensors, medical equipment, communication infrastructure and data analytics techniques together. This chapter provided a detailed insight into the architecture and core components of IoMT including the medical devices, sensors, communication architecture and data analytics. The benefits and challenges of integrating CPS with IoMT are discussed and some common use cases exhibiting the fusion of these two technologies have been presented. It has been seen that there are endless possibilities for revolutionizing the operation of healthcare sector through enabling intelligent CPS. However, there are also serious challenges that relate to the interoperability of devices and maintaining security and confidentiality of patients.

References

1. S. Siddiqui, A. A. Khan and I. Dey, "Internet Technologies for Personalized Care," in *Information and Communication Technology (ICT) Frameworks in Telehealth*, Cham: Springer International Publishing, 2022, pp. 173–189.
2. S. Razdan and S. Sharma, "Internet of medical things (IoMT): Overview, emerging technologies, and case studies," *IETE technical review,* vol. 39, pp. 775–788, 2022.
3. S. Siddiqui, A. A. Khan and I. Dey, "Body sensor networks—recent advances and challenges," in *Wireless Mesh Networks for IoT and Smart Cities: Technologies and Applications*, 2022.
4. A. Sharma, "Cloud Computing for Complex IoMT Data," in *Data Modelling and Analytics for the Internet of Medical Things*, CRC Press, 2023.
5. S. Hamid, N. Z. Bawany, A. H. Sodhro, A. Lakhan and S. Ahmed, "A systematic review and IoMT based big data framework for COVID-19 prevention and detection," *Electronics,* vol. 11, no. 17, 2022.
6. F. Al-Dhaen, J. Hou, N. P. Rana and V. Weerakkody, "Advancing the Understanding of the Role of Responsible AI in the Continued Use of IoMT in Healthcare," *Information Systems Frontiers,* vol. 25, no. 6, pp. 2159–2178, 2023.
7. R. Akter, M. Golam, V.-S. Doan, J.-M. Lee and D.-S. Kim, "IOMT-NET: Blockchain-integrated unauthorized uav localization using lightweight convolution neural network for internet of military things," *IEEE Internet of Things Journal,* vol. 10, no. 8, 2022.

8. B. Cunha and L. Gonçalves, "An IoMT architecture for patient rehabilitation based on low-cost hardware and interoperability standards," in *Exploring the Convergence of Computer and Medical Science Through Cloud Healthcare*, IGI Global, 2023, pp. 37–59.
9. X. Li, Y. Lu, X. Fu and Y. Qi, "Building the Internet of Things platform for smart maternal healthcare services with wearable devices and cloud computing," *Future Generation Computer Systems,* vol. 118, no. 2021, pp. 282–296, 2021.
10. A. S. Albahri, A. M. Duhaim, M. A. Fadhel, A. Alnoor, N. S. Baqer, L. Alzubaidi and O. S. Albahri, "A systematic review of trustworthy and explainable artificial intelligence in healthcare: Assessment of quality, bias risk, and data fusion," *Information Fusion,* 2023.
11. M. W. Bhatt and S. Sharma, "An IoMT-Based Approach for Real-Time Monitoring Using Wearable Neuro-Sensors," *Journal of Healthcare Engineering,* 2023.
12. S. Siddiqui, A. A. Khan and I. Dey, "Internet Technologies for Personalized Care," in *Information and Communication Technology (ICT) Frameworks in Telehealth*, Springer, 2022, pp. 173–189.
13. D. Sharma, A. Z. B. Nawab and M. Alam, "Integrating M-health with IoMT to counter COVID-19," in *Computational intelligence methods in COVID-19: Surveillance, prevention, prediction and diagnosis*, 2021, pp. 373–396.
14. S. Siddiqui, A. A. Khan, F. Nait-Abdesselam and I. Dey, "Anxiety and depression management for elderly using internet of things and symphonic melodies," in *IEEE International Conference on Communications*, 2021.
15. P. Manickam, S. A. Mariappan, S. M. Murugesan, S. Hansda, A. Kaushik, R. Shinde and S. P. Thipperudraswamy, "Artificial intelligence (AI) and internet of medical things (IoMT) assisted biomedical systems for intelligent healthcare," *Biosensors,* vol. 12, no. 8, 2022.
16. L. Syed, S. Jabeen, S. Manimala and A. Alsaeedi, "Smart healthcare framework for ambient assisted living using IoMT and big data analytics techniques," *Future Generation Computer Systems,* vol. 101, no. 2019, pp. 136–151, 2019.
17. A. I. Awad, M. M. Fouda, M. M. Khashaba, E. R. Mohamed and K. M. Hosny, "Utilization of mobile edge computing on the Internet of Medical Things: A survey," *ICT Express,* 2022.
18. A. M. Joshi, P. Jain and S. P. Mohanty, "iglu 3.0: A secure noninvasive glucometer and automatic insulin delivery system in IoMT," *IEEE Transactions on Consumer Electronics,* vol. 68, no. 1, pp. 14-22, 2022.
19. W. Liu, F. Zhao, A. Shankar, C. Maple, J. D. Peter, B.-G. Kim, A. Slowik, B. D. Parameshachari and J. Lv, "Explainable AI for Medical Image Analysis in Medical Cyber-Physical Systems: Enhancing Transparency and Trustworthiness of IoMT," *IEEE Journal of Biomedical and Health Informatics,* 2023.
20. F. Chen, Y. Tang, C. Wang, J. Huang, C. Huang, D. Xie, T. Wang and C. Zhao, "Medical cyber–physical systems: A solution to smart health and the state of the art," *IEEE Transactions on Computational Social Systems,* vol. 9, no. 5, pp. 1359–1386, 2021.
21. M. Mohamed, N. Mohamed and J. G. Kim, "Advancements in Wearable EEG Technology for Improved Home-Based Sleep Monitoring and Assessment: A Review," *Biosensors,* vol. 12, no. 202, 2023.
22. A. Ç. Seçkin, B. Ateş and M. Seçkin, "Review on Wearable Technology in sports: Concepts, Challenges and opportunities," *Applied Sciences,* vol. 13, no. 18, 2023.
23. N.-N. Dao, "Internet of wearable things: Advancements and benefits from 6G technologies," *Future Generation Computer Systems,* vol. 138, no. 2023, pp. 172–184, 2023.
24. Y. Yuan, B. Liu, H. Li, M. Li, Y. Song, R. Wang, T. Wang and H. Zhang, "Flexible wearable sensors in medical monitoring," *Biosensors,* vol. 12, no. 2022, 2022.
25. A. Merabet, A. Saighi, Z. Laboudi and M. A. Ferradji, "Multiple Diseases Forecast Through AI and IoMT Techniques: Systematic Literature Review," in *International Conference on Intelligent Systems and Pattern Recognition*, 2024.
26. K. K. Baseer, K. Sivakumar, D. Veeraiah, G. Chhabra, P. K. Lakineni, M. J. Pasha, R. Gandikota and G. Harikrishnan, "Healthcare diagnostics with an adaptive deep learning model integrated with the Internet of medical Things (IoMT) for predicting heart disease," *Biomedical Signal Processing and Control,* vol. 92, no. 2024, 2024.

27. J. Almalki, W. A. Shehri, R. Mehmood, K. Alsaif, S. M. Alshahrani, N. Jannah and N. A. Khan, “Enabling blockchain with IoMT devices for healthcare,” *Sensors,* vol. 13, no. 10, 2022.
28. F. Pelekoudas-Oikonomou, G. Zachos, M. Papaioannou, M. d. Ree, J. C. Ribeiro, G. Mantas and J. Rodriguez, “Blockchain-based security mechanisms for IoMT Edge networks in IoMT-based healthcare monitoring systems,” *Sensors,* vol. 22, no. 7, 2022.
29. A.-u. Rahman, M. U. Nasir, M. Gollapalli, S. A. Alsaif, A. S. Almadhor, S. Mehmood, M. A. Khan and A. Mosavi, “IoMT-based mitochondrial and multifactorial genetic inheritance disorder prediction using machine learning,” *Computational Intelligence and Neuroscience,* no. 2022, 2022.
30. R. Thirunavukarasu, R. Gnanasambandan, M. Gopikrishnan and V. Palanisamy, “Towards computational solutions for precision medicine based big data healthcare system using deep learning models: A review,” *Computers in Biology and Medicine,* vol. 149, no. 2022, 2022.
31. B. Zhou, G. Yang, Z. Shi and S. Ma, “Natural language processing for smart healthcare,” *IEEE Reviews in Biomedical Engineering,* 2022.
32. D. Mishra, P. Singh and S. Agarwal, “AI-and IoT-Based Architecture in Healthcare,” in *Transformation in Healthcare with Emerging Technologies*, Chapman and Hall/CRC, 2022, pp. 1–18.
33. S. Aminizadeh, A. Heidari, S. Toumaj, M. Darbandi, N. J. Navimipour, M. Rezaei, S. Talebi, P. Azad and M. Unal, “The applications of machine learning techniques in medical data processing based on distributed computing and the Internet of Things,” *Computer methods and programs in biomedicine,* 2023.

Addressing Healthcare Challenges with IoMT in Intelligent Cyber-Physical Systems

Pankaj Mudholkar, Megha Mudholkar, Chirag Bhalodia, and Pranav Tank

Abstract The advent of Internet of Things (IoT) technologies in the medical industry has given rise to the concept of the Internet of Medical Things (IoMT), leading to the development of intelligent and interconnected cyber-physical systems in healthcare. The integration of the Internet of Medical Things (IoMT) in Intelligent Cyber-Physical Systems (CPS) is revolutionizing healthcare by enabling advanced monitoring, diagnosis, and treatment solutions. IoMT devices, such as wearable sensors, medical implants, and smart healthcare equipment, collect real-time data and communicate with CPS platforms to provide personalized and proactive healthcare services. This has significantly improved healthcare access for remote communities through telemedicine and virtual consultations, while also encouraging patient engagement. This chapter provides an all-encompassing overview of the Internet of Medical Things and its potential to revolutionize healthcare by creating intelligent and interconnected cyber-physical systems.

Keywords IoMT (Internet of medical things) · CPS (Cyber physical system) · IoT (Internet of things) · Healthcare · Security

1 Introduction

Cyber-Physical Systems (CPS) is a new generation of systems that integrate computational (software) and physical components. In healthcare, CPS involves the synergy between medical hardware (like robotic surgery systems) and software (such as AI algorithms), creating an interactive and responsive healthcare environment [1]. Cyber-Physical Systems (CPS) comprise physical processes, networking, and computation. Physical processes are typically monitored and controlled by embedded computers and networks via feedback loops in which physical processes influence computations and vice versa. CPS is an integration of physical and computational processes utilizing Internet of Things technology [2].

P. Mudholkar · M. Mudholkar (✉) · C. Bhalodia · P. Tank
Marwadi University, Rajkot, Gujarat, India
e-mail: mudholkarmegha1984@gmail.com

M. Mittal and J. Narayan (eds.), *Intelligent Cyber-Physical Systems for Healthcare Solutions*, https://doi.org/10.1007/978-981-97-8983-2_8

The Internet of Things (IoT) is a cutting-edge technology that is developing quickly and has the potential to transform the interaction of objects with devices in surroundings [3–5]. It is projected that there will be more than 75 billion linked devices globally by 2025 [6]. One of the areas that stand to gain the most from this expansion is the healthcare sector. IoT refers to the process of connecting various physical entities, equipment types, and sensors via the Internet so they may exchange data and communicate with one another [7, 8]. IoT technologies are already being employed in the healthcare industry to enhance patient outcomes and care by providing new avenues for individualized treatment regimens [9], remote monitoring [10, 11], and effective healthcare delivery [12].

The Internet of Medical Things (IoMT) for Intelligent Cyber-Physical Systems (CPS) represents a significant advancement in healthcare technology. This concept integrates the Internet of Things (IoT) within the medical field, emphasizing the interconnectivity of medical devices and systems. In the context of CPS, IoMT devices interact with computing processes to enable advanced functionalities. This includes automated decision-making based on health data, remote medical interventions, and predictive analytics for healthcare. The CPS composed of computational and physical capability that engages with humans. The smart grid, smart automobile system, medical monitoring, robotics system are some of the examples of CPS.

Key Components of CPS and their Characteristics are [13]:

- Embedded Systems: These are at the core of CPS, providing the computing power necessary for control and feedback.
- Sensors and Actuators: Sensors gather data from the physical world, while actuators effect changes in it.
- Connectivity: Networks facilitate communication between the system's components, often involving wireless technology.
- Intelligence and Autonomy: CPS often possess some level of intelligence, capable of autonomous decision-making based on data analysis.
- Interoperability: These systems are designed to work with various protocols and standards, ensuring compatibility and integration across different platforms.

The usage of smart devices is increasing day by day. Internet of Things facilitates in the production of the smart devices by integrating devices, network and cloud services and also exchanges the data in between these devices. The usage of IoT is exploding in the consumer sector. Dishwashers, refrigerators, smart TVs, smart watches, cars and trucks, heating and cooling systems, fitness machines and trackers are some of the examples of IoT-enabled smart devices.

IoMT is a subset of IoT, focusing specifically on the application of connected devices in the realm of healthcare and medicine. It includes interconnected devices with sensors, data exchange and enabling better patient care through improved data accessibility and analysis. The common examples include wearable fitness trackers, remote patient monitoring devices, and advanced prosthetics with sensors. These devices collect, analyze, and transmit health data, offering real-time monitoring and data-driven insights into patient health. CPS in healthcare often relies on data from IoMT devices. This symbiotic relationship enables sophisticated functionalities like automated clinical decision-making, real-time health monitoring, and advanced therapeutic interventions.

IoMT for Intelligent Cyber-Physical Systems (CPS) represents a significant advancement in healthcare technology. This concept integrates the Internet of Things (IoT) within the medical field, emphasizing the interconnectivity of medical devices and systems.

In the context of CPS, IoMT devices interact with computing processes to enable advanced functionalities. This includes automated decision-making based on health data, remote medical interventions, and predictive analytics for healthcare.

Figure 1 shows the relationship between CPS, IoT and IoMT, however, effectively designing, building, and assuring CPS/IoT systems requires consideration of the system's functional context, including how the system is used and for what purpose or outcome. In all the cases, every system uses the combination of sensors, networks, applications and analytics to build a product, but only difference is the usage of those applications in varied sectors. IoT and CPS may be considered equivalent, or IoT as a subset of CPS or vice versa depending on the context of the application [14]. IoMT is built upon the foundational principles and technologies of IoT. Both IoT and IoMT use similar technologies such as sensors, data analytics, cloud computing, and machine learning for predictive insights. IoMT specifically aimed at improving healthcare delivery, patient outcomes, and healthcare cost efficiency by using the principles of IoT, the components and the protocols. In addition to the general regulations of IoT regarding data security, privacy [15], and device standards IoMT must adhere to stricter regulatory standards due to the sensitive nature of health data and the critical importance of medical devices. This includes compliance with healthcare-specific regulations like HIPAA in the U.S. [16], GDPR in Europe [17], and others. IoT encompasses a wide range of applications across multiple sectors, IoMT is a focused application within the realm of healthcare. Both are interconnected and share many technological similarities, but IoMT is subject to more stringent regulations due to its direct impact on human health.

The chapter begins by introducing the terms Cyber-Physical Systems (CPS), Internet of Things (IoT) and Internet of Medical Things (IoMT) and its primary characteristics. It then delves into IoMT's various applications in intelligent cyber-physical systems within healthcare. These applications encompass enhanced patient monitoring, telehealth services, and personalized medicine. Moreover, IoMT plays a crucial role in optimizing resource allocation, refining diagnostic and therapeutic decisions, and promoting preventive and prognostic care. However, the chapter also addresses the challenges and considerations associated with IoMT implementation in intelligent cyber-physical systems. Key concern include data security and privacy concerns, interoperability standards and the potential for IoMT-enabled CPS to transform healthcare delivery models. The findings highlight the transformative impact of IoMT in CPS on healthcare systems, paving the way for innovative and patient-centric care approaches in the digital health era.

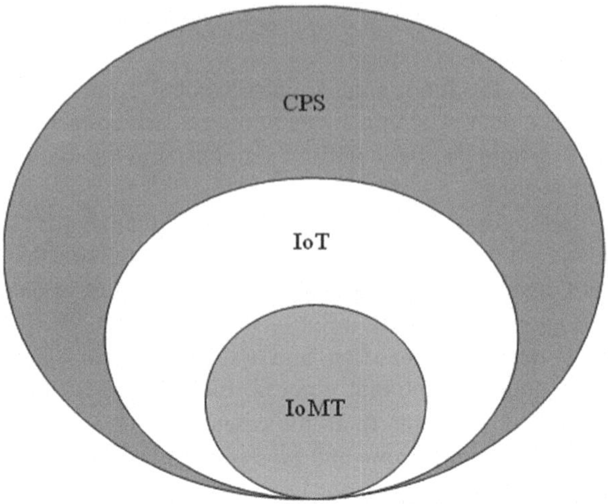

Fig. 1 Relationship between CPS, IoT and IoMT

2 Overview of CPS, IoT and IoMT

CPS provides the infrastructure having the ability to integrate the physical and digital realms, coupled with real-time responsiveness, makes it crucial in advancing healthcare delivery, improving patient outcomes, and ushering in new medical innovations. Cyber Physical Systems give IoT all the support it needs to function robustly and intelligently across applications, industries, and the healthcare sector. Within the Internet of Things, the Internet of Medical Things (IoMT) handles all of the forecasts and services related to the healthcare system [18]. The integration of the Internet of Medical Things (IoMT) with Cyber-Physical Systems (CPS) in healthcare represents a transformative approach to medical care. This convergence enhances healthcare delivery through advanced data collection, analysis, and system-wide integration, leading to more effective, efficient, and personalized patient care. The integration of IoMT with CPS facilitates in improving the healthcare services which provides the following benefits:

Complementary Functions: IoMT devices collect health-related data, while CPS processes this data in real-time, allowing for immediate response and interaction with the physical world.

Enhanced Data Utilization: IoMT's data collection capabilities combined with CPS's data processing and feedback loops create a more dynamic and responsive healthcare system.

Remote Monitoring and Telehealth: CPS technology enables remote health monitoring and telehealth services, allowing for continuous care outside traditional clinical settings.

Improved Patient Outcomes: The integrated system enables more accurate diagnoses, timely interventions, and personalized treatment plans.

Operational Efficiency: It streamlines healthcare operations, reducing costs and improving resource allocation.
Predictive Analytics: Leveraging AI and machine learning, the integrated system can predict health trends, potential crises, and patient-specific health risks.
Remote Patient Management: It facilitates remote monitoring and telehealth, especially crucial for chronic disease management and elderly care.
Precision Medicine: They facilitate precision medicine through advanced diagnostics and patient-specific treatment strategies.
Surgical Automation and Robotics: CPS is integral in surgical robotics, enhancing precision in procedures and reducing human error.
Patient Data Management: These systems manage vast amounts of patient data, streamlining processes and improving healthcare delivery.
Emergency Response: CPS can enhance emergency medical responses by enabling faster, more coordinated, and effective interventions.
Chronic Disease Management: They are particularly beneficial in managing chronic conditions, offering real-time monitoring and proactive management strategies.

Some of the examples of Successful Integrations of IoMT with CPS are:

- **Smart Hospitals:** Hospitals are integrating IoMT devices (like smart beds and connected monitoring equipment) with CPS for real-time patient monitoring, improving patient care and operational efficiency.
- **Wearable Health Devices:** Integration of wearable devices with CPS enables continuous monitoring of vital signs, alerting healthcare providers and patients to potential health issues.
- **Surgical Robotics:** In surgery, the combination of IoMT (for data collection) and CPS (for precise control) is enhancing surgical accuracy and reducing human error.
- **Emergency Response Systems:** Integrated systems in ambulances and emergency response teams allow for real-time patient monitoring and data transmission to hospitals, enabling immediate care decisions enroute.

The integration of IoMT with CPS in healthcare is a significant advancement, offering numerous benefits from operational efficiencies to enhanced patient care. This synergy is driving the future of healthcare, leading to more proactive, personalized, and efficient medical services.

As shown in Fig. 2, the medical devices, sensors, data processing units, and connectivity infrastructure are connected together. It visually communicates the interconnected nature of medical devices and systems in the IoMT, emphasizing data flow, processing, and security. It includes various medical devices like a heart rate monitor, blood pressure monitor, and glucose meter. These devices are equipped with sensors to collect patient data. Figure 2 also shows a central data processing unit, symbolizing a computer or server, where data from these devices is aggregated and analyzed. This unit represents the 'brain' of the IoMT, equipped with advanced algorithms for data processing and decision making.

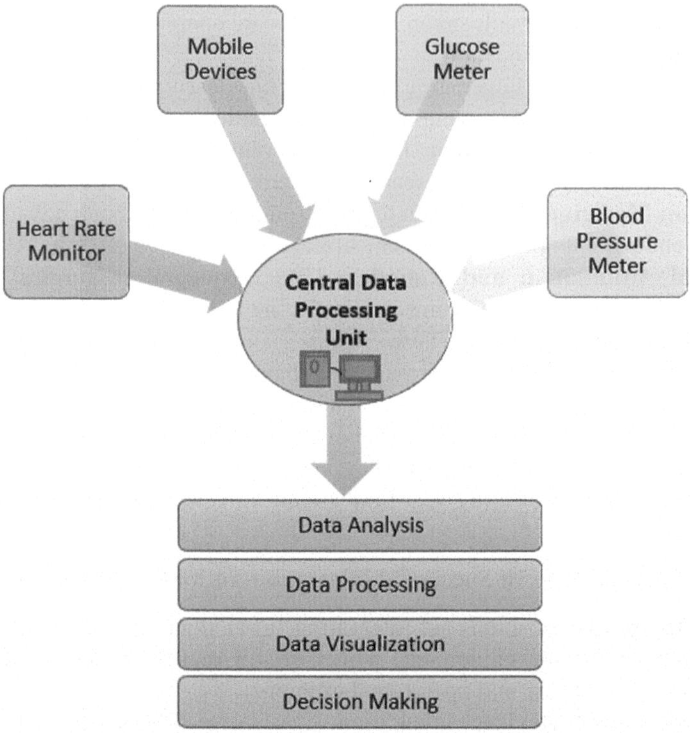

Fig. 2 A conceptual illustration of the architecture for IoMT and CPS

3 Sensing Technologies in Healthcare

Sensing technologies in intelligent medical devices, especially within the Internet of Medical Things (IoMT), play a crucial role in modern healthcare. These technologies enable the collection of vital health data, providing insights into patient health and improving the quality of care. Sensing technologies are essential for real-time monitoring, diagnosis, and management of health conditions. They collect physiological data, which is then analyzed for medical insights. These technologies are used in various settings, from hospitals to home care, and in different forms, including wearable devices, implantable, and stationary monitoring equipment. Various sensors used in building IoMT Devices capable of collecting, processing and analyzing the healthcare data are [19, 20]:

- **Wearable Sensors:** These are integrated into devices like smartwatches and fitness bands to monitor heart rate, sleep patterns, and physical activity. The number of advancements pertaining to wearable and flexible sensors designed for health surveillance and disease prediction has increased substantially over the last few years. Within this particular framework, man-made wearable sensors have been affixed to the wrist or thorax in order to capture or identify various critical physiological parameters. These sensors are capable of notifying the user in the event of an anomalous circumstance. This can safeguard human health by affording an opportunity to implement preventative measures [21] (Fig. 3).

- **Implantable Sensors:** Implanted into the body, these sensors monitor internal health metrics such as glucose levels in diabetic patients or cardiac rhythms.

Implantable medical devices, such as pacemakers, cardiac defibrillators, insulin pumps, and neurostimulators that have wireless connectivity have made it possible to remotely monitor patients and assist the delivery of timely treatment, which has contributed to an improvement in the health care system [22].

Different types of implantable sensors (Mechanical and electrophysiological cardiac monitors, Pressure and gas sensors, Electrophysiological probes etc.) are used

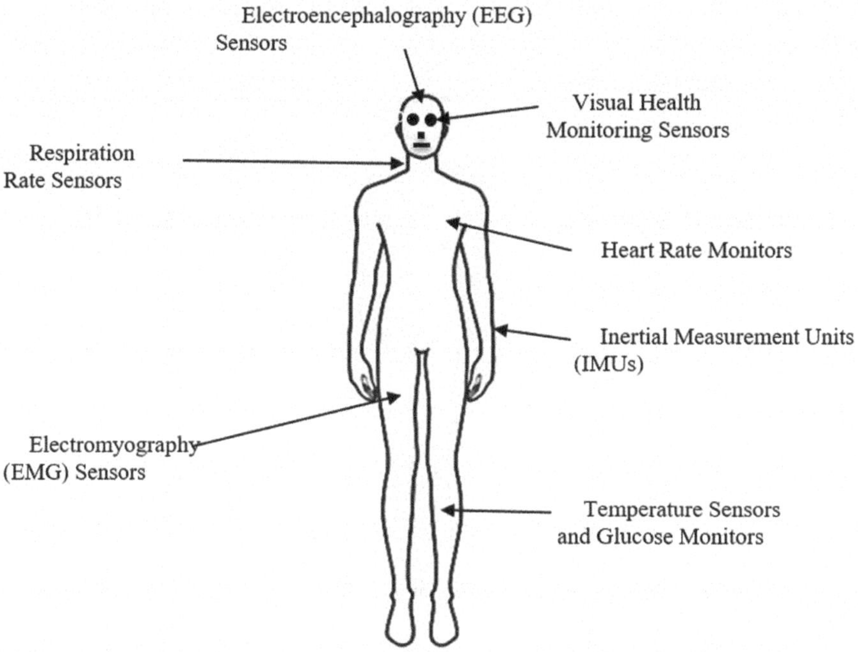

EEG Sensors	• Measure electrical activity in the brain
Visual Health Monitoring Sensors	• Provide continuous monitoring and real time data on eye health
Respiration Rate Sensors	• Measure breathing rate
Heart Rate Monitors	• Measure heart rate using eletcrical signals
Inertial Measurement Units (IMUs)	• Track motion by combining using accelerometer, gyroscope and magenetometers

Fig. 3 Wearable sensors

for different medical fields such as cardiology, pulmonology, neurology, oncology, diabetes etc. Figure 4 shows the different types of implantable sensors used for different types of medical fields [23].

- **Environmental Sensors:** Used to monitor environmental factors like room temperature and air quality, which can affect patient health. It is mandatory for hospitals to uphold a humidity level of at least 30%, with operating rooms (ORs) being the specific area that must be maintained within the humidity range of 20–60% [24].
- **Biochemical Sensors:** These detect specific chemical markers in bodily fluids, playing a crucial role in diagnosing and monitoring diseases.
- **Motion Sensors:** Used to monitor and analyze patient movement, especially important in physical therapy and rehabilitation. There is a wide selection of motion trackers available, such as magnetometers, gyroscopic sensors, and

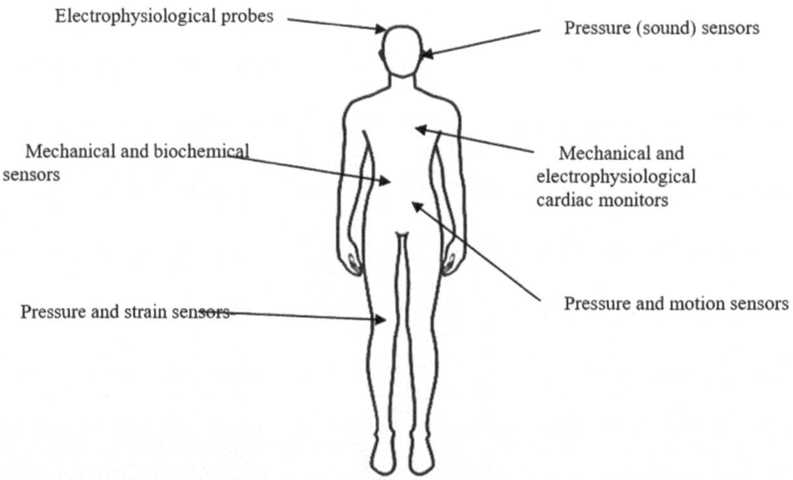

Electrophysiological probes	• Monitors neural activity
Mechanical and electrophysiological cardiac monitors	• Monitors heart activity
Mechanical and biochemical sensors	• Monitors gastrointestinal motility, food, or medication intake
Pressure (sound) sensors	• Treatment of severe-to-profound sensorineural hearing loss
Pressure and motion sensors	• Detect small-scale autonomous movements (micromotions) in the bladder relevant to bladder physiology
Pressure and strain sensors	• Monitor mechanical forces to track tendon healing after surgical repair, potential for improved diagnosis and personalized treatment of orthopedic conditions

Fig. 4 Implantable sensors

accelerometers that measure motion on three axes. The majority of the time, wrist wearable gadgets are utilized for the purpose of monitoring daily activities. Movement, acceleration, rotation, and gestures are some of the activity signals that these devices are able to measure [25].

Ongoing advancements are leading to smaller, more comfortable, and less invasive sensors, improving patient compliance and comfort. The development of wireless sensors has facilitated continuous, real-time monitoring without restricting patient mobility. Further, the integration of AI and machine learning enables smart diagnostic capabilities, with sensors providing predictive analytics for preventive healthcare. Some of the characteristics of these sensors are:

- Biocompatibility and Durability: Innovations in materials and design are enhancing sensor biocompatibility and durability, crucial for implantable and long-term use devices.
- Multiparametric Monitoring: Modern sensors are capable of monitoring multiple parameters simultaneously, offering a more comprehensive health overview.
- Energy Efficiency and Self-Powered Sensors: Development of energy-efficient and self-powered sensors addresses the challenge of battery life in long-term monitoring.

The advancements in sensing technologies are revolutionizing the field of healthcare, making IoMT devices smarter and more capable. This leads to better patient outcomes, more efficient healthcare delivery, and opens new avenues for medical research and treatment methods.

4 Communication Protocols for IoMT Devices

The communication protocols are fundamental to the efficacy and security of Medical IoT devices. The right balance of speed, reliability, scalability, and security in these protocols is crucial for advancing healthcare technology and improving patient outcomes. The usage of protocols in the IoMT depends on various factors. Some of the considerations for the protocol selection for reliable data transmission are:

- Scalability: Protocols must be scalable to accommodate the growing number of IoT devices in healthcare.
- Energy Efficiency: Particularly for wearable and implantable devices, protocols should minimize power consumption to extend battery life.
- Latency and Speed: In critical healthcare applications, the latency should be minimal, and data transmission speeds must be high to ensure timely delivery of vital health information.
- Security and Compliance: Protocols must adhere to healthcare regulations and standards (like HIPAA in the U.S.) to ensure data privacy and security.

Communication protocols for IoMT devices are critical for the seamless and secure transmission of medical data. These protocols ensure that the vast amount of data generated by various medical devices is transmitted efficiently, accurately, and securely, facilitating improved patient care and healthcare operations. Some of the protocols which facilitates the communication between the devices are [26]:

- ZigBee and Z-Wave: Utilized for creating personal area networks with small, low-power digital radios; suitable for sensor networks in hospitals.
- Radio Frequency Identification (RFID): RFID is a wireless object identification technology that enables extremely short-range communications via radio frequency signals.
- Near Field Communication (NFC): The NFC protocol facilitates communication between devices over extremely short distances (no more than a few centimeters).
- Bluetooth Low Energy (BLE): Popular for wearable health devices due to its low power consumption and efficient short-range communication capabilities.
- Wireless Fidelity (WiFi): WiFi is a protocol with a maximum range of 100 meters and is based upon the IEEE 802.11 family of standards. WiFi is extensively implemented in support of local area networks and transportable devices, enabling Internet.
- Long Range Wide Area Network (LoRaWAN): Used for long-range communications with minimal power consumption, ideal for large-scale health monitoring applications.
- Hypertext Transfer Protocol Secure (HTTPS): Often used for secure communication over a computer network within a web browser, essential for protecting patient data.
- The Constrained Application Protocol (COAP): COAP is a web transmission protocol that is designed to operate efficiently on IoT nodes that have memory and processing limitations. Its intended application is in lossy and power-constrained networks.
- Message Queuing Telemetry Transport (MQTT): A lightweight messaging protocol, designed for low-bandwidth, high-latency, or unreliable networks, often used in remote patient monitoring devices.
- Advanced Message Queuing Protocol (AMQP): AMQP is an open source Message-Oriented Middleware (MOM) protocol. Designed to facilitate communications among applications, devices, and systems from various vendors, this platform was not initially developed with the Internet of Things in mind.
- Data Distribution Service (DDS): DDS protocol is an interoperable, real-time communication protocol that is specifically engineered for applications that demand substantial coordination, dependable transmissions, and decentralized processing among the devices.
- WebSocket: WebSocket is a bidirectional communication protocol developed for web applications to rapidly transmit large amounts of data. A WebSocket facilitates the establishment of a connection between a client and a server; consequently, subsequent to the initial connection establishment, each individual message incurs minimal latency. This protocol enables servers and devices to transmit and receive

Table 1 Protocols for IoMT devices

Layers	Protocols
Perception layer	ZigBee, Z-Wave, RFID, NFC, Bluetooth/BLE
Network layer	ZigBee, Z-Wave, NFC, Bluetooth/BLE, WiFi, LoRaWAN
Application layer	COAP, MQTT, HTTP, WebSocket, DDS, AMQP

data simultaneously in real-time, rendering it most suitable for Internet of Things (IoT) applications that prioritize frequent communication, low latency, and data consumption.

All the above mentioned protocols worked in different layers (the perception, the network and the application layer) of IoT architecture. Table 1 briefs the protocols according to the IoT architecture layers.

5 Data Security and Privacy in IoMT-CPS

Data security and privacy in the integration of the Internet of Medical Things (IoMT) and Cyber-Physical Systems (CPS) is a critical area in healthcare technology. As IoMT-CPS systems collect, process, and transmit sensitive health data, ensuring their security and maintaining patient privacy are paramount.

5.1 Challenges and Concerns in Healthcare Data Security

In this digital era, each and every industry has a very high priority on data security, no matter which field you consider. Provide a security to the data is essential components of the health care. Protect the sensitive patient data and adhere its rules is a crucial thing. However, IoMT devices and existing networks improved their security over a period of time, there are still numerous security challenges when it comes to protect the patient health information. Medical services have also raised the population's risk of losing their privacy.

The following are the vital challenges [27, 28]:

(a) Technical Heterogeneity of IoMT networks Challenge.
(b) Administrative Challenge.
(c) Societal Challenge (Fig. 5).

(a) **Technical Heterogeneity Challenges in IoMT**

For the Internet of Medical Things (IoMT) to be successfully implemented and widely used in the healthcare industry, a number of technological issues must be resolved. Among these difficulties are:

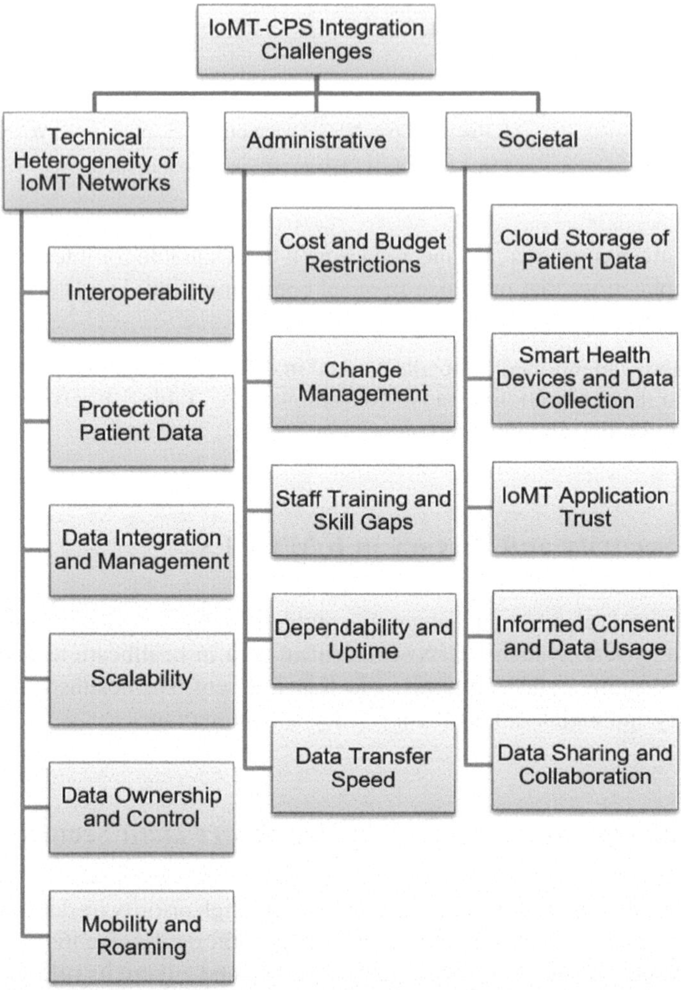

Fig. 5 Challenges in IoMT-CPS integration

Interoperability: IoMT devices may employ proprietary data formats or communication protocols, and they frequently originate from multiple vendors. It is crucial for these disparate devices to become interoperable in order to facilitate smooth data integration and interchange between healthcare systems.

Protection of Patient Data: It is critical to guarantee the protection of patient data transferred and stored by IoMT devices. Strong security measures, encryption methods, and authentication procedures are required for these devices because they are vulnerable to cyberattacks, data leaks, and unauthorized access.

Data Integration and Management: Aggregating, storing, processing, and analyzing the massive amounts of data produced by IoMT devices presents difficulties. In order to properly handle a variety of data kinds, formats, and sources, healthcare organizations require excellent data management policies and infrastructure.

Scalability: As more IoMT devices are being used in healthcare settings, scalability is becoming a major challenge. Network infrastructure, data storage, computing resources, and system architecture all provide scalability difficulties that call for scalable solutions to handle growing device deployments and data volumes.

Data Ownership and Control: When there are several parties involved, it can be difficult to decide who owns and has control over data that is kept in the cloud. Establishing explicit data governance standards and defining rights to data ownership are crucial.

Mobility and Roaming: Since IoMT devices are frequently portable or mobile, they must have smooth connectivity and handoff when they travel between or inside healthcare institutions. It is essential to guarantee support for mobility and roaming via Wi-Fi roaming protocols and mobile network technologies.

(b) **Administrative Challenges in IoMT**

Cost and Budget Restrictions: Investing in IoMT technologies frequently necessitates large upfront expenditures for staff training, infrastructure upgrades, and device acquisition. Allocating resources for IoMT activities might be difficult for healthcare organizations due to financial and budgetary limits.

Change management: Implementing IoMT technology necessitates modifying organizational structures, workflows, and procedures. Healthcare workers may run into people who are resistant to change, fear that technology will take the place of people in their jobs, or worry that their routines will be disturbed. Adoption and resistance reduction require effective change management techniques.

Staff Training and Skill Gaps: The implementation of IoMT necessitates the acquisition of new competences and abilities by healthcare workers in the areas of data administration, device operation, and technology use. To guarantee that employees are competent in utilizing IoMT devices and platforms, healthcare institutions must fund extensive training initiatives.

Dependability and Uptime: In order to provide continuous access to medical data and services, cloud-based IoMT systems must possess high availability and dependability. It's critical to put service level agreements (SLAs), redundancy, and disaster recovery into place with cloud providers.

Data Transfer Speed: It can be bandwidth-intensive and can cause latency problems to transfer massive amounts of medical data between IoMT devices and the cloud. Real-time monitoring and analysis depend on maximizing data transfer rates and reducing latency.

(c) **Societal Challenges in IoMT**

Cloud Storage of Patient Data: Privacy and security issues are brought up when patient health data is stored on the cloud. Patients might be concerned about data breaches, illegal access, and the misuse of their private medical records.

Smart Health Devices and Data Collection: Wearables and home monitoring systems are examples of smart health devices that continuously gather and send patient data to the cloud. Patients could be worried about how this continuous data sharing and monitoring will affect their privacy.

IoMT Application Trust: Patients and healthcare professionals require reassurance regarding the accuracy, security, and dependability of IoMT apps, including telemedicine platforms and remote monitoring. It is necessary to show that IoMT applications are functional, respect privacy, and adhere to ethical guidelines in order to gain users' trust.

Informed Consent and Data Usage: Patients ought to be in charge of how IoMT systems gather, store, and utilize the health data they provide. Ethical IoMT deployments depend on getting informed consent for data gathering and making sure data procedures are transparent.

Data Sharing and Collaboration: In order to conduct joint research and analysis, healthcare organizations and researchers may look to exchange patient data. It is essential to make sure that data sharing policies uphold privacy laws, safeguard patient confidentiality, and put patients' needs first.

Other challenges in healthcare data security and privacy. Following are some of the challenges in healthcare:

Data Breaches [29]**:** With the increasing amount of sensitive health data being transmitted, IoMT-CPS systems are attractive targets for cyberattacks, leading to potential data breaches. Healthcare data breaches can result from a variety of causes, including purpose of harmful behaviour and careless use of electronic health records (EHRs). The confidentiality of patients and the integrity of healthcare systems are seriously jeopardized by these breaches. The following is a summary of the main vulnerabilities and cyberthreats that are frequently connected to breaches of healthcare data:

Ransomware attacks: Malicious malware known as ransomware encrypts data on a victim's computer and prevents it from being accessed unless a ransom is paid. Attacks using ransomware have the potential to seriously impair healthcare operations, contaminate patient records, and cause large financial losses.

E-health records vulnerabilities: Attackers may use weaknesses in electronic health record systems to obtain sensitive patient data without authorization.

Insider threats from disgruntled employees: Employees who have been granted permission to access healthcare systems could be dangerous if they were to steal or leak patient information on purpose due to personal grudges or malicious intent.

Unintentional disclosure of patient information: Inadvertent disclosures may result from carelessness or human mistake when managing patient data. This could involve exposing data accidentally through incorrect storage or disposal procedures, providing private information to the wrong person, or incorrectly configuring security settings.

Email phishing scams: Phishing attempts that use email to target healthcare staff have the ability to fool them into revealing their login credentials, downloading harmful files, or clicking on dubious links.

DDoS attacks: Healthcare services may become unavailable due to Distributed Denial of Service (DDoS) attacks, which cause a deluge of malicious traffic to overwhelm network infrastructure or web servers. These assaults may cause outages, denying patients access to vital medical information or services.

Device Vulnerabilities: Many IoMT devices may not have robust built-in security features, making them vulnerable to hacking and unauthorized access. The Internet of Medical Things (IoMT) device vulnerabilities provide serious threats to patient safety, data security, and healthcare operations. Malicious actors may use these vulnerabilities to hack IoMT devices, obtain private patient information, and interfere with the provision of healthcare services.

Data Integrity: Ensuring the accuracy and integrity of health data throughout its lifecycle is challenging but essential for reliable patient care. The Internet of Medical Things (IoMT) depends on data integrity to guarantee the correctness, consistency, and credibility of medical data that is gathered, sent, and stored by networked devices.

5.2 Privacy Regulations and Compliance

The Internet of Medical Things (IoMT) refers to interconnected medical devices and systems that gather, transmit, and share health-related data via the internet. Privacy regulations and compliance are crucial aspects of IoMT to ensure the protection of sensitive health information. Several regulations and standards play a significant role in governing the privacy and security of health data in IoMT. It's important to note that the regulatory landscape may evolve, so it's advisable to stay updated on the latest developments. Some key regulations include:

Health Insurance Portability and Accountability Act (HIPAA): Within the USA [30], HIPAA primarily governs the privacy and security of personally identifiable health statistics held or transmitted through covered entities (healthcare providers, fitness plans, and healthcare clearinghouses) and their commercial enterprise associates. IoMT devices and systems utilized by protected entities are issue to HIPAA guidelines. Producers, builders, and providers can also be considered enterprise pals and must follow HIPAA if they cope with included fitness statistics (PHI).

General Data Protection Regulation (GDPR): In the European Union (EU) [31] and the European Economic Area (EEA), GDPR applies to the processing of personal data and grants individuals control over their data. IoMT devices and services that process personal data of EU/EEA residents must comply with GDPR.

This includes obtaining explicit consent, ensuring data security, and providing individuals with the right to access and delete their data.

Medical Device Regulation (MDR): Within the EU [32], MDR regulates the marketing and use of medical devices. IoMT devices fall under the scope of MDR if they meet the definition of a medical device. Compliance involves meeting safety and performance requirements, as well as addressing data protection concerns.

Food and Drug Administration (FDA) Regulations: In the United States [33], the FDA regulates medical devices, including IoMT devices. IoMT devices must adhere to FDA regulations, including pre-market approval or clearance processes. The FDA also emphasizes cybersecurity considerations to protect patient data and device functionality.

Compliance with these regulations involves adopting security measures, conducting risk assessments, implementing privacy policies, and staying informed about updates in the regulatory landscape. Organizations involved in IoMT should also consider ethical considerations and best practices for data protection beyond the legal requirements. It's advisable to consult legal and compliance experts for the most current and relevant guidance.

5.3 Strategies for Securing IoMT-CPS Ecosystem

Securing the Internet of Medical Things (IoMT) within Cyber-Physical Systems (CPS) is crucial to safeguard sensitive health data, ensure patient safety, and maintain the integrity of medical devices. The IoMT-CPS ecosystem involves the integration of medical devices, networks, and software systems, creating a complex environment that requires comprehensive security strategies. Here are some key strategies for securing the IoMT-CPS ecosystem:

Risk Assessment and Management: Risk assessment and management are essential things to identify vulnerabilities and threats in IoMT-CPS ecosystem. Apply risk mitigation strategies based on their impact on patient data safety, integrity and functionalities of system.

Authentication and Access Control: Multi-factor strong authentication mechanisms are required to ensure only authorized users can access patient data, medical equipment and related systems. Also define users' roles and responsibilities to restrict the users' privileges for access control.

Device Identity Management: Provide device identity management to authenticate and uniquely identify device in the IoMT-CPS ecosystem. To prevent unauthorized access, manage and monitor the lifecycle of device identities.

Security Training and Awareness: To access the IoMT devices and avoid vulnerabilities, security training and awareness about cyber security practices are required. Provide a training to the employees, professionals (healthcare) and other person who are involves to use and access the data related to IoMT devices.

Also encourage and learn security awareness, if any kind of suspicious activities are happened.

Continuous Monitoring and Auditing: To identify security dangers and take immediate action against them, constant monitoring is necessary. Regular audits are also conducted to guarantee risk reduction and pinpoint areas in need of improvement.

By adopting a multi-layered and holistic approach to security, organizations can enhance the resilience of the IoMT-CPS ecosystem and mitigate potential risks and threats effectively. It's essential to regularly update security measures in response to evolving cybersecurity landscapes and emerging threats. Additionally, collaboration with cybersecurity experts and adherence to industry best practices contribute to a robust security posture for the IoMT-CPS ecosystem.

6 Real Time Data Analytics for Healthcare Monitoring

6.1 Significance of Real-Time Analytics in Healthcare

Real-time data analytics for healthcare monitoring represents a significant advancement in medical technology, particularly in the realm of the Internet of Medical Things (IoMT) and Cyber-Physical Systems (CPS). The ability to analyze health data as it is collected transforms how healthcare providers monitor and respond to patient needs. Below are some of the significances of real-time data analytics in healthcare:

- Timely Decision Making: Real-time analytics enable healthcare providers to make immediate decisions based on the latest data, crucial in emergency and critical care situations.
- Predictive Insights: Analyzing data as it's collected allows for predictive insights, potentially identifying health issues before they become critical.
- Personalized Patient Care: Continuous analysis of patient data facilitates personalized healthcare, tailoring treatments and interventions to individual patient needs.
- Efficiency in Healthcare Operations: Real-time data analysis can streamline operations, reduce costs, and improve the overall efficiency of healthcare services.

6.2 Applications of Analytics in IoMT-CPS

IoMT enables individuals to transmit medical information from their residence to a hospital or healthcare provider. For example, Remote Patient Monitoring (RPM), which involves the transmission of vital signs (e.g., blood pressure or oxygen saturation) of the patient who might got discharged from the hospital after the treatment to their hospital for the purpose of review by their attending doctor. This may reduce re-admissions to the hospital by identifying problems before they become severe.

Some of the applications of analytics in IoMT-CPS are:

- Remote Patient Monitoring: IoMT devices like wearable health monitors use real-time analytics to monitor vital signs and notify healthcare providers of any alarming changes.
- Chronic Disease Management: For chronic conditions like diabetes or heart disease, real-time data analysis allows for ongoing adjustment of treatment plans.
- Hospital Resource Management: In hospitals, real-time analytics help in managing resources, like beds and staff, by analyzing patient flow and care requirements.
- Surgical and Rehabilitation Monitoring: Real-time analysis during surgeries and rehabilitation processes provides immediate feedback, enhancing patient outcomes.
- Predictive Maintenance for Medical devices: Predictive analytics is used to estimate maintenance requirements by analysing data from medical equipment. Predicting when maintenance is needed, reducing downtime, and enhancing equipment lifecycle management to ensure the dependability of medical devices.
- Infection Control and Surveillance: Tracking and identifying trends linked to infections by analysing data from connected devices. Preventive measures are put in place to control the spread of illnesses within healthcare facilities, early outbreak identification, and infection rate tracking.

6.3 Case Studies Demonstrating Real-Time Monitoring

Data analytics in IoMT helps in monitoring the patients, their health parameters remotely. Some of the prominent case studies are given below:

- **Remote Patient Monitoring** [34]**:** Imagine that the patient is reading a book in a rocking chair while a smart device sends the healthcare professional (doctors) an information about his heart rate and blood sugar level. This is possible because of progress made in remote patient tracking systems. A lot has changed in health care over the years. Remote Patient Monitoring (RPM) is a new way to help patients that was made possible by advances in technology. With this technology, people can share their health information safely from the comfort of their own homes. In turn, doctors have a better idea of the illness of their patients and may provide medications or suggestions, if, required.
- **Real-Time Health Monitoring System Using IoT** [35]**:** A real-time health monitoring system was developed to record, analyze, and decode patients' vital signs and psychological factors. It comprises an IoT application that is coupled with a wearable wireless device comprising sensors, such as a bracelet, to enable a physician to access medical information.

- **Heart function Monitoring and Alert System** [36]**:** There are several technologies in place that measure a person's heart rate in real time and alert them to any serious cardiac issues. Nevertheless, there isn't a mechanism in place that can identify a person's actual cardiac status and notify the patient and their loved ones to see a cardiologist in an emergency. To get around the aforementioned restrictions, a system that monitors a person's cardiac health and alerts them to any major illnesses must be developed. Additionally, the system should be able to pinpoint the person's precise location in real time so that they may be contacted in an emergency.
- **Glucose Monitoring in Diabetic Patients** [37]**:** Increase in the number of peoples with diabetes chooses Continuous Glucose Monitor (CGM) as their preferred method of glucose measurement, healthcare professionals will be challenged to become proficient in incorporating this technology into their practices CGM enables patients and clinicians to identify blood glucose trends, making it easier to adapt diets and manage medications, as well as offering motivation to improve physical activity. The usage of CGM system in the medical practice provides the healthcare professionals assistance on data interpretation and decision-making strategies.

  Some other case studies are as follows:

- **"HealthPlus"** A regional hospital, [11] aimed to improve patient care by leveraging emerging technologies. They recognized the potential of IoMT and its ability to transform their existing infrastructure into an intelligent CPS. HealthPlus embarked on implementing an IoMT-based solution to enhance patient monitoring and care.

  - **Sensor Integration:** HealthPlus deployed a range of sensors across patient rooms, monitoring vital signs, motion, and environmental factors. These sensors were integrated with the hospital's network infrastructure, creating a connected ecosystem for data collection.
  - **Predictive Analytics:** Advanced analytics algorithms were employed to analyze the collected data, generating insights and predictions about patient health conditions. Machine learning models were trained to identify patterns and anomalies, enabling early detection of deteriorating patient conditions.
  - **Remote Patient Monitoring:** HealthPlus extended their patient care beyond the hospital walls through remote monitoring capabilities. Patients were provided with wearable devices that continuously tracked their vital signs and transmitted the data to the CPS platform. Healthcare providers could remotely monitor patients' health conditions and intervene when necessary, reducing the need for unnecessary hospital visits.

- **A home healthcare service provider, "CareLink,"** [13] aimed to improve patient care and enable remote monitoring of patients' health conditions. They recognized the potential of IoMT and intelligent CPS to enhance their services, ensuring better patient outcomes and reducing hospital readmissions. CareLink embarked on implementing an IoMT-based solution for their home healthcare operations.

  - **Care Coordination and Telehealth:** The intelligent CPS facilitated seamless care coordination among healthcare providers, patients, and caregivers. Telehealth services were provided, allowing virtual consultations, remote monitoring, and medication management. This reduced the need for in-person visits and improved access to healthcare services.
  - **Patient Engagement and Education:** CareLink utilized the IoMT capabilities to engage and educate patients about their health conditions. Patients had access to personalized dashboards that displayed their health data, trends, and educational resources.

- **A large hospital system, "HealthTech,"** [24] recognized the need for innovative technologies to enhance patient care, streamline processes, and improve operational efficiency. To achieve these goals, they implemented an IoMT-based intelligent CPS solution. HealthTech, a prominent healthcare system, acknowledged the necessity of cutting-edge technologies to enhance patient care, streamline processes, and boost operational efficiency. In order to accomplish these objectives, they put into effect an Intelligent Cyber-Physical System (CPS) based on the Internet of Medical Things (IoMT). Connected Medical Devices of HealthTech gathered real-time patient information, such as vital signs, medication adherence, and mobility patterns.

7 Summary

Intelligent Cyber-Physical Systems (CPS) in healthcare depend on the Internet of Medical Things (IoMT). Medical gadgets, wearables, and sensors that collect and share health data form the IoMT network. IoMT allows for easy data integration and interoperability among medical devices, providing a single healthcare environment. Interoperability across devices and systems streamlines data flow, enabling patient monitoring and analysis. IoMT empowers people by enabling access to health data via wearables and mobile apps. This emphasizes active healthcare management, preventive measures, and tailored treatment.

Real-time data analytics in healthcare monitoring, enabled by IoMT and CPS, are revolutionizing the way healthcare is delivered. By providing timely, data-driven insights, these technologies are enhancing patient care, improving outcomes, and making healthcare systems more efficient.

IoMT transmits critical health data, requiring extensive security procedures. Intelligent CPS must protect patient data via encryption, privacy, and regulatory compliance. Still, patient health data security remains a major concern even with improvements in security protocols for Internet of Medical Things (IoMT) devices and networks.

IoMT and Intelligent CPS can transform healthcare delivery. Medical equipment, data analytics, and networking provide a dynamic ecosystem that improves patient care, operational efficiency, and healthcare system innovation. To maximize its potential, this breakthrough technology must overcome security, privacy, and standards issues.

References

1. Amit Kumar Tyagi, N. Sreenath, Cyber Physical Systems: Analyses, challenges and possible solutions, ScienceDirect—Internet of Things and Cyber-Physical Systems, Volume 1, 2021, Pages 22–33.
2. Husham I. AL-Salman and Muataz H. Salih, A review Cyber of Industry 4.0 (Cyber-Physical Systems (CPS), the Internet of Things (IoT) and the Internet of Services (IoS)): Components, and Security Challenges, Journal of Physics: Conference Series, Volume 1424, 2nd International Conference on Advance & Scientific Innovation 19–20 July 2019, Medan, Indonesia.
3. V.A. Dang, et al., Intelligent healthcare: integration of emerging technologies and internet of things for humanity, Sensors 23 (9) (2023) 4200.
4. M. Mansour, et al., Internet of things: a comprehensive overview on protocols, architectures, technologies, simulation tools, and future directions, Energies 16 (8) (2023) 3465.
5. Z. Haitaamar, et al., Lower inclination orbit concept for direct-communication-to satellite internet-of-things using lean satellite standard in near-equatorial regions, Appl. Sci. 13 (9) (2023) 5654.
6. D. Shehada, et al., Fog-based distributed trust and reputation management system for internet of things, J. King Saud. Univ. Comput. Inf. Sci. 34 (10) (2022) 8637–8646.
7. B. Tekinerdogan, O. Koksal, T. Çelik, System architecture design of IoT-based smart cities, Appl. Sci. 13 (7) (2023) 4173.
8. M. Ryalat, H. ElMoaqet, M. AlFaouri, Design of a smart factory based on cyberphysical systems and internet of things towards industry 4.0, Appl. Sci. 13 (4) (2023) 2156.
9. S. Tiwari, K. Nahak, A. Mishra, Revolutionizing healthcare: the power of IoT in health monitoring, J. Data Acquis. Process. 38 (2) (2023) 2416.
10. H.H. Alshammari, The internet of things healthcare monitoring system based on MQTT protocol, Alex. Eng. J. 69 (2023) 275–287.
11. B.G. Mohammed, D.S. Hasan, Smart healthcare monitoring system using IoT, iJIM 17 (01) (2023) 141.
12. S. Krishnamoorthy, A. Dua, S. Gupta, Role of emerging technologies in future IoT driven Healthcare 4.0 technologies: a survey, current challenges and future directions, J. Ambient Intell. Humaniz. Comput. 14 (1) (2023) 361–407.
13. Mohd Javaid, Abid Haleem, Ravi Pratap Singh, Rajiv Suman, An integrated outlook of Cyber–Physical Systems for Industry 4.0: Topical practices, architecture, and applications, Journal on Green Technologies and Sustainability, Volume 1, Issue 1, 2023.
14. Christopher Greer Martin Burns David Wollman Edward Griffor, Cyber-Physical Systems and Internet of Things, National Institute of Standards and Technology (NIST) Special Publication 1900-202, 2019.
15. E.P. Kelly, F. Unsal, Health information privacy and e-healthcare, International Journal of Healthcare Technology and Management, 4 (2002), pp. 41–52.
16. M. Rhahla, T. Abdellatif, R. Attia, W. Berrayana, A gdpr controller for iot systems: application to e-health, 2019 IEEE 28th International Conference on Enabling Technologies: Infrastructure for Collaborative Enterprises (WETICE), IEEE (2019), pp. 170–173.
17. Y. Sun, Security and privacy for the internet of medical things enabled healthcare systems: A survey, IEEE Access, 7 (2019), pp. 183339-183355
18. J. Deepa, J. Jayashree, J. Vijayashree, Mohamed Yousuff, IoT CPS Interpretation for Healthcare Systems, CRC Press, ISBN: 9781003262527, 2023.

19. Mohd Javaid, Abid Haleem, Shanay Rab, Ravi Pratap Singh, Rajiv Suman, Sensors for daily life: A review, https://doi.org/10.1016/j.sintl.2021.100121 Received 4 July 2021; Received in revised form 19 July 2021; Accepted 19 July 2021 Available online 24 July 2021 2666-3511/ © 2021 The Authors. Publishing services by Elsevier B.V. on behalf of KeAi Communications Co. Ltd. This is an open access article under the CC BY license.
20. George Vasilev Angelov, Dimitar Petrov Nikolakov, Ivelina Nikolaeva Ruskova, Elitsa Emilova Gieva, and Maria Liubomirova Spasova, Healthcare Sensing and Monitoring, I. Ganchev et al. (Eds.): Enhanced Living Environments, LNCS 11369, pp. 226–262, 2019.
21. Nasiri, S., & Khosravani, M. R. (2020). Progress and challenges in fabrication of wearable sensors for health monitoring. *Sensors and Actuators. A, Physical, 312*, 112105. https://doi.org/10.1016/j.sna.2020.112105.
22. Shyamnath Gollakota, Haitham Al Hassanieh, Ben Ransford, Dina Katabi, Kevin Fu, IMD Shield: Securing Implantable Medical Devices, Massachusetts Institute of Technology, URL: https://groups.csail.mit.edu/netmit/IMDShield/.
23. Yogev D, Goldberg T, Arami A, Tejman-Yarden S, Winkler TE, Maoz BM. Current state of the art and future directions for implantable sensors in medical technology: Clinical needs and engineering challenges. APL Bioeng. 2023 Sep 27;7(3):031506. https://doi.org/10.1063/5.0152290. PMID: 37781727; PMCID: PMC10539032.
24. The Importance of Environmental Monitoring in Healthcare, https://www.golighthouse.com/en/knowledge-center/environmental-monitoring-healthcare/.
25. Xiaoming Wang, Hongliu Yu, Søren Kold, Ole Rahbek, Shaoping Bai, "Wearable sensors for activity monitoring and motion control: A review", Biomimetic Intelligence and Robotics 3 (2023) 100089.
26. Dimitris Koutras, George Stergiopoulos, Thomas Dasaklis, Panayiotis Kotzanikolaou, Dimitris Glynos, and Christos Douligeris, Security in IoMT Communications: A Survey, Sensors—An Open Access Journal from MDPI, 2020.
27. Smart Network Division, Telecommunication Engineering Centre, Security and Privacy in the Internet of Medical things (IoMT), security and privacy in M2M for e Health.pdf (tec.gov.in).
28. Cybersecurity Technologies for the Internet of Medical Wearable Devices (IoMWD), Advances in Cyber Security Analytics and Decision Systems pp 117–140.
29. Fortra: Digital Guardian and Data Protection, https://www.digitalguardian.com/blog/healthcare-data-security.
30. HIPAA Privacy Rule Accounting of Disclosures Under the Health Information Technology for Economic and Clinical Health Act, Federal Register, US Government, https://www.federalregister.gov/documents/2011/05/31/2011-13297/hipaa-privacy-rule-accounting-of-disclosures-under-the-health-information-technology-for-economic.
31. Data protection under GDPR, https://europa.eu/youreurope/business/dealing-with-customers/data-protection/data-protection-gdpr/index_en.htm.
32. Medical device regulation: landscape and trends, https://www.elsevier.com/en-in/industry/medical-device-regulation.
33. Cyber Security, US Food and Drug Administration, https://www.fda.gov/medical-devices/digital-health-center-excellence/cybersecurity.
34. Case Study of Remote Patient Monitoring Solution Development, empeek, https://empeek.com/case-studies/remote-patient-monitoring-solution-development/.
35. Real-Time Health Monitoring System Using IoT, empeek, https://empeek.com/case-studies/case-studies-wireless-medical-monitoring-in-real-time/.
36. Rajiv Ranjan, Case Study: Heart function Monitoring and Alert System, ITSEC International Journal of Engineering Sciences, Vol. 1, No. 1, January 2020, Greater Noida pp. 24–27.
37. Jeff Unger, and Denise R. Franco, Practical Application of Continuous Glucose Monitoring in Clinical Practice: Case Studies, Diabetes Technology & Therapeutics, Vol. 25, No. S3, 2023.

Towards Smarter, Interconnected Futures: The Crucial Role of Data in Cyber-Physical Systems

Kathiravan Pannerselvam and Saranya Rajiakodi

Abstract Cyber-physical systems (CPS) integrate computational elements with physical entities and are prevalent across diverse domains. Effective data collection, analysis, and management are important to enhancing their potential. CPS data collection involves gathering information from physical and digital sources through sensing, digitization, and communication. Sensors are responsible for sensing the properties of the physical world, circumstances, and machines. CPS converts data into digital format before transmitting it to the computational components. The data analysis in CPS employs statistical analysis, machine learning, and data mining to process collected data, identify patterns, and make predictions. It includes data cleaning, transformation, analysis, interpretation, and visualization. Data management in CPS involves storage, maintenance, security, and governance. Data is stored efficiently in databases or warehouses, undergoes regular maintenance for integrity, and is protected through encryption and access control. Governance establishes policies and procedures for data use and management. These processes enable intelligent decision-making and informed predictions, ensuring data integrity and security. Successful implementation of data collection, analysis, and management enhances the efficiency and performance of CPS, nurturing their widespread adoption. Transportation, healthcare, energy, and smart city applications can benefit from these advancements, contributing to a more intelligent, interconnected future. By addressing challenges and exploring future directions, this chapter expands the understanding and practice of data collection, analysis, and management in intelligent CPS. It serves as a valuable resource for researchers, engineers, and policymakers, promoting the integration and utilization of CPS across diverse sectors.

Keywords Cyber-physical system · Sensory data · Edge AI · Data process · Distributed system · IoT

K. Pannerselvam · S. Rajiakodi (✉)
Department of Computer Science, Central University of Tamil Nadu, Thiruvarur, Tamil Nadu, India
e-mail: saranya@acad.cutn.ac.in

M. Mittal and J. Narayan (eds.), *Intelligent Cyber-Physical Systems for Healthcare Solutions*, https://doi.org/10.1007/978-981-97-8983-2_9

1 Introduction

The contemporary era is witnessing an intersection of technological innovation and societal change, boosted by the rise of Cyber-Physical Systems (CPS). At the core of this transformative paradigm lies a pervasive and vital element called data. This introduction sets the stage for exploring the relationship between data and cyber-physical systems. Cyber-physical systems represent a fusion of computational algorithms and physical processes, creating an ecosystem where the digital and physical worlds congregate flawlessly [1, 2]. The CPS framework, thus, acts as a channel for many applications across diverse sectors, from healthcare and transportation to manufacturing and energy [3, 4]. In the context of CPS, the data-driven paradigm becomes increasingly evident. The traditional boundary between the digital and physical realms dissolves, creating an environment where data is not merely a byproduct but a vital constituent of the entire system [5].

1.1 The Role of Data in Cyber-Physical Systems

Sensors continuously acquire real-time data from the physical environment. This process, often called sensing, lays the foundational groundwork for the subsequent data synthesis, integration, communication, and analysis phases. The data deriving from sensors becomes the essential for decision-making, system adaptation, and optimization within the CPS framework [6]. In the context of CPS, data is not a uniform entity but rather a multi-faceted construct that undergoes various transformations throughout its lifecycle within the system. From the initial stages of data acquisition, where raw information is gathered from sensors to the consequent phases of integration and synthesis, where disparate data sources merge to provide a comprehensive representation of the physical environment—the course of data within CPS is inherently dynamic and complex [7].

Moreover, sophisticated algorithms have driven the data-centric paradigm to unprecedented heights. Advanced analytics and processing techniques enable CPS to collect insights, patterns, and trends from the voluminous sensor-generated datasets. This analytical layer empowers CPS to respond intelligently to dynamic changes in the physical environment and optimize its operations based on the distinguished patterns [8].

1.2 The Interdisciplinary Implications of Data in CPS

The interaction between data and Cyber-Physical Systems extends beyond the technological province, infusing diverse disciplines. Ethical considerations surrounding data usage, privacy implications, and societal impacts merit analysis in the era of data-centric CPS [9]. Additionally, the interdisciplinary nature of CPS implies a convergence of engineering, computer science, data science, ethics, and social sciences [10]. This chapter describes a structured exploration of the pivotal role of data in Cyber-Physical Systems. Following this introductory section, subsequent segments will delve into specific facets of this relationship, encompassing the nuances of sensing, data fusion, communication, processing, and the associated challenges. Each section aims to contribute to a general comprehension of the relationship between data and CPS.

2 Understanding Cyber-Physical Systems

Cyber-Physical Systems (CPS) significantly advance how we understand and interact with the physical and digital worlds. These systems integrate computational algorithms and physical processes, enabling a seamless interaction between the digital and physical realms. This integration is vital to digital transformation in various sectors [11, 12].

Healthcare: In healthcare, CPS can transform patient care through advanced monitoring systems, personalized medicine, and robotic surgery. By integrating real-time data with physical processes, CPS enhances diagnosis, treatment, and patient monitoring, leading to better health outcomes [13].

Transportation: CPS transforms transportation through intelligent transportation systems, autonomous vehicles, and smart infrastructure. This integration improves safety, efficiency, and sustainability in transportation. For example, CPS can optimize traffic flow, reduce accidents, and enable more efficient logistics and supply chain management [14].

Manufacturing: In manufacturing, CPS is at the heart of Industry 4.0. It enables smart factories where machines communicate and adapt in real time. This leads to increased efficiency, reduced downtime, and a more flexible production process. CPS allows for predictive maintenance, real-time quality control, and customized manufacturing, enhancing productivity and innovation [15].

Energy: CPS plays a crucial role in the energy sector by enabling the integration of art grids and renewable energy i. It allows for better management of energy resources, improves grid reliability, and facilitates the use of renewable sources. CPS in energy contributes to more sustainable and efficient energy systems, adapting to real-time changes in demand and supply [16].

In each of these sectors, the role of data is critical. Data acts as the bridge between the digital computations and the physical processes. It provides the necessary information for the algorithms to make informed decisions and adapt to changes in the physical environment. This continuous data exchange makes CPS so powerful and transformative in various industries.

3 Handling Data in Cyber-Physical Systems

Managing data within Cyber-Physical Systems is essential to maintaining unified functionality and making informed decisions. This process entails gathering, analyzing, and processing data derived from physical operations and converting this data into meaningful information that can guide actionable decisions.

3.1 Sensing and Data Acquisition

In Cyber-Physical Systems (CPS), standard sensors include electrochemical sensors, semiconductors like Metal Oxide Semiconductors (MOS), and conductivity sensors with conductive polymers. These sensors vary across domains based on the specific requirements of different applications. For instance, in environmental monitoring and food quality assessment, chemiresistive sensors are frequently employed to detect odors and volatile organic compounds [17]. In medicine, fiber-optic sensors are integrated into surgical instruments to enhance procedure precision. Furthermore, sensors based on organic field-effect transistors (OFETs) may be utilized for gas detection applications. Each domain necessitates sensors tailored to its unique needs, highlighting the diversity of sensor types and their applications within CPS. This miniaturization is pivotal as it enables the widespread deployment of sensors, facilitating the capture and relay of data across various contexts and environments. Additionally, modern sensors are now equipped with multi-sensing capabilities, which means a single device can detect and measure diverse data types such as temperature, pressure, and motion. This multiplicity streamlines the data acquisition process and enriches the data pool, providing a more comprehensive understanding of the monitored conditions. Finally, the precision of sensors has seen significant enhancement. The ability to obtain precise measurements ensures that CPS can operate with the finesse required for automated and critical decision-making processes, thereby elevating the reliability and efficiency of these integrated systems.

3.2 Integrating and Synthesizing Data

In Cyber-Physical Systems (CPS), the conversion and transmission of data from physical sources to computational components are pivotal processes for system functionality [2]. This begins with the digitization of analog signals through analog-to-digital converters (ADCs), allowing sensors to capture physical data and convert it into digital form. These sensors, strategically positioned within the physical environment, continuously measure relevant parameters and transmit the data to computational units. The digitized data is then transmitted to computational components for analysis using wired or wireless communication protocols like Ethernet, Wi-Fi, or Bluetooth [18]. Here, microcontrollers, processors, or dedicated computing units process and analyze the data, extracting valuable insights through computations, algorithms, or machine learning techniques. Subsequently, decisions are made based on this analysis, enabling control actions such as parameter adjustments, actuator activation, or system alerts to optimize performance or respond to changing environmental conditions. These processes facilitate real-time monitoring, analysis, and control of physical processes, enhancing efficiency, safety, and autonomy across diverse CPS applications [3]. Integrating and fusing data within Cyber-Physical Systems (CPS) enhances decision-making capabilities. Data fusion merges disparate strands of information from multiple sources, yielding a unified and accurate depiction of the physical environment. This process fosters a comprehensive understanding of the system's current state and supports the development of more effective strategies. Additionally, data aggregation is a critical step that consolidates individual data points into a coherent summary form, simplifying complex data sets for easy analysis. By distilling vast data arrays into more manageable summaries, decision-makers can more readily discern patterns and trends, essential for informed decision-making [2].

The unification of these processes significantly elevates the overall efficiency of CPS. By synthesizing various data sources, CPS can achieve optimized system performance and more intelligent allocation of resources [5]. Moreover, the integrated data is instrumental in the realm of predictive analysis. The insights gained from a full spectrum of data allow for the creation of predictive models that enable researchers and professionals to identify potential issues before they arise, allowing for a proactive stance in system management. This forward-looking approach is crucial in the preemptive maintenance and Management of CPS, ensuring that systems remain robust and functional. In conclusion, data fusion and aggregation practices are fundamental to the intelligent operation and strategic foresight required to manage Cyber-Physical Systems.

3.3 Communicating and Networking Data

The continuous data exchange between the CPS and its physical and digital components relies on robust communication and networking. Data must be secure and reliable to support real-time decision-making and control, whether wired or wireless.

In Cyber-Physical Systems (CPS), safeguarding sensitive data and communications security are paramount. Robust security measures are critical to protect against breaches and attacks, ensuring that data integrity and privacy are maintained. As wireless technologies continue to advance, as illustrated in Fig. 1, the evolution of standards such as 5G and Wi-Fi 6 is crucial, providing the high-speed and reliable communication needed for CPS to operate effectively in distributed environments. These technologies enable faster data transfer rates and improve system reliability and connectivity range, essential for CPS networks' continuous operation. Moreover, developing interoperable communication standards is a foundational aspect of CPS design. It ensures that different components and networks can work together without

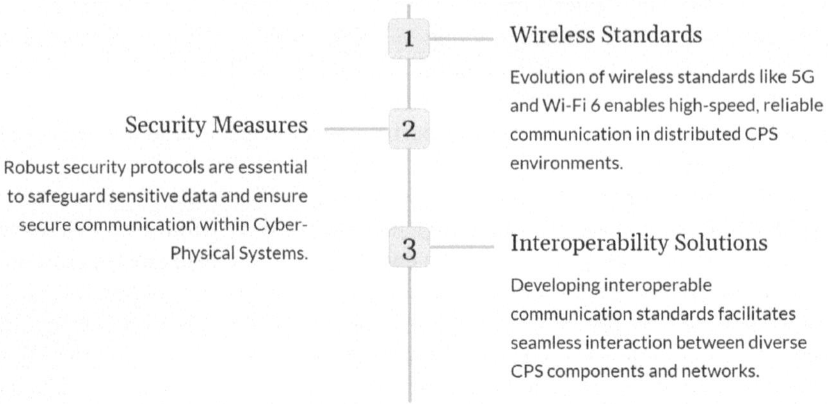

Fig. 1 Communication protocol for CPS

compatibility issues, facilitating the interaction across diverse CPS components. Such interoperability is not just about technology. It is about creating an ecosystem where devices, regardless of their make or model, can communicate and function cohesively, driving efficiency and enabling more sophisticated and coordinated CPS functionalities [19].

3.4 Processing and Analyzing Data

Once data is acquired and transmitted, the next crucial step is processing and analysis. Advanced algorithms analyze the data, extracting meaningful insights and patterns. This analytical layer empowers CPS to adapt and respond intelligently to changes in the physical environment. Figure 2 illustrates the processes and analysis of CPS data.

Integrating edge computing into modern data management systems presents a transformative approach to handling information. By processing data at its source, edge computing significantly reduces latency, resulting in the swift execution of tasks and rapid responses to imperative situations. This decentralized model distributes computational workloads and circumvents the need for data to travel to centralized data centers, conserving bandwidth and accelerating the decision-making process [20]. The proximity of data processing to data generation points ensures that critical services and applications operate with minimal delay, a crucial factor in scenarios such as autonomous vehicle navigation, real-time health monitoring systems, and automated manufacturing processes, where milliseconds can determine the efficacy of outcomes [21]. Addressing challenges like latency and reliability in real-time data collection for Cyber-Physical Systems (CPS) involves implementing various strategies and technologies. This includes selecting communication protocols like MQTT

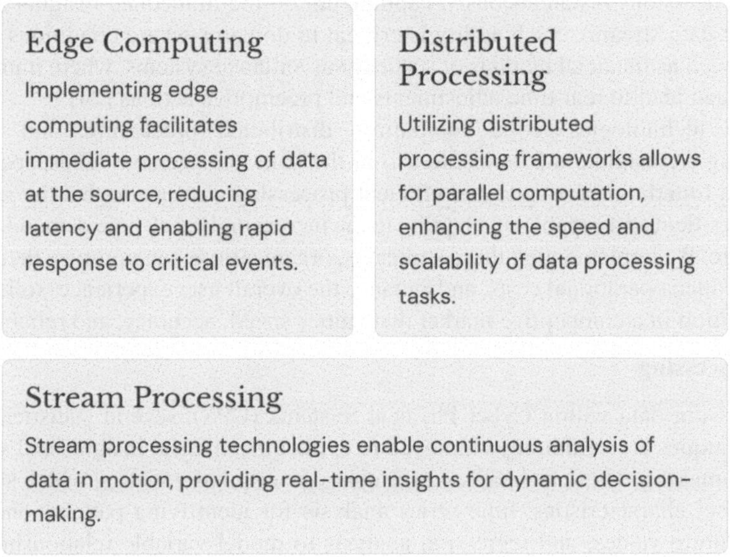

Fig. 2 Data processing and analysis

or CoAP designed for low latency and high reliability, leveraging edge computing capabilities to preprocess data locally and reduce transmission distance, and prioritizing critical data transmission over non-critical data. Additionally, building redundancy and fault tolerance into the system architecture, implementing quality of service (QoS) management techniques, and utilizing predictive analytics and proactive monitoring help mitigate potential issues before they impact system performance [22]. Continuous optimization of the CPS infrastructure based on performance feedback and evolving requirements is also essential, involving fine-tuning communication protocols, adjusting data processing algorithms, and upgrading hardware components to ensure optimal real-time data collection while maintaining reliability.

Distributed processing frameworks come into play to enhance the capabilities of edge computing further. These frameworks are adept at dividing complex computing tasks across multiple nodes, which work in parallel to analyze and process large volumes of data. This method not only quickens the data processing but also scales up the system's capacity to handle expansive datasets, thereby reinforcing the robustness and efficiency of computational operations. By its nature, distributed processing provides redundancy and increases reliability, as the failure of a single node does not incapacitate the entire system. This resilience is indispensable for critical infrastructure systems and large-scale industrial operations, where uptime and reliability are paramount [23]. Complementing both edge computing and distributed processing is stream processing technology. Unlike traditional batch processing, stream processing is designed to evaluate and act upon data in real time as it flows into the system. This continuous analysis empowers businesses and organizations to make informed and dynamic decisions instantaneously, capitalizing on the immediate insights derived from live data streams. Such agility is critical in domains where conditions evolve rapidly, such as financial markets or security surveillance systems, where immediate analysis can lead to real-time adjustments and preemptive actions [24].

These technologies—edge computing, distributed processing, and stream processing—constitute a formidable trio in the data management landscape. They provide a foundation for agile and efficient processing and ensure that the systems remain resilient and capable of adapting to the increasingly real-time demands of the digital age. By implementing these strategies, organizations can optimize their operations, reduce operational costs, and enhance the overall user experience, solidifying their position in a competitive market that values speed, accuracy, and reliability.

Data processing

In processing data within Cyber-Physical Systems (CPS), several statistical analysis techniques are commonly employed to extract meaningful insights and support decision-making. These techniques encompass descriptive statistics, which summarize dataset characteristics, time series analysis for identifying patterns and forecasting future values, and regression analysis to model variable relationships [2]. Anomaly detection methods are utilized to identify irregularities indicative of system faults or security breaches, while classification and clustering techniques categorize data into groups for fault diagnosis and event detection [25]. Bayesian inference aids decision-making under uncertainty, while spatial analysis handles data with geographical attributes for applications like environmental monitoring [26]. By integrating these statistical techniques, CPS can effectively analyze vast data volumes, derive actionable insights, and enhance system performance and reliability [4, 13].

Data analysis

Machine Learning algorithms play a pivotal role in identifying patterns and making predictions in CPS. Examples of commonly used algorithms include Support Vector Machines (SVM) for fault detection and anomaly detection, Random Forest for fault diagnosis and event detection, Recurrent Neural Networks (RNN) and Long Short-Term Memory (LSTM) networks for time series prediction tasks, Convolutional Neural Networks (CNN) for object detection and image classification, Gaussian Process Regression (GPR) for predictive modeling, and Autoencoders for anomaly detection and data denoising [27]. These algorithms analyze sensor data to detect patterns, trends, and anomalies, enabling CPS to make informed decisions, predict future events, and optimize system performance. Depending on the application, algorithms such as decision trees, gradient boosting machines, and deep reinforcement learning may also address specific challenges in CPS data analysis and prediction.

Data storing and management

Efficiently storing and maintaining data within databases or warehouses in Cyber-Physical Systems (CPS) demands thoroughly considering critical factors [5]. Firstly, scalability is paramount to accommodate the vast volumes of data generated by myriad sensors and devices, necessitating a flexible infrastructure capable of scaling horizontally or vertically. Additionally, designing an appropriate data model tailored to CPS requirements is essential, ensuring optimal storage, retrieval, and relationship management [28]. Striking the right balance between data granularity and storage overhead is crucial, alongside implementing compression and encoding techniques to minimize storage space. Furthermore, partitioning and sharding data across multiple nodes can enhance scalability and performance, while efficient indexing and query optimization techniques facilitate swift data retrieval. Robust backup and disaster recovery mechanisms are imperative to safeguard against data loss or corruption, complemented by stringent security measures to protect sensitive information. Regular monitoring and maintenance are vital to identify and mitigate potential issues promptly, ensuring CPS data storage systems' uninterrupted availability and reliability. By addressing these considerations, CPS can efficiently manage data, empowering data-driven decision-making and system operation [29].

4 Ensuring Security and Privacy

As data takes center stage in CPS, ensuring its security and protecting user privacy are paramount. Robust encryption, secure communication, and strict access control mechanisms are essential to safeguard the integrity and confidentiality of data within these systems.

4.1 Data Encryption

Contemporary encryption algorithms like AES (Advanced Encryption Standard), RSA (Rivest–Shamir–Adleman), and ECC (Elliptic Curve Cryptography) are fundamental to the security infrastructure of data management. These sophisticated algorithms are designed to encode information so only authorized parties can decipher it, protecting it from unauthorized access. In conjunction with these, end-to-end encryption offers an enhanced level of security. It ensures that data is encoded at the origin point, typically on the sender's device, and remains encrypted during transit, only to be decoded at its final destination on the recipient's device. This method ensures no intermediaries can intercept and read the data [30].

Additionally, Transparent Data Encryption (TDE) provides a layer of security for businesses by encrypting data stored within databases. This type of encryption operates behind the scenes, allowing companies to secure their sensitive data against unauthorized access, which is critical in preventing data breaches and information theft. These encryption methodologies are vital in preserving data privacy and protecting sensitive information across various platforms and channels [31].

Access Control Mechanisms

Role-Based Access Control (RBAC) is a robust mechanism governing access to information, as it confines data accessibility exclusively to authorized individuals according to their designated roles within the organization [32]. This approach effectively thwarts unauthorized entry into sensitive data repositories, ensuring data security. Multi-factor authentication (MFA) amplifies security measures by requiring users to validate their identity through multiple means before being granted access. This multi-pronged authentication system is a formidable deterrent against illicit login attempts, substantially diminishing the risk of unauthorized access. Attribute-Based Access Control (ABAC) introduces a dynamic layer of control over data access, allowing organizations to formulate access policies based on many attributes, including user roles, temporal factors, geographic location, and data sensitivity. This nuanced approach affords organizations unprecedented precision in regulating data access, promoting a highly tailored and secure environment for information management [33].

Secure Communication Protocols

Transport Layer Security (TLS) is the cornerstone of secure communication across computer networks, guaranteeing data privacy and integrity in various applications, including web browsing, email exchanges, and messaging services. In tandem with TLS, Secure Hypertext Transfer Protocol (HTTPS) fortifies web security by encrypting and decrypting user interactions with websites, preserving the confidentiality of online communications. Furthermore, Internet Protocol Security (IPsec) augments data security by authenticating and encrypting each IP packet in Internet communication, ensuring data remains confidential and unaltered during transit [34]. Collectively, these protocols form a robust security framework, safeguarding sensitive information across a wide array of online interactions and data transmissions.

User Privacy Protection

User Data Anonymization, a fundamental practice in safeguarding privacy, transforms personal information into an unidentifiable format, effectively thwarting any attempts at tracking or profiling individuals without authorization. Concurrently, Privacy-Preserving Data Processing employs cutting-edge techniques like secure multiparty computation and homomorphic encryption, facilitating valuable data analysis while preserving the confidentiality of raw data. This innovative approach ensures that user privacy is maintained even during data analysis. Additionally, Consent Management systems empower users by providing transparent information on data usage and allowing them to grant or withdraw consent, granting individuals control over their data and reinforcing their privacy rights. These measures constitute a robust framework for protecting user privacy in data-driven contexts.

Comprehension and compliance with data security laws and regulations, such as the General Data Protection Regulation (GDPR), Health Insurance Portability and Accountability Act (HIPAA), and California Consumer Privacy Act (CCPA), are fundamental to maintaining legal conformity and avoiding any regulatory penalties. These frameworks guide how systems should handle sensitive data [35]. Additionally, conducting regular risk assessments is a key practice that enables the identification of vulnerabilities and potential threats within the system. Such assessments are vital as they lead to the implementation of proactive strategies that safeguard sensitive data and reduce the risk of security breaches [36, 37]. Furthermore, investing in comprehensive security training and fostering employee awareness is essential. This training ensures that all organization members know about data protection best practices and contribute to a culture that prioritizes security. These collective efforts ensure that sensitive information within Cyber-Physical Systems remains secure and that privacy is upheld.

5 Challenges and Future Directions

While integrating data in Cyber-Physical Systems (CPS) presents immense opportunities, several challenges must be mitigated to harness its transformative potential fully.

Data Interoperability is a prominent issue. CPS often involves many sensors, devices, and platforms from diverse manufacturers. Ensuring seamless data exchange and interoperability between these components is non-trivial. Developing universal data standards and protocols is essential to overcome this challenge, enabling different CPS elements to communicate effectively.

Standardization is another hurdle. The absence of standardized frameworks for data collection, storage, and analysis hampers the scalability and efficiency of CPS. Establishing industry-wide standards is imperative to streamline operations and promote compatibility among CPS systems.

Ethical Considerations loom large in the age of data-driven CPS. The collection and utilization of vast amounts of data raise concerns about individual privacy, security, and data ownership. Ethical frameworks and regulations must be developed and enforced to safeguard against potential data misuse, ensuring that CPS development aligns with ethical principles.

Looking ahead, the future of data-driven CPS is promising. Artificial intelligence (AI) and machine learning (ML) advancements are poised to revolutionize CPS. These technologies will enable CPS to collect and process data and learn from it, make autonomous decisions, and adapt to changing environments in real-time.

Moreover, the future holds the potential for more sophisticated and intelligent CPS. These systems will be capable of predictive analysis, anomaly detection, and self-optimization. For example, in healthcare, CPS can predict patient health deterioration and trigger timely interventions. In transportation, they can optimize traffic flow to reduce congestion and accidents.

In brief, while challenges like data interoperability, standardization, and ethical considerations persist, the future of data-driven CPS is marked by unprecedented advancements in AI and ML, paving the way for more intelligent and responsive systems that have the potential to revolutionize a wide range of industries. Proactively and responsibly addressing these challenges is crucial to realize this potential fully.

6 Conclusion

In conclusion, the role of data in Cyber-Physical Systems (CPS) is central. From sensing the physical world to making informed decisions, the entire CPS ecosystem hinges on data quality, reliability, and security. Data extraction is critical to this process, ensuring that relevant information is collected efficiently. As technology evolves, understanding and harnessing the power of data will be key to unlocking the full potential of Cyber-Physical Systems in shaping the future of industries and societies. Challenges such as data interoperability, standardization, ethical considerations, and data extraction must be addressed proactively to ensure that the benefits of CPS are realized while preserving individual privacy and data integrity. Looking ahead, advancements in artificial intelligence (AI) and machine learning (ML) promise more sophisticated and intelligent CPS that is capable of predictive analysis and proactive interventions. To navigate this rapidly evolving landscape, it is imperative to strike a balance between innovation and responsibility, guided by ethical frameworks and regulations, to harness the transformative potential of data-driven CPS for the betterment of society.

References

1. M. Lombardi and S. Vannuccini, "Understanding emerging patterns and dynamics through the lenses of the cyber-physical universe," *Patterns*, vol. 3, no. 11, p. 100601, Nov. 2022, https://doi.org/10.1016/J.PATTER.2022.100601.
2. T. Sobb, B. Turnbull, and N. Moustafa, "A Holistic Review of Cyber–Physical–Social Systems: New Directions and Opportunities," *Sensors (Basel).*, vol. 23, no. 17, Sep. 2023, https://doi.org/10.3390/S23177391.
3. R. Singh and S. S. Gill, "Edge AI: A survey," *Internet Things Cyber-Physical Syst.*, vol. 3, pp. 71–92, Dec. 2023, https://doi.org/10.1016/J.IOTCPS.2023.02.004.
4. S. Wolfert, L. Ge, C. Verdouw, and M. J. Bogaardt, "Big data in smart farming—a review," *Agric Syst*, vol. 153, pp. 69–80, May 2017, https://doi.org/10.1016/j.agsy.2017.01.023.
5. D. Humeniuk, G. Antoniol, and F. Khomh, "Data Driven Testing of Cyber Physical Systems," *Proc. - 2021 IEEE/ACM 14th Int. Work. Search-Based Softw. Testing, SBST 2021*, pp. 16–19, 2021, https://doi.org/10.1109/SBST52555.2021.00010.
6. "Sensors | Special Issue : Real-Time and Cyber-Physical Systems." https://www.mdpi.com/journal/sensors/special_issues/cyber_physical_system (accessed Jan. 14, 2024).
7. Y. Liu, X. Wang, Y. Liu, and S. Cui, "Data-Aware Retrodiction for Asynchronous Harmonic Measurement in a Cyber-Physical Energy System," *Sensors 2016, Vol. 16, Page 1316*, vol. 16, no. 8, p. 1316, Aug. 2016, https://doi.org/10.3390/S16081316.
8. M. Elahi, S. O. Afolaranmi, J. L. Martinez Lastra, and J. A. Perez Garcia, *A comprehensive literature review of the applications of AI techniques through the lifecycle of industrial equipment*, vol. 3, no. 1. Springer International Publishing, 2023.
9. L. Van Woensel *et al.*, *Ethical Aspects of Cyber-Physical Systems*. 2016.

10. M. Mohammad Amini, M. Jesus, D. Fanaei Sheikholeslami, P. Alves, A. Hassanzadeh Benam, and F. Hariri, "Artificial Intelligence Ethics and Challenges in Healthcare Applications: A Comprehensive Review in the Context of the European GDPR Mandate," *Mach. Learn. Knowl. Extr.*, vol. 5, no. 3, pp. 1023–1035, 2023, https://doi.org/10.3390/make5030053.
11. S. A. Haque, S. M. Aziz, and M. Rahman, "Review of Cyber-Physical System in Healthcare," https://doi.org/10.1155/2014/217415, vol. 2014, Apr. 2014, https://doi.org/10.1155/2014/217415.
12. M. S. Farooq *et al.*, "A Survey on the Role of Industrial IoT in Manufacturing for Implementation of Smart Industry," *Sensors (Basel)*, vol. 23, no. 21, pp. 1–38, 2023, https://doi.org/10.3390/s23218958.
13. M. Sony, J. Antony, and O. McDermott, "The impact of medical cyber–physical systems on healthcare service delivery," *TQM J.*, vol. 34, no. 7, pp. 73–94, 2022, https://doi.org/10.1108/TQM-01-2022-0005.
14. A. Pundir, S. Singh, M. Kumar, A. Bafila, and G. J. Saxena, "Cyber-Physical Systems Enabled Transport Networks in Smart Cities: Challenges and Enabling Technologies of the New Mobility Era," *IEEE Access*, vol. 10, pp. 16350–16364, 2022, https://doi.org/10.1109/ACCESS.2022.3147323.
15. N. H. Tran, H. S. Park, Q. V. Nguyen, and T. D. Hoang, "Development of a smart cyber-physical manufacturing system in the Industry 4.0 context," *Appl. Sci.*, vol. 9, no. 16, 2019, https://doi.org/10.3390/app9163325.
16. P. Pandiyan, S. Saravanan, K. Usha, R. Kannadasan, M. H. Alsharif, and M. K. Kim, "Technological advancements toward smart energy management in smart cities," *Energy Reports*, vol. 10, pp. 648–677, 2023, https://doi.org/10.1016/j.egyr.2023.07.021.
17. A. John, K. Murugappan, D. Nisbet, and A. Tricoli, "An outlook of recent advances in chemiresistive sensor-based electronic nose systems for food quality and environmental monitoring," *Sensors*, vol. 21, no. 7, p. 2271, 2021, https://doi.org/10.3390/s21072271.
18. J. Criado, J. A. Asensio, N. Padilla, and L. Iribarne, "Integrating cyber-physical systems in a component-based approach for smart homes," *Sensors*, vol. 18, no. 7, p. 2156, 2018.
19. J. P. A. Yaacoub, O. Salman, H. N. Noura, N. Kaaniche, A. Chehab, and M. Malli, "Cyber-physical systems security: Limitations, issues and future trends," *Microprocess. Microsyst.*, vol. 77, p. 103201, Sep. 2020, https://doi.org/10.1016/J.MICPRO.2020.103201.
20. "Edge computing is transforming the way we process data." https://blog.seeburger.com/what-is-edge-computing-and-why-is-it-important/ (accessed Jan. 14, 2024).
21. E. Badidi, K. Moumane, and F. El Ghazi, "Opportunities, Applications, and Challenges of Edge-AI Enabled Video Analytics in Smart Cities: A Systematic Review," *IEEE Access*, vol. 11, pp. 80543–80572, 2023, https://doi.org/10.1109/ACCESS.2023.3300658.
22. H. N. S. Aldin, M. R. Ghods, F. Nayebipour, and M. N. Torshiz, "A comprehensive review of energy harvesting and routing strategies for IoT sensors sustainability and communication technology," *Sensors Int.*, p. 100258, 2023.
23. S. Moin, A. Karim, Z. Safdar, K. Safdar, E. Ahmed, and M. Imran, "Securing IoTs in distributed blockchain: Analysis, requirements and open issues," *Futur. Gener. Comput. Syst.*, vol. 100, pp. 325–343, 2019, https://doi.org/10.1016/j.future.2019.05.023.
24. F. Al-Doghman, N. Moustafa, I. Khalil, N. Sohrabi, Z. Tari, and A. Y. Zomaya, "AI-Enabled Secure Microservices in Edge Computing: Opportunities and Challenges," *IEEE Trans. Serv. Comput.*, vol. 16, no. 2, pp. 1485–1504, Mar. 2023, https://doi.org/10.1109/TSC.2022.3155447.
25. "AI in anomaly detection." https://www.leewayhertz.com/ai-in-anomaly-detection/ (accessed Oct. 24, 2023).
26. N. Qazi and B. L. W. Wong, "An interactive human centered data science approach towards crime pattern analysis," *Inf. Process. Manag.*, vol. 56, no. 6, 2019, https://doi.org/10.1016/j.ipm.2019.102066.
27. Z. Hasan and N. Roy, "Trending machine learning models in cyber-physical building environment: A survey," *Wiley Interdiscip. Rev. Data Min. Knowl. Discov.*, vol. 11, no. 5, p. e1422, 2021.

28. L. Da Xu and L. Duan, "Big data for cyber physical systems in industry 4.0: a survey," *Enterp. Inf. Syst.*, vol. 13, no. 2, pp. 148–169, 2019.
29. B. Boulekrouche, N. Jabeur, and Z. Alimazighi, "Toward integrating grid and cloud-based concepts for an enhanced deployment of spatial data warehouses in cyber-physical system applications," *J. Ambient Intell. Humaniz. Comput.*, vol. 7, pp. 475–487, 2016.
30. N. J. Parmar and P. K. Verma, "A comparative evaluation of algorithms in the implementation of an ultra-secure router-to-router key exchange system," *Secur. Commun. Networks*, vol. 2017, 2017, https://doi.org/10.1155/2017/1467614.
31. P. Williams, I. K. Dutta, H. Daoud, and M. Bayoumi, "A survey on security in internet of things with a focus on the impact of emerging technologies," *Internet of Things (Netherlands)*, vol. 19, p. 100564, 2022, https://doi.org/10.1016/j.iot.2022.100564.
32. "What is RBAC? | Definition from TechTarget." https://www.techtarget.com/searchsecurity/definition/role-based-access-control-RBAC (accessed Jan. 14, 2024).
33. U. Upadhyay *et al.*, "Mitigating Risks in the Cloud-Based Metaverse Access Control Strategies and Techniques," *Int. J. Cloud Appl. Comput.*, vol. 14, no. 1, 2023, https://doi.org/10.4018/IJCAC.334364.
34. Y. Himeur *et al.*, "Blockchain-based recommender systems: Applications, challenges and future opportunities," *Comput. Sci. Rev.*, vol. 43, p. 100439, 2022, https://doi.org/10.1016/j.cosrev.2021.100439.
35. H. Onc, "Guide to Privacy and Security of Electronic Health Information," 2015.
36. "HIPAA, CCPA, and GDPR: Privacy or Information Security? - ControlCase." https://www.controlcase.com/hipaa-ccpa-and-gdpr-privacy-or-information-security/ (accessed Jan. 14, 2024).
37. "Privacy | HHS.gov." https://www.hhs.gov/hipaa/for-professionals/privacy/index.html (accessed Oct. 26, 2023).

Restoring Human Grasp Functionality Through Soft Hand Exoskeletons

Subhash Pratap, Sanjib Saikia, Kazuaki Ito, and Shyamanta M. Hazarika

Abstract This work analyzes existing soft hand exoskeleton models in-depth, points out their drawbacks and difficulties, and offers design suggestions that prioritize adaptability, comfort, and compactness. The key areas of interest are the tendon-driven mechanism, tendon routing, and dynamics analysis because they provide essential knowledge for selecting the optimum design, material, and functional features to improve the exoskeleton's usefulness and usability for persons with hand impairments. To choose the best materials for 3D printing and ensure structural integrity, the task starts by determining the maximum forces and tendon tensions that the exoskeleton must withstand. When evaluating the flexibility and efficiency of the design, tendon routing is a crucial factor. The functioning and responsiveness of the tendon-driven fingers are further evaluated using a thorough dynamics study. This paper offers valuable information on design considerations, material choices, and functional elements of the soft hand exoskeleton by focusing on these crucial areas. The results of these studies and the novel insights they offer open the door to the creation of more useful and effective designs that will enhance usability and functionality for people with hand restrictions.

Keywords Soft hand exoskeleton · Tendon-driven mechanism · Design optimization

---

S. Pratap (✉) · S. Saikia · S. M. Hazarika
Indian Institute of Technology Guwahati, Guwahati, India
e-mail: subhash18@iitg.ac.in

S. Saikia
e-mail: ssaikia@alumni.iitg.ac.in

S. M. Hazarika
e-mail: s.m.hazarika@iitg.ac.in

S. Pratap · K. Ito
Gifu University, Gifu, Japan
e-mail: ito.kazuaki.x5@f.gifu-u.ac.jp

M. Mittal and J. Narayan (eds.), *Intelligent Cyber-Physical Systems for Healthcare Solutions*, https://doi.org/10.1007/978-981-97-8983-2_10

1 Introduction

The hand plays a pivotal role in our physical interaction with the world around us. Many of our daily activities, known as Activities of Daily Living (ADL), require intricate hand movements, such as precise manipulation, grasping, and tool usage. For individuals who have experienced a complete or partial loss of motor function in their hands, the restoration of these abilities is essential for improving their overall quality of life. From both a mechanical and neural perspective, the hand is exceptionally complex. Research indicates that, on average, an individual engages in approximately 1500 hand grasping actions per day [1]. Unfortunately, the global population facing hand function impairments is growing significantly, with millions of individuals affected. Hand functionality and coordination can be compromised for a variety of reasons, with common causes including traumatic incidents, injuries such as spinal cord injuries, degenerative diseases, strokes, various motor disabilities, and age-related muscle weakness. For instance, studies have highlighted that among survivors of stroke, the hand is frequently the limb most impacted by the impairment [2, 3]. When hand function is compromised, it can severely limit an individual's ability to perform daily tasks, ultimately leading to a diminished quality of life [4]. Consequently, therapists and medical professionals have been actively developing diverse approaches and methodologies aimed at restoring normal function to impaired body parts.

The primary method for enhancing hand functionality is through rehabilitation administered via physical therapy. However, the prevalence of individuals with hand impairments is continually rising in contemporary society, driven in part by the increasing aging population. Consequently, it becomes challenging to provide every affected patient with the level of therapist involvement required for effective rehabilitation. Furthermore, the extensive repetition of exercises during therapy sessions can render the work of healthcare professionals monotonous and underutilize their qualifications and expertise. To alleviate the burden on specialists and address these challenges, engineers have developed various robotic devices aimed at automating the rehabilitation process. These devices not only lighten the workload of therapists but also enhance the overall therapy experience for patients. Numerous experimental studies have substantiated the effectiveness of employing robotic systems, while under the supervision of medical professionals, to enhance the motor functions of patients recovering from post-stroke and post-trauma conditions [5]. To date, a variety of hand rehabilitation systems have been developed for this purpose. The utilization of exoskeletons in the context of extreme upper limb rehabilitation exhibits significant potential. Exoskeletons represent wearable robotic systems that can be affixed to the human body, engineered to operate harmoniously with the limbs. These devices have the capability to function across multiple degrees of freedom, thereby enhancing the efficiency and effectiveness of rehabilitation processes by reducing the labor-intensive aspects associated with physical therapy.

Understanding the biomechanical characteristics of the human hand is paramount for the design of effective hand exoskeletons. By comprehensively studying these characteristics, designers can develop exoskeletons that seamlessly integrate with the natural movement patterns of the hand, enhancing user comfort and usability. Incorporating biomechanical insights ensures that hand exoskeletons provide optimal support and assistance while minimizing strain or discomfort during use.

2 Biomechanical Characteristics of Human Hands

A human hand comprises 27 bones: five distal phalanges, four middle phalanges, five proximal phalanges, five metacarpals, and eight carpals (see Fig. 1a). The index, middle, ring, and little fingers each have three revolute joints for angular movement (Fig. 1b). These include the metacarpal-phalangeal (MCP) joint between the metacarpal and proximal phalange bones, and the proximal and distal interphalangeal (PIP and DIP) joints that separate the phalangeal bones. The thumb has MCP and interphalangeal (IP) joints. In terms of degrees of freedom (DOFs), each finger has four (two at MCP, one at PIP, and one at DIP), the thumb has three (two at MCP and one at IP), the wrist has two, and the carpometacarpal (CMC) joint has two [6, 7]. The Fig. 2 illustrates the range of motion achievable by the human hand. Despite its relatively small size, the hand commands a significant portion of our central nervous system's (CNS) capacity, accounting for approximately 30% [8]. Additionally, the hand plays a substantial role in our sense of touch. The combination of this sensory capability and the intricate mobility of its joints contributes to hand dexterity and the ability to perceive tactile sensations [9].

The movement capabilities of the human finger are defined by distinct attributes that impact its functionality and range of motion. Within specified limits of range

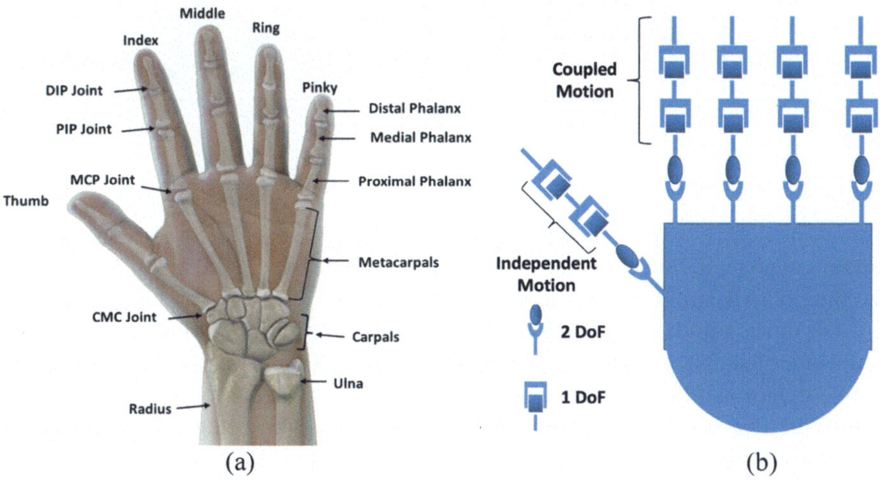

Fig. 1 **a** Human hand anatomy **b** hand model showing DoF at joints

Fingers	Motion direction	Range of Motion (degree)	Description
Thumb	MCP Flexion MCP Extension	60 10	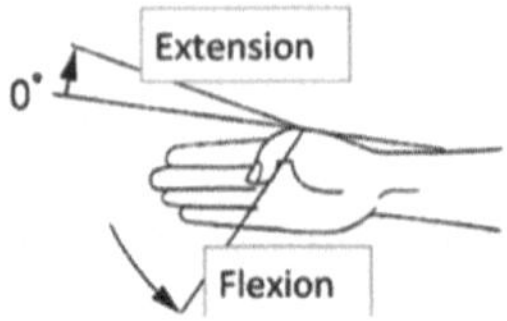
	IP Flexion IP Extension	80 10	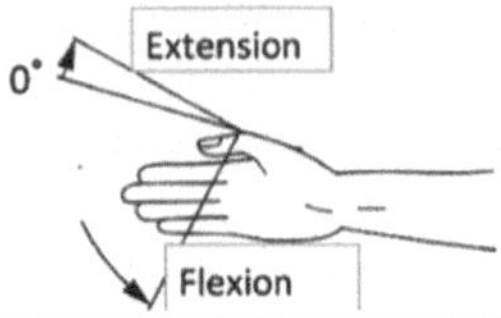
Index Middle Ring Pinky	MCP Flexion MCP Extension	90 45	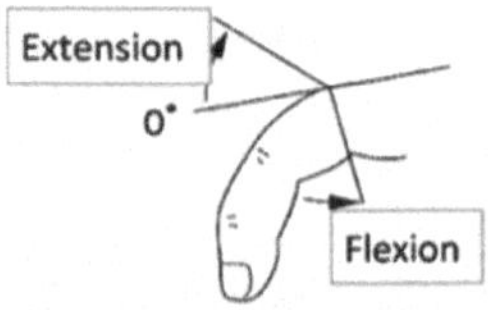
	PIP Flexion PIP Extension	100 0	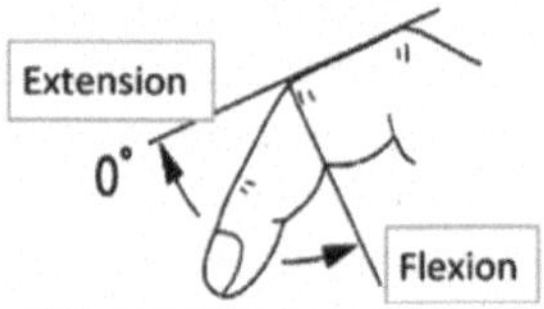
	DIP Flexion DIP Extension	80 0	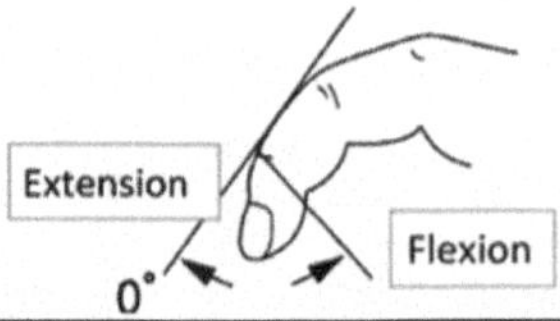

Fig. 2 Range of motion of fingers

of motion (ROM) [10], as shown in Fig. 2, the finger joints are constrained in their bending angles , delineating the scope of flexion, extension, and lateral movement. The thumb's MCP and IP joints flex up to 60° and 80°, respectively, and extend up to 10°. The index, middle, ring, and pinky finger's MCP flexes up to 90° and extends 45° on the other hand their PIP and DIP joints flex up to 100° and 80°, with no extension. Simple diagrams illustrate these movements in Fig. 2. Furthermore, except for the thumb, the two bones of each finger align within the same plane when extended, fostering coordinated motion and stability during activities such as grasping and manipulation. Moreover, the MCP joint's flexion axis is nearly perpendicular to the adduction-abduction axis, facilitating precise finger positioning and dexterity across multiple planes of movement. Lastly, the interdependence between the PIP and DIP joints (refer Fig. 1b) ensures synchronized motion and stability throughout the finger's range, wherein bending at one joint can influence bending at another due to their interconnected structure. Together, these characteristics orchestrate the intricate and synchronized movements of the human finger, enabling precise interaction with objects in the surrounding environment.

3 Hand Assistive Systems

In the study conducted by Du Plessis et al. [11], they categorized hand exoskeletons into primarily two types that have evolved over the years: rigid and soft exoskeletons, or a combination of both. They distinguished rigid exoskeletons as those wherein forces or torques are conveyed to the targeted joints through a mechanical structure. On the other hand, soft exoskeletons utilize flexible materials or elastic structures to transmit forces to the fingers' joints. In contrast, Güçlü and Cora [12] identified a more comprehensive classification, distinguishing among three classes: rigid (linkage-based) exoskeletons, cable-driven exoskeletons, and soft exoskeletons (see Fig. 3). They characterized rigid exoskeletons as those in which the movement generated by actuators is transferred to the joints using hard and inelastic materials. Hybrid exoskeletons, including those driven by cables and pulleys or tendons, fall into this category. Soft exoskeletons, as per their definition, are devices crafted from materials that align with the human anatomy.

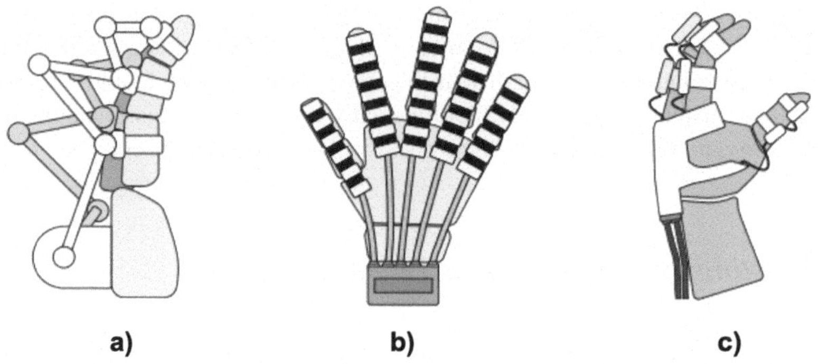

Fig. 3 Illustrative depictions showcasing the three categories of exoskeletons designed for robotic hand rehabilitation: **a** rigid, **b** soft, and **c** hybrid (from [5], licensed under CC-BY 4.0)

3.1 Requirements and Challanges for Hand-Assistance Devices

This section outlines the major prerequisites for devices designed to provide assistance for hand-related activities in the context of Activities of Daily Living (ADL). We have compiled this list of essential characteristics through a comprehensive review of the existing literature [11], as well as consultations with rehabilitation specialists and medical professionals. These requirements are pivotal for the effective development and deployment of hand-assistance devices:

1. **Bidirectionality**: Ideally, the system should offer support for both finger flexion and extension, allowing precise control of each finger individually.
2. **Wearability**: The device must be designed to be wearable, enabling complete portability. Users should have the freedom to move around without hindrance while wearing the device.
3. **High Power-to-Weight Ratio**: It is essential for the system to maintain a balance between weight and power, striving to be lightweight and compact while generating sufficient force and velocity. This necessitates the development of an exoskeleton with an exceptional power-to-weight ratio.
4. **Unrestricted Wrist and Palm**: The device should facilitate object grasping without imposing constraints on the mobility of other arm joints, particularly the wrist. Users should be able to maintain full dexterity and flexibility.
5. **Safety and Comfort**: Above all, the device must prioritize safety and comfort for the wearer. It should be free from any potential hazards or discomfort that could arise during use.

Expanding upon these requirements, it is crucial to recognize that addressing these challenges in the design and development of hand-assistive systems holds the key to significantly enhancing the quality of life for individuals with hand impairments. Meeting these criteria will not only facilitate daily tasks but also foster independence and autonomy, thereby improving the overall well-being of the users.

3.2 Existing Models and Their Limitations

Rigid exoskeletons are renowned for their capacity to apply significant and precise forces at various contact points. However, their rigidity poses challenges in accommodating diverse hand sizes, often leading to joint misalignment and kinematic mismatches. Such issues can detract from the device's comfort and practicality, as noted in previous studies [13]. Carbone et. al. introduces two-degrees-of-freedom rigid finger exoskeleton mechanism designed for assisting human finger motions [14, 15], but it has complexity due to its rigid structure. To address these limitations, innovative approaches like underactuated self-aligning kinematics and intrinsically adaptive mechanisms that incorporate the finger's own kinematics into a parallel arrangement have been introduced [16]. These strategies enhance the system's adaptability to various hand sizes but necessitate a more careful attachment of the exoskeleton segments to the finger bones to ensure effective force transmission [17]. The advent of soft robotics has spurred the creation of hand exoskeletons that prioritize adaptability, wearing comfort, and a lightweight design [5]. Such soft exoskeletons leverage the natural kinematics of the finger, supplemented by an external actuation mechanism. Designs like pneumatic actuated soft gloves use inflatable sections on the back of the fingers to aid in hand movements, such as closing or opening [18]. Innovations have led to designs with a modular fishbone structure for enhanced compactness and adaptability [19].

Hybrid designs merging rigid and soft components have emerged, providing a balanced approach to hand exoskeleton development [20]. Bützer et al. [21] employed semi-rigid elements within a layered spring mechanism to facilitate hand movements. Another compact design utilizes cable-driven mechanisms, echoing the natural muscle-tendon structure of the hand, and has been extensively explored [22–24]. This approach, however, introduces challenges in force transmission, necessitating higher forces to move the tendons effectively and ensuring stable guide paths without causing discomfort. A notable design features open-ring finger supports and dual tendon paths to maintain soft support firmness only during tendon engagement [24]. Actuator placement strategies have varied, with some designs opting for remote motor locations connected via Bowden cables [16, 24, 25] reducing hand weight but impacting wearability and force efficiency. Alternatives include mounting actuators on the hand's dorsal side to improve force distribution and comfort, aiming for an optimized balance of functionality and user adaptation.

Furthermore, enhancing the wearability and comfort of these systems remains a critical challenge, especially for patients with limited hand mobility. Traditional rehabilitation gloves, for example, feature an open design for easier application but translating this to soft exoskeletons, which require intricate cable and tendon routing, proves more complex. Despite these obstacles, strategic design modifications can still enhance the practicality and ease of use for soft exoskeletons, allowing for more accessible finger module application and potentially detachable components [24]. This area of research continues to evolve, seeking to merge the benefits of both rigid and soft system designs for improved user experience.

In this work, a thorough investigation of current soft hand exoskeleton models is conducted, identifying existing limitations and challenges while proposing design modifications that emphasize adaptability, comfort, and compactness. The focus areas of this study include the tendon-driven mechanism, the intricacies of tendon routing, and a comprehensive analysis of dynamics, as these aspects are crucial in determining the optimal design, materials, and functional features that enhance the exoskeleton's effectiveness and ease of use for individuals with hand disabilities. The process begins with an assessment of the maximum forces and tendon tensions the exoskeleton must accommodate, informing the selection of suitable materials for 3D printing to ensure durability and structural integrity using Finite Element Analysis (FEA). The design's flexibility and operational efficiency hinge significantly on effective tendon routing strategies. Additionally, the functionality and responsiveness of the tendon-driven fingers are evaluated through detailed dynamic studies. This work provides valuable insights into design considerations, material selections, and functional features of the soft hand exoskeleton, setting the stage for the creation of more functional and user-friendly designs that aim to improve the daily experiences of individuals with hand limitations.

4 Design of Tendon-Driven Soft Hand Exoskeleton

On assessing the shortcomings and difficulties of existing soft hand exoskeleton models, this work up with design standards based on adaptability, comfort, and compactness, and making use of cutting-edge additive manufacturing methods like fused deposition modelling. It concentrates on the tendon-driven mechanism, tendon routing, and dynamics analysis, offering insights for optimum design, material selection, and functional features, boosting functionality and usability for people with hand impairments. This section concentrates on the design and analysis of the tendon-driven mechanism found in the soft hand exoskeleton. The maximal forces and tendon tensions that the exoskeleton must withstand are determined. This analysis aids in the selection of suitable materials using finite element analysis, ensuring the structural integrity of the exoskeleton. We investigate the tendon routing system's design while taking efficiency and flexibility into account. In order to assess the performance and responsiveness of the tendon-driven fingers, a thorough dynamics study is also performed on them. This section offers insightful information regarding the design considerations, material choice, and functional properties of the soft hand exoskeleton by focusing on these important aspects. These studies open the door for a more effective and efficient design, resulting in improved functionality and usability for helping people with hand impairments.

4.1 Design Approach

Most cable-actuated soft exoskeletons [26–28] exhibit two significant issues: lack of compactness and constrained hand size and shape flexibility. These exoskeletons are frequently built to independently move specific joints or several fingers, which necessitates more actuators and more room for their installation. As a result, the actuator unit is frequently placed far from the hand. Additionally, gloves with covered fingers cannot be used by all patients due to size restrictions. Due to this restriction, more elaborate models must be produced at a higher cost for potential clinical facilities.

Designing a soft exoskeleton that addresses the issues with conventional models was the goal of this project. The objective was to develop a small, flexible gadget that could fit hands of various sizes and shapes. The mechanical structure's parameters have been considered taking into account the hand sizes of the right-handed Indian population. These dimensions have been derived from established studies in the field,

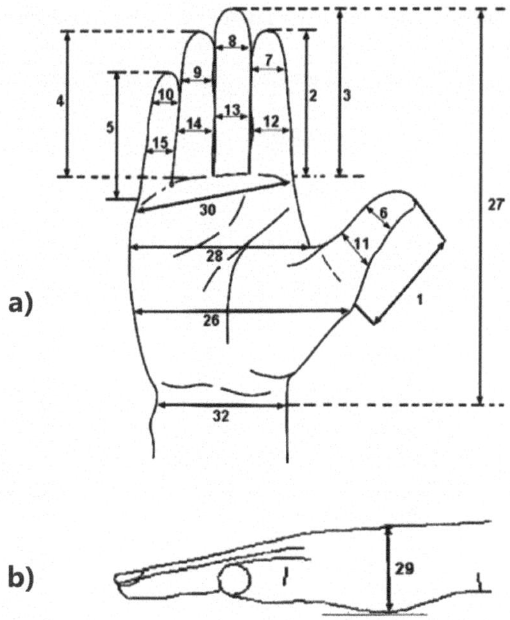

Fig. 4 Hand measurements **a** palmer view; **b** side view

ensuring that the exoskeleton design is tailored to the target demographic [29, 30]. Figure 4 illustrates the various parameters used to measure the human hand, while Table 1 provides the corresponding dimensions derived for the exoskeleton design.

The actuation system was initially decided upon as a tendon type operated by cables. By controlling all joint movements with a single actuator and coordinating with ADLs, this design enables assistance with hand opening and closing. The choice was made not to create a closed, one-piece glove in order to increase versatility. An open half-glove design with modular finger units was chosen as an alternative. The finger unit was built using a thimble, many rings, and other components. Depending on the size of the finger, this modular method enables adjustments in the number and size of rings. The length of the finger unit can be changed without using a fixed-size glove by passing the cables through the rings and fastening them at the tip of the thimble. SOLIDWORKS software was utilized in order to create the model. The separate components that cover each phalanx have spaces between them to make the flexion work easier, and these components will be connected to each other with flexible strips.The structure of one finger with the flexible strip is shown in Fig. 6. Cable guides are provided on both the dorsal and palmer sides of the exoskeleton so that cables can pass through them and complete the process of flexing or extending the fingers. The cables originating from the dorsal side and palmer side were wound upon the spool that was coupled to the motor shaft in such a way that the bidirectional movement of the finger could be performed simply by changing the direction that the motor rotated in. In this manner, only one motor will be required for each finger in order to accomplish both flexing and extending movements. In order to provide a

Table 1 Hand dimensions (mm) for the Indian population

No.	Dimension	Mean	SD	No.	Dimension	Mean	SD
1	Fingertip to MCP joint thumb	64.1	6.3	18	Circumference at DIP joint middle	48	4.2
2	Fingertip to MCP joint index	69.2	5.5	19	Circumference at DIP joint ring	44.42	3.09
3	Fingertip to MCP joint middle	76	5.7	20	Circumference at DIP joint pinky	40.86	3.20
4	Fingertip to MCP joint ring	70.2	5.4	21	Circumference at PIP joint thumb	60.75	3.64
5	Fingertip to MCP joint pinky	56.3	5.4	22	Circumference at PIP joint index	57	3.1
6	Breadth at DIP joint thumb	18.17	1.74	23	Circumference at PIP joint middle	59.2	3.6
7	Breadth at DIP joint index	10.4	1.6	24	Circumference at PIP joint ring	55.59	3.28
8	Breadth at DIP joint middle	10.4	1.5	25	Circumference at PIP joint pinky	49.59	2.74
9	Breadth at DIP joint ring	14.12	0.88	26	Handbreadth across thumb	35.63	2.53
10	Breadth at DIP joint pinky	12.85	0.68	27	Hand length	169.6	9.4
11	Breadth at PIP joint thumb	18.65	1.15	28	Palm breadth	34.2	5.2
12	Breadth at PIP joint index	13.3	1.5	29	Hand depth	34.2	5.2
13	Breadth at PIP joint middle	17.71	1.01	30	Handbreadth at metacarpals	68	5.1
14	Breadth at PIP joint ring	16.71	0.96	31	Wrist circumference	15.35	0.78
15	Breadth at PIP joint pinky	15.21	0.69	32	Wrist breadth	46.1	4.8
16	Circumference at DIP joint thumb	48	4.2	33	Elbow-wrist length	251.52	16.92
17	Circumference at DIP joint index	49.1	2.5				

high level of lateral stability, the finger is equipped with two cable guides on either side. At the end of each section, several cuts have been made that increase the number of people who can use that section with varying hand sizes (Fig. 5).

4.2 *Finger Unit*

To accommodate the cable actuation model, open rings were specifically designed to provide support. In previous designs, such as the one proposed by In et al. [26], the cables were secured within a leather-like glove, where they were sewn into appropriate sheaths. Another innovative approach, as demonstrated by Kang et al. [24], involved the creation of a semi-open glove composed entirely of a soft polymer. In

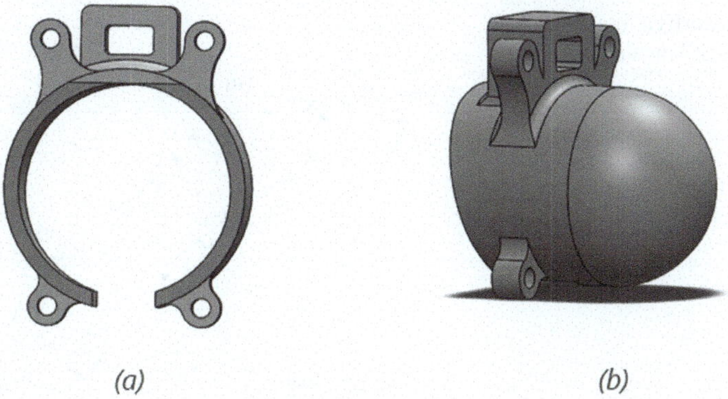

Fig. 5 Designed part for finger units: **a** flexible open ring; **b** thimble

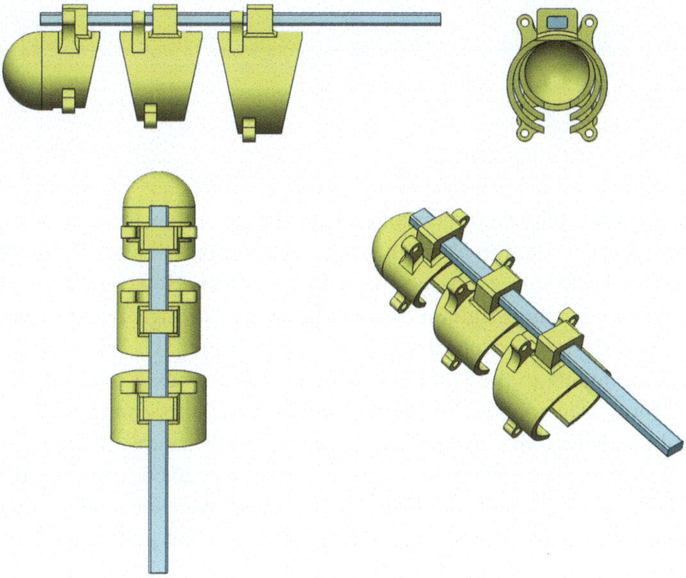

Fig. 6 Finger with the flexible strip

both cases, the cables were guided through specific channels to facilitate finger flexion and extension. However, these models share a limitation: they require knowledge of the finger length and precise positioning of the cable support along the phalanges. To overcome this constraint, a novel approach was adopted in this study. Rings were designed independently, without any connection to fabric or polymer supports. These rings are capable of adaptation to different finger lengths.

To secure the cables at the fingertip and enable parallel sliding, two components were designed: the open ring and the thimble (Fig. 5). The upper and lower holes of these parts accommodate the cables. The open ring plays a crucial role in modular-

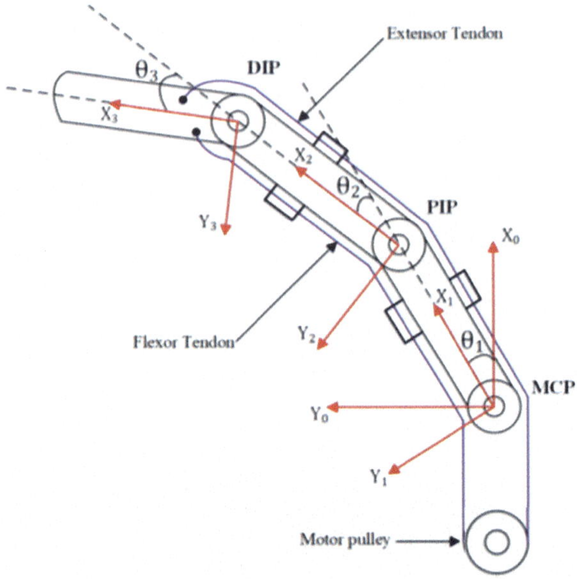

Fig. 7 Tendon-driven finger and schematic of kinematics

izing the finger unit. Its design combines two ellipses to ensure a better fit around the finger and prevent rotation along the finger's longitudinal axis. When the flexion cables are relaxed, the ring exerts no force on the finger. However, when the cables are pulled, the ring's edges tighten around the finger through friction, maintaining its position. This design concept draws inspiration from [31]. Ensuring a firm fixation of the components to the hand is a critical aspect of exoskeletons, as it allows for efficient force transmission to the limbs. However, this can pose challenges as conventional bands tend to constantly tighten around the limbs. In contrast, the proposed ring design reduces stress on the fingers when relaxed. Figure 7 illustrates a tendon-driven finger. Through the flexor tendon and extensor tendon, respectively, and by spinning the flexor motor pulley and extensor motor pulley, the finger can be bent and extended using this mechanism. The MCP, PIP, and DIP joints serve as the links connecting the separate phalanges to form an open chain mechanism.

4.3 Tendon Routing and the Complete Assembly of the Exoskeleton

Every digit on the human hand has four degrees of freedom (DoFs), encompassing three for bending and straightening and one for movement towards or away from the hand's midline. These actions are driven by the muscular and tendinous systems. Specifically, there are two primary tendon groups: one aiding in bending (flexion) and the other in straightening (extension) of the fingers. The muscles that facilitate the bending of fingers include the "flexor digitorum profundus" (a deeper muscle) and the "flexor digitorum superficialis" (a more superficial muscle), which extend along the length of the fingers. The flexor digitorum profundus, extending to the distal interphalangeal (DIP) joint, passes through the flexor digitorum superficialis, which attaches near the proximal interphalangeal (PIP) joint, with both muscles extending towards the metacarpophalangeal (MCP) joint [27]. Conversely, the muscles that enable finger straightening are simpler in structure and located on the back (dorsal side) of the fingers.

The chosen design, inspired by In et al. [26], employs two parallel cables for flexion, which are fastened laterally to the finger and joined at the tip using a thimble. This arrangement prevents the deformation of the glove. Furthermore, to divide the weight and promote stability, two cables are also utilized for an extension. To enhance the stability of the finger units, the decision was made to incorporate four cables per finger. This design choice was driven by the need to mitigate glove deformation issues that can arise in fabric exoskeletons equipped with only two cables per finger, typically used for extension and flexion [28] (Fig. 8).

Leveraging the anatomical understanding, a new soft exoskeleton design has been conceptualized, incorporating essential simplifications for practical application. To enhance the stability of the finger segments and address the issue of material deformation seen in fabric-based exoskeletons that typically use two cables per finger for bending and straightening, our design integrates four cables per finger. This approach not only aligns with the biomechanical principles of finger movement but also aims to improve the functionality and reliability of the glove [28]. Figure 9 shows the computer-aided design (CAD) model of the proposed hand exo-glove that incorporates the actuators.

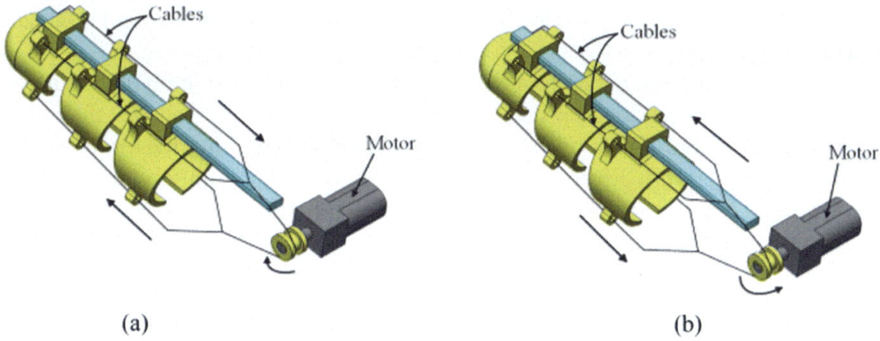

Fig. 8 Finger actuation: **a** extension, **b** flexion

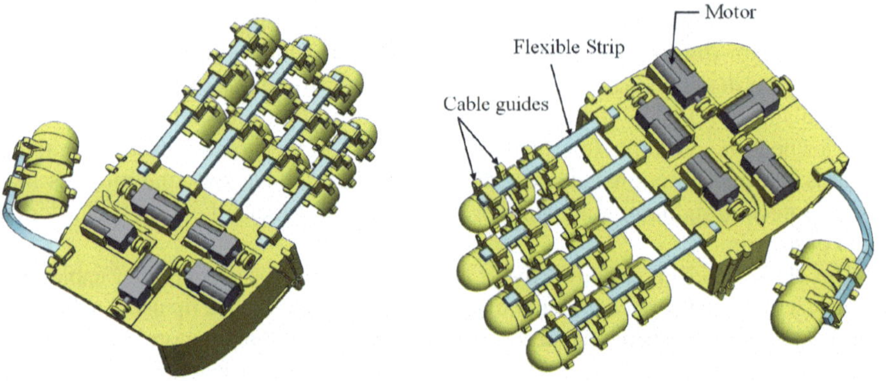

Fig. 9 Exoskeleton design model

5 Dynamics Study for Functionality

The positions of the soft anchors were determined based on a model that considered the forces exerted on the anchors by the tendons. Figure 10 provides an illustration of this model. In the illustration, J_1, J_2, and J_3 denote the articulations of the fingers, with L_1, L_2, and L_3 indicating the lengths of the proximal, intermediate, and distal segments, respectively. The parameters d and t refer to the measurements from the nearest joint to the attachment point along the sagittal plane and the perpendicular distance from this attachment to the sagittal plane, respectively. The variable θ describes the angular relationship between adjacent segments, while α and β outline the angles formed by the tendon with respect to the tangential plane at the attachment points. These specific angles, pertinent to the model for each articulation, are depicted in Fig. 10.

Upon integrating the anchors into the exoskeleton glove and applying a tension force T through the tendon, it produces a perpendicular force TN against the finger and a tangential force TT along the finger's direction. To maximize the torque across all three finger joints effectively, the placement of these anchor points requires careful optimization. This optimization is achieved by maximizing the sum of the torques τ_1, τ_2, and τ_3, as expressed in Eq. 1.

$$\sum_{n=1}^{3} \tau_n = \tau_1 + \tau_2 + \tau_3 \tag{1}$$

$$\tau_1 = T_{N1}d_{12} - T_{T1}t_1 + T_{N2}(L_1 - d_{21}) + T_{T2}t_1 \tag{2}$$

$$\tau_2 = T_{N3}d_{22} - T_{T3}t_2 + T_{N4}(L_2 - d_{31}) + T_{T4}t_2 \tag{3}$$

$$\tau_3 = T_{N5}d_{32} + T_{T5}t_3 \tag{4}$$

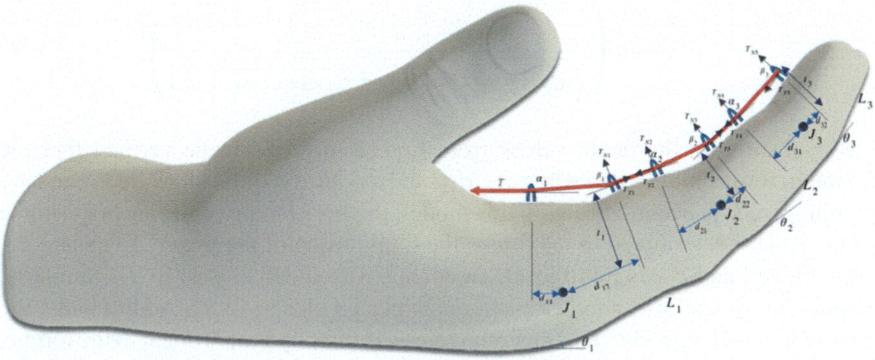

Fig. 10 The diagram illustrates the tendon routing of a typical finger, where L_1, L_2, and L_3 denote the proximal, middle, and distal phalanges, respectively. The black circles labeled as J_1, J_2, and J_3 represent the finger joints. The brown line represents the artificial tendon utilized, while the green rectangles depict the anchor points

$$T_{N1} = T \sin \beta_1 \qquad T_{T1} = -T \cos \beta_1 \tag{5}$$
$$T_{N2} = T \sin \alpha_2 \qquad T_{T2} = -T \cos \alpha_2 \tag{6}$$
$$T_{N3} = T \sin \beta_2 \qquad T_{T3} = -T \cos \beta_2 \tag{7}$$
$$T_{N4} = T \sin \alpha_3 \qquad T_{T4} = -T \cos \alpha_3 \tag{8}$$
$$T_{N5} = T \sin \beta_3 \qquad T_{T5} = T \cos \beta_3 \tag{9}$$

The tangential and perpendicular forces can be written in terms of the angles α and β and tension T (Eqs. 6–8).

$$\tau_1 = T\,\sin(\beta_1)d_{12} + T\,\cos(\beta_1)t_1 + T\,\sin(\alpha_2)(L_1 - d_{21}) - T\,\cos(\alpha_2)t_1 \tag{10}$$

$$\tau_2 = T\,\sin(\beta_2)d_{22} + T\,\cos(\beta_2)t_2 + T\,\sin(\alpha_3)(L_2 - d_{31}) - T\,\cos(\alpha_3)t_2 \tag{11}$$

$$\tau_3 = T\,\sin(\beta_3)d_{32} + T\,\cos(\beta_3)t_3 \tag{12}$$

Using the sines and cosines laws, the angles α and β can be written as-

$$\alpha_n = \arcsin\left(\frac{d_{n1}\sin(180 - \theta_n)}{\sqrt{d_{n2}^2 + d_{n1}^2 - 2d_{n2}\sqrt{d_{n1}}\cos(180 - \theta_n)}}\right) \tag{13}$$

$$\beta_n = \arcsin\left(\frac{d_{n2}\sin(180-\theta_n)}{\sqrt{d_{n2}^2 + d_{n1}^2 - 2d_{n2}\sqrt{d_{n1}}\cos(180-\theta_n)}}\right) \quad (14)$$

By substituting the angle values from Eqs. 2 to 8, it can be verified that the maximum torque is achieved when d_{12}, d_{22}, and d_{32} are maximized, while d_{21} and d_{31} are minimized. In accordance with this model, the positioning of the anchors shown in Fig. 10 was determined to maximize the total torque of the finger. To ensure d_{12} is maximized and d_{21} is minimized, an anchor was added closest to J_2. Similarly, to optimize d_{22} and d_{31}, another anchor was placed closest to J_3. Additionally, the distance h, which relates to the finger thickness, is directly proportional to the torque. Hence, the tendon should be positioned as far as possible from the sagittal plane.

5.1 Determination of Maximum Forces and Tendon Tensions

The tendon tensions are measured with the use of a load cell. The tendons at each end are coupled with the load cell, and the fingers are permitted to execute flexion movements with the help of the load cell through the tendons. The tendon tensions are directly related to establishing the arrangement of the motor necessary to drive the fingers through the exoskeleton. As between the mechanical unit and the control unit, the tendon is the common link that communicates the rotation of the motor into the flexion or extension of the finger. After determining the maximum, lowest, and average values of the tendon tension, we have determined the parameters of the motor. We have also measured the required RPM (97.27) through the period for bending of the finger and the pulley radius (2.75 mm) of the device through which the tending travels. Figure 11 shows the tendon tensions measured by strain gauge for each finger in repeated cycles It has been discovered that the tendon tension in the thumb is the highest on average with a value of 10.03 N. This is followed by the ring and index fingers with values of 8.32 N and 8.39 N respectively, the middle finger with a value of 7.08 N, and the pinky finger with a value of 6.97 N, which is the lowest.

5.2 Finite Element Analysis (FEA) of the Design

A qualitative computational assessment of the structural integrity of the finger components in the exoskeleton was carried out using ANSYS Workbench. The finite element analysis (FEA) was conducted in an annular ring subjected to physiological loads during the assistive rehabilitation process. The finger unit comprises the rings which are interconnected by means of tendons and linked to the thimble at the fingertip. The components were subjected to forces via the cables. The worst-case scenario was taken into account in the FEM study, concentrating on the lower portions of the

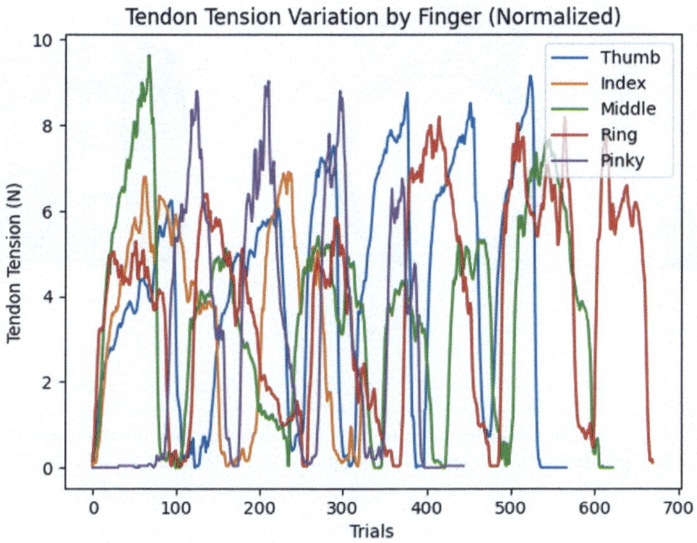

Fig. 11 Tendon tensions measured by strain gauge for each finger

rings and the overhanging, less confined thimble, and utilizing force values double the recorded values from the load cell. The top interface of the finger and the ring were fixed for analysis.

The worst-case scenario entailed a force applied at a 45° angle to the axis of the ring holes, which is equivalent to finger closure. In addition, the force perpendicular to the hole axis was taken into account and considered to be zero, taking into account the presence of sheaths designed to lessen friction. As a result, the force that was generated was perpendicular to the axis of the hole. The diagram exhibiting the applied forces and constraints on the rings and thimble is shown in Fig. 12. A static torque of 1.375 Nm (the average torque of frequently used gear motors) was taken into account for the FEM study. By dividing the torque by the 2.75 mm tendon pulley's radius, the torque was transformed into a force. Refer to Fig. 13 for the statistical load diagram of the mesh ring structure. The outcomes, shown in Fig. 14, showed that despite elastic deformations, the components stayed in a safety range considerably below the yield stress. For the 3D printing of the design, we have taken into account three alternative materials. A parametric study was carried out using 3 different materials for 3D printing. The materials are Acrylonitrile Butadiene Styrene (ABS), Polylactic Acid (PLA), and Thermoplastic Polyurethane (TPU). It has been noted that the TPU material has a larger maximum stress value than the other two materials, although it is still within the allowable strain range. However, due to the structure's ability to slightly expand circumferentially during finger flexion due to the minor expansion of the finger's muscles, the ABS and PLA materials have very slight deformation, which is not particularly favourable. The outcomes of the study infer that a ring made of TPU exhibits maximal elastic strain as compared to the

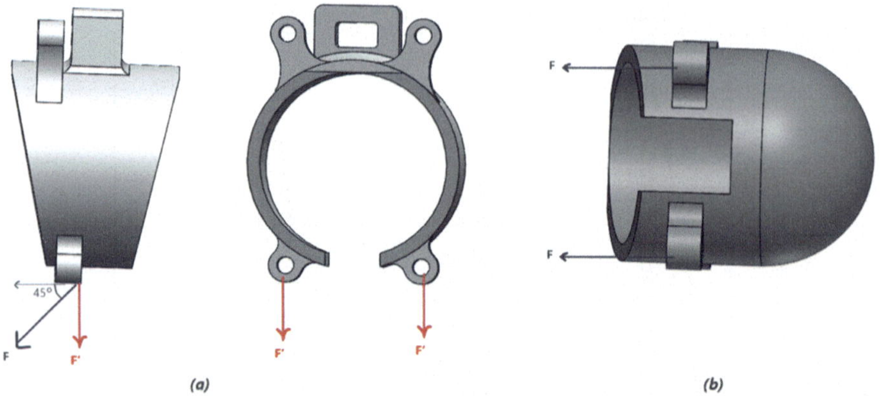

Fig. 12 Figures illustrating the distribution of forces and constraints applied to the different components: **a** forces applied to the ring and **b** forces applied to the thimble

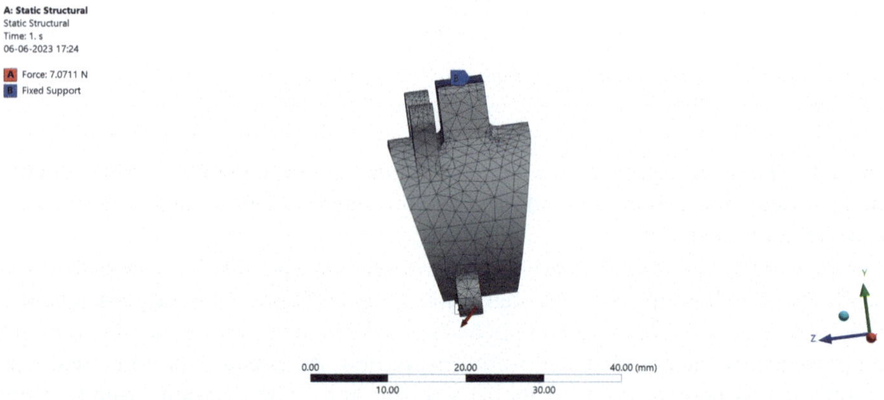

Fig. 13 Statical load diagram of meshed ring structure

other two materials using the same reload regime. Even though the TPU-based ring shows deflection superior to others, it lies within the permissible extension range, which allowed us to choose TPU material for the final printing of the structure.

6 Discussions and Conclusion

This study embarked on a comprehensive exploration of soft hand exoskeletons, delving into their current models, identifying the inherent limitations and challenges, and proposing innovative design modifications. Our focus was on enhancing adaptability, comfort, and compactness, through meticulous attention to the tendon-driven mechanism, optimal tendon routing, and dynamic analysis. The research findings

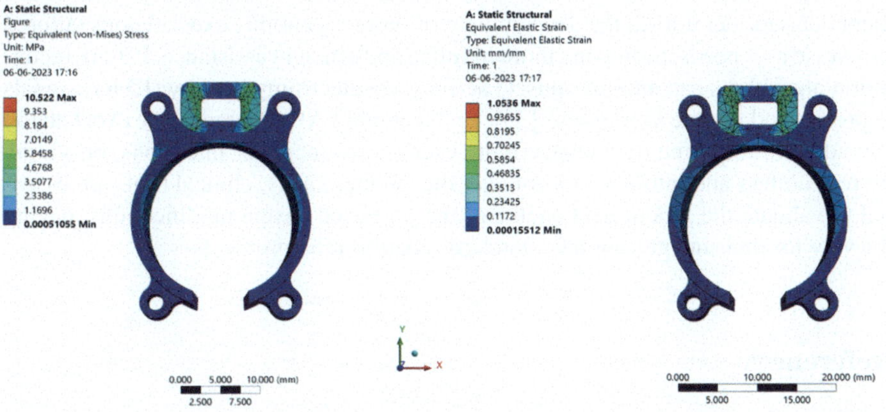

Fig. 14 Finite element analysis for the ring structure with equivalent stress and equivalent strain for TPU material

underscore the critical role these elements play in refining the exoskeleton's design to better meet the needs of individuals with hand disabilities. A key contribution of our work is the development of a design framework that significantly improves the usability and functionality of soft hand exoskeletons. By incorporating advanced tendon routing strategies and leveraging dynamic analysis, we have laid a foundation for creating devices that not only align with the natural kinematics of the human hand but also offer enhanced structural integrity and operational efficiency. This approach facilitates the selection of suitable materials for 3D printing, ensuring the durability of the exoskeletons under physiological loads encountered during rehabilitation activities.

The implications of our findings extend beyond the technical advancements in exoskeleton design. By enhancing the adaptability and comfort of these devices, we open new avenues for rehabilitation, offering individuals with hand impairments a means to regain functionality and independence in their daily lives. The modular and customizable nature of the proposed design addresses a wide range of hand sizes and shapes, thereby broadening the applicability of soft hand exoskeletons across diverse patient populations. Furthermore, our study highlights the importance of interdisciplinary collaboration in the field of soft robotics. The integration of insights from biomechanics, material science, and rehabilitation therapy is crucial for the iterative design process, ensuring that the developed exoskeletons are not only technologically sophisticated but also clinically relevant. Looking ahead, several avenues for further research emerge from our study. First, the exploration of novel materials and fabrication techniques holds promise for enhancing the performance and wearability of soft exoskeletons. Second, the implementation of postural and force synergy-based intelligent grasp control systems [32], could significantly improve the efficacy of these devices in rehabilitation settings. Thirdly, integrating machine learning and deep learning algorithms for grasp classification and synergy-based control systems will enhance hand exoskeleton design [33, 34]. Analyzing extensive hand movement datasets can inform the development of more ergonomic exoskeletons tailored to diverse user needs, promising more intuitive and efficient assistance. Pattern recognition algorithms can analyze muscle activity via electromyography (EMG) signals to predict and initiate movements [35]. By leveraging AI techniques, the exoskeleton can adapt in real-time to changes in the user's movements or intentions, providing more seamless and intuitive control over the device. Lastly, clinical trials are essential to validate the functional benefits of the proposed design modifications, paving the way for their integration into standard rehabilitation protocols.

References

1. J. Z. Zheng, S. De La Rosa, and A. M. Dollar, "An investigation of grasp type and frequency in daily household and machine shop tasks," in *2011 IEEE international conference on robotics and automation*. IEEE, 2011, pp. 4169–4175.
2. M. V. Radomski and C. A. T. Latham, *Occupational therapy for physical dysfunction*. Lippincott Williams & Wilkins, 2008.
3. S. S. Rathore, A. R. Hinn, L. S. Cooper, H. A. Tyroler, and W. D. Rosamond, "Characterization of incident stroke signs and symptoms: findings from the atherosclerosis risk in communities study," *Stroke*, vol. 33, no. 11, pp. 2718–2721, 2002.
4. G. J. Snoek, M. J. IJzerman, H. J. Hermens, D. Maxwell, and F. Biering-Sorensen, "Survey of the needs of patients with spinal cord injury: impact and priority for improvement in hand function in tetraplegics," *Spinal cord*, vol. 42, no. 9, pp. 526–532, 2004.
5. G. M. Achilli, C. Amici, M. Dragusanu, M. Gobbo, S. Logozzo, M. Malvezzi, M. Tiboni, and M. C. Valigi, "Soft, rigid, and hybrid robotic exoskeletons for hand rehabilitation: Roadmap with impairment-oriented rationale for devices design and selection," *Applied Sciences*, vol. 13, no. 20, p. 11287, 2023.
6. N. R. Council *et al.*, "Artificial limbs. a review of current developments: September 1955," 2023.
7. B. Buchholz and T. J. Armstrong, "An ellipsoidal representation of human hand anthropometry," *Human factors*, vol. 33, no. 4, pp. 429–441, 1991.
8. M. Aman, M. E. Sporer, C. Gstoettner, C. Prahm, C. Hofer, W. Mayr, D. Farina, and O. C. Aszmann, "Bionic hand as artificial organ: Current status and future perspectives," *Artificial organs*, vol. 43, no. 2, pp. 109–118, 2019.
9. G. Robles-De-La-Torre, "The importance of the sense of touch in virtual and real environments," *IEEE Multimedia*, vol. 13, no. 3, pp. 24–30, 2006.
10. H. Kawasaki, *Robot Hands and Multi-Fingered Haptic Interfaces: Fundamentals and Applications*. World Scientific, 2015.
11. T. Du Plessis, K. Djouani, and C. Oosthuizen, "A review of active hand exoskeletons for rehabilitation and assistance," *Robotics*, vol. 10, no. 1, p. 40, 2021.
12. H. Güçlü and A. Cora, "A survey on wearable hand robotics design for assistive, rehabilitative, and haptic applications," *International Journal of Intelligent Robotics and Applications*, pp. 1–26, 2023.
13. M. Almenara, M. Cempini, C. Gómez, M. Cortese, C. Martín, J. Medina, N. Vitiello, and E. Opisso, "Usability test of a hand exoskeleton for activities of daily living: an example of user-centered design," *Disability and Rehabilitation: Assistive Technology*, vol. 12, no. 1, pp. 84–96, 2017.
14. G. Carbone, E. C. Gerding, B. Corves, D. Cafolla, M. Russo, and M. Ceccarelli, "Design of a two-dofs driving mechanism for a motion-assisted finger exoskeleton," *Applied Sciences*, vol. 10, no. 7, p. 2619, 2020.

15. G. Carbone, M. Ceccarelli, C. Capalbo, G. Caroleo, and C. Morales-Cruz, "Numerical and experimental performance estimation for a exofing-2 dofs finger exoskeleton," *Robotica*, vol. 40, no. 6, pp. 1820–1832, 2022.
16. M. Cempini, M. Cortese, and N. Vitiello, "A powered finger–thumb wearable hand exoskeleton with self-aligning joint axes," *IEEE/ASME Transactions on mechatronics*, vol. 20, no. 2, pp. 705–716, 2014.
17. M. Sarac, M. Solazzi, D. Leonardis, E. Sotgiu, M. Bergamasco, and A. Frisoli, "Design of an underactuated hand exoskeleton with joint estimation," in *Advances in Italian Mechanism Science: Proceedings of the First International Conference of IFToMM Italy*. Springer, 2017, pp. 97–105.
18. H. K. Yap, J. H. Lim, F. Nasrallah, and C.-H. Yeow, "Design and preliminary feasibility study of a soft robotic glove for hand function assistance in stroke survivors," *Frontiers in neuroscience*, vol. 11, p. 547, 2017.
19. Y. Jiang, D. Chen, P. Liu, X. Jiao, Z. Ping, Z. Xu, J. Li, and Y. Xu, "Fishbone-inspired soft robotic glove for hand rehabilitation with multi-degrees-of-freedom," in *2018 IEEE International Conference on Soft Robotics (RoboSoft)*. IEEE, 2018, pp. 394–399.
20. V. Nazari, M. Pouladian, Y.-P. Zheng, and M. Alam, "A compact and lightweight rehabilitative exoskeleton to restore grasping functions for people with hand paralysis," *Sensors*, vol. 21, no. 20, p. 6900, 2021.
21. T. Bützer, O. Lambercy, J. Arata, and R. Gassert, "Fully wearable actuated soft exoskeleton for grasping assistance in everyday activities," *Soft robotics*, vol. 8, no. 2, pp. 128–143, 2021.
22. M. Xiloyannis, L. Galli, D. Chiaradia, A. Frisoli, F. Braghin, and L. Masia, "A soft tendon-driven robotic glove: Preliminary evaluation," in *Converging Clinical and Engineering Research on Neurorehabilitation III: Proceedings of the 4th International Conference on NeuroRehabilitation (ICNR2018), October 16–20, 2018, Pisa, Italy 5*. Springer, 2019, pp. 329–333.
23. D. H. Kim, Y. Lee, and H.-S. Park, "Bioinspired high-degrees of freedom soft robotic glove for restoring versatile and comfortable manipulation," *Soft Robotics*, vol. 9, no. 4, pp. 734–744, 2022.
24. B. B. Kang, H. Choi, H. Lee, and K.-J. Cho, "Exo-glove poly ii: A polymer-based soft wearable robot for the hand with a tendon-driven actuation system," *Soft robotics*, vol. 6, no. 2, pp. 214–227, 2019.
25. A. Ribas Neto, J. Fajardo, W. H. A. da Silva, M. K. Gomes, M. C. F. de Castro, E. Fujiwara, and E. Rohmer, "Design of tendon-actuated robotic glove integrated with optical fiber force myography sensor," *Automation*, vol. 2, no. 3, pp. 187–201, 2021.
26. H. In, B. B. Kang, M. Sin, and K.-J. Cho, "Exo-glove: A wearable robot for the hand with a soft tendon routing system," *IEEE Robotics & Automation Magazine*, vol. 22, no. 1, pp. 97–105, 2015.
27. N. Takahashi, S. Furuya, and H. Koike, "Soft exoskeleton glove with human anatomical architecture: production of dexterous finger movements and skillful piano performance," *IEEE Transactions on Haptics*, vol. 13, no. 4, pp. 679–690, 2020.
28. M. Decker and Y. Kim, "A hand exoskeleton device for robot assisted sensory-motor training after stroke," in *2017 IEEE World Haptics Conference (WHC)*. IEEE, 2017, pp. 436–441.
29. A. Nag, P. Nag, and H. Desai, "Hand anthropometry of indian women," *Indian Journal of Medical Research*, vol. 117, pp. 260–269, 2003.
30. E. Cakit, B. Durgun, O. Cetik, and O. Yoldas, "A survey of hand anthropometry and biomechanical measurements of dentistry students in turkey," *Human Factors and Ergonomics in Manufacturing & Service Industries*, vol. 24, no. 6, pp. 739–753, 2014.
31. B. B. Kang, H. Lee, H. In, U. Jeong, J. Chung, and K.-J. Cho, "Development of a polymer-based tendon-driven wearable robotic hand," in *2016 IEEE International Conference on Robotics and Automation (ICRA)*. IEEE, 2016, pp. 3750–3755.
32. S. Pratap, K. Ito, and S. M. Hazarika, "Grasp synergies in activities of daily living: A cross-sectional study using a multi-sensory data glove," in *Proceedings of the 2023 6th International Conference on Advances in Robotics*, 2023, pp. 1–7.

33. S. Pratap, J. Narayan, Y. Hatta, K. Ito, and S. M. Hazarika, "From tactile signals to grasp classification: Exploring patterns with machine learning," in *2024 IEEE International Conference on Interdisciplinary Approaches in Technology and Management for Social Innovation (IATMSI)*, vol. 2. IEEE, 2024, pp. 1–6.
34. S. Briouza, H. Gritli, N. Khraief, S. Belghith, and D. Singh, "An auto-ann for emg classification for the motion recognition of the human hand," in *2022 IEEE Information Technologies & Smart Industrial Systems (ITSIS)*. IEEE, 2022, pp. 1–6.
35. S. Briouza, H. Gritli, N. Khraief, S. Belghith, and D. Singh, "Classification of semg biomedical signals for upper-limb and hand rehabilitation using a hybrid cnn-svm architecture," in *2022 International Conference on Data Analytics for Business and Industry (ICDABI)*. IEEE, 2022, pp. 467–471.

Human-Robot Interaction in Lower Limb Rehabilitation: A Scoping Review

Sadia Younis, Jyotindra Narayan, and Mamta Mittal

Abstract The rising prevalence of chronic diseases and an aging population have led to a significant increase in disability rates worldwide. Stroke, a major cause of disability, necessitates effective rehabilitation strategies to restore lost motor functions in the lower limbs. Human-robot interaction (HRI) in lower limb rehabilitation offers promising solutions, providing personalized feedback and intensive, repetitive training to enhance motor recovery. While personalized feedback and adaptive assistance have shown promise in enhancing rehabilitation outcomes, there remains limited exploration of how these elements can be optimized through machine learning and other advanced technologies. This review aims to bridge these gaps by systematically examining the design criteria for effective human-robot interaction (HRI) systems, evaluating various modalities employed in robotic rehabilitation, and analyzing control strategies that enhance user outcomes. By delving into these areas, our review seeks to provide a comprehensive understanding of HRI in lower limb rehabilitation, offering a foundation for future research and development in this critical field. By integrating advanced technologies with personalized rehabilitation approaches, HRI systems can adapt more effectively to individual patient needs, maximizing their potential to improve rehabilitation outcomes. Finally, our review emphasizes the importance of interdisciplinary collaboration in advancing HRI systems for lower limb rehabilitation.

S. Younis
Department of Biomedical Engineering, Government College of Engineering and Technology Ganderbal, Ganderbal, India

J. Narayan (✉)
Mechatronics and Robotics Laboratory, Department of Mechanical Engineering, Indian Institute of Technology Guwahati, Guwahati, Assam, India
e-mail: n.jyotindra@gmail.com

Department of Computing, Imperial College London, London, UK

Chair of Digital Health, Universität Bayreuth, Bayreuth, Germany

M. Mittal
Data Analytics and Data Science at Delhi Skill and Entrepreneur University, New Delhi, India

M. Mittal and J. Narayan (eds.), *Intelligent Cyber-Physical Systems for Healthcare Solutions*, https://doi.org/10.1007/978-981-97-8983-2_11

1 Introduction

With the increase in life expectancy and the prevalence of chronic diseases, the disability rate is on the rise. Recent statistics indicate a significant global need for rehabilitation services, with an estimated 2.41 billion people, or one in every three individuals, requiring these services at some point [16]. Neurological damage following a stroke often results in hemiparesis or partial paralysis on one side of the body, impacting the individual's capacity to carry out daily activities like walking and eating. Ambulatory disability is considered the most prevalent type; its leading causes are limb deformities and dysfunction in limb joints, which significantly contribute to locomotor disability. It is important to note that rehabilitation is not limited to the elderly, as it is also crucial for the well-being and independence of younger individuals [16, 23, 38]. Therefore, the healthcare system must be adaptable to address the growing challenges posed by the increasing number of patients, a rise in chronic diseases, escalating costs, and shortages in skilled personnel. Physical therapy, including rehabilitation, assists in regaining lost functions. The objective of rehabilitation exercises is to engage in targeted movements that stimulate motor plasticity in patients, thereby enhancing motor recovery and reducing functional impairments. However, evidence-based physical interventions are lacking—one-third of stroke survivors fail to regain the ability to walk independently, and among those who do, many exhibit a typical asymmetric gait pattern. Over two decades, the field of robotics for rehabilitation treatment is emerging and is anticipated to expand as a solution for automating training. Robotic rehabilitation has the potential to (i) substitute the physical training efforts of a therapist, enabling more intensive repetitive movements and providing therapy at a reasonable cost, and (ii) quantitatively evaluate motor recovery levels by assessing force and movement patterns [11].

Enhancing lower limb rehabilitation through Human-Robot Interaction (HRI) presents a transformative avenue for addressing the diverse needs of individuals recovering from lower limb impairments. Personalized feedback and motivation are essential to HRI systems and provide real-time encouragement based on individual progress. By customizing tasks and challenges according to user abilities, robots foster a sense of accomplishment crucial for sustaining engagement in rehabilitation activities. Robots intended for rehabilitation were developed as a clinical tool to automate labor-intensive, repetitive training techniques, particularly beneficial during the initial stage of neurological recovery when patients often need considerable support. With their programmable force-producing capability, robotic devices facilitate task-oriented movements and offer more accurate afferent feedback by guiding the limb to encourage heel strike and hip extension during the initial contact and midstance phases of walking [14]. The intensive and repetitive training facilitated by HRI devices, such as robotic exoskeletons and gait trainers, accelerates neuroplasticity and functional recovery and neuroplasticity and functional recovery [45]. Precise control over movement patterns enables individuals to achieve a higher number of repetitions, contributing to accelerated progress. Furthermore, incorporating multimodal sensory stimulation synchronizes sensory cues with movement tasks, enhancing proprioception and spatial awareness [33]. This integration promotes neural reorganization and functional recovery in the lower limbs. Long-term studies have demonstrated sustained improvements in functional outcomes, including gait speed and balance control, highlighting the effectiveness of HRI in achieving meaningful long-term functional gains.

Exploring methods, limitations, and the scope of Human-Robot Interaction (HRI) in lower limb rehabilitation reveals a dynamic landscape poised for advancement. Robotic exoskeletons offer customizable assistance levels, facilitating gait training for individuals with lower limb impairments [2, 37]. Gait training robots provide real-time feedback, enhancing gait parameters and promoting motor relearning [6]. Virtual Reality (VR) systems merge immersive environments with robotic assistance, fostering engagement and cognitive involvement in rehabilitation [21, 49]. However, cost and accessibility hinder the widespread adoption of HRI-based approaches. User acceptance and adaptation remain critical considerations, impacting engagement and compliance with therapy protocols. Moreover, the limited clinical evidence underscores the need for robust research supporting the efficacy and long-term outcomes of HRI in lower limb rehabilitation. Looking ahead, personalized and adaptive systems leveraging machine learning algorithms hold promise for optimizing treatment outcomes. In navigating these challenges and opportunities, HRI-based approaches stand poised to revolutionize rehabilitation practices and enhance outcomes for individuals with lower limb impairments.

Despite the HRI for lower limb rehabilitation, significant gaps remain in the literature. Current studies predominantly focus on the development and application of robotic systems, yet there is a lack of comprehensive research addressing the integration of design criteria, types of modalities, and control strategies within HRI. Furthermore, while personalized feedback and adaptive assistance have shown promise, there is limited exploration of how these elements can be optimized through machine learning and other advanced technologies. This review aims to bridge these gaps by systematically examining the design criteria for effective HRI systems, evaluating various modalities employed in robotic rehabilitation, and analyzing control strategies that enhance user outcomes. By addressing these areas, our review seeks to provide a holistic understanding of HRI in lower limb rehabilitation, offering a foundation for future research and development in this critical field. Through this synthesis, we highlight the need for innovative approaches that combine design, technology, and personalized care, ensuring that HRI systems can fully realize their potential in improving rehabilitation outcomes.

2 Design Criteria

In this section, we explore the multifaceted design criteria essential for optimizing the interaction between humans and robots in the context of lower limb assistance and rehabilitation. As the field of robotics advances, the design of exoskeleton systems for HRI becomes increasingly crucial. Exoskeleton systems represent a cutting-edge

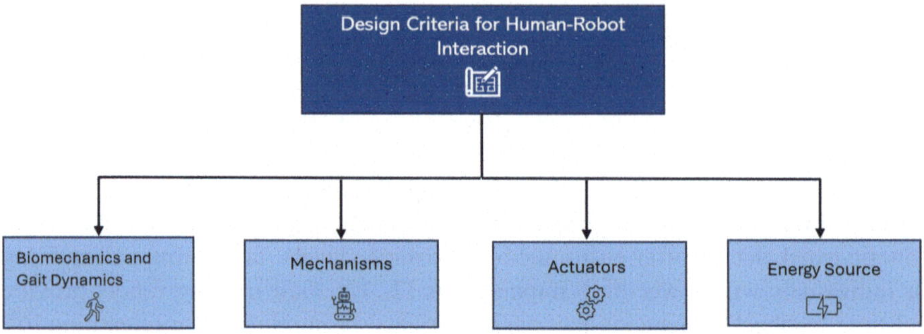

Fig. 1 Design criteria for human-robot interaction

approach to augmenting human mobility and rehabilitation, offering promising solutions for individuals with lower limb impairments. The design and implementation of these systems require a nuanced understanding of biomechanics and gait dynamics, mechanisms, actuators, and energy sources to ensure optimal performance and user experience as shown in Fig. 1.

2.1 Gait Biomechanics

The foundation of designing effective lower limb exoskeletons lies in understanding human biomechanics and gait dynamics. The exoskeleton systems must align with the human body's anatomical structure and movement patterns to ensure optimal functionality and user comfort. One crucial aspect of this alignment involves accurately modeling the Degrees of Freedom (DoF) and movement limitations of the human body. Such models serve as the basis for developing control algorithms that drive assistive devices with precision and efficiency. While modeling upper limb movements can be complex, lower limb models are often simpler due to the fewer DoF in joints like the hip, ankle, and knee [41]. A well-known study by Dollar and Herr [13] has shed light on the biomechanical nuances of lower limb movement during activities like level walking and weight-climbing. Weight-climbing poses additional challenges as it necessitates raising the body's Center of Mass (CoM), emphasizing the importance of understanding biomechanical principles in designing assistive devices [28]. By comprehensively studying the biomechanical impact of exoskeletons on users, researchers can assess effectiveness through various metrics such as average maximum load, joint moment, muscle torque reduction, muscle activity, and metabolic cost.

Lower limb exoskeleton robots play a vital role in assisting individuals with mobility impairments, necessitating thorough consideration of human walking characteristics during the design process. Referred to as gait in biomedicine and sports science, understanding the dynamics of human locomotion forms the cornerstone of effective exoskeleton design. Gait dynamics encompass a broad spectrum of research activities, predominantly focused on gait quantitative analysis and pattern recognition [50]. The quantitative analysis relies heavily on sensor technology to measure various gait parameters, including gait cycle, balance, symmetry, and mobility, facilitating objective gait assessment [22]. Inertial measurement units (IMUs) play a critical role in various gait analysis studies. Lefeber et al. [27] validate their use in stroke patients, showing reliable spatiotemporal gait parameter measurements. Silsupadol et al. [52] utilize smartphone-based IMUs for assessing gait in multiple environments, proving their versatility. Martindale et al. [31] employ IMUs in a mobile gait analysis system for hereditary spastic paraplegia, highlighting their technical efficacy. Wang et al. [55] develop an IMU-based gait normalcy index for clinical evaluation of impaired gait, demonstrating their clinical utility. In another study, Zhou et al. [60] integrate IMUs into a smart walking stick, enhancing gait analysis for the elderly and disabled. Electromyography (EMG) sensors were employed by Castagneri et al. [8] to measure muscle activations, facilitating the asymmetry analysis. In another study, Xi et al. [56] present an advanced method for the simultaneous and continuous estimation of joint angles based on surface electromyography (sEMG) signals. Utilizing a state-space model, the research effectively processes sEMG data to predict joint movements accurately. The methodology incorporates Hidden Markov models and sophisticated feature extraction techniques to enhance the precision of the estimations. Applying sEMG sensors is pivotal, as they capture the electrical activity of muscles, thereby facilitating accurate joint angle prediction. The summarization of these gait quantification studies, having significant implications for improving motion tracking in prosthetics and rehabilitation devices, is given in Table 1.

2.2 Mechanisms

The intricate mechanisms integrated into lower limb rehabilitation exoskeleton robots are pivotal for fostering effective human-robot interaction (HRI) during therapy sessions. This section delves into the mechanisms utilized to achieve anatomical fidelity and optimize movement synchronization between the robot and the wearer. Lower limb rehabilitation exoskeletons are engineered to replicate human lower limb movements through meticulous mechanism design. The Berkeley lower extremity exoskeleton (BLEEX) is a foundational model for subsequent robots, emphasizing safety and user compatibility while emulating human joint movements. Notably, BLEEX incorporates rotary joints at critical points such as the hip, knee, and ankle, facilitating a range of motion akin to human joints. This design enables fluid and natural movements during rehabilitation exercises. Furthermore, BLEEX adopts a parallel structure for the hip joints, bolstering stability and enabling three rotational motions while ensuring automatic centering with the human hip, thereby enhancing biomechanical alignment and therapy effectiveness [61]. In another fundamental study by Banala et al. [5], the active leg exoskeleton employs sophisticated mechanisms to facilitate natural gait adaptation and neuromotor training. These mechanisms

Table 1 Recent studies in gait quantification with wearable sensors

Sensor	Year	Authors	Methods	Gait parameters extracted
IMU	2019	Nina et al.	Statistical analysis	Gait cycle, cadence, stride length, stride velocity, stance phase, swing phase, double support phase
IMU	2020	Patima et al.	Statistical analysis	Gait velocity, step time, step length, cadence, step time symmetry, step length symmetry
IMU	2020	Christine et al.	Hierarchical hidden Markov models	Stride time, swing duration
IMU	2021	Wang et al.	ZUPT+Thresholding	Gait cycle, stride length, swing phase, ankle velocity and height, range of motion, ankle abduction and adduction
IMU	2022	Zhou et al.	EKF+Thresholding	No. of steps, stride time, step length, step speed
EMG	2019	Castagneri et al.	Statistical analysis	Asymmetry of muscle activations
EMG	2020	Yin et al.	Machine learning	Joint angle
EMG	2020	Gui et al.	Assist as needed	Torque
EMG	2021	Xi et al.	Hill-type muscle model	Knee joint angles
EMG	2022	Jung et al.	Musculoskeletal modelling	Joint torques
EEG	2022	Roy et al.	Feature extraction	Trigger movement
EEG	2023	Quiles et al.	Transfer learning	Head acceleration, right foot acceleration, left acceleration

include joint structures and linkages mirroring the anatomical movements of human lower limbs. The exoskeleton enables dynamic movements with enhanced biomechanical compatibility by replicating the kinematics of hip, knee, and ankle joints. Adjustable mechanisms are incorporated to accommodate individual variations in gait patterns, thereby enabling personalized rehabilitation protocols tailored to user needs.

The robotic device used for gait training in Srivastava et al. [53] integrates mechanisms that emulate human joint movements to promote naturalistic walking patterns. These mechanisms, such as articulated joints and support structures, are designed to provide assistance and support during gait training sessions. Adjustable components allow customization based on gait impairment severity and rehabilitation progress. The research by Malcom et al. [30] investigates the interaction between actuation timing and power in reducing the metabolic cost of walking with an ankle exoskeleton. The ankle exoskeleton described in this study incorporates mechanical mechanisms to augment ankle joint movements [30]. A recent study by Zhao et al. [59]

employs a series elastic actuator mechanism. This mechanism incorporates elastic elements, such as springs, between the actuator and the load to measure force through spring deflection. This design enhances the force control accuracy, improves safety by adding compliance, and reduces the impact of external disturbances during lower limb rehabilitation exercises. In the study by Gong et al. [17], the mechanisms utilized include omnidirectional wheels, which enhance maneuverability, and a pelvic assist mechanism designed to support and guide the user's movements effectively. These mechanisms, including articulated joints and springs, mimic natural ankle biomechanics, optimizing walking efficiency and reducing muscular effort.

2.3 Actuators

Choosing the right actuators is essential in exoskeleton design, as it involves balancing mechanical strength with minimal weight and transparency. Many traditional robotic actuators face difficulties meeting exoskeletons' high torque and speed requirements, which affects their range and maneuverability. Electric actuators, such as servo motors, provide precise position control, making them suitable for devices that assist injured body parts, including those with spinal cord injuries [58]. However, various configurations pose challenges, from bulky direct drive setups to friction issues with geared solutions. Load cells in closed-loop systems can help address these challenges by measuring force and adjusting accordingly, although they are prone to shocks. Series elastic actuators present an alternative, using spring deflection for force measurement and offering energy-saving benefits [43]. BLEEX employs advanced actuation systems to drive movements at the hip, knee, and ankle joints, aiding therapeutic exercises and supporting individuals with lower limb impairments [5]. Electric motors are the primary actuators, providing the necessary torque and power to initiate and control joint movements. Specifically, motors with linear ball screws are used at the hip and knee joints, enhancing precision and efficiency in motion control. Additionally, series elastic drives are integrated into the design, particularly at the knee joint, to achieve precise force control and improve drive flexibility. This combination of electric motors and specialized drive mechanisms ensures robust and responsive actuation, crucial for effective rehabilitation outcomes. The active leg exoskeleton used for gait adaptation and neuromotor training developed by Banala et al. [4] incorporates electric motors as the primary actuators, delivering precise torque and power to actuate the hip, knee, and ankle joints. These motors include innovative transmission mechanisms, such as gears or belts, to optimize efficiency and control.

Furthermore, the exoskeleton may feature sensors and feedback mechanisms to dynamically adjust actuator output based on real-time measurements of user movement and biomechanical parameters. This ensures smooth and responsive assistance during gait rehabilitation exercises, enhancing the effectiveness of the training regimen. The model developed by Gong et al. [17] The system employs force sensors and control levers for precise feedback and control, along with a real sense camera for predicting user intentions [17]. Zhao et al. [59] investigate a series of elastic actuator structures for lower limb exoskeleton rehabilitation robots. The study explores the design and implementation of these actuators in the context of improving rehabilitation outcomes for lower limb impairments. In the study of Malcom et al. [30], it can be inferred that the device uses electric motors or pneumatic actuators to generate controlled forces and movements at the ankle joint. These actuators are integrated into the exoskeleton's structure and strategically positioned to deliver assistance or resistance during different gait cycle phases.

2.4 Energy Source

Exoskeletons necessitate an energy source capable of providing the necessary range of motion for a given task duration without compromising system mobility. While some designs rely on external power sources, others utilize internal options such as batteries, small internal combustion engines, electrochemical fuel cells, or wireless energy transfer. Lithium batteries, renowned for their high energy-to-weight density, are commonly employed in exoskeletons, enabling active functionality for durations ranging from one to five hours with current technology. Regenerative braking solves energy limitations, as demonstrated in ankle foot orthosis systems by Oymagil et al. [42]. Nevertheless, energy constraints may impose restrictions on exoskeletons and their applications, necessitating the development of more efficient energy transfer, storage, processing, and actuation techniques.

3 Human-Robot Interaction Modalities

In the realm of rehabilitation robotics, HRI encompasses three primary modalities: patient-robot interaction, therapist-robot interaction, and robot learning (Fig. 2). Therapist-robot interactions typically involve the monitoring, customization, and parameter control of therapeutic interventions. Patient-robot interactions include collecting performance assessment data and control system feedback, disseminating procedural and progress information to the patient, and operating a closed-loop control system that manages motion planning and the robot's compliant behavior in response to the patient's movements. An example of these interaction modalities can be seen in a lower limb rehabilitation robot in Fig. 3 [34]. Robot learning is pivotal in rehabilitation robotics, allowing machines to adapt and respond dynamically to patient needs and conditions.

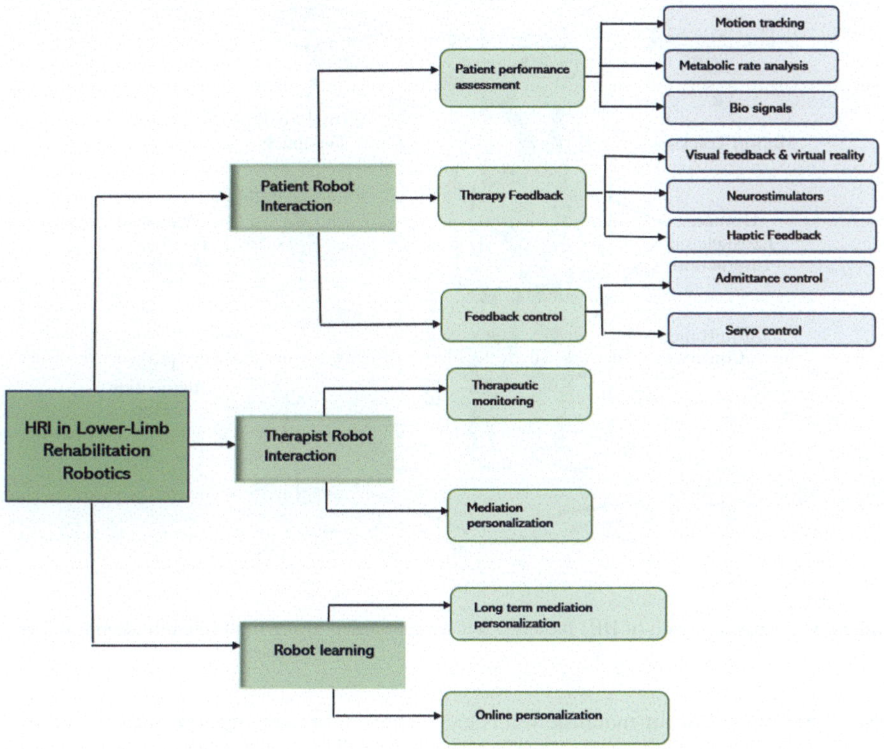

Fig. 2 Human-robot interaction modalities for lower-limb rehabilitation robotics

3.1 Patient-Robot Interaction

Patient-robot interaction is a crucial aspect of rehabilitation robotics, focusing on the data exchange between the patient and the robotic system. This interaction involves collecting movement and performance data through various sensing devices, which is then used to inform and adapt the control systems of the robots to enhance therapeutic outcomes. Serpelloni et al. [48] developed a sophisticated hand rehabilitation robotic system that leverages sEMG measurements. This system is particularly innovative in that it mirrors the movements of a healthy hand to guide the rehabilitation of the affected hand. The primary sensing device used in this system is the sEMG sensor, which measures the electrical activity produced by skeletal muscles. By capturing the muscle activity of the healthy hand, the robotic system can replicate these movements in the impaired hand, facilitating a natural and intuitive rehabilitation process. This method provides real-time feedback to the patient and ensures that the rehabilitation exercises are tailored to the individual's specific needs and capabilities. Sarasola-Sanz et al. [47] presented a control method for a 7-degree-of-freedom (DOF) upper limb rehabilitation robot, integrating electroencephalography (EEG),

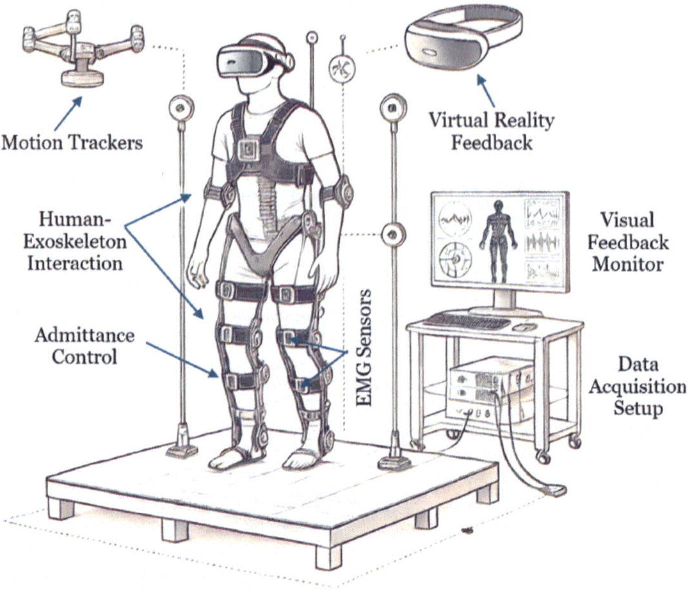

Fig. 3 A schematic sketch of HRI modalities in a robot-aided lower-limb rehabilitation training

EMG, and hybrid brain-machine interfaces. Their approach incorporates a comprehensive data acquisition system that taps into central and peripheral nervous system structures. EEG sensors monitor brain activity, providing insights into the patient's intent and cognitive state [20]. EMG sensors capture muscle activity, offering precise data on the physical actions of the patient. This combination allows the robotic system to create a biologically inspired hierarchical control scheme, where the robot can adapt its movements and resistance levels based on the patient's neural and muscular feedback. This hierarchical control enhances the effectiveness of the rehabilitation exercises and promotes a more natural interaction between the patient and the robot, closely mimicking voluntary movements [47].

3.2 Therapist-Robot Interaction

Therapist-robot interaction plays a pivotal role in enhancing the effectiveness of rehabilitation interventions by leveraging intelligent algorithms and machine learning methods. This interaction encompasses monitoring the therapeutic process, quantifying patient performance and progress, and designing adaptive interventions tailored to individual patient needs. Intelligent algorithms enable therapists to conduct detailed analyses of patients' conditions and adaptability, facilitating faster and more comprehensive restoration of lost or diminished functions. By exploiting co-adaptation between the robot and patients, these algorithms utilize training data composed of synthetic kinematic features and bio-signal activation patterns, such as EMG signals, based on known motor functions. This allows the robotic therapist to adapt interventions to each patient's specific needs, optimizing the rehabilitation process [7]. Concurrently, machine learning methods play a crucial role in therapist-robot interaction by enabling the classification of patients' motor functions and health conditions. Analyzing data collected during therapy sessions provides valuable insights into patients' progress and enables therapists to tailor interventions accordingly. Furthermore, these machine learning algorithms can be integrated into intelligent rehabilitation systems, suggesting interventions based on patient conditions and adjusting assessment methods in real time. This dynamic adaptation ensures that therapy remains responsive to the evolving needs of each patient, maximizing the potential for successful outcomes [15].

3.3 Robot Learning

This section explores how machine learning techniques enhance various aspects of rehabilitation therapy. Dolatabadi et al. [12] utilized machine learning methods with an affordable sensing approach to differentiate between healthy and pathological gait patterns resulting from stroke or brain injuries. They collected gait features, including the orientations of key body parts such as the hip, spine, shoulders, neck, knee, and ankle, during walking using a motion tracking system. Subsequently, they applied a Gaussian process latent variable model to analyze these features and discern the role of each body part in distinguishing between pathological and healthy gait patterns. This approach highlights the use of machine learning to identify subtle variations in gait patterns, enabling more accurate diagnosis and tailored rehabilitation strategies [12]. Cui et al. [10] developed an intelligent gait analysis system to identify and assess gait abnormalities among post-stroke hemiparetic patients. They recorded marker trajectory, ground reaction forces, and EMG signals during walking and employed machine learning methods on multimodal sensor fusion data to distinguish hemiparetic gait patterns from healthy ones. By leveraging machine learning algorithms, they could detect subtle deviations in gait patterns associated with post-stroke hemiparesis, facilitating early intervention and personalized rehabilitation strategies [10]. Badesa et al. [3] presented an adaptive robot-aided therapy system that utilizes machine learning classification to dynamically apply modifications to the intervention and feedback provided to the subject, following the specific state of each patient. The system can continuously adapt its therapeutic approach based on real-time patient feedback and progress by incorporating machine learning algorithms. This adaptive framework ensures that therapy remains tailored to individual patient needs, maximizing therapeutic effectiveness and promoting patient engagement and motivation throughout the rehabilitation process [3].

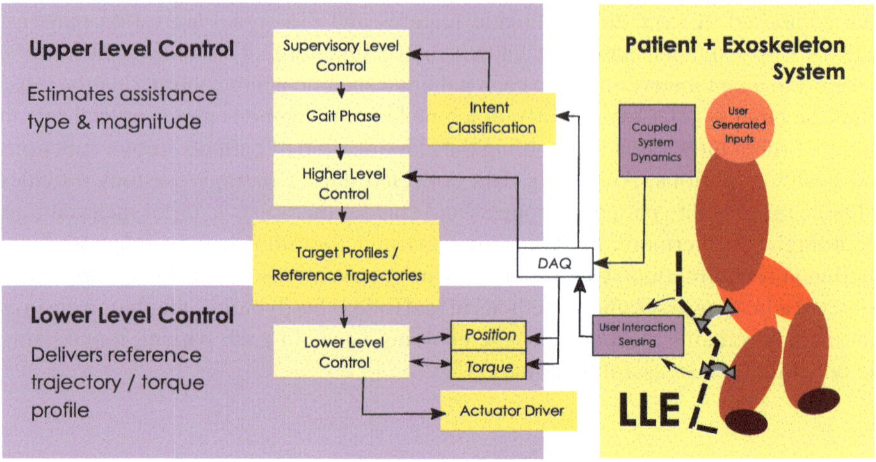

Fig. 4 Hierarchical classification of control strategies (from [37], licensed under CC-BY 4.0)

4 Control Strategies

Control techniques govern a coupled subject-exoskeleton system's joint torques and positions, driven by actuators. Hierarchical-level control schemes are widely acknowledged in lower-limb exoskeleton robots, comprising upper- and lower-level control [37]. Upper-level control focuses on decision-making algorithms that consider human intent and facilitate "assist-as-needed" interactions between the user and the exoskeleton robot during gait rehabilitation. Lower-level control ensures accurate position and torque tracking. Lower-level control schemes utilize actuator-driven position or torque strategies, with joint position sensors from the DAQ serving as feedback devices. One such architecture is shown in Fig. 4. The data from the user-exoskeleton environment are categorized into user interaction sensing inputs and user-generated inputs, processed for intent classification or interaction assessment using a data acquisition system (DAQ). Gait phase updates are incorporated into high-level control for interaction assessment, leading to a modified gait trajectory controlled by lower-level schemes [37].

4.1 Upper-Level Control

In robotic exoskeletons, upper-level control orchestrates decision-making algorithms to determine the overarching set of instructions for the actuation systems, which are executed by the lower-level control schema. Its primary function involves collecting information from both the user and the environment to discern the intended actions and requisite conditions for usage. Subsequently, it selects the mode of functionality needed for the system's operation. Within this tier, the supervisory level furnishes supplementary feedback to the high-level control while overseeing the functionality of the lower-level control schema [51]. The high-level control component assumes responsibility for choosing the appropriate functionality mode based on inputs from the user and environmental cues. This ensures the safe and reliable operation of the exoskeleton system while optimizing its performance.

4.1.1 Supervisory Control

The supervisory control layer is vital for managing exoskeletons in lower limb rehabilitation. It switches between operational modes based on intent estimation or direct user inputs, identifying gait phases and activities like walking, running, and sitting. This layer generates joint reference trajectories for high-level control, ensuring the exoskeleton aligns with the desired activity and phase. Inputs come from user commands or sensors, enhancing user experience. Motion and force sensors, including IMUs and encoders, track the user-exoskeleton system's state, measuring segment positions, orientations, and interaction forces. These sensors are crucial across all control levels, helping monitor actuators and determine gait features like phase, step length, and cadence, essential for effective rehabilitation [37].

Surface EMG has been used in exoskeletons for over two decades to implement closed-loop control. EMG sensors detect the electrical activity of muscles before intended movements, allowing for effective control of lower limb exoskeletons. For example, Yin et al. [57] extracted gait cycle duration (GCD) from sEMG signals at various walking speeds, which they used to program the motion of their exoskeleton system. In another study, Gui et al. [18] used unsupervised learning of the EMG-torque relationship to estimate a subject's voluntary joint torque, enabling precise movement and active participation during training. The control strategies discussed by Jung et al. [24] involve using intramuscular EMG signals to drive musculoskeletal models. These strategies aim to precisely interpret muscle activation for improving movement control in spinal cord injury patients. These sensors are integral in providing real-time feedback and adjusting motor control inputs. On the other hand, EEG signals help determine user intent and direct the exoskeleton system accordingly. For instance, Roy et al. [46] developed a real-time guideline for controlling an assistive robotics device using motor imagery EEG signals, achieving high accuracy in signal classification. Quiles et al. [44] used EEG to detect the intention to stop in response to obstacles, showing improved detection rates in both treadmill and exoskeleton experiments. However, they have low spatial resolution and weak signals with poor signal-to-noise ratios, requiring extensive signal processing to extract cortical electrical activity rhythms.

4.1.2 Higher-Level Control

Effective rehabilitation necessitates patient participation, hence, high-level control strategies leverage the admittance/impedance model to provide active involvement to users in gait training, under the premise of "assist-as-needed". Understanding the essential components of this level of control, namely admittance and impedance, is crucial. Recent research has witnessed active exploration of impedance/admittance controllers for gait exoskeletons [29]. Admittance control, extensively used in user-robot interaction environments, operates by adjusting motion output based on measured forces, with force sensors and disturbance observers enabling measurement of coupled exoskeleton human-interaction forces [35, 40]. Impedance control, on the other hand, is deployed in scenarios where robots interact physically with their surroundings, adapting force/torque outputs based on measured displacements or deviations from motion trajectories [9]. Recent advancements have seen the application of soft computing and deep learning techniques for enabling various levels of assistance and resistance in patient care [35]. These strategies hold promise in enhancing the efficacy and safety of exoskeleton systems during rehabilitation.

4.2 Lower-Level Control

In lower-level control, the focus is on tracking a reference torque/position based on the actuator's electric current as the input state. Position control ensures that the exoskeleton robot accurately tracks the desired gait trajectory, typically utilizing potentiometers for movement information measurement. The existing research underscores the importance of robust and intelligent control schemes to address the limitations of classical control approaches due to parametric perturbations and unwanted interference [37]. Robust gait tracking control is essential to maintain stability and performance despite uncertainties or disturbances inherent in exoskeleton-human interactions [25]. Incorporating robust control strategies enables exoskeletons to adapt to changing conditions and disturbances, providing consistent assistance or resistance to the user during rehabilitation and assistance tasks. Various methods such as adaptive and swarm-fuzzy logic control [1] and backstepping sliding control with nonlinear disturbance observer [26] have been proposed and tested to improve tracking behavior and disturbance rejection. Additionally, adaptive high-order super-twisting SMC [19] and adaptive backstepping control have been explored to enhance robustness against uncertainties.

In recent years, there has been a surge in robust intelligent control strategies to mitigate uncertain effects by leveraging effective approximation capabilities. Techniques such as neuro-fuzzy compensated PID control [39] and periodic event-triggered SMC with motion intention estimation using EMG signals [54] have demonstrated improved tracking performance and robustness against disturbances. Additionally, computed torque control with an RBF network compensator has shown promising results in reducing frictional effects and ensuring stable control performance despite uncertainties [36]. However, the initial selection of network hyperparameters remains challenging in intelligent control techniques. Combining these robust and intelligent control strategies creates a comprehensive approach that ensures stability, adaptability, and high performance in exoskeleton-assisted rehabilitation.

4.3 Learning from Demonstrators

Learning From Demonstration (LfD), also known as imitation learning, mainly realizes robot learning of the instructor's actions through teaching, action coding, motion learning, and robot reproduction. The main goal of LfD is to automatically learn the optimal strategy by learning the instructor's behavior without requiring a deep understanding of the robot. Although LfD has been widely used in robot motion planning research, there are always some challenges. A large amount of learning data should be provided by humans in LfD, which can lead to poor control accuracy when there are few teaching tracks, especially in tasks with restrictions on obtaining data. Additionally, human limitations in complex motion control tasks can result in low control accuracy of LfD. Furthermore, the principle of LfD limits its adaptability and autonomy, making it ineffective in tasks with few teaching trajectories. However, it can be used to learn the initial strategy model and then improve it through other methods, like reinforcement learning (RL) [32].

5 Discussions and Future Directions

In this comprehensive exploration of the multifaceted realm of lower limb exoskeleton technology, drawing insights from seminal works such as Nazari et al. [41], Li et al. [28], Mohebbi [34] and Narayan et al. [37], our work commenced with an overview of the evolving landscape of human-robot interaction (HRI) within the context of lower limb assistance, laying the groundwork for an in-depth examination of key thematic areas. Biomechanics and gait dynamics emerged as central pillars underpinning the design and efficacy of lower limb exoskeletons. We uncovered invaluable insights into optimizing gait performance and rehabilitation outcomes by elucidating the intricate interplay between human biomechanics and exoskeleton mechanics. Furthermore, we shed light on mechanisms, actuators, and energy sources utilized in wearable lower extremity, driving innovation in this domain. From pneumatic actuators to electric motors, the selection of actuation technology plays a pivotal role in shaping the functionality, efficiency, and user experience of exoskeleton systems. Thereafter, we focused on three primary modalities: patient-robot interaction, therapist-robot interaction, and robot learning. Future advancements could enhance robot learning, enabling machines to dynamically adapt to patient needs and conditions more effectively. Transitioning to control strategies, we delved into hierarchical classification frameworks for subject-cooperative control strategies in lower limb exoskeletons. By synthesizing a spectrum of control paradigms, from centralized to decentralized approaches, we underscored the pivotal role of adaptive control mechanisms in facilitating seamless interaction between users and exoskeleton devices. Leveraging insights from control theory and human motor control, researchers can devise sophisticated control algorithms that seamlessly adapt to user intent and physiological dynamics, thereby enhancing the efficacy and usability of exoskeleton systems in rehabilitation settings.

Looking ahead, future directions and emerging trends in lower limb exoskeleton technology will include biomechanically informed design methodologies, advanced sensor technologies, and machine learning-driven control algorithms. The landscape of HRI is poised for transformative advancements. By embracing interdisciplinary collaboration, user-centric design principles, and innovative research methodologies, we can fully harness the potential of lower limb exoskeleton technology. This will empower individuals with mobility impairments and drive positive societal impacts in the field of assistive technology.

6 Conclusion

In conclusion, our review highlighted the transformative potential of lower limb exoskeleton technology in enhancing mobility, independence, and quality of life for individuals with mobility impairments. Starting with an overview of the evolving landscape of human-robot interaction (HRI) in lower limb assistance, we reviewed biomechanics, gait dynamics, and design principles of exoskeletons. We outlined the intricate interplay between human biomechanics and exoskeleton mechanics to optimize gait performance and rehabilitation outcomes. Additionally, we discussed actuation technologies and control strategies, emphasizing the importance of adaptive control mechanisms in enhancing user interaction and device efficacy. Future research should prioritize advanced biomechanical modeling, innovative actuation technologies, and energy-efficient power sources to enhance exoskeleton design. Advancements in robot learning and control algorithms are further essential for better adaptation to patient needs. Addressing user acceptance, usability, and safety is crucial for broader adoption, and interdisciplinary collaboration and user-centric design can drive positive societal impact in human-robot interaction.

References

1. Amiri, M.S., Ramli, R., Aliman, N.: Adaptive swarm fuzzy logic controller of multi-joint lower limb assistive robot. Machines **10**(6), 425 (2022). https://doi.org/10.3390/machines10060425
2. Awad, L.N., Bae, J., O'donnell, K., De Rossi, S.M., Hendron, K., Sloot, L.H., Kudzia, P., Allen, S., Holt, K.G., Ellis, T.D., et al.: A soft robotic exosuit improves walking in patients after stroke. Science translational medicine **9**(400), eaai9084 (2017)

3. Badesa, F.J., Morales, R., Garcia-Aracil, N., Sabater, J.M., Casals, A., Zollo, L.: Auto-adaptive robot-aided therapy using machine learning techniques. Computer methods and programs in biomedicine **116**(2), 123–130 (2014)
4. Banala, S.K., Agrawal, S.K., Kim, S.H., Scholz, J.P.: Novel gait adaptation and neuromotor training results using an active leg exoskeleton. IEEE/ASME Transactions on mechatronics **15**(2), 216–225 (2010)
5. Banala, S.K., Kim, S.H., Agrawal, S.K., Scholz, J.P.: Robot assisted gait training with active leg exoskeleton (alex). IEEE transactions on neural systems and rehabilitation engineering **17**(1), 2–8 (2008)
6. Basteris, A., Nijenhuis, S.M., Stienen, A.H., Buurke, J.H., Prange, G.B., Amirabdollahian, F.: Training modalities in robot-mediated upper limb rehabilitation in stroke: a framework for classification based on a systematic review. Journal of neuroengineering and rehabilitation **11**, 1–15 (2014)
7. Cabitza, F., Locoro, A., Banfi, G.: Machine learning in orthopedics: a literature review. Frontiers in bioengineering and biotechnology **6**, 75 (2018)
8. Castagneri, C., Agostini, V., Rosati, S., Balestra, G., Knaflitz, M.: Asymmetry index in muscle activations. IEEE Transactions on Neural Systems and Rehabilitation Engineering **27**(4), 772–779 (2019)
9. Cifuentes, C.A., Múnera, M., Arciniegas-Mayag, L., Rodriguez-Guerrero, C., Rocon, E., Múnera, M., Cifuentes, C.A.: Impedance control strategies for lower-limb exoskeletons. Interfacing Humans and Robots for Gait Assistance and Rehabilitation pp. 213–236 (2022)
10. Cui, C., Bian, G.B., Hou, Z.G., Zhao, J., Su, G., Zhou, H., Peng, L., Wang, W.: Simultaneous recognition and assessment of post-stroke hemiparetic gait by fusing kinematic, kinetic, and electrophysiological data. IEEE Transactions on Neural Systems and Rehabilitation Engineering **26**(4), 856–864 (2018)
11. Díaz, I., Gil, J.J., Sánchez, E., et al.: Lower-limb robotic rehabilitation: literature review and challenges. Journal of Robotics **2011** (2011)
12. Dolatabadi, E., Taati, B., Mihailidis, A.: An automated classification of pathological gait using unobtrusive sensing technology. IEEE Transactions on Neural Systems and Rehabilitation Engineering **25**(12), 2336–2346 (2017)
13. Dollar, A.M., Herr, H.: Lower extremity exoskeletons and active orthoses: Challenges and state-of-the-art. IEEE Transactions on robotics **24**(1), 144–158 (2008)
14. Esquenazi, A., Talaty, M.: Robotics for lower limb rehabilitation. Physical Medicine and Rehabilitation Clinics **30**(2), 385–397 (2019)
15. Fong, J., Ocampo, R., Gross, D.P., Tavakoli, M.: Intelligent robotics incorporating machine learning algorithms for improving functional capacity evaluation and occupational rehabilitation. Journal of occupational rehabilitation **30**(3), 362–370 (2020)
16. Frontera, W.R., De Groote, W., Ghaffar, A., for Rehabilitation Group, H.P..S.R.: Importance of health policy and systems research for strengthening rehabilitation in health systems: a call to action to accelerate progress. Frontiers in Rehabilitation Sciences **4**, 1303135 (2023)
17. Gong, T., Chen, D., Wang, G., Zhang, W., Zhang, J., Ouyang, Z., Zhang, F., Sun, R., Ji, J.C., Chen, W.: Multimodal fusion and human-robot interaction control of an intelligent robot. Frontiers in Bioengineering and Biotechnology **11** (2024). https://doi.org/10.3389/fbioe.2023.1310247
18. Gui, K., Tan, U.X., Liu, H., Zhang, D.: Electromyography-driven progressive assist-as-needed control for lower limb exoskeleton. IEEE Transactions on Medical Robotics and Bionics **2**(1), 50–58 (2020)
19. Hasan, S., Dhingra, A.K.: Biomechanical design and control of an eight dof human lower extremity rehabilitation exoskeleton robot. Results in Control and Optimization **7**, 100107 (2022)
20. Herath, H., de Mel, W., Mittal, M.: Brain-computer interfacing for flexion and extension of bio-inspired robot fingers. International Journal of Cognitive Computing in Engineering **4**, 89–99 (2023)

21. Herath, H., Mittal, M., Kataria, A.: Navigating the metaverse: A technical review of emerging virtual worlds. Wiley Interdisciplinary Reviews: Data Mining and Knowledge Discovery p. e1538 (2024)
22. Hutabarat, Y., Owaki, D., Hayashibe, M.: Recent advances in quantitative gait analysis using wearable sensors: A review. IEEE Sensors Journal **21**(23), 26470–26487 (2021)
23. James, S.L., Abate, D., Abate, K.H., Abay, S.M., Abbafati, C., Abbasi, N., Abbastabar, H., Abd-Allah, F., Abdela, J., Abdelalim, A., et al.: Global, regional, and national incidence, prevalence, and years lived with disability for 354 diseases and injuries for 195 countries and territories, 1990–2017: a systematic analysis for the global burden of disease study 2017. The Lancet **392**(10159), 1789–1858 (2018)
24. Jung, M.K., Muceli, S., Rodrigues, C., Megía-García, Á., Pascual-Valdunciel, A., Del-Ama, A.J., Gil-Agudo, A., Moreno, J.C., Barroso, F.O., Pons, J.L., et al.: Intramuscular emg-driven musculoskeletal modelling: Towards implanted muscle interfacing in spinal cord injury patients. IEEE Transactions on Biomedical Engineering **69**(1), 63–74 (2021)
25. Kalita, B., Narayan, J., Dwivedy, S.K.: Development of active lower limb robotic-based orthosis and exoskeleton devices: a systematic review. International Journal of Social Robotics **13**, 775–793 (2021)
26. Khamar, M., Edrisi, M.: Designing a backstepping sliding mode controller for an assistant human knee exoskeleton based on nonlinear disturbance observer. Mechatronics **54**, 121-132 (2018). https://doi.org/10.1016/j.mechatronics.2018.07.010
27. Lefeber, N., Degelaen, M., Truyers, C., Safin, I., Beckwée, D.: Validity and reproducibility of inertial physilog sensors for spatiotemporal gait analysis in patients with stroke. IEEE transactions on neural systems and rehabilitation engineering **27**(9), 1865–1874 (2019)
28. Li, B., Yuan, B., Tang, S., Mao, Y., Zhang, D., Huang, C., Tan, B.: Biomechanical design analysis and experiments evaluation of a passive knee-assisting exoskeleton for weight-climbing. Industrial Robot: An International Journal **45**(4), 436–445 (2018)
29. Luo, R., Sun, S., Zhao, X., Zhang, Y., Tang, Y.: Adaptive CPG-based impedance control for assistive lower limb exoskeleton. In: 2018 IEEE International Conference on Robotics and Biomimetics (ROBIO), pp. 685–690. IEEE (2018)
30. Malcolm, P., Derave, W., Galle, S., De Clercq, D.: A simple exoskeleton that assists plantarflexion can reduce the metabolic cost of human walking. PLoS ONE **8**(2), e56137 (2013)
31. Martindale, C.F., Roth, N., Gaßner, H., List, J., Regensburger, M., Eskofier, B.M., Kohl, Z.: Technical validation of an automated mobile gait analysis system for hereditary spastic paraplegia patients. IEEE journal of biomedical and health informatics **24**(5), 1490–1499 (2019)
32. Michini, B., Walsh, T.J., Agha-Mohammadi, A.A., How, J.P.: Bayesian nonparametric reward learning from demonstration. IEEE Transactions on Robotics **31**(2), 369-386 (2015). https://doi.org/10.1109/tro.2015.2405593
33. Mirelman, A., Rochester, L., Maidan, I., Del Din, S., Alcock, L., Nieuwhof, F., Rikkert, M.O., Bloem, B.R., Pelosin, E., Avanzino, L., et al.: Addition of a non-immersive virtual reality component to treadmill training to reduce fall risk in older adults (v-time): a randomised controlled trial. The Lancet **388**(10050), 1170–1182 (2016)
34. Mohebbi, A.: Human-robot interaction in rehabilitation and assistance: a review. Current Robotics Reports **1**(3), 131–144 (2020)
35. Narayan, J., Abbas, M., Dwivedy, S.K.: Adaptive backstepping sliding mode subject-cooperative control for a pediatric lower-limb exoskeleton robot. Transactions of the Institute of Measurement and Control p. 01423312241245764 (2024)
36. Narayan, J., Abbas, M., Patel, B., Dwivedy, S.K.: Adaptive RBF neural network-computed torque control for a pediatric gait exoskeleton system: an experimental study. Intelligent Service Robotics **16**(5), 549–564 (2023)
37. Narayan, J., Auepanwiriyakul, C., Jhunjhunwala, S., Abbas, M., Dwivedy, S.K.: Hierarchical classification of subject-cooperative control strategies for lower limb exoskeletons in gait rehabilitation: a systematic review. Machines **11**(7), 764 (2023)
38. Narayan, J., Dwivedy, S.K.: Lower limb exoskeletons for pediatric gait rehabilitation: A brief review of design, actuation, and control schemes. In: 2023 IEEE International Conference on Advanced Systems and Emergent Technologies (IC_ASET), pp. 1–6. IEEE (2023)

39. Narayan, J., Dwivedy, S.K.: Towards neuro-fuzzy compensated PID control of lower extremity exoskeleton system for passive gait rehabilitation. IETE Journal of Research **69**(2), 778–795 (2023)
40. Narayan, J., Kalita, B., Dwivedy, S.K.: Adaptive backstepping human-cooperative control of a pediatric gait exoskeleton system with high-and low-level admittance. Proceedings of the Institution of Mechanical Engineers, Part I: Journal of Systems and Control Engineering **238**(3), 545–562 (2024)
41. Nazari, F., Mohajer, N., Nahavandi, D., Khosravi, A., Nahavandi, S.: Applied exoskeleton technology: A comprehensive review of physical and cognitive human-robot interaction. IEEE Transactions on Cognitive and Developmental Systems **15**(3), 1102–1122 (2023). https://doi.org/10.1109/tcds.2023.3241632
42. Oymagil, A.M., Hitt, J.K., Sugar, T., Fleeger, J.: Control of a regenerative braking powered ankle foot orthosis. In: 2007 IEEE 10th International Conference on Rehabilitation Robotics, pp. 28–34. IEEE (2007)
43. Pratt, J., Krupp, B., Morse, C.: Series elastic actuators for high fidelity force control. Industrial Robot: An International Journal **29**(3), 234–241 (2002)
44. Quiles, V., Ferrero, L., Iáñez, E., Ortiz, M., Gil-Agudo, Á., Azorín, J.M.: Brain-machine interface based on transfer-learning for detecting the appearance of obstacles during exoskeleton-assisted walking. Frontiers in Neuroscience **17**, 1154480 (2023)
45. Reinkensmeyer, D.J., Burdet, E., Casadio, M., Krakauer, J.W., Kwakkel, G., Lang, C.E., Swinnen, S.P., Ward, N.S., Schweighofer, N.: Computational neurorehabilitation: modeling plasticity and learning to predict recovery. Journal of neuroengineering and rehabilitation **13**, 1–25 (2016)
46. Roy, G., Bhoi, A.K., Das, S., Bhaumik, S.: Cross-correlated spectral entropy-based classification of eeg motor imagery signal for triggering lower limb exoskeleton. Signal, Image and Video Processing **16**(7), 1831–1839 (2022)
47. Sarasola-Sanz, A., Irastorza-Landa, N., López-Larraz, E., Bibián, C., Helmhold, F., Broetz, D., Birbaumer, N., Ramos-Murguialday, A.: A hybrid brain-machine interface based on eeg and emg activity for the motor rehabilitation of stroke patients. In: 2017 International conference on rehabilitation robotics (ICORR), pp. 895–900. IEEE (2017)
48. Serpelloni, M., Tiboni, M., Lancini, M., Pasinetti, S., Vertuan, A., Gobbo, M.: Preliminary study of a robotic rehabilitation system driven by emg for hand mirroring. In: 2016 IEEE International Symposium on Medical Measurements and Applications (MeMeA), pp. 1–6. IEEE (2016)
49. Serrano-Vergel, R., Morillo, P., Casas-Yrurzum, S., Cruz-Neira, C.: Exploring the suitability of using virtual reality and augmented reality for anatomy training. IEEE Transactions on Human-Machine Systems **53**(2), 378–389 (2023)
50. Shankar, S.R., Battineni, G., Mittal, M.: Cognitive computing in human activity recognition with a focus on healthcare. In: Cognitive Computing for Human-Robot Interaction, pp. 51–67. Elsevier (2021)
51. Shi, D., Zhang, W., Zhang, W., Ding, X.: A review on lower limb rehabilitation exoskeleton robots. Chinese Journal of Mechanical Engineering **32**(1), 1–11 (2019)
52. Silsupadol, P., Prupetkaew, P., Kamnardsiri, T., Lugade, V.: Smartphone-based assessment of gait during straight walking, turning, and walking speed modulation in laboratory and free-living environments. IEEE journal of biomedical and health informatics **24**(4), 1188–1195 (2019)
53. Srivastava, S., Kao, P.C., Kim, S.H., Stegall, P., Zanotto, D., Higginson, J.S., Agrawal, S.K., Scholz, J.P.: Assist-as-needed robot-aided gait training improves walking function in individuals following stroke. IEEE Transactions on Neural Systems and Rehabilitation Engineering **23**(6), 956–963 (2014)
54. Wang, J., Liu, J., Zhang, G., Guo, S.: Periodic event-triggered sliding mode control for lower limb exoskeleton based on human–robot cooperation. ISA transactions **123**, 87–97 (2022)
55. Wang, L., Sun, Y., Li, Q., Liu, T., Yi, J.: Imu-based gait normalcy index calculation for clinical evaluation of impaired gait. IEEE Journal of Biomedical and Health Informatics **25**(1), 3–12 (2020)

56. Xi, X., Jiang, W., Hua, X., Wang, H., Yang, C., Zhao, Y.B., Miran, S.M., Luo, Z.: Simultaneous and continuous estimation of joint angles based on surface electromyography state-space model. IEEE Sensors Journal **21**(6), 8089–8099 (2021)
57. Yin, G., Zhang, X., Chen, D., Li, H., Chen, J., Chen, C., Lemos, S.: Processing surface emg signals for exoskeleton motion control. Frontiers in Neurorobotics **14**, 40 (2020)
58. Young, A.J., Ferris, D.P.: State of the art and future directions for lower limb robotic exoskeletons. IEEE Transactions on Neural Systems and Rehabilitation Engineering **25**(2), 171–182 (2016)
59. Zhao, C., Liu, Z., Zhu, L., Wang, Y.: Design and research of series actuator structure and control system based on lower limb exoskeleton rehabilitation robot. Actuators **13**(1), 20 (2024). https://doi.org/10.3390/act13010020
60. Zhou, J.L., Li, W.F., Zhang, Q., Xie, F., Wang, Q.: A smart walking stick for gait analysis of elderly and people with disabilities. IEEE Sensors Journal **22**(9), 9035–9045 (2022)
61. Zoss, A.B., Kazerooni, H., Chu, A.: Biomechanical design of the berkeley lower extremity exoskeleton (bleex). IEEE/ASME Transactions on mechatronics **11**(2), 128–138 (2006)

LMI-Based Robust Control Strategy for a Knee Rehabilitation Exoskeleton: Addressing State Constraints, Parameter Uncertainties and External Disturbances

Sahar Jenhani and Hassène Gritli

Abstract Exoskeletons, or wearable robotics, are gaining popularity for assisting the elderly and individuals with limb disorders in regaining mobility. This study focuses on lower limb exoskeletons designed for physical movement assistance and rehabilitation. Our main objective is to introduce a robust control strategy tailored for a 1-DoF knee rehabilitation exoskeleton robot, with a focus on precise position control. Our approach utilizes an affine state-feedback controller to address challenges such as state constraints, parameter uncertainties, and external disturbances. We employ a quadratic Lyapunov function and utilize mathematical tools such as the Schur complement, Young's inequality, matrix inversion lemma, and the S-procedure lemma to formulate Linear Matrix Inequality (LMI) stability conditions on the feedback gains of the adopted controller. These conditions are developed through two different design methods. They ensure robust stabilization of the 1-DoF knee exoskeleton robot, even in the presence of uncertainties and external disruptions. Furthermore, a comparison between these methods is conducted. Finally, simulation studies validate the efficiency of the proposed LMI stability conditions and demonstrate the controller's effectiveness in achieving robust position control of the knee exoskeleton robot, providing valuable insights for the advancement of rehabilitation exoskeleton control strategies.

1 Introduction

The global landscape is currently undergoing a transformative demographic shift, characterized by a steady rise in the aging population. This trend has significant implications for healthcare, social welfare, and labor markets [24, 40, 53]. While

S. Jenhani · H. Gritli (✉)
Laboratory of Robotics, Informatics and Complex Systems (RISC Lab—LR16ES07), National Engineering School of Tunis, University of Tunis El Manar, Le Belvédère, 1002 Tunis, Tunisia
e-mail: hassene.gritli@istic.ucar.tn

H. Gritli
Higher Institute of Information and Communication Technologies, University of Carthage, Technopole of Borj Cédria, Route de Soliman, BP 123, Hammam Chatt, 1164 Ben Arous, Tunisia

M. Mittal and J. Narayan (eds.), *Intelligent Cyber-Physical Systems for Healthcare Solutions*, https://doi.org/10.1007/978-981-97-8983-2_12

advancements in healthcare and living conditions have extended the quality of life for the elderly, they have also brought challenges due to the shrinking population of younger caregivers. This presents societies with complex challenges and unprecedented opportunities to address the needs of an aging population. According to United Nations data, the percentage of those aged 60 and above has substantially increased in the last two decades and is projected to reach 21.1% by 2050. Population aging significantly affects the mobility and functional capabilities of older individuals [11, 15, 47]. Age-related physiological changes, such as reduced physical capacities and increased mobility-related vulnerabilities, underscore the importance of assistive technologies. In this context, exoskeletons, especially those designed for rehabilitation purposes, have emerged as a promising intersection of robotics and assistive technology. They offer transformative possibilities for addressing the declining physical capabilities associated with aging and even for pediatric therapy [34, 39, 40, 42]. These wearable devices have demonstrated their potential not only in enhancing mobility but also in reshaping the landscape of elderly and pediatric care when integrated with personalized healthcare strategies [4, 6, 13, 34, 40, 46].

Exoskeletons offer a promising solution for addressing mobility challenges encountered by the aging population. By enhancing mobility, balance, and independence in daily activities, and when combined with personalized healthcare, exoskeletons have the potential to revolutionize elderly care and support [4, 6, 9, 13, 40]. A crucial focus within the exoskeleton field revolves around the development of specialized robotic systems for rehabilitation, intended to assist individuals with disabilities and the elderly in walking and improving mobility [12, 51].

One of the critical factors influencing the effectiveness of exoskeletons is their control strategies. The robustness and adaptability of these strategies are paramount to ensure the safe and effective operation of exoskeleton systems. The exploration of diverse control methodologies, ranging from classical methods to sophisticated model-based, adaptive, and neural network-based approaches, reflects the multidisciplinary nature of this research domain [14, 36, 39, 40, 49]. Trajectory tracking, impedance control, robust control, neural networks, and fuzzy logic are among the strategies pursued [2, 8, 10, 25, 38, 41]. Nowhere is this more evident than in the realm of lower limb exoskeletons, where the pursuit of precise joint movement has led to research in trajectory tracking, impedance control, robust control, neural networks, and fuzzy logic [10, 25, 38, 41, 42]. The aim is to achieve precise joint movement, user adaptability, and overall safety. These control approaches underscore the need for adaptable and personalized exoskeleton systems tailored to individual user needs. The evolution of control strategies holds significant potential to impact rehabilitation and mobility enhancement for the elderly and those with mobility limitations.

This study explores the multifaceted landscape of rehabilitation exoskeleton robotics, with a specific focus on the knee joint-a crucial joint with significant implications for mobility and stability [3, 26, 28, 29, 37, 44, 52]. The knee joint plays a pivotal role in essential activities such as walking and weight-bearing. Therefore, designing exoskeletons tailored for rehabilitation and support places paramount importance on the efficacy of the knee joint. Our primary objective is to design and implement a robust control strategy explicitly tailored for a one-degree-of-freedom

(1-DoF) knee rehabilitation exoskeleton robot [27, 28, 30, 32]. This strategic focus arises from recognizing that many wearable exoskeletons commonly exhibit one to three degrees of freedom per leg in the sagittal plane [7, 44, 52].

The complexity of achieving robust control in the 1-DoF knee exoskeleton stems from the intricate interplay of factors, including state constraints, parameter uncertainties, solid and viscous frictions, and external disturbances. Therefore, we propose an affine state-feedback controller to effectively address these challenges. By leveraging the Lyapunov stability theory and employing the Linear Matrix Inequality (LMI) approach, we aim to ensure stability and robustness in the presence of uncertainties and external disturbances. To achieve this, we utilize mathematical tools such as the S-procedure, the Young's inequality, the Schur complement, and the matrix inversion lemma [16–18, 20, 50]. These LMI conditions are carefully formulated using two different methods, laying the foundation for achieving precise and robust control of the 1-DoF knee exoskeleton robot. Finally, we will present simulation results that demonstrate the effectiveness of the controller in robustly controlling the active 1-DoF knee exoskeleton robot.

The main contributions of this chapter are summarized as follows:

- Development of an effective affine state-feedback control law tailored to stabilize the 1-DoF knee exoskeleton robot. This control law addresses the complexities of nonlinear dynamics, incorporating key factors such as state constraints, parameter uncertainties, solid and viscous frictions, and external disturbances.
- Formulation of stability conditions using Linear Matrix Inequalities (LMIs) based on various mathematical tools including the Lyapunov approach, S-procedure, Young's inequality, Schur complement, and matrix inversion lemma. These LMIs are derived using two distinct methods, laying the groundwork for achieving precise and robust control of the 1-DoF knee exoskeleton robot.
- Improvement of stability criteria expressed in LMI form by introducing optimization problems. These optimization problems enable the maximization or minimization of two critical parameters: the highest magnitude of the lumped disturbance and the parameter added to the constraint on the controller.
- Conducting numerical simulations to validate the effectiveness of the controller in robustly controlling the active 1-DoF knee exoskeleton robot. These simulations serve to demonstrate the efficiency of the proposed control strategy.

The subsequent sections of this chapter are structured as follows. Section 2 describes the dynamic model of the knee exoskeleton rehabilitation robot. Section 3 covers the robust control of the knee exoskeleton robotic system. The design of the LMI stability condition is detailed in Sect. 4. Section 5 demonstrates the results of the simulations. Finally, in Sect. 6, we provide the conclusion and discuss some future works.

2 Dynamic Model of the Adopted Knee Exoskeleton Robot

2.1 Adopted Knee Exoskeleton Structure

Our research centers on wearable exoskeletons, typically equipped with one to three degrees of freedom (DoF) per leg in the sagittal plane, accommodating passive, active, or fixed joints. The primary focus lies in investigating and controlling a rehabilitation exoskeleton robot tailored for the knee joint level, specifically designed to support or rehabilitate a single degree of freedom [7, 44, 52]. The 1-DoF knee exoskeleton robot, as depicted in Fig. 1 and adopted from [21, 23, 31, 44, 45], offers simplicity and user-friendliness, aligning with the research objectives. Its straightforward design facilitates ease of use during both donning and removal, catering to individuals with knee joint mobility limitations [44, 45].

In addressing the multifaceted challenges associated with wearable exoskeletons, our study extends to exoskeletons and orthoses with a single degree of freedom. This design approach aims to minimize size, weight, and electrical component requirements, encompassing sensors, actuators, processors, and batteries. Figure 1 illustrates the exoskeleton orthosis adopted for this research, featuring a single degree of freedom at the knee joint level [21, 31, 32, 44, 45]. The selection of this orthosis is grounded in its simplicity and user-friendliness, making it an optimal choice for the study's objectives. Its uncomplicated design ensures straightforward donning and removal, catering to individuals with knee joint limitations [44, 45].

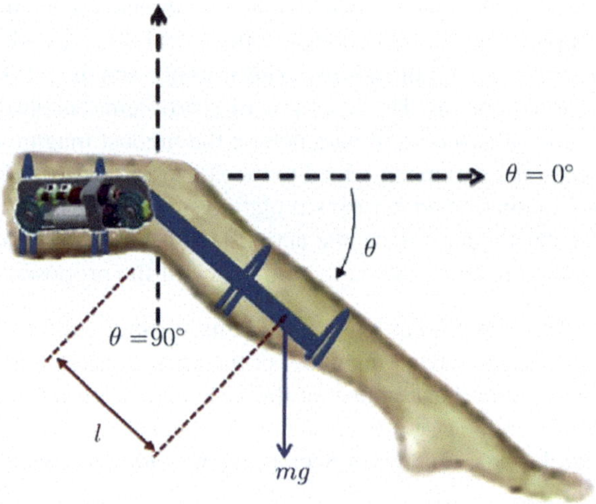

Fig. 1 Visualization of the actuated knee exoskeleton robot system (adapted from [45])

2.2 Dynamic Modeling of the Knee Exoskeleton Robot

This section delineates the nonlinear dynamics inherent in the 1-DoF knee rehabilitation exoskeleton robotic system, as depicted in Fig. 1. The formulation of the nonlinear dynamic model for this exoskeleton takes into consideration various factors, including external disturbances such as solid and viscous frictions, along with the incorporation of parameter uncertainties.

$$\vartheta_\star \ddot{\theta} = u - f_v^\star \dot{\theta} + a_\star \cos(\theta) - f_s^\star \mathrm{sgn}(\dot{\theta}) + \Delta_t \tag{1}$$

where $a_\star = g m_\star l_\star$, with $m_\star$ representing the system's mass, g denoting the gravitational constant, and $l_\star$ representing a length (refer to Fig. 1). Additionally, the terms $\vartheta_\star$, $f_v^\star$ and $f_s^\star$ respectively signify the inertia, the coefficient of viscous friction, and the coefficient of solid friction. Furthermore, u signifies the torque input or the controller to be designed subsequently.

Moreover, Δ_t denotes the lumped disturbance and is given by:

$$\Delta_t = \Delta_{pu} + \Delta_{ed} + \Delta_{ud} + \Delta_{hl} \tag{2}$$

where Δ_{pu} denotes the term for parametric uncertainties, Δ_{ed} represents the term for external disturbances, Δ_{ud} stands for the term for unmodeled dynamics, and Δ_{hl} indicates the term for the force exerted by the human leg.

Next, let us assume that Δ_t follows the following constraint:

$$|\Delta_t| \leq \bar{\delta}, \qquad \bar{\delta} > 0 \tag{3}$$

Consider $\phi = \theta - \theta_d$, where θ_d represents the intended state. Subsequently, model (1) transforms into:

$$\vartheta_\star \ddot{\phi} = u - f_v^\star \dot{\phi} + a_\star \cos(\phi + \theta_d) - f_s^\star \mathrm{sgn}(\dot{\phi}) + \Delta_t \tag{4}$$

3 Robust Control of the Knee Exoskeleton

3.1 Problem Formulation

Recent advancements in technology have fueled extensive research in the design and control of exoskeleton robots, aiming to enhance human capabilities in tasks such as object transportation and neuro-muscular rehabilitation. These robots serve diverse demographics, including the elderly and individuals with injuries or disabilities. Over the decades, various control methodologies, such as PID controllers [41, 44], reduced adaptive fuzzy decoupling control [48], Fuzzy PID control [2], sliding mode controllers [1], and other nonlinear controllers [5], have been developed to address position control challenges in exoskeleton robotic systems.

Our goal is to create robust control strategies for lower limb exoskeletons used in rehabilitation, addressing the complexities of human-robot interaction [6, 43]. We aim to design control laws that prioritize safety and ensure natural joint movement during rehabilitation. This includes considering limited knee and foot movement ranges and incorporating these constraints into the control system. Our approach accounts for motion constraints across the entire system, which includes both the exoskeleton and the wearer's lower limb.

In the present work, we consider a rehabilitation exoskeleton with only one degree of freedom at the knee joint level. Thus, as shown in Fig. 1, the exoskeleton robotic system is configured to have an operating interval of 90°. Notably, the position 0° represents the full extension of the knee joint, and the position 90° represents the resting position. Therefore, we adopt the following constraint:

$$0 \leq \theta \leq \frac{\pi}{2} \tag{5}$$

Therefore, to accomplish the control purpose of the knee exoskeleton robot defined by its nonlinear dynamics (1) or equivalently (4), we should design such a simple, efficient, and appropriate controller by taking into consideration the state constraint (5).

3.2 Intended Control Effort at Equilibrium

After implementing the control law u to position the robotic system at the desired angle θ_d effectively, the robot must exert continuous control effort to maintain this equilibrium position, where $\dot{\theta}_d = 0$. Let u_d denote the required control input at the equilibrium position. Utilizing the equation of motion (1), we can deduce the expression for the desired control input u_d at the equilibrium as follows:

$$u_d = -a_\star \cos(\theta_d) \tag{6}$$

3.3 State Space Representation

As mentioned earlier, the dynamic model (1) of the robotic system introduces a state constraint. This constraint delineates the operational space of the system, represented as Ω, and can be mathematically expressed like so:

$$\Omega = \left\{\theta \in \mathbb{R} : 0 \leq \theta \leq \frac{\pi}{2}\right\} \tag{7}$$

Furthermore, considering $\phi = \theta - \theta_d$ and the fact that $0 \leq \theta \leq \frac{\pi}{2}$, we can easily demonstrate the subsequent expression:

$$-\gamma_1 \leq \phi \leq \gamma_2 \tag{8}$$

with

$$\gamma_1 = \theta_d \qquad \gamma_2 = \frac{\pi}{2} - \theta_d \tag{9}$$

Taking $\chi = \begin{bmatrix} \phi \\ \dot{\phi} \end{bmatrix}$ to represent the state vector, and by considering the expression (6), we can recast the equation of motion (4) as follows:

$$\begin{aligned} \dot{\chi} &= \mathcal{A}\chi + \mathcal{B}\Delta u + \mathcal{D}_1\Psi_1(\chi) + \mathcal{D}_2\Psi_2(\chi) + \mathcal{B}\Delta_t \\ \text{where} \quad & -\gamma_1 \leq \mathcal{C}^{\mathrm{T}}\chi \leq \gamma_2 \end{aligned} \tag{10}$$

The matrices $\mathcal{A}$, $\mathcal{B}$, $\mathcal{D}_1$, $\mathcal{D}_2$ and $\mathcal{C}$ are represented by the following expressions:

$$\mathcal{A} = \begin{bmatrix} 0 & 1 \\ 0 & -\frac{f_v^\star}{\vartheta_\star} \end{bmatrix} \qquad \mathcal{B} = \begin{bmatrix} 0 \\ \frac{1}{\vartheta_\star} \end{bmatrix} \qquad \mathcal{D}_1 = \begin{bmatrix} 0 \\ -\frac{f_s^\star}{\vartheta_\star} \end{bmatrix} \tag{11a}$$

$$\mathcal{D}_2 = \begin{bmatrix} 0 \\ \frac{a_\star}{\vartheta_\star} \end{bmatrix} \qquad \mathcal{C} = \begin{bmatrix} 1 \\ 0 \end{bmatrix} \tag{11b}$$

Furthermore, the functions $\Psi_1(\chi)$ and $\Psi_2(\chi)$ in Eq. (10) are defined as follows:

$$\Psi_1(\chi) = \mathrm{sgn}(\dot{\phi}) \tag{12a}$$

$$\Psi_2(\chi) = \cos(\phi + \theta_d) - \cos(\theta_d) \tag{12b}$$

Moreover, the term Δu defines the control error as expressed below:

$$\Delta u = u - u_d \tag{13}$$

3.4 Adopted Affine State-Feedback Control Law

To accomplish the control objectives for the knee exoskeleton robot, the design of the controller u takes into account the state constraint (5). In this study, we employ the following affine state-feedback controller:

$$u = u_d + \Delta u \tag{14}$$

The term Δu is defined as follows:

$$\Delta u = \begin{cases} \mathcal{K}\chi & \text{if } \|\chi\|^2 \geq \epsilon^2 \\ 0 & \text{if } \|\chi\|^2 < \epsilon^2 \end{cases} \tag{15}$$

where ϵ is a small constant that will be determined later.

3.5 Controlled Nonlinear Dynamics

The nonlinear dynamic model of the knee exoskeleton robot under the adopted control law (14) is expressed as follows:

$$\begin{aligned} &\dot{\chi} = (\mathcal{A} + \mathcal{B}\mathcal{K})\chi + \mathcal{D}_1\Psi_1(\chi) + \mathcal{D}_2\Psi_2(\chi) + \mathcal{B}\Delta_t \\ &\text{such that} \quad -\gamma_1 \leq \mathcal{C}^{\mathrm{T}}\chi \leq \gamma_2 \quad \text{and} \quad \|\chi\|^2 \geq \epsilon^2 \end{aligned} \tag{16}$$

Notice that, the constraints within the expression (16) can be rephrased in the following manner:

$$\begin{bmatrix} \chi \\ 1 \end{bmatrix}^{\mathrm{T}} \begin{bmatrix} \mathcal{O} & \mathcal{C} \\ \star & -2\gamma_2 \end{bmatrix} \begin{bmatrix} \chi \\ 1 \end{bmatrix} \leq 0 \tag{17a}$$

$$\begin{bmatrix} \chi \\ 1 \end{bmatrix}^{\mathrm{T}} \begin{bmatrix} \mathcal{O} & -\mathcal{C} \\ \star & -2\gamma_1 \end{bmatrix} \begin{bmatrix} \chi \\ 1 \end{bmatrix} \leq 0 \tag{17b}$$

$$\begin{bmatrix} \chi \\ 1 \end{bmatrix}^{\mathrm{T}} \begin{bmatrix} \mathcal{I} & \mathcal{O} \\ \star & -\epsilon^2 \end{bmatrix} \begin{bmatrix} \chi \\ 1 \end{bmatrix} \geq 0 \tag{17c}$$

Here and in the subsequent discussions, the notation $\star$ appended to a matrix denotes the element obtained through its transpose, while the symbol $\mathcal{O}$ signifies a null matrix. Furthermore, $\mathcal{I}$ represents the identity matrix.

Remark 1 In this research, we opted for the LMI approach to determine the feedback gain for the proposed control law (14). This method presents advantages over both linear and nonlinear controllers. While linear controllers such as the Linear Quadratic Regulator (LQR) are conventionally employed for linear systems, our study introduces nonlinear dynamics to govern the movement of the knee exoskeleton robotic system [33]. Unlike the Proportional-Derivative (PD) controller with gravity compensation, which relies on nonlinear dynamics but often requires extensive computation time and imposes constraints on control parameter selection, our approach using the LMI technique effectively addresses these challenges [33]. By leveraging the LMI approach, our control strategy offers a more adaptable solution for knee exoskeleton robotic system control. Moreover, the LMI method enables the integration of conditions aimed at minimizing the feedback gain magnitude $\mathcal{K}$, enhancing the practicality and suitability of the controller for real-world implementation.

4 Design of the LMI Stability Conditions

This section is devoted to formulating an LMI condition for the feedback gains $\mathcal{K}$ of the proposed controller (14), serving the dual purpose of controlling and stabilizing knee exoskeleton robots.

Our approach involves leveraging the Lyapunov technique to achieve this objective. Therefore, we will adopt the subsequent candidate Lyapunov function:

$$\mathcal{V}(\chi) = \chi^{\mathrm{T}}\mathcal{P}\chi \tag{18}$$

The second stability condition, accounting for the constraints in the model (16), is given like so:

$$\dot{\mathcal{V}}(\chi) + \alpha\mathcal{V}(\chi) < 0 \quad \text{such that} - \gamma_1 \leq \mathcal{C}^{\mathrm{T}}\chi \leq \gamma_2 \quad \text{and} \quad \|\chi\|^2 \geq \epsilon^2 \tag{19}$$

where α is a predetermined positive scalar, satisfying $\alpha > 0$.

Employing (16), the derivative of $\mathcal{V}(\chi)$ can be expressed as follows:

$$\begin{aligned}\dot{\mathcal{V}}(\chi) = {} & 2\chi^{\mathrm{T}}\mathcal{P}\left(\mathcal{A}+\mathcal{B}\mathcal{K}\right)\chi + 2\chi^{\mathrm{T}}\mathcal{P}\mathcal{D}_1\Psi_1(\chi) \\ & + 2\chi^{\mathrm{T}}\mathcal{P}\mathcal{D}_2\Psi_2(\chi) + 2\chi^{\mathrm{T}}\mathcal{P}\mathcal{B}\Delta_t\end{aligned} \tag{20}$$

In the following, we will proceed to formulate two distinct methods for designing LMI conditions on the feedback gain $\mathcal{K}$ for stabilization, based on the developed expression (20).

4.1 First LMI Design Approach

In our first approach, let us assume that the function $\Psi_2(\chi)$ can be bounded by a second-degree equation.

Our primary objective is to ensure the stability of the controlled robotic system, utilizing the expanded expression (20). Subsequently, we will proceed to formulate a dedicated LMI constraint for the gain $\mathcal{K}$.

Applying the Young inequality lemma [16–18, 20, 50] to Eq. (20), we obtain:

$$2\chi^{\mathrm{T}}\mathcal{P}\mathcal{D}_1\Psi_1(\chi) \leq \chi^{\mathrm{T}}\mathcal{P}\mathcal{M}_1\mathcal{P}\chi + \mathcal{D}_1^{\mathrm{T}}\mathcal{M}_1^{-1}\mathcal{D}_1\Psi_1(\chi)^2 \tag{21}$$

where $\mathcal{M}_1 = \mathcal{M}_1^{\mathrm{T}} > 0$.

Additionally, with the utilization of (12b), inequality (21) can be expressed as:

$$2\chi^{\mathrm{T}}\mathcal{P}\mathcal{D}_1\Psi_1(\chi) \leq \chi^{\mathrm{T}}\mathcal{P}\mathcal{M}_1\mathcal{P}\chi + \mathcal{D}_1^{\mathrm{T}}\mathcal{M}_1^{-1}\mathcal{D}_1 \tag{22}$$

Similarly, employing the Young inequality, we obtain:

$$2\chi^{\mathrm{T}}\mathcal{P}\mathcal{D}_2\Psi_2(\chi) \leq \tau_2\chi^{\mathrm{T}}\mathcal{P}\mathcal{D}_2\mathcal{D}_2^{\mathrm{T}}\mathcal{P}\chi + \tau_2^{-1}\Psi_2(\chi)^2 \tag{23}$$

with $\tau_2 = \tau_2^{\mathrm{T}} > 0$.

By utilizing (12b), we can deduce that:

$$\Psi_2(\chi)^2 = \cos^2(\theta) - 2\cos(\theta_d)\cos(\theta) + \cos^2(\theta_d) \tag{24}$$

We can illustrate the subsequent two expressions:

$$\cos^2(\theta) \leq 1 \tag{25a}$$

$$-2\cos(\theta) \leq a_2\theta + b_2 \tag{25b}$$

where

$$a_2 = \frac{4}{\pi} \quad \text{and} \quad b_2 = -2 \tag{26}$$

Thus, we can demonstrate the subsequent condition:

$$-2\cos(\theta_d)\cos(\theta) \leq a_2\cos(\theta_d)\phi + a_2\cos(\theta_d)\theta_d + b_2\cos(\theta_d) \tag{27}$$

Hence, we get:

$$\Psi_2(\chi)^2 \leq 2\mu_1\phi + \mu_2 \tag{28}$$

where

$$\mu_1 = \frac{a_2}{2}\cos(\theta_d) > 0 \tag{29a}$$

$$\mu_2 = 1 + a_2\cos(\theta_d)\theta_d + b_2\cos(\theta_d) + \cos^2(\theta_d) \tag{29b}$$

Taking $\phi = \mathcal{C}_1\chi$, where $\mathcal{C}_1 = \begin{bmatrix} 1 & 0 \end{bmatrix}$, inequality (28) can be reformulated as:

$$\Psi_2(\chi)^2 \leq 2\mu_1\mathcal{C}_1\chi + \mu_2 \tag{30}$$

Therefore, (21) can be expressed as:

$$2\chi^{\mathrm{T}}\mathcal{P}\mathcal{D}_2\Psi_2(\chi) \leq \tau_2\chi^{\mathrm{T}}\mathcal{P}\mathcal{D}_2\mathcal{D}_2^{\mathrm{T}}\mathcal{P}\chi + 2\mu_1\tau_2^{-1}\mathcal{C}_1\chi + \mu_2\tau_2^{-1} \tag{31}$$

Utilizing (3), we get $\Delta_t^2 \leq \bar{\delta}^2$, and applying the Young inequality, we derive:

$$2\chi^{\mathrm{T}}\mathcal{P}\mathcal{B}\Delta_t \leq \chi^{\mathrm{T}}\mathcal{P}\mathcal{M}_3\mathcal{P}\chi + \bar{\delta}^2\mathcal{B}^{\mathrm{T}}\mathcal{M}_3^{-1}\mathcal{B} \tag{32}$$

for which the matrix $\mathcal{M}_3$ is such that $\mathcal{M}_3 = \mathcal{M}_3^{\mathrm{T}}$.

By substituting (22), (31), and (32) into (20) and integrating the constraints from (19), we arrive at:

$$\dot{\mathcal{V}}(\chi) + \alpha\mathcal{V}(\chi) \leq \begin{bmatrix} \chi \\ 1 \end{bmatrix}^{\mathrm{T}} \begin{bmatrix} \Upsilon_{11} & \mu_1\tau_2^{-1}\mathcal{C}_1^{\mathrm{T}} \\ \star & \Upsilon_{22} \end{bmatrix} \begin{bmatrix} \chi \\ 1 \end{bmatrix} < 0 \tag{33}$$

with

$$\begin{aligned} \Upsilon_{11} &= (\mathcal{PA} + \mathcal{PBK}) + (\mathcal{PA} + \mathcal{PBK})^{\mathrm{T}} + \mathcal{PM}_1\mathcal{P} \\ &\quad + \tau_2\mathcal{PD}_2\mathcal{D}_2^{\mathrm{T}}\mathcal{P} + \mathcal{PM}_3\mathcal{P} + \alpha\mathcal{P} && \text{(34a)} \\ \Upsilon_{22} &= \mathcal{D}_1^{\mathrm{T}}\mathcal{M}_1^{-1}\mathcal{D}_1 + \mu_2\tau_2^{-1} + \bar{\delta}^2\mathcal{B}^{\mathrm{T}}\mathcal{M}_3^{-1}\mathcal{B} && \text{(34b)} \end{aligned}$$

Applying the S-procedure lemma [16–18, 20, 50] and taking into account inequality (33) along with the conditions in (17), we derive:

$$\begin{bmatrix} \Upsilon_{11} + \beta_3\mathcal{I} & \mu_1\tau_2^{-1}\mathcal{C}_1^{\mathrm{T}} - (\beta_1 - \beta_2)\mathcal{C} \\ \star & \Upsilon_{22} + 2\gamma_2\beta_1 + 2\gamma_1\beta_2 - \epsilon^2\beta_3 \end{bmatrix} < 0 \tag{35}$$

with $\beta_1 > 0$, $\beta_2 > 0$ and $\beta_3 > 0$.

Let $\mathcal{S} = \mathcal{P}^{-1}$. By multiplying both sides of condition (35) on the right and left by diag $(\mathcal{S}, \mathcal{I})$, we obtain:

$$\begin{bmatrix} \Gamma_{11} & \mu_1\tau_2^{-1}\mathcal{SC}_1^{\mathrm{T}} - (\beta_1 - \beta_2)\mathcal{SC} \\ \star & \Gamma_{22} \end{bmatrix} < 0 \tag{36}$$

where

$$\begin{aligned} \Gamma_{11} &= (\mathcal{AS} + \mathcal{BR}) + (\mathcal{AS} + \mathcal{BR})^{\mathrm{T}} + \mathcal{M}_1 + \tau_2\mathcal{D}_2\mathcal{D}_2^{\mathrm{T}} \\ &\quad + \mathcal{M}_3 + \alpha\mathcal{S} + \beta_3\mathcal{S}^2 && \text{(37a)} \\ \Gamma_{22} &= \mathcal{D}_1^{\mathrm{T}}\mathcal{M}_1^{-1}\mathcal{D}_1 + \mu_2\tau_2^{-1} + \bar{\delta}^2\mathcal{B}^{\mathrm{T}}\mathcal{M}_3^{-1}\mathcal{B} + 2\gamma_2\beta_1 + 2\gamma_1\beta_2 - \epsilon^2\beta_3 && \text{(37b)} \end{aligned}$$

and where the matrix $\mathcal{R}$ is defined like so:

$$\mathcal{R} = \mathcal{KS} \tag{38}$$

Let us pose:

$$\mathcal{M} = \begin{bmatrix} \mathcal{M}_1 & \mathcal{O} & \mathcal{O} \\ \mathcal{O} & \tau_2 & \mathcal{O} \\ \mathcal{O} & \mathcal{O} & \mathcal{M}_3 \end{bmatrix} \qquad \mathcal{D} = \begin{bmatrix} \mathcal{D}_1 \\ \mathcal{O} \\ \mathcal{B} \end{bmatrix} \tag{39a}$$

$$\mathcal{F}^{-1} = \begin{bmatrix} \mathcal{I} & \mathcal{O} & \mathcal{O} \\ \mathcal{O} & \mu_2\mathcal{I} & \mathcal{O} \\ \mathcal{O} & \mathcal{O} & \bar{\delta}^2\mathcal{I} \end{bmatrix} \qquad \mathcal{J} = \begin{bmatrix} \mathcal{I} \\ \mathcal{D}_2^{\mathrm{T}} \\ \mathcal{I} \end{bmatrix} \tag{39b}$$

Consequently, inequality (36) can be expressed as:

$$\begin{bmatrix} \Theta_{11} & \mu_1\tau_2^{-1}\mathcal{S}\mathcal{C}_1^{\mathrm{T}} - (\beta_1 - \beta_2)\mathcal{S}\mathcal{C} \\ \star & \Theta_{22} \end{bmatrix} < 0 \tag{40}$$

with

$$\Theta_{11} = (\mathcal{A}\mathcal{S} + \mathcal{B}\mathcal{R}) + (\mathcal{A}\mathcal{S} + \mathcal{B}\mathcal{R})^{\mathrm{T}} + \mathcal{J}^{\mathrm{T}}\mathcal{M}\mathcal{J} + \alpha\mathcal{S} + \beta_3\mathcal{S}^2 \tag{41a}$$

$$\Theta_{22} = \mathcal{D}^{\mathrm{T}}\mathcal{M}^{-1}\mathcal{F}^{-1}\mathcal{D} + 2\gamma_2\beta_1 + 2\gamma_1\beta_2 + \mu_2\tau_2^{-1} - \epsilon^2\beta_3 \tag{41b}$$

Therefore, employing the Schur complement [16–18, 20, 50], we can express inequality (40) as:

$$\begin{bmatrix} \Theta_{11} & \mu_1\tau_2^{-1}\mathcal{S}\mathcal{C}_1^{\mathrm{T}} - (\beta_1 - \beta_2)\mathcal{S}\mathcal{C} & \mathcal{O} \\ \star & \mu_2\tau_2^{-1} + 2\gamma_2\beta_1 + 2\gamma_1\beta_2 - \epsilon^2\beta_3 & \mathcal{D}^{\mathrm{T}} \\ \star & \star & -\mathcal{F}\mathcal{M} \end{bmatrix} < 0 \tag{42}$$

Multiplying (42) on the right and left sides by $\mathcal{V} = \begin{bmatrix} \mathcal{I} & \mathcal{O} & \mathcal{O} \\ \mathcal{O} & \mathcal{O} & \mathcal{I} \\ \mathcal{O} & \mathcal{I} & \mathcal{O} \end{bmatrix}$, we get:

$$\begin{bmatrix} \Theta_{11} & \mathcal{O} & \mu_1\tau_2^{-1}\mathcal{S}\mathcal{C}_1^{\mathrm{T}} - (\beta_1 - \beta_2)\mathcal{S}\mathcal{C} \\ \star & -\mathcal{F}\mathcal{M} & \mathcal{D} \\ \star & \star & \mu_2\tau_2^{-1} + 2\gamma_2\beta_1 + 2\gamma_1\beta_2 - \epsilon^2\beta_3 \end{bmatrix} < 0 \tag{43}$$

To facilitate our discussion, let us introduce some new variables:

$$\kappa^{-1} = -\epsilon^2\beta_3, \qquad \sigma_1 = \beta_1^{-1}, \qquad \sigma_2 = \beta_2^{-1} \tag{44a}$$

$$\mathcal{T} = \begin{bmatrix} \mathcal{S} \\ \mathcal{O} \end{bmatrix}, \quad \mathcal{G} = \begin{bmatrix} -\mathcal{S}\mathcal{C} & \mathcal{S}\mathcal{C} & \mathcal{S}\mathcal{C}_1^{\mathrm{T}} \\ \mathcal{O} & \mathcal{O} & \mathcal{O} \end{bmatrix}, \quad \mathcal{Z} = \begin{bmatrix} \mathcal{O} \\ \mathcal{D} \end{bmatrix} \tag{44b}$$

$$\Lambda = \begin{bmatrix} (\mathcal{A}\mathcal{S} + \mathcal{B}\mathcal{R}) + (\mathcal{A}\mathcal{S} + \mathcal{B}\mathcal{R})^{\mathrm{T}} + \mathcal{J}^{\mathrm{T}}\mathcal{M}\mathcal{J} + \alpha\mathcal{S} & \mathcal{O} \\ \star & -\mathcal{F}\mathcal{M} \end{bmatrix} \tag{44c}$$

$$\mathcal{L} = \begin{bmatrix} \mathcal{I} \\ \mathcal{I} \\ \mathcal{I} \end{bmatrix}, \quad \mathcal{N} = \begin{bmatrix} \sigma_1 & \mathcal{O} & \mathcal{O} \\ \mathcal{O} & \sigma_2 & \mathcal{O} \\ \mathcal{O} & \mathcal{O} & \frac{1}{\mu_1}\tau_2 \end{bmatrix}, \quad \mathcal{Q}^{-1} = \begin{bmatrix} 2\gamma_2 & \mathcal{O} & \mathcal{O} \\ \mathcal{O} & 2\gamma_1 & \mathcal{O} \\ \mathcal{O} & \mathcal{O} & \frac{\mu_2}{\mu_1} \end{bmatrix} \tag{44d}$$

Subsequently, we can reformulate inequality (43) as follows:

$$\begin{bmatrix} \Lambda - (\epsilon^2\kappa)^{-1}\mathcal{T}\mathcal{T}^{\mathrm{T}} & \mathcal{Z} + \mathcal{G}\mathcal{N}^{-1}\mathcal{L} \\ \star & \kappa^{-1} + \mathcal{L}^{\mathrm{T}}(\mathcal{Q}\mathcal{N})^{-1}\mathcal{L} \end{bmatrix} < 0 \tag{45}$$

Applying the Schur lemma and taking into account (45), we obtain:

$$\kappa^{-1} + \mathcal{L}^{\mathrm{T}}(\mathcal{Q}\mathcal{N})^{-1}\mathcal{L} < 0 \tag{46a}$$

$$\begin{aligned} \Lambda - (\epsilon^2\kappa)^{-1}\mathcal{T}\mathcal{T}^{\mathrm{T}} - \left(\mathcal{Z} + \mathcal{G}\mathcal{N}^{-1}\mathcal{L}\right)\left(\kappa^{-1} + \mathcal{L}^{\mathrm{T}}(\mathcal{Q}\mathcal{N})^{-1}\mathcal{L}\right)^{-1} \\ \times \left(\mathcal{Z} + \mathcal{G}\mathcal{N}^{-1}\mathcal{L}\right)^{\mathrm{T}} < 0 \end{aligned} \tag{46b}$$

Utilizing the matrix inversion lemma [16, 18], we have:

$$\left(\kappa^{-1} + \mathcal{L}^{\mathrm{T}}(\mathcal{Q}\mathcal{N})^{-1}\mathcal{L}\right)^{-1} = \kappa - \kappa^2\mathcal{L}^{\mathrm{T}}\mathcal{W}^{-1}\mathcal{L} \tag{47}$$

with

$$\mathcal{W} = \kappa\mathcal{L}\mathcal{L}^{\mathrm{T}} + \mathcal{Q}\mathcal{N} \tag{48}$$

Referring to (47), we can express inequality (46b) as follows:

$$\Lambda - (\epsilon^2\kappa)^{-1}\mathcal{T}\mathcal{T}^{\mathrm{T}} - \left(\mathcal{Z} + \mathcal{G}\mathcal{N}^{-1}\mathcal{L}\right)\left(\kappa - \kappa^2\mathcal{L}^{\mathrm{T}}\mathcal{W}^{-1}\mathcal{L}\right)\left(\mathcal{Z} + \mathcal{G}\mathcal{N}^{-1}\mathcal{L}\right)^{\mathrm{T}} < 0 \tag{49}$$

Considering

$$\Pi = \left(\mathcal{Z} + \mathcal{G}\mathcal{N}^{-1}\mathcal{L}\right)\left(\kappa - \kappa^2\mathcal{L}^{\mathrm{T}}\mathcal{W}^{-1}\mathcal{L}\right)\left(\mathcal{Z} + \mathcal{G}\mathcal{N}^{-1}\mathcal{L}\right)^{\mathrm{T}} \tag{50}$$

and therefore

$$\begin{aligned} \Pi = {} & \kappa\mathcal{Z}\mathcal{Z}^{\mathrm{T}} + \kappa\mathcal{Z}\mathcal{L}^{\mathrm{T}}\mathcal{N}^{-1}\mathcal{G}^{\mathrm{T}} + \kappa\mathcal{G}\mathcal{N}^{-1}\mathcal{L}\mathcal{Z}^{\mathrm{T}} + \kappa\mathcal{G}\mathcal{N}^{-1}\mathcal{L}\mathcal{L}^{\mathrm{T}}\mathcal{N}^{-1}\mathcal{G}^{\mathrm{T}} \\ & - \kappa^2\mathcal{G}\mathcal{N}^{-1}\mathcal{L}\mathcal{L}^{\mathrm{T}}\mathcal{W}^{-1}\mathcal{L}\mathcal{Z}^{\mathrm{T}} - \kappa^2\mathcal{G}\mathcal{N}^{-1}\mathcal{L}\mathcal{L}^{\mathrm{T}}\mathcal{W}^{-1}\mathcal{L}\mathcal{L}^{\mathrm{T}}\mathcal{N}^{-1}\mathcal{G}^{\mathrm{T}} \\ & - \kappa^2\mathcal{Z}\mathcal{L}^{\mathrm{T}}\mathcal{W}^{-1}\mathcal{L}\mathcal{Z}^{\mathrm{T}} - \kappa^2\mathcal{Z}\mathcal{L}^{\mathrm{T}}\mathcal{W}^{-1}\mathcal{L}\mathcal{L}^{\mathrm{T}}\mathcal{N}^{-1}\mathcal{G}^{\mathrm{T}} \end{aligned} \tag{51}$$

By utilizing the expression for $\mathcal{W}$, we can simplify (50) as follows:

$$\Pi = \kappa\mathcal{Z}\mathcal{Z}^{\mathrm{T}} - \left(\kappa\mathcal{Z}\mathcal{L}^{\mathrm{T}} - \mathcal{G}\mathcal{Q}\right)\mathcal{W}^{-1}\left(\kappa\mathcal{Z}\mathcal{L}^{\mathrm{T}} - \mathcal{G}\mathcal{Q}\right)^{\mathrm{T}} + \mathcal{G}\mathcal{Q}\mathcal{N}^{-1}\mathcal{G}^{\mathrm{T}} \tag{52}$$

Therefore, Substituting (52) into (49), we get:

$$\begin{aligned} \Lambda - (\epsilon^2\kappa)^{-1}\mathcal{T}\mathcal{T}^{\mathrm{T}} - \kappa\mathcal{Z}\mathcal{Z}^{\mathrm{T}} + \left(\kappa\mathcal{Z}\mathcal{L}^{\mathrm{T}} - \mathcal{G}\mathcal{Q}\right)\mathcal{W}^{-1}\left(\kappa\mathcal{Z}\mathcal{L}^{\mathrm{T}} - \mathcal{G}\mathcal{Q}\right)^{\mathrm{T}} \\ - \mathcal{G}\mathcal{Q}\mathcal{N}^{-1}\mathcal{G}^{\mathrm{T}} < 0 \end{aligned} \tag{53}$$

As $\mathcal{Q}\mathcal{N} > 0$, inequality (53) can be simplified to:

$$\varLambda - (\epsilon^2\kappa)^{-1}\mathcal{T}\mathcal{T}^{\mathrm{T}} - \kappa\mathcal{Z}\mathcal{Z}^{\mathrm{T}} + \left(\kappa\mathcal{Z}\mathcal{L}^{\mathrm{T}} - \mathcal{G}\mathcal{Q}\right)\mathcal{W}^{-1}\left(\kappa\mathcal{Z}\mathcal{L}^{\mathrm{T}} - \mathcal{G}\mathcal{Q}\right)^{\mathrm{T}} < 0 \quad (54)$$

Since $\kappa < 0$, we conclude that $\mathcal{W} > 0$. Therefore, inequality (54) becomes:

$$\begin{bmatrix} \varLambda - \kappa\mathcal{Z}\mathcal{Z}^{\mathrm{T}} & \mathcal{T} & \kappa\mathcal{Z}\mathcal{L}^{\mathrm{T}} - \mathcal{G}\mathcal{Q} \\ \star & \epsilon^2\kappa\mathcal{I} & \mathcal{O} \\ \star & \star & -\mathcal{W} \end{bmatrix} < 0 \quad (55)$$

Introducing $\sigma_3 = \beta_3^{-1}$, $\mathcal{M}_3 = m_3\mathcal{I}$, $\lambda = \frac{m_3}{\delta^2}$ and $\rho = \frac{\sigma_3}{\epsilon^2}$, we can express the ensuing LMI as follows:

$$\begin{bmatrix} \Xi_{11} & \mathcal{O} & \mathcal{O} & \mathcal{O} & \mathcal{S} & \frac{1}{2\gamma_2}\mathcal{S}\mathcal{C} & -\frac{1}{2\gamma_1}\mathcal{S}\mathcal{C} & -\frac{\mu_1}{\mu_2}\mathcal{S}\mathcal{C}_1^{\mathrm{T}} \\ \star & \Xi_{22} & \mathcal{O} & \rho\mathcal{D}_1\mathcal{B}^{\mathrm{T}} & \mathcal{O} & -\rho\mathcal{D}_1 & -\rho\mathcal{D}_1 & -\rho\mathcal{D}_1 \\ \star & \star & \Xi_{33} & \mathcal{O} & \mathcal{O} & \mathcal{O} & \mathcal{O} & \mathcal{O} \\ \star & \star & \star & \Xi_{44} & \mathcal{O} & -\rho\mathcal{B} & -\rho\mathcal{B} & -\rho\mathcal{B} \\ \star & \star & \star & \star & \Xi_{55} & \mathcal{O} & \mathcal{O} & \mathcal{O} \\ \star & \star & \star & \star & \star & \Xi_{66} & \rho & \rho \\ \star & \star & \star & \star & \star & \star & \Xi_{77} & \rho \\ \star & \star & \star & \star & \star & \star & \star & \Xi_{88} \end{bmatrix} < 0 \quad (56)$$

with

$$\Xi_{11} = (\mathcal{A}\mathcal{S} + \mathcal{B}\mathcal{R}) + (\mathcal{A}\mathcal{S} + \mathcal{B}\mathcal{R})^{\mathrm{T}} + \mathcal{M}_1 + \tau_2\mathcal{D}_2\mathcal{D}_2^{\mathrm{T}} + m_3\mathcal{I} + \alpha\mathcal{S} \quad (57a)$$

$$\Xi_{22} = -\mathcal{M}_1 + \rho\mathcal{D}_1\mathcal{D}_1^{\mathrm{T}} \quad (57b)$$

$$\Xi_{33} = -\frac{1}{\mu_2}\tau_2 \quad (57c)$$

$$\Xi_{44} = -\lambda\mathcal{I} + \rho\mathcal{B}\mathcal{B}^{\mathrm{T}} \quad (57d)$$

$$\Xi_{55} = -\sigma_3\mathcal{I} \quad (57e)$$

$$\Xi_{66} = \rho - \frac{\sigma_1}{2\gamma_2} \quad (57f)$$

$$\Xi_{77} = \rho - \frac{\sigma_2}{2\gamma_1} \quad (57g)$$

$$\Xi_{88} = \rho - \frac{1}{\mu_2}\tau_2 \quad (57h)$$

Furthermore, by multiplying (46a) by κ^2, we can deduce the following:

$$\kappa + \kappa^2\mathcal{L}^{\mathrm{T}}(\mathcal{Q}\mathcal{N})^{-1}\mathcal{L} < 0 \quad (58)$$

Given that $\kappa < 0$ and invoking the Schur complement lemma, we can derive the subsequent LMI condition:

$$\begin{bmatrix} -\rho & -\rho & -\rho & -\rho \\ \star & -\frac{1}{2\gamma_2}\sigma_1 & \mathcal{O} & \mathcal{O} \\ \star & \star & -\frac{1}{2\gamma_1}\sigma_2 & \mathcal{O} \\ \star & \star & \star & -\frac{1}{\mu_2}\tau_2 \end{bmatrix} < 0 \tag{59}$$

It is crucial to highlight that $\rho = \frac{\sigma_3}{\epsilon^2}$ implies $\epsilon = \sqrt{\frac{\sigma_3}{\rho}}$. To minimize ϵ, we aim to minimize $\left(\sigma_3 + \rho^{-1}\right)$. Consequently, let us examine the subsequent condition:

$$\sigma_3 + \rho^{-1} < \nabla_1 \tag{60}$$

Therefore, we deduce that minimizing ϵ corresponds to minimizing ∇_1. It is evident that inequality (60) can be recast like so:

$$\nabla_1 - \sigma_3 - \rho^{-1} > 0 \tag{61}$$

By employing (61) and applying the Schur complement lemma, we derive the subsequent LMI stability condition:

$$\begin{bmatrix} \nabla_1 - \sigma_3 & 1 \\ 1 & \rho \end{bmatrix} > 0 \tag{62}$$

with $\sigma_3 > 0$.

Furthermore, it is noteworthy that $\lambda = \frac{m_3}{\bar{\delta}^2}$. Consequently, $\bar{\delta} = \sqrt{\frac{m_3}{\lambda}}$. Let us also consider $\Omega = \bar{\delta}^{-1} = \sqrt{\frac{\lambda}{m_3}}$. To maximize $\bar{\delta}$, we aim to minimize Ω, and consequently, minimize $\lambda + m_3^{-1}$. Then, let us introduce the subsequent constraint:

$$\lambda + m_3^{-1} < \nabla_2 \tag{63}$$

We establish that maximizing $\bar{\delta}$ involves minimizing ∇_2. Hence, it is evident that inequality (63) can be reformulated as follows:

$$\nabla_2 - \lambda - m_3^{-1} > 0 \tag{64}$$

By utilizing (64) and applying the Schur complement lemma, we can formulate the following LMI stability condition:

$$\begin{bmatrix} \nabla_2 - \lambda & 1 \\ 1 & m_3 \end{bmatrix} > 0 \tag{65}$$

with $\lambda > 0$.

Consequently, the LMI stability condition expressed by (56), (59), (62) and (65) are derived. These conditions are formulated in terms of the unknown variables $\mathcal{S}$, $\mathcal{R}$, $\mathcal{M}_1$, τ_2, m_3, σ_1, σ_2, σ_3, ρ, ∇_1, ∇_2 and λ.

Theorem 1 *Supposing the existence of matrices $\mathcal{S}$, $\mathcal{R}$, $\mathcal{M}_1$, τ_2, m_3, σ_1, σ_2, σ_3, ρ, ∇_1, ∇_2 and λ, the subsequent LMI-based problem is considered:*

$$\begin{array}{ll} min & \nabla_1 + \nabla_2 \\ s.t. & LMI\ (56),\ LMI\ (59),\ LMI\ (62)\ and\ LMI\ (65). \end{array} \tag{66}$$

is feasible, we can conclude that the proposed controller (14) stabilizes the dynamic model (1). Furthermore, the gain matrix $\mathcal{K}$ for the adopted control law can be computed using the following expression:

$$\mathcal{K} = \mathcal{R}\mathcal{S}^{-1} \tag{67}$$

Moreover, the minimum value of the parameter ϵ can be determined like so:

$$\epsilon_{min} = \sqrt{\frac{\sigma_3}{\rho}} \tag{68}$$

Furthermore, the maximum value of the parameter $\bar{\delta}$ can be computed as follows:

$$\bar{\delta}_{max} = \sqrt{\frac{m_3}{\lambda}} \tag{69}$$

4.2 Second LMI Design Approach

In our second method of designing the LMI conditions, we operate under the assumption that the function $\Psi_2(\chi)$ is consistently bounded by a constant value.

As previously highlighted, we redefine the constraint applied to the potential Lyapunov function (18) by incorporating the expression (17). Furthermore, we will retain the same formulation (20) to derive specific LMI conditions related to the feedback gain matrix $\mathcal{K}$.

It is important to note that $\Psi_1(\chi) = \text{sgn}(\dot{\phi}) = \pm 1$. This implies $\Psi_1(\chi)^2 = 1$, therefore, we demonstrate the expression (22).

Considering $\Psi_2(\chi)$ as a scalar function defined in (12b), we can utilize the Young inequality on Eq. (20) to obtain the subsequent expression:

$$2\chi^{\mathrm{T}}\mathcal{P}\mathcal{D}_2\Psi_2(\chi) \leq \chi^{\mathrm{T}}\mathcal{P}\mathcal{M}_2\mathcal{P}\chi + \mathcal{D}_2^{\mathrm{T}}\mathcal{M}_2^{-1}\mathcal{D}_2\Psi_2(\chi)^2 \tag{70}$$

with $\mathcal{M}_2 = \mathcal{M}_2^{\mathrm{T}} > 0$.

Utilizing the expression of $\Psi_2(\chi)$ as defined in (12b), we find that

$$\Psi_2(\chi)^2 = \cos^2(\theta) - 2\cos(\theta_d)\cos(\theta) + \cos^2(\theta_d) \tag{71}$$

Consequently, we can demonstrate the following expressions:

$$\cos^2(\theta) \leq 1 \tag{72a}$$

$$-2\cos(\theta) \leq 0 \tag{72b}$$

Referring to the prior evaluations in (72), we can establish the subsequent inequality:

$$\Psi_2(\chi)^2 \leq \mu_1 \tag{73}$$

where the constant μ_1 is defined by the following relation:

$$\mu_1 = 1 + \cos^2(\theta_d) \tag{74}$$

Therefore, the expression (70) can be reformulated as:

$$2\chi^{\mathrm{T}}\mathcal{P}\mathcal{D}_2\Psi_2(\chi) \leq \chi^{\mathrm{T}}\mathcal{P}\mathcal{M}_2\mathcal{P}\chi + \mu_1\mathcal{D}_2^{\mathrm{T}}\mathcal{M}_2^{-1}\mathcal{D}_2 \tag{75}$$

Furthermore, considering Δ_t as a scalar function, we can apply the Young inequality lemma to the term $2\chi^{\mathrm{T}}\mathcal{P}\mathcal{B}\Delta_t$ in Eq. (20). Assuming that Δ_t adheres to the constraint outlined in (3), we can subsequently derive the inequalities as depicted in (32).

By substituting (22), (75), and (32) into the inequality (20) and subsequently integrating constraint (19), we arrive at the resulting inequality:

$$\begin{aligned}\dot{\mathcal{V}}(\chi) \leq\, & 2\chi^{\mathrm{T}}\mathcal{P}(\mathcal{A} + \mathcal{B}\mathcal{K})\chi + \chi^{\mathrm{T}}\mathcal{P}\mathcal{M}_1\mathcal{P}\chi + \mathcal{D}_1^{\mathrm{T}}\mathcal{M}_1^{-1}\mathcal{D}_1 + \chi^{\mathrm{T}}\mathcal{P}\mathcal{M}_2\mathcal{P}\chi \\ & + \mu_1\mathcal{D}_2^{\mathrm{T}}\mathcal{M}_2^{-1}\mathcal{D}_2 + \chi^{\mathrm{T}}\mathcal{P}\mathcal{M}_3\mathcal{P}\chi + \bar{\delta}^2\mathcal{B}^{\mathrm{T}}\mathcal{M}_3^{-1}\mathcal{B} + \alpha\chi^{\mathrm{T}}\mathcal{P}\chi\end{aligned} \tag{76}$$

Suppose $\mathcal{Y}(\chi) = 2\chi^{\mathrm{T}}\mathcal{P}(\mathcal{A} + \mathcal{B}\mathcal{K})\chi + \chi^{\mathrm{T}}\mathcal{P}\mathcal{M}_1\mathcal{P}\chi + \mathcal{D}_1^{\mathrm{T}}\mathcal{M}_1^{-1}\mathcal{D}_1 + \chi^{\mathrm{T}}\mathcal{P}\mathcal{M}_2\mathcal{P}\chi + \mu_1\mathcal{D}_2^{\mathrm{T}}\mathcal{M}_2^{-1}\mathcal{D}_2 + \chi^{\mathrm{T}}\mathcal{P}\mathcal{M}_3\mathcal{P}\chi + \bar{\delta}^2\mathcal{B}^{\mathrm{T}}\mathcal{M}_3^{-1}\mathcal{B} + \alpha\chi^{\mathrm{T}}\mathcal{P}\chi$. This leads to the following result:

$$\mathcal{Y}(\chi) = \begin{bmatrix}\chi \\ 1\end{bmatrix}^{\mathrm{T}}\begin{bmatrix}\Upsilon_{11} & \mathcal{O} \\ \star & \Upsilon_{22}\end{bmatrix}\begin{bmatrix}\chi \\ 1\end{bmatrix} < 0 \tag{77}$$

with

$$\begin{aligned}\Upsilon_{11} =\, & (\mathcal{P}\mathcal{A} + \mathcal{P}\mathcal{B}\mathcal{K}) + (\mathcal{P}\mathcal{A} + \mathcal{P}\mathcal{B}\mathcal{K})^{\mathrm{T}} \\ & + \mathcal{P}\mathcal{M}_1\mathcal{P} + \mathcal{P}\mathcal{M}_2\mathcal{P} + \mathcal{P}\mathcal{M}_3\mathcal{P} + \alpha\mathcal{P}\end{aligned} \tag{78a}$$

$$\Upsilon_{22} = \mathcal{D}_1^{\mathrm{T}}\mathcal{M}_1^{-1}\mathcal{D}_1 + \mu_1\mathcal{D}_2^{\mathrm{T}}\mathcal{M}_2^{-1}\mathcal{D}_2 + \bar{\delta}^2\mathcal{B}^{\mathrm{T}}\mathcal{M}_3^{-1}\mathcal{B} \tag{78b}$$

By employing the S-procedure, and incorporating the inequalities (77), (17a), (17b), and (17c), we deduce the subsequent stability condition:

$$\begin{bmatrix} \Upsilon_{11} + \beta_3\mathcal{I} & -(\beta_1 - \beta_2)\mathcal{C} \\ \star & \Upsilon_{22} + 2\gamma_2\beta_1 + 2\gamma_1\beta_2 - \epsilon^2\beta_3 \end{bmatrix} < 0 \tag{79}$$

with $\beta_1 > 0$, $\beta_2 > 0$ and $\beta_3 > 0$.

Multiplying both sides of the obtained condition (79) by the matrix $\mathcal{Q} = \begin{bmatrix} \mathcal{S} & \mathcal{O} \\ \mathcal{O} & \mathcal{I} \end{bmatrix}$, where $\mathcal{S} = \mathcal{P}^{-1}$, yields:

$$\begin{bmatrix} \Gamma_{11} & -(\beta_1 - \beta_2)\mathcal{S}\mathcal{C} \\ \star & \Gamma_{22} \end{bmatrix} < 0 \tag{80}$$

where

$$\Gamma_{11} = (\mathcal{A}\mathcal{S} + \mathcal{B}\mathcal{R}) + (\mathcal{A}\mathcal{S} + \mathcal{B}\mathcal{R})^{\mathrm{T}} + \mathcal{M}_1 + \mathcal{M}_2 + \mathcal{M}_3 + \alpha\mathcal{S} + \beta_3\mathcal{S}^2 \tag{81a}$$

$$\Gamma_{22} = \mathcal{D}_1^{\mathrm{T}}\mathcal{M}_1^{-1}\mathcal{D}_1 + \mu_1\mathcal{D}_2^{\mathrm{T}}\mathcal{M}_2^{-1}\mathcal{D}_2 + \bar{\delta}^2\mathcal{B}^{\mathrm{T}}\mathcal{M}_3^{-1}\mathcal{B} + 2\gamma_2\beta_1 + 2\gamma_1\beta_2 - \epsilon^2\beta_3 \tag{81b}$$

where the matrix $\mathcal{R}$ is defined by expression (38).

Let's pose the following matrix variables:

$$\mathcal{M} = \begin{bmatrix} \mathcal{M}_1 & \mathcal{O} & \mathcal{O} \\ \mathcal{O} & \mathcal{M}_2 & \mathcal{O} \\ \mathcal{O} & \mathcal{O} & \mathcal{M}_3 \end{bmatrix} \qquad \mathcal{D} = \begin{bmatrix} \mathcal{D}_1 \\ \mathcal{D}_2 \\ \mathcal{B} \end{bmatrix} \tag{82a}$$

$$\mathcal{F}^{-1} = \begin{bmatrix} \mathcal{I} & \mathcal{O} & \mathcal{O} \\ \mathcal{O} & \mu_1\mathcal{I} & \mathcal{O} \\ \mathcal{O} & \mathcal{O} & \bar{\delta}^2\mathcal{I} \end{bmatrix} \qquad \mathcal{J} = \begin{bmatrix} \mathcal{I} \\ \mathcal{I} \\ \mathcal{I} \end{bmatrix} \tag{82b}$$

The inequality (80) is thus modified to:

$$\begin{bmatrix} \Upsilon_{11} & -(\beta_1 - \beta_2)\mathcal{S}\mathcal{C} \\ \star & \Upsilon_{22} \end{bmatrix} < 0 \tag{83}$$

with

$$\Upsilon_{11} = (\mathcal{A}\mathcal{S} + \mathcal{B}\mathcal{R}) + (\mathcal{A}\mathcal{S} + \mathcal{B}\mathcal{R})^{\mathrm{T}} + \mathcal{J}^{\mathrm{T}}\mathcal{M}\mathcal{J} + \alpha\mathcal{S} + \beta_3\mathcal{S}^2 \tag{84a}$$

$$\Upsilon_{22} = \mathcal{D}^{\mathrm{T}}\mathcal{M}^{-1}\mathcal{F}^{-1}\mathcal{D} + 2\gamma_2\beta_1 + 2\gamma_1\beta_2 - \epsilon^2\beta_3 \tag{84b}$$

Utilizing the Schur complement and taking into account the positive definiteness of $\mathcal{F}\mathcal{M}$, the expression (83) can be rephrased as:

$$\begin{bmatrix} \Upsilon_{11} & -(\beta_1 - \beta_2)\mathcal{SC} & \mathcal{O} \\ \star & 2\gamma_2\beta_1 + 2\gamma_1\beta_2 - \epsilon^2\beta_3 & \mathcal{D}^{\mathrm{T}} \\ \star & \star & -\mathcal{FM} \end{bmatrix} < 0 \tag{85}$$

Furthermore, by performing both pre- and post-multiplication on Eq. (85) with the matrix $\mathcal{V} = \begin{bmatrix} \mathcal{I} & \mathcal{O} & \mathcal{O} \\ \mathcal{O} & \mathcal{O} & \mathcal{I} \\ \mathcal{O} & \mathcal{I} & \mathcal{O} \end{bmatrix}$, we obtain the subsequent expression:

$$\begin{bmatrix} \Upsilon_{11} & \mathcal{O} & -(\beta_1 - \beta_2)\mathcal{SC} \\ \star & -\mathcal{FM} & \mathcal{D} \\ \star & \star & 2\gamma_2\beta_1 + 2\gamma_1\beta_2 - \epsilon^2\beta_3 \end{bmatrix} < 0 \tag{86}$$

To simplify, we define the following variables:

$$\xi^{-1} = -\epsilon^2\beta_3, \qquad \sigma_1 = \beta_1^{-1}, \qquad \sigma_2 = \beta_2^{-1} \tag{87a}$$

$$\mathcal{T} = \begin{bmatrix} \mathcal{S} \\ \mathcal{O} \end{bmatrix}, \qquad \mathcal{G} = \begin{bmatrix} -\mathcal{SC} & \mathcal{SC} \\ \mathcal{O} & \mathcal{O} \end{bmatrix}, \qquad \mathcal{Z} = \begin{bmatrix} \mathcal{O} \\ \mathcal{D} \end{bmatrix} \tag{87b}$$

$$\Lambda = \begin{bmatrix} (\mathcal{AS} + \mathcal{BR}) + (\mathcal{AS} + \mathcal{BR})^{\mathrm{T}} + \mathcal{J}^{\mathrm{T}}\mathcal{MJ} + \alpha\mathcal{S} & \mathcal{O} \\ \star & -\mathcal{FM} \end{bmatrix} \tag{87c}$$

$$\mathcal{L} = \begin{bmatrix} \mathcal{I} \\ \mathcal{I} \end{bmatrix}, \qquad \mathcal{N} = \begin{bmatrix} \sigma_1 & \mathcal{O} \\ \mathcal{O} & \sigma_2 \end{bmatrix}, \qquad \mathcal{Q}^{-1} = \begin{bmatrix} 2\gamma_2 & \mathcal{O} \\ \mathcal{O} & 2\gamma_1 \end{bmatrix} \tag{87d}$$

Consequently, the expression (86) transforms into:

$$\begin{bmatrix} \Lambda - (\epsilon^2\xi)^{-1}\mathcal{TT}^{\mathrm{T}} & \mathcal{Z} + \mathcal{GN}^{-1}\mathcal{L} \\ \star & \xi^{-1} + \mathcal{L}^{\mathrm{T}}(\mathcal{QN})^{-1}\mathcal{L} \end{bmatrix} < 0 \tag{88}$$

By applying the Schur complement lemma and considering (88), we can derive the subsequent inequalities:

$$\xi^{-1} + \mathcal{L}^{\mathrm{T}}(\mathcal{QN})^{-1}\mathcal{L} < 0 \tag{89a}$$

$$\Lambda - (\epsilon^2\xi)^{-1}\mathcal{TT}^{\mathrm{T}} - \left(\mathcal{Z} + \mathcal{GN}^{-1}\mathcal{L}\right)\left(\xi^{-1} + \mathcal{L}^{\mathrm{T}}(\mathcal{QN})^{-1}\mathcal{L}\right)^{-1} \times \left(\mathcal{Z} + \mathcal{GN}^{-1}\mathcal{L}\right)^{\mathrm{T}} < 0 \tag{89b}$$

Applying the the matrix inversion lemma to the term on the left-hand side of expression (89b), we derive:

$$\left(\xi^{-1} + \mathcal{L}^{\mathrm{T}}(\mathcal{QN})^{-1}\mathcal{L}\right)^{-1} = \xi - \xi^2\mathcal{L}^{\mathrm{T}}\mathcal{W}^{-1}\mathcal{L} \tag{90}$$

with

$$\mathcal{W} = \xi\mathcal{LL}^{\mathrm{T}} + \mathcal{QN} \tag{91}$$

Subsequently, referring to expression (90), we can establish that the Eq. (89b) is equivalent to:

$$\Lambda - (\epsilon^2\xi)^{-1}\mathcal{T}\mathcal{T}^{\mathrm{T}} - \left(\mathcal{Z} + \mathcal{G}\mathcal{N}^{-1}\mathcal{L}\right)\left(\xi - \xi^2\mathcal{L}^{\mathrm{T}}\mathcal{W}^{-1}\mathcal{L}\right)\left(\mathcal{Z} + \mathcal{G}\mathcal{N}^{-1}\mathcal{L}\right)^{\mathrm{T}} < 0 \quad (92)$$

Let us consider

$$\Pi = \left(\mathcal{Z} + \mathcal{G}\mathcal{N}^{-1}\mathcal{L}\right)\left(\xi - \xi^2\mathcal{L}^{\mathrm{T}}\mathcal{W}^{-1}\mathcal{L}\right)\left(\mathcal{Z} + \mathcal{G}\mathcal{N}^{-1}\mathcal{L}\right)^{\mathrm{T}} \quad (93)$$

As both $\mathcal{N}$ and $\mathcal{W}$ are symmetric, the expansion of Eq. (93) results in the following:

$$\begin{aligned}\Pi = &\xi\mathcal{Z}\mathcal{Z}^{\mathrm{T}} + \xi\mathcal{Z}\mathcal{L}^{\mathrm{T}}\mathcal{N}^{-1}\mathcal{G}^{\mathrm{T}} + \xi\mathcal{G}\mathcal{N}^{-1}\mathcal{L}\mathcal{Z}^{\mathrm{T}} + \xi\mathcal{G}\mathcal{N}^{-1}\mathcal{L}\mathcal{L}^{\mathrm{T}}\mathcal{N}^{-1}\mathcal{G}^{\mathrm{T}}\\ &- \xi^2\mathcal{G}\mathcal{N}^{-1}\mathcal{L}\mathcal{L}^{\mathrm{T}}\mathcal{W}^{-1}\mathcal{L}\mathcal{Z}^{\mathrm{T}} - \xi^2\mathcal{G}\mathcal{N}^{-1}\mathcal{L}\mathcal{L}^{\mathrm{T}}\mathcal{W}^{-1}\mathcal{L}\mathcal{L}^{\mathrm{T}}\mathcal{N}^{-1}\mathcal{G}^{\mathrm{T}}\\ &- \xi^2\mathcal{Z}\mathcal{L}^{\mathrm{T}}\mathcal{W}^{-1}\mathcal{L}\mathcal{Z}^{\mathrm{T}} - \xi^2\mathcal{Z}\mathcal{L}^{\mathrm{T}}\mathcal{W}^{-1}\mathcal{L}\mathcal{L}^{\mathrm{T}}\mathcal{N}^{-1}\mathcal{G}^{\mathrm{T}} \end{aligned} \quad (94)$$

Given that $\mathcal{W} = \xi\mathcal{L}\mathcal{L}^{\mathrm{T}} + \mathcal{Q}\mathcal{N}$, we can straightforwardly present the subsequent equations:

$$\xi\mathcal{G}\mathcal{N}^{-1}\mathcal{L}\mathcal{L}^{\mathrm{T}}\mathcal{N}^{-1}\mathcal{G}^{\mathrm{T}} = \mathcal{G}\mathcal{N}^{-1}\mathcal{W}\mathcal{N}^{-1}\mathcal{G}^{\mathrm{T}} - \mathcal{G}\mathcal{Q}\mathcal{N}^{-1}\mathcal{G}^{\mathrm{T}} \quad (95a)$$

$$\begin{aligned}\xi^2\mathcal{G}\mathcal{N}^{-1}\mathcal{L}\mathcal{L}^{\mathrm{T}}\mathcal{W}^{-1}\mathcal{L}\mathcal{L}^{\mathrm{T}}\mathcal{N}^{-1}\mathcal{G}^{\mathrm{T}} &= \mathcal{G}\mathcal{N}^{-1}\mathcal{W}\mathcal{N}^{-1}\mathcal{G}^{\mathrm{T}}\\ &- 2\mathcal{G}\mathcal{Q}\mathcal{N}^{-1}\mathcal{G}^{\mathrm{T}} + \mathcal{G}\mathcal{Q}\mathcal{W}^{-1}\mathcal{Q}\mathcal{G}^{\mathrm{T}}\end{aligned} \quad (95b)$$

$$\xi^2\mathcal{G}\mathcal{N}^{-1}\mathcal{L}\mathcal{L}^{\mathrm{T}}\mathcal{W}^{-1}\mathcal{L}\mathcal{Z}^{\mathrm{T}} = \xi\mathcal{G}\mathcal{N}^{-1}\mathcal{L}\mathcal{Z}^{\mathrm{T}} - \xi\mathcal{G}\mathcal{Q}\mathcal{W}^{-1}\mathcal{L}\mathcal{Z}^{\mathrm{T}} \quad (95c)$$

By utilizing (95), we can streamline the expression (93) as follows:

$$\Pi = \xi\mathcal{Z}\mathcal{Z}^{\mathrm{T}} - \left(\xi\mathcal{Z}\mathcal{L}^{\mathrm{T}} - \mathcal{G}\mathcal{Q}\right)\mathcal{W}^{-1}\left(\xi\mathcal{Z}\mathcal{L}^{\mathrm{T}} - \mathcal{G}\mathcal{Q}\right)^{\mathrm{T}} + \mathcal{G}\mathcal{Q}\mathcal{N}^{-1}\mathcal{G}^{\mathrm{T}} \quad (96)$$

Hence, by replacing this ultimate expression (96) into inequality (92), we obtain:

$$\begin{aligned}\Lambda - (\epsilon^2\xi)^{-1}\mathcal{T}\mathcal{T}^{\mathrm{T}} - \xi\mathcal{Z}\mathcal{Z}^{\mathrm{T}} + \left(\xi\mathcal{Z}\mathcal{L}^{\mathrm{T}} - \mathcal{G}\mathcal{Q}\right)\mathcal{W}^{-1}\left(\xi\mathcal{Z}\mathcal{L}^{\mathrm{T}} - \mathcal{G}\mathcal{Q}\right)^{\mathrm{T}}&\\ - \mathcal{G}\mathcal{Q}\mathcal{N}^{-1}\mathcal{G}^{\mathrm{T}} < 0&\end{aligned} \quad (97)$$

As $\mathcal{Q}\mathcal{N} > 0$, we can restate inequality (97) like so:

$$\Lambda - (\epsilon^2\xi)^{-1}\mathcal{T}\mathcal{T}^{\mathrm{T}} - \xi\mathcal{Z}\mathcal{Z}^{\mathrm{T}} + \left(\xi\mathcal{Z}\mathcal{L}^{\mathrm{T}} - \mathcal{G}\mathcal{Q}\right)\mathcal{W}^{-1}\left(\xi\mathcal{Z}\mathcal{L}^{\mathrm{T}} - \mathcal{G}\mathcal{Q}\right)^{\mathrm{T}} < 0 \quad (98)$$

Moreover, considering that $\xi < 0$, $\mathcal{L}\mathcal{L}^{\mathrm{T}} > 0$, and $\mathcal{N} > 0$, we can deduce that $\mathcal{W} = \xi\mathcal{L}\mathcal{L}^{\mathrm{T}} + \mathcal{Q}\mathcal{N} > 0$. Therefore, by utilizing the Schur complement, inequality (98) can be reformulated as follows:

$$\begin{bmatrix} \Lambda - \xi \mathcal{Z}\mathcal{Z}^{\mathrm{T}} & \mathcal{T} & \xi \mathcal{Z}\mathcal{L}^{\mathrm{T}} - \mathcal{G}\mathcal{Q} \\ \star & \epsilon^2 \xi \mathcal{I} & \mathcal{O} \\ \star & \star & -\mathcal{W} \end{bmatrix} < 0 \tag{99}$$

By substituting expressions of $\Lambda, \xi, \mathcal{L}\mathcal{T}, \mathcal{Z}, \mathcal{G}, \mathcal{Q}$ and $\mathcal{W}$ into (99) and introducing $\sigma_3 = \beta_3^{-1}$, $\mathcal{M}_3 = m_3\mathcal{I}$, $\lambda = \frac{m_3}{\delta^2}$ and $\rho = \frac{\sigma_3}{\epsilon^2}$ we obtain the subsequent LMI:

$$\begin{bmatrix} \Xi_{11} & \mathcal{O} & \mathcal{O} & \mathcal{O} & \mathcal{S} & \frac{1}{2\gamma_2}\mathcal{S}\mathcal{C} & -\frac{1}{2\gamma_1}\mathcal{S}\mathcal{C} \\ \star & \Xi_{22} & \rho\mathcal{D}_1\mathcal{D}_2^{\mathrm{T}} & \rho\mathcal{D}_1\mathcal{B}^{\mathrm{T}} & \mathcal{O} & -\rho\mathcal{D}_1 & \rho\mathcal{D}_1 \\ \star & \star & \Xi_{33} & \rho\mathcal{D}_2\mathcal{B}^{\mathrm{T}} & \mathcal{O} & -\rho\mathcal{D}_2 & \rho\mathcal{D}_2 \\ \star & \star & \star & \Xi_{44} & \mathcal{O} & -\rho\mathcal{B} & \rho\mathcal{B} \\ \star & \star & \star & \star & \Xi_{55} & \mathcal{O} & \mathcal{O} \\ \star & \star & \star & \star & \star & \Xi_{66} & \rho \\ \star & \star & \star & \star & \star & \star & \Xi_{77} \end{bmatrix} < 0 \tag{100}$$

with

$$\Xi_{11} = (\mathcal{A}\mathcal{S} + \mathcal{B}\mathcal{R}) + (\mathcal{A}\mathcal{S} + \mathcal{B}\mathcal{R})^{\mathrm{T}} + \mathcal{M}_1 + \mathcal{M}_2 + m_3\mathcal{I} + \alpha\mathcal{S} \tag{101a}$$

$$\Xi_{22} = -\mathcal{M}_1 + \rho\mathcal{D}_1\mathcal{D}_1^{\mathrm{T}} \tag{101b}$$

$$\Xi_{33} = -\frac{1}{\mu_1}\mathcal{M}_2 + \rho\mathcal{D}_2\mathcal{D}_2^{\mathrm{T}} \tag{101c}$$

$$\Xi_{44} = -\lambda\mathcal{I} + \rho\mathcal{B}\mathcal{B}^{\mathrm{T}} \tag{101d}$$

$$\Xi_{55} = -\sigma_3\mathcal{I} \tag{101e}$$

$$\Xi_{66} = \rho - \frac{\sigma_1}{2\gamma_2} \tag{101f}$$

$$\Xi_{77} = \rho - \frac{\sigma_2}{2\gamma_1} \tag{101g}$$

Moreover, employing (89a) and multiplying it by the quantity ξ^2, we deduce the following inequality:

$$\xi + \xi^2\mathcal{L}^{\mathrm{T}}(\mathcal{Q}\mathcal{N})^{-1}\mathcal{L} < 0 \tag{102}$$

Given that $\xi < 0$ and $\mathcal{Q}\mathcal{N} > 0$, the application of the Schur complement to expression (102), yields the equivalent form:

$$\begin{bmatrix} \xi & \xi\mathcal{L}^{\mathrm{T}} \\ \star & -\mathcal{Q}\mathcal{N} \end{bmatrix} < 0 \tag{103}$$

As a result, we arrive at the following LMI:

$$\begin{bmatrix} -\rho & -\rho & -\rho \\ \star & -\frac{1}{2\gamma_2}\sigma_1 & \mathcal{O} \\ \star & \star & -\frac{1}{2\gamma_1}\sigma_2 \end{bmatrix} < 0 \tag{104}$$

Notably, $\rho = \frac{\sigma_3}{\epsilon^2}$ implies $\epsilon = \sqrt{\frac{\sigma_3}{\rho}}$. The goal is to minimize ϵ, consequently minimizing $(\sigma_3 + \rho^{-1})$. Therefore, by considering (60), we derive the LMI stability condition (62). Thus, we deduce that minimizing ϵ entails minimizing ∇_1.

Furthermore, expressing λ as $\lambda = \frac{m_3}{\bar{\delta}^2}$ results in $\bar{\delta} = \sqrt{\frac{m_3}{\lambda}}$. Assuming $\Omega = \bar{\delta}^{-1} = \sqrt{\frac{\lambda}{m_3}}$, the objective is to maximize $\bar{\delta}$ by minimizing Ω, equivalent to minimizing $\lambda + m_3^{-1}$. To accomplish this, we consider condition (63) and derive the LMI stability condition presented in (65). Thus, it is clear that to maximize $\bar{\delta}$, we need to minimize ∇_2.

Hence, we deduce the LMI stability conditions given by (100), (104), (62), and (65). These conditions are formulated with respect to the unknown variables $\mathcal{S}$, $\mathcal{R}$, $\mathcal{M}_1$, $\mathcal{M}_2$, m_3, σ_1, σ_2, σ_3, ρ, ∇_1, ∇_2, and λ.

Theorem 2 *Supposing the existence of matrices $\mathcal{S}$, $\mathcal{R}$, $\mathcal{M}_1$, $\mathcal{M}_2$, along with scalar values m_3, σ_1, σ_2, σ_3, ρ, ∇_1, ∇_2, and λ, which satisfy the subsequent LMI-based problem:*

$$\begin{array}{ll} \textit{min} & \nabla_1 + \nabla_2 \\ \textit{s.t.} & \textit{LMI}\ (100),\ \textit{LMI}\ (104),\ \textit{LMI}\ (62)\ \textit{and LMI}\ (65) \end{array} \tag{105}$$

Thus, we can deduce that the proposed control law (14) ensures the stabilization of the dynamic model (1). The gain matrix $\mathcal{K}$ of the adopted control law can be determined using the equation (67). Moreover, the maximum value of the parameter $\bar{\delta}$ can be computed using the expression (69), and the minimum value of the parameter ϵ can be calculated using the relation (68).

4.3 LMI Criteria for Minimizing Controller Gain Size

Emphasizing the significance of the preceding theorems, it becomes evident that solving the LMI problem holds the potential for a significant gain $\mathcal{K}$. Consequently, the primary focus revolves around minimizing the magnitude of $\mathcal{K}$. In pursuit of this goal, two supplementary LMIs will be presented in the upcoming theorems, serving to augment the practicality and real-world relevance of the proposed control methodology. These additional LMIs are explicitly detailed like so [18]:

$$\begin{bmatrix} \ell_1 \mathcal{I} & \mathcal{R}^{\mathrm{T}} \\ \mathcal{R} & \mathcal{I} \end{bmatrix} > 0 \tag{106a}$$

$$\begin{bmatrix} \ell_2 \mathcal{I} & \mathcal{I} \\ \mathcal{I} & \mathcal{S} \end{bmatrix} > 0 \tag{106b}$$

In the preceding two LMIs outlined in (106b), the optimization focus lies on minimizing the two parameters, ℓ_1 and ℓ_2, with the ultimate aim of reducing the magnitude of $\mathcal{K}$.

Remark 2 Our objective in this study is to enhance the precise control of a lower limb exoskeleton, with a specific focus on the critical knee joint [27, 29, 30, 32, 52]. To achieve this, we have implemented a control strategy based on state feedback, tailored to address the inherent challenges in this domain. What distinguishes our research from other studies [3, 21, 28, 31, 35, 44] is the utilization of the LMI technique, ensuring efficient control and stability of the knee rehabilitation exoskeleton robot. This innovation significantly contributes to the existing body of knowledge and enhances control performance by demonstrating its adeptness in managing parametric uncertainties and disturbances.

5 Simulation Results

In this section, we showcase the simulation outcomes for the two implemented control methods in this study. Our main goal is to demonstrate the efficacy of the formulated LMI criteria in determining the controller gain $\mathcal{K}$ to ensure the stability of the knee exoskeleton, as depicted in Fig. 1. The diverse parameters of the robot, described by the dynamic equation (1), are provided in detail in Table 1.

It is crucial to emphasize that our attention is centered on presenting numerical simulation results for the diverse control methods utilized in this study. A subsequent comparative analysis between these methods will be undertaken. To enable a meaningful comparison of the controlled robotic system's behavior, we will present two simulation scenarios involving identical external disturbances applied to the knee exoskeleton robotic system. Furthermore, all simulations employing the proposed

Table 1 The parameter's adopted values of the knee exoskeleton robot

Parameter	Value	Nominal parameter	Nominal value	Unit
ϑ	0.323 + 0.1	$\vartheta_\star$	0.323	kg m^2/rad
m	0.000105 + 0.01	$m_\star$	0.000105	kg
l	0.25 + 0.05	$l_\star$	0.25	m
f_v	0.35 + 0.1	$f_v^\star$	0.35	N m s/rad
f_s	0.059 + 0.05	$f_s^\star$	0.059	N m/A
g	9.8			

control law will start from the same initial position, with the same desired position chosen for the experiments.

5.1 First Simulation Results

In the first simulation results, we will set the desired angular position θ_d to a constant value, specifically $\theta_d = 50°$. Furthermore, in this simulation scenario, an external disturbance Δ_t will be introduced in the form of a sinusoidal input, defined as follows:

$$\Delta_t = \bar{\delta} \times \sin(\omega_f \times t) \tag{107}$$

with ω_f representing the angular frequency of the signal, in our case, we will set $\omega_f = 10\pi$. Additionally, this disturbance input will only be active between 2 and 7 seconds. Beyond this time interval, $\Delta_t = 0$.

5.1.1 Results Obtained Using the First Design Methodology

Applying the established LMI conditions from Theorem 1, we address the LMI-based minimization problem derived from this theorem. Additionally, we integrate two supplementary LMI conditions outlined in (106b), with the selection of $\alpha = 1$. This yields:

$$\mathcal{K} = \begin{bmatrix} -1.6302 & -0.7302 \end{bmatrix} \tag{108a}$$

$$\epsilon_{\min} = 2.5616 \tag{108b}$$

$$\bar{\delta}_{\max} = 0.5004 \tag{108c}$$

Incorporating the feedback gain specified in (108) into the utilized controller (14), the simulation results presented in Fig. 2 illustrate our achieved outcomes. Evidently, the robot successfully attains the desired state θ_d. Moreover, the control effort u converges to the desired control input as the robot stabilizes.

5.1.2 Results Obtained Using the Second Design Methodology

Utilizing the LMI stability conditions outlined in Theorem 2, we address the LMI problem derived from this theorem. Moreover, we incorporate the two supplementary LMI conditions described in (106b) with $\alpha = 1$. We obtain:

$$\mathcal{K} = \begin{bmatrix} -1.6116 & -0.7237 \end{bmatrix} \tag{109a}$$

$$\epsilon_{\min} = 2.5661 \tag{109b}$$

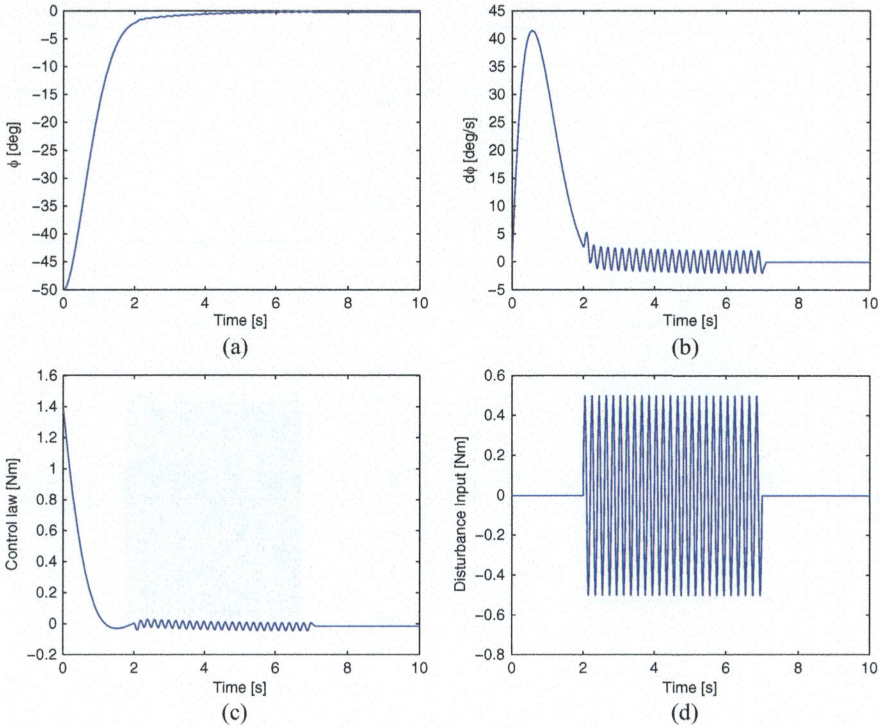

Fig. 2 First simulation results obtained utilizing the first design methodology. Evolution of: **a** the angular position error ϕ, **b** the angular velocity error $\dot{\phi}$, **c** the adopted controller u, and **d** the external disturbance Δ_t

$$\bar{\delta}_{\max} = 0.5016 \tag{109c}$$

Applying the feedback gains $\mathcal{K}$ as described in (109) to the adopted control law (14), we get the graphical results depicted in Fig. 3. These figures illustrate that the robot is effectively controlled and successfully reaches the desired state. Furthermore, at the equilibrium point, the control effort u is zero.

5.2 *Second Simulation Results*

In the second simulation results, we will choose a different desired position, specifically $\theta_d = 20°$. However, we will employ a distinct form of external disturbance compared to the first simulation. In this case, the external disturbance Δ_t will be in the form of a random signal, active only between 2 and 7 seconds. Outside this time interval, Δ_t will be set to zero. Thus, the expression for Δ_t is as follows:

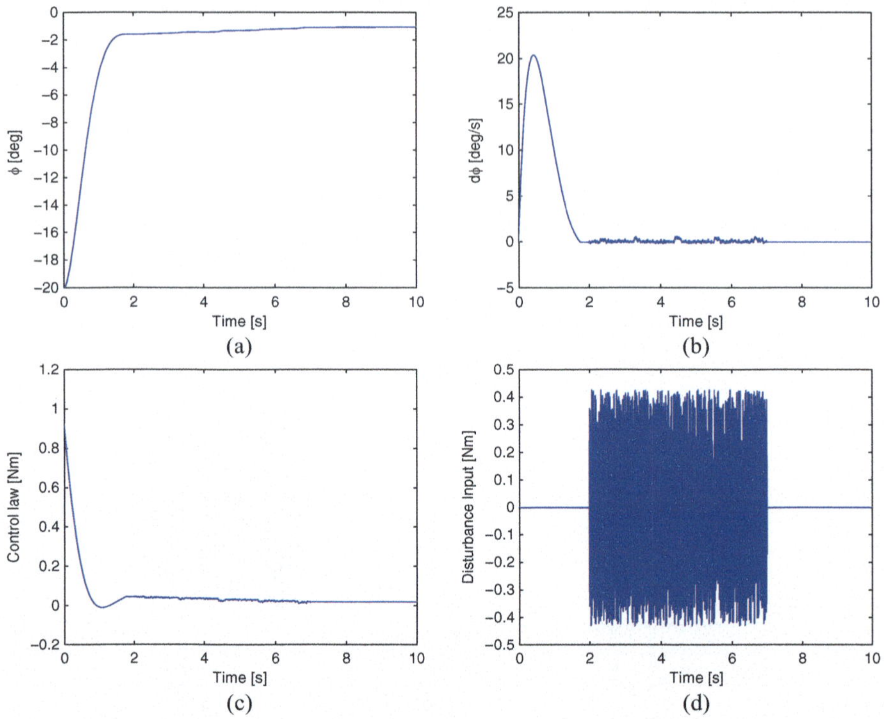

Fig. 3 First simulation results obtained utilizing the second design methodology. Evolution of: **a** the angular position error ϕ, **b** the angular velocity error $\dot{\phi}$, **c** the proposed controller u, and **d** the external disturbance Δ_t

$$\Delta_t = \bar{\delta} \times (2 \times \text{rand} - 1) \tag{110}$$

where the function rand represents a random signal ranging between 0 and 1.

5.2.1 Results Obtained Using the First Design Methodology

Utilizing the LMI conditions established in Theorem 1 and addressing the LMI-based minimization problem derived from this theorem, incorporating the two additional LMI conditions described in (106b), and setting $\alpha = 2$, we get the following outcomes:

$$\mathcal{K} = \begin{bmatrix} -2.7314 & -1.0864 \end{bmatrix} \tag{111a}$$

$$\epsilon_{\min} = 2.9544 \tag{111b}$$

$$\bar{\delta}_{\max} = 0.4287 \tag{111c}$$

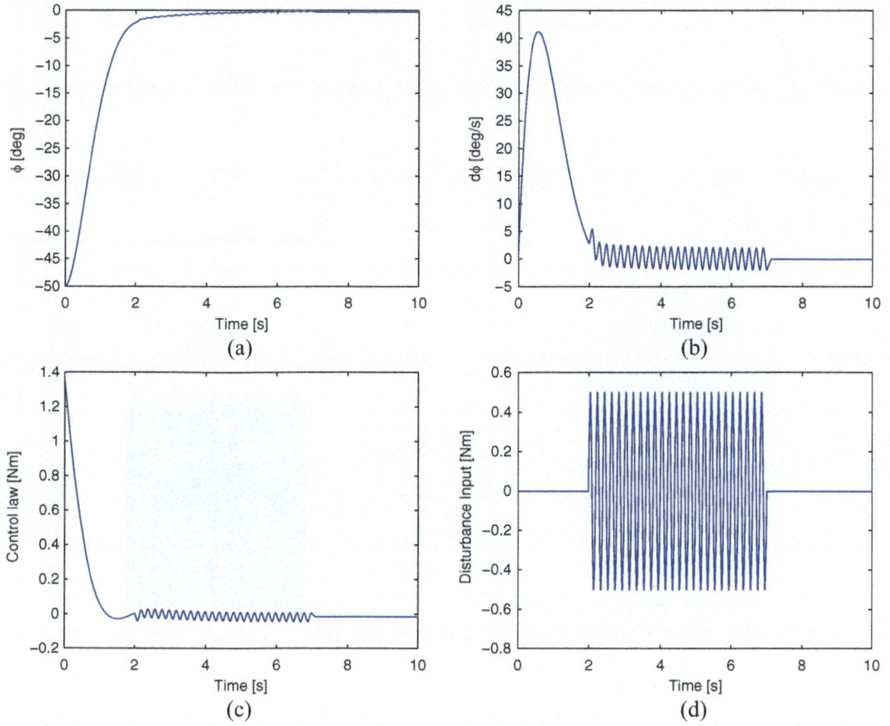

Fig. 4 Second simulation results obtained using the first design methodology. Evolution of: **a** the angular position error ϕ, **b** the angular velocity error $\dot{\phi}$, **c** the proposed controller u, and **d** the external disturbance Δ_t

Using the feedback gain $\mathcal{K}$ outlined in (111) within the proposed control law (14), we derive the graphical results showcased in Fig. 4. These figures demonstrate the successful control of the robot achieving the desired state. Furthermore, at the equilibrium point, the control effort u reaches zero.

5.2.2 Results Obtained Using the Second Design Methodology

Utilizing the improved design methodology based on the LMI conditions presented in Theorem 2 and solving the LMI problem outlined in this theorem while incorporating the two supplementary LMI conditions described in (106b), with $\alpha = 2$, the obtained results are as follows:

$$\mathcal{K} = \begin{bmatrix} -2.6799 & -1.0746 \end{bmatrix} \tag{112a}$$

$$\epsilon_{\min} = 2.9784 \tag{112b}$$

$$\bar{\delta}_{\max} = 0.4309 \tag{112c}$$

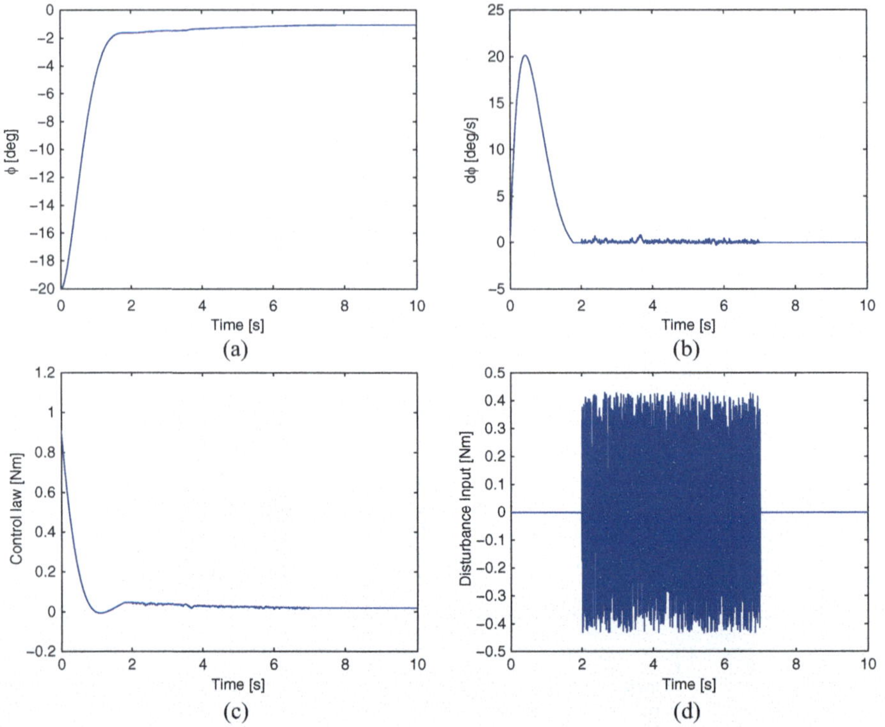

Fig. 5 Second simulation results obtained utilizing the second design methodology. Evolution of: **a** the angular position error ϕ, **b** the angular velocity error $\dot{\phi}$, **c** the proposed controller u, and **d** the external disturbance Δ_t

Utilizing the feedback gain $\mathcal{K}$ specified in (112) within the control law (14), we derived the graphical representations depicted in Fig. 5. Consequently, these figures demonstrate the successful control of the exoskeleton robot, achieving the desired state. Moreover, the control effort u reaches zero upon the stabilization of the exoskeleton robot at the intended location.

5.3 Discussion

The proposed controller effectively addresses the challenge of regulating the position of the knee exoskeleton robotic system depicted in Fig. 1. This accomplishment is realized through the application of two distinct approaches to compute the feedback gain. Across all simulations, the robot is precisely guided to achieve the target position denoted as θ_d. Consequently, the angular position error ϕ converges to zero, as evidenced by Figs. 2a, 3a, 4a, and 5a. Likewise, in these simulations, the angular velocity error $\dot{\phi}$ also converges to zero, as illustrated in Figs. 2b, 3b, 4b, and 5b. It is important to note that some fluctuations occur due to the presence of a disturbing torque Δ_t. Nevertheless, these outcomes demonstrate the robustness of the controller against external disturbances.

Moreover, visual representations of the external disturbance applied to the knee exoskeleton in each of the two simulations are depicted in Figs. 2d, 3d, 4d, and 5d. This disturbance is illustrated by the torque load Δ_t. In the initial simulation, the lumped disturbance is characterized as a sinusoidal signal with a range between $-\bar{\delta}$ and $\bar{\delta}$, with the torque applied only during the time interval from 2 to 7 s. Subsequently, the simulation outcomes influenced by this lumped disturbing torque Δ_t are illustrated in Figs. 2 and 3. It is evident that the knee exoskeleton system displays oscillatory behavior around its equilibrium position. As the impact of the perturbing torque diminishes, the controlled knee exoskeleton robot returns to its desired state. Notably, the first approach yields $\bar{\delta} = 0.5004$, while the second approach yields $\bar{\delta} = 0.5016$. In the subsequent simulation, the disturbing torque is characterized as a randomly time-varying signal within the range of $-\bar{\delta}$ to $\bar{\delta}$, with the torque applied exclusively between 2 and 7 s. The results influenced by the lumped disturbing torque Δ_t are presented in Figs. 4 and 5. Once again, the oscillatory behavior of the knee exoskeleton system around its equilibrium position is observed. Upon the reduction of the perturbing torque's influence, the controlled knee exoskeleton robot resumes its desired state. As previously mentioned, the first approach yields $\bar{\delta} = 0.4287$, while the second approach yields $\bar{\delta} = 0.4309$.

Additionally, Figs. 2c, 3c, 4c and 5c display the temporal progression of the implemented control law u across all scenarios. It is observable that upon stabilization of the knee exoskeleton robot under the influence of the torque load acting as an external disturbance, the control input u converges to the desired controller u_d.

Moreover, it is crucial to emphasize that the applied control effort u to the joint, in both developed approaches across the two distinct simulations, is notably minimal, as observed in Figs. 2c, 3c, 4c, and 5c. Nevertheless, in both simulations, the second design method consistently produces a lower initial value for the control effort compared to the first design method. For instance, in the first simulation results using the initial approach, the control effort at the beginning of the simulation equals 1.387 (as depicted in Fig. 2), whereas the second approach yields a control effort at the start of the simulation equal to 1.404 (as shown in Fig. 3c).

Additionally, it is noteworthy that the minimum value of ϵ and the maximum value of $\bar{\delta}$ are nearly identical for both developed approaches, as presented in (108) and (109) for the first simulation, and in (111) and (112) for the second simulation. However, the first simulation results provide a slightly smaller value for $\epsilon_{\min}$ compared to that obtained in the second simulation. Nonetheless, the second simulation yields a slightly larger value for $\bar{\delta}$ than what was obtained in the first simulation.

Hence, the outcomes from the two design methodologies demonstrate the effective control of the actuated knee exoskeleton, successfully attaining the desired position. Consequently, the controller for the knee exoskeleton robot proves to be effective in all scenarios.

Table 2 Assessment of the effectiveness of the proposed affine state-feedback controller across two design methodologies using various performance metrics

	First simulation		Second simulation	
Indicator	Approach 1	Approach 2	Approach 1	Approach 2
MAE (ϕ)	0.0801	0.0808	0.0422	0.0431
MAE ($\dot{\phi}$)	0.0956	0.0956	0.0334	0.0333
MSE (ϕ)	0.0440	0.0443	0.0061	0.0062
MSE ($\dot{\phi}$)	0.0456	0.0453	0.0085	0.0084
RMSE (ϕ)	0.2098	0.2105	0.0780	0.0786
RMSE ($\dot{\phi}$)	0.2136	0.2128	0.0923	0.0915
CEI (u)	0.2203	0.2187	0.1255	0.1242
MATI (u)	1.4036	1.3873	0.9255	0.9076

Moreover, the performance of the proposed affine state-feedback controller was evaluated using various indicators across two design methodologies and two simulation scenarios, as shown in Table 2. The Mean Absolute Error (MAE) for joint angle (ϕ) was found to be 0.0801 and 0.0808 for approaches 1 and 2, respectively, in the first simulation, while in the second simulation, it decreased to 0.0422 and 0.0431 for approaches 1 and 2, respectively. Similarly, the MAE for joint velocity ($\dot{\phi}$) remained consistent at 0.0956 for both approaches in the first simulation. while in the second simulation, it decreased to 0.0334 and 0.0333 for approaches 1 and 2, respectively.

Moving to the Mean Squared Error (MSE), for joint angle (ϕ), the values were 0.0440 and 0.0443 for approaches 1 and 2, respectively, in the first simulation, and 0.0061 and 0.0062 in the second simulation. For joint velocity ($\dot{\phi}$), the MSE values were 0.0456 and 0.0453 for approaches 1 and 2, respectively, in the first simulation, and 0.0085 and 0.0084 in the second simulation.

The Root Mean Squared Error (RMSE) followed a similar trend, with values of 0.2098 and 0.2105 for joint angle (ϕ) in the first simulation and 0.0780 and 0.0786 in the second simulation for approaches 1 and 2, respectively. For joint velocity ($\dot{\phi}$), the RMSE values were 0.2136 and 0.2128 in the first simulation and 0.0923 and 0.0915 in the second simulation for approaches 1 and 2, respectively.

Furthermore, the Control Effort Indicator (CEI) and Maximum Absolute Torque Indicator (MATI) were also evaluated. The CEI values were 0.2203 and 0.2187 for approaches 1 and 2, respectively, in the first simulation, and 0.1255 and 0.1242 in the second simulation. Similarly, the MATI values were 1.4036 and 1.3873 for approaches 1 and 2, respectively, in the first simulation, and 0.9255 and 0.9076 in the second simulation.

These results underscore the effectiveness of the controller in achieving precise and robust control in knee exoskeleton systems.

6 Conclusion and Future Works

In this research, we introduced a novel control strategy tailored for a 1-DoF knee rehabilitation exoskeleton robot [21, 27, 28], focusing on precise position control to address challenges such as state constraints, parameter uncertainties, and external disturbances. Two different design methods were employed to formulate LMI stability conditions on the feedback gains of the adopted affine state-feedback controller. Our approach utilizes a quadratic Lyapunov function and incorporates mathematical tools, including the Schur complement, Young's inequality, matrix inversion lemma, and the S-procedure lemma. The derived LMIs ensure robust stabilization of the knee exoskeleton, even in the presence of uncertainties and external disruptions.

Simulation studies were conducted to validate the efficiency of the proposed LMI stability conditions. The results demonstrated the controller's effectiveness in achieving robust position control of the knee exoskeleton, providing valuable insights for the advancement of rehabilitation exoskeleton control strategies.

Looking ahead, our future work aims to implement a filtering mechanism to further reduce the amplitude or duration of observed oscillations in the controlled system. Additionally, our focus is on conducting extensive experimental tests to validate the proposed LMI approach in real-world applications, assessing its robustness in various scenarios, and addressing challenges in existing lower limb exoskeletons, such as actuator saturation, similar to the approach presented in [19]. Furthermore, we plan to explore the design of a static output feedback controller using the LMI approach, as discussed in [22].

References

1. Ahmed, S., Wang, H., Tian, Y.: Robust adaptive fractional-order terminal sliding mode control for lower-limb exoskeleton. Asian Journal of Control **21**(1), 473–482 (2019)
2. Al Rezage, G., Tokhi, M.: Fuzzy PID control of lower limb exoskeleton for elderly mobility. In: 2016 IEEE International Conference on Automation, Quality and Testing, Robotics (AQTR), pp. 1–6 (2016)
3. Aljuboury, A.S., Hameed, A.H., Ajel, A.R., Humaidi, A.J., Alkhayyat, A., Mhdawi, A.K.A.: Robust adaptive control of knee exoskeleton-assistant system based on nonlinear disturbance observer. Actuators **11**(3) (2022)
4. Baragash, R.S., Aldowah, H., Ghazal, S.: Virtual and augmented reality applications to improve older adults' quality of life: A systematic mapping review and future directions. Digital health **8**, 20552076221132099 (2022)
5. Baud, R., Manzoori, A.R., Ijspeert, A., Bouri, M.: Review of control strategies for lower-limb exoskeletons to assist gait. Journal of NeuroEngineering and Rehabilitation **18**(1), 119 (2021)
6. Bergmann, L., Voss, D., Leonhardt, S., Ngo, C.: Lower-limb exoskeleton with compliant actuators: Human cooperative control. IEEE Transactions on Medical Robotics and Bionics **5**(3), 717–729 (2023)
7. Bkekri, R., Benamor, A., Alouane, M.A., Fried, G., Messaoud, H.: Robust adaptive super twisting controller: methodology and application of a human-driven knee joint orthosis. Industrial Robot **46**(4), 481–489 (2019)

8. Brahmi, B., Saad, M., Luna, C.O., Archambault, P.S., Rahman, M.H.: Passive and active rehabilitation control of human upper-limb exoskeleton robot with dynamic uncertainties. Robotica **36**(11), 1757–1779 (2018)
9. Clemson, L., Singh, M.A.F., Bundy, A., Cumming, R.G., Manollaras, K., O'Loughlin, P., Black, D.: Integration of balance and strength training into daily life activity to reduce rate of falls in older people (the life study): randomised parallel trial. Bmj **345** (2012)
10. Daachi, M.E., Madani, T., Daachi, B., Djouani, K.: A radial basis function neural network adaptive controller to drive a powered lower limb knee joint orthosis. Applied Soft Computing **34**, 324–336 (2015)
11. de Araujo, T.B., Martins, W.R., Freitas, M.P., Camargos, E., Mota, J., Safons, M.P.: An exploration of equine-assisted therapy to improve balance, functional capacity, and cognition in older adults with alzheimer disease. Journal of geriatric physical therapy **42**(3), E155–E160 (2019)
12. Esquenazi, A., Talaty, M., Jayaraman, A.: Powered exoskeletons for walking assistance in persons with central nervous system injuries: a narrative review. PM&R **9**(1), 46–62 (2017)
13. Fareh, R., Elsabe, A., Baziyad, M., Kawser, T., Brahmi, B., Rahman, M.H.: Will your next therapist be a robot?-a review of the advancements in robotic upper extremity rehabilitation. Sensors **23**(11) (2023)
14. Gambhire, S., Kishore, D.R., Londhe, P., Pawar, S.: Review of sliding mode based control techniques for control system applications. International Journal of dynamics and control **9**, 363–378 (2021)
15. Gerber, A.M., Botes, R., Mostert, A., Vorster, A., Buskens, E.: A cohort study of elderly people in bloemfontein, south africa, to determine health-related quality of life and functional abilities. South African Medical Journal **106**(3), 298–301 (2016)
16. Gritli, H.: Robust master-slave synchronization of chaos in a one-sided 1-DoF impact mechanical oscillator subject to parametric uncertainties and disturbances. Mechanism and Machine Theory **142**, 103610 (2019)
17. Gritli, H.: LMI-based robust stabilization of a class of input-constrained uncertain nonlinear systems with application to a helicopter model. Complexity **2020**, 7025761 (2020)
18. Gritli, H., Belghith, S.: Robust feedback control of the underactuated Inertia Wheel Inverted Pendulum under parametric uncertainties and subject to external disturbances: LMI formulation. Journal of The Franklin Institute **355**(18), 9150–9191 (2018)
19. Gritli, H., Belghith, S.: LMI-based synthesis of a robust saturated controller for an underactuated mechanical system subject to motion constraints. European Journal of Control **57**, 179–193 (2021)
20. Gritli, H., Jenhani, S.: LMI-based state feedback control of the underactuated inertia wheel inverted pendulum to the unstable upright position. Journal of Vibration Testing and System Dynamics **8**(2), 207–234 (2024). https://doi.org/10.5890/JVTSD.2024.06.005
21. Gritli, H., Jenhani, S.: Position control of robotic systems via linear controllers with application to a lower limb rehabilitation exoskeleton robot: Design and comparative analysis. In: E. Campos-Cantón, G. Huerta-Cuellar, E. Zambrano-Serrano, E. Tlelo-Cuautle (eds.) Complex Systems and Their Applications, pp. 123–151. Springer Nature Switzerland, Cham (2024)
22. Gritli, H., Zemouche, A., Belghith, S.: On LMI conditions to design robust static output feedback controller for continuous-time linear systems subject to norm-bounded uncertainties. International Journal of Systems Science **52**(1), 12–46 (2021)
23. Hassani, W., Mohammed, S., Rifaï, H., Amirat, Y.: Powered orthosis for lower limb movements assistance and rehabilitation. Control Engineering Practice **26**, 245–253 (2014)
24. Herrmann, M.: Population aging and economic development: anxieties and policy responses. Journal of Population Ageing **5**, 23–46 (2012)
25. Islam, M.R., Assad-Uz-Zaman, M., Rahman, M.H.: Design and control of an ergonomic robotic shoulder for wearable exoskeleton robot for rehabilitation. International Journal of Dynamics and Control **8**, 312–325 (2020)
26. Jansen, C.M., Windau, J.E., Bonutti, P.M., Brillhart, M.V.: Treatment of a knee contracture using a knee orthosis incorporating stress-relaxation techniques. Physical therapy **76**(2), 182–186 (1996)

27. Jenhani, S., Gritli, H.: A composite robust position control design for an actuated knee rehabilitation exoskeleton. In: 2023 20th International Multi-Conference on Systems, Signals & Devices (SSD), pp. 129–134 (2023)
28. Jenhani, S., Gritli, H.: Enhancing knee rehabilitation exoskeleton control via a robust LMI-based strategy and by considering state constraints. In: 2023 IEEE 11th International Conference on Systems and Control (ICSC), pp. 905–911 (2023)
29. Jenhani, S., Gritli, H.: LMI-based design of an affine PD controller for the robust stabilization of the knee joint of a lower-limb rehabilitation exoskeleton. In: 2023 IEEE International Conference on Advanced Systems and Emergent Technologies (IC_ASET), pp. 1–7. IEEE (2023)
30. Jenhani, S., Gritli, H.: Robust LMI-based state-feedback control of a knee exoskeleton robotic system. In: 2023 20th International Multi-Conference on Systems, Signals & Devices (SSD), pp. 121–128 (2023)
31. Jenhani, S., Gritli, H.: LMI-based design of a robust affine control law for the position control of a knee exoskeleton robot: Comparative analysis of stability conditions. In: E. Campos-Cantón, G. Huerta-Cuellar, E. Zambrano-Serrano, E. Tlelo-Cuautle (eds.) Complex Systems and Their Applications, pp. 95–122. Springer Nature Switzerland, Cham (2024)
32. Jenhani, S., Gritli, H.: An LMI-based robust state-feedback controller design for the position control of a knee rehabilitation exoskeleton robot: Comparative analysis. Measurement and Control **57**(9), 1326–1346 (2024). https://doi.org/10.1177/00202940241236295
33. Jenhani, S., Gritli, H., Carbone, G.: Comparison between some nonlinear controllers for the position control of Lagrangian-type robotic systems. Chaos Theory and Applications **4**(4), 179–196 (2022)
34. Kalita, B., Narayan, J., Dwivedy, S.K.: Development of active lower limb robotic-based orthosis and exoskeleton devices: A systematic review. International Journal of Social Robotics **3**(4), 775–793 (2021)
35. Khamar, M., Edrisi, M.: Designing a backstepping sliding mode controller for an assistant human knee exoskeleton based on nonlinear disturbance observer. Mechatronics **54**, 121–132 (2018)
36. Liu, J., Fang, H., Xu, J.: Online adaptive pid control for a multi-joint lower extremity exoskeleton system using improved particle swarm optimization. Machines **10**(1), 21 (2021)
37. Lysholm, J., Nordin, M., Ekstrand, J., Gillquist, J.: The effect of a patella brace on performance in a knee extension strength test in patients with patellar pain. The American Journal of Sports Medicine **12**(2), 110–112 (1984)
38. Madani, T., Daachi, B., Djouani, K.: Adaptive controller based on uncertainty parametric estimation using backstepping and sliding mode techniques: Application to an active orthosis. In: 2014 European Control Conference (ECC), pp. 1869–1874 (2014)
39. Narayan, J., Dwivedy, S.K.: Preliminary design and development of a low-cost lower-limb exoskeleton system for paediatric rehabilitation. Proceedings of the Institution of Mechanical Engineers, Part H: Journal of Engineering in Medicine **235**(5), 530–545 (2021)
40. Narayan, J., Dwivedy, S.K.: Lower limb exoskeletons for pediatric gait rehabilitation: A brief review of design, actuation, and control schemes. In: 2023 IEEE International Conference on Advanced Systems and Emergent Technologies (IC_ASET), pp. 1–6 (2023)
41. Narayan, J., Dwivedy, S.K.: Towards neuro-fuzzy compensated PID control of lower extremity exoskeleton system for passive gait rehabilitation. IETE Journal of Research **69**(2), 778–795 (2023)
42. Narayan, J., Gritli, H., Dwivedy, S.K.: Fast terminal sliding mode control with rapid reaching law for a pediatric gait exoskeleton system. International Journal of Intelligent Robotics and Applications **8**, 76–95 (2024)
43. Narayan, J., Kalita, B., Dwivedy, S.K.: Adaptive backstepping human-cooperative control of a pediatric gait exoskeleton system with high-and low-level admittance. Proceedings of the Institution of Mechanical Engineers, Part I: Journal of Systems and Control Engineering p. 09596518231191390 (2023)

44. Rifai, H., Mohammed, S., Daachi, B., Amirat, Y.: Adaptive control of a human-driven knee joint orthosis. In: 2012 IEEE International Conference on Robotics and Automation, pp. 2486–2491 (2012)
45. Rifaï, H., Mohammed, S., Hassani, W., Amirat, Y.: Nested saturation based control of an actuated knee joint orthosis. Mechatronics **23**(8), 1141–1149 (2013)
46. Rupal, B.S., Rafique, S., Singla, A., Singla, E., Isaksson, M., Virk, G.S.: Lower-limb exoskeletons: Research trends and regulatory guidelines in medical and non-medical applications. International Journal of Advanced Robotic Systems **14**(6), 1729881417743554 (2017)
47. Sun, F., Norman, I.J., While, A.E.: Physical activity in older people: a systematic review. BMC public health **13**(1), 1–17 (2013)
48. Sun, W., Lin, J.W., Su, S.F., Wang, N., Er, M.J.: Reduced adaptive fuzzy decoupling control for lower limb exoskeleton. IEEE transactions on cybernetics **51**(3), 1099–1109 (2020)
49. Topini, A., Sansom, W., Secciani, N., Bartalucci, L., Ridolfi, A., Allotta, B.: Variable admittance control of a hand exoskeleton for virtual reality-based rehabilitation tasks. Frontiers in neurorobotics **15**, 789743 (2022)
50. Turki, F., Gritli, H., Belghith, S.: An LMI-based design of a robust state-feedback control for the master-slave tracking of an impact mechanical oscillator with double-side rigid constraints and subject to bounded-parametric uncertainty. Communications in Nonlinear Science and Numerical Simulation **82**, 105020 (2020)
51. Van der Loos, H.M., Reinkensmeyer, D.J., Guglielmelli, E.: Rehabilitation and health care robotics. Springer handbook of robotics pp. 1685–1728 (2016)
52. Wang, Z., Yang, C., Zhang, S., Zhang, S., Yi, C., Ding, Z., Wei, B., Jiang, F.: Knee flexion-assisted method for human-exoskeleton system. IEEE Transactions on Neural Systems and Rehabilitation Engineering **31**, 2800–2808 (2023)
53. Zhao, Y.: The impact of population ageing on the economy. International Journal of Social Sciences and Public Administration **2**(2), 108–121 (2024)

Robust Position Control of an Exoskeleton Robot for Knee Rehabilitation Utilizing an LMI-Based Affine State-Feedback Controller

Sahar Jenhani and Hassène Gritli

Abstract Rehabilitation exoskeleton robots are designed to assist individuals with lower limb dysfunction. This work proposes a robust control strategy to regulate the position of a rehabilitation exoskeleton system at the knee joint level, employing an LMI-based linear state-feedback controller. The methodology involves the utilization of the nonlinear dynamics that incorporates elements such as frictions and uncertainties in the system parameters. Additionally, the expanded dynamics is formulated to encapsulate the difference between the nonlinear dynamic model and its linearized approximation. Subsequently, a Lyapunov function conducive to the context is selected to formulate the LMI conditions governing the feedback gain of the proposed control law via two distinct design approaches, thereby ensuring the stabilization of the regulated dynamics at the desired position. We validate the robustness of the controller through the introduction of external disturbances. Furthermore, a comparison between the two proposed control strategies is achieved. Finally, simulation results and performance indexes show that the formulated controller effectively controls the position of the knee exoskeleton robot under the effects of uncertainties and external disturbances.

1 Introduction

During the past few years, robotics has made significant advancements, sparking a technological revolution that extends far beyond factories and is reshaping healthcare dramatically. One particularly noteworthy advancement in this technological progress is the development of rehabilitation exoskeleton robots. These robots have the potential to restore movement and independence to individuals, significantly

S. Jenhani · H. Gritli (✉)
Laboratory of Robotics, Informatics and Complex Systems (RISC Lab—LR16ES07), National Engineering School of Tunis, University of Tunis El Manar, Le Belvédère, 1002 Tunis, Tunisia
e-mail: hassene.gritli@istic.ucar.tn

H. Gritli
Higher Institute of Information and Communication Technologies, University of Carthage, Technopole of Borj Cédria, Route de Soliman, BP 123, Hammam Chatt, 1164 Ben Arous, Tunisia

M. Mittal and J. Narayan (eds.), *Intelligent Cyber-Physical Systems for Healthcare Solutions*, https://doi.org/10.1007/978-981-97-8983-2_13

improving their quality of life [37, 44, 47]. Rehabilitation exoskeleton robots are a blend of cutting-edge technologies like bionics, robotics, and medicine. They are not just about providing assistance; they're tailored to each individual's needs and aid in recovery from conditions such as strokes, spinal injuries, and muscle weakness in the legs. By integrating these technologies, these robots aim to restore people's independence and enhance mobility. Technology is revolutionizing healthcare, and smart healthcare is the current trend. These devices enable healthcare professionals to obtain more accurate data promptly and deliver improved treatments. They also facilitate remote patient monitoring, benefiting patients and streamlining the work of healthcare providers. Additionally, utilizing these devices may potentially reduce hospital expenditures and enhance overall efficiency. Rehabilitation exoskeleton robots play a significant role in smart healthcare, as they are continuously advancing in understanding human locomotion and devising strategies to assist individuals with impaired mobility. They incorporate innovative concepts from robotics, bionics, and medicine to enhance strength and activity levels [13, 21, 45]. The accurate control of exoskeleton positions is crucial for assisting individuals with mobility challenges, particularly the elderly, during their rehabilitation process. Exoskeletons show promise in addressing mobility, balance, and independence issues, potentially enhancing the overall quality of life for these individuals. However, the field of position control in exoskeletons encounters several challenges, including system non-linearity, uncertainties related to factors such as friction, and external disturbances. Overcoming these obstacles is essential to ensure precise and stable control, especially during rehabilitation. Researchers have explored various control methods, including traditional approaches, model-based control, adaptive control, and neural networks, all with the goal of enhancing exoskeleton functionality, adaptability, stability, and user safety [6, 35, 39, 41, 42].

The evolving domain of exoskeleton robotic systems' control is heavily influenced by the intricate dynamics of human-robot interaction [7, 20, 34, 39, 42]. Specifically focusing on lower limb exoskeletons, a multitude of investigations has been dedicated to uncovering an array of control strategies, all aimed at optimizing walking support and enhancing gait rehabilitation outcomes [6, 31, 38, 39, 46]. This dynamic landscape has witnessed the emergence of diverse methodologies, including trajectory tracking, impedance control, robust control, neural networks, and fuzzy logic, each offering significant promise as pivotal avenues for exploration [3, 9, 22]. The crux of these endeavors revolves around achieving precision in joint motions, ensuring seamless alignment with individual user preferences, and prioritizing an overarching commitment to user safety. Furthermore, a parallel line of inquiry has directed its attention towards a critical facet: position control within actuated lower limb exoskeleton robotic systems, with a particular emphasis on the knee joint [4, 23, 25, 26, 28, 40, 43, 50]. Given the knee joint's indispensable role in fundamental activities such as walking and bearing weight, its significance in the design of exoskeletons for rehabilitation and assistance cannot be overstated. By honing in on refining knee joint control, researchers strive to enhance the functionality and effectiveness of these systems, forging a path towards more intuitive and impactful human-machine interaction in the field of exoskeleton technology [7, 39, 40].

Our primary focus in this work revolves around enhancing precise control of a lower limb exoskeleton, with specific emphasis on the crucial knee joint [4, 19, 24, 25, 27, 50]. To achieve this goal, we have introduced an innovative control strategy based on state feedback, purposefully designed to overcome the unique challenges inherent in this field. What sets our research apart from previous studies is our application of a Linear Matrix Inequality (LMI) approach, which ensures efficient control and stabilization of the knee rehabilitation exoskeleton robot. This innovation significantly contributes to the existing body of knowledge by demonstrating its ability to better handle uncertainties and disturbances, thereby enhancing control performance. At the heart of our approach is the core objective of maintaining the exoskeleton precisely at its intended position, even when faced with uncertainties and external disturbances. Our research is dedicated to refining position control in knee rehabilitation exoskeletons, with a strong focus on the knee joint's pivotal role in activities such as walking and bearing weight. Achieving precise and stable motion control is paramount to facilitating effective and safe rehabilitation exercises.

To achieve robust position control, we propose a control strategy based on a state-feedback controller. We consider the nonlinear dynamics of the knee exoskeleton robot, accounting for factors such as friction and uncertain parameters. Moreover, we develop the expanded dynamics that outline the distinction between the nonlinear dynamic model and its linearized approximation. Subsequently, the Lyapunov stability theory serves as the foundation for our control strategy, enabling us to design conditions through LMIs based on the feedback gain of the adopted controller via two different approaches. The first design approach utilizes the nonlinear dynamics of the exoskeleton, while the second design method is based on the linearized dynamic model. These LMI conditions ensure the stabilization of the controlled system at the desired position. The efficacy and robustness of the proposed control strategy are evaluated through extensive simulations, including scenarios with external disturbances. A comparative analysis between the two proposed control techniques will be conducted. Finally, we will illustrate several simulation outcomes that demonstrate the effectiveness and performance of our developed controller for robust position control of the active knee exoskeleton robot under uncertainties and external disturbances.

In our study, we have placed a strong focus on pushing the boundaries of lower limb exoskeleton technology by enhancing precise position control, with a particular emphasis on the critical knee joint. What sets our work apart from prior research is the introduction of a groundbreaking control strategy rooted in state feedback. This strategy has been finely tuned to address the challenges we have identified, aiming for the exact stabilization of the exoskeleton at its intended position, even in the presence of uncertainties and disturbances. Crucially, our innovative approach capitalizes on the LMI methodology, marking a significant leap in our field [15–17, 25, 30, 49]. It is worth noting that the utilization of the LMI approach significantly boosts control stability, surpassing the effectiveness of traditional methods. Our methodology also excels in handling uncertainties and disturbances, surpassing the capabilities of conventional techniques. This forward-thinking approach ultimately elevates control performance, cementing our contribution as a valuable advancement in the realm of exoskeleton control systems.

The main contributions of this chapter may be summarized as follows:

- Proposal of a control strategy based on a state-feedback controller to achieve robust position control of the knee exoskeleton robot, taking into consideration factors such as friction and uncertain parameters.
- Through the Lyapunov approach, the Young inequality, and the S-procedure Lemma [14–16, 18, 49], some stabilization conditions, formulated as nonlinear matrix inequalities that are nontraceable, are developed.
- Development of expanded dynamics that distinguish between the nonlinear dynamic model and its linearized approximation.
- Utilization of Lyapunov stability theory as the foundation for the control strategy, facilitating the design of conditions through LMIs based on the feedback gain of the adopted controller via two different approaches. The first approach utilizes the nonlinear dynamics of the exoskeleton, while the second approach is based on the linearized dynamic model. These LMI conditions ensure the stabilization of the controlled system at the desired position.
- Evaluation of the effectiveness and robustness of the proposed control strategy through extensive simulations, including scenarios with external disturbances.
- Conducting a comparative analysis between the two proposed control techniques.

The remainder of this study is structured in the subsequent manner: Sect. 2 presents a brief overview of some examples of lower limb rehabilitation exoskeletons robotic systems. We describe the nonlinear dynamics of the knee exoskeleton in Sect. 3. Section 4 provides the linearized dynamic model and the adopted affine state-feedback controller. The position control using the nonlinear dynamics is described in Sect. 5. Section 6 presents the position control using the expanded dynamics. Section 7 demonstrates the results of the simulations. Finally, in Sect. 8, we provide the conclusion and discuss some future works.

2 A Brief Review on Lower Limb Rehabilitation Exoskeleton Robotic Systems

In recent decades, the field of lower-limb rehabilitation exoskeleton robotic systems has witnessed substantial growth, garnering increasing attention and research efforts [11, 52]. This surge in interest can be largely attributed to the utilization of groundbreaking devices like Lokomat in clinical rehabilitation settings. These exoskeleton systems play a pivotal role in assisting individuals, particularly the elderly and those with lower limb motor impairments, in their journey toward recovery and enhanced mobility. Within this realm, two distinct rehabilitation approaches come to the forefront. The first approach revolves around passive rehabilitation [2, 53], where the user's effort is minimized. This method involves repetitively guiding the limbs along pre-defined trajectories set by rehabilitation professionals. It is particularly applicable to individuals who have undergone procedures such as spinal cord injuries or total knee arthroplasty. On the other hand, the second approach, known as active rehabilitation, centers on fostering a symbiotic interaction between the exoskeleton and the user. This approach empowers users to voluntarily initiate lower limb movements by generating torque through their own efforts.

The development of wearable mechanical devices like exoskeleton robots necessitates a fusion of multiple disciplines, encompassing sensing, control mechanisms, information technology, and computer science. Notable contributions from both industry and academia have led to significant progress in both the theoretical understanding and practical implementation of these rehabilitation exoskeleton robotic systems. Categorically, these therapeutic robots are classified into two main categories based on their intended applications: overground systems and treadmill-based setups [46]. This segmentation underscores the diversity of exoskeleton technology and its diverse applications in the field of rehabilitation and enhanced mobility.

The field of exoskeleton robotics, exemplified by notable creations such as ALEX, Lokomat, and LOPES (depicted in Fig. 1), is specifically tailored to provide targeted gait training to patients, a fact that becomes particularly pronounced when coupled with treadmill-based exercises. These innovator robots encompass an exoskeleton framework that assists and augments leg movements while being complemented by a body weight support mechanism. This ingenious body weight support system efficiently counteracts the pull of gravity on the legs, thereby enhancing safety, equilibrium, and stability throughout the training regimen [11, 46].

Over the treadmill field, the landscape of exoskeleton innovation further extends. Figure 2 showcases a cadre of overground exoskeleton robots poised to aid patients in the restoration of overground walking functionality. Noteworthy exemplars include eLEGS, a product of meticulous research [10, 48]. Additionally, the MINDWALKER [46], ReWalk [51], Indego [5], and HAL (Hybrid Assistive Limb) [32] exoskeletons are manifest embodiments of this paradigm shift towards supporting natural locomotion.

The view widens further with Fig. 3, which reveals a range of lower limb rehabilitation exoskeletons in static environments. Among them is the EksoWalker and the

Fig. 1 Examples of treadmill-based lower limb rehabilitation exoskeletons (from [46], licensed under CC-BY 4.0)

Fig. 2 Examples of overground lower limb rehabilitation exoskeletons (from [46], licensed under CC-BY 4.0)

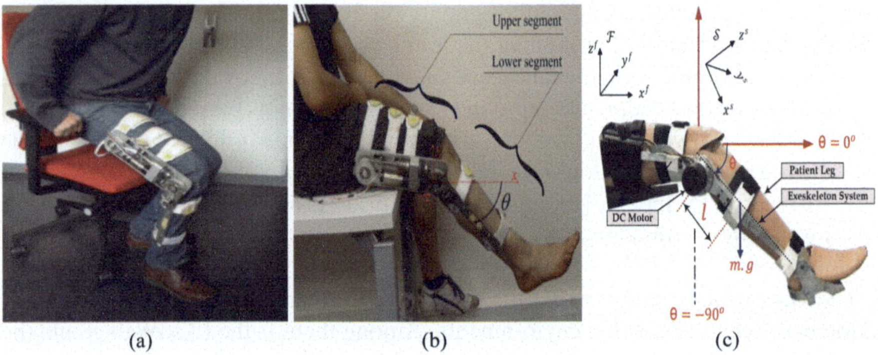

Fig. 3 Examples of lower limb rehabilitation exoskeletons in the setting position. **a** [12], **b** [36], and **c** [1]

orthosis EICOSI [1, 8, 12, 36], an innovative creation designed to facilitate complex rehabilitation maneuvers while securing the user in a fixed posture. This wide array of exoskeleton innovations underscores the ever-changing landscape of robotics in healthcare, illuminating the myriad ways technology can be harnessed to improve mobility, restore independence, and improve quality of life.

3 Nonlinear Dynamics of the Knee Rehabilitation Exoskeleton

3.1 Adopted Knee Exoskeleton

This study examines a seated knee exoskeleton, illustrated in Fig. 4, with a movable shank allowing knee joint flexion and extension [43]. At $\theta = 0°$, the knee is fully extended, while at $\theta = 90°$, full flexion is achieved. The exoskeleton consists of two connected segments (Fig. 4): the upper part houses the actuator and represents the thigh, while the lower part signifies the shank. Straps secure both parts to the wearer's lower limb. The exoskeleton imitates human knee joint movement in the sagittal plane. This one-degree-of-freedom knee exoskeleton is chosen for its simplicity and restricted range of motion, making it appropriate for the study.

3.2 Nonlinear Dynamics of the Exoskeleton Robot

Considering the effects of solid and viscous frictions, the nonlinear dynamics of the exoskeleton robotic system is given as follows:

$$\nu_\star \ddot{\theta} = u - f_v^\star \dot{\theta} + a_\star \cos(\theta) - f_s^\star \text{sgn}(\dot{\theta}) + \Delta_t \tag{1}$$

Here, the scalar value $a_\star$ is defined as mgl, with m representing the system's mass, g standing for the acceleration due to gravity, and l indicating a characteristic length, the system's inertia is denoted as $\nu_\star$, and the applied torque is indicated by u. The

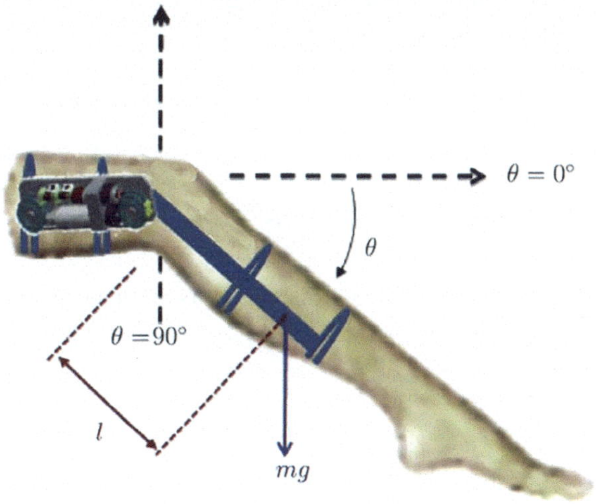

Fig. 4 Visual depiction of the knee exoskeleton's geometry, adopted from [43]

coefficient for viscous friction is represented by $f_v^\star$. while $f_s^\star$ corresponds to the solid friction coefficient. Furthermore, Δ_t represents the term for total or lumped disturbance and is given by:

$$\Delta_t = \Delta_{pu} + \Delta_{ed} + \Delta_{ud} + \Delta_{hl} \tag{2}$$

where Δ_{pu} represents the term for parametric uncertainties, Δ_{ed} represents the term for external disturbances, Δ_{ud} represents the term for unmodeled dynamics, and Δ_{hl} represents the term for the force exerted by the human leg.

Taking into account that $\phi = \theta - \theta_d$, then $\dot{\theta} = \dot{\phi}$ and $\ddot{\theta} = \ddot{\phi}$, where θ_d represents the predicted state where the knee exoskeleton robotic system will be regulated. Thus, the expression (1) becomes:

$$\nu_\star \ddot{\phi} = u - f_v^\star \dot{\phi} - f_s^\star \mathrm{sgn}(\dot{\phi}) + a_\star \cos(\phi + \theta_d) + \Delta_t \tag{3}$$

4 Linearized Dynamics and Adopted Control Law

4.1 Intended Controller at the Equilibrium

The robotic system has to exert some control effort to keep itself in this equilibrium position, where $\dot{\theta}_d = 0$, after the controller u has successfully moved it to the intended state θ_d. Let the required control input at the desired state be represented by u_d. Then, we may construct the following equation using the expression (3):

$$0 = u_d + a_\star \cos(\theta_d) \tag{4}$$

We can demonstrate that the required control input u_d is dictated by the following equation at the equilibrium point:

$$u_d = -a_\star \cos(\theta_d) \tag{5}$$

4.2 Linearized Dynamic Model

The primary objective of this section is to linearize the nonlinear dynamics (3) at the intended state (θ_d, u_d). Taking $f_s^\star \mathrm{sgn}(\dot{\theta}) = 0$ and $\Delta_t = 0$, we can demonstrate the subsequent expression:

$$\nu_\star \ddot{\phi} = u - f_v^\star \dot{\phi} + a_\star \cos(\theta) \tag{6}$$

Furthermore, by using the following approximation

$$\cos(\theta) \approx \cos(\theta_d) - \sin(\theta_d)\phi \tag{7}$$

we can rewrite the previous Eq. (6) as follows:

$$\nu_\star \ddot{\phi} = u - f_v^\star \dot{\phi} + a_\star \cos(\theta_d) - a_\star \sin(\theta_d)\phi \tag{8}$$

Hence, utilizing the derived intended controller (5) and considering $\Delta u = u - u_d$, we can express the linear approximation of the nonlinear dynamics (3) as follows:

$$\nu_\star \ddot{\phi} = \Delta u - f_v^\star \dot{\phi} - a_\star \sin(\theta_d)\phi \tag{9}$$

4.3 Expanded Nonlinear Dynamic Model

We may create a dynamic model to represent the distinction between the nonlinear dynamics (3) and its linear approximation given by (9), as follows:

$$\begin{aligned} \nu_\star \ddot{\phi} = {} & \Delta u - f_v^\star \dot{\phi} + a_\star \cos(\phi + \theta_d) - f_s^\star \operatorname{sgn}(\dot{\phi}) + \Delta_t \\ & - a_\star \sin(\theta_d)\phi + u_d + a_\star \sin(\theta_d)\phi \end{aligned} \tag{10}$$

Furthermore, by utilizing the linearized dynamic model (5), the previous expression (10) becomes:

$$\begin{aligned} \nu_\star \ddot{\phi} = {} & \Delta u - f_v^\star \dot{\phi} - a_\star \sin(\theta_d)\phi \\ & - f_s^\star \operatorname{sgn}(\dot{\phi}) + a_\star \left(\cos(\phi + \theta_d) - \cos(\theta_d) + \sin(\theta_d)\phi\right) + \Delta_t \end{aligned} \tag{11}$$

4.4 Adopted Affine State-Feedback Control Law

Our primary goal in this study is to solve the position control problem of the knee exoskeleton robot. Then, we will design a linear controller for the robot, described by its equation of motion (1). For this purpose, we will consider an affine state-feedback controller described by:

$$u = u_d + \Delta u \tag{12}$$

where Δu is described as follows:

$$\Delta u = \begin{cases} \mathcal{K}\mathcal{X} & \text{if } \|\mathcal{X}\|^2 \geq \epsilon^2 \\ 0 & \text{if } \|\mathcal{X}\|^2 < \epsilon^2 \end{cases} \tag{13}$$

where ϵ is a tiny constant that will later be established and fixed.

Remark 1 In this study, we chose to employ the LMI approach to determine the feedback gain for our proposed control law (12). This approach brings several advantages over both linear and nonlinear controllers. While linear control laws, such as the Linear Quadratic Regulator (LQR), are typically applied to linear systems, our work takes a novel approach by utilizing a nonlinear dynamic model to describe the motion of the knee exoskeleton robotic system. Furthermore, our selected method proves to be more suitable than the Proportional-Derivative (PD) controller with gravity compensation, even though the PD controller is based on the nonlinear dynamic model [29]. In practical application, the PD controller often demands a significant amount of computation time, and the choice of controller gains is subject to constraints, resulting in a limited and somewhat specialized selection of control parameters. Our use of the LMI approach overcomes these challenges and provides a more efficient and adaptable solution for controlling knee exoskeleton robotic systems.

The next objective is to develop the controller u that allows the configuration state θ of the robotic system to move to its intended position θ_d. To achieve this objective, we will design a state-feedback controller utilizing two methods. In the first method, we will use the nonlinear dynamics (3), and in the second method, we will use the expanded dynamics (11).

5 Position Control Using the Nonlinear Dynamics

As previously mentioned, the primary goal of this section is to address the position control issue for the exoskeleton robot under consideration. To effectively control this type of robotic system and ensure stability at the desired state, we will utilize the nonlinear dynamic model to develop a state-feedback control law.

5.1 State Space Representation

Let define $\mathcal{X} = \begin{bmatrix} \phi \\ \dot{\phi} \end{bmatrix}$ as the state vector. Thus, the robotic system's nonlinear dynamics (3) may be stated using the state space representation shown below:

$$\dot{\mathcal{X}} = \mathcal{A}\mathcal{X} + \mathcal{B}\Delta u + \mathcal{D}_1\Phi_1(\mathcal{X}) + \mathcal{D}_2\Phi_2(\mathcal{X}) + \mathcal{B}\Delta_t \tag{14}$$

The functions $\Phi_1(\mathcal{X})$ and $\Phi_2(\mathcal{X})$ in Eq. (14) are described as follows:

$$\Phi_1(\mathcal{X}) = \text{sgn}(\dot{\phi}) \tag{15a}$$

$$\Phi_2(\mathcal{X}) = \cos(\phi + \theta_d) - \cos(\theta_d) \tag{15b}$$

The matrices $\mathcal{A}$, $\mathcal{B}$, $\mathcal{D}_1$, and $\mathcal{D}_2$ are represented by the following expression:

$$\mathcal{A} = \begin{bmatrix} 0 & 1 \\ 0 & -\frac{f_v^\star}{\nu_\star} \end{bmatrix} \quad \mathcal{B} = \begin{bmatrix} 0 \\ \frac{1}{\nu_\star} \end{bmatrix} \quad \mathcal{D}_1 = \begin{bmatrix} 0 \\ -\frac{f_s^\star}{\nu_\star} \end{bmatrix} \quad \mathcal{D}_2 = \begin{bmatrix} 0 \\ \frac{a_\star}{\nu_\star} \end{bmatrix} \tag{16}$$

According to the proposed control law (12), the nonlinear dynamic model (14) of the exoskeleton robotic system may be expressed like so:

$$\dot{\mathcal{X}} = (\mathcal{A} + \mathcal{B}\mathcal{K})\,\mathcal{X} + \mathcal{D}_1\Phi_1(\mathcal{X}) + \mathcal{D}_2\Phi_2(\mathcal{X}) + \mathcal{B}\Delta_t \quad \text{where} \quad \|\mathcal{X}\|^2 \geq \epsilon^2 \tag{17}$$

5.2 *Design of LMI Stability Conditions*

This section is dedicated to establishing conditions on the gain of the proposed control law (12) to achieve control and, consequently, stability of the knee exoskeleton robot. Our approach revolves around using the Lyapunov technique. Then, the proposed Lyapunov function defined below will be used for this purpose:

$$\mathcal{V}(\mathcal{X}) = \mathcal{X}^{\mathrm{T}}\mathcal{P}\mathcal{X} > 0 \;\text{ such that }\; \|\mathcal{X}\|^2 \geq \epsilon^2 \tag{18}$$

Then, it is evident that its time-dependent derivative is provided like so:

$$\dot{\mathcal{V}}(\mathcal{X}) = 2\mathcal{X}^{\mathrm{T}}\mathcal{P}\dot{\mathcal{X}} < 0 \;\text{ such that }\; \|\mathcal{X}\|^2 \geq \epsilon^2 \tag{19}$$

Note that we can recast the restriction on the Lyapunov function (18) as follows:

$$\mathcal{Z}(\mathcal{X}) = \begin{bmatrix} \mathcal{X} \\ 1 \end{bmatrix}^{\mathrm{T}} \begin{bmatrix} \mathcal{I} & \mathcal{O} \\ \star & -\epsilon^2 \end{bmatrix} \begin{bmatrix} \mathcal{X} \\ 1 \end{bmatrix} \geq 0 \tag{20}$$

where here and in the sequel $\mathcal{I}$ and $\mathcal{O}$ are respectively the identity and zero matrices with appropriate dimensions.

According to the nonlinear dynamics under controller (17), the established expression (19) becomes:

$$\begin{aligned} \dot{\mathcal{V}}(\mathcal{X}) &= 2\mathcal{X}^{\mathrm{T}}\mathcal{P}\,(\mathcal{A} + \mathcal{B}\mathcal{K})\,\mathcal{X} + 2\mathcal{X}^{\mathrm{T}}\mathcal{P}\mathcal{D}_1\Phi_1(\mathcal{X}) \\ &\quad + 2\mathcal{X}^{\mathrm{T}}\mathcal{P}\mathcal{D}_2\Phi_2(\mathcal{X}) + 2\mathcal{X}^{\mathrm{T}}\mathcal{P}\mathcal{B}\Delta_t \end{aligned} \tag{21}$$

Let us apply the subsequent requirements for exponential stabilization to further improve the control results:

$$\dot{\mathcal{V}}(\mathcal{X}) + \zeta\mathcal{V}(\mathcal{X}) < 0 \tag{22}$$

where $\zeta > 0$ is a fixed positive scalar.

To guarantee the stability of the controlled robot, we will rely mainly on the expanded expression (21). Therefore, a specific LMI constraint on the gain matrix $\mathcal{K}$ will be developed in the following. According to the Young inequality [14–16, 18, 49], it is easy to demonstrate that in the expression (21), we obtain:

$$2\mathcal{X}^{\mathrm{T}}\mathcal{P}\mathcal{D}_1\Phi_1(\mathcal{X}) \leq \mathcal{X}^{\mathrm{T}}\mathcal{P}\mathcal{M}_1\mathcal{P}\mathcal{X} + \mathcal{D}_1^{\mathrm{T}}\mathcal{M}_1^{-1}\mathcal{D}_1\Phi_1(\mathcal{X})^2 \quad (23)$$

with $\mathcal{M}_1 = \mathcal{M}_1^{\mathrm{T}} > 0$, and $\Phi_1(\mathcal{X})$ represents a scalar function.

In addition, using expression (15a) of the function $\Phi_1(\mathcal{X})$, it follows that: $\Phi_1(\mathcal{X}) = \mathrm{sgn}(\dot{\phi}) = \pm 1$, and therefore $\Phi_1(\mathcal{X})^2 = 1$. Hence, the previously found inequality (23) is expressed as follows:

$$2\mathcal{X}^{\mathrm{T}}\mathcal{P}\mathcal{D}_1\Phi_1(\mathcal{X}) \leq \mathcal{X}^{\mathrm{T}}\mathcal{P}\mathcal{M}_1\mathcal{P}\mathcal{X} + \mathcal{D}_1^{\mathrm{T}}\mathcal{M}_1^{-1}\mathcal{D}_1 \quad (24)$$

As $\Phi_2(\mathcal{X})$ is a scalar function (see expression (15b)), therefore, using the Young inequality in (21), we may demonstrate the subsequent expression:

$$2\mathcal{X}^{\mathrm{T}}\mathcal{P}\mathcal{D}_2\Phi_2(\mathcal{X}) \leq \tau_2\mathcal{X}^{\mathrm{T}}\mathcal{P}\mathcal{D}_2\mathcal{D}_2^{\mathrm{T}}\mathcal{P}\mathcal{X} + \tau_2^{-1}\Phi_2(\mathcal{X})^2 \quad (25)$$

with $\tau_2 > 0$.

Since $\Phi_2(\mathcal{X})$ is defined by expression (15b), and as $\theta = \phi + \theta_d$, then we obtain $\Phi_2(\mathcal{X}) = \cos(\theta) - \cos(\theta_d)$, and therefore we obtain the following expression:

$$\Phi_2(\mathcal{X})^2 = \cos^2(\theta) - 2\cos(\theta)\cos(\theta_d) + \cos^2(\theta_d) \quad (26)$$

Thus, let us assume that:

$$\cos^2(\theta) \leq a_1\theta^2 + 1 \quad (27a)$$

$$-2\cos(\theta) \leq a_2\theta - 2 \quad (27b)$$

with $a_1 \geq \frac{-4}{\pi^2}$ and $a_2 = \frac{4}{\pi}$. In the next, we will take $a_1 = \frac{-4}{\pi^2}$.

As $\theta = \phi + \theta_d$, then we get:

$$\Phi_2(\mathcal{X})^2 \leq \mu_1\phi^2 + 2\mu_2\phi + \mu_3 \quad (28)$$

where

$$\mu_1 = a_1 \quad (29a)$$

$$\mu_2 = a_1\theta_d + \frac{a_2}{2}\cos(\theta_d) \quad (29b)$$

$$\mu_3 = a_1\theta_d^2 + a_2\cos(\theta_d)\theta_d + (\cos(\theta_d) - 1)^2 \quad (29c)$$

It is important to note that for all values of θ_d between 0 and $\frac{\pi}{2}$, we get

$$\mu_1 < 0 \qquad \mu_2 < 0 \qquad \mu_3 > 0 \tag{30}$$

Taking $\phi = \mathcal{C}_1\mathcal{X}$, where $\mathcal{C}_1 = \begin{bmatrix} 1 & 0 \end{bmatrix}$. Therefore, the inequality (28) may be written as follows:

$$\Phi_2(\mathcal{X})^2 \leq \mu_1\mathcal{X}^{\mathrm{T}}\mathcal{C}_1^{\mathrm{T}}\mathcal{C}_1\mathcal{X} + 2\mu_2\mathcal{C}_1\mathcal{X} + \mu_3 \tag{31}$$

As a result, (23) becomes:

$$\begin{aligned} 2\mathcal{X}^{\mathrm{T}}\mathcal{P}\mathcal{D}_2\Phi_2(\mathcal{X}) \leq\ & \tau_2\mathcal{X}^{\mathrm{T}}\mathcal{P}\mathcal{D}_2\mathcal{D}_2^{\mathrm{T}}\mathcal{P}\mathcal{X} + \mu_1\tau_2^{-1}\mathcal{X}^{\mathrm{T}}\mathcal{C}_1^{\mathrm{T}}\mathcal{C}_1\mathcal{X} \\ & + 2\mu_2\tau_2^{-1}\mathcal{C}_1\mathcal{X} + \mu_3\tau_2^{-1} \end{aligned} \tag{32}$$

Moreover, as Δ_t denotes a scalar function, using the Young inequality in (21), the following equation is established:

$$2\mathcal{X}^{\mathrm{T}}\mathcal{P}\mathcal{B}\Delta_t \leq \mathcal{X}^{\mathrm{T}}\mathcal{P}\mathcal{M}_3\mathcal{P}\mathcal{X} + \mathcal{B}^{\mathrm{T}}\mathcal{M}_3^{-1}\mathcal{B}\Delta_t^2 \tag{33}$$

with $\mathcal{M}_3 = \mathcal{M}_3^{\mathrm{T}} > 0$.

Assuming that Δ_t adheres to the subsequent condition:

$$|\Delta_t| \leq \bar{\delta}, \qquad \bar{\delta} > 0 \tag{34}$$

Hence, $\Delta_t^2 \leq \bar{\delta}^2$, and therefore (33) becomes:

$$2\mathcal{X}^{\mathrm{T}}\mathcal{P}\mathcal{B}\Delta_t \leq \mathcal{X}^{\mathrm{T}}\mathcal{P}\mathcal{M}_3\mathcal{P}\mathcal{X} + \bar{\delta}^2\mathcal{B}^{\mathrm{T}}\mathcal{M}_3^{-1}\mathcal{B} \tag{35}$$

Replacing (24), (32) and (35) in the resulting expression (21) and using the constraint (22), the following inequality is derived:

$$\begin{aligned} \dot{\mathcal{V}}(\mathcal{X}) + \zeta\mathcal{V}(\mathcal{X}) \leq\ & 2\mathcal{X}^{\mathrm{T}}\mathcal{P}\left(\mathcal{A} + \mathcal{B}\mathcal{K}\right)\mathcal{X} + \mathcal{X}^{\mathrm{T}}\mathcal{P}\mathcal{M}_1\mathcal{P}\mathcal{X} + \mathcal{D}_1^{\mathrm{T}}\mathcal{M}_1^{-1}\mathcal{D}_1 \\ & + \tau_2\mathcal{X}^{\mathrm{T}}\mathcal{P}\mathcal{D}_2\mathcal{D}_2^{\mathrm{T}}\mathcal{P}\mathcal{X} + \mu_1\tau_2^{-1}\mathcal{X}^{\mathrm{T}}\mathcal{C}_1^{\mathrm{T}}\mathcal{C}_1\mathcal{X} + 2\mu_2\tau_2^{-1}\mathcal{C}_1\mathcal{X} \\ & + \mu_3\tau_2^{-1} + \mathcal{X}^{\mathrm{T}}\mathcal{P}\mathcal{M}_3\mathcal{P}\mathcal{X} + \bar{\delta}^2\mathcal{B}^{\mathrm{T}}\mathcal{M}_3^{-1}\mathcal{B} + \zeta\mathcal{X}^{\mathrm{T}}\mathcal{P}\mathcal{X} \end{aligned} \tag{36}$$

Let us consider $\mathcal{Y}(\mathcal{X}) = 2\mathcal{X}^{\mathrm{T}}\mathcal{P}\left(\mathcal{A} + \mathcal{B}\mathcal{K}\right)\mathcal{X} + \mathcal{X}^{\mathrm{T}}\mathcal{P}\mathcal{M}_1\mathcal{P}\mathcal{X} + \mathcal{D}_1^{\mathrm{T}}\mathcal{M}_1^{-1}\mathcal{D}_1 + \tau_2\mathcal{X}^{\mathrm{T}}\mathcal{P}\mathcal{D}_2\mathcal{D}_2^{\mathrm{T}}\mathcal{P}\mathcal{X} + \mu_1\tau_2^{-1}\mathcal{X}^{\mathrm{T}}\mathcal{C}_1^{\mathrm{T}}\mathcal{C}_1\mathcal{X} + 2\mu_2\tau_2^{-1}\mathcal{C}_1\mathcal{X} + \mu_3\tau_2^{-1} + \mathcal{X}^{\mathrm{T}}\mathcal{P}\mathcal{M}_3\mathcal{P}\mathcal{X} + \bar{\delta}^2\mathcal{B}^{\mathrm{T}}\mathcal{M}_3^{-1}\mathcal{B} + \zeta\mathcal{X}^{\mathrm{T}}\mathcal{P}\mathcal{X}$. Hence, we get $\dot{\mathcal{V}}(\mathcal{X}) + \zeta\mathcal{V}(\mathcal{X}) \leq \mathcal{Y}(\mathcal{X})$, and therefore in order to satisfy the constraint (22), we need to have the following inequality condition:

$$\mathcal{Y}(\mathcal{X}) = \begin{bmatrix} \mathcal{X} \\ 1 \end{bmatrix}^{\mathrm{T}} \begin{bmatrix} \Upsilon_{11} & \Upsilon_{12} \\ \star & \Upsilon_{22} \end{bmatrix} \begin{bmatrix} \mathcal{X} \\ 1 \end{bmatrix} < 0 \tag{37}$$

where

$$\begin{aligned}\mathcal{Y}_{11} &= (\mathcal{P}\mathcal{A}+\mathcal{P}\mathcal{B}\mathcal{K})+(\mathcal{P}\mathcal{A}+\mathcal{P}\mathcal{B}\mathcal{K})^{\mathrm{T}}+\mathcal{P}\mathcal{M}_1\mathcal{P}\\ &\quad+\tau_2\mathcal{P}\mathcal{D}_2\mathcal{D}_2^{\mathrm{T}}\mathcal{P}+\mu_1\tau_2^{-1}\mathcal{C}_1^{\mathrm{T}}\mathcal{C}_1+\mathcal{P}\mathcal{M}_3\mathcal{P}+\zeta\mathcal{P} \quad (38a)\\ \mathcal{Y}_{12} &= \mu_2\tau_2^{-1}\mathcal{C}_1^{\mathrm{T}} \quad (38b)\\ \mathcal{Y}_{22} &= \mathcal{D}_1^{\mathrm{T}}\mathcal{M}_1^{-1}\mathcal{D}_1+\mu_3\tau_2^{-1}+\bar{\delta}^2\mathcal{B}^{\mathrm{T}}\mathcal{M}_3^{-1}\mathcal{B} \quad (38c)\end{aligned}$$

Based on the S-procedure [14–16, 18, 49] and using the expressions (37) and (20), we develop the following stability condition:

$$\begin{bmatrix}\mathcal{Y}_{11}+\tau_4\mathcal{I} & \mathcal{Y}_{12}\\ \star & \mathcal{Y}_{22}-\tau_4\epsilon^2\end{bmatrix}<0 \quad (39)$$

with $\tau_4>0$.

Therefore, multiplying the extended condition defined by (39) at the right side and the left side by $\mathcal{Q}=\begin{bmatrix}\mathcal{S} & \mathcal{O}\\ \star & \mathcal{I}\end{bmatrix}$ where $\mathcal{S}=\mathcal{P}^{-1}$, we obtain:

$$\begin{bmatrix}\Gamma_{11} & \Gamma_{12}\\ \star & \Gamma_{22}\end{bmatrix}<0 \quad (40)$$

where

$$\begin{aligned}\Gamma_{11} &= (\mathcal{A}\mathcal{S}+\mathcal{B}\mathcal{R})+(\mathcal{A}\mathcal{S}+\mathcal{B}\mathcal{R})^{\mathrm{T}}+\mathcal{M}_1+\tau_2\mathcal{D}_2\mathcal{D}_2^{\mathrm{T}}\\ &\quad+\mu_1\tau_2^{-1}\mathcal{S}\mathcal{C}_1^{\mathrm{T}}\mathcal{C}_1\mathcal{S}+\mathcal{M}_3+\zeta\mathcal{S}+\tau_4\mathcal{S}^2 \quad (41a)\\ \Gamma_{12} &= \mu_2\tau_2^{-1}\mathcal{S}\mathcal{C}_1^{\mathrm{T}} \quad (41b)\\ \Gamma_{22} &= \mathcal{D}_1^{\mathrm{T}}\mathcal{M}_1^{-1}\mathcal{D}_1+\mu_3\tau_2^{-1}+\bar{\delta}^2\mathcal{B}^{\mathrm{T}}\mathcal{M}_3^{-1}\mathcal{B}-\tau_4\epsilon^2 \quad (41c)\end{aligned}$$

with

$$\mathcal{R}=\mathcal{K}\mathcal{S} \quad (42)$$

For the sake of simplicity, let us set $\beta^{-1}=\tau_4\epsilon^2$, $\mathcal{J}=\begin{bmatrix}\mathcal{O} & \mu_2\mathcal{S}\mathcal{C}_1^{\mathrm{T}} & \mathcal{O}\end{bmatrix}$, $\mathcal{D}=\begin{bmatrix}\mathcal{D}_1\\ 1\\ \mathcal{B}\end{bmatrix}$, $\mathcal{M}=\begin{bmatrix}\mathcal{M}_1 & \mathcal{O} & \mathcal{O}\\ \star & \tau_2 & \mathcal{O}\\ \star & \star & \mathcal{M}_3\end{bmatrix}$, $\mathcal{Q}^{-1}=\begin{bmatrix}\mathcal{I} & \mathcal{O} & \mathcal{O}\\ \star & \mu_3 & \mathcal{O}\\ \star & \star & \bar{\delta}^2\mathcal{I}\end{bmatrix}$. Therefore, the inequality (40) becomes:

$$\begin{bmatrix}\Gamma_{11} & \mathcal{J}\mathcal{M}^{-1}\mathcal{D}\\ \star & -\beta^{-1}+\mathcal{D}^{\mathrm{T}}\mathcal{M}^{-1}\mathcal{Q}^{-1}\mathcal{D}\end{bmatrix}<0 \quad (43)$$

According to the Schur complement Lemma [14–16, 18, 49], the matrix inequality (43) may be recast like so:

$$-\beta^{-1} + \mathcal{D}^{\mathrm{T}}\mathcal{M}^{-1}\mathcal{Q}^{-1}\mathcal{D} < 0 \tag{44a}$$

$$\Gamma_{11} + \mathcal{J}\mathcal{M}^{-1}\mathcal{D}\left(\beta^{-1} - \mathcal{D}^{\mathrm{T}}\mathcal{M}^{-1}\mathcal{Q}^{-1}\mathcal{D}\right)^{-1}\left(\mathcal{J}\mathcal{M}^{-1}\mathcal{D}\right)^{\mathrm{T}} < 0 \tag{44b}$$

Applying the Matrix Inversion Lemma [14–16, 18, 49] to the quantity in the left-hand side of the expression (44a), we get:

$$\left(\beta^{-1} - \mathcal{D}^{\mathrm{T}}\mathcal{M}^{-1}\mathcal{Q}^{-1}\mathcal{D}\right)^{-1} = \beta - \beta^{2}\mathcal{D}^{\mathrm{T}}\mathcal{H}^{-1}\mathcal{D} \tag{45}$$

with

$$\mathcal{H} = \beta\mathcal{D}\mathcal{D}^{\mathrm{T}} - \mathcal{Q}\mathcal{M} \tag{46}$$

Then, according to the Eq. (45), the inequality (44b) is equivalent to:

$$\Gamma_{11} + \mathcal{J}\mathcal{M}^{-1}\mathcal{D}\left(\beta - \beta^{2}\mathcal{D}^{\mathrm{T}}\mathcal{H}^{-1}\mathcal{D}\right)\left(\mathcal{J}\mathcal{M}^{-1}\mathcal{D}\right)^{\mathrm{T}} < 0 \tag{47}$$

Posing

$$\Psi = \beta\mathcal{J}\mathcal{M}^{-1}\mathcal{D}\mathcal{D}^{\mathrm{T}}\mathcal{M}^{-1}\mathcal{J}^{\mathrm{T}} - \beta^{2}\mathcal{J}\mathcal{M}^{-1}\mathcal{D}\mathcal{D}^{\mathrm{T}}\mathcal{H}^{-1}\mathcal{D}\mathcal{D}^{\mathrm{T}}\mathcal{M}^{-1}\mathcal{J}^{\mathrm{T}} \tag{48}$$

As $\mathcal{H} = \beta\mathcal{D}\mathcal{D}^{\mathrm{T}} - \mathcal{Q}\mathcal{M}$ (relying on expression (46)), we demonstrate then the following expressions:

$$\beta\mathcal{J}\mathcal{M}^{-1}\mathcal{D}\mathcal{D}^{\mathrm{T}}\mathcal{M}^{-1}\mathcal{J}^{\mathrm{T}} = \mathcal{J}\mathcal{M}^{-1}\mathcal{H}\mathcal{M}^{-1}\mathcal{J}^{\mathrm{T}} + \mathcal{J}\mathcal{M}^{-1}\mathcal{Q}\mathcal{M}\mathcal{M}^{-1}\mathcal{J}^{\mathrm{T}} \tag{49a}$$

$$\begin{aligned}&\beta^{2}\mathcal{J}\mathcal{M}^{-1}\mathcal{D}\mathcal{D}^{\mathrm{T}}\mathcal{H}^{-1}\mathcal{D}\mathcal{D}^{\mathrm{T}}\mathcal{M}^{-1}\mathcal{J}^{\mathrm{T}} = \mathcal{J}\mathcal{M}^{-1}\mathcal{H}\mathcal{M}^{-1}\mathcal{J}^{\mathrm{T}}\\&+ 2\mathcal{J}\mathcal{M}^{-1}\mathcal{Q}\mathcal{M}\mathcal{M}^{-1}\mathcal{J}^{\mathrm{T}} + \mathcal{J}\mathcal{M}^{-1}\mathcal{Q}\mathcal{M}\mathcal{H}^{-1}\mathcal{Q}\mathcal{M}\mathcal{M}^{-1}\mathcal{J}^{\mathrm{T}}\end{aligned} \tag{49b}$$

Then, using these previous equations, the expression (48) can be simplified as follows:

$$\Psi = -\mathcal{J}\mathcal{Q}\mathcal{M}^{-1}\mathcal{J}^{\mathrm{T}} - \mathcal{J}\mathcal{Q}\mathcal{H}^{-1}\mathcal{Q}\mathcal{J}^{\mathrm{T}} \tag{50}$$

Using (50) in (47), we obtain:

$$\begin{aligned}&(\mathcal{A}\mathcal{S} + \mathcal{B}\mathcal{R}) + (\mathcal{A}\mathcal{S} + \mathcal{B}\mathcal{R})^{\mathrm{T}} + \mathcal{M}_1 + \tau_2\mathcal{D}_2\mathcal{D}_2^{\mathrm{T}} + \mu_1\tau_2^{-1}\mathcal{S}\mathcal{C}_1^{\mathrm{T}}\mathcal{C}_1\mathcal{S} + \mathcal{M}_3\\&+ \zeta\mathcal{S} + \tau_4\mathcal{S}^2 - \mathcal{J}\mathcal{Q}\mathcal{M}^{-1}\mathcal{J}^{\mathrm{T}} - \mathcal{J}\mathcal{Q}\mathcal{H}^{-1}\mathcal{Q}\mathcal{J}^{\mathrm{T}} < 0\end{aligned} \tag{51}$$

For simplicity, we take the following terms:

$$\rho\mathcal{J}\mathcal{M}^{-1}\mathcal{J}^{\mathrm{T}} = \mu_1\tau_2^{-1}\mathcal{S}\mathcal{C}_1^{\mathrm{T}}\mathcal{C}_1\mathcal{S} \tag{52a}$$

$$\mathcal{J}\mathcal{Q}\mathcal{M}^{-1}\mathcal{J}^{\mathrm{T}} = \frac{1}{\mu_3}\mathcal{J}\mathcal{M}^{-1}\mathcal{J}^{\mathrm{T}} \tag{52b}$$

with $\rho = \frac{\mu_1}{\mu_2^2}$.

Therefore, using these expressions, it is easy to demonstrate the subsequent expression:

$$\begin{aligned}&(\mathcal{A}\mathcal{S}+\mathcal{B}\mathcal{R})+(\mathcal{A}\mathcal{S}+\mathcal{B}\mathcal{R})^{\mathrm{T}}+\mathcal{M}_1+\tau_2\mathcal{D}_2\mathcal{D}_2^{\mathrm{T}}+\mathcal{M}_3+\zeta\mathcal{S}+\tau_4\mathcal{S}^2\\&+(\rho-\frac{1}{\mu_3})\mathcal{J}\mathcal{M}^{-1}\mathcal{J}^{\mathrm{T}}-\mathcal{J}\mathcal{Q}\left(\beta\mathcal{D}\mathcal{D}^{\mathrm{T}}-\mathcal{Q}\mathcal{M}\right)^{-1}\mathcal{Q}\mathcal{J}^{\mathrm{T}}<0\end{aligned} \tag{53}$$

Thus, by considering $\bar{\mathcal{C}}_1 = \begin{bmatrix}\mathcal{C}_1\\ \mathcal{O}\end{bmatrix}$, it is easy to show that:

$$\mathcal{J}\mathcal{M}^{-1}\mathcal{J}^{\mathrm{T}} = \mu_2^2\tau_2^{-1}\mathcal{S}\mathcal{C}_1^{\mathrm{T}}\mathcal{C}_1\mathcal{S} = \mu_2^2\tau_2^{-1}\mathcal{S}\bar{\mathcal{C}}_1^{\mathrm{T}}\bar{\mathcal{C}}_1\mathcal{S} \tag{54}$$

Therefore, using (54), the inequality (53) may be expressed by:

$$\begin{aligned}&(\mathcal{A}\mathcal{S}+\mathcal{B}\mathcal{R})+(\mathcal{A}\mathcal{S}+\mathcal{B}\mathcal{R})^{\mathrm{T}}+\mathcal{M}_1+\tau_2\mathcal{D}_2\mathcal{D}_2^{\mathrm{T}}+\mathcal{M}_3+\zeta\mathcal{S}+\tau_4\mathcal{S}^2\\&+\mu_5^{-1}\tau_2^{-1}\mathcal{S}\bar{\mathcal{C}}_1^{\mathrm{T}}\bar{\mathcal{C}}_1\mathcal{S}-\mathcal{J}\mathcal{Q}\left(\beta\mathcal{D}\mathcal{D}^{\mathrm{T}}-\mathcal{Q}\mathcal{M}\right)^{-1}\mathcal{Q}\mathcal{J}^{\mathrm{T}}<0\end{aligned} \tag{55}$$

where μ_5 is defined as follows:

$$\mu_5^{-1} = (\rho - \frac{1}{\mu_3})\mu_2^2 \tag{56}$$

Notice that $\mu_5^{-1} < 0$ and $\tau_2^{-1} > 0$, then $\mu_5^{-1}\tau_2^{-1}\mathcal{S}\bar{\mathcal{C}}_1^{\mathrm{T}}\bar{\mathcal{C}}_1\mathcal{S} < 0$. Hence, using the young inequality, we get:

$$\mu_5^{-1}\tau_2^{-1}\mathcal{S}\bar{\mathcal{C}}_1^{\mathrm{T}}\bar{\mathcal{C}}_1\mathcal{S} \leq -\mu_5\tau_2\mathcal{I} - \bar{\mathcal{C}}_1\mathcal{S} - \mathcal{S}\bar{\mathcal{C}}_1^{\mathrm{T}} \tag{57}$$

Then, relying to (57), the Eq. (55) may be expressed as follows:

$$\begin{aligned}&(\mathcal{A}\mathcal{S}+\mathcal{B}\mathcal{R})+(\mathcal{A}\mathcal{S}+\mathcal{B}\mathcal{R})^{\mathrm{T}}+\mathcal{M}_1+\tau_2\mathcal{D}_2\mathcal{D}_2^{\mathrm{T}}+\mathcal{M}_3+\zeta\mathcal{S}+\tau_4\mathcal{S}^2\\&-\mu_5\tau_2\mathcal{I}-\bar{\mathcal{C}}_1\mathcal{S}-\mathcal{S}\bar{\mathcal{C}}_1^{\mathrm{T}}-\mathcal{J}\mathcal{Q}\left(\beta\mathcal{D}\mathcal{D}^{\mathrm{T}}-\mathcal{Q}\mathcal{M}\right)^{-1}\mathcal{Q}\mathcal{J}^{\mathrm{T}}<0\end{aligned} \tag{58}$$

Moreover, according to the inequality (44a), as $\beta > 0$ and $\mathcal{M} > 0$, then, using the Schur complement, we can write:

$$\begin{bmatrix}-\beta^{-1} & \mathcal{D}^{\mathrm{T}}\\ \star & -\mathcal{M}\mathcal{Q}\end{bmatrix} < 0 \tag{59}$$

Therefore, based on the Schur complement, we demonstrate that $\beta \mathcal{D}\mathcal{D}^{\mathrm{T}} - \mathcal{Q}\mathcal{M} < 0$. Therefore, we get $-\left(\beta \mathcal{D}\mathcal{D}^{\mathrm{T}} - \mathcal{Q}\mathcal{M}\right)^{-1} > 0$. Hence, posing $\gamma_1 = \tau_4^{-1}$ and based on the Schur complement, we expand:

$$\begin{bmatrix} \Xi & \mathcal{S} & \mathcal{J}\mathcal{Q} \\ \star & -\gamma_1 \mathcal{I} & \mathcal{O} \\ \star & \star & \beta \mathcal{D}\mathcal{D}^{\mathrm{T}} - \mathcal{Q}\mathcal{M} \end{bmatrix} < 0 \tag{60}$$

with

$$\begin{aligned} \Xi = & (\mathcal{A}\mathcal{S} + \mathcal{B}\mathcal{R}) + (\mathcal{A}\mathcal{S} + \mathcal{B}\mathcal{R})^{\mathrm{T}} + \mathcal{M}_1 + \tau_2 \mathcal{D}_2 \mathcal{D}_2^{\mathrm{T}} + \mathcal{M}_3 \\ & + \zeta \mathcal{S} - \mu_5 \tau_2 \mathcal{I} - \bar{\mathcal{C}}_1 \mathcal{S} - \mathcal{S} \bar{\mathcal{C}}_1^{\mathrm{T}} \end{aligned} \tag{61}$$

In addition, assuming that $\kappa = \frac{\gamma_1}{\epsilon^2}$, $\mathcal{M}_3 = m_3 \mathcal{I}$, and $\lambda = \frac{m_3}{\delta^2}$, we can rephrase the expression (60) as an LMI stability condition, which can be stated as follows:

$$\begin{bmatrix} \Xi_1 & \mathcal{S} & \mathcal{O} & \frac{\mu_2}{\mu_3} \mathcal{S}\mathcal{C}_1^{\mathrm{T}} & \mathcal{O} \\ \star & -\gamma_1 \mathcal{I} & \mathcal{O} & \mathcal{O} & \mathcal{O} \\ \star & \star & \kappa \mathcal{D}_1 \mathcal{D}_1^{\mathrm{T}} - \mathcal{M}_1 & \kappa \mathcal{D}_1 & \kappa \mathcal{D}_1 \mathcal{B}^{\mathrm{T}} \\ \star & \star & \star & \kappa \mathcal{I} - \frac{1}{\mu_3} \tau_2 & \kappa \mathcal{B}^{\mathrm{T}} \\ \star & \star & \star & \star & \kappa \mathcal{B}\mathcal{B}^{\mathrm{T}} - \lambda \mathcal{I} \end{bmatrix} < 0 \tag{62}$$

where

$$\begin{aligned} \Xi_1 = & (\mathcal{A}\mathcal{S} + \mathcal{B}\mathcal{R}) + (\mathcal{A}\mathcal{S} + \mathcal{B}\mathcal{R})^{\mathrm{T}} + \mathcal{M}_1 + \tau_2 \mathcal{D}_2 \mathcal{D}_2^{\mathrm{T}} + m_3 \mathcal{I} \\ & + \zeta \mathcal{S} - \mu_5 \tau_2 \mathcal{I} - \bar{\mathcal{C}}_1 \mathcal{S} - \mathcal{S} \bar{\mathcal{C}}_1^{\mathrm{T}} \end{aligned} \tag{63}$$

It is important to note that $\kappa = \frac{\gamma_1}{\epsilon^2}$, which implies $\epsilon = \sqrt{\frac{\gamma_1}{\kappa}}$. In order to minimize ϵ, we need to minimize $\left(\gamma_1 + \kappa^{-1}\right)$. Therefore, let us consider the following condition:

$$\gamma_1 + \kappa^{-1} < \nabla_1 \tag{64}$$

Hence, we conclude that to minimize ϵ, we should minimize ∇_1. It is clear that the inequality (64) can be reformulated as follows:

$$\nabla_1 - \gamma_1 - \kappa^{-1} > 0 \tag{65}$$

By utilizing the expression (65) and based on the Schur complement lemma, the following LMI stability condition is obtained:

$$\begin{bmatrix} \nabla_1 - \gamma_1 & 1 \\ \star & \kappa \end{bmatrix} > 0 \tag{66}$$

with $\gamma_1 > 0$.

Moreover, it is worth noting that $\lambda = \frac{m_3}{\bar{\delta}^2}$. Thus, $\bar{\delta} = \sqrt{\frac{m_3}{\lambda}}$. Furthermore, let assume $\Omega = \bar{\delta}^{-1} = \sqrt{\frac{\lambda}{m_3}}$. In order to maximize $\bar{\delta}$, we should minimize Ω, and consequently minimize $\lambda + m_3^{-1}$. Therefore, let us impose the following constraint:

$$\lambda + m_3^{-1} < \nabla_2 \tag{67}$$

We conclude that to maximize $\bar{\delta}$, we should minimize ∇_2. Thus, it is clear that the inequality (67) can be recast like so:

$$\nabla_2 - \lambda - m_3^{-1} > 0 \tag{68}$$

By employing the expression (68) and using the Schur complement lemma, we can establish the subsequent LMI stability condition:

$$\begin{bmatrix} \nabla_2 - \lambda & 1 \\ \star & m_3 \end{bmatrix} > 0 \tag{69}$$

with $\lambda > 0$.

As a result, the LMI stability requirements stated by (62), (66), and (69) are obtained. These conditions are described with regard to the unknowable variables $\mathcal{S}$, $\mathcal{R}$, $\mathcal{M}_1$, τ_2, m_3, γ_1, λ, ∇_1, ∇_2, and κ.

Theorem 1 *Assuming the existence of matrices $\mathcal{S}$, $\mathcal{R}$ and $\mathcal{M}_1$, as well as scalar values τ_2, m_3, γ_1, λ, ∇_1, ∇_2, and κ, such that the following LMI-based problem:*

$$\begin{array}{ll} \min & \nabla_1 + \nabla_2 \\ s.t. & LMI\ (62),\ LMI\ (66)\ and\ LMI\ (69). \end{array} \tag{70}$$

is feasible, it can be concluded that the proposed controller defined in (12) stabilizes the nonlinear dynamics (1). Additionally, the gain matrix $\mathcal{K}$ of the adopted control law can be calculated using the subsequent expression:

$$\mathcal{K} = \mathcal{R}\mathcal{S}^{-1} \tag{71}$$

Furthermore, the minimum value of the parameter ϵ can be computed as follows:

$$\epsilon_{min} = \sqrt{\frac{\gamma_1}{\kappa}} \tag{72}$$

Moreover, the maximum value of the parameter $\bar{\delta}$ can be calculated like so:

$$\bar{\delta}_{max} = \sqrt{\frac{m_3}{\lambda}} \tag{73}$$

6 Position Control Using the Expanded Nonlinear Dynamics

As mentioned earlier, the primary goal of this part is to solve the position control problem for the knee exoskeleton robot. To achieve effective control and ensure stability at the desired point, we will use the expanded nonlinear dynamics (11).

6.1 State Space Representation

The state vector will be defined as $\mathcal{X} = \begin{bmatrix} \phi \\ \dot{\phi} \end{bmatrix}$. Hence, we can express the expanded dynamic model (11) of the robotic system in the subsequent state space representation:

$$\dot{\mathcal{X}} = \mathcal{A}_1\mathcal{X} + \mathcal{B}\Delta u + \mathcal{D}_1\Phi_1(\mathcal{X}) + \mathcal{D}_2\Phi_3(\mathcal{X}) + \mathcal{B}\Delta_t \tag{74}$$

In this context, the terms $\Phi_1(\mathcal{X})$ and $\Phi_3(\mathcal{X})$ mentioned in Eq. (74) can be described as follows:

$$\Phi_1(\mathcal{X}) = \mathrm{sgn}(\dot{\phi}) \tag{75a}$$
$$\Phi_3(\mathcal{X}) = \cos(\phi + \theta_d) + \sin(\theta_d)\phi - \cos(\theta_d) \tag{75b}$$

and the matrices $\mathcal{A}_1$, $\mathcal{B}$, $\mathcal{D}_1$, and $\mathcal{D}_2$ are represented by the following expression:

$$\mathcal{A}_1 = \begin{bmatrix} 0 & 1 \\ -\frac{a_\star}{\mathcal{J}_\star}\sin(\theta_d) & -\frac{f_v^\star}{\mathcal{J}_\star} \end{bmatrix} \quad \mathcal{B} = \begin{bmatrix} 0 \\ \frac{1}{\mathcal{J}_\star} \end{bmatrix} \quad \mathcal{D}_1 = \begin{bmatrix} 0 \\ -\frac{f_s^\star}{\mathcal{J}_\star} \end{bmatrix} \quad \mathcal{D}_2 = \begin{bmatrix} 0 \\ \frac{a_\star}{\mathcal{J}_\star} \end{bmatrix} \tag{76}$$

Using the proposed affine state-feedback controller (12), the nonlinear dynamic model (74) becomes:

$$\dot{\mathcal{X}} = (\mathcal{A}_1 + \mathcal{B}\mathcal{K})\,\mathcal{X} + \mathcal{D}_1\Phi_1(\mathcal{X}) + \mathcal{D}_2\Phi_3(\mathcal{X}) + \mathcal{B}\Delta_t \quad \text{where} \quad \|\mathcal{X}\|^2 \geq \epsilon^2 \tag{77}$$

6.2 Design of LMI Stability Conditions

This section is dedicated to establishing LMI conditions on the feedback gain of the proposed control law (12) to achieve control and, consequently, stability of the knee exoskeleton robot. We adopt the same statement of the candidate Lyapunov function defined by (18), with its time derivative being expressed by (19). Moreover, we will enforce the constraint on $\mathcal{V}(\mathcal{X})$ presented in (20) that will be applied. Therefore, according to the controlled nonlinear dynamics described by (77), the expression (19) can be reformulated as follows:

$$\dot{\mathcal{V}}(\mathcal{X}) = 2\mathcal{X}^{\mathrm{T}}\mathcal{P}\left(\mathcal{A}_1 + \mathcal{B}\mathcal{K}\right)\mathcal{X} + 2\mathcal{X}^{\mathrm{T}}\mathcal{P}\mathcal{D}_1\Phi_1(\mathcal{X}) + 2\mathcal{X}^{\mathrm{T}}\mathcal{P}\mathcal{D}_2\Phi_3(\mathcal{X}) + 2\mathcal{X}^{\mathrm{T}}\mathcal{P}\mathcal{B}\Delta_t \tag{78}$$

Furthermore, to further enhance the control results, we apply the same requirement for exponential stability defined by (22). To ensure the stability of the controlled robot, we will primarily rely on the expanded expression (78). Consequently, a specific LMI constraint on the gain matrix $\mathcal{K}$ will be formulated.

By applying the Young inequality lemma to the term $2\mathcal{X}^{\mathrm{T}}\mathcal{P}\mathcal{D}_1\Phi_1(\mathcal{X})$ in Eq. (78), we can demonstrate the equivalent expression (24). Moreover, as $\Phi_3(\mathcal{X})$ is a scalar function (expression (75b)), therefore, using the Young inequality lemma on the term $2\mathcal{X}^{\mathrm{T}}\mathcal{P}\mathcal{D}_2\Phi_3(\mathcal{X})$ presented in Eq. (78), we can demonstrate the following expression:

$$2\mathcal{X}^{\mathrm{T}}\mathcal{P}\mathcal{D}_2\Phi_3(\mathcal{X}) \leq \tau_2\mathcal{X}^{\mathrm{T}}\mathcal{P}\mathcal{D}_2\mathcal{D}_2^{\mathrm{T}}\mathcal{P}\mathcal{X} + \tau_2^{-1}\Phi_3(\mathcal{X})^2 \tag{79}$$

with $\tau_2 > 0$.

By considering expression (75b) of the function $\Phi_3(\mathcal{X})$, it follows that $\Phi_3(\mathcal{X}) = \cos(\theta) + \sin(\theta_d)\phi - \cos(\theta_d)$, and then we can express $\Phi_3(\mathcal{X})^2$ as follows:

$$\Phi_3(\mathcal{X})^2 = \cos^2(\theta) + \sin^2(\theta_d)\phi^2 + \cos^2(\theta_d) + 2\cos(\theta)\sin(\theta_d)\phi - 2\cos(\theta_d)\cos(\theta) - 2\sin(\theta_d)\cos(\theta_d)\phi \tag{80}$$

Next, we illustrate the subsequent expressions:

$$\cos^2(\theta) \leq a_1\theta^2 + 1 \qquad 2\cos(\theta)\theta \leq 2\theta \qquad -2\cos(\theta) \leq a_2\theta + b_2 \tag{81}$$

where

$$a_1 = \frac{-4}{\pi^2} \qquad a_2 = \frac{4}{\pi} \qquad b_2 = -2 \tag{82}$$

Using the inequalities in (81), we demonstrate the following expression:

$$-2\cos(\theta)\sin(\theta_d)\theta_d \leq (a_2\theta + b_2)\sin(\theta_d)\theta_d \tag{83a}$$

$$2\cos(\theta)\sin(\theta_d)\theta \leq 2\sin(\theta_d)\theta \tag{83b}$$

Thus, as $2\cos(\theta)\sin(\theta_d)\phi = 2\cos(\theta)\sin(\theta_d)\theta - 2\cos(\theta)\sin(\theta_d)\theta_d$, then we obtain:

$$2\cos(\theta)\sin(\theta_d)\phi \leq 2\sin(\theta_d)\theta + (a_2\theta + b_2)\sin(\theta_d)\theta_d \tag{84}$$

Considering that $\theta = \phi + \theta_d$ and using the previously derived inequalities (81) and (84), we get:

$$\cos^2(\theta) \leq a_1\phi^2 + 2a_1\theta_d\phi + a_1\theta_d^2 + 1 \tag{85a}$$
$$-2\cos(\theta_d)\cos(\theta) \leq a_2\cos(\theta_d)\phi + (a_2\theta_d + b_2)\cos(\theta_d) \tag{85b}$$
$$\begin{aligned} 2\cos(\theta)\sin(\theta_d)\phi \leq{}& 2\sin(\theta_d)\theta_d + 2\sin(\theta_d)\phi + a_2\sin(\theta_d)\theta_d\phi \\ &+ (a_2\theta_d + b_2)\sin(\theta_d)\theta_d \end{aligned} \tag{85c}$$

Therefore, based on the above evaluations, we can conclude:

$$\Phi_3(\mathcal{X})^2 \leq \eta_1\phi^2 + 2\eta_2\phi + \eta_3 \tag{86}$$

where

$$\eta_1 = a_1 + \sin^2(\theta_d) \tag{87a}$$
$$\eta_2 = a_1\theta_d + \frac{a_2}{2}\cos(\theta_d) - \sin(\theta_d)\cos(\theta_d) + \sin(\theta_d) + \frac{a_2}{2}\sin(\theta_d)\theta_d \tag{87b}$$
$$\begin{aligned} \eta_3 ={}& a_1\theta_d^2 + \cos^2(\theta_d) + (a_2\theta_d + b_2)\cos(\theta_d) + 1 + 2\sin(\theta_d)\theta_d \\ &+ (a_2\theta_d + b_2)\sin(\theta_d)\theta_d \end{aligned} \tag{87c}$$

It is important to note that for all values of θ_d between 0 and $\frac{\pi}{2}$, we get

$$\eta_3 > 0 \qquad\qquad \eta_2 > 0 \tag{88}$$

Taking $\phi = \mathcal{C}_1\mathcal{X}$, where $\mathcal{C}_1 = \begin{bmatrix} 1 & 0 \end{bmatrix}$, we can rewrite the inequality (86) as follows:

$$\Phi_3(\mathcal{X})^2 \leq \eta_1\mathcal{X}^{\mathrm{T}}\mathcal{C}_1^{\mathrm{T}}\mathcal{C}_1\mathcal{X} + 2\eta_2\mathcal{C}_1\mathcal{X} + \eta_3 \tag{89}$$

Consequently, the expression (79) can be reformulated as:

$$\begin{aligned} 2\mathcal{X}^{\mathrm{T}}\mathcal{P}\mathcal{D}_2\Phi_3(\mathcal{X}) \leq{}& \tau_2\mathcal{X}^{\mathrm{T}}\mathcal{P}\mathcal{D}_2\mathcal{D}_2^{\mathrm{T}}\mathcal{P}\mathcal{X} + \eta_1\tau_2^{-1}\mathcal{X}^{\mathrm{T}}\mathcal{C}_1^{\mathrm{T}}\mathcal{C}_1\mathcal{X} \\ &+ 2\eta_2\tau_2^{-1}\mathcal{C}_1\mathcal{X} + \eta_3\tau_2^{-1} \end{aligned} \tag{90}$$

Furthermore, considering that Δ_t represents a scalar function, we can apply the Young inequality lemma to the term $2\mathcal{X}^{\mathrm{T}}\mathcal{P}\mathcal{B}\Delta_t$ in Eq. (78). Assuming that Δ_t satisfies the constraint specified by (34), we can then establish the inequalities as presented in (35).

By substituting the expressions (24), (90), and (35) into the resulting equation (78) and using (22), we get:

$$\begin{aligned}\dot{\mathcal{V}}(\mathcal{X})+\zeta\mathcal{V}(\mathcal{X}) \leq\ & 2\mathcal{X}^{\mathrm{T}}\mathcal{P}\left(\mathcal{A}_1+\mathcal{B}\mathcal{K}\right)\mathcal{X}+\mathcal{X}^{\mathrm{T}}\mathcal{P}\mathcal{M}_1\mathcal{P}\mathcal{X}+\mathcal{D}_1^{\mathrm{T}}\mathcal{M}_1^{-1}\mathcal{D}_1\\ &+\tau_2\mathcal{X}^{\mathrm{T}}\mathcal{P}\mathcal{D}_2\mathcal{D}_2^{\mathrm{T}}\mathcal{P}\mathcal{X}+\eta_1\tau_2^{-1}\mathcal{X}^{\mathrm{T}}\mathcal{C}_1^{\mathrm{T}}\mathcal{C}_1\mathcal{X}+2\eta_2\tau_2^{-1}\mathcal{C}_1\mathcal{X}\\ &+\eta_3\tau_2^{-1}+\mathcal{X}^{\mathrm{T}}\mathcal{P}\mathcal{M}_3\mathcal{P}\mathcal{X}+\bar{\delta}^2\mathcal{B}^{\mathrm{T}}\mathcal{M}_3^{-1}\mathcal{B}+\zeta\mathcal{X}^{\mathrm{T}}\mathcal{P}\mathcal{X}\end{aligned}\tag{91}$$

It is crucial to highlight that the derived expression (91) exhibits significant similarity to the obtained expression (36). Consequently, by employing the same technical strategies used previously to manipulate the developed inequality (91) and assuming $\kappa=\frac{\gamma_1}{\epsilon^2}$, $\mathcal{M}_3=m_3\mathcal{I}$, and $\lambda=\frac{m_3}{\bar{\delta}^2}$, we can establish the following LMI stability condition:

$$\begin{bmatrix}\Xi_2 & \mathcal{S} & \mathcal{O} & \frac{\eta_2}{\eta_3}\mathcal{S}\mathcal{C}_1^{\mathrm{T}} & \mathcal{O}\\ \star & -\gamma_1\mathcal{I} & \mathcal{O} & \mathcal{O} & \mathcal{O}\\ \star & \star & \kappa\mathcal{D}_1\mathcal{D}_1^{\mathrm{T}}-\mathcal{M}_1 & \kappa\mathcal{D}_1 & \kappa\mathcal{D}_1\mathcal{B}^{\mathrm{T}}\\ \star & \star & \star & \kappa\mathcal{I}-\frac{1}{\mu_3}\tau_2 & \kappa\mathcal{B}^{\mathrm{T}}\\ \star & \star & \star & \star & \kappa\mathcal{B}\mathcal{B}^{\mathrm{T}}-\lambda\mathcal{I}\end{bmatrix}<0\tag{92}$$

where

$$\begin{aligned}\Xi_2=\ &(\mathcal{A}_1\mathcal{S}+\mathcal{B}\mathcal{R})+(\mathcal{A}_1\mathcal{S}+\mathcal{B}\mathcal{R})^{\mathrm{T}}+\mathcal{M}_1+\tau_2\mathcal{D}_2\mathcal{D}_2^{\mathrm{T}}\\ &+m_3\mathcal{I}+\zeta\mathcal{S}-\mu_5\tau_2\mathcal{I}-\bar{\mathcal{C}}_1\mathcal{S}-\mathcal{S}\bar{\mathcal{C}}_1^{\mathrm{T}}\end{aligned}\tag{93}$$

It is important to note that $\kappa=\frac{\gamma_1}{\epsilon^2}$, which implies $\epsilon=\sqrt{\frac{\gamma_1}{\kappa}}$, the objective is to minimize ϵ, which in turn minimizes $\left(\gamma_1+\kappa^{-1}\right)$. Therefore, we consider the condition (64) and derive the LMI stability condition presented in (66). Then, we conclude that to minimize ϵ, we should minimize ∇_1.

Furthermore, we can express λ as $\lambda=\frac{m_3}{\bar{\delta}^2}$, leading to $\bar{\delta}=\sqrt{\frac{m_3}{\lambda}}$. Assuming $\Omega=\bar{\delta}^{-1}=\sqrt{\frac{\lambda}{m_3}}$, the objective is to maximize $\bar{\delta}$ by minimizing Ω, which corresponds to minimizing $\lambda+m_3^{-1}$. To achieve this, we consider the condition (67) and develop the LMI stability condition presented in (69). Hence, it is clear that to maximize $\bar{\delta}$, we should minimize ∇_2.

Consequently, we derive the LMI stability conditions denoted by (92), (66), and (69). These conditions are expressed in terms of the unknown variables $\mathcal{S}$, $\mathcal{R}$, $\mathcal{M}_1$, τ_2, m_3, γ_1, λ, ∇_1, ∇_2, and κ.

Theorem 2 *Assuming the existence of matrices $\mathcal{S}$, $\mathcal{R}$ and $\mathcal{M}_1$, as well as scalar values τ_2, m_3, γ_1, λ, ∇_2, ∇_1, and κ, that satisfy the following LMI-based problem:*

$$\begin{aligned}&\textit{min} && \nabla_1+\nabla_2\\ &\textit{s.t.} && \textit{LMI}\ (92),\ \textit{LMI}\ (66)\ \textit{and}\ \textit{LMI}\ (69).\end{aligned}\tag{94}$$

we can conclude that the proposed controller defined in (12) stabilizes the nonlinear dynamics (1). The gain matrix $\mathcal{K}$ of the proposed control law can be computed using the expression (71). Additionally, the maximum value of the parameter $\bar{\delta}$ can be calculated using relation (73), and the lowest value of the parameter ϵ can be computed using expression (72).

6.3 LMI Requirements for Reducing Controller Gain Size

Highlighting the importance of the previous theorems, it's notable that the LMI problem can lead to a substantial gain $\mathcal{K}$. Thus, the key objective is to minimize the size of $\mathcal{K}$. To achieve this, two additional LMIs will be introduced in the preceding theorems, enhancing the practicality and real-life applicability of the control approach. These extra LMIs are illustrated as follows [16]:

$$\begin{bmatrix} \ell_1 \mathcal{I} & \mathcal{R}^{\mathrm{T}} \\ \star & \mathcal{I} \end{bmatrix} > 0 \qquad \begin{bmatrix} \ell_2 \mathcal{I} & \mathcal{I} \\ \star & \mathcal{S} \end{bmatrix} > 0 \tag{95}$$

In these previous two LMIs in (95), the two parameters ℓ_1 and ℓ_2 must be minimized to decreased the size of $\mathcal{K}$.

Remark 2 Our study focuses on the key knee joint and aims to enhance the precise control of a lower limb exoskeleton [19, 24, 25, 50]. To achieve this, we have implemented a state feedback-based control method specifically designed to address the challenges typically encountered in this field. By employing the LMI approach, which ensures efficient control and stability of the exoskeleton robot for knee rehabilitation, our research distinguishes itself from previous studies [4, 33, 43]. This innovation significantly expands existing knowledge and improves control performance by demonstrating a more effective approach to managing parametric uncertainties and disturbances.

7 Simulation Results

In this section, we present simulation results for the two distinct control methods used in this study. The main aim is to demonstrate the effectiveness of the designed LMI criteria for the controller gain $\mathcal{K}$ in ensuring the stability of the knee exoskeleton, as shown in Fig. 4. The robot's various parameters, modeled using dynamic equation (1), are listed in Table 1.

Importantly, our focus is on showcasing numerical simulation outcomes for the different control methods employed in this study. A subsequent comparative analysis between these methods will be performed. For the purpose of comparing the controlled robotic system's behavior, we'll present two simulation scenarios involving

Table 1 Parameter values for the knee exoskeleton system (from [4, 28], licensed under CC-BY 4.0)

Parameter	Value	Unit
$\nu_\star$	0.323	kg m^2/rad
$m_\star$	0.000105	kg
$l_\star$	0.25	m
$f_v^\star$	0.35	N m s/rad
$f_s^\star$	0.059	N m/A
g	9.8	N

the same type of external disturbance applied to the knee exoskeleton robotic system. Furthermore, all simulations with the proposed control law will begin from the same initial position while selecting the same desired position for the experiments.

7.1 *First Simulation Results*

In the first simulation results, we will choose the desired angular position θ_d to be fixed at $\theta_d = 30°$. Moreover, for this simulation, we will introduce an external disturbance Δ_t in the form of a sinusoidal input defined like so:

$$\Delta_t = \bar{\delta} \times \sin(\omega_f \times t) \tag{96}$$

with ω_f represents the pulsation of the signal. In our case, we will use $\omega_f = 10\pi$. Moreover, this disturbance input will be active only between 2 and 7 s. Outside this time interval, $\Delta_t = 0$.

7.1.1 Results Obtained Utilizing the First Design Approach

Using the developed LMI conditions in Theorem 1, we solve the LMI-based minimization problem derived from this theorem. Moreover, we incorporate two additional LMI conditions defined in (95), and selecting $\zeta = 3$, we get then the following results:

$$\mathcal{K} = \begin{bmatrix} -3.3956 & -1.3455 \end{bmatrix} \tag{97a}$$

$$\epsilon_{\min} = 5.0391 \tag{97b}$$

$$\bar{\delta}_{\max} = 0.3368 \tag{97c}$$

By adding the feedback gain defined in (97c) to the adopted controller (12), the simulation outcomes shown in Fig. 5 demonstrate our achieved results. Clearly,

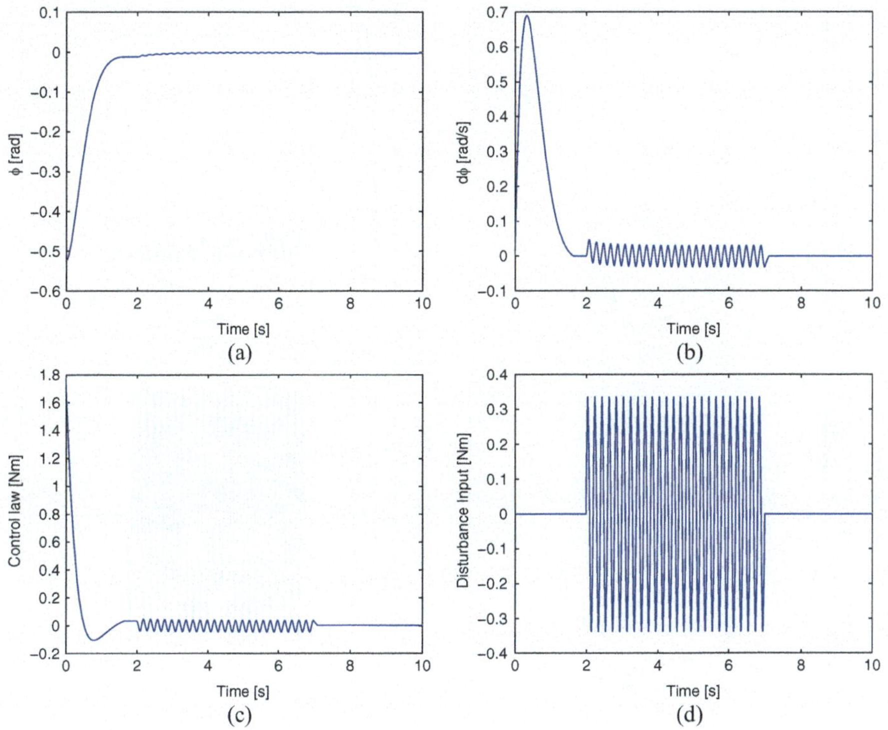

Fig. 5 First simulation outcomes obtained using the first design method. Evolution of: **a** the angular position error ϕ, **b** the angular velocity error $\dot{\phi}$, **c** the adopted controller u, and **d** the external disturbance Δ_t

the robot effectively reached the desired state θ_d. Additionally, the control effort u diminishes to zero upon the stabilization of the robotic system.

7.1.2 Results Obtained Utilizing the Second Design Approach

Based on the LMI stability conditions formulated in Theorem 2, we will solve the LMI issue derived from this theorem. Additionally, we integrate the two additional LMI conditions defined in (95) with $\zeta = 3$. we get:

$$\mathcal{K} = \begin{bmatrix} -2.6764 & -1.3434 \end{bmatrix} \tag{98a}$$

$$\epsilon_{\min} = 6.6025 \tag{98b}$$

$$\bar{\delta}_{\max} = 0.3632 \tag{98c}$$

By using the feedback gains $\mathcal{K}$ as defined in (98c) to the proposed controller (12), we obtained the graphical results shown in Fig. 6. These figures show that the robot

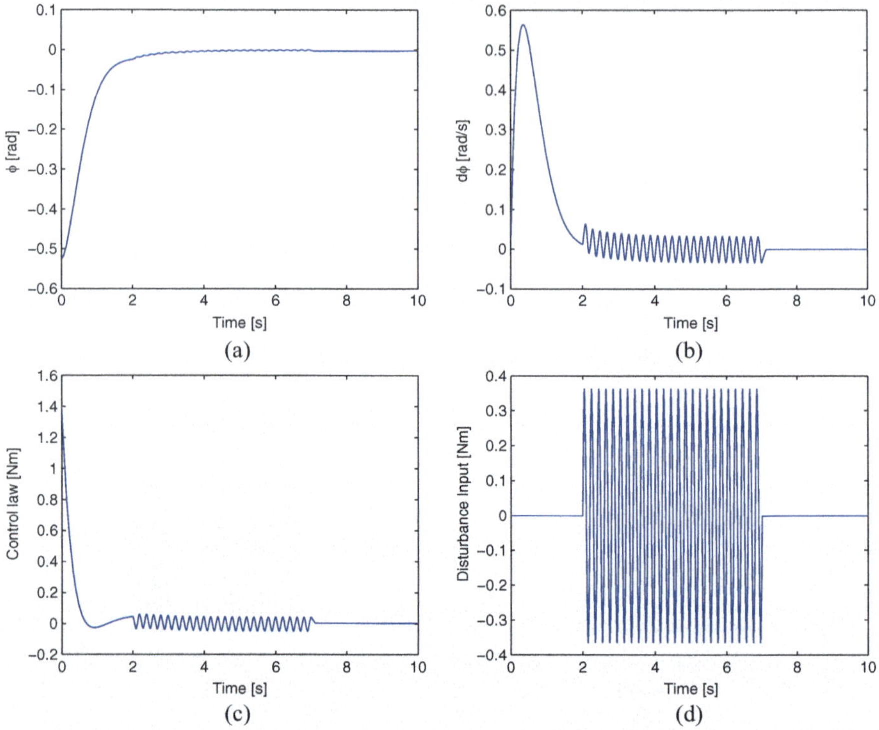

Fig. 6 First simulation results obtained using the second design method. Evolution of: **a** the angular position error ϕ, **b** the angular velocity error $\dot{\phi}$, **c** the proposed controller u, and **d** the external disturbance Δ_t

is effectively controlled and successfully reaching the intended state. Moreover, at the equilibrium point, the control effort u is zero.

7.2 Second Simulation Results

In the second simulation results, we will take a different desired position to be $\theta_d = 20°$. However, we will adopt a different kind of external disturbance used in the first simulation results. Indeed, we will introduce an external disturbance Δ_t in the form of a random signal, which will only be active between 2 and 7 s. Nevertheless, outside this time interval, Δ_t will be set to zero. Thus, Δ_t has the following expression:

$$\Delta_t = \bar{\delta} \times (2 \times \text{rand} - 1) \qquad (99)$$

where the function rand stands for the random signal between 0 and 1.

7.2.1 Results Obtained Utilizing the First Design Approach

Based on the LMI requirements developed in Theorem 1 and resolving the LMI-based minimization issue derived from this theorem, using the two additional LMI conditions defined in (95), and by setting $\zeta = 4$, we obtain the following results:

$$\mathcal{K} = \begin{bmatrix} -5.6961 & -1.7423 \end{bmatrix} \tag{100a}$$

$$\epsilon_{\min} = 5.2728 \tag{100b}$$

$$\bar{\delta}_{\max} = 0.2831 \tag{100c}$$

By applying the feedback gain $\mathcal{K}$ presented in (100c) in the adopted controller (12), we obtain the graphical results depicted in Fig. 7. The results in this figure illustrate the successful control of the robot at the intended state. In addition, at the equilibrium point, the control effort u is zero.

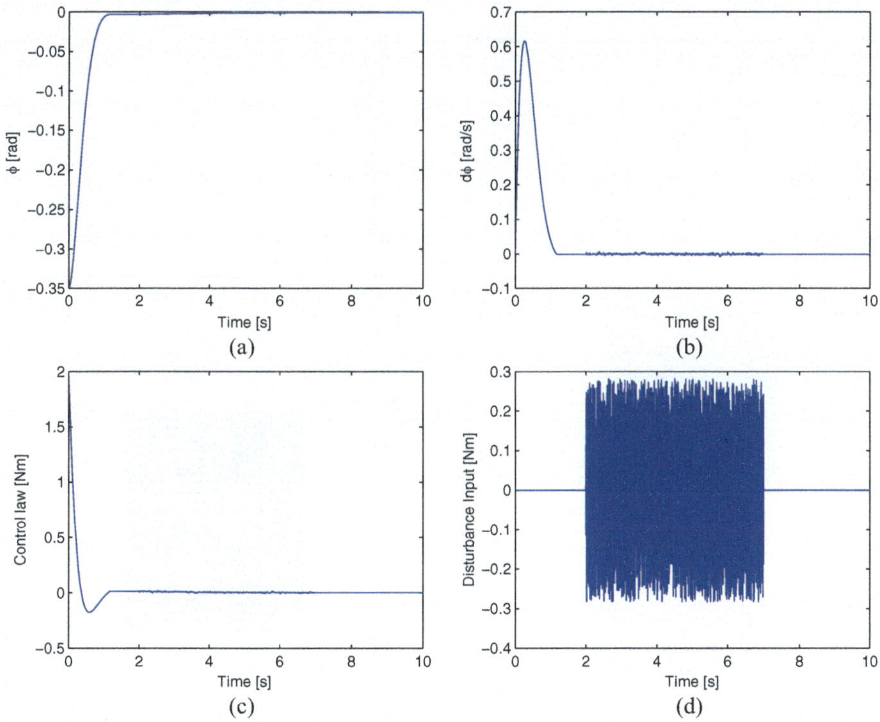

Fig. 7 Second simulation results obtained according to the first design method. Evolution of: **a** the angular position error ϕ, **b** the angular velocity error $\dot{\phi}$, **c** the proposed controller u, and **d** the external disturbance Δ_t

7.2.2 Results Obtained Utilizing the Second Design Approach

According to the enhanced design approach of the LMI conditions formulated in Theorem 2 and by resolving the LMI issue presented in this theorem, and by integrating the two additional LMI conditions defined in (95), with $\zeta = 4$, we get:

$$\mathcal{K} = \begin{bmatrix} -4.9902 & -1.7140 \end{bmatrix} \tag{101a}$$

$$\epsilon_{\min} = 6.0535 \tag{101b}$$

$$\bar{\delta}_{\max} = 0.2940 \tag{101c}$$

By applying the feedback gain $\mathcal{K}$ as defined in (101c) to the controller (12), we achieved the graphical results illustrated in Fig. 8. Therefore, these figures show that the exoskeleton robot was successfully controlled to the intended state. Additionally, the control effort u is zero when the exoskeleton robot has been stabilized at the intended location.

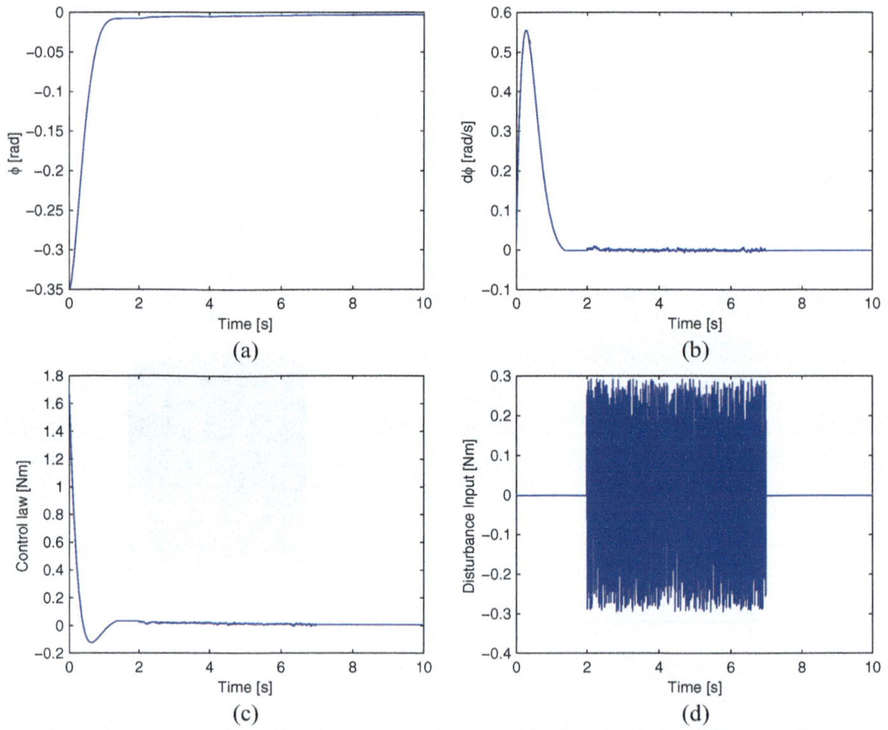

Fig. 8 Second simulation results obtained using the second design method. Evolution of: **a** the angular position error ϕ, **b** the angular velocity error $\dot{\phi}$, **c** the proposed controller u, and **d** the external disturbance Δ_t

7.3 Discussion

Notice that the proposed controller effectively handles the challenge of controlling the position of the knee exoskeleton robotic system of Fig. 4. This is achieved by using two different approaches to compute the feedback gain. As a result, in all simulations, the robot is accurately regulated to reach the intended position, denoted as θ_d. This causes the angular position error ϕ to converge to zero, as shown in Figs. 5a, 6a, 7a, and 8a. Additionally, in these simulations, the angular velocity error $\dot{\phi}$ also converges to zero, as depicted in Figs. 5b, 6b, 7b, and 8b. However, variations occur, attributed to the presence of the perturbing torque Δ_t. These outcomes demonstrate the resilience of the controller to lumped disturbances.

The disturbance affecting the knee exoskeleton robot is represented by the torque load Δ_t in Figs. 5d, 6d, 7d, and 8d. In the first simulation, this lumped disturbance is characterized as a sinusoidal signal ranging between $-\bar{\delta}$ and $\bar{\delta}$, with the torque applied only between 2 and 7 s. Consequently, the simulation results under the influence of this lumped disturbing torque Δ_t are depicted in Figs. 5 and 6. It is evident that the knee exoskeleton system exhibits oscillations around its equilibrium position. When the perturbing torque's impact diminishes, the controlled knee exoskeleton robot returns to its desired state. It's worth noting that we obtain $\bar{\delta} = 0.3368$ in the first approach and $\bar{\delta} = 0.3632$ in the second approach. In the second simulation, the disturbing torque is modeled as a randomly time-varying signal ranging between $-\bar{\delta}$ and $\bar{\delta}$, with the torque applied solely between 2 and 7 s. The results under the lumped disturbing torque Δ_t are shown in Figs. 7 and 8. Again, we observe the oscillatory behavior of the knee exoskeleton system around its equilibrium position. When the perturbing torque's influence diminishes, the controlled knee exoskeleton robot returns to its desired state. As previously mentioned, $\bar{\delta} = 0.2831$ in the first approach, while in the second approach, $\bar{\delta} = 0.2940$.

Moreover, in Figs. 5c, 6c, 7c and 8c, the temporal evolution of the proposed control law u for all cases is depicted. It is evident that when the knee exoskeleton robot was stabilized under the influence of the charge load as an external disturbance, the control input u converged to zero.

Additionally, it is worth noting that in all cases, the time taken for the exoskeleton to stabilize varies between the two approaches. Notably, the first design method usually results in shorter stabilization times compared to the second design method. For instance, in the simulation results, the first approach stabilizes the robot in approximately 2 s (as shown in Fig. 5a), while the second approach achieves stability in less than 3 s (as presented in Fig. 6a).

Furthermore, it is essential to highlight that the control effort u applied to the joint for both developed approaches in the two different simulations is significantly small, as depicted in Figs. 5c, 6c, 7c, and 8c. However, in the two simulations, the second design method consistently yields a smaller value of the control effort at the start of the simulation compared to the first design method. For example, in the first simulation results, using the first developed approach, the control effort at the start of the simulation is equal to 1.8 (as illustrated in Fig. 5c), while the second approach results in a control effort at the start of the simulation is equal to 1.4 (as shown in Fig. 6c).

Therefore, the results from the two design methods showed that the actuated knee exoskeleton is effectively controlled, achieving the desired position. Therefore, in all cases, the controller for the knee exoskeleton robot proves to be effective.

8 Conclusion and Future Directions

The position control of an exoskeleton knee assistance system for the rehabilitation of lower limbs was the main topic of this work [23, 26, 28]. To achieve this goal, we employed an affine state-feedback controller tailored to the dynamics of the rehabilitation robot, which includes considerations for external disturbances. Using the Lyapunov methodology and technical lemmas, we developed two different methods to establish LMI requirements on the gain of the adopted controller, ensuring the stability of the regulated knee exoskeleton. Through a comparative analysis, we evaluated the efficiency of each method. Moreover, numerical and simulation results showcased the successful stabilization of the knee exoskeleton robotic system, validating the developed LMI requirements and demonstrating the efficacy of the affine state-feedback control law in solving the robust control problem addressed in this work. Our goal going forward is to create a robust control law capable of handling uncertainties and external perturbations. Additionally, we intend to explore the development of alternative controllers using the LMI techniques. By integrating movement constraints of various lower limb articulations into the controller design, we aim to minimize control effort and reduce energy consumption, ultimately advancing the capabilities of the knee exoskeleton robotic system.

References

1. Al-Dujaili, A.Q., Hasan, A.F., Humaidi, A.J., Al-Jodah, A.: Anti-disturbance control design of exoskeleton knee robotic system for rehabilitative care. Heliyon **10**(9) (2024). https://doi.org/10.1016/j.heliyon.2024.e28911
2. Al-Hayali, N.K., Chiad, J.S., Nacy, S.M., Hussein, O.: A review of passive and quasi-passive lower limb exoskeletons for gait rehabilitation. vol **44**, 428–439 (2021)
3. Al Rezage, G., Tokhi, M.: Fuzzy PID control of lower limb exoskeleton for elderly mobility. In: 2016 IEEE International Conference on Automation, Quality and Testing, Robotics (AQTR), pp. 1–6 (2016)
4. Aljuboury, A.S., Hameed, A.H., Ajel, A.R., Humaidi, A.J., Alkhayyat, A., Mhdawi, A.K.A.: Robust adaptive control of knee exoskeleton-assistant system based on nonlinear disturbance observer. Actuators **11**(3) (2022)
5. Arazpour, M., Hutchins, S.W., Ahmadi Bani, M.: The efficacy of powered orthoses on walking in persons with paraplegia. Prosthetics and orthotics international **39**(2), 90–99 (2015)
6. Baud, R., Manzoori, A.R., Ijspeert, A., Bouri, M.: Review of control strategies for lower-limb exoskeletons to assist gait. Journal of NeuroEngineering and Rehabilitation **18**(1), 119 (2021)

7. Bergmann, L., Voss, D., Leonhardt, S., Ngo, C.: Lower-limb exoskeleton with compliant actuators: Human cooperative control. IEEE Transactions on Medical Robotics and Bionics **5**(3), 717–729 (2023)
8. Bkekri, R., Benamor, A., Alouane, M.A., Fried, G., Messaoud, H.: Robust adaptive super twisting controller: methodology and application of a human-driven knee joint orthosis. Industrial Robot **46**(4), 481–489 (2019)
9. Brahmi, B., Saad, M., Luna, C.O., Archambault, P.S., Rahman, M.H.: Passive and active rehabilitation control of human upper-limb exoskeleton robot with dynamic uncertainties. Robotica **36**(11), 1757–1779 (2018)
10. Chen, B., Zhong, C.H., Zhao, X., Ma, H., Qin, L., Liao, W.H.: Reference joint trajectories generation of cuhk-exo exoskeleton for system balance in walking assistance. IEEE Access **7**, 33809–33821 (2019)
11. Chen, G., Chan, C.K., Guo, Z., Yu, H.: A review of lower extremity assistive robotic exoskeletons in rehabilitation therapy. Critical Reviews™ in Biomedical Engineering **41**(4-5) (2013)
12. Daachi, M.E., Madani, T., Daachi, B., Djouani, K.: A radial basis function neural network adaptive controller to drive a powered lower limb knee joint orthosis. Applied Soft Computing **34**, 324–336 (2015)
13. Grimmer, M., Riener, R., Walsh, C.J., Seyfarth, A.: Mobility related physical and functional losses due to aging and disease-a motivation for lower limb exoskeletons. Journal of neuroengineering and rehabilitation **16**(1), 1–21 (2019)
14. Gritli, H.: Robust master-slave synchronization of chaos in a one-sided 1-DoF impact mechanical oscillator subject to parametric uncertainties and disturbances. Mechanism and Machine Theory **142**, 103610 (2019)
15. Gritli, H.: LMI-based robust stabilization of a class of input-constrained uncertain nonlinear systems with application to a helicopter model. Complexity **2020**, 7025761 (2020)
16. Gritli, H., Belghith, S.: Robust feedback control of the underactuated Inertia Wheel Inverted Pendulum under parametric uncertainties and subject to external disturbances: LMI formulation. Journal of The Franklin Institute **355**(18), 9150–9191 (2018)
17. Gritli, H., Belghith, S.: LMI-based synthesis of a robust saturated controller for an underactuated mechanical system subject to motion constraints. European Journal of Control **57**, 179–193 (2021)
18. Gritli, H., Jenhani, S.: LMI-based state feedback control of the underactuated inertia wheel inverted pendulum to the unstable upright position. Journal of Vibration Testing and System Dynamics **8**(2), 207–234 (2024). https://doi.org/10.5890/JVTSD.2024.06.005
19. Gritli, H., Jenhani, S.: Position control of robotic systems via linear controllers with application to a lower limb rehabilitation exoskeleton robot: Design and comparative analysis. In: E. Campos-Cantón, G. Huerta-Cuellar, E. Zambrano-Serrano, E. Tlelo-Cuautle (eds.) Complex Systems and Their Applications, pp. 123–151. Springer Nature Switzerland, Cham (2024)
20. Hedayati, H., Suzuki, R., Rees, W., Leithinger, D., Szafir, D.: Designing expandable-structure robots for human-robot interaction. Frontiers in Robotics and AI **9**, 719639 (2022)
21. Hobbs, B., Artemiadis, P.: A review of robot-assisted lower-limb stroke therapy: unexplored paths and future directions in gait rehabilitation. Frontiers in neurorobotics **14**, 19 (2020)
22. Islam, M.R., Assad-Uz-Zaman, M., Rahman, M.H.: Design and control of an ergonomic robotic shoulder for wearable exoskeleton robot for rehabilitation. International Journal of Dynamics and Control **8**, 312–325 (2020)
23. Jenhani, S., Gritli, H.: A composite robust position control design for an actuated knee rehabilitation exoskeleton. In: 2023 20th International Multi-Conference on Systems, Signals & Devices (SSD), pp. 129–134 (2023)
24. Jenhani, S., Gritli, H.: Enhancing knee rehabilitation exoskeleton control via a robust LMI-based strategy and by considering state constraints. In: 2023 IEEE 11th International Conference on Systems and Control (ICSC), pp. 905–911 (2023)
25. Jenhani, S., Gritli, H.: Lmi-based design of an affine PD controller for the robust stabilization of the knee joint of a lower-limb rehabilitation exoskeleton. In: 2023 IEEE International

Conference on Advanced Systems and Emergent Technologies (IC_ASET), pp. 1–7. IEEE (2023)
26. Jenhani, S., Gritli, H.: Robust LMI-based state-feedback control of a knee exoskeleton robotic system. In: 2023 20th International Multi-Conference on Systems, Signals & Devices (SSD), pp. 121–128 (2023)
27. Jenhani, S., Gritli, H.: LMI-based design of a robust affine control law for the position control of a knee exoskeleton robot: Comparative analysis of stability conditions. In: E. Campos-Cantón, G. Huerta-Cuellar, E. Zambrano-Serrano, E. Tlelo-Cuautle (eds.) Complex Systems and Their Applications, pp. 95–122. Springer Nature Switzerland, Cham (2024)
28. Jenhani, S., Gritli, H.: An LMI-based robust state-feedback controller design for the position control of a knee rehabilitation exoskeleton robot: Comparative analysis. Measurement and Control **57**(9), 1326–1346 (2024). https://doi.org/10.1177/00202940241236295
29. Jenhani, S., Gritli, H., Carbone, G.: Comparison between some nonlinear controllers for the position control of Lagrangian-type robotic systems. Chaos Theory and Applications **4**(4), 179 – 196 (2022)
30. Jenhani, S., Gritli, H., Carbone, G.: Position control of Lagrangian robotic systems via an affine PID-based controller and using the LMI approach. In: V. Niola, A. Gasparetto, G. Quaglia, G. Carbone (eds.) Advances in Italian Mechanism Science, pp. 727–737. Springer International Publishing, Cham (2022)
31. Kalita, B., Narayan, J., Dwivedy, S.K.: Development of active lower limb robotic-based orthosis and exoskeleton devices: A systematic review. International Journal of Social Robotics **3**(4), 775–793 (2021)
32. Kawamoto, H., Kandone, H., Sakurai, T., Ariyasu, R., Ueno, Y., Eguchi, K., Sankai, Y.: Development of an assist controller with robot suit hal for hemiplegic patients using motion data on the unaffected side. In: 2014 36th Annual International Conference of the IEEE Engineering in Medicine and Biology Society, pp. 3077–3080 (2014)
33. Khamar, M., Edrisi, M.: Designing a backstepping sliding mode controller for an assistant human knee exoskeleton based on nonlinear disturbance observer. Mechatronics **54**, 121–132 (2018)
34. Li, Y., Sena, A., Wang, Z., Xing, X., Babic, J., van Asseldonk, E.H., Burdet, E.: A review on interaction control for contact robots through intent detection. Progress in Biomedical Engineering (2022)
35. Liu, J., Fang, H., Xu, J.: Online adaptive pid control for a multi-joint lower extremity exoskeleton system using improved particle swarm optimization. Machines **10**(1), 21 (2021)
36. Mefoued, S.: A robust adaptive neural control scheme to drive an actuated orthosis for assistance of knee movements. Neurocomputing **140**, 27–40 (2014)
37. Mekki, M., Delgado, A.D., Fry, A., Putrino, D., Huang, V.: Robotic rehabilitation and spinal cord injury: a narrative review. Neurotherapeutics **15**, 604–617 (2018)
38. Narayan, J., Dwivedy, S.K.: Preliminary design and development of a low-cost lower-limb exoskeleton system for paediatric rehabilitation. Proceedings of the Institution of Mechanical Engineers, Part H: Journal of Engineering in Medicine **235**(5), 530–545 (2021)
39. Narayan, J., Dwivedy, S.K.: Lower limb exoskeletons for pediatric gait rehabilitation: A brief review of design, actuation, and control schemes. In: 2023 IEEE International Conference on Advanced Systems and Emergent Technologies (IC_ASET), pp. 1–6 (2023)
40. Narayan, J., Gritli, H., Dwivedy, S.K.: Fast terminal sliding mode control with rapid reaching law for a pediatric gait exoskeleton system. International Journal of Intelligent Robotics and Applications **8**, 76–95 (2024)
41. Narayan, J., Kalita, B., Dwivedy, S.K.: Adaptive backstepping human-cooperative control of a pediatric gait exoskeleton system with high- and low-level admittance. Proceedings of the Institution of Mechanical Engineers, Part I: Journal of Systems and Control Engineering p. 09596518231191390 (2023). https://doi.org/10.1177/09596518231191390
42. Narayan, J., Patel, B.M., Abbas, M., Shivhare, G., Dwivedy, S.K.: Cooperative control of a pediatric exoskeleton system for active-assist gait rehabilitation. In: 2022 IEEE International Conference on Electronics, Computing and Communication Technologies (CONECCT), pp. 1–6 (2022)

43. Rifaï, H., Mohammed, S., Hassani, W., Amirat, Y.: Nested saturation based control of an actuated knee joint orthosis. Mechatronics **23**(8), 1141–1149 (2013)
44. Rodríguez-Fernández, A., Lobo-Prat, J., Font-Llagunes, J.M.: Systematic review on wearable lower-limb exoskeletons for gait training in neuromuscular impairments. Journal of neuroengineering and rehabilitation **18**(1), 1–21 (2021)
45. Rupal, B.S., Rafique, S., Singla, A., Singla, E., Isaksson, M., Virk, G.S.: Lower-limb exoskeletons: Research trends and regulatory guidelines in medical and non-medical applications. International Journal of Advanced Robotic Systems **14**(6), 1729881417743554 (2017)
46. Shi, D., Zhang, W., Zhang, W., Ding, X.: A review on lower limb rehabilitation exoskeleton robots. Chinese Journal of Mechanical Engineering **32**(1), 74 (2019)
47. Starczyńska, M., Sacharuk, A.: Rehabilitation exoskeleton-the perspective of improving the quality of life for people with disabilities. Archives of Physiotherapy & Global Researches **24**(2) (2020)
48. Tan, K., Koyama, S., Sakurai, H., Teranishi, T., Kanada, Y., Tanabe, S.: Wearable robotic exoskeleton for gait reconstruction in patients with spinal cord injury: A literature review. Journal of orthopaedic translation **28**, 55–64 (2021)
49. Turki, F., Gritli, H., Belghith, S.: An LMI-based design of a robust state-feedback control for the master-slave tracking of an impact mechanical oscillator with double-side rigid constraints and subject to bounded-parametric uncertainty. Communications in Nonlinear Science and Numerical Simulation **82**, 105020 (2020)
50. Wang, Z., Yang, C., Zhang, S., Zhang, S., Yi, C., Ding, Z., Wei, B., Jiang, F.: Knee flexion-assisted method for human-exoskeleton system. IEEE Transactions on Neural Systems and Rehabilitation Engineering **31**, 2800–2808 (2023)
51. Yang, A., Asselin, P., Knezevic, S., Kornfeld, S., Spungen, A.: Assessment of in-hospital walking velocity and level of assistance in a powered exoskeleton in persons with spinal cord injury. Topics in spinal cord injury rehabilitation **21**(2), 100–109 (2015)
52. Zhou, J., Yang, S., Xue, Q.: Lower limb rehabilitation exoskeleton robot: A review. Advances in Mechanical Engineering **13**(4), 16878140211011862 (2021)
53. Zhou, L., Chen, W., Chen, W., Bai, S., Zhang, J., Wang, J.: Design of a passive lower limb exoskeleton for walking assistance with gravity compensation. Mechanism and Machine Theory **150**, 103840 (2020)

LMI-Based Design of an Affine PD Controller for the Position Control of Robotic Systems with Application to Human Upper-Limb Rehabilitation via an Exoskeleton Robot

Hassène Gritli

Abstract Controlling the motion dynamics of robotic systems, notably exoskeleton robots for the rehabilitation of human's upper/lower limbs, has piqued the interest of researchers as a potential healthcare strategy for treating impairment problems in disabled persons. The controller design methodology can appropriately rely on linearizing the nonlinear dynamics around some desired point. In this chapter, we use the difference between the robotic system's nonlinear dynamic model and the approximate linear model to generate a nonlinear dynamical system that meets a specific Lipschitz constraint. Using this scaled nonlinear dynamics, we propose an affine PD controller to construct certain LMI conditions ensuring the closed-loop stability of the controlled robotic system using three approaches. Minimization problems based on LMI constraints are then created to determine the maximal Lipschitz constant. Some new LMI conditions are recommended to limit the extent of the controller's feedback gains. We suggest a two-degree-of-freedom (2-DoF) upper-limb exoskeleton robot as an application. The three methods are used to provide a portfolio of numerical findings for evaluating the feasibility of the designed LMI challenges. Furthermore, some simulation results demonstrating the efficacy of the adopted affine PD control law in the stabilization of the robotic system, and therefore of the 2-DoF upper-limb exoskeleton robot, are accomplished.

H. Gritli (✉)
Higher Institute of Information and Communication Technologies, University of Carthage, Borj Cedria 1164, Tunis, Tunisia
e-mail: hassene.gritli@istic.ucar.tn

Laboratory of Robotics, Informatics and Complex Systems (RISC Lab—LR16ES07), National Engineering School of Tunis, University of Tunis El Manar, Technopole of Borj Cédria, Route de Soliman, BP 123, Hammam Chatt, 1164 Ben Arous, Tunisia

M. Mittal and J. Narayan (eds.), *Intelligent Cyber-Physical Systems for Healthcare Solutions*, https://doi.org/10.1007/978-981-97-8983-2_14

1 Introduction

Robotic systems are utilized in a variety of applications where they must be controlled in order to achieve a certain purpose [34, 51]. The construction of some specific mathematical models, like transformation models between Cartesian space and joint one, and also dynamic models describing the robot's equations of motion, is required for the control of robots. Secondly, robotic system control was regarded as an essential subject in the field of study. Several control approaches for robotic systems may be found in the literature, such as [1, 7, 33, 37, 39, 50]. A robotic system can use linear and nonlinear control approaches to realize a specific objective, like position control or trajectory tracking. Among the most useful controllers that can be found in the literature are the PID controller, the computed-torque controller, the sliding-mode controller, and the gravity compensated controller, as in [17, 28, 34, 51, 53], just to name a few. Furthermore, we regard robot position control to be one of the most crucial topics in robotics [28, 35, 53, 59].

In medicine, robotic systems have made important contributions to healthcare by providing revolutionary solutions for diagnosis, surgery, rehabilitation, and a variety of medical treatments [4, 41, 54]. Some significant applications of robotic systems in healthcare are robotic surgery, diagnostic and imaging robotics, laboratory automation, robotic prosthetics and orthotics, robotic patient assistants, and rehabilitation robotics [32, 40, 41, 46, 60]. For rehabilitation robotics, we can find two main types of robots used for the rehabilitation therapy of lower and upper limbs [4, 54, 61]: (1) Robotic exoskeletons are devices that help people with mobility issues by providing support and enabling movement during rehabilitation exercises [3, 22, 25, 42, 47–49], (2) Robots for physical therapy assistance, for which robots are used to help patients recover from strokes, spinal cord injuries, and other neurological diseases [19, 21, 38, 40, 44].

Upper and lower limb rehabilitation exoskeletons are robotic devices that help people with upper limb disabilities restore strength, mobility, and functioning. These devices are especially beneficial for patients who have had a stroke, spinal cord injury, or other neurological or musculoskeletal diseases that impair the arms, hands, knees, and legs. We can note two main essential elements of upper limb rehabilitation exoskeletons: (1) Assistance and support, for which exoskeletons provide mechanical support to help disabled users perform daily activities and rehabilitation exercises [19, 21, 46], and (2) Neuromuscular rehabilitation, for which the rehabilitation exoskeletons are often used for neuromuscular retraining, helping individuals regain control and coordination of their upper limbs [9, 19, 38, 48]. Several control methods have been developed in the literature as those in [2, 6, 32, 42, 43, 45, 49, 61].

Linear Matrix Inequalities (LMIs) are an extremely useful tool in control theory, especially for analyzing and constructing control systems [5]. Many problems related to stability analysis and controller synthesis can be tackled as feasibility or optimization problems using LMI constraints. They offer a computationally efficient paradigm for addressing complicated control problems. Moreover, they allow the formulation of many constraints and objectives as LMIs, which may be solved effectively with convex optimization techniques. In fact, this efficiency of LMIs is especially useful when working with large-scale systems or real-time control applications, which have limited computational resources. Furthermore, LMIs enable the development of robust controllers that provide stability and performance in the face of parametric uncertainties and external disturbances. Several works in the literature have used the LMIs for the analysis and synthesis problems, as in [10–14, 18, 55–58], just to mention a few. The LMIs have been also considered recently for the control of lower-limb exoskeleton robots for the rehabilitation purpose [15, 23–27]. Different approaches have been proposed for the design of the controller based on different forms of the Lipschitz constraint imposed on the non-linearity presented in the nonlinear dynamics of the exoskeleton robot.

Furthermore, it is well known that high feedback gains are unrealizable in practice to control robotic systems. Moreover, the presence of high gains might cause instability in the closed-loop robotic system. Furthermore, they can increase noise and disturbances, resulting in oscillations or even instability in the controlled system. Therefore, the objective is to limit the controller's gains in order to ensure that the closed-loop system is stable and it does not display undesired behavior, and will be certainly realizable in real-world applications. Several works and approaches have been achieved to deal with such problems, especially using the LMI approach. See for example [11, 13, 20, 52] and references inside.

We are interested in this study in the control of the position of robotic systems, and we use a two-degree-of-freedom (2-DoF) upper-limb rehabilitation exoskeleton robot as an application example. We use an affine PD controller with a dynamical model characterizing the difference between nonlinear and approximate linear systems. Thus, relying on the resized nonlinear dynamical model, which will be supposed to verify some specific Lipschitz condition characterized by an unknown Lipschitz constant to be maximized, we use LMI techniques to build inequality conditions on the feedback gains of the controller guaranteeing the closed-loop stability of the controlled robotic system at the required point via three different methods. In addition, and to establish the LMI requirements, we will resort to the S-procedure lemma, the Schur complement, and the Young inequality [10, 12]. To concertize this objective while also finding the maximal Lipschitz constant, an LMI-based minimization problem to determine the optimum value of the controller's feedback gains will be built. Furthermore, we impose some conditions to limit the amount of the feedback gains [10, 12].

The rest of this chapter is organized like so: Sect. 2 presents the nonlinear dynamics of robotic systems and the 2-DoF exoskeleton robot as an application. The problem of this work is also examined in this previous section. Sect. 3 presents the resized nonlinear dynamics based on the linear dynamic system and the proposed affine PD control law. The three design methodologies of the LMI conditions without considering the problem of high feedback gains, are presented in Sect. 4. Some numerical simulations are also realized in this same section. The development of the improved LMI design methods by considering the problem of reducing the size of the matrix feedback gains is realized in Sect. 5. Some numerical results of the enhanced LMI problems are realized in Sect. 6. The dependence of the intended position of the robotic system on the Lipschitz condition is also achieved in the previous section. The study of the evolution of the robotic system's states is also realized in Sect. 6. A conclusion is lastly presented in Sect. 7.

2 Nonlinear Dynamical Model of Robotic Systems

2.1 General Nonlinear Dynamics

Relying on the Lagrangian mechanical system concept, the dynamic model characterizing the motion of robotic systems can be developed as follows:

$$\frac{d}{dt}\left(\frac{\partial \mathcal{L}_g(\theta,\dot{\theta})}{\partial \dot{\theta}}\right) - \frac{\partial \mathcal{L}_g(\theta,\dot{\theta})}{\partial \theta} + \frac{\partial \mathcal{R}(\dot{\theta})}{\partial \dot{\theta}} = \mathcal{D}(\theta)u \tag{1}$$

where the quantity $\mathcal{L}_g(\theta,\dot{\theta})$ stands for the Lagrangian and has the following definition:

$$\mathcal{L}_g(\theta,\dot{\theta}) = \mathcal{K}_e(\theta,\dot{\theta}) - \mathcal{P}_e(\theta) \tag{2}$$

where $\mathcal{K}_e$ stands for the kinetic energy, and $\mathcal{P}_e$ represents the potential energy.

Furthermore, in the nonlinear dynamical model (1), we have the following notations:

- $\theta \in \mathbb{R}^n$ represents the vector of angular positions,
- $\dot{\theta} \in \mathbb{R}^n$ represents the vector of angular velocities,
- $u \in \mathbb{R}^n$ represents the vector of inputs, and stands for the controller to design in this chapter to control the position of the robotic system,
- $\mathcal{R}(\dot{\theta})$ represents the frictional dissipation term, and
- $\mathcal{D}(\theta) \in \mathbb{R}^{n\times m}$ is an external force matrix that represents the distribution of control inputs.

The model's vector form (1) can be written and reformed using the following form:

$$\mathcal{M}(\theta)\ddot{\theta} + \mathcal{H}(\theta,\dot{\theta})\dot{\theta} + \mathcal{G}(\theta) + \mathcal{F}_f + \mathcal{F}_e + \mathcal{F}_d = \mathcal{D}(\theta)u \tag{3}$$

where

- $\mathcal{M}(\theta)$ is the inertia matrix such that $\mathcal{M}(\theta) = \mathcal{M}^{\mathrm{T}}(\theta)$.
- $\mathcal{H}(\theta,\dot{\theta})\dot{\theta}$ is a vector containing Centrifugal and Coriolis forces.
- $\mathcal{G}(\theta)$ is the gravity vector.

- $\mathcal{F}_f$ is a vector that represents forces induced by friction losses, and is like so:

$$\mathcal{F}_f = \mathcal{F}_v\dot{\theta} + \mathcal{F}_c\text{sign}(\dot{\theta}) \tag{4}$$

where the square matrix $\mathcal{F}_v$ contains viscous frictions, the square matrix $\mathcal{F}_c$ contains Coulomb frictions, and "sign" represents the signum function.
- $\mathcal{F}_e$ is a vector that represents elastic element forces, and is defined as follows:

$$\mathcal{F}_e = \mathcal{F}_k\theta \tag{5}$$

where $\mathcal{F}_k$ is a square stiffness matrix that contains stiffness coefficients of elastic elements such as springs.
- $\mathcal{F}_d$ is a vector representing external disturbances.

2.2 Simplified Nonlinear Dynamics

Assuming in the sequel that $\tau_f = 0$, $\tau_k = 0$, and $\tau_d = 0$. Then, the general nonlinear dynamical model (3) is recast:

$$\mathcal{M}(\theta)\ddot{\theta} + \mathcal{H}(\theta, \dot{\theta})\dot{\theta} + \mathcal{G}(\theta) = \mathcal{D}(\theta)u \tag{6}$$

It is worth noting that the nonlinear dynamical model (6) has been described in various research articles in the literature, including [33, 36, 37]. This canonical form (6) can represent a variety of robotic systems.

2.3 A 2-DoF Upper-Limb Exoskeleton Robot as an Application

As an example of application, we propose the 2-DoF exoskeleton robot of the human upper extremity, illustrated in Fig. 1. In this plot, θ_1 and θ_2 correspond to the absolute angular positions of the two rotating joints. Such exoskeleton is composed of two active joints actuated by the two controllers u_1 and u_2. The different parameters, their specifications, and values are provided in Table 1.

The following matrices of the adopted robotic system are defined using the nonlinear model (6):

$$\mathcal{M}(\theta) = \begin{bmatrix} m_1a_1^2 + m_2l_1^2 + I_1 & m_2l_1a_2\cos(\theta_1 - \theta_2) \\ m_2l_1a_2\cos(\theta_1 - \theta_2) & m_2a_2^2 + I_2 \end{bmatrix} \tag{7a}$$

$$\mathcal{H}(\theta, \dot{\theta}) = \sin(\theta_1 - \theta_2)\begin{bmatrix} 0 & m_2l_1a_2\dot{\theta}_2 \\ -m_2l_1a_2\dot{\theta}_1 & 0 \end{bmatrix} \tag{7b}$$

Table 1 Description and values of the different parameters of the 2-DoF upper-limb rehabilitation exoskeleton robot illustrated in Fig. 1

Parameter	Specification	Value
m_1	Mass of the exoskeleton robot's first segment	2 kg
m_2	Mass of the exoskeleton robot's second segment	1 kg
l_1	Length of the exoskeleton robot's first segment	0.5 m
l_2	Length of the exoskeleton robot's second segment	0.4 m
a_1	Distance to the center of mass of the first segment	0.375 m
a_2	Distance to the center of mass of the second segment	0.25 m
I_1	Rotational inertia of the exoskeleton robot's first segment	0.02
I_2	Rotational inertia of the exoskeleton robot's second segment	0.01 kg m^2
g	Constant of the gravity acceleration	9.81 m/s^2

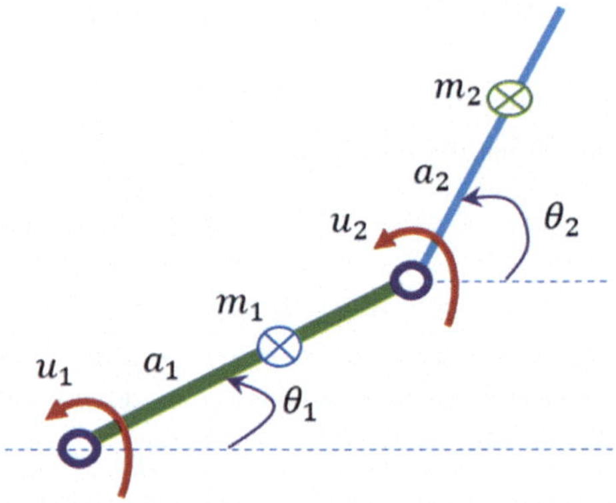

Fig. 1 The robotic system adopted as an application: a 2-DoF exoskeleton robot for upper-limb rehabilitation

$$\mathcal{G}(\theta) = g \begin{bmatrix} (m_1 a_1 + m_2 l_1)\cos(\theta_1) \\ m_2 a_2 \cos(\theta_2) \end{bmatrix} \tag{7c}$$

$$\mathcal{D}(\theta) = \begin{bmatrix} 1 & -1 \\ 0 & 1 \end{bmatrix} \tag{7d}$$

where $\theta = \begin{bmatrix} \theta_1 & \theta_2 \end{bmatrix}^{\mathrm{T}}$ is the vector of generalized absolute angular positions.

2.4 *Problem Statement*

The control process of robots is primarily concerned with building an efficient controller u and, as a result, selecting the suitable value of the matrix feedback gains to accomplish the intended result. The main objective is to use the nonlinear dynamic model defined by expression (6) to control the position of the robotic system, and then the 2-DoF exoskeleton robot in Fig. 1, and maintain its stability at the required position [8, 51].

Therefore, the goal of the position control of robots is to design a function u satisfying the following objective:

$$\lim_{t \to +\infty} \theta(t) = \theta_d \tag{8}$$

where $\theta_d \in \mathbb{R}^n$ represents the desired position. It is worth noting that at θ_d, we have $\dot{\theta}_d = 0$ and $\ddot{\theta}_d = 0$.

In this chapter, we adopt the design of an affine controller based on the Proportional and Derivative (PD) actions, to ensure the control of the robot to the intended position θ_d and hence satisfies the control objective (8). Such controller u will depend mainly on two matrix gains, namely $\mathcal{K}_1$ and $\mathcal{K}_2$.

Relying on the work in [30, 31], we will design LMI conditions on $\mathcal{K}_1$ and $\mathcal{K}_2$ to be designed using the dynamical model describing the difference between the nonlinear dynamic system (6) and its linear model (9); which will be developed in the next section.

Remark 1 In the sequel, the following notations will be considered: $\mathcal{O}$ represents the zero-matrix, and $\mathcal{I}$ represents the identity matrix,, both with appropriate dimensions. Moreover, He $\{\mathcal{X}\} = \mathcal{X} + \mathcal{X}^{\mathrm{T}}$.

3 Resized Nonlinear Dynamics Based on the Linear Dynamic Model

3.1 *Approximate Linearized Dynamic Model*

Let $\epsilon = \theta - \theta_d$ represents the position error. Relying on [16, 29], a linear dynamical approximation model of the nonlinear dynamics (6) was developed. A linear model of this type is defined by the following expression and is approximated about the target position θ_d:

$$\ddot{\epsilon} = \mathcal{A}_d \epsilon + \mathcal{B}_d (u - u_d) \tag{9}$$

where $\mathcal{A}_d$, $\mathcal{B}_d$, and u_d (the desired control effort at the intended position θ_d) are defined as follows:

$$\mathcal{A}_d = \mathcal{M}^{-1}(\theta_d)\left(\mathcal{D}_\theta(\theta_d)\widehat{u_d} - \mathcal{G}_\theta(\theta_d)\right) \tag{10a}$$

$$\mathcal{B}_d = \mathcal{M}^{-1}(\theta_d)\mathcal{D}(\theta_d) \tag{10b}$$

$$u_d = \mathcal{D}^{-1}(\theta_d)\mathcal{G}(\theta_d) \tag{10c}$$

where

$$\mathcal{G}_\theta(\theta_d) = \frac{\partial \mathcal{G}(\theta)}{\partial \theta}|_{(\theta_d)} \tag{11a}$$

$$\mathcal{D}_\theta(\theta_d) = \frac{\partial \mathcal{D}(\theta)}{\partial \theta}|_{(\theta_d)} \tag{11b}$$

$$\widehat{u_d} = \text{diag}\left(\underbrace{u_d, u_d, \ldots, u_d}_{n \text{ times}}\right) \tag{11c}$$

As an illustrative application, consider the following target location θ_d for the robot's stabilization:

$$\theta_d = \begin{bmatrix} 90^\circ \\ -45^\circ \end{bmatrix} \tag{12}$$

Using the desired state (12), expression of matrices $\mathcal{M}(\theta_d)$, $\mathcal{G}(\theta_d)$, $\mathcal{D}(\theta_d)$, $\mathcal{G}_\theta(\theta_d)$, $\mathcal{D}_\theta(\theta_d)$ and $\widehat{u_d}$ presented in the linear system (9), are equal to:

$$\mathcal{M}(\theta_d) = \begin{bmatrix} 0.5513 & -0.0884 \\ -0.0884 & 0.0725 \end{bmatrix} \tag{13a}$$

$$\mathcal{G}(\theta_d) = \begin{bmatrix} 0.0000 \\ 1.7342 \end{bmatrix} \tag{13b}$$

$$\mathcal{D}(\theta_d) = \begin{bmatrix} 1 & -1 \\ 0 & 1 \end{bmatrix} \tag{13c}$$

$$\mathcal{G}_\theta(\theta_d) = \begin{bmatrix} -12.2625 & 0 \\ 0 & 1.7342 \end{bmatrix} \tag{13d}$$

$$\mathcal{D}_\theta(\theta_d) = \begin{bmatrix} 0 & 0 & 0 & 0 \\ 0 & 0 & 0 & 0 \end{bmatrix} \tag{13e}$$

$$\widehat{u_d} = \begin{bmatrix} 1.7342 & 0 \\ 1.7342 & 0 \\ 0 & 1.7342 \\ 0 & 1.7342 \end{bmatrix} \tag{13f}$$

Moreover, the matrices $\mathcal{A}_d$ and $\mathcal{B}_d$ presented in the model (9), and which were defined by expressions (10a) and (10b), and the desired control effort u_d defined by expression (10c), are computed like so:

$$\mathcal{A}_d = \begin{bmatrix} 0 & 0 & 1 & 0 \\ 0 & 0 & 0 & 1 \\ 27.6499 & -4.7672 & 0 & 0 \\ 33.7094 & -29.7317 & 0 & 0 \end{bmatrix} \tag{14a}$$

$$\mathcal{B}_d = \begin{bmatrix} 0 & 0 \\ 0 & 0 \\ 2.2548 & 0.4941 \\ 2.7490 & 14.3955 \end{bmatrix} \tag{14b}$$

$$u_d = \begin{bmatrix} 1.7342 \\ 1.7342 \end{bmatrix} \tag{14c}$$

3.2 *Resized Nonlinear Dynamical Model*

Since $\epsilon = \theta - \theta_d$, then $\dot{\epsilon} = \dot{\theta}$ and $\ddot{\epsilon} = \ddot{\theta}$. As a result, the nonlinear model (6) can be rewritten as follows:

$$\mathcal{M}(\epsilon)\ddot{\epsilon} + \mathcal{H}(\epsilon, \dot{\epsilon})\dot{\epsilon} + \mathcal{G}(\epsilon) = \mathcal{D}(\epsilon)u \tag{15}$$

We will look at the difference between the nonlinear model and its approximate linearized part using the linear dynamical model (9). Therefore, we obtain the following resized nonlinear dynamical model:

$$\ddot{\epsilon} = \mathcal{A}_d\epsilon + \mathcal{B}_d\,(u - u_d) + \Psi(\epsilon, \dot{\epsilon}) \tag{16}$$

where the term $\Psi(\epsilon, \dot{\epsilon})$ is defined as follows:

$$\begin{aligned} \Psi(\epsilon, \dot{\epsilon}) = {} & \mathcal{M}^{-1}(\epsilon)(-\mathcal{H}(\epsilon, \dot{\epsilon})\dot{\epsilon} - \mathcal{G}(\epsilon) + \mathcal{D}(\epsilon)U) \\ & - (\mathcal{A}_d\epsilon + \mathcal{B}_d\,(u - u_d)) \end{aligned} \tag{17}$$

We suppose that the quantity $\Psi(\epsilon, \dot{\epsilon})$ meets the Lipschitz condition:

$$\Psi(\epsilon, \dot{\epsilon})^{\mathrm{T}}\Psi(\epsilon, \dot{\epsilon}) \leq \ell^2\left(\epsilon^{\mathrm{T}}\epsilon + \dot{\epsilon}^{\mathrm{T}}\dot{\epsilon}\right) \tag{18}$$

where $\ell > 0$ defines the Lipschitz constant that will be determined and maximized simultaneously.

Remark 2 It is worth noting that imposing the Lipschitz condition (18) on the nonlinear function $\Psi(\epsilon, \dot{\epsilon})$ of the dynamical model of the robot allows to mainly simplify the design of the controller ensuring the stabilization of the controlled robotic system. Since the main idea behind the synthesis of the controller is the use of the LMI techniques, then the approach is to transform the nonlinear function into a quadratic one. Such quadratic form will be then used by virtue of the Lyapunov method to design the LMI conditions ensuring the stability of the position error of the robotic system. Furthermore, the Lipschitz condition allows to add some degree of robustness against uncertainties and disturbances, making hence the controller more robust against external circumstances and parameters' variation.

3.3 Adopted Affine PD Controller

Relying on the approximated linearized dynamical system (9), we propose the following PD control law having an affine structure:

$$u = u_d + \mathcal{K}_1\epsilon + \mathcal{K}_2\dot{\epsilon} \tag{19}$$

It is important to note that in [16, 29], the same expression (19) of the controller was proposed. However, such a controller was solely built and utilized to stabilize the zero equilibrium point of the linearized model (9). In this chapter, such a controller will be used for the nonlinear dynamics (16). Such a controller (19) was solely built and utilized to stabilize the linear model's zero state (9). It will be employed in this work for the nonlinear dynamics (15) or (16).

Remark 3 It is worth mentioning that the affine PD controller outperforms alternative control techniques in a variety of applications. One key advantage is the simplicity and convenience of implementation in a real-world application. Indeed, the PD controller's structure is relatively simple, with only proportional and derivative terms, making it easy to construct and tune for a variety of applications. In addition, the proposed PD controller effectively damps oscillations and stabilizes the system by modifying the control effort based on the position error and the velocity error. Furthermore, the affine PD controller can achieve fast response times while minimizing overshoot, making it ideal for applications needing rapid and precise control actions, such as robotics, aircraft, and industrial automation. Moreover, its linear structure makes analysis and stability verification easier, allowing us to more correctly forecast and optimize system performance.

3.4 Resized Nonlinear Dynamical model Under the Controller

The nonlinear dynamics (16) of the robotic system under the adopted affine PD control law (19), becomes:

$$\ddot{\epsilon} = (\mathcal{A}_d + \mathcal{B}_d\mathcal{K}_1)\epsilon + \mathcal{B}_d\mathcal{K}_2\dot{\epsilon} + \Psi(\epsilon, \dot{\epsilon}) \tag{20}$$

Let $z = \begin{bmatrix} \epsilon \\ \dot{\epsilon} \end{bmatrix}$ be the state vector. Then, the system (20) can be recast into the following form:

$$\dot{z} = (\mathcal{A} + \mathcal{B}\mathcal{K})z + \mathcal{C}\Psi(z) \tag{21}$$

where $\mathcal{A}$, $\mathcal{B}$ and $\mathcal{C}$ are expressed like so:

$$\mathcal{A} = \begin{bmatrix} \mathcal{O} & \mathcal{I} \\ \mathcal{A}_d & \mathcal{O} \end{bmatrix} \qquad \mathcal{B} = \begin{bmatrix} \mathcal{O} \\ \mathcal{B}_d \end{bmatrix} \qquad \mathcal{C} = \begin{bmatrix} \mathcal{O} \\ \mathcal{I} \end{bmatrix} \tag{22}$$

and the matrix gain $\mathcal{K}$ is defined like so:

$$\mathcal{K} = \begin{bmatrix} \mathcal{K}_1 & \mathcal{K}_2 \end{bmatrix} \tag{23}$$

Our major goal is to construct the conditions on the feedback gain $\mathcal{K}$, or systematically $\mathcal{K}_1$ and $\mathcal{K}_2$ according to expression (23), to ensure the stability of the zero equilibrium point of the controlled system (21). As a result, we will propose three methodologies to realize this objective and therefore to compare them to choose the best methodology for designing the stability conditions.

4 LMI Design of Stability Conditions

Let us first consider the following Lyapunov function:

$$\mathcal{L}(z) = z^{\mathrm{T}}\mathcal{P}z \tag{24}$$

for which $\mathcal{P} = \mathcal{P}^{\mathrm{T}} > 0$.

Relying on this expression (24), let us consider also the following stability condition:

$$\dot{\mathcal{L}}(z) + \alpha\mathcal{L}(z) < 0 \tag{25}$$

for which the parameter α is a fixed positive scalar defining the decay rate of the Lyapunov function.

From the dynamic model (21), we get the following relation:

$$\dot{\mathcal{L}}(z) + \alpha\mathcal{L}(z) = z^{\mathrm{T}}\left(\mathrm{He}\left\{\mathcal{P}\mathcal{A} + \mathcal{P}\mathcal{B}\mathcal{K}\right\} + \alpha\mathcal{P}\right)z + 2z^{\mathrm{T}}\mathcal{P}\mathcal{C}\Psi(z) \tag{26}$$

Then, relying on condition (25), the stability condition that will be considered and to be converted into LMI constraints, is defined as follows:

$$z^{\mathrm{T}}\left(\mathrm{He}\left\{\mathcal{P}\mathcal{A} + \mathcal{P}\mathcal{B}\mathcal{K}\right\} + \alpha\mathcal{P}\right)z + 2z^{\mathrm{T}}\mathcal{P}\mathcal{C}\Psi(z) < 0 \tag{27}$$

We will use three alternative ways in the following to derive the LMI stability criteria from (26) or (27) and using the Lipschitz condition (18), and also to find the admissible maximal value of the Lipschitz constant ℓ.

4.1 Used Lemmas for the Development of LMI Conditions

In order to develop the LMI conditions using the inequality constraint (27), we will use the following technical Lemmas.

Lemma 1 (Young inequality lemma [10, 12, 14]) *Let $\mathcal{Q}$ and $\mathcal{R}$ be matrices with appropriate dimensions, and a positive-definite symmetric matrix $\mathcal{H} = \mathcal{H}^{\mathrm{T}} > 0$. Then, the following inequality condition holds:*

$$\mathcal{Q}^{\mathrm{T}}\mathcal{R} + \mathcal{R}^{\mathrm{T}}\mathcal{Q} \leq \mathcal{Q}^{\mathrm{T}}\mathcal{H}\mathcal{Q} + \mathcal{R}^{\mathrm{T}}\mathcal{H}^{-1}\mathcal{R} \tag{28}$$

Lemma 2 (Schur complement lemma [10, 12, 14]) *Let $\mathcal{Q} = \mathcal{Q}^{\mathrm{T}}$, $\mathcal{R} = \mathcal{R}^{\mathrm{T}}$ and $\mathcal{S}$ be matrices with appropriate dimensions. Then, the following inequality statements are equivalent:*

$$\begin{bmatrix} \mathcal{Q} & \mathcal{S} \\ \mathcal{S}^{\mathrm{T}} & \mathcal{R} \end{bmatrix} > 0 \tag{29a}$$

$$\begin{cases} \mathcal{R} > 0 \\ \mathcal{Q} - \mathcal{S}\mathcal{R}^{-1}\mathcal{S}^{\mathrm{T}} > 0 \end{cases} \tag{29b}$$

$$\begin{cases} \mathcal{Q} > 0 \\ \mathcal{R} - \mathcal{S}^{\mathrm{T}}\mathcal{Q}^{-1}\mathcal{S} > 0 \end{cases} \tag{29c}$$

Lemma 3 (S-procedure Lemma [10, 12, 14]) *Let $\mathcal{H}_0 \in \mathbb{R}^{n\times n}$, $\mathcal{H}_1 \in \mathbb{R}^{n\times n}$, ..., $\mathcal{H}_p \in \mathbb{R}^{n\times n}$ be symmetric matrices having the same dimension. Let consider the following condition on $\mathcal{H}_0$, ..., $\mathcal{H}_p$,*

$$\xi^{\mathrm{T}}\mathcal{H}_0\xi > 0 \quad \textit{for all} \quad \xi \neq 0 \quad \textit{such that} \quad \xi^{\mathrm{T}}\mathcal{H}_i\xi > 0, \quad i = 1, \ldots, p \tag{30}$$

where $\xi \in \mathbb{R}^{n\times 1}$.

If there exist scalar variables $\tau_1 > 0$, $\tau_2 > 0$, ..., $\tau_p > 0$ such that the following inequality condition holds:

$$\mathcal{H}_0 - \sum_{i=1}^{p} \tau_i\mathcal{H}_i > 0 \tag{31}$$

then the quadratic condition subject to quadratic constraints (30) is satisfied.

4.2 First LMI Condition Designing Method

Relying on Young relation (see Lemma 1), the following inequality is then derived:

$$2z^{\mathrm{T}}\mathcal{P}\mathcal{C}\Psi(z) \leq z^{\mathrm{T}}\mathcal{P}\mathcal{C}\mathcal{N}\mathcal{C}^{\mathrm{T}}\mathcal{P}z + \Psi(z)^{\mathrm{T}}\mathcal{N}^{-1}\Psi(z) \tag{32}$$

with $\mathcal{N} = \mathcal{N}^{\mathrm{T}} > 0$.

Using condition (32), expression (26) can be written like so:

$$\begin{aligned}\dot{\mathcal{L}}(z) + \alpha\mathcal{L}(z) \leq z^{\mathrm{T}}\,(\mathrm{He}\,\{\mathcal{P}\mathcal{A} + \mathcal{P}\mathcal{B}\mathcal{K}\} + \alpha\mathcal{P})\,z \\ + z^{\mathrm{T}}\mathcal{P}\mathcal{C}\mathcal{N}\mathcal{C}^{\mathrm{T}}\mathcal{P}z + \Psi(z)^{\mathrm{T}}\mathcal{N}^{-1}\Psi(z)\end{aligned} \tag{33}$$

In addition, using relation (33), the condition ensuring stability is then formulated like so:

$$\begin{bmatrix} z \\ \Psi(z) \end{bmatrix}^{\mathrm{T}} \begin{bmatrix} \mathrm{He}\,\{\mathcal{P}\mathcal{A} + \mathcal{P}\mathcal{B}\mathcal{K}\} + \mathcal{P}\mathcal{C}\mathcal{N}\mathcal{C}^{\mathrm{T}}\mathcal{P} + \alpha\mathcal{P} & \mathcal{O} \\ \mathcal{O} & \mathcal{N}^{-1} \end{bmatrix} \begin{bmatrix} z \\ \Psi(z) \end{bmatrix} < 0 \tag{34}$$

Furthermore, the Lipschitz condition (18) can be expressed as follows:

$$\begin{bmatrix} z \\ \Psi(z) \end{bmatrix}^{\mathrm{T}} \begin{bmatrix} -\ell^2\mathcal{I} & \mathcal{O} \\ \mathcal{O} & \mathcal{I} \end{bmatrix} \begin{bmatrix} z \\ \Psi(z) \end{bmatrix} \leq 0 \tag{35}$$

Relying on the S-procedure lemma (see Lemma 3), and based on expressions (34) and (35), we get:

$$\begin{bmatrix} \mathrm{He}\,\{\mathcal{P}\mathcal{A} + \mathcal{P}\mathcal{B}\mathcal{K}\} + \mathcal{P}\mathcal{C}\mathcal{N}\mathcal{C}^{\mathrm{T}}\mathcal{P} + \alpha\mathcal{P} + \tau\ell^2\mathcal{I} & \mathcal{O} \\ \mathcal{O} & \mathcal{N}^{-1} - \tau\mathcal{I} \end{bmatrix} < 0 \tag{36}$$

where $\tau > 0$.

The matrix inequality (36) is simplified and rephrased as follows:

$$\mathrm{He}\,\{\mathcal{P}\mathcal{A} + \mathcal{P}\mathcal{B}\mathcal{K}\} + \mathcal{P}\mathcal{C}\mathcal{N}\mathcal{C}^{\mathrm{T}}\mathcal{P} + \alpha\mathcal{P} + \tau\ell^2\mathcal{I} < 0 \tag{37}$$

$$\mathcal{N}^{-1} - \tau\mathcal{I} < 0 \tag{38}$$

Thus, multiplying condition (37) right and left by $\mathcal{S} = \mathcal{P}^{-1}$, we get:

$$\mathrm{He}\,\{\mathcal{A}\mathcal{S} + \mathcal{B}\mathcal{R}\} + \alpha\mathcal{S} + \mathcal{C}\mathcal{N}\mathcal{C}^{\mathrm{T}} + \tau\ell^2\mathcal{S}^2 < 0 \tag{39}$$

with $\mathcal{R} = \mathcal{K}\mathcal{S}$.

Furthermore, defining $\beta = \tau^{-1}\ell^{-2}$. The inequality (39) is reformulated as follows using the Schur complement (see Lemma 2):

$$\begin{bmatrix} \text{He}\{\mathcal{AS}+\mathcal{BR}\}+\alpha\mathcal{S}+\mathcal{CNC}^{\mathrm{T}} & \mathcal{S} \\ \mathcal{S} & -\beta\mathcal{I} \end{bmatrix} < 0 \tag{40}$$

In addition, the inequality (38) can be recast like so:

$$\begin{bmatrix} \tau\mathcal{I} & \mathcal{I} \\ \mathcal{I} & \mathcal{N} \end{bmatrix} > 0 \tag{41}$$

As a result, two LMIs (40) and (41) are obtained. Since $\beta = \tau^{-1}\ell^{-2}$, then it yields $\ell = \sqrt{\frac{1}{\tau\beta}}$. Therefore, to maximize the Lipschitz constant ℓ, we need to minimize the two parameters β and τ. Accordingly, the maximal Lipschitz constant, $\ell_{\max}$, is expressed by expression $\ell_{\max} = \sqrt{\frac{1}{\tau\beta}}$. Therefore, let us establish the following Theorem associated with the first design methodology of the LMI conditions.

Theorem 1 *Assuming that there are matrices $\mathcal{S}$, $\mathcal{R}$, and $\mathcal{N}$ such that $\mathcal{S} = \mathcal{S}^{\mathrm{T}}$ and $\mathcal{N} = \mathcal{N}^{\mathrm{T}}$, and two scalars τ and β, with some fixed scalar $\alpha > 0$, the following minimization problem subject to LMI constraints, is feasible.*

$$\min \quad \beta + \tau \tag{42a}$$

s.t.

$$\mathcal{S} > 0 \tag{42b}$$

$$\begin{bmatrix} He\{\mathcal{AS}+\mathcal{BR}\}+\alpha\mathcal{S}+\mathcal{CNC}^{\mathrm{T}} & \mathcal{S} \\ \mathcal{S} & -\beta\mathcal{I} \end{bmatrix} < 0 \tag{42c}$$

$$\begin{bmatrix} \tau\mathcal{I} & \mathcal{I} \\ \mathcal{I} & \mathcal{N} \end{bmatrix} > 0 \tag{42d}$$

Therefore, the affine PD controller (19) stabilizes the robotic system's nonlinear dynamics (6) at the intended point θ_d. The two matrix gains $\mathcal{K}_1$ and $\mathcal{K}_2$ of the controller are computed using the matrix $\mathcal{K}$ by considering expression (23), which can be calculated via the subsequent relation:

$$\mathcal{K} = \mathcal{R}\mathcal{S}^{-1} \tag{43}$$

Furthermore, the maximal Lipschitz constant ℓ_{max} is obtained using the following expression:

$$\ell_{max} = \sqrt{\frac{1}{\tau\beta}} \tag{44}$$

4.3 Second LMI Condition Designing Method

Let us reconsider the same Lyapunov function (24). The goal is to develop some other sets of LMI conditions allowing the computation of the matrix $\mathcal{K}$ that guarantees the stability of the robotic system under the controller (19).

The Lipschitz constraint (18) is reformulated as follows:

$$\Psi(z)^{\mathrm{T}}\Psi(z) \leq \ell^2 z^{\mathrm{T}} z \tag{45}$$

In the inequality condition (32), let us assume that $\mathcal{N} = \varepsilon\mathcal{I}$ with $\varepsilon > 0$, and by considering the quadratic Lipschitz condition (45), the constraint (32) becomes:

$$2z^{\mathrm{T}}\mathcal{P}\mathcal{C}\Psi(z) \leq \varepsilon z^{\mathrm{T}}\mathcal{P}\mathcal{C}\mathcal{C}^{\mathrm{T}}\mathcal{P}z + \varepsilon^{-1}\ell^2 z^{\mathrm{T}} z \tag{46}$$

Then, based on constraint (46), we get from the inequality (26) the following result:

$$\mathrm{He}\,\{\mathcal{P}\mathcal{A} + \mathcal{P}\mathcal{B}\mathcal{K}\} + \alpha\mathcal{P} + \varepsilon\mathcal{P}\mathcal{C}\mathcal{C}\mathcal{T}\mathcal{P} + \ell^2\varepsilon^{-1} < 0 \tag{47}$$

Let us pose $\mathcal{S} = \mathcal{P}^{-1}$. Multiplying inequality (47) from the right and the left by the matrix $\mathcal{S}$ gives the following inequality:

$$\mathrm{He}\,\{\mathcal{A}\mathcal{S} + \mathcal{B}\mathcal{R}\} + \alpha\mathcal{S} + \varepsilon\mathcal{C}\mathcal{C}^{\mathrm{T}} + \ell^2\varepsilon^{-1}\mathcal{S}^2 < 0 \tag{48}$$

where the unknown matrix $\mathcal{R}$ is expressed like so: $\mathcal{R} = \mathcal{K}\mathcal{S}$.

Posing $\beta = \ell^{-2}\varepsilon$. Thus, based on the Schur complement (Lemma 2), the condition (48) becomes:

$$\begin{bmatrix} \mathrm{He}\,\{\mathcal{A}\mathcal{S} + \mathcal{B}\mathcal{R}\} + \alpha\mathcal{S} + \varepsilon\mathcal{C}\mathcal{C}^{\mathrm{T}} & \mathcal{S} \\ \mathcal{S} & -\beta\mathcal{I} \end{bmatrix} < 0 \tag{49}$$

Therefore, we obtain the LMI condition (49), which is described in terms of the unknown matrix variables $\mathcal{S}$ and $\mathcal{R}$, and unknown scalar variables β and ε.

As $\beta = \ell^{-2}\varepsilon$, it follows then that $\ell = \sqrt{\frac{\varepsilon}{\beta}}$. Therefore, to maximize the Lipschitz constant ℓ, we must minimize the parameter β and maximize together the parameter ε. Note that the maximization of ε can be converted back to minimizing (ε^{-1}), and so the optimization/maximization goal of the scalar ℓ becomes the minimization of the quantity $(\beta + \varepsilon^{-1})$. Notice that this last quality is not linear and is not solvable using LMI techniques. To solve such problem, and since $\beta > 0$ and $\varepsilon > 0$, it follows to transform the minimization of the quantity $(\beta + \varepsilon^{-1})$ into the minimization of a new variable, saying λ, with respect to the following condition:

$$\lambda > \beta + \varepsilon^{-1} \tag{50}$$

Using the Schur complement lemma (see Lemma 2), this last condition (50) is rewritten under the following LMI condition:

$$\begin{bmatrix} \lambda - \beta & 1 \\ 1 & \varepsilon \end{bmatrix} > 0 \tag{51}$$

As a result, maximization of the Lipschitz parameter ℓ becomes minimization of the variable λ. Furthermore, once the minimization issue under the two LMIs (49) and (51) has been solved, we may calculate the gain $\mathcal{K}$ using expression (43). Furthermore, the maximal Lipschitz constant $\ell_{\max}$ is described by $\ell_{\max} = \sqrt{\frac{\varepsilon}{\beta}}$. Finally, let us state the following Theorem.

Theorem 2 *For some constant parameter $\alpha > 0$, If there are matrices $\mathcal{S}$, such that $\mathcal{S} = \mathcal{S}^{\mathrm{T}}$, and $\mathcal{R}$, and scalars β, ε and λ, so that the following LMI-based minimization problem*

$$\text{min} \quad \lambda \tag{52a}$$

$$\text{s.t.}$$

$$\mathcal{S} > 0 \tag{52b}$$

$$\begin{bmatrix} He\{\mathcal{AS} + \mathcal{BR}\} + \alpha\mathcal{S} + \varepsilon\mathcal{CC}^{\mathrm{T}} & \mathcal{S} \\ \mathcal{S} & -\beta\mathcal{I} \end{bmatrix} < 0 \tag{52c}$$

$$\begin{bmatrix} \lambda - \beta & 1 \\ 1 & \varepsilon \end{bmatrix} > 0 \tag{52d}$$

is feasible. Hence, the affine PD controller (19) permits controlling and stabilizing the nonlinear dynamics (6) at the intended position θ_d. The controller's gains $\mathcal{K}_1$ and $\mathcal{K}_2$ are derived from the matrix $\mathcal{K}$ (from relation (23)), which may be determined using relation (43). Furthermore, the maximal Lipschitz constant ℓ_{max} is defined and determined using the following expression:

$$\ell_{max} = \sqrt{\frac{\varepsilon}{\beta}} \tag{53}$$

4.4 Third LMI Condition Designing Method

As before, to build another LMI condition, we will use the same Lyapunov function (24). Expression (26) can be rewritten as follows:

$$\dot{\mathcal{L}}(z) + \alpha\mathcal{L}(z) = \begin{bmatrix} z \\ \Psi(z) \end{bmatrix}^{\mathrm{T}} \begin{bmatrix} \text{He}\{\mathcal{PA} + \mathcal{PBK}\} + \alpha\mathcal{P} & \mathcal{PC} \\ \mathcal{C}^{\mathrm{T}}\mathcal{P} & \mathcal{O} \end{bmatrix} \begin{bmatrix} z \\ \Psi(z) \end{bmatrix} \tag{54}$$

Based on the S-procedure (Lemma 3), and based on inequality constraints (35) and (54), we get for all $\tau > 0$ the following inequality:

$$\begin{bmatrix} \mathrm{He}\{\mathcal{PA} + \mathcal{PBK}\} + \alpha\mathcal{P} + \tau\ell^2\mathcal{I} & \mathcal{PC} \\ \mathcal{C}^{\mathrm{T}}\mathcal{P} & -\tau\mathcal{I} \end{bmatrix} < 0 \tag{55}$$

Multiplying expression (55) on the right and the left by the diagonal matrix $\mathcal{Q} = \mathrm{diag}(\mathcal{S}\ ,\ \mathcal{I})$, where $\mathcal{S} = \mathcal{P}^{-1}$, we get then the following matrix condition:

$$\begin{bmatrix} \mathrm{He}\{\mathcal{AS} + \mathcal{BR}\} + \alpha\mathcal{S} + \tau\ell^2\mathcal{S}^2\mathcal{I} & \mathcal{C} \\ \mathcal{C}^{\mathrm{T}} & -\tau\mathcal{I} \end{bmatrix} < 0 \tag{56}$$

Let us pose $\beta = \ell^{-2}\tau^{-1}$. Based on the Schur complement (Lemma 2), the inequality (56) can be recast as follows:

$$\begin{bmatrix} \mathrm{He}\{\mathcal{AS} + \mathcal{BR}\} + \alpha\mathcal{S} & \mathcal{C} & \mathcal{S} \\ \mathcal{C}^{\mathrm{T}} & -\tau\mathcal{I} & \mathcal{O} \\ \mathcal{S} & \mathcal{O} & -\beta\mathcal{I} \end{bmatrix} < 0 \tag{57}$$

Accordingly, the condition (57) is an LMI expressed about the two unknown matrices $\mathcal{S}$ and $\mathcal{R}$, and the two unknown scalars τ and β, ensuring the stability of the closed-loop system. It is worth noting that since $\beta = \ell^{-2}\tau^{-1}$, it follows that $\ell = \sqrt{\frac{1}{\beta\tau}}$. As a result, in order to maximize the Lipschitz constant ℓ, both the variables β and τ must be minimized.

When the minimization problem subject to the LMI (57) is solved, the gain $\mathcal{K}$ is calculated using relation (43). Furthermore, the maximal Lipschitz constant $\ell_{\max}$ is expressed in this third design methodology like so: $\ell_{\max} = \sqrt{\frac{1}{\beta\tau}}$.

Theorem 3 *For some constant $\alpha > 0$, suppose that the following LMI minimization problem:*

$$\mathit{min} \qquad \beta + \tau \tag{58a}$$

$$\mathit{s.t.}$$

$$\mathcal{S} > 0 \tag{58b}$$

$$\begin{bmatrix} \mathit{He}\{\mathcal{AS} + \mathcal{BR}\} + \alpha\mathcal{S} & \mathcal{C} & \mathcal{S} \\ \mathcal{C}^{\mathrm{T}} & -\tau\mathcal{I} & \mathcal{O} \\ \mathcal{S} & \mathcal{O} & -\beta\mathcal{I} \end{bmatrix} < 0 \tag{58c}$$

is feasible for matrices $\mathcal{S}$ and $\mathcal{R}$, and scalars β and τ. Then, the adopted affine PD controller (19) controls the dynamics (6) to the intended state θ_d. The gains $\mathcal{K}_1$ and $\mathcal{K}_2$ of the adopted affine PD controller are derived from the matrix $\mathcal{K}$ (by considering Equation (23)), which may be determined using relation (43). Moreover, the maximal Lipschitz constant ℓ_{max} is calculated using the following expression:

$$\ell_{max} = \sqrt{\frac{1}{\beta_{\mathcal{T}}}} \tag{59}$$

4.5 Numerical Results

Some numerical results to show the feasibility of the developed LMI conditions in the three design methods will be carried out in this Section. For each design method, we will fix some values of the decay parameter α and compute the resulting solutions of the different LMI-based problems in the previous theorems. Thus, we will illustrate the values of the two feedback gains $\mathcal{K}_1$ and $\mathcal{K}_2$ (or systematically the feedback gain $\mathcal{K}$ according to expressions in (23)), and the maximal Lipschitz constant $\ell_{\max}$.

4.5.1 Numerical Results Obtained via the First Design Approach

Let us consider the first design approach of the LMI conditions presented in Sect. 4.2 and then the LMI-based minimization problem developed in Theorem 1. According to this Theorem, we present in Table 2 the numerical results of the two matrix gains $\mathcal{K}_1$ and $\mathcal{K}_2$, and the maximal Lipschitz constant $\ell_{\max}$. By varying the value of the decay rate α, it is obvious that the obtained values of the two gains $\mathcal{K}_1$ and $\mathcal{K}_2$ are very high, and then they are not practicable for real-life robotic systems. In addition, the value of $\ell_{\max}$ is very high, around 10^9. Nevertheless, since $\mathcal{K}_1$ and $\mathcal{K}_2$ can not be considered, these high values of $\ell_{\max}$ are not taken in consideration.

4.5.2 Numerical Results Obtained via the Second LMI Design Approach

In this part, we consider the second design methodology of the LMI conditions and then the LMI minimization problem developed in Theorem 2. The numerical results ($\mathcal{K}_1$, $\mathcal{K}_2$, and $\ell_{\max}$) are illustrated in Table 3. As previously, for the four adopted values of the decay rate α, the feedback gains $\mathcal{K}_1$ and $\mathcal{K}_2$ are found to be a very huge

Table 2 Numerical results obtained using the first design methodology, and then by solving the LMI-based minimization problem developed in Theorem 1

	$\alpha = 0$	$\alpha = 5$	$\alpha = 10$	$\alpha = 20$
$\mathcal{K}_1 \times 10^{10}$	$\begin{bmatrix} -2.3436 & 0.1255 \\ 0.4623 & -0.1356 \end{bmatrix}$	$\begin{bmatrix} -4.3272 & 0.2059 \\ 0.8451 & -0.3986 \end{bmatrix}$	$\begin{bmatrix} -9.3030 & 0.4418 \\ 1.8166 & -0.8475 \end{bmatrix}$	$\begin{bmatrix} -18.498 & 0.892 \\ 3.617 & -1.610 \end{bmatrix}$
$\mathcal{K}_2 \times 10^{9}$	$\begin{bmatrix} -13.531 & 0.724 \\ 2.669 & -0.783 \end{bmatrix}$	$\begin{bmatrix} -4.2047 & 0.2001 \\ 0.8211 & -0.3873 \end{bmatrix}$	$\begin{bmatrix} -4.6172 & 0.2193 \\ 0.9016 & -0.4206 \end{bmatrix}$	$\begin{bmatrix} -4.6160 & 0.2226 \\ 0.9024 & -0.4018 \end{bmatrix}$
$\ell_{\max} \times 10^9$	8.4013	4.4592	4.5444	4.6864

Table 3 Numerical results obtained using the second design methodology of the LMI conditions and by solving the LMI-based minimization problem developed in Theorem 2

	$\alpha = 0$	$\alpha = 5$	$\alpha = 10$	$\alpha = 20$
$\mathcal{K}_1 \times 10^6$	$\begin{bmatrix} -2.9181 & 0.1002 \\ 0.5572 & -0.4571 \end{bmatrix}$	$\begin{bmatrix} -13.619 & 0.467 \\ 2.601 & -2.133 \end{bmatrix}$	$\begin{bmatrix} -43.048 & 1.478 \\ 8.220 & -6.743 \end{bmatrix}$	$\begin{bmatrix} -65.903 & 2.262 \\ 12.585 & -10.323 \end{bmatrix}$
$\mathcal{K}_2 \times 10^6$	$\begin{bmatrix} -1.6848 & 0.0578 \\ 0.3217 & -0.2639 \end{bmatrix}$	$\begin{bmatrix} -1.3234 & 0.0454 \\ 0.2527 & -0.2073 \end{bmatrix}$	$\begin{bmatrix} -2.1365 & 0.0733 \\ 0.4080 & -0.3347 \end{bmatrix}$	$\begin{bmatrix} -1.6446 & 0.0565 \\ 0.3141 & -0.2576 \end{bmatrix}$
$\ell_{max} \times 10^6$	1.7369	1.3748	2.1672	1.7479

size and then they are not realizable in real-life robotic applications and then to the robotic system.

It is obvious that the values of $\mathcal{K}_1$ and $\mathcal{K}_2$, and also the value of the maximal Lipschitz constant ℓ_{max} are smaller (around 10^6) than those obtained in the first design method (around 10^{10}). Nevertheless, these values are very high and should be imperatively reduced to be realizable and hence applicable in practice.

4.5.3 Numerical Results Obtained via the Third LMI Design Approach

We explore the LMI-based minimization problem presented in Theorem 3 in this third design methodology of the LMI constraints. The obtained numerical results are illustrated in Table 4. The acquired outcomes of the gains $\mathcal{K}_1$ and $\mathcal{K}_2$ are not adequate, as in the first and second LMI design methodologies. Indeed, the values of these improvements are discovered to be quite large, making them unattainable in practice.

To remedy these impracticable values of the two matrix feedback gains $\mathcal{K}_1$ and $\mathcal{K}_2$ resulting from the three design methodologies of the LMI stability conditions, the goal is to reduce their size. This objective will be considered in the sequel as improved results where additional LMI conditions will be considered.

Table 4 Numerical results obtained by using the third design methodology of the LMI conditions and by solving the LMI-based minimization problem provided in Theorem 3

	$\alpha = 0$	$\alpha = 5$	$\alpha = 10$	$\alpha = 20$
$\mathcal{K}_1 \times 10^{10}$	$\begin{bmatrix} -7.5190 & 0.4176 \\ 1.4880 & -0.3854 \end{bmatrix}$	$\begin{bmatrix} -10.555 & 0.549 \\ 2.077 & -0.683 \end{bmatrix}$	$\begin{bmatrix} -21.053 & 1.066 \\ 4.133 & -1.590 \end{bmatrix}$	$\begin{bmatrix} -139.541 & 7.599 \\ 27.560 & -8.148 \end{bmatrix}$
$\mathcal{K}_2 \times 10^{10}$	$\begin{bmatrix} -4.3411 & 0.2411 \\ 0.8591 & -0.2225 \end{bmatrix}$	$\begin{bmatrix} -1.0256 & 0.0533 \\ 0.2018 & -0.0663 \end{bmatrix}$	$\begin{bmatrix} -1.0449 & 0.0529 \\ 0.2051 & -0.0789 \end{bmatrix}$	$\begin{bmatrix} -3.4820 & 0.1896 \\ 0.6877 & -0.2033 \end{bmatrix}$
$\ell_{max} \times 10^{10}$	1.8517	0.79835	0.80186	1.6410

5 Improved LMI Design Methods

In this section, the main idea lies in imposing some conditions to limit the controller's feedback gains. Such a step is crucial for maintaining stability, robustness, performance, and practicality in the control system, to ensure that the closed-loop system operates effectively and reliably in real-world applications. Thus, in this part, we will present some additional LMI constraints to reduce the size of the feedback gains of the adopted affine PD controller.

5.1 Additional LMI Constraints for Reducing the Size of Feedback Gains

The previously constructed minimization problems under LMI conditions provided us with very high gains $\mathcal{K}_1$ and $\mathcal{K}_2$ of the controller, which are then not realizable in reality. As a result, the goal of this section is to provide improved LMI conditions that permit a reduction in the magnitude of $\mathcal{K}_1$ and $\mathcal{K}_2$, or systemically $\mathcal{K}$. Because the matrix gain $\mathcal{K}$ is determined via relation (43), the aim is to put restrictions on $\mathcal{R}$ and $\mathcal{S}^{-1}$. As a result, the two constraints conditions listed below are imposed:

$$\mathcal{S}^{-1} < \ell_2 \mathcal{I}_n \tag{60a}$$

$$\mathcal{R}^{\mathrm{T}}\mathcal{R} < \ell_1 \mathcal{I}_n \tag{60b}$$

where $\ell_1 > 0$ and $\ell_2 > 0$.

These two restrictions on the two matrices $\mathcal{R}$ and $\mathcal{S}^{-1}$ defined by the two inequality constraints (60a) and (60b) can be rewritten as follows:

$$\begin{bmatrix} \ell_2 \mathcal{I} & \mathcal{I} \\ \mathcal{I} & \mathcal{S} \end{bmatrix} > 0 \tag{61a}$$

$$\begin{bmatrix} \ell_1 \mathcal{I} & \mathcal{R}^{\mathrm{T}} \\ \mathcal{R} & \mathcal{I} \end{bmatrix} > 0 \tag{61b}$$

In these previous LMI constraints (61a) and (61b), to reduce the size of $\mathcal{K}$, and so of $\mathcal{K}_1$ and $\mathcal{K}_2$, the two parameters ℓ_1 and ℓ_2 must be minimized.

Remark 4 It is important to note that including the required LMI constraints (61a) and (61b) to limit the controller's feedback gains poses many challenges. One significant challenge is developing some LMIs that accurately represent the desired restrictions on the controller's feedback gains $\mathcal{K}_1$ and $\mathcal{K}_2$. Certainly, these conditions represent accurately the desired limitation of the size of the feedback gain $\mathcal{K}$ and then of $\mathcal{K}_1$ and $\mathcal{K}_2$. Moreover, another challenge behind designing such LMIs that limit feedback gains lies in maintaining the stability of the controlled robotic system.

These two LMI conditions (61a) and (61b) will be added to the other LMI that were already designed to ensure the stability of the closed-loop system.

5.2 Enhanced LMI Conditions Design Methods

In this part, we will provide the enhanced LMI conditions obtained by merging the previously developed LMIs with the two additional LMI conditions (61a) and (61b).

5.2.1 Enhanced Conditions Developed via the First LMI Design Approach

In this section, we describe the LMI constraints that are enhanced from those presented in Sect. 4.2 while also taking into account the two new LMI constraints (61a) and (61b). Consider then the following theorem, which states the augmented LMI-based minimization problem.

Theorem 4 *Assume that, with unknown matrix variables $\mathcal{S}$, $\mathcal{N}$ and $\mathcal{R}$, such that $\mathcal{S} = \mathcal{S}^{\mathrm{T}}$ and $\mathcal{N} = \mathcal{N}^{\mathrm{T}}$, and scalar variables τ, β and ℓ_1 and ℓ_2 exists for some scalar $\alpha > 0$, the subsequent LMI-based minimization problem is realizable.*

$$\min \quad \beta + \tau + \ell_1 + \ell_2 \tag{62a}$$

$$\text{s.t.}$$

$$\begin{bmatrix} He\{\mathcal{AS} + \mathcal{BR}\} + \alpha\mathcal{S} + \mathcal{CNC}^{\mathrm{T}} & \mathcal{S} \\ \mathcal{S} & -\beta\mathcal{I} \end{bmatrix} < 0 \tag{62b}$$

$$\begin{bmatrix} \tau\mathcal{I} & \mathcal{I} \\ \mathcal{I} & \mathcal{N} \end{bmatrix} > 0 \tag{62c}$$

$$\begin{bmatrix} \ell_2\mathcal{I} & \mathcal{I} \\ \mathcal{I} & \mathcal{S} \end{bmatrix} > 0 \tag{62d}$$

$$\begin{bmatrix} \ell_1\mathcal{I} & \mathcal{R}^{\mathrm{T}} \\ \mathcal{R} & \mathcal{I} \end{bmatrix} > 0 \tag{62e}$$

The adopted affine PD controller (19) then control the dynamics (6) to the intended point θ_d. The matrix gain $\mathcal{K}$ is computed using expression (43). Furthermore, the expression (44) is used to compute the greatest Lipschitz constant ℓ_{max}.

5.2.2 Enhanced Conditions Developed via the Second LMI Design Approach

The outputs reported for this second enhanced methodology for the development of the LMI conditions are derived from those shown in Sect. 3.3. These enhanced results are obtained by combining the LMI-based minimization problem developed in Theorem 2 with the addition LMI constraints (61a) and (61b). As a result, we announce the following Theorem providing the enhanced LMI-based minimization problem.

Theorem 5 *If there are matrices $\mathcal{S}$ and $\mathcal{R}$, such that $\mathcal{S} = \mathcal{S}^{\mathrm{T}}$, and five positive scalars λ, β, ε, ℓ_1 and ℓ_2, so that the subsequent minimization problem subject to LMIs, is realizable.*

$$\min \quad \lambda + \ell_1 + \ell_2 \tag{63a}$$

s.t.

$$\begin{bmatrix} He\{\mathcal{AS} + \mathcal{BR}\} + \alpha\mathcal{S} + \varepsilon\mathcal{CC}^{\mathrm{T}} & \mathcal{S} \\ \mathcal{S} & -\beta\mathcal{I} \end{bmatrix} < 0 \tag{63b}$$

$$\begin{bmatrix} \lambda - \beta & 1 \\ 1 & \varepsilon \end{bmatrix} > 0 \tag{63c}$$

$$\begin{bmatrix} \ell_2\mathcal{I} & \mathcal{I} \\ \mathcal{I} & \mathcal{S} \end{bmatrix} > 0 \tag{63d}$$

$$\begin{bmatrix} \ell_1\mathcal{I} & \mathcal{R}^{\mathrm{T}} \\ \mathcal{R} & \mathcal{I} \end{bmatrix} > 0 \tag{63e}$$

Therefore, the dynamical model (6) is stabilized by the controller (19) at the required configuration θ_d. Moreover, the matrix gain $\mathcal{K}$ is calculated using expression (43), and the highest Lipschitz constant ℓ_{max} is calculated using expression (53).

5.2.3 Enhanced Conditions Developed via the Third LMI Design Approach

As before, we provide an improved LMI-based minimization problem for calculating the matrix gain $\mathcal{K}$ and therefore $\mathcal{K}_1$ and $\mathcal{K}_2$ of the affine PD controller (19). This enhanced LMI problem is based on the design strategy described in Sect. 4.4 and subsequently on Theorem 3, as well as by taking into account the extra LMI conditions (61a) and (61b) meant to lower the size of the matrix gain $\mathcal{K}$. Let us state the following theorem.

Theorem 6 *Assuming that for some constant $\alpha > 0$, it exists a square symmetric matrix $\mathcal{S}$, a non-square matrix $\mathcal{R}$, and four positive scalars β, τ, ℓ_1 and ℓ_2, so that the following improved LMI minimization problem is realizable.*

$$\min \quad \beta + \tau + \ell_1 + \ell_2 \tag{64a}$$

s.t.

$$\begin{bmatrix} He\{\mathcal{AS} + \mathcal{BR}\} + \alpha\mathcal{S} & \mathcal{C} & \mathcal{S} \\ \mathcal{C}^{\mathrm{T}} & -\tau\mathcal{I} & \mathcal{O} \\ \mathcal{S} & \mathcal{O} & -\beta\mathcal{I} \end{bmatrix} < 0 \tag{64b}$$

$$\begin{bmatrix} \ell_2 \mathcal{I} & \mathcal{I} \\ \mathcal{I} & \mathcal{S} \end{bmatrix} > 0 \tag{64c}$$

$$\begin{bmatrix} \ell_1 \mathcal{I} & \mathcal{R}^{\mathrm{T}} \\ \mathcal{R} & \mathcal{I} \end{bmatrix} > 0 \tag{64d}$$

As a result, the suggested affine controller (19) controls the nonlinear dynamical model (6) to the required location θ_d. The matrix gain $\mathcal{K}$ is calculated using relation (43). Moreover, the maximal Lipschitz parameter ℓ_{max} is calculated using an expression (59).

6 Numerical Results Obtained via the Enhanced LMI Problems

In this part, some numerical results of the enhanced developed LMI-based minimization problems are presented. We will vary the value of the decay rate α and provide the results of the two feedback gains $\mathcal{K}_1$ and $\mathcal{K}_2$ (or systematically the feedback gain $\mathcal{K}$) and the maximal value of the Lipschitz constant $\ell_{\max}$. Such numerical results will be compared to those illustrated in Tables 2, 3 and 4.

6.1 *Results of the First Enhanced LMI Design Approach*

Consider the first enhanced design method of the LMI-based minimization problem presented in Sect. 5.2.1 and then in Theorem 4. Table 5 reveals the obtained results of the matrix gains $\mathcal{K}_1$ and $\mathcal{K}_2$, and the maximal Lipschitz constant $\ell_{\max}$ by varying the value of the decay rate α. Compared to the numerical results illustrated in Table 2, the results presented in Table 5 are satisfactory. Indeed, the obtained values of $\mathcal{K}_1$ and $\mathcal{K}_2$ have small and acceptable sizes and then are all realizable in practice. Furthermore, the value of $\ell_{\max}$ is small and could be reasonable. By increasing the value of the parameter α, the value of the maximal Lipschitz constant $\ell_{\max}$ decreases. In addition, the elements of $\mathcal{K}_1$ and $\mathcal{K}_2$ increases slightly with respect to the increase of α.

Table 5 Numerical results obtained using the first enhanced design methodology of the LMI conditions and therefore by solving the LMI-based minimization problem developed in Theorem 4

	$\alpha = 0$	$\alpha = 5$	$\alpha = 10$	$\alpha = 20$
$\mathcal{K}_1$	$\begin{bmatrix} -13.5790 & 1.7393 \\ 0.2240 & 0.9093 \end{bmatrix}$	$\begin{bmatrix} -20.1494 & 4.3116 \\ 1.4249 & -0.4521 \end{bmatrix}$	$\begin{bmatrix} -30.9606 & 4.0136 \\ 2.7472 & -5.9466 \end{bmatrix}$	$\begin{bmatrix} -103.4652 & -19.3341 \\ 16.4119 & -30.1167 \end{bmatrix}$
$\mathcal{K}_2$	$\begin{bmatrix} -2.6028 & 0.1594 \\ 0.4550 & -0.7950 \end{bmatrix}$	$\begin{bmatrix} -3.3458 & 0.2334 \\ 0.5204 & -0.5178 \end{bmatrix}$	$\begin{bmatrix} -4.9087 & 0.3440 \\ 0.6919 & -1.1351 \end{bmatrix}$	$\begin{bmatrix} -8.9882 & -0.8957 \\ 2.3620 & -2.6144 \end{bmatrix}$
$\ell_{\max}$	2.7851	1.0909	0.3307	0.2613

6.2 Results of the Second Enhanced LMI Design Approach

Let us consider now the second improved design methodology of LMI conditions and then the LMI-based minimization problem developed in Theorem 5. The numerical results of the two feedback gains $\mathcal{K}_1$ and $\mathcal{K}_2$, and the allowable maximal Lipschitz constant $\ell_{\max}$, using this LMI-based minimization problem and concerning the different values of the decay parameter α, are illustrated in Table 6. As in the previous methodology, and for the different values of the decay parameter α, the values of $\mathcal{K}_1$ and $\mathcal{K}_2$ are found to be low and then satisfactory and applicable to the robotic system.

It is obvious that, for the four fixed values of the parameter α, the values of $\mathcal{K}_1$ and $\mathcal{K}_2$ obtained in this second enhanced design methodology (illustrated in Table 6) are almost equal to those obtained in the first design method, that is those presented in Table 3. Moreover, the value of $\ell_{\max}$ is found to be decreased slightly for $\alpha = 0$ and, in contrast, increased for the three other values: $\alpha = 5$, $\alpha = 10$ and $\alpha = 20$.

6.3 Results of the Third Enhanced LMI Design Approach

In this third enhanced design method, we consider the LMI-based minimization problem provided in Theorem 6. The obtained numerical results resulting from this LMI problem are illustrated in Table 7. As in the first and second LMI design methodologies, the results obtained for the two matrices $\mathcal{K}_1$ and $\mathcal{K}_2$ are satisfactory and can be realizable in practice and then applied to the robotic system.

Table 6 Numerical results obtained using the second enhanced design methodology of the LMI conditions and then by solving the LMI-based minimization problem developed in Theorem 5

	$\alpha = 0$	$\alpha = 5$	$\alpha = 10$	$\alpha = 20$
$\mathcal{K}_1$	$\begin{bmatrix} -13.5701 & 1.7255 \\ 0.2404 & 1.0244 \end{bmatrix}$	$\begin{bmatrix} -20.1548 & 4.2948 \\ 1.4288 & -0.4574 \end{bmatrix}$	$\begin{bmatrix} -30.9390 & 4.0421 \\ 2.7972 & -5.4321 \end{bmatrix}$	$\begin{bmatrix} -103.3258 & -16.6895 \\ 16.7515 & -26.1406 \end{bmatrix}$
$\mathcal{K}_2$	$\begin{bmatrix} -2.6062 & 0.1582 \\ 0.4122 & -0.6156 \end{bmatrix}$	$\begin{bmatrix} -3.3419 & 0.2383 \\ 0.5207 & -0.5184 \end{bmatrix}$	$\begin{bmatrix} -4.9059 & 0.3680 \\ 0.7084 & -1.0359 \end{bmatrix}$	$\begin{bmatrix} -9.0201 & -0.7249 \\ 2.3341 & -2.2432 \end{bmatrix}$
$\ell_{\max}$	2.7775	1.1089	0.3321	0.2768

Table 7 Numerical results obtained by using the third enhanced design methodology of the LMI conditions and by solving the LMI-based minimization problem proposed in Theorem 6

	$\alpha = 0$	$\alpha = 5$	$\alpha = 10$	$\alpha = 20$
$\mathcal{K}_1$	$\begin{bmatrix} -13.5859 & 1.7219 \\ 0.2455 & 1.0246 \end{bmatrix}$	$\begin{bmatrix} -20.1276 & 4.3157 \\ 1.4425 & -0.4456 \end{bmatrix}$	$\begin{bmatrix} -30.9003 & 4.0628 \\ 2.7843 & -5.4656 \end{bmatrix}$	$\begin{bmatrix} -103.2558 & -16.4686 \\ 16.7009 & -26.1022 \end{bmatrix}$
$\mathcal{K}_2$	$\begin{bmatrix} -2.6067 & 0.1507 \\ 0.4071 & -0.6161 \end{bmatrix}$	$\begin{bmatrix} -3.3321 & 0.2251 \\ 0.5239 & -0.5152 \end{bmatrix}$	$\begin{bmatrix} -4.9012 & 0.3699 \\ 0.7053 & -1.0357 \end{bmatrix}$	$\begin{bmatrix} -9.0237 & -0.7103 \\ 2.3169 & -2.2487 \end{bmatrix}$
$\ell_{\max}$	2.8180	1.1048	0.3247	0.2641

Compared to the previous numerical results illustrated in Tables 5 and 6, the maximal Lipschitz constant $\ell_{\max}$ increases. However, for the other values of the decay parameter α, the values of $\ell_{\max}$ are found to be decreased slightly.

6.4 *Discussion*

In these previous numerical results, we have fixed the desired position θ_d to a single fixed value (12). According to these results, it appears that the third design approach of the LMI conditions is the best one for the decay rate $\alpha = 0$. However, for the other values $\alpha = 5, \alpha = 10$, and $\alpha = 20$, the second LMI design methodology is the best one. At this level, the question is whether the optimum LMI design approaches remain the same when different values of the desired location θ_d are used. This issue will be addressed in the following section.

6.5 *Effect of the Desired Position on the Maximum Lipschitz Constant*

The major goal of this part is to make a comparison between the three methodologies for the design of the LMIs employed in this study to illustrate the most efficient approach. To accomplish this, each minimization problem will be studied for different pints θ_d in the admissible interval $\left[-180^\circ\ ,\ 180^\circ\right]$, and therefore compute the admissible highest value of the Lipschitz constant ℓ_{max} for the three cases with a step size equal to 2°. We will consider the our values of the decay parameter α, that is $\alpha = 0$, $\alpha = 5$, $\alpha = 10$ and $\alpha = 20$.

6.5.1 Comparison for a Decay Rate $\alpha = 0$

We consider the three improved LMI design methods and we take a decay rate as $\alpha = 0$. Figure 2 depicts the evolution shape of the allowable Lipschitz constant $\ell_{\max}$ with regard to the target location θ_d for the three LMI design approaches. Figure 2a depicts $\ell_{\max}$ versus θ_1^d and θ_2^d, while Fig. 2b depicts the 2D portrait relative to θ_1^d.

From Fig. 2, it yields that the second LMI design method of the stability condition gives generally values of $\ell_{\max}$ slightly greater than those obtained by means of the first or third design approaches. Moreover, it seems also that the third LMI design methodology is the best one for some value of the desired vector θ_d. This statement can be revealed from the 2D plot of Fig. 2b.

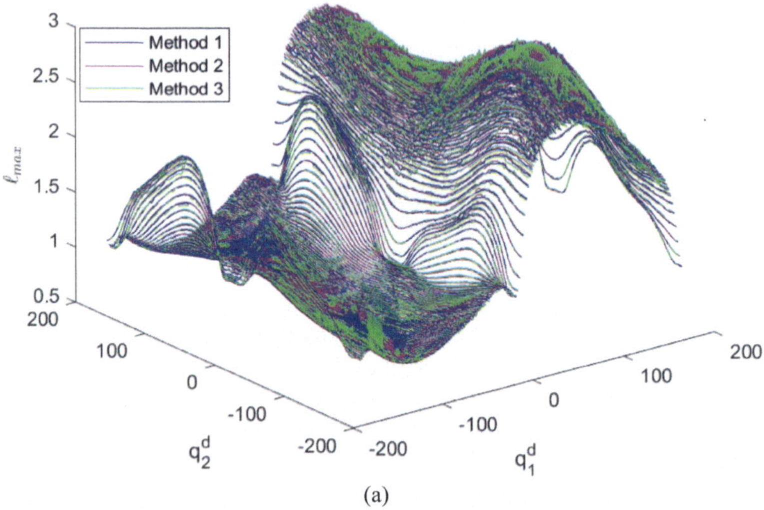

Fig. 2 Variation of the value of the admissible maximal Lipschitz constant $\ell_{\max}$ versus the desired position θ_d by taking $\alpha = 5$ and for the three enhanced LMI design methods. **a** Depicts the 3D portrait, and **b** depicts the 2D plot versus the state θ_1^d

6.5.2 Comparison for a Decay Rate $\alpha = 5$

Let us consider now a decay rate $\alpha = 5$. Variation of the parameter $\ell_{\max}$ versus θ_d is depicted in Fig. 3. As previously, it appears that the second enhanced LMI design methodology is slightly better than the first and third design methods. In

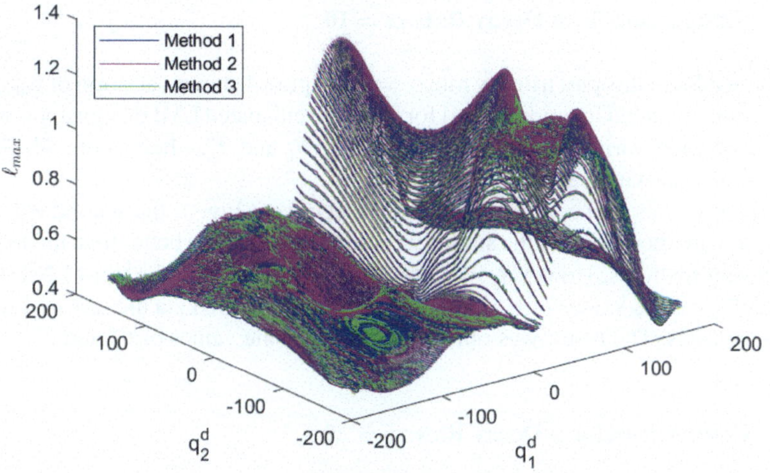

(a)

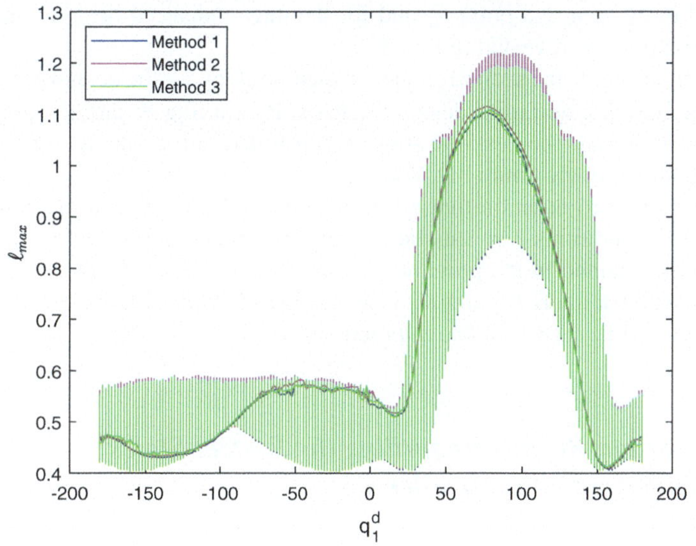

(b)

Fig. 3 Evolution of $\ell_{\max}$ versus θ_d for the three enhanced LMI design methods and by taking $\alpha = 5$. **a** Reveals the 3D portrait, while **b** reveals the 2D portrait in function of the state θ_1^d

some circumstances, the third design approach yields higher values of $\ell_{\max}$ than the first or second design methodologies.

6.5.3 Comparison for a Decay Rate $\alpha = 10$

Let us consider in this part a decay rate $\alpha = 10$. Figure 4 shows variation of $\ell_{\max}$ with regard to the intended location θ_d and for the three enhanced LMI design approaches. Figure 4a depicts variation of $\ell_{\max}$ with regard to θ_1^d and θ_2^d, whereas Fig. 4b depicts variation of $\ell_{\max}$ with respect to only θ_1^d.

As the previous two comparisons, and as seen from Fig. 4, the second enhanced LMI design methodology of the stability conditions is slightly better than the first and third design methods. However, we can see from Fig. 4b that the third LMI design methodology gives values of $\ell_{\max}$ bigger than those obtained via the first and second design methods. The result was obtained only for some values of θ_1^d and θ_2^d.

6.5.4 Comparison for a Decay Rate $\alpha = 20$

We take now a decay rate $\alpha = 20$. Evolution of the maximal Lipschitz constant $\ell_{\max}$ with regard to the required point θ_d and for the three enhanced design methods of the LMI conditions, is revealed in Fig. 5.

As seen from Fig. 5, the second enhanced methodology for the design of the LMIs is better than the first and third design methods. By varying θ_1^d and θ_2^d, the second design methodology is the best one since as illustrated in Fig. 5a, the pink curve is the most dominant in the entire 3D plot.

It is noteworthy to mention that all three enhanced LMI design methodologies of the stability conditions give satisfactory results. Indeed, the value of $\ell_{\max}$ is not (very) high as obtained in the previous investigation in Sect. 4.5. Thus, the size of the matrix feedback gains $\mathcal{K}_1$ and $\mathcal{K}_2$ of the affine PD control law (19) will be not high, and hence they are realizable in practice.

6.6 Simulation Results Regarding the System States and the Applied Controller

In this part, we show some simulation/graphical results illustrating the evolution of the four states of the robotic system under the affine PD controller (19). Since the three design methods of the LMI conditions gave us almost the same values of the feedback gains $\mathcal{K}_1$ and $\mathcal{K}_2$ as illustrated in Tables 5, 6 and 7, and by taking into consideration the previous comparison, we adopt here the second design methodology for these simulations results. In addition, we consider another desired position θ_d different to that in (12), to be like so:

$$\theta_d = \begin{bmatrix} -45^\circ \\ 45^\circ \end{bmatrix} \tag{65}$$

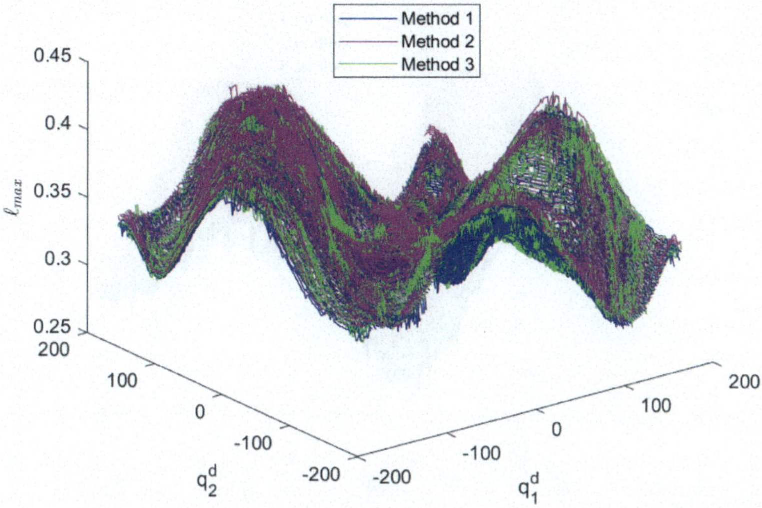

(a)

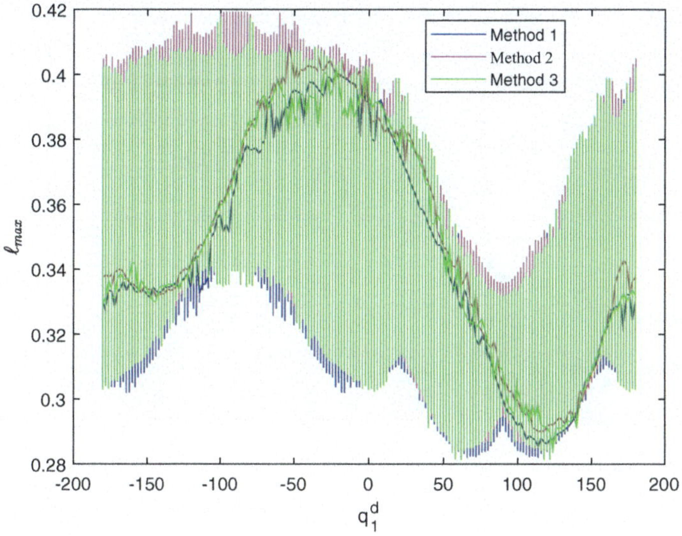

(b)

Fig. 4 Evolution of the maximal Lipschitz constant $\ell_{\max}$ with regard to the required position θ_d by considering the three enhanced LMI design methods and by taking a decay rate $\alpha = 10$. **a** Reveals $\ell_{\max}$ versus θ_1^d and θ_2^d, and **b** reveals $\ell_{\max}$ versus θ_1^d

Moreover, the initial point at which the robot will be emanated is defined by the two following vectors θ_0 and $\dot{\theta}_0$:

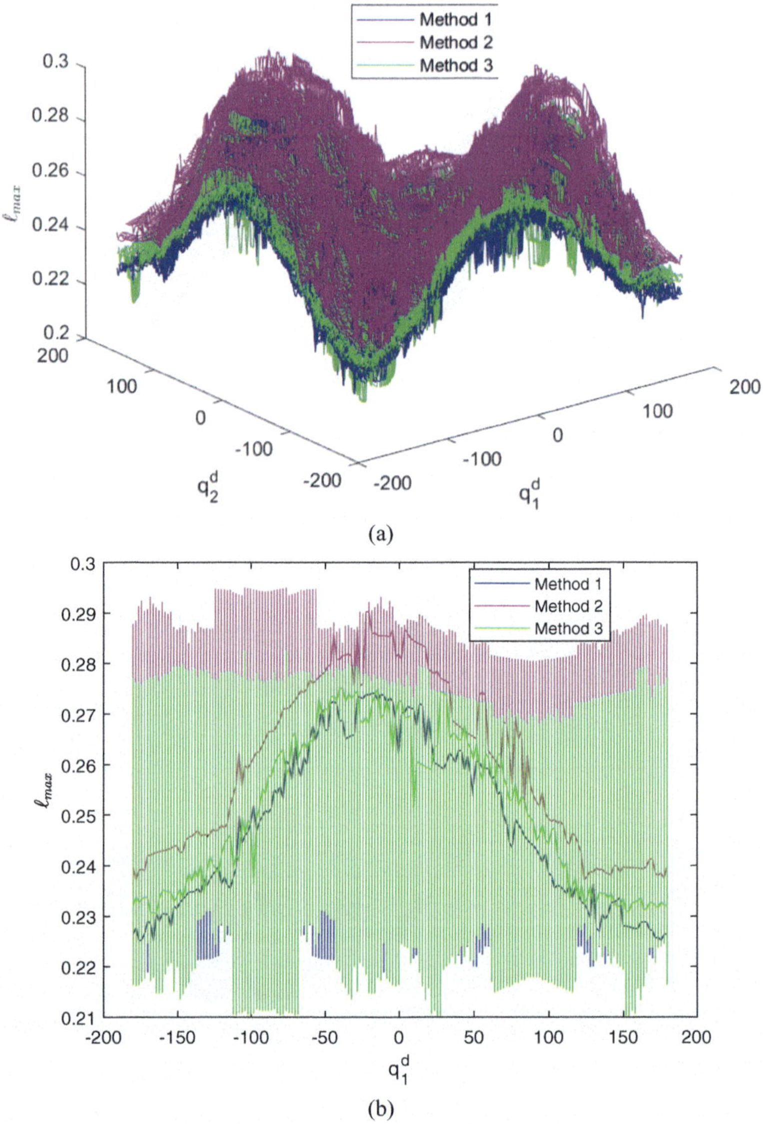

Fig. 5 Variation of $\ell_{\max}$ versus θ_d by considering the three enhanced LMI design methods and by taking $\alpha = 20$. **a** Reveals the 3D portrait: $\ell_{\max}$ versus θ_1^d and θ_2^d, whereas **b** shows the 2D portrait: $\ell_{\max}$ versus θ_1^d

$$\theta_0 = \begin{bmatrix} 0^\circ \\ 0^\circ \end{bmatrix} \qquad \dot{\theta}_0 = \begin{bmatrix} 0^{\circ/s} \\ 0^{\circ/s} \end{bmatrix} \tag{66}$$

Table 8 Numerical results obtained using the second enhanced LMI design methodology by resolving the LMI-based minimization problem in Theorem 5 and by considering the desired position θ_d in (65)

	$\alpha = 0$	$\alpha = 5$	$\alpha = 10$	$\alpha = 20$
$\mathcal{K}_1$	$\begin{bmatrix} 4.5555 & -2.0643 \\ 0.5319 & -2.0076 \end{bmatrix}$	$\begin{bmatrix} -0.5775 & -6.2277 \\ 2.7578 & -3.3487 \end{bmatrix}$	$\begin{bmatrix} -24.3589 & 9.6939 \\ 4.8418 & -9.8832 \end{bmatrix}$	$\begin{bmatrix} -122.0654 & 96.2406 \\ 8.1981 & -52.2446 \end{bmatrix}$
$\mathcal{K}_2$	$\begin{bmatrix} -0.6504 & -0.3989 \\ 0.0955 & -0.3693 \end{bmatrix}$	$\begin{bmatrix} -3.8729 & -1.3596 \\ 0.3615 & -0.6535 \end{bmatrix}$	$\begin{bmatrix} -2.9865 & 1.0162 \\ -0.8435 & -1.5926 \end{bmatrix}$	$\begin{bmatrix} -0.9196 & 5.8044 \\ -4.4296 & -4.1747 \end{bmatrix}$
$\ell_{\max}$	0.9866	0.4839	0.3386	0.2571

Using this desired position θ_d and by adopting the second enhanced LMI design approach and then the LMI-minimization problem in Theorem 5, we obtain the numerical results in Table 8 for the four values of the decay parameter α, as in the previous Tables 5, 6 and 7.

Remark 5 In this part, the affine PD-based control law will be evaluated for its efficacy in stabilizing the exoskeleton robotic system using mainly the position error between the actual position of the robot and the desired position. Moreover, we will consider the stabilization (settling) time and the overshoot with respect to the four values of the parameter α. In addition, we will assess the control effort required to achieve the stabilization to the intended position. These studies will be achieved by means of the graphical results and then via the depicted curves of the different state variables θ_1, θ_2, $\dot{\theta}_1$ and $\dot{\theta}_2$, and the applied controller u, or systematically the two sub-controllers u_1 and u_2 applied to the two joints of the exoskeleton robot.

Using these matrix gains $\mathcal{K}_1$ and $\mathcal{K}_2$ in Table 8 and for the four cases of the parameter α, we depict the evolution of the four states of the controlled robot using its dynamics (6) and the applied affine PD controller (19). The simulation results of the four states are presented in Figs. 6 and 7, and those of the two sub-controllers u_1 and u_2 are presented in Fig. 9. Figure 6a (resp. Fig. 6b) shows the time variation of the angular position θ_1 (resp. θ_2) of the controlled robot. Moreover, Fig. 7a (resp. Fig. 7b) shows the temporal variation of the angular velocity $\dot{\theta}_1$ (resp. $\dot{\theta}_2$).

These plots in Figs. 6, 7 and 9 reveal that for the four values of the parameter α, the robot has been controlled to the desired position θ_d defined by expression (65). It is clear from Fig. 7a, b that the two angular velocities $\dot{\theta}_1$ and $\dot{\theta}_2$ converge to zero, leading to the stabilization of the robot at the intended position θ_1. In addition, it is obvious from Fig. 6a, b that, by increasing the value of the parameter α, the robot will be controlled rapidly to the desired point. From Fig. 6a, and for $\alpha = 0$, some oscillations around the desired position θ_1^d occur their attenuation and convergence to θ_1^d. These oscillations are eliminated for the three other values of the parameter α. Nevertheless, from Fig. 7a, b, the increase of α leads to the increase of the angular velocities $\dot{\theta}_1$ and $\dot{\theta}_2$ of the two joints of the robot. Figure 8a (resp. Fig. 8b) is an enlargement of Fig. 7a (resp. Fig. 7b) showing the temporal evolution during only the first second. It is clear that for $\alpha = 0$ and $\alpha = 5$ (and also for $\alpha = 10$ but with a slight difference), there is a smooth variation of the angular velocities $\dot{\theta}_1$ and $\dot{\theta}_2$.

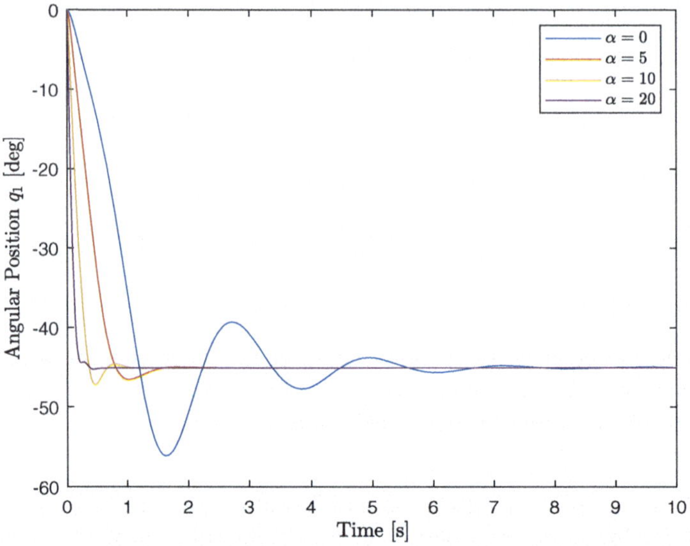

(a) θ_1

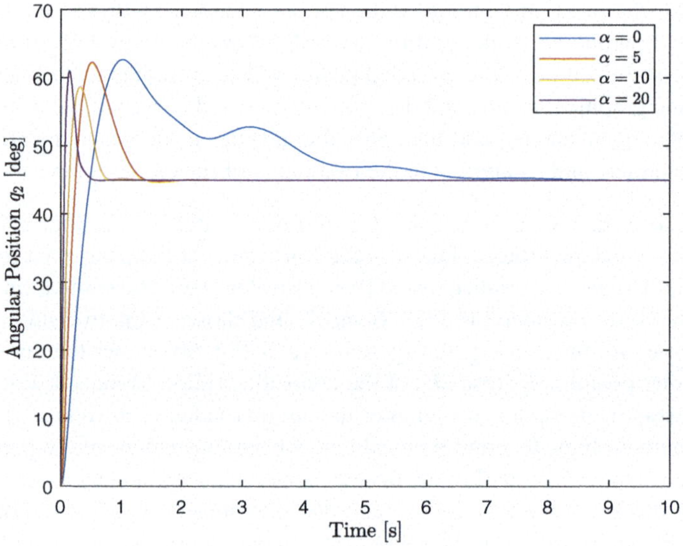

(b) θ_2

Fig. 6 Simulation results showing the temporal evolution of the two states θ_1 and θ_2 of the controlled robot for the four different values of the decay parameter α

However, for $\alpha = 20$, these angular velocities, and from the zero state, reach very high values. Indeed, $\dot{\theta}_1$ reaches the angular velocity around $-420°/s$, and $\dot{\theta}_2$ reaches the value around $950°/s$.

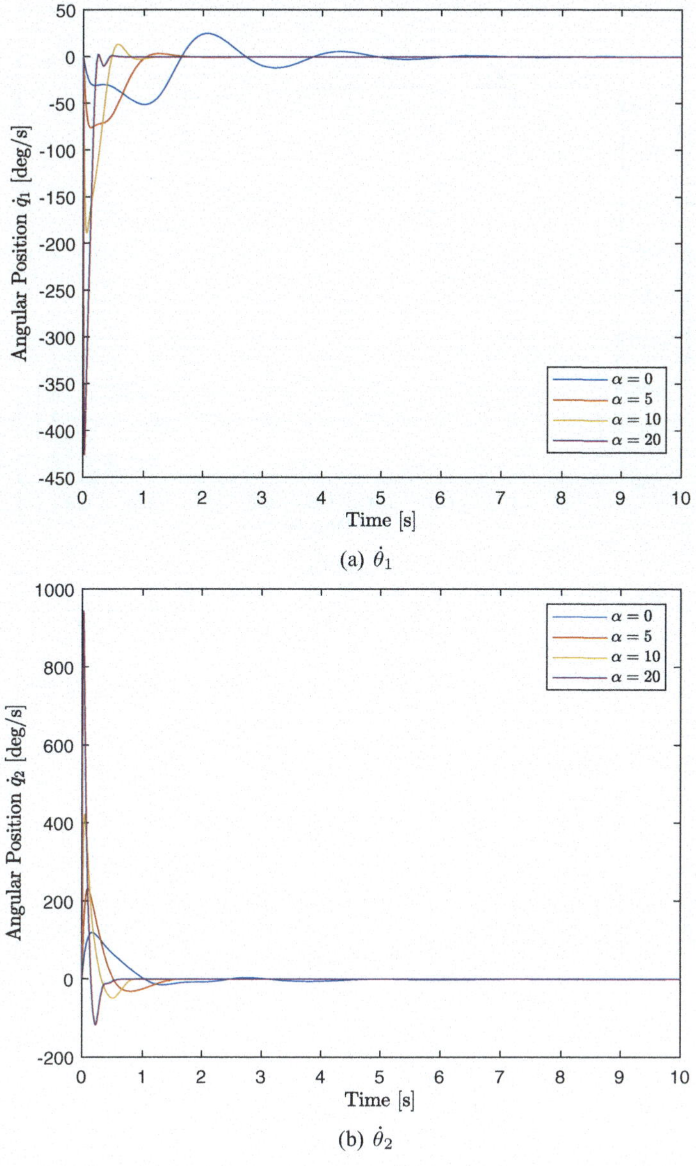

Fig. 7 Simulation results showing the temporal evolution of the two states $\dot{\theta}_1$ and $\dot{\theta}_2$ of the controlled robot for the four different values of the decay parameter α

Moreover, Fig. 9 shows the evolution of the applied sub-controllers u_1 and u_2 applied to the robot. Figure 9a shows the applied controller u_1, whereas Fig. 9b depicts the applied controller u_2 for a simulation between 0 and 1 s. It is clear that for the four cases of the parameter α, when the robot is controlled to and therefore stabilized at the

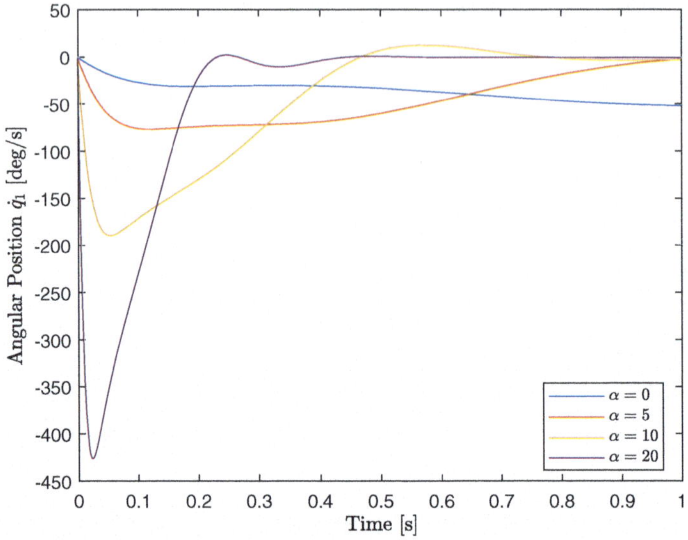

(a) $\dot{\theta}_1$

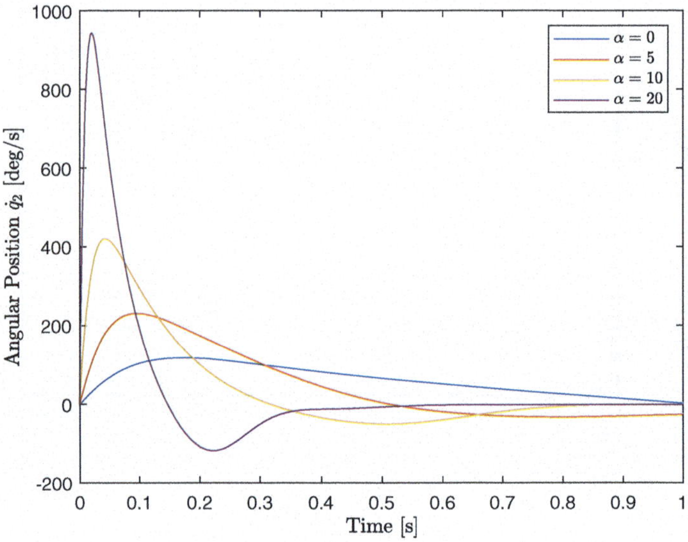

(b) $\dot{\theta}_2$

Fig. 8 Enlargement of the two plots of Fig. 7a, b showing the simulation during the first second

intended position θ_d, the two controllers u_1 and u_2 tend to a constant value. Indeed, the sub-controller u_1 converges to $u_1^\infty = 10.4051\,\text{N}$, whereas the sub-controller u_2 converges to $u_2^\infty = 1.7342\,\text{N}$.

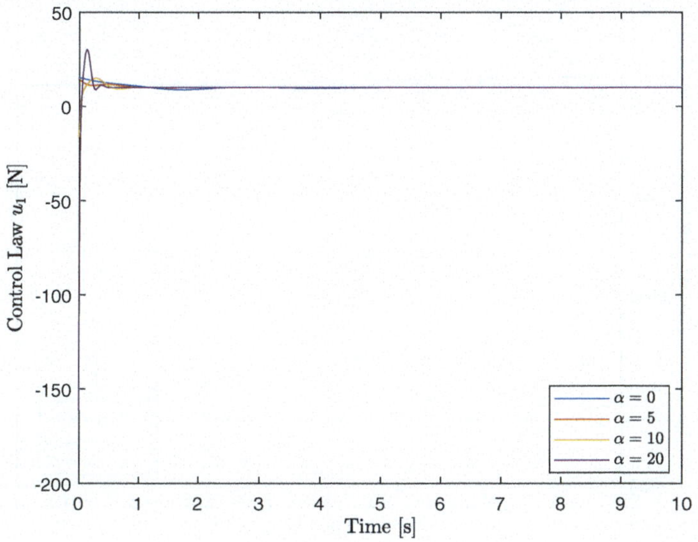

(a) u_1

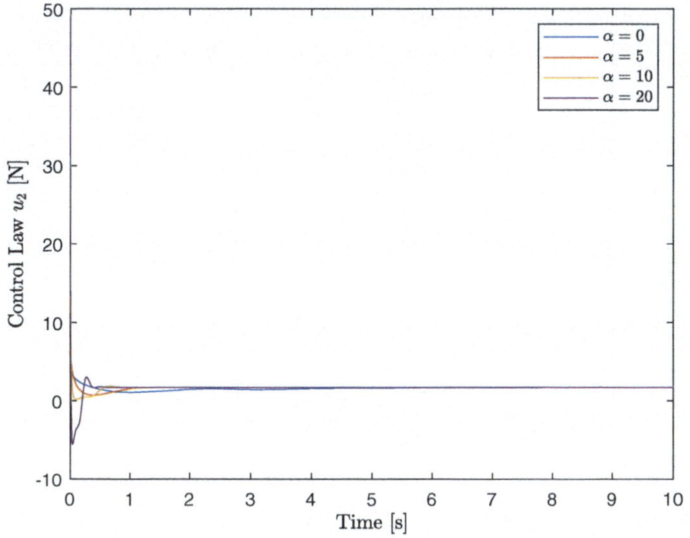

(b) u_2

Fig. 9 Evolution of the two controllers u_1 and u_2 applied to the robot and for the four different values of the decay parameter α

Figure 10 shows the curves of u_1 and u_2 during the first one second of the simulation. It is obvious that by increasing the parameter α, the robot requires more control effort to be controlled to the desired position θ_d. Notice that for $\alpha = 20$, the controller u_1 (resp. u_2) reaches the minimum (resp. maximal) value around -160 N

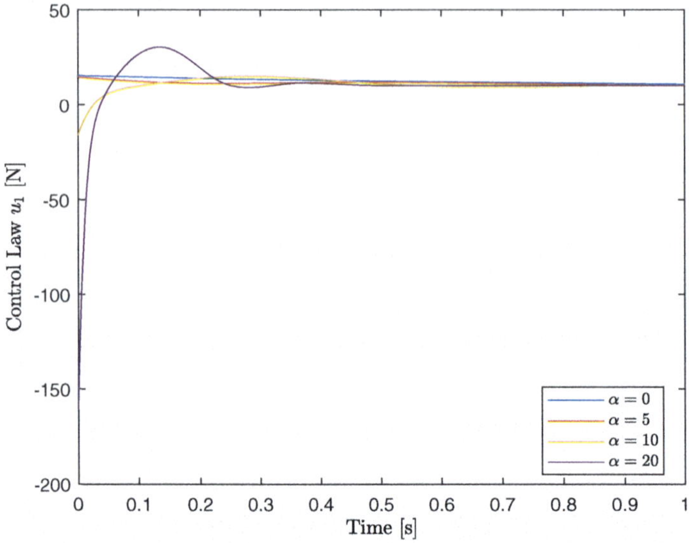

(a) u_1

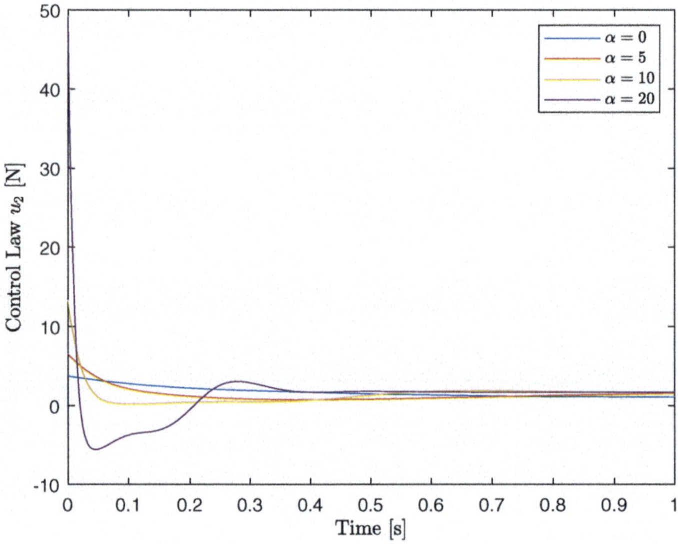

(b) u_2

Fig. 10 Enlargement of the two plots of Fig. 9a, b showing the simulation during the first second

(resp. 50 N). In contrast, for the other values of the parameter α, the controller u_1 reaches the maximal value around ± 15 N, and the controller u_2 reaches the maximal value around 3.7 N for $\alpha = 0$, around 6.5 N for $\alpha = 5$, and around 13.3 N for $\alpha = 10$.

However, these high values of the controllers contribute to the rapid stabilization of the robot at the intended position θ_d.

7 Conclusion

In this chapter, we suggested an affine PD controller for controlling the position of robotic systems, with an application to a 2-DoF exoskeleton robot for upper extremity rehabilitation. As a result, we investigated the dynamical system that describes the difference between the robot's nonlinear dynamics and the approximation linear system, and we assumed that the difference satisfied a particular Lipschitz condition. Furthermore, we derived several LMI conditions with the Lipschitz constant maximized utilizing three design methodologies and some theoretical tools and lemmas. We demonstrated that computing such a Lipschitz constant results in resolving a minimization problem with LMI constraints. We also added two more LMI constraints to limit the magnitude of the gain of the feedback controller. Several numerical results comparing the three LMI design techniques have been achieved. Furthermore, we performed some simulation and graphic results to demonstrate the effectiveness of the designed LMIs for computing the feedback gains of the proposed affine PD controller and thus of such controller in controlling the adopted 2-DoF rehabilitation exoskeleton to the required point.

References

1. Abbas, M., Al Issa, S., Dwivedy, S.K.: Event-triggered adaptive hybrid position-force control for robot-assisted ultrasonic examination system. Journal of Intelligent & Robotic Systems **102**(4) (2021)
2. Baud, R., Manzoori, A.R., Ijspeert, A., Bouri, M.: Review of control strategies for lower-limb exoskeletons to assist gait. Journal of NeuroEngineering and Rehabilitation **18**(1), 119 (2021)
3. Bhujel, S., Hasan, S.K.: A comparative study of end-effector and exoskeleton type rehabilitation robots in human upper extremity rehabilitation. Human-Intelligent Systems Integration **5**(1), 11–42 (2023)
4. Boubaker, O.: Medical and Healthcare Robotics. New Paradigms and Recent Advances, 1 edn. Medical Robots and Devices: New Developments and Advances. Elsevier, Academic Press (2023)
5. Boyd, S., El-Ghaoui, L., Feron, E., Balakrishnan, V.: Linear matrix inequalities in system and control theory, *Studies in Applied and Numerical Mathematics*, vol. 15, 1 edn. Society for Industrial and Applied Mathematics (SIAM), Philadelphia, PA. (1994)
6. Brahmi, B., Saad, M., Luna, C.O., Archambault, P.S., Rahman, M.H.: Passive and active rehabilitation control of human upper-limb exoskeleton robot with dynamic uncertainties. Robotica **36**(11), 1757–1779 (2018)
7. Chawla, I., Singla, A.: Real-time stabilization control of a rotary inverted pendulum using LQR-based sliding mode controller. Arabian Journal for Science and Engineering **46**(3), 2589–2596 (2021)
8. Choukchou-Braham, A., Cherki, B., Djemai, M., Busawon, K.: Analysis and Control of Underactuated Mechanical Systems. Springer-Verlag, New York (2014)

9. Deng, W., Papavasileiou, I., Qiao, Z., Zhang, W., Lam, K.Y., Han, S.: Advances in automation technologies for lower extremity neurorehabilitation: A review and future challenges. IEEE reviews in biomedical engineering **11**, 289–305 (2018)
10. Gritli, H.: Robust master-slave synchronization of chaos in a one-sided 1-DoF impact mechanical oscillator subject to parametric uncertainties and disturbances. Mechanism and Machine Theory **142**, 103610 (2019)
11. Gritli, H.: LMI-based robust stabilization of a class of input-constrained uncertain nonlinear systems with application to a helicopter model. Complexity **2020**, 7025761 (2020)
12. Gritli, H., Belghith, S.: Robust feedback control of the underactuated Inertia Wheel Inverted Pendulum under parametric uncertainties and subject to external disturbances: LMI formulation. Journal of The Franklin Institute **355**(18), 9150–9191 (2018)
13. Gritli, H., Belghith, S.: LMI-based synthesis of a robust saturated controller for an underactuated mechanical system subject to motion constraints. European Journal of Control **57**, 179–193 (2021)
14. Gritli, H., Jenhani, S.: LMI-based state feedback control of the underactuated inertia wheel inverted pendulum to the unstable upright position. Journal of Vibration Testing and System Dynamics **8**(2), 207–234 (2024). https://doi.org/10.5890/JVTSD.2024.06.005
15. Gritli, H., Jenhani, S.: Position control of robotic systems via linear controllers with application to a lower limb rehabilitation exoskeleton robot: Design and comparative analysis. In: E. Campos-Cantón, G. Huerta-Cuellar, E. Zambrano-Serrano, E. Tlelo-Cuautle (eds.) Complex Systems and Their Applications, pp. 123–151. Springer Nature Switzerland, Cham (2024)
16. Gritli, H., Jenhani, S., Carbone, G.: Position control of robotic systems via an affine PD-based controller: Comparison between two design approaches. In: 2022 5th International Conference on Advanced Systems and Emergent Technologies (IC_ASET), pp. 424–432 (2022)
17. Gu, E.Y.L.: Control of Robotic Systems, vol. 1, pp. 293–396. Springer, Berlin, Heidelberg (2013)
18. Hassène Gritli, A.Z., Belghith, S.: On LMI conditions to design robust static output feedback controller for continuous-time linear systems subject to norm-bounded uncertainties. International Journal of Systems Science **52**(1), 12–46 (2021)
19. Hobbs, B., Artemiadis, P.: A review of robot-assisted lower-limb stroke therapy: unexplored paths and future directions in gait rehabilitation. Frontiers in neurorobotics **14**, 19 (2020)
20. Hu, T., Lin, Z.: Control Systems with Actuator Saturation: Analysis and Design, 1 edn. Control Engineering. Birkhauser Basel (2011)
21. Hussain, F., Goecke, R., Mohammadian, M.: Exoskeleton robots for lower limb assistance: A review of materials, actuation, and manufacturing methods. Proceedings of the Institution of Mechanical Engineers, Part H: Journal of Engineering in Medicine **235**(12), 1375–1385 (2021)
22. Islam, M.R., Brahmi, B., Ahmed, T., Assad-Uz-Zaman, M., Rahman, M.H.: Chapter 9 - exoskeletons in upper limb rehabilitation: A review to find key challenges to improve functionality. In: O. Boubaker (ed.) Control Theory in Biomedical Engineering, pp. 235–265. Academic Press (2020)
23. Jenhani, S., Gritli, H.: A composite robust position control design for an actuated knee rehabilitation exoskeleton. In: 2023 20th International Multi-Conference on Systems, Signals & Devices (SSD), pp. 129–134 (2023)
24. Jenhani, S., Gritli, H.: Enhancing knee rehabilitation exoskeleton control via a robust LMI-based strategy and by considering state constraints. In: 2023 IEEE 11th International Conference on Systems and Control (ICSC), pp. 905–911 (2023)
25. Jenhani, S., Gritli, H.: LMI-based design of an affine PD controller for the robust stabilization of the knee joint of a lower-limb rehabilitation exoskeleton. In: 2023 IEEE International Conference on Advanced Systems and Emergent Technologies (IC_ASET), pp. 1–7. IEEE (2023)
26. Jenhani, S., Gritli, H.: LMI-based design of a robust affine control law for the position control of a knee exoskeleton robot: Comparative analysis of stability conditions. In: E. Campos-Cantón, G. Huerta-Cuellar, E. Zambrano-Serrano, E. Tlelo-Cuautle (eds.) Complex Systems and Their Applications, pp. 95–122. Springer Nature Switzerland, Cham (2024)

27. Jenhani, S., Gritli, H.: An LMI-based robust state-feedback controller design for the position control of a knee rehabilitation exoskeleton robot: Comparative analysis. Measurement Control **57**(9), 1326–1346 (2024). https://doi.org/10.1177/00202940241236295
28. Jenhani, S., Gritli, H., Carbone, G.: Comparison between some nonlinear controllers for the position control of Lagrangian-type robotic systems. Chaos Theory and Applications **4**(4), 179–196 (2022)
29. Jenhani, S., Gritli, H., Carbone, G.: Design of an affine control law for the position control problem of robotic systems based on the development of a linear dynamic model. In: 2022 5th International Conference on Advanced Systems and Emergent Technologies (IC_ASET), pp. 403–411 (2022)
30. Jenhani, S., Gritli, H., Carbone, G.: Position feedback control of lagrangian robotic systems via an affine PD-based control law. Part 1: Design of LMI conditions. In: 2022 IEEE 2nd International Maghreb Meeting of the Conference on Sciences and Techniques of Automatic Control and Computer Engineering (MI-STA 2022) (2022)
31. Jenhani, S., Gritli, H., Carbone, G.: Position feedback control of lagrangian robotic systems via an affine PD-based control law. Part 2: Improved results. In: 2022 IEEE 2nd International Maghreb Meeting of the Conference on Sciences and Techniques of Automatic Control and Computer Engineering (MI-STA 2022) (2022)
32. Kalita, B., Narayan, J., Dwivedy, S.K.: Development of active lower limb robotic-based orthosis and exoskeleton devices: A systematic review. International Journal of Social Robotics **3**(4), 775–793 (2021)
33. Krafes, S., Chalh, Z., Saka, A.: A review on the control of second order underactuated mechanical systems. Complexity **2018**, 9573514 (2018)
34. Kurdila, A.J., Ben-Tzvi, P.: Dynamics and Control of Robotic Systems, 1 edn. Control Process & Measurements. Wiley (2019)
35. Li, X., Liu, B., Wang, L.: Control system of the six-axis serial manipulator based on active disturbance rejection control. International Journal of Advanced Robotic Systems **17**(4), 1729881420939476 (2020)
36. Liu, P., Huda, M.N., Sun, L., Yu, H.: A survey on underactuated robotic systems: Bio-inspiration, trajectory planning and control. Mechatronics **72**, 102443 (2020)
37. Liu, Y., Yu, H.: A survey of underactuated mechanical systems. IET Control Theory Applications **7**(7), 921–935 (2013)
38. Mekki, M., Delgado, A.D., Fry, A., Putrino, D., Huang, V.: Robotic rehabilitation and spinal cord injury: a narrative review. Neurotherapeutics **15**, 604–617 (2018)
39. Mobayen, S., Tchier, F., Ragoub, L.: Design of an adaptive tracker for n-link rigid robotic manipulators based on super-twisting global nonlinear sliding mode control. International Journal of Systems Science **48**(9), 1990–2002 (2017)
40. Narayan, J., Abbas, M., Dwivedy, S.K.: Design and validation of a pediatric gait assistance exoskeleton system with fast non-singular terminal sliding mode controller. Medical Engineering & Physics **123**, 104080 (2024)
41. Narayan, J., Auepanwiriyakul, C., Jhunjhunwala, S., Abbas, M., Dwivedy, S.K.: Hierarchical classification of subject-cooperative control strategies for lower limb exoskeletons in gait rehabilitation: A systematic review. Machines **11**(7) (2023)
42. Narayan, J., Dwivedy, S.K.: Lower limb exoskeletons for pediatric gait rehabilitation: A brief review of design, actuation, and control schemes. In: 2023 IEEE International Conference on Advanced Systems and Emergent Technologies (IC_ASET), pp. 1–6 (2023)
43. Narayan, J., Dwivedy, S.K.: Towards neuro-fuzzy compensated PID control of lower extremity exoskeleton system for passive gait rehabilitation. IETE Journal of Research **69**(2), 778–795 (2023)
44. Narayan, J., Gritli, H., Dwivedy, S.K.: Fast terminal sliding mode control with rapid reaching law for a pediatric gait exoskeleton system. International Journal of Intelligent Robotics and Applications **8**, 76–95 (2024)
45. Narayan, J., Kalita, B., Dwivedy, S.K.: Adaptive backstepping human-cooperative control of a pediatric gait exoskeleton system with high- and low-level admittance. Proceedings of the

Institution of Mechanical Engineers, Part I: Journal of Systems and Control Engineering **0**(0), 09596518231191390 (2024). https://doi.org/10.1177/09596518231191390
46. Qiu, S., Pei, Z., Pei, Z., Wang, C., Tang, Z.: Systematic review on wearable lower extremity robotic exoskeletons for assisted locomotion. Journal of Bionic Engineering **20**(2), 436–469 (2023)
47. Rehmat, N., Zuo, J., Meng, W., Liu, Q., Xie, S.Q., Liang, H.: Upper limb rehabilitation using robotic exoskeleton systems: A systematic review. International Journal of Intelligent Robotics and Applications **2**, 283–295 (2018)
48. Rodríguez-Fernández, A., Lobo-Prat, J., Font-Llagunes, J.M.: Systematic review on wearable lower-limb exoskeletons for gait training in neuromuscular impairments. Journal of neuroengineering and rehabilitation **18**(1), 1–21 (2021)
49. Shi, D., Zhang, W., Zhang, W., Ding, X.: A review on lower limb rehabilitation exoskeleton robots. Chinese Journal of Mechanical Engineering **32**(1), 74 (2019)
50. Singla, A., Singh, G.: Real-time swing-up and stabilization control of a cart-pendulum system with constrained cart movement. International Journal of Nonlinear Sciences and Numerical Simulation **18**(6), 525–539 (2017)
51. Spong, M.W., Hutchinson, S., Vidyasagar, M.: Robot Modeling and Control, 2 edn. Robotics. John Wiley & Sons Inc (2020)
52. Tarbouriech, S., Garcia, G., Gomes da Silva Jr., J.M., Queinnec, I.: Stability and Stabilization of Linear Systems with Saturating Actuators, 1 edn. Springer, London (2011)
53. Tipary, B., Erdos, G.: Generic development methodology for flexible robotic pick-and-place workcells based on digital twin. Robotics and Computer-Integrated Manufacturing **71**, 102140 (2021)
54. Van der Loos, H.M., Reinkensmeyer, D.J., Guglielmelli, E.: Rehabilitation and health care robotics. In: B. Siciliano, O. Khatib (eds.) Springer Handbook of Robotics, pp. 1685–1728. Springer International Publishing, Cham (2016)
55. Wang, Y., Rajamani, R., Zemouche, A.: Sequential LMI approach for the design of a BMI-based robust observer state feedback controller with nonlinear uncertainties. International Journal of Robust and Nonlinear Control **28**(4), 1246–1260 (2018)
56. Wang, Y., Zemouche, A., Rajamani, R.: A sequential LMI approach to design a BMI-based multi-objective nonlinear observer. European Journal of Control **44**, 50–57 (2018)
57. Zemouche, A., Aitouche, A., Alma, M., Bezzaoucha-Rebai, S.: Advanced control and observer design for nonlinear systems via LMIs. European Journal of Control **44**, 1–2 (2018)
58. Zemouche, A., Rajamani, R., Kheloufi, H., Bedouhene, F.: Robust observer-based stabilization of Lipschitz nonlinear uncertain systems via LMIs - discussions and new design procedure. International Journal of Robust and Nonlinear Control **27**(11), 1915–1939 (2017)
59. Zhang, C., Wu, Y.: P-Rob six-degree-of-freedom robot manipulator dynamics modeling and anti-disturbance control. IEEE Access **9**, 141403–141420 (2021)
60. Zhang, Y.P., Cao, G.Z., Li, L.L., Diao, D.F.: Interactive control of lower limb exoskeleton robots: A review. IEEE Sensors Journal **24**(5), 5759–5784 (2024)
61. Zhu, Y., Tong, X., Yang, R., Li, Y., Du, M., Su, C.Y.: A survey on modeling mechanism and control strategy of rehabilitation robots: Recent trends, current challenges, and future developments. International Journal of Control, Automation and Systems **20**(8), 2724–2748 (2022)

Smart Hospitals and Healthcare Facilities for CPS

Urvi Bhatt, Monisha Mohan, Aswathy R. Nair, Santushti Santosh Betgeri, and Twinkle Keshvani

Abstract A robust and intelligent healthcare system that can properly monitor patients and deal with situations like disease outbreaks is essential in light of the recent surge in technological advancements. Smart hospitals and healthcare facilities are leading a technological revolution that is reshaping the healthcare industry. Cyber-Physical System (CPS) in Smart Healthcare have emerged as a result of developments in areas such as the Internet of Things (IoT), artificial intelligence (AI), big data analytics, and automation systems. Aim of all these technologies is to create an interconnected intelligent healthcare environment. Smart healthcare uses advanced CPS technology. It tracks and controls a patient's physical dynamics using highly complicated embedded systems with network connection skills. This chapter begins with an overview of CPS and the key components that make up CPS, such as sensors, actuators, communication networks, and data analytics. After that, we'll discuss how CPS is being used in healthcare facilities specifically, with an emphasis on the transformative potential of "smart hospitals," their distinguishing features, the contributions of various technologies to their creation, and the primary obstacles standing in the way of widespread adoption of "cyber physical medication systems." Increasingly pervasive technologies such as wireless sensor networks (WSN), wearable sensor devices, and ambient systems make CPS a reality by interconnecting with the IoT, which facilitates the exchange and collection of data. The physical and cyber worlds are integrated in smart healthcare cyber physical systems for efficient treatment by externally monitoring and controlling medical devices and equipment for constant communication and physiological data transaction.

Keywords CPS · IoT · WSN

U. Bhatt · M. Mohan (✉) · A. R. Nair · T. Keshvani
Marwadi University, Rajkot, Gujarat, India
e-mail: monisha.mohan@marwadieducation.edu.in

A. R. Nair
e-mail: aswathy.nair@marwadieducation.edu.in

S. S. Betgeri
Vishwakarma Institute of Technology, Pune, Maharashtra, India
e-mail: santushti.betgeri@vit.edu

M. Mittal and J. Narayan (eds.), *Intelligent Cyber-Physical Systems for Healthcare Solutions*, https://doi.org/10.1007/978-981-97-8983-2_15

1 Introduction to CPS in Healthcare

Cyber physical systems, which are also called "smart systems," use information technologies to link the physical world to the cyber world, which is the computing part. This paves the way for the development of smart services and enhances existing ones. Health care, transportation, emergency response, intelligent production, sustainable development, and countless other fields rely on cyber physical systems [1]. In recent years, CPS have become increasingly important in the medical field. In the face of the present pandemic, a strong healthcare system is the backbone of every smart city. Patient monitoring, drug delivery, and medical equipment maintenance are all more likely to run smoothly and efficiently if the system can keep up with the demand for them. This is achievable because of a predictive mechanism that can foresee the state of healthcare and immediately put into action measures to deal with medical emergencies.

This integration of physical and digital elements has the potential to revolutionize patient care and treatment methodologies. In this introduction, we will explore the implications and benefits of CPS in healthcare, highlighting its impact on medical advancements, patient monitoring, and data-driven decision-making.

Computing and physical processes define a CPS, which consists of networked devices [2]. In dynamic temporal and geographical contexts, these processes act upon material constituents and systems of finite resources [3]. Any computational system's main objective is to control and communicate with physical processes via contact points (sensors and actuators). The substantial connectivity between networks of physical and computational components that define complex physical systems in CPS. Additionally, how people behave in these situations has a big impact on the group as a whole. It has received high praise for being a smart, real-time, flexible, predictive, and decentralized feedback system. Its implementation in heterogeneous environments is what allows it to be interoperable and scalable, as seen in Table 1. An equivalent concept to a CPS is a "system of systems." These systems often operate autonomously and optimize themselves [4]. Healthcare, smart homes, autonomous vehicles, and business are just a few of the many fields that can benefit from these systems [5]. Sensor- and actuator-equipped autonomous cars are one sort of this technology. The ability to perceive and interpret its surroundings, form its own conclusions, and act on those conclusions autonomously using actuators. Some examples of CPS are intelligent home management systems, healthcare robots, and medical monitoring gadgets. The economic and social impacts of a CPS are substantial, and so is the potential for it to leave a sizable energy footprint that may be minimized with some careful planning.

Table 1 Devices found in CPS

Sr. no	Devices	Technology
1	Microcontrollers	Zigbee
2	Smart appliances	API
3	ICT equipments	Ethernet/WIFI
4	Smart gadgets	Bluetooth
5	Smart vehicle	LTE/5G
6	Surveillance system	TCP/IP

1.1 Understanding CPS and Their Significance in Healthcare

CPS are technological marvels that bridge the gap between the physical and digital realms, holding immense potential to transform the healthcare landscape. In this discussion, we will delve into the fundamentals of CPS, their relevance in the medical field, and the myriad ways they can revolutionize patient care, diagnostics, treatment, and overall healthcare efficiency. By understanding CPS and their significant impact, we can unlock a new era of advanced healthcare solutions that benefit both medical professionals and patients alike [6].

Real-time patient monitoring through CPS significantly enhances healthcare delivery by offering continuous monitoring of patients. This system collects and analyzes vital signs, symptoms, and other relevant data, enhancing patient safety and enabling timely interventions in critical situations. Additionally, access to comprehensive medical records allows medical personnel to tailor treatment plans more precisely to individual patient needs, considering their health and medical history. CPS also facilitates remote healthcare services, extending the reach of healthcare providers to patients in remote areas and improving care for those with chronic conditions through better follow-up and management. Moreover, the integration of advanced analytics into CPS enables predictive analytics and early detection, identifying potential health hazards early to prevent catastrophic outcomes.

The incorporation of CPS in medical devices not only improves their functionality but also increases their reliability, leading to more accurate diagnoses and safer medical procedures. This technology supports data-driven decision-making, enhancing quality improvement activities and contributing to medical research, which in turn promotes innovations in healthcare practices. Furthermore, CPS helps healthcare facilities optimize resource allocation, streamline workflows, and reduce medical errors, thus boosting operational efficiency and enabling cost savings. As healthcare increasingly relies on digital technology, the importance of cyber security measures grows, emphasizing the need to secure patient data and protect against cyber threats. Lastly, the data generated by CPS is invaluable for medical research, facilitating breakthroughs in treatments, drug development, and medical technology innovations, which continues to push the boundaries of what is possible in healthcare.

1.2 Key Components of CPS: Sensors, Actuators, Communication Networks, and Data Analytics

The key component of CPS includes:

Sensors and actuaries play pivotal roles in CPS, particularly in the context of healthcare. Sensors are devices capable of detecting and measuring a wide range of environmental and physiological information, such as temperature, pressure, humidity, motion and biochemical indicators including glucose levels and heart rate. They are crucial for the acquisition of real-time data from the physical environment, which is fundamental to effective monitoring and response systems.

Actuators, on the other hand, control or influence physical processes based on data received from sensors. They can initiate actions, perform tasks, or make adjustments in response to gathered information, thus directly impacting patient care through automated actions and responses. Examples of actuators used in healthcare include electric motors, which are integral to devices like robotic surgery systems and rehabilitation devices; pumps, essential for precise drug delivery in insulin pumps and IV fluid systems; and valves, which regulate gas and liquid flow in devices such as ventilators. Other types include linear actuators used in hospital beds, solenoids in automated external defibrillators (AEDs), piezoelectric actuators in ultrasound probes, thermal actuators in incubators, and artificial muscles in prosthetics and exoskeletons. Each type of actuator enhances the functionality and efficacy of medical devices and systems, allowing for precise and responsive patient care.

In addition to sensors and actuaries, communication networks are vital in CPS, enabling seamless data exchange between sensors, actuators, and central processing units. This connectivity ensures real-time data transmission and coordinated responses across the system, which is essential for maintaining continuous monitoring and timely interventions.

Lastly, data analytics plays a transformative role in interpreting the vast amounts of data collected by sensors. Employing advanced analytics techniques such as machine learning and artificial intelligence helps to identify patterns, trends, and anomalies, enhancing decision-making and predictive capabilities. This analytical process is critical in advancing healthcare practices, leading to more informed strategies and improved patient outcomes. Together, these components integrate to form a sophisticated CPS that enhances healthcare delivery through technology-driven solutions.

1.3 The Role of CPS in Reshaping the Healthcare Industry and the Need for Intelligent Healthcare Systems

The investigation of cyber physical systems within the healthcare domain is necessary to facilitate the integration of intelligent medical and healthcare services (Table 2). The field of cyber physical system research in healthcare is now at its nascent stage.

Table 2 Real time cyber healthcare application [7]

Sr. no	Healthcare application	Sensor and operations
01	Monitoring and control of heart rate	Heartbeat sensors are used to track changes in the volume of blood in the body. If the changes, go up to a threshold them alarm is send to doctors and patient to take corrective actions
02	Diabetic patient monitoring	Glucose sensor is used to monitor level of sugar in body and real time alert system is developed
03	Asthma patient monitoring	Asthma tracker is used to track the patient asthma level and updates the real time information to cloud
04	Skin disease monitoring and control	Smart cameras take images of akin, processes and updates if any skin disorder
05	Eye monitoring and control	Smart cameras take pictures of eyes. Mobile app processes images of eyes and send real time eye information to doctor
06	Pulse rate monitoring	Oximeter is used to monitor pulse rate
07	Temperature monitoring system	Temperature sensor used to monitor temperature of patients and store information in the cloud
08	Blood pressure monitoring	BP sensor is used to monitor the real time value of blood pressure
09	Cough monitoring system	Microphone is used to processes cough sound and voice processing is used track the real time cough analysis
10	Remote surgery	Robot surgical system and augmented reality sensor used to perform remote surgery on real time

CPS within the context of smart healthcare systems encompass various components, including patient monitoring, real-time control and feedback mechanisms, digital storage of patient and doctors' records, and real-time analytics for informed decision-making. CPS are employed within the healthcare sector to effectively coordinate and manage adaptive medical devices [8]. Several CPS architectures have been proposed in the past; however, only a limited number of these have been specifically focused on healthcare applications. The utilization of service-oriented architecture in the development of CPS. An integrated architecture for cyber-physical healthcare systems that utilizes cloud computing and wireless sensor networks. Several research articles propose the utilization of artificial intelligence in the development of CPS for patient healthcare. The user's text is already academic and does not require any rewriting.

CPS are revolutionizing the healthcare industry, ushering in a new era of intelligent healthcare systems that significantly impact patient care and medical practices. By seamlessly integrating physical and digital elements, CPS enables real-time patient monitoring, providing healthcare providers with continuous data on a patient's health status. Improved patient outcomes and increased safety are the results of this ongoing monitoring that enables for early detection of health concerns and timely interventions. Moreover, CPS empowers personalized treatment plans by analyzing vast amounts of patient data, tailoring medical approaches to individual needs and medical histories, and optimizing treatment effectiveness.

One of the most remarkable contributions of CPS in healthcare is the extension of medical services to remote areas. Telemedicine and remote patient monitoring are made possible through CPS, enabling healthcare access for individuals in underserved regions. This expansion of healthcare services enhances follow-up care for patients with chronic conditions and reduces the burden of travel for routine medical consultations, ultimately improving overall patient satisfaction and adherence to treatment plans. Additionally, CPS-driven predictive analytics aids in identifying patterns and trends in patient data, allowing for proactive healthcare measures that can prevent the onset of diseases and optimize disease management, leading to better health outcomes and cost savings.

Intelligent healthcare systems powered by CPS also optimize resource management and streamline healthcare workflows, leading to increased operational efficiency within healthcare facilities. Through the utilization of data-driven decision-making, medical professionals are able to make educated decisions on patient diagnosis and treatment, thereby elevating the standard of care provided to patients and expanding the field of medical research. However, as CPS-driven healthcare relies heavily on digital infrastructure, robust cyber security measures become paramount to protect patient data and ensure privacy. Through the continuous contribution of CPS-generated data to medical research and innovations, healthcare is propelled towards new horizons, driving advancements in treatments, therapies, and medical technologies, ultimately benefiting patients and healthcare providers alike.

1.4 Real Time Cyber Physical System in Healthcare

Different monitoring and control tasks need to be done and scheduled in real time for the cyber- physical healthcare system. Timing restrictions are challenging to implement in a cyber-physical healthcare system due of:

In the realm of cyber-physical healthcare systems, the real-time jobs essential for monitoring and managing patient health are subject to varying release times and deadlines. This variation arises because computing nodes, which are crucial for processing and transmitting health data, are often dispersed across different locations and may be mobile, moving in distinct patterns. This complex setup requires precise coordination to ensure timely data handling and decision-making.

Real-time jobs within these systems are typically associated with hard deadlines, underscoring the critical nature of timely and accurate task completion. Failing to meet these deadlines could lead to dire consequences, including the loss of lives, as these systems often support life-critical functions. For example, a delay in processing data from heart monitoring sensors could delay urgent medical interventions.

A cyber-physical healthcare system integrates various technological components to maintain efficiency and reliability in real-time healthcare delivery. This includes an array of sensors monitoring vital health metrics, which continuously gather data and relay it to medical staff. These sensors are connected to embedded processing units that operate on real-time operating systems designed specifically for handling such high-stakes data seamlessly. These systems utilize real-time schedulers to manage multiple processes simultaneously, ensuring that all data is processed promptly and accurately.

Further enhancing the system's capabilities, fog computing plays a crucial role by processing data at or near the source, reducing latency and allowing for immediate response to critical health changes (Fig. 1). The Kafka pipeline supports robust data handling and streaming capabilities, enabling efficient healthcare data processing. Additionally, the Spark framework is employed to manage and analyze health data effectively, ensuring that healthcare providers can make informed decisions quickly. Together, these components form a sophisticated architecture that supports dynamic and responsive healthcare delivery, catering to the urgent needs of patients in real-time environments.

1.5 How do CPS Technologies Facilitate Real-Time Data Analytics in Healthcare?

CPS technologies significantly enhance real-time data analytics in healthcare settings by integrating physical processes with computational resources. This integration enables advanced monitoring, analysis, and decision-making capabilities, particularly in patient monitoring and disease outbreak detection. Here's how CPS technologies facilitate these critical functions.

Seamless Data Integration

CPS technologies integrate data from various sources, including wearable sensors, medical devices, and Electronic health records (EHR). This integration allows for the continuous collection of patient data such as vital signs, movement, and other health indicators in real time, enabling healthcare providers to monitor patient conditions more accurately and efficiently.

Real-Time Monitoring and Alerts

Through the use of sensors and networked devices, CPS enables real-time monitoring of patients' health status. This continuous monitoring can detect changes in physiological parameters, triggering alerts for healthcare providers when abnormal

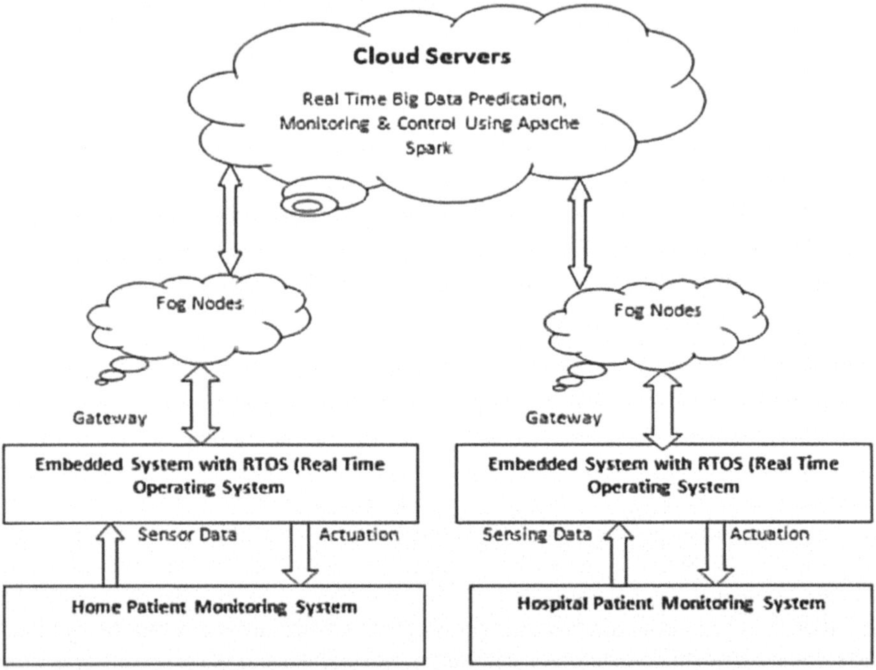

Fig. 1 System for real-time cyber-physical healthcare

values are detected. For instance, in the case of a patient with heart conditions, CPS can immediately alert medical staff if cardiac irregularities are observed, facilitating rapid response.

Predictive Analytics for Early Intervention

CPS technologies apply machine learning and data analytics to the vast amounts of data collected, identifying patterns and trends that may not be immediately apparent to human observers. By analyzing this data, CPS can predict potential health issues before they become critical, enabling preventative measures or early interventions, which is especially useful in managing chronic diseases and preventing hospital readmissions.

Disease Outbreak Detection

In the context of public health, CPS technologies can play a pivotal role in disease surveillance and outbreak detection. By aggregating and analyzing data from multiple healthcare facilities and sources, CPS can help identify trends and clusters of illnesses, signaling potential outbreaks much earlier than traditional methods. This real-time analysis allows health authorities to implement containment measures promptly, minimizing the spread of infectious diseases.

Telehealth and Remote Care

CPS technologies enable telehealth services by allowing real-time communication and data exchange between patients and healthcare providers. This capability is particularly beneficial for remote patient monitoring, where healthcare providers can track patients' health status and provide consultations without the need for physical visits. During disease outbreaks, such as the COVID-19 pandemic, this aspect of CPS becomes invaluable in reducing exposure risks and ensuring continuous care for patients with chronic conditions.

Data Security and Privacy

Implementing CPS in healthcare requires stringent data security and privacy measures to protect sensitive patient information. CPS technologies incorporate advanced encryption methods, secure data transmission protocols, and compliance with healthcare regulations like HIPAA (Health Insurance Portability and Accountability Act) to ensure data integrity and confidentiality.

By leveraging these capabilities, CPS technologies not only improve patient care and outcomes through enhanced monitoring and predictive analytics but also help in public health responses to emerging health threats and disease outbreaks, showcasing the transformative potential of integrating physical and digital worlds in healthcare.

2 Technological Foundations of Smart Healthcare

2.1 Exploring Advancements in the Internet of Things (IoT) for Healthcare Applications

The Internet of Things (IoT) innovations have had a significant impact on healthcare applications, altering patient care and the way medical services are provided. The seamless integration of devices, sensors, and data analytics made possible by IoT technology promotes a more networked and data-driven healthcare ecosystem.

The Internet of Things (IoT) has brought about significant advancements in healthcare, revolutionizing the way patient care is delivered and managed. Remote patient monitoring has become increasingly feasible with wearable sensors and IoT-enabled devices that continuously track vital signs such as heart rate, blood pressure, and glucose levels. This technology enables medical professionals to monitor patients remotely, allowing for timely interventions, particularly beneficial for those recovering from chronic conditions or recent surgeries [9]. Moreover, IoT has facilitated the creation of smart healthcare devices like smart inhalers, pill dispensers, and glucometers, which not only collect data but also provide real-time feedback to both patients and healthcare providers.

Telemedicine and virtual consultations have also been enhanced through IoT advancements, with high-definition cameras and other connected medical devices making it possible for doctors to conduct remote examinations and diagnoses, thus improving the quality of care delivered virtually. Predictive analytics, another critical advancement, uses IoT data combined with machine learning algorithms to model patient health trends, enabling early detection of health risks and preventive measures that help reduce readmissions and improve patient outcomes.

In addition to patient care, IoT technology aids in healthcare asset tracking, ensuring that medical equipment is readily available and efficiently managed within facilities, thereby improving operational efficiency. The concept of "smart hospitals" has emerged, integrating patient monitoring, EHR, and facility management systems to optimize resource allocation and enhance patient experiences. Furthermore, as healthcare becomes increasingly digitized, ensuring data security and privacy is paramount; IoT applications address these concerns through advanced encryption and secure communication protocols.

Beyond the scope of medical care, IoT also supports general health and wellness monitoring. Devices such as fitness trackers and health apps allow individuals to keep tabs on their physical activity, sleep patterns, and overall well-being, empowering them to make informed health decisions. These advancements in IoT for healthcare not only improve the efficiency of healthcare delivery but also open up new possibilities for early intervention and preventive care, solidifying IoT's role as a crucial element in the modern healthcare ecosystem. As technology evolves, the potential for further enhancing healthcare services and outcomes through IoT continues to expand.

2.2 Leveraging Artificial Intelligence (AI) and Machine Learning in Smart Healthcare Systems

Machine learning (ML) and artificial intelligence (AI) have developed into potent tools in smart healthcare systems, changing how medical services are provided and how patient care is managed. By using the power of AI and ML, smart healthcare systems can process large amounts of data, find useful insights, and make decisions based on the data to improve patient outcomes and make healthcare operations run more smoothly. Here are some key ways that AI and ML are changing smart healthcare systems.

Artificial intelligence (AI) and machine learning (ML) are transforming the landscape of healthcare through various innovative applications [10]. Personalized medicine is one such area where AI and ML algorithms analyze vast amounts of patient data, including medical history, genetic information, lifestyle factors, and responses to previous treatments. This analysis allows healthcare providers to tailor interventions specifically for each patient, thereby maximizing treatment efficacy and minimizing adverse effects. Additionally, AI-powered diagnostic systems utilize patient symptoms, test results, and medical imaging to facilitate rapid and accurate disease diagnosis. ML models further enhance this by predicting disease progression and prognosis, enabling early intervention and more effective management of chronic conditions.

Predictive analytics is another critical application, where AI and ML models sift through large datasets from EHR, wearables, and other sources to detect patterns and trends [10]. This capability aids in identifying potential health risks, predicting disease outbreaks, and optimizing resource allocation within healthcare facilities. In the realm of drug discovery and development, AI and ML accelerate the process by analyzing molecular datasets and simulating drug interactions, significantly reducing the time and cost associated with bringing new drugs to market.

Remote patient monitoring has also benefited from AI integration, with wearable devices that monitor health metrics continuously and detect anomalies in real time. This technology enhances patient safety, enables timely interventions, and decreases the frequency of hospital visits. Virtual health assistants powered by AI provide personalized healthcare advice, answer medical queries, and help patients manage their health, improving patient engagement and facilitating better communication with healthcare providers.

Furthermore, AI systems employ natural language processing (NLP) to understand and interpret human language, making them invaluable in analyzing unstructured medical texts such as doctor's notes and research papers. This analysis helps extract crucial insights and knowledge. AI-driven decision support systems compile patient data and medical literature to assist doctors in making informed decisions, providing evidence-based recommendations and treatment guidelines. Lastly, AI and ML algorithms play a significant role in detecting fraudulent activities within the healthcare system, such as insurance fraud and billing irregularities, leading to cost savings and enhanced security. Together, these AI and ML applications are crucial in advancing healthcare, making it more efficient, personalized, and secure.

The integration of AI and ML in smart healthcare systems has opened up new horizons in patient care, medical research, and healthcare management. By enabling personalized medicine, improving disease diagnosis, and enhancing predictive analytics, AI and ML are propelling the healthcare industry towards more efficient, effective, and patient-centric services [10]. As these technologies continue to evolve, the potential for smarter and more innovative healthcare solutions remains promising, driving advancements and transformations in the field of medicine.

2.3 Utilizing Big Data Analytics for Medical Insights and Predictive Healthcare

The advent of Big Data analytics has been a game-changer in the medical field, providing doctors with insights and predictive powers that were previously unavailable to them. Big data analytics is reshaping medical research, patient treatment, and healthcare administration by making use of huge amounts of data from a variety of sources, including wearables, genomics, medical imaging, and EHR. Key ways in which big data analytics is changing healthcare include the following:

Big data analytics has become an indispensable tool in modern healthcare, transforming the landscape by providing medical professionals with invaluable insights, predictive capabilities, and evidence-based decision support. By mining and analyzing massive datasets, researchers can identify patterns, correlations, and new medical insights, which accelerate drug discovery, genetic research, and other medical breakthroughs. This leads to more effective treatments and therapies. Predictive healthcare and preventive medicine leverage historical patient data to predict disease risks and outcomes, enabling healthcare providers to implement preventive measures, design personalized interventions, and improve population health management.

Real-time patient monitoring uses big data analytics to continuously monitor patients' vitals, allowing for early detection of anomalies or potential dangers, which enhances the ability to intervene swiftly and reduce hospital readmissions. Precision medicine is another area where big data analytics plays a crucial role by tailoring medicines to patients' genetics, lifestyle, and other factors, thus improving therapeutic efficacy and minimizing side effects. Furthermore, big data facilitates health information exchanges that improve care coordination, decision-making, and patient safety while reducing redundant tests and treatments.

In terms of population health management, healthcare organizations utilize big data analytics to assess health trends, identify at-risk groups, and implement targeted interventions to enhance community health [5]. Additionally, big data helps manage healthcare costs by analyzing utilization patterns and cost data to pinpoint inefficiencies and optimize resource allocation, leading to significant cost savings and better financial management. In medical imaging, big data enhances the analysis by automating image interpretation, speeding up diagnosis, and aiding radiologists in making faster, more accurate decisions.

Lastly, big data analytics is crucial for quality improvement initiatives within healthcare organizations. It aids in measuring and monitoring healthcare quality measures, identifying improvement opportunities, and implementing evidence-based practices to enhance patient safety and satisfaction. Overall, by harnessing the power of big data, healthcare systems can deliver more personalized and effective care, drive advancements in medical research, and transform healthcare into a more efficient, cost-effective, and patient-centric industry.

2.4 Sensor Used in Healthcare Sector

For medical purposes, wearable gadgets can incorporate a variety of sensors. These sensors are made to record a wide range of information about a person's health and surroundings, allowing for constant monitoring and tracking wearable medical devices are equipped with a variety of sensors that play crucial roles in monitoring health and fitness. These include heart rate monitors, which assess cardiovascular health and track exercise intensity, and electrocardiogram (ECG/EKG) sensors that record the electrical activity of the heart to detect rhythm abnormalities [11]. Blood pressure sensors allow for non-invasive, continuous monitoring, crucial for managing hypertension and other cardiovascular issues, while pulse oximeters measure blood oxygen saturation levels, important for respiratory monitoring and during physical activity. Body temperature sensors help in detecting fevers and assessing overall health, and respiratory rate sensors track breathing frequency, aiding in the management of respiratory conditions.

Devices also include blood glucose sensors that are vital for diabetics to monitor their sugar levels effectively. Electrodermal activity (EDA) sensors measure skin conductance, indicating emotional arousal and stress levels. For motion and orientation tracking, accelerometers, gyroscopes, and magnetometers are used, the latter also serving in applications like compasses. Ambient light sensors adjust device display brightness based on environmental light, and UV sensors help monitor exposure to ultraviolet radiation to prevent skin damage.

Moreover, capacitive touch sensors detect interactions with the device, and inertial measurement units combine several sensing capabilities for comprehensive motion tracking. Gas and chemical sensors detect environmental pollutants, crucial for occupational health, while electroencephalogram (EEG) sensors measure brainwave activity, useful in neurological monitoring and research. Electromyogram (EMG) sensors are employed in muscle rehabilitation and prosthetic control by recording electrical activity from skeletal muscles.

These sensors are integrated into various wearable forms like smart watches, fitness trackers, patches, and even smart clothing, allowing for extensive health monitoring. The data collected is transmitted to smartphones or cloud-based platforms for analysis, providing valuable insights to individuals and healthcare professionals alike [2]. As sensor technology advances, wearable devices are expected to become even more sophisticated, enhancing their capability to monitor a wider range of health parameters. This progression is set to further drive the growth of personalized and preventive healthcare, making it more accessible and effective.

2.5 *Real-Time Healthcare Systems Using Fog Computing*

The data of patients is collected through sensors and then communicated to fog nodes for immediate processing, as illustrated in Fig. 2 [12]. The data collected by the sensor is transmitted to the embedded CPU, which performs real-time data processing and subsequently transmits it to the fog nodes. In contrast to other cyber physical systems, medical applications are unable to utilise cloud computing due to the necessity for dependable and secure remote monitoring, as well as the requirement for real-time execution of all procedures [2]. Therefore, the utilization of fog computing is highly advantageous in healthcare and other time-sensitive domains

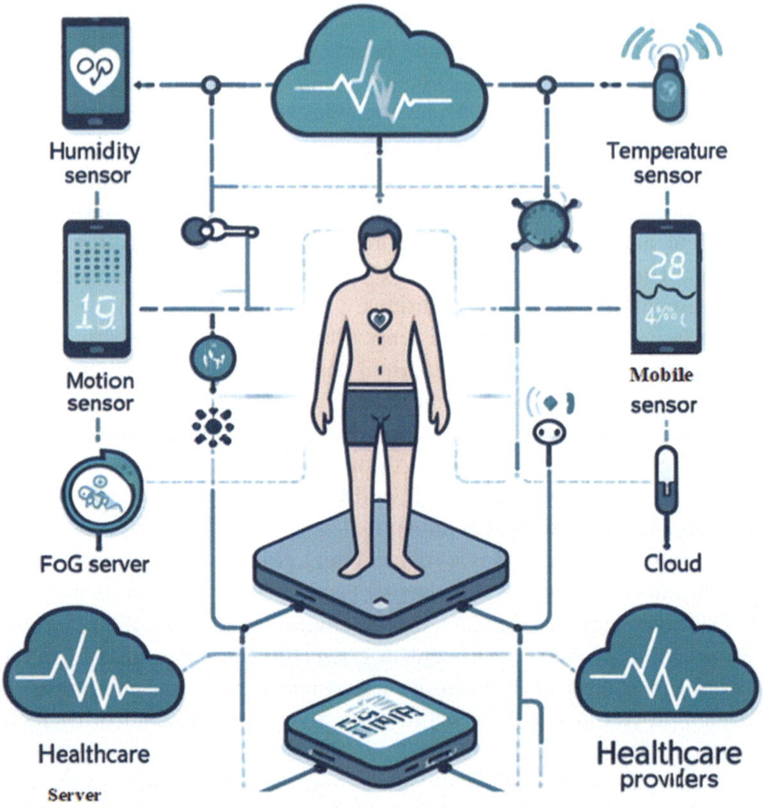

Fig. 2 Use case of real time healthcare monitoring services using fog computing

for the purpose of executing real-time analytics. The further advantages that fog computing can offer to a real-time healthcare system are as follows [3].

The dispersed nature of Fog Computing architecture significantly enhances the reliability and efficiency of healthcare applications. By providing direct connectivity with devices at the network's edge, fog computing enables near-real-time data exchange crucial for medical environments. This immediacy in data handling is critical for applications where time-sensitive decisions can have significant implications on patient outcomes. Additionally, fog computing processes data close to its source, which not only speeds up response times but also reduces the bandwidth needed for transferring large volumes of data to centralized cloud servers.

The architecture facilitates the interconnection of multiple nodes, which is essential for developing robust CPS in healthcare. These systems rely on seamless integration and communication between various components to function effectively, making the decentralized nature of fog computing highly beneficial. Moreover, by minimizing the lag time required for analyzing data in real-time healthcare systems, fog computing ensures that medical professionals can access the critical information they need without delay, enhancing the overall responsiveness of the system.

Compared to traditional cloud computing, fog computing offers distinct advantages such as support for multiple communication protocols and enhanced security measures. These features are particularly important in healthcare settings where the privacy and security of patient data are paramount, and diverse device ecosystems require robust interoperability. Thus, fog computing's ability to provide quick, secure, and reliable data processing and communication supports more effective and efficient healthcare delivery.

One potential application of real-time monitoring services facilitated by fog computing, as shown in Fig. 2, is the continuous monitoring of patients who are undergoing treatment with critical drugs, including those affected by the covid-19 virus. Steps 1 and 2, respectively, show how significant sensor data is transmitted from the fog node to the fog server [2]. In step 3, a complex data analysis algorithm is applied to data saved on the fog server, and the actuator is engaged at fog nodes to take corrective action depending on the findings. Any situation that requires immediate medical attention is considered abnormal. This includes the following: a fall by an elderly person, a sudden increase in blood sugar or blood pressure, and any other indications of a disease that is currently spreading throughout the community. If nothing unusual occurs, the data will be uploaded to a cloud server for archival and upcoming analysis, as explained in step 4. In step 5, the information is saved on the cloud in an unchangeable manner so that it may be analyzed by machine learning algorithms to determine the patient's current state of health. With a real-time communication mechanism in place, problems may be addressed immediately.

Assume that a fall has been detected by the accelerometer and gyroscope, and that the values of the blood pressure and EEG sensors have exceeded the appropriate thresholds. After the fall is captured on camera, the photos are sent to a fog sensor where they are processed to identify the extent of the injury and where appropriate action is taken in the form of notifications to medical professionals, loved ones, and emergency services [12].

3 Smart Hospitals: Transformative Potential and Distinguishing Features

Healthcare systems have gone through a number of changes, including the transition from institutionalized settings to homes and daily life. Smart healthcare is becoming more widely recognized as a significant advancement for society that will provide 24-h healthcare for elderly patients, rural residents, working populations, etc. Smart home healthcare cannot, however, completely take the role of hospitals. Smart hospitals are needed as a result of the ongoing rise in healthcare expenditures since they are anticipated to be more cost-effective, patient-friendly, and efficient. Emerging technologies like AI, ML, IoHT [11], and big data analytical techniques will hasten the transition to smart hospitals. Smart healthcare technologies are widely used to prevent and detect diseases early, and they play a key role in the shift from traditional medical treatment to patient-centered care. Home health systems, however, cannot completely replace conventional hospitals; rather, they must force them to advance. The doctors will just have the managing role in the future's smart hospitals, which might be done even remotely using touch-screen devices, with robots doing surgery and artificial intelligence (AI) systems performing patient diagnosis [13].

The majority of conventional hospitals are enormously complex businesses built on a vast network of resources, people, and operations. It may be difficult to balance and improve this trinity of factors to create a smarter structure, but technology now offers a variety of tools to improve every facet of patient care and clinical workflow, including the ability to launch fully functional digital or smart hospitals. Incorporating all of the aforementioned technologies Internet of Things (IoT), artificial intelligence (AI), process automation, virtual reality (VR), healthcare data governance, and analytics, smart hospitals represent the holistic embodiment of these instruments.

3.1 Smart Hospitals and Their Characteristics

Smart hospitals are hospitals that use innovative technologies and data-driven solutions that enhance operational effectiveness, improve the treatment of patients, and offer a smooth, integrated healthcare experience. These medical facilities include a range of digital innovations and smart technologies that create an intelligent and interconnected healthcare ecosystem. There are several unique characteristics that distinguishes the smart hospitals, which could serve as the basis for developing a framework for a smart hospital [13].

Patient-centric healthcare: Patient-centric healthcare: While designing a medical treatment plan, smart hospitals give equal consideration to the mental and physical well-being of their patients. The comfort of patients can be greatly improved and recovery may speed up through the proper design of both digital and physical places, along with patient interaction initiatives. Consider telemedicine programs or applications for self-checking, AI driven—smart diagnostic solutions, healthcare gadgets, and other telemedicine technology to constantly track patients from the comfort of their homes in terms of online assistance, scheduling and full-time clinical record accessibility, taking advantage of mobile apps as well. Smart hospital care also includes a data-driven medical service system. For more precise in risk assessment and diagnosis; it integrates reputable data analytics techniques with the expertise and judgment of doctors. To do this, it is critical to gather patient data from wearable or EHR and use analytical tools driven by machine learning to understand the patients' conditions. The same reasoning holds true for medical equipment, which may be monitored by suitable sensors to identify any issues and initiate the necessary maintenance procedures.

Decentralization of healthcare: Rather than being inflexible, all-inclusive institutions, smart hospitals are cooperative hubs and data aggregators that exchange a steady stream of data with other establishments within the same digital environment. These involve the sharing of clinical data and task collaboration between tech companies and other healthcare actors, like labs and clinics. These technologies include EHR, mobile health apps, virtual care, and IoT-enabled health gadgets. The service collaboration and externalization can be possible also.

Workflow automation: Workflow automation: Using virtual (RPA bots and digital assistants) or physical (real robots) assistants is another approach for smart hospitals to reduce their operational and administrative strain. Integration of RFID technology for the medical inventory administrations with robotics and RPA to optimize clinical procedures are used. Accuracy and efficiency are significantly increased, allowing the clinicians to concentrate more on patient care.

Smart healthcare harmonization: Harmonization of smart healthcare: Hospitals are complex systems that integrate systems, professionals, and technologies; they are not just a collection of technical assets. As a smart subject, healthcare can easily be digitized, but it also demands a complete harmonization of clinical procedures, workers doing them, and technologies used to speed them up.

3.1.1 Certain Unique Characteristics of a Smart Hospital System Listed Below

Smart hospitals leverage the Internet of Things (IoT) to achieve interconnectivity among medical devices, wearable's, and other healthcare technologies, enabling the seamless exchange of real-time data and facilitating communication between different systems. This interconnectivity allows healthcare personnel to remotely monitor patients, assess their essential physiological indicators, and respond promptly to medical crises. Smart hospitals also employ robust and secure EHR systems, which centralize patient data storage and allow healthcare workers from various departments to access patient medical histories, medication documentation, and diagnostic findings swiftly, thus enhancing patient safety and care coordination.

Incorporating artificial intelligence (AI) and data analytics, smart hospitals can process vast amounts of medical data efficiently, facilitating predictive analysis, disease identification, personalized treatment strategies, and resource allocation, which all contribute to improved diagnosis and patient outcomes. Telemedicine and remote monitoring systems enable patients to receive medical consultations and access healthcare services remotely, reducing the need for physical hospital visits and readmissions while facilitating early intervention. Automation and robotics are utilized in smart hospitals to perform a range of functions including drug delivery, sample collection, and surgical procedures, enhancing precision, reducing human error, and optimizing routine tasks.

Patient engagement is also a priority, with the use of mobile apps, patient portals, and interactive interfaces that improve the overall patient experience by allowing individuals to access medical records, book appointments, and receive personalized health advice, thus enhancing satisfaction and treatment compliance. Furthermore, smart hospitals focus on environmental sustainability by implementing energy-efficient systems and practices, which lower operational costs, reduce carbon emissions, and positively impact community welfare. Security and privacy are paramount, with significant resources devoted to robust cyber security measures that protect patient data and hospital systems from potential attacks, ensuring the confidentiality and security of sensitive information.

Real-Time Location Services (RTLS) in smart hospitals precisely track medical equipment, patients, and staff, optimizing asset management, simplifying operations, and enhancing patient flow. Predictive maintenance utilizes data analytics to foresee equipment malfunctions and schedule proactive maintenance, minimizing downtime and ensuring continuous operational effectiveness. Overall, smart hospitals aim to enhance healthcare outcomes, increase efficiency, and improve patient satisfaction through the use of advanced technologies and data-driven initiatives.

3.2 Integration of CPS Technologies in Healthcare Facilities

The use of CPS technologies in healthcare facilities has the capacity to transform patient care and enhance overall healthcare results. CPS stands for CPS, which involves the smooth integration of physical and digital elements to create interconnected systems capable of real-time data monitoring, analysis, and response. Here are several methods in which CPS technologies can improve patient care in healthcare settings. These are some prominent real-time examples of CPS that are observable in a smart hospital setting [14].

Computer vision: By utilizing AI-powered computer vision, it is possible to quickly detect signs of potential health risks in medical images or other clinical sources. This is achieved through the combination of anomaly identification and pattern recognition based on machine learning. The use of computer vision in this manner assists medical professionals in making more accurate diagnoses. A collaborative effort between Cambridge University Hospitals and the Inner-Eye team at Microsoft has resulted in the creation of a computer vision system that accelerates radiation planning and automates tumor mapping which can be considered as an example for the above scenario [10].

Natural language processing: Natural language processing (NLP) is another discipline of AI that can be effectively used in smart hospitals for numerous AI applications. NER, or named entity recognition, is not only employed for identifying specific concepts in written texts, but also for organizing such content to facilitate classification. Moreover, it is frequently utilized for the digitization of medical records and their preservation in clinical databases. The Australian e-Health Research Centre developed a Natural Language Processing (NLP) technology to convert unstructured medical data from pathology reports into digital format, in order to effectively monitor cancer incidence trends.

Chatbots: These employ Natural Language Processing (NLP) and machine learning algorithms that are specifically tailored for the healthcare sector to mimic human communication and interact with patients and clinical personnel. They embody an exceedingly loquacious form of AI that is closely linked to the preceding idea. Chatbots and virtual assistants have the ability to aid employees in smart hospitals by performing various tasks, such as simplifying call centre routing and they can provide continuous care to patients in need.

Robotics: In the present reality, physical robots serve as the counterparts to chatbots. Although human-operated machines used in remote surgery are considered as robots, they do not necessarily rely on artificial intelligence. However, the incorporation of cognitive AI-related technologies such as natural language processing (NLP) and computer vision has significantly enhanced their ability to interact with humans. Currently, modern hospitals can depend on artificial intelligence (AI)-driven robotic surgeons to do surgery without human assistance, as well as robotic helpers to handle administrative tasks such as transporting test items or ensuring sanitation in rooms.

Less paperwork with RPA: RPA bots require less paperwork compared to the robots discussed earlier and may have a lower tendency to engage in conversation. However, they have demonstrated significant utility in a smart hospital setting due to their ability to be trained in emulating human interactions with software applications. They can also autonomously learn when powered by artificial intelligence, thereby substituting or aiding clinical staff in various challenging administrative tasks.

Healthcare RPA applications encompass several tasks such as scheduling patient appointments, maintaining and updating medical records, providing self-service triage, managing claims administration, and more.

Physician's second sight is data analytics: Machine learning plays a crucial role in cognitive technologies, enabling medical devices to perceive, interpret, and communicate in a manner that closely resembles human capabilities. Regarding medical analytics, this highly developed field of artificial intelligence has a multitude of benefits to provide. Smart hospitals utilize machine learning algorithms, particularly their ability to recognise patterns and detect anomalies, to constantly monitor patient health and medical equipment performance. They also identify risk factors and provide personalized treatments or targeted interventions. The medical datasets necessary to fuel these algorithms can also be obtained from patient-generated health data (PGHD) and health wearables that were previously collected and analyzed using a data repository or a data-intensive solution. Laboratory findings and patient-generated health data (PGHD) can be utilized, along with EHR that were previously maintained in hospital databases.

The internet of (medical) things: The concept of the Internet of Things (IoT) applied to the medical field: Considering the previously established fact that smart hospitals prioritize a data-centric approach to medical care and have streamlined clinical workflows, it is not unexpected that a technology such as the Internet of Things has great importance. Healthcare IoT devices, which are commonly integrated with cloud computing for data storage and sharing, collect data through hands-on interactions with the ground. The data is then analyzed by data analytics systems, serving as the brain in this process. Smart hospitals can utilize health wearable's equipped with sensors, GPS asthma inhalers, video conferencing tools, and mobile health apps on smartphones to provide remote patient monitoring and consulting. This can be done both within the hospital premises and beyond their usual geographical boundaries [15].

4 Interconnecting the Physical and Cyber Worlds in Smart Healthcare

CPS is a concept that aims to seamlessly merge the real and virtual worlds by fusing computing and communication capabilities with physical processes (Fig. 3). A CPS is required to link the actual hospital equipment for healthcare monitoring and to assess the data saved in the cloud. Furthermore, for the world to efficiently provide healthcare, an internet-of-things (IoT) analytics platform is required. Scholars and medical experts can exchange data online for analysis and future-needs decision-making. Through IoT, wireless communication, cloud and edge computing, APIs, interoperability standards, telehealth platforms, data security techniques, and AI integration, physical devices in smart healthcare are connected to the cyber world [9].

4.1 IoT

The emergence of the Internet of Things introduced a new era in which radio transmission, Bluetooth, wireless sensor networks, Near Field Communication, and other technologies are used to facilitate machine-to-machine communication. At the integration level, where sensor networks produce massive amounts of data that are transmitted to remote computers for processing and regulating operations, the Internet of Things (IOT) makes smart, cyber-physical healthcare systems possible. Some Medical Internet of Things (IOT) gadgets have limited processing capacity and memory, thus cryptographic techniques and lightweight authentication are essential for maintaining data integrity and confidentiality and information sharing. The present pandemic has benefited from the Medical IOT's ability to provide remote patient monitoring. Patient temperature, blood pressure, and heart rate have all been

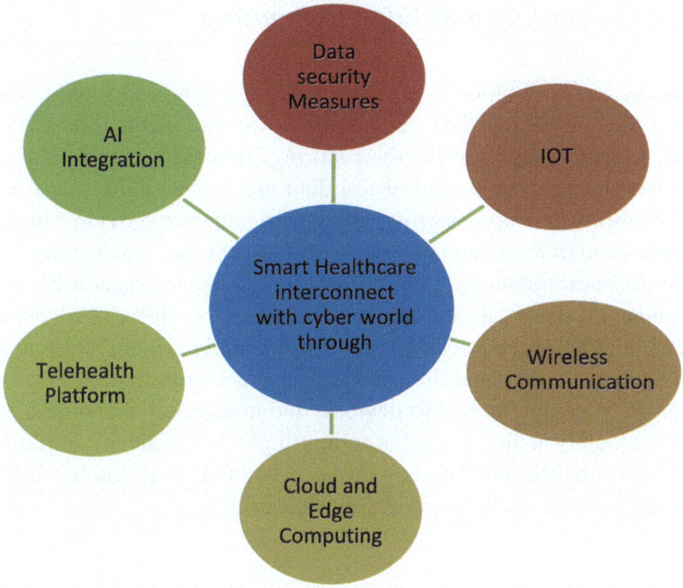

Fig. 3 Physical devices in smart healthcare

tracked using wearable's like smart watches and smart bands. These devices are connected to cellphones, which send the information to cloud servers for health analytics [16].

4.2 Wireless Communication Protocols

In smart healthcare, various wireless communication protocols are employed to enable seamless connectivity and data exchange between devices, sensors, and systems. Bluetooth Low Energy (BLE) facilitates continuous monitoring and data transmission, while Wi-Fi networks provide high-speed internet connectivity for medical devices and EHR systems. Zigbee's mesh networking capability enables self-organizing networks for patient monitoring and home healthcare applications, while RFID and NFC technologies are utilized for asset tracking, inventory management, and patient identification. Cellular networks support remote patient monitoring and telemedicine, LoRaWAN offers long-range communication for IoT deployments, and Thread ensures reliable and secure connectivity among IoT devices. These protocols collectively contribute to enhancing patient care, operational efficiency, and healthcare outcomes in smart healthcare ecosystems.

4.3 Cloud Computing and Edge Computing

In smart healthcare, both cloud computing and edge computing play crucial roles in processing and managing data generated by various medical devices, sensors, and systems. Cloud computing involves storing, processing, and analyzing large volumes of healthcare data in centralized data centers over the internet. It offers scalability, flexibility, and accessibility, allowing healthcare providers to store EHR, medical images, and other patient data securely in the cloud. On the other hand, edge computing brings computational power closer to the data source, enabling real-time processing and analysis of data at the edge of the network, closer to where it is generated. In smart healthcare, edge computing is particularly beneficial for applications requiring low latency, high reliability, and real-time decision-making, such as remote patient monitoring, wearable health devices, and emergency response systems. By processing data locally at the edge, edge computing reduces latency, minimizes bandwidth usage, and enhances data privacy and security, making it suitable for healthcare use cases where immediate action or response is critical.

4.4 Telehealth Platforms

In smart healthcare Telehealth platforms enable remote delivery of healthcare services through telecommunications technology. They offer features like video consultations, secure messaging, remote monitoring, electronic prescriptions, and integration with EHR. These platforms empower patients to access care conveniently, improve communication with healthcare providers, and enable proactive monitoring of health conditions. Overall, telehealth platforms play a crucial role in expanding access to healthcare services, enhancing care delivery efficiency, and promoting patient-centered care in smart healthcare systems.

4.5 Data Security Measures

Ensuring regulatory compliance and safeguarding confidential patient data are essential concerns in the realm of smart healthcare. Data protection strategies include data segregation, encryption, access control, and routine auditing [17]. These strategies assist prevent breaches and unwanted access to data. Security defenses are further strengthened by putting secure development techniques, staff training, and vendor risk management into practice. Healthcare organizations that prioritize data security measures can uphold patient trust, minimize data breaches, and guarantee the confidentiality, integrity, and accessibility of patient data.

4.6 AI Integration

By using cutting-edge algorithms and data, AI integration in smart healthcare transforms patient care, diagnosis, and treatment. It provides recommendations for individualized treatment regimens, forecasts the course of diseases, and aids in proper diagnosis. AI streamlines healthcare processes, permits remote patient monitoring, and speeds up medication discovery. Healthcare providers can improve patient outcomes and operational efficiency in smart healthcare systems by utilizing AI to deliver more effective, precise, and personalized care.

4.7 Seamless Communication and Data Exchange

In the realm of smart healthcare, efficient communication and safe data interchange with the online community are critical to promoting fast decision-making, productive teamwork, and the security of private patient data. Interoperability standards, secure communication protocols, data governance principles, encryption methods, access control mechanisms, cybersecurity precautions, and blockchain technology are all used to accomplish this. Secure communication protocols like SSL/TLS are utilized to encrypt data transmitted over networks, ensuring that patient information remains confidential and protected from unauthorized access or interception by cyber threats. Additionally, role-based access control (RBAC) mechanisms are implemented to manage access to healthcare data and resources based on users' roles and permissions. This helps mitigate the risk of data breaches and unauthorized disclosure by ensuring that only authorized personnel can access and exchange patient information.

Sensitive information is encrypted both in transit and at rest using data encryption techniques, protecting patient privacy and confidentiality when information is shared between healthcare systems and the internet. This guarantees that without the encryption keys, data will remain unreadable even if it is intercepted by cybercriminals.

Strong cyber security measures are put in place to guard against online dangers including malware, ransom ware, and phishing scams. These methods include firewalls, intrusion detection/prevention systems, and endpoint security solutions. To find and fix security flaws and guarantee the integrity and security of smart healthcare systems, regular security assessments, vulnerability scans, and penetration tests are carried out.

Blockchain technology is being used more and more to guarantee the immutability and integrity of medical data that is shared online. Blockchain technology offers a decentralized, impenetrable ledger for securely recording transactions. This not only increases confidence and transparency in data transmission but also guards against unauthorized modifications or tampering.

In smart healthcare systems, policies and procedures for data governance are created to specify guidelines, expectations, and roles in the management and exchange of healthcare data. To maintain legal compliance and safeguard patient privacy and confidentiality, this also involves data classification, retention, and sharing procedures.

Smart healthcare systems may ensure the security, privacy, and integrity of patient data while facilitating smooth communication and data interchange with the cyber world by putting these thorough procedures into place. This makes it possible for healthcare organizations to take advantage of technological breakthroughs and work productively with online stakeholders to enhance patient care and results.

5 Cyber-Physical Medication Systems: Advancements and Challenges

Healthcare technology has advanced significantly with the introduction of Cyber-Physical Medicine Systems (CPMS), which combine digital and biological components to enhance medicine administration and delivery. These systems monitor patient health, deliver medication, and offer individualised care by combining sensors, actuators, computing devices, and communication networks. Although CPMS have many advantages, there are a number of issues that must be resolved before they can be widely used and effectively implemented.

5.1 Advancements in Cyber-Physical Medication

Some advancements in cyber-physical medication are as follow [18]:

The Clinical Pharmacy Management System (CPMS) significantly enhances medication management by tailoring medication delivery to each patient's unique characteristics, such as age, weight, medical history, and genetics. This system adjusts medication dosages and regimens to maximize therapeutic outcomes and minimize side effects, integrating patient data with real-time monitoring capabilities. Additionally, CPMS enables remote monitoring and management, allowing medical professionals to track patient compliance, monitor vital signs, and adjust treatment plans as necessary. This capability not only enhances drug adherence and effectiveness but also engages patients more actively, reduces hospital readmissions, and enables preemptive actions to prevent complications.

CPMS also provides real-time feedback and alerts about medication adherence, dose errors, drug interactions, and adverse reactions, enhancing patient safety and treatment efficacy. Utilizing advanced analytics and AI algorithms, the system can analyze sensor data and patient responses to detect issues and initiate timely interventions. Furthermore, CPMS systems are designed to integrate seamlessly with EHR, ensuring accurate documentation of drug delivery, dose modifications, and patient responses. This integration facilitates continuity of care across various healthcare settings, improves care coordination, and simplifies communication between healthcare providers.

Overall, CPMS enhances treatment outcomes and patient satisfaction through precise dosing, real-time monitoring, and improved adherence, leading to fewer side effects, quicker recovery, and improved overall health. Moreover, by streamlining pharmaceutical workflows, CPMS reduces administrative burden on healthcare professionals and maximizes resource allocation, resulting in cost savings and increased productivity for healthcare facilities. This comprehensive management system thus represents a significant advancement in the efficiency and effectiveness of healthcare delivery.

5.2 Challenges in Cyber-Physical Medication

Cyber-physical medication systems (CPMS) [19] face several significant challenges that can impact their effectiveness and adoption within the healthcare sector. One of the primary issues is interoperability and integration. CPMS needs to integrate seamlessly with existing healthcare IT platforms, devices, and systems to maximize their efficiency and avoid creating information silos. This requires robust connectivity and data exchange protocols to ensure that all systems can communicate effectively and work together harmoniously.

Security and privacy concerns are also paramount, given the sensitive nature of health information and the risks associated with cyberattacks and unauthorized access. To safeguard patient data and minimize the risk of breaches or misuse, it is crucial to implement strong encryption methods, enforce strict access controls, and maintain rigorous cybersecurity measures. Additionally, user acceptance and adoption play critical roles in the successful implementation of CPMS. It is essential to educate both patients and healthcare providers about the benefits of CPMS while addressing concerns related to privacy, usability, and reliability. Providing adequate training and support can also help in fostering acceptance and promoting widespread adoption.

Lastly, the deployment and maintenance of CPMS involve significant investments in infrastructure, technology, and resources. Healthcare organizations must consider the cost-effectiveness, scalability, and sustainability of these systems, especially in settings where resources are limited. Balancing these factors is critical for ensuring that CPMS can be successfully integrated and utilized to improve healthcare delivery and patient outcomes.

6 Ethical and Privacy Considerations in Smart Healthcare CPS

In the progression and merging of Smart Healthcare CPS, ethical and privacy factors play a crucial role. The difficulties experienced in the design, development, and implementation of CPS in healthcare and various other sectors are intricate. A multitude of elements must be taken into account during the design process of CPS for healthcare, encompassing aspects such as software robustness and system interoperability. Computational intelligence, privacy, and security. Hardware and software have a close interaction within the functioning of medical devices [20]. Certain challenges typical of CPS are initially presented. These systems merge different technologies such as sensors, communication networks, and data analytics to enhance healthcare procedures and patient outcomes. Nonetheless, they also present significant ethical and privacy challenges that must be addressed to protect the well-being of patients and the ethical use of technology.

Let us discuss the primary challenges associated with ensuring the security and privacy of patient data in CPS-enabled healthcare environments.

The transmission of data between devices, patients, and healthcare providers over networks can be vulnerable to interception and unauthorized access by cyber attackers. This risk is exacerbated by the use of wireless communication technologies, which, if not properly secured, can provide entry points for attackers to access sensitive health information. CPS for healthcare typically involves a wide variety of devices, ranging from wearable health monitors to advanced imaging equipment. Ensuring the security of these devices is challenging due to their diverse operating systems, protocols, and levels of security. This heterogeneity makes it difficult to implement uniform security measures across all devices.

Maintaining the integrity and authenticity of patient data is crucial. Any unauthorized modification of data, whether during transmission or storage, can lead to incorrect diagnoses, inappropriate treatment decisions, and other serious health repercussions. Ensuring that data remains unchanged and is from a trustworthy source is a significant challenge in CPS environments. As CPS in healthcare environments grows in size and complexity, security solutions must scale accordingly. However, scalable security mechanisms that can efficiently manage the encryption, access control, and real-time monitoring of an expanding network of devices and data flows are challenging to implement and manage.

Ensuring patient privacy involves not only protecting data from unauthorized access but also ensuring that the use of data complies with privacy regulations such as the General Data Protection Regulation (GDPR) in the EU or the Health Insurance Portability and Accountability Act (HIPAA) in the US. Achieving compliance requires robust data governance policies and practices that are often difficult to maintain in a dynamic and distributed CPS environment. The risk of insider threats where individuals within the healthcare system maliciously or negligently compromise data security is amplified in CPS environments. This can happen through actions such as mishandling of data, improper access controls, or intentional data breaches.

The absence of widely accepted security standards for CPS in healthcare complicates the implementation of security measures. While there are general cybersecurity frameworks and specific regulations governing healthcare data, the unique characteristics of CPS require specialized standards that are still under development. Many CPS devices, especially wearable and implantable medical devices, are resource-constrained in terms of processing power, memory, and battery life. Implementing sophisticated security algorithms, which often require significant computational resources, is challenging on such devices.

6.1 Key Considerations for Ethical and Privacy Challenges

The key considerations for ethical and privacy challenges in the development and implementation of Smart Healthcare CPS include Software Reliability. Essential for the functionality of medical equipment, software plays a crucial role in ensuring the device's capabilities within the organization and maintaining the connection with patients. The design, development, and management of software directly impact the reliability and effectiveness of the system.

The acquisition of informed consent from patients is imperative for the collection and processing of their data. Patients must possess a clear comprehension of the objectives, extent, and possible hazards associated with data collection, as well as how their data will be utilized to facilitate informed choices regarding their involvement. It is vital to establish stringent security measures to defend sensitive patient data from unauthorized access, breaches, and cyber-attacks. Utilizing encryption, secure authentication, and conducting regular security audits are crucial steps to protect patient information. The collection of data is kept to a minimum to fulfill the healthcare purpose intended, ensuring that unnecessary or excessive personal information is not gathered in order to reduce the potential for privacy breaches. Complying with the guidelines to anonymize or de-identify patient data is crucial to prevent the identification of individuals from the data. This practice safeguards patient privacy while still allowing for valuable analysis to take place.

Patients should be educated on the procedures involved in data collection, the authorized personnel with access to their personal details, and the period of storage. Direct communication is important in cultivating trust among patients, healthcare providers, and technology experts. It is imperative to establish a clear definition of data ownership, indicating whether patients, healthcare institutions, or technology providers have ownership of the data collected. Patients are entitled to engage in decisions regarding the utilization and sharing of their data.

Maintaining interoperability standards within Smart Healthcare CPS is vital to support the secure transfer of data among different systems and healthcare providers, enhancing the continuity of patient care and avoiding data segregation. It is essential to conduct thorough testing on algorithms utilized in Smart Healthcare CPS to identify and address biases that may result in unjust treatment of specific demographic groups. Ongoing audits and adjustments are vital to mitigate the presence of such biases.

Providing patients with the tools to access their personal health data and manage its distribution can lead to enhanced patient participation and collaboration. This empowerment can enhance patient engagement and facilitate collaborative decision-making processes. Crucial to establish transparent guidelines that outline the responsibilities and accountability of technology developers, healthcare providers, and patients in the occurrence of data breaches or system malfunctions.

Ethical reflections must be integrated into the developmental stages of Smart Healthcare CPS. Independent ethics review committees should evaluate the potential risks and advantages associated with the implementation of these systems. Envision and plan for the possible long-term outcomes of data storage, particularly considering the ever-changing landscape of technology and healthcare practices. Acknowledge and honor cultural variances in patient expectations, preferences for sharing data, and healthcare methods. Also following institute guidelines for managing patient data when Smart Healthcare CPS are retired or upgraded to guarantee data security and privacy.

In addition to digital concerns, healthcare systems encounter the significant physical obstacle of effective waste disposal. Hospitals, for the benefit of the city's environment, produce a concerning volume of waste, necessitating proper waste management strategies like source segregation, transportation, and disposal methods. Addressing these ethical and privacy issues is crucial to ensure that Smart Healthcare CPS effectively enhances healthcare outcomes while upholding patient rights and fostering trust in the healthcare system. Cooperation among healthcare professionals, technology innovators, policymakers, and patients is essential to navigate these intricate challenges.

6.2 Addressing Ethical Dilemmas in Using AI and Autonomous Systems for Healthcare Decisions

Addressing moral quandaries when utilizing AI and self-governing systems for healthcare choices involves navigating through various ethical challenges that demand thorough consideration and resolution. Here are some crucial ethical issues and possible approaches to alleviate them [21]. The utilization of AI and self-governing systems in healthcare decisions may result in decisions that are complex to elucidate to patients, healthcare professionals, and regulators. By formulating AI models and algorithms that are transparent and capable of providing rationales for their decisions. Incorporate methodologies like interpretable machine learning to enhance the comprehensibility of the decision-making procedure.

AI systems necessitate vast amounts of confidential patient data, sparking concerns regarding privacy breaches and unauthorized entry. Approach: Enforce stringent data safeguarding protocols, including anonymization, encryption, and rigorous access management. Contemplate the utilization of federated learning to educate AI models using decentralized data sources without sharing raw data. AI algorithms also have the potential to perpetuate or worsen existing biases in healthcare, resulting in unequal treatment across different demographic categories. Using routine scrutinize AI systems for bias and fairness, both in the developmental phase and real-world implementation. Utilize varied and inclusive datasets for model training and adopt methodologies like fairness-aware learning to counteract bias.

When an AI system makes a wrong decision, determining who is responsible and liable can be complex. Strategy: Clearly define the roles and responsibilities of human professionals and AI systems in healthcare decision-making. Establish legal frameworks that allocate responsibility appropriately and hold developers, healthcare providers, and users accountable. The advent of AI systems has the potential to impact the doctor-patient relationship, possibly diminishing the personal connection and empathy in healthcare interactions. Present AI tools as supportive aids for healthcare professionals rather than substitutes. Focus on the evolution of AI systems that enhance and support the abilities of human clinicians, enabling them to provide more tailored care.

Patients may lack a full understanding of the role of AI in their healthcare choices, leading to difficulties in obtaining informed consent. By ensuring that patients receive education on the capabilities, limitations, and potential effects of AI systems on their care. Establish transparent consent procedures that incorporate details about AI involvement.

The extensive utilization of AI in healthcare may spark concerns about job displacement among healthcare professionals. Dedicating resources to ongoing training and advancement programs for healthcare professionals to adapt to AI technologies and promoting the incorporation of AI as a tool to enrich clinical practice, rather than replacing human expertise can be hopeful.

AI systems could make decisions leading to unintended adverse consequences, and foreseeing these outcomes can be intricate. By enforcing thorough testing and validation processes to foresee and mitigate potential risks. Continuously supervise AI systems in real-world settings and be prepared to intervene if unforeseen consequences emerge.

Smart healthcare CPS are innovative digital platforms expected to dominate the future. These systems need to have the ability to effectively confront and minimize cyber threats, thus highlighting the importance of their forensic preparedness [17, 22]. Artificial intelligence, also referred to as machine intelligence, plays a crucial role in self-sustaining systems that can carry out tasks like pinpointing abnormal activities resulting from malfunctions or cyber intrusions [23]. Uncovering malicious software is an essential endeavor to uphold the smooth and efficient operation of CPS. Various machine learning approaches relying on system calls, operation codes, and energy usage patterns have been utilized for the purpose of identifying malware [24].

7 Future Trends and Applications of CPS in Healthcare

CPS are poised to induce considerable shifts in the healthcare field in the immediate future, fostering enhanced, individualized, and patient-oriented healthcare. The incorporation of CPS into healthcare, through the use of interconnected medical equipment and wearable sensors, will enable the delivery of services in real time.

The surveillance and examination of patients' vital signs, medical histories, and progress in therapy are of utmost importance. This will contribute to a reduction in hospitalization rates and an improvement in overall patient outcomes by detecting health issues early, intervening promptly, and monitoring patients remotely. Additionally, leveraging CPS-driven predictive analytics and machine learning algorithms will enable healthcare providers to make well-informed decisions through the extraction of valuable insights from the extensive patient data gathered. As a result, this will lead to enhanced treatment approaches and individualized medical strategies. However, as the integration of CPS and healthcare continues to grow, it is crucial to implement strong cyber security measures and prioritize patient confidentiality to protect sensitive medical information.

The diverse impacts of Clinical Pharmacy Services (CPS) on various stakeholders can be ascribed to the distinct effects experienced by each group. It is therefore advisable for future research efforts to conduct a qualitative analysis to explore the perspectives of stakeholders concerning their firsthand involvement with the implementation of MCPS. The primary contributors in this study should be patients, physicians, EMTs, nurses, and other individuals who possess direct or indirect connections to the patient or healthcare provider. The diverse impacts of Clinical Pharmacy Services (CPS) on various stakeholders can be ascribed to the distinct effects experienced by each group. Additionally, it is essential to integrate an empirical inquiry into the study.

In the healthcare sector, CPS technologies are reshaping the functioning of medical devices, systems, and procedures, thereby enhancing patient care, diagnostics, treatment, and overall healthcare administration. The incorporation of IoMT (Internet of Medical Things), Predictive Analytics and AI, Robotics and Surgical Automation, Telemedicine and Remote Patient Monitoring, Wearable Health Tech, Personalized Treatment Plans, Drug Delivery and Adherence, as well as Genomic Medicine Integration are indicative of some of the emerging trends and potential advancements in CPS for healthcare. To fully leverage the impact of CPS technologies in healthcare, challenges like regulatory obstacles, data privacy concerns, and ethical dilemmas must be effectively tackled.

8 Conclusion

The chapter encompasses a thorough investigation of CPS in the healthcare sector. It commences with a concise explanation of CPS, followed by a detailed exploration of their application in healthcare. The taxonomy is viewed through eight lenses: application, architecture, sensing, data management, computing, communication, challenges, and security. Technologies like Blockchain, Artificial Intelligence, cloud computing, Big Data, and wearable devices have not only advanced smart health but also escalated the demand for smart healthcare employing CPS. Major hurdles include establishing a secure and efficient identity authentication system, integrating diverse networks, securely sharing medical data, and achieving seamless network integration.

References

1. Amit Kumar Tyagi, N. Sreenath, Cyber Physical Systems: Analyses, challenges and possible solutions, ScienceDirect—Internet of Things and CPS, Volume 1, 2021, Pages 22–33.
2. A. Alamri, W. S. Ansari, M. M. Hassan, M. S. Hossain, A. Alelaiwi, and M. A. Hossain, "A survey on sensor-cloud: Architecture, applications, and approaches," Int. J. Distrib. Sens. Networks, vol. 2013, https://doi.org/10.1155/2013/917923.
3. M. S. Kamal, S. Parvin, A. S. Ashour, F. Shi, and N. Dey, "De-Bruijn graph with MapReduce framework towards metagenomic data classification," Int. J. Inf. Technol., vol. 9, no. 1, pp. 59–75, 2017, https://doi.org/10.1007/s41870-017-0005-z.
4. L. Gu, D. Zeng, S. Guo, A. Barnawi, and Y. Xiang, "Cost efficient resource management in fog computing supported medical CPS," IEEE Trans. Emerg. Top.Comput., vol. 5, no. 1, pp. 108–119, 2017, https://doi.org/10.1109/TETC.2015.2508382.
5. J. Shi, J. Wan, H. Yan, and H. Suo, "A survey of CPS," 2011 Int. Conf. Wirel. Commun. Signal Process. WCSP 2011, no. November 2011, 2011, https://doi.org/10.1109/WCSP.2011.6096958.
6. A. Lounis, A. Hadjidj, A. Bouabdallah, and Y. Challal, "Secure and scalable cloud-based architecture for e-Health wireless sensor networks," 2012 21st Int. Conf. Comput. Commun. Networks, ICCCN 2012 - Proc., 2012, https://doi.org/10.1109/ICCCN.2012.6289252.
7. L. Hu, N. Xie, Z. Kuang, and K. Zhao, "Review of CPS architecture," Proc. - 2012 15th IEEE Int. Symp. Object/Component/Service-Oriented Real-Time Distrib. Comput. Work. ISORCW 2012, pp. 25–30, 2012, https://doi.org/10.1109/ISORCW.2012.15.
8. A. M. Rahmani et al., "Smart e-Health Gateway: Bringing intelligence to Internet-of-Things based ubiquitous healthcare systems," 2015 12th Annu. IEEE Consum. Commun.Netw.Conf. CCNC 2015, no. July, pp. 826–834, 2015. https://doi.org/10.1109/CCNC.2015.7158084.
9. F. Chen et al., "Medical CPS: A Solution to Smart Health and the State of the Art," IEEE Trans. Comput. Soc. Syst., vol. 9, no. 5, pp. 1359–1386, 2022, https://doi.org/10.1109/TCSS.2021.3122807.
10. F. Farivar, M. S. Haghighi, A. Jolfaei, and M. Alazab, "Artificial Intelligence for Detection, Estimation, and Compensation of Malicious Attacks in Nonlinear CPS and Industrial IoT," IEEE Trans. Ind. Informatics, vol. 16, no. 4, pp. 2716–2725, 2020, https://doi.org/10.1109/TII.2019.2956474.
11. G. Hackmann, W. Guo, G. Yan, Z. Sun, C. Lu, and S. Dyke, "Cyber-physical codesign of distributed structural health monitoring with wireless sensor networks," IEEE Trans. Parallel Distrib. Syst., vol. 25, no. 1, pp. 63–72, 2014, https://doi.org/10.1109/TPDS.2013.30.

12. Griffor et al., "Framework for CPS: Volume 2, Working Group Reports," NIST Spec. Publ., vol. 2, pp. 1500–202, 2017, [Online]. Available: https://nvlpubs.nist.gov/nistpubs/SpecialPublications/NIST.SP.1500-202.pdf.
13. E. N. Nwobodo-Anyadiegwu, M. N. Ditend, and A. K. Lumbwe, "The benefits and challenges of Implementing Smart hospital projects: A systematic Review," 2022 IEEE 28th Int. Conf. Eng. Technol. Innov. ICE/ITMC 2022 31st Int. Assoc. Manag.Technol. IAMOT 2022 Jt. Conf. - Proc., no. January, 2022, https://doi.org/10.1109/ICE/ITMC-IAMOT55089.2022.10033238.
14. https://www.itransition.com/blog/smart-hospital.
15. https://www.microsoft.com/en-us/research/project/medical-image-analysis/.
16. S. Chaudhary et al., "A Taxonomy on Smart Healthcare Technologies: Security Framework, Case Study, and Future Directions," J. Sensors, vol. 2022, 2022, https://doi.org/10.1155/2022/1863838.
17. K. J. Park, R. Zheng, and X. Liu, "CPS: Milestones and research challenges," Comput. Commun., vol. 36, no. 1, pp. 1–7, 2012, https://doi.org/10.1016/j.comcom.2012.09.006.
18. M. M. Nair, A. K. Tyagi, and R. Goyal, "Medical Cyber Physical Systems and Its Issues," ProcediaComput. Sci., vol. 165, no. 2019, pp. 647–655, 2019, https://doi.org/10.1016/j.procs.2020.01.059.
19. R. Verma, "Smart City Healthcare Cyber Physical System: Characteristics, Technologies and Challenges," Wirel. Pers. Commun., vol. 122, no. 2, pp. 1413–1433, 2022, https://doi.org/10.1007/s11277-021-08955-6.
20. R. Alguliyev, Y. Imamverdiyev, and L. Sukhostat, "CPS and their security issues," Comput.Ind., vol. 100, no. April, pp. 212–223, 2018, https://doi.org/10.1016/j.compind.2018.04.017.
21. H. HaddadPajouh, A. Dehghantanha, R. Khayami, K.-K. Raymond Choo, "This is a repository copy of A Deep Recurrent Neural Network Based Approach for Internet of Things Malware Threat Hunting. White Rose Research Online URL for this paper: Version: Accepted Version Article", 2018.
22. J. Wang, H. Abid, S. Lee, L. Shu, and F. Xia, "A secured health care application architecture for CPS," Control Eng. Appl. Informatics, vol. 13, no. 3, pp. 101–108, 2011.
23. Q. Do, B. Martini, and K. K. R. Choo, "CPS information gathering: A smart home case study," Comput. Networks, vol. 138, pp. 1–12, 2018, https://doi.org/10.1016/j.comnet.2018.03.024.
24. Y. Lu, "Cyber physical system (CPS)-based industry 4.0: A survey," J. Ind. Integr. Manag., vol. 2, no. 3, pp. 1–57, 2017, https://doi.org/10.1142/S2424862217500142.

Advancing Patient-Centric Care: Harnessing CPS for Smart Hospitals and Healthcare Facilities

Anwar Ahmed Khan, Shama Siddiqui, Ausaf Ahmed Khan, and Karima Karam

Abstract In this chapter, we explore the pivotal role of Cyber-Physical Systems (CPS) in advancing patient-centric care within smart hospitals and healthcare facilities. These systems have been revolutionizing healthcare through offering facilities of real time monitoring, automation, and data analytics. We provide a comprehensive overview of smart hospitals, detailing their key components and functionalities. The chapter sheds light on the smart technologies being used for seamless integration of physical infrastructure, medical devices, data systems, and decision-making processes that truly has a potential to revolutionize the delivery of healthcare services. Various applications of CPS have been examined such as patient safety, streamlining workflows, resource management and personalized care. We also present the challenges encountered during the implementation of CPS in healthcare environments, including security, privacy, interoperability, and scalability. There is an immense need for robust infrastructure, effective data governance, and collaborative engagement among stakeholders. Finally, we outline the prospects and emerging trends for deploying CPS in the healthcare domain. This chapter would serve as a valuable resource for researchers, healthcare professionals, and policymakers as it highlights the future of healthcare integrated with smart computing technologies.

Keywords Cyber-physical systems (CPS) · Smart hospitals · Resource management · Real-time monitoring

---

A. A. Khan
Department of Computer Science, Millennium Institute of Technology and Entrepreneurship, Karachi, Pakistan
e-mail: anwar.ahmed@mite.edu.pk

S. Siddiqui (✉)
Department of Computer Science, DHA Suffa University, Karachi, Pakistan
e-mail: shamasid@hotmail.com

A. A. Khan
Department of Anesthesiology, Aga Khan University Hospital, Karachi, Pakistan
e-mail: ausaf.khan@aku.edu

K. Karam
Department of Anesthesiology, Aga Khan University Hospital, Karachi, Pakistan
e-mail: karima.karam@aku.edu

M. Mittal and J. Narayan (eds.), *Intelligent Cyber-Physical Systems for Healthcare Solutions*, https://doi.org/10.1007/978-981-97-8983-2_16

1 Smart Hospitals: An Overview

Smart hospitals integrate Cyber Physical Systems (CPS) within medical equipment to increase automation, improve operational efficiency and enhance the quality of overall patient care. These hospitals integrate a range of medical infrastructure with data processing systems and decision support systems and utilize the cutting-edge technologies of Internet of Things (IoT), Machine Learning (ML) and Artificial Intelligence (AI). The conventional devices have been made smart through integrating them with information processing and communication technologies; some of the devices which have been launched with a smarted version include sphygmomanometers, glucometers, thermometers, pulse oximeters, ECG monitors, inhalers among others [1]. Through collecting, analyzing, and interpreting patient's data, smart hospitals aim at realizing proactive personalized care and improving health outcomes by empowering patients as well as the physicians.

The major components of smart hospitals include medical devices and equipment, communication architecture, Health Information Systems (HIS), patient engagement platforms, data analytics platforms, digital twin, cybersecurity infrastructure.

1.1 *Medical Devices and Equipment*

Smart medical devices are developed to provide continuous and real-time data from patients to anyone, anywhere. In the context of smart hospitals, these devices are expected to transmit data from patients to the physicians/nursing staff/nursing counters/centralized dashboards such that the need for staff to visit each patient repeatedly, reduces. In addition to the wearable equipment, there is also a range of implantable medical devices which offer assistance in real-time data collection.

1.2 *Communication Architecture*

There are several components of the communication architecture that ensure transmission of data from patients' devices to the physicians' handheld devices/cloud-based dashboards, as illustrated in Fig. 1. These components are listed below:

Edge Devices are either patient devices themselves or are placed close to the patient devices. The responsibility of these devices is to preprocess and aggregate data so that only crucial data is transmitted to the cloud. The role of edge devices is pivotal for managing the bandwidth requirement. For example, the consulting physicians may set threshold values for vital parameters for the patients admitted in the critical care units; the data may only be transmitted if the threshold value is reached. This approach significantly reduces the amount of data transmitted to the cloud, dealing simultaneously with the issues of bandwidth wastage and information overload.

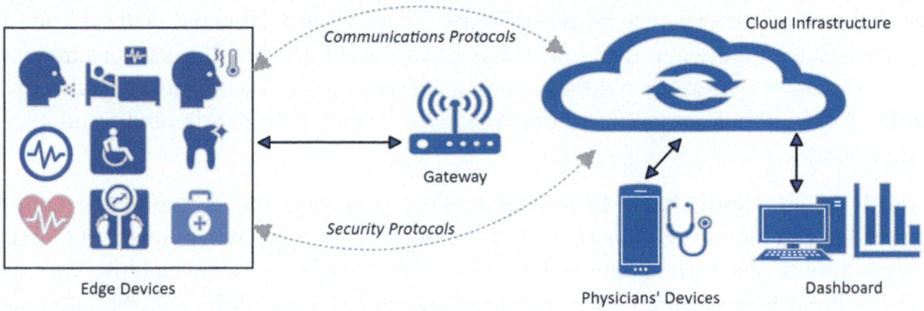

Fig. 1 Communication architecture for smart hospitals

Gateways: These gateways/routers filter, preprocess and transmit data from the patients' (edge) devices to the cloud. Also, in case alerts are to be generated, gateways also transmit the response commands from the cloud to the devices.

Communication Protocols: On the software side, there are hundreds of communication protocols that govern the transmission of data between different layers of smart hospital communication architecture. In this regard, Bluetooth, Wi-Fi and Zigbee exemplify the commonly used standard protocols; however, there are various other protocols being developed for specific healthcare applications. For example, FROG-MAC has been developed for transmitting the prioritized heterogenous data for critical care applications, where wearable devices are not even allowed to sleep [2]. The focus of healthcare protocols is mainly on transmitting patient data with high reliability, low latency, and excellent level of security.

Cloud Infrastructure: The CPS cloud infrastructure for smart hospitals comprises of servers and databases, used for processing, storing, and analyzing the data received from the patients' devices. The servers incorporate technologies such as ML, data analytics and to conduct real-time analysis and risk prediction on healthcare data.

Security Measures: Just like communication protocols, security measures are also inherent in smart hospital software with the overall goal of assuring confidentiality, integrity, and privacy of patient information. Encryption, authentication, anomaly detection, firewall, all components are embedded at the different levels of communication architecture. The sensitive patient data is safeguarded throughout the lifecycle including all the stages of transmission, storage, and processing. It is always ensured that only authorized users can access the patient information through implementing user roles. The audit trails and logging mechanisms are implemented to track access to patient data, record user activities, and monitor system interactions; this includes regular security audits and risk assessment activities; In fact, the regulatory compliances at most countries require to manage the events of unauthorized access.

The conventional methods of anonymization are also used to ensure that patients cannot be identified, while still ensuring that data remains fully useful for the analytics purpose. Similarly, data minimization is implemented across all the HIS; it not only reduces the risk for patients' data breach, but at the same time also improves the processing performance of the systems. Secured protocols and APIs are used for data sharing between different stakeholders and HIS. Finally, user awareness programs and trainings are regularly conducted with a focus on educating healthcare professionals about data privacy best practices, security protocols, and regulatory requirements.

Cloud Based Centralized Dashboard: This is mostly the endpoint for smart hospital's data journey. Customized dashboards are developed where medical practitioners may access patient data and historical trends and may receive alerts. Various IoT dashboards are available for patient monitoring, for example, a dashboard was developed for monitoring anxiety risk among the patient during COVID-19 [3].

1.3 Health Information Systems (HIS)

HIS are largely benefited by the integration of CPS because of integrating large amounts of data. The efficient flow and optimization of patient information becomes possible by utilizing integrated devices, sensors, and decision support systems. Some of the major areas in which HIS improve with the advent of CPS are discussed below, and summarized in Fig. 2.

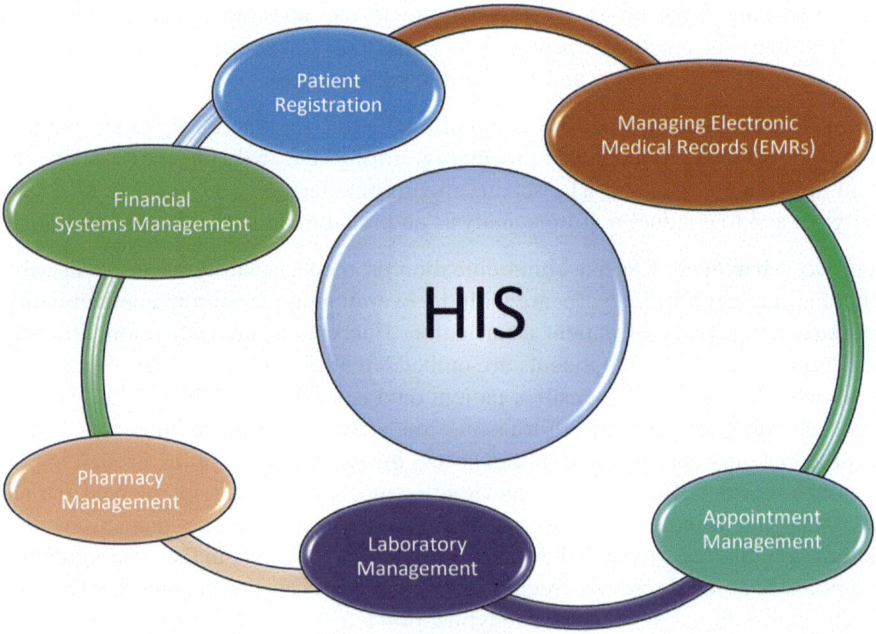

Fig. 2 Key application areas of hospital information systems

Patient Registration: The patients may register to the hospital using smart kiosks installed at the hospitals, or through their smart phone applications. The patients can either pre-register before their actual visit to the facility, or they may use various option such as by using a biometric authentication method, scanning a QR code, or through manual data entry at smart kiosks, instead of waiting at the registration counters. These platforms provide user-friendly interfaces for collecting basic demographic information, insurance details, medical history, and consent forms digitally.

Managing Electronic Medical Records (EMRs): Through CPS, the process of managing EMRs can be improved to a large extent. Due to collection of real-time data and interconnectivity between the medical equipment, the scope of EMR can be enhanced to maintaining historical trends, rather than just storing, and updating demographic information. Synchronization of patient data across various departments of the smart hospital is an important feature offered. As soon as the information is entered/updated at any one point, the same is replicated across the network; thus, the consistency, integrity and accuracy of patient information is maintained. To ensure security of patient information, technologies such as blockchain are proposed which would reduce the risk of unauthorized access, breach, or tampering.

It is to be noted that there are several indirect benefits of integrating EMRs and CPS as well; for example, collection of large and continuous datasets would benefit the clinical research as availability of big population data would be possible [4]. Therefore, instead of relying on evidence-based studies which are mostly conducted for other populations, the medical researchers and practitioners shall become able to conduct research on their own population and develop customized diagnostics and treatment strategies.

Appointment Management: Based on the CPS data, the appointment management process can be optimized. Particularly for facilities with limited resources and high patient flow, the data may be used to identify various factors and the appointments may be scheduled accordingly. Some of these factors could be the risk factor for each patient, the availability of resources, the availability of physicians, etc. Similarly, the follow-up visits for patients may also be adjusted based on the treatment response for each patient. Therefore, integrating CPS with HIS for appointment management may optimize the appointments in a way that the required medical care is provided to each patient as per their requirements.

Laboratory Management: By using CPS, the facilities of smart hospitals are automated. If we consider a laboratory which remains equipped all the time with the testing requests of in- and out-patients, the CPS reduces the work burden and optimizes the workflow by automating the processes. Firstly, the routine laboratory processes such as sample collection, analysis and reporting can be automated. There have been numerous proposals on using robots, RFID tags and IoT protocols like NB-IoT to collect and deliver specimen [5]. Such techniques promise to increase reliability and reduce the latency of sample collection, as human intervention is minimized. Moreover, the connection between wearable devices of patients, laboratory equipment and decision support systems help to streamline the testing operations. As CPS plays a critical role in maintaining the quality of equipment, compliance to standards and predictive maintenance of the hospital's equipment also becomes easier.

The accuracy of the laboratory tests can increase through the use of CPS. As the manual intervention and activities reduce, the increased automation improves the reliability and reduces errors. Furthermore, the resource allocation may be improved by managing inventory and scheduling the tasks; for example, the risk level for each patient may be used to process the queued requests to assure quality and timely care delivery for each patient. In addition, CPS also offers an opportunity to smart hospitals for scaling and adapting their laboratory departments as per the evolving needs. By providing real-time data about workload, performance of staff and equipment, accuracy, etc., smart hospitals may decide to expand the laboratory services or adapt newer technologies.

Pharmacy Management: There are several key areas in which CPS supports smart hospitals to optimize their pharmacy processes. Some of these are discussed in the following:

- *Inventory Management*: IoT sensors and networks are used to track the availability of medicines on the shelves and in the warehouse. The integration of these networks with the pharmacy information system provides access to information about sales data and hence, helps to maintain the optical stock. Thus, the problems of over or understocking are reduced.
  The reordering process may also be automated based on the availability of stock, and its predicted demand over a certain period. Robots are also used at some facilities for managing inventory as they automate warehousing, shipping, and transportation processes [6]. Also, robots can perform sorting of medicines/equipment at much higher rate as compared to their human counterparts. Various approaches of integrating customized hardware and software have been developed in this context.
- *Automation of Medicine Dispensing*: Some advanced medical facilities have started to deploy robots for dispensing medicine to the wards, or patients as per the prescriptions. Although mostly in the research phase, use of robots for dispensing medicine would result in overcoming pharmacy staff shortage and human errors.
- *Customized Medication Management*: Since CPS integrates all the components of HIS together, the data from EHRs may be used by the pharmacy information systems to access the patient's medical history. This could identify any possible allergies to the medication suggested in the prescription. The adverse drug reactions could be minimized through such analysis.
- *Dosage Adherence and Compliance*: Finally, CPS can also manage the medication for patients through sending them reminders. Moreover, smart medicine bottles (integrated with technologies such as Bluetooth) also have the capability to inform the patients as well as the pharmacy about any missed dosages, the remaining dosages in the bottle, etc.

Radiology Management: Through deployment of CPS, the advanced imaging technologies equipped with ML and AI functionalities are integrated into the smart hospital. Smart imaging machines including those performing X-rays, MRIs, CT-Scans, and others are integrated into the hospital's network for real-time data collection. The radiologists and consulting physicians can directly access the data from advanced imaging equipment to derive quick insights into the patients' diagnosis. The use of AI algorithms assists the physicians in detecting the anomalies [7]. Moreover, due to the connection with EHR, the radiologists have readily available access to the patient's medical history and medications, which assists them in decision making about the image. At the same time, the interconnection of imaging equipment with the decision support system ensures that population history is maintained, which in turn provides an opportunity of utilizing big data analytics algorithms.

CPS improves the workflow and resource allocation at the radiology departments. These systems also enable the smart hospital to enhance their network of experts [8]. Without the provisions of CPS and smart imaging systems, the hospitals had only to rely on the in-house expertise; however, with the help of CPS, it becomes possible for the physicians to seek suggestions from their collaborative network via internet.

Financial Systems Management: Since all physical systems and the reports generated by them are interconnected at the smart hospitals, the financial processes become smooth. All the financial transactions conducted with the patients, suppliers and other stakeholders provide a quick financial insight into the revenue, expenses etc. the stakeholders may timely be informed about their bills and ML algorithms may be used for predicting the future amount [9]. For example, a patient may get an alert on their smart phone application informing them about the amount due with the break-up of all the items. The insurance agencies could also remain informed about the limits, usage, and excess for each patient.

Similarly, the historical and current financial data about each department is available due to the connectivity of CPS. Based on these insights, the hospital could make real-time and informed financial decisions. Moreover, the predictions can be more efficient due to the analysis of a vast number of financial trends or patterns identified from all the hospital's operations. As a result, activities such as budget planning, resource allocation, and future expansion can be smoothly executed.

The fraud detection also becomes easier when all the transactions along with their trail can be tracked. The discrepancies can be identified, which leads to identification of possible frauds from the network of patients, insurance agencies, suppliers, and other stakeholders. Also, the audit and compliance activities become efficient as accurate data for compliance with healthcare financial standards is available.

1.4 Patient Engagement Platforms

These platforms provide an interface for the patients to interact with the hospital's information systems and physical equipment (according to the authority assigned).

The core objectives of these systems include offering patients to connect with their physicians, get real-time health insights and overall, get more control over managing their health; for example, if a patient is aware of his health risks such as diabetes, he will be encouraged to consume lesser carbohydrates via smartphone app. Some of the key components of patient engagement platforms and advantage of their integration with CPS are discussed next:

Personal Health Portals: The patients may access their health records, history, test results and system's recommendations to maintain their risk level by accessing digital health portals. When integrated with CPS, these portals provide real-time and accurate data.

Remote Monitoring System: The basic service provided by CPS to the patients and physicians is continuous, remote monitoring. Not only the patients may access their real-time data (collected via wearable or implantable devices) on their smart phone, but also physicians may access this information from anytime anywhere. The CPS also integrates the hospital's equipment with the patients' and physicians' dashboards ensuring that real-time data remains updated in both the portals.

Tele-Health: The concept of teleclinics has increasingly been realized for the far-off places where healthcare services are not as accessible. Often, smart wearable devices are embedded within the digital clinic booths, where patients may use them to enter data into the system. Also, the patients may engage in virtual consultation with the doctors via these booths. Alternatively, the patients may also use their smart phone applications to avail the facility of online consultation. This facility (although in infancy stage for most of the world), promises to reduce the healthcare cost, improve the patients' access, and improve the overall health quality of people.

Appointment Scheduling: The apps provided by hospitals provide various functionalities ranging from simple appointment management to complex customized recommendations. The patients may schedule appointments as per their convenience, may reschedule or even cancel. Similarly, physicians are also allowed to update their details in real-time; for example, a physician may mark themselves unavailable for clinic on any given day. In such a situation, the app interface of patient generates an alert intimating the patient about the appointment cancellation, and mostly offering them a chance to reschedule on the first immediate availability of the physician. On one hand, this helps the patients by providing them with an online appointment facility, and on the other hand, the hospital also benefits as the rate of no-show reduces which optimizes the working hours of physicians.

Patient Awareness and Opinion Mining: Today, social media and influencers play a critical role in conducting awareness campaigns. Unlike the past, when Television and print media used to be considered as the major sources of information dissemination, social media has slowly replaced them. Therefore, social media platforms have widely been used to raise awareness among populations regarding spread of viruses, prevention of diseases etc. [10]. Various such campaigns were launched by public and private sector organizations, during the surge of COVID-19. In addition to raising awareness about the requirements of social distancing and isolation, the technologies such as opinion mining and big data analytics provide insight on various social issues like impact of isolation on mental health of various demographic sectors [11].

1.5 Data Analytics Platforms

Data analytics platforms provide the backbone functionality for the CPS enabled smart hospitals. In these platforms, advanced analytics and machine learning algorithms are deployed for processing the massive real-time data obtained from interconnected medical equipment. Based on the crucial insights, informed decision-making is performed by the physicians; there are various objectives of advanced data analytics; first and foremost, it becomes possible for the medical practitioners to timely detect the events based on patients' or environmental data. Secondly, based on the historical trends and big data algorithms, the analytics platforms actively engage in predictive analytics; be it for the patients, medical equipment, or critical care units. Thus, it becomes possible to identify the high-risk patients, optimize the workflow, maintain the equipment, manage the staffing, and resource allocation. Similarly, the patient flow through various departments of the hospital can easily be predicted using CPS, which optimizes the scheduling of tasks and streamlines all the processes, starting from the admission, and ending at the discharge of patients.

The clinical decision support systems (DSS) at a smart hospital are largely governed by data analytics platforms. Conventionally, the role of DSS was to provide expert insight into the issues faced by the patient by providing guidance into the evidence-based practices from across the world [12]; however, the scope of DSS significantly increases for the case of smart hospital; in a smart hospital, DSS collects data from various CPS equipment and offers detailed insight to the physicians, which in turn offer them guidance for efficient diagnosis and treatment strategies for each patient.

Another important benefit of having data analytics platforms at a hospital is continuous performance monitoring of equipment and services offered. The managers of facilities can easily keep an eye on their staff performance by monitoring the online dashboards and observing the indicators such as number of hours maintained, number of complaints received, number of errors made, etc. At the same time, the patients can also provide their feedback through interactive mobile apps or smart pods installed at the facilities.

1.6 Data Analytics Techniques

Today, the major application areas for which modern data analytics techniques used for smart hospital settings include predictive analytics, diagnostic support, clinical decision support systems, anomaly detection, continuous surveillance, resource allocation, supply chain management, genomic analysis, clinical trial optimization and behavioral analytics. The overall objectives of these techniques to derive insights, optimize operations, and improve patient outcomes. Some of the emerging techniques employed within CPS in healthcare environments are detailed below:

Machine Learning: Various machine learning techniques are used in the healthcare settings. Some of these are classification, regression, clustering, and anomaly detection; the focus of these techniques has mainly been on the processes of disease diagnosis, risk stratification, and personalized medicine. Moreover, due to the integration of ML algorithms with the data collected from CPS health monitors, it has also become possible to perform anomaly detection in medical devices.

Deep Learning: Deep learning techniques in the smart hospital settings are mainly used for signal processing (e.g., physiological data from wearable devices), natural language processing (e.g., clinical notes, medical literature) and medical imaging analysis (e.g., MRI, CT scans). Since deep learning algorithms are based on using neural networks with multiple layers to extract intricate patterns from large datasets, the technique has been regarded ideal for health data due to the complex patterns.

Time Series Analysis: Time series analysis is used for monitoring patient vital signs, analyzing medication adherence, forecasting patient admissions, and optimizing resource allocation.

Natural Language Processing (NLP): The use of NLP has been increasing due to the increased automation of hospital facilities and a higher degree of support for the interactive platforms for patients. NLP techniques help to extract information from the patient-doctor conversations, medical literature and clinical notes. Thus, the clinical knowledge base improves a lot and quickly with the help of NLP.

Sentiment Analysis: It is an emerging data analytics technique for smart hospitals. It mainly involved collecting patient's opinion through channels such as social media posts, online reviews, patients feedback during interview or routine conversations with the hospital staff. This technique helps to measure the patient's satisfaction level, to monitor public health trends and to identify areas for improvement.

Network Analysis: Network analysis facilitates the decision support systems of a smart hospital through offering an insight into the healthcare provider networks, patient referral patterns, disease transmission networks, and social determinants of health. By having data about the connections between networks related to smart hospital, not only the patient outcomes will improve, but also the chances of marketing and building a positive reputation for the hospital.

Simulation and Optimization: Simulation and optimization techniques are used to model complex healthcare systems, simulate different scenarios, and optimize processes to improve efficiency and quality of care. In healthcare CPS, simulation and optimization are used for capacity planning, resource allocation, scheduling, and healthcare delivery redesign.

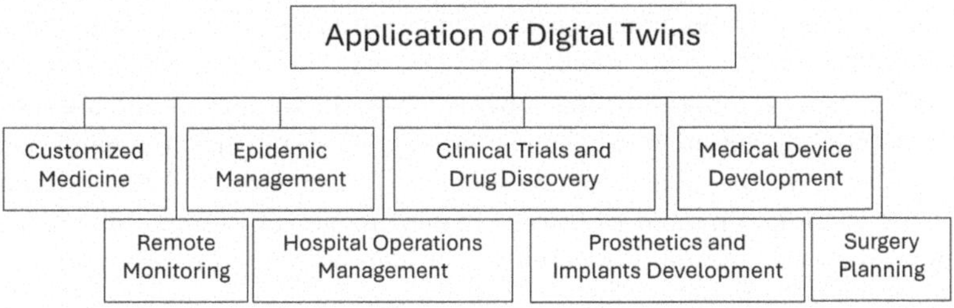

Fig. 3 Digital twins for smart hospitals

1.7 Digital Twins

Digital twins refer to virtual replicas of physical objects, equipment, processes, or systems. For the case of a smart hospital, various sources, and technologies such as IoT devices, sensors and medical equipment is used to replicate actual healthcare processes, such as surgeries. Digital twins are created to simulate the hospital environment to create, monitor and analyze the real-world process, without putting actual patients or medical equipment at risk. For example, each of the costly and crucial medical equipment such as MRI machines, monitors etc. can have a digital twin which helps the designers and users to understand the operating parameters and needs of maintenance.

Digital twins can replicate the layout of smart hospitals and the features such as rooms, wards, operation theaters along with the placement of their associated medical equipment. They could also be used to extend critical healthcare services to the patients. For example, a digital twin can function at emergency department of a smart hospital [13], where patient authentication is done using biometrics, previous history is provided by the connected EMR, and the robot doctors can provide the early intervention.

There could be numerous other applications of digital twins in hospital's environment as well. Some of them are illustrated in Fig. 3.

2 Benefits of CPS for Smart Hospitals

2.1 Facility Automation

The first and simplest application of CPS For smart hospitals is the automation of facilities. Considering the patient centric care, the fundamental objective of any healthcare facility is to provide a comfortable environment to hospitalized and outpatients. Various IoT sensors can be used for maintaining the comfortable physical conditions [14]; for example, thermostats, pressure sensors, door switches, light sensors are just few of the many sensors that are used by advanced smart hospitals today.

The IoT sensors at smart hospitals operate stand-alone devices and are also integrated with building automation systems for collecting statistics and optimizing the resources. The real-time data about environmental parameters and activities provide key insights about facility and workforce management; for example, the data about occupancy of rooms and other locations may help to adjust the room temperature and lights, which could reduce energy consumption.

2.2 *Workflow Automation*

CPS aids in various ways for workflow automation at the smart hospital, due to its core focus on real-time data generation and analysis. This data helps to automate all the major healthcare processes, starting from the patient's admission, continuing to develop personalized diagnostics and treatment plans, and ending at billing and management of smooth discharge process. The interconnected nature of CPS devices ensure that each department of the hospital remains aware about the expected influx of the tasks; for example, the laboratory department may have advance information on the number of tests they may expect to conduct on any given day; as a result, the lab in charge may develop the duty roaster accordingly. Similarly, the nursing department, due to the integration with EHR and data analytics algorithms, shall have an accurate insight into the number of patients to be discharged and admitted each evening [15]. Such real-time data helps the nursing heads to overcome the long prevailing staffing shortages by optimizing the work schedules while taking care of staff burn out and work-life balance.

2.3 *Seamless Data Integration*

Data from various sources are integrated and displayed in the form of customized reports to the authorized users; these sources may include but are not limited to Electronic Health Records (EHRs), IoT sensors, mobile applications, and smart medical equipment. Thus, an integrated eco-system is developed where information may smoothly flow between departments and stakeholders, for optimization of resources and workflow.

2.4 *Realtime Decision Making*

Due to the availability of real-time data and advanced analytics methods, it becomes possible for the administration to identify the bottlenecks in the workflow processes.

The problems at various levels such as staffing, equipment, external stakeholders or even policies may quickly be identified. For example, if a request from patient is taking more than expected time at the pharmacy, quick decisions may be taken to ensure smooth transition of patient's service from one department to the other [16]. The wait time at various departments could be reduced by providing advance information to the staff so they may schedule activities accordingly.

Moreover, patient centric care also becomes a reality when CPS integrates with decision support systems. The readily available patients' data (collected through CPS sensors) and its analysis are provided to the decision support systems for diagnostics, customized treatment plans, and alerts. With the integration of advanced AI and Ml models with the CPS systems, there could be a variety of predictions generated; these may include patient outcomes, diseases progression rate, expected risk levels and potential complications.

Some of the ways in which CPS could facilitate the decision-making capability of a smart hospital is illustrated in Fig. 4.

Resource Allocation: The resources can efficiently be allocated to various departments/processes in the light of data generated through CPS. In this context, various parameters are analyzed such as rate of patient admission/discharge, availability of staff, equipment usage etc. Activities such as bed management, staff management, inventory ordering can be supported through identifying the trends of real-time data collected over a certain period. Inventory management is also improved as through RFID tags, sensors, and real-time tracking systems, hospitals can optimize inventory levels, reduce wastage, and ensure that critical items are always available when needed. Energy consumption is optimized by integrating smart meters, sensors, and control systems. These systems monitor energy usage patterns, adjust lighting, heating, and cooling systems based on occupancy and environmental conditions.

Moreover, the patient's data is collected through connected wearable devices, which not only reduces the manual resources needed for continuous monitoring, but also improves resource allocation due to timely interventions. Similarly, due to the integration of CPS with HIS, Patients can receive medical consultations, follow-up appointments, and continuous monitoring from the comfort of their homes, reducing the need for hospital visits. This not only improves patient convenience but also

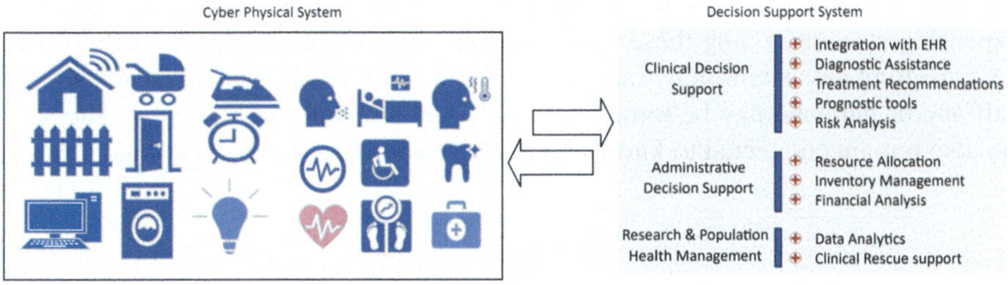

Fig. 4 Applications of decision support systems enhanced with CPS

reduces the strain on hospital resources, allowing healthcare providers to focus on more critical cases.

Automation of Routine Tasks: Various tasks which are repeatedly performed in a hospital environment can easily be automated through efficient deployment of CPS. For example, the staff required for entry of patients' bio or vitals' data may be reduced. The patients may automatically book the appointment by using interfaces provided at the facility or using their smart phone applications. Similarly, as previously discussed, the data about patients' vitals may automatically be entered into the system through wearable devices, which reduces the need for staff to collect this information at regular intervals.

Compliance and Quality: Using CPS data collection and analytics capability, it becomes possible for the healthcare facility to automate the routine quality check activities. For example, adopting the conventional industrial IoT procedures, medical equipment engages in predictive maintenance activities which ensures that the quality of equipment is maintained through continuous yet automated testing. Thus, a culture of continuous improvement nourishes smart hospitals through the CPS integration.

Patient Safety: The conventional role of real-time monitoring has been to observe the patient's health state through collecting data about various parameters such as blood pressure, pulse rate, oxygen saturation etc. While at smart hospital, all and particularly critical patients can be monitored continuously for their deterioration. The critical conditions can be quickly communicated to the medical staff via timely alerts, due to which early intervention becomes possible. These alerts cannot only be transmitted to the centralized counters, but also to mobile apps of nurses and doctors, leading to an even quicker service time.

Moreover, with the help of ambient and environmental sensors, the hospital staff can easily track the movement and safety of patients. The critical patients may be placed in rooms occupied with cameras, proximeters, gyroscopes, etc. which may detect the position, mobility, and posture of the patients. In case any event such as fall occurs, the hospital staff may timely be informed through generating an alert. Also, the patient may be guided through automated audible commands to remain safe.

There are also various developments in the area of smart medicine bottles, insulin pens and intravenous infusion bottles for realizing the use of automated medicine dispensing systems. Using these variants, drug administration becomes efficient as the consulting physicians may track the intake of medications remotely. The nursing staff and/or patients may be reminded timely about any missed dosages. The staff can also remain connected to know about any reactions of the medications.

3 Challenges for Implementing CPS

3.1 Security

There are various security risks for the critical CPS implementation scenarios such as smart hospitals due to the sensitivity of patient data, interconnected devices and systems, and the potential life-threatening situations that may occur as a result of breach or intrusions. Some of the major security risks applied to the implementation of CPS in a smart hospital setting are detailed in this section:

Vulnerabilities in Connected Devices: There could be hundreds of connected devices at a smart hospital because multiple devices may be connected to collect data from a single patient. As the points connected to a network increase, so do the points of possible attacks. There is always a chance that vulnerabilities present in a small wearable may compromise entire network, which could risk hundreds of lives at a time due to disruption in service, delay in response, or propagation of false information, discussed next.

False Alerts: One of the major risks for smart hospital networks is false alert generation which could have various negative effects such as wastage of resources, disruption of routine operations, causing fear etc. therefore, it has to be ensured that the alerts are only generated when an event happens (in terms of patient or environmental data).

Lack of Standardization: As previously discussed in this chapter, managing heterogeneity of devices and data formats is one of the core challenges for smart hospitals. The use of varying communication and operating standards does not only create complexities in the communication process, but also results in needing a complex security framework. The security measures cannot be consistent across the entire network due to diverse needs of each device/department. Thus, it becomes easier for the attackers to find the weakest link in the hospital network; for example, the one link for which recent patch is not available could serve as the favorite point of entry for the intruders.

Malware Attacks: Due to the high risk of healthcare sector, smart hospitals are always at risk of malware or ransomware attacks. Such attacks involve encryption of entire hospital's data to make the information inaccessible [17]. Often, the attackers ask for a ransom in return of the data. Such attacks can cause life-threatening risks for patients.

Compliance with Regulations: Generally, the regulations are not very frequently updated, whereas the network attacks evolve at a very rapid rate. Novel network attack methods as well as vulnerabilities at device levels keep on emerging continuously [18]. As a result, the hospital needs to implement the security protocol which may not be defined in any regulation such as HIPAA. Therefore, it is often challenging for a healthcare facility to achieve a balance between required compliance to the regulation and implementation of security measure.

Factors Affecting Decision-making: Although the integration of CPS helps in real-time decision making, there are some factors which could affect the decision-making process. First of all, the availability of clinical evidence and best practice data shall strongly govern the decision-making process, particularly when AI is integrated. Similarly, the data about patients' medical history, current health state, and other demographic information should also be available.

Secondly, the level of expertise and experience of the hospital staff with the conventional and CPS based systems will serve as a major factor for affecting the quality of decision-making process. The staff should be able to manage and optimize the resources in order to ensure availability and usability of technology, including clinical decision support systems, electronic health records, and medical devices. Thirdly, the staff should also be knowledgeable in adopting CPS in line with the healthcare policies, regulations, and clinical guidelines. Finally, the cultural beliefs and norms about the use of technology in healthcare systems would limit the decision-making process. For example, the staff, patients or their families may not be comfortable in sharing their data online. This would significantly limit the scope of CPS implementation.

3.2 Privacy

CPS integrates physical hospital equipment across various departments, wearable devices, implantable sensors, and hospital information systems together. It is crucial to protect patient data from unauthorized access, misuse, or breaches. Since the data is shared across various heterogenous platforms within and outside the hospital network, maintaining the privacy of information is much more complex as compared to the conventional EHRs.

In addition to the major stakeholders of health information systems (patients and medical practitioners), the data may also be accessible to the third-party vendors/ technology service providers for maintenance or similar activities. It is the responsibility of the hospital to manage these third-party relationships without violating patients' data privacy. In this context, the regulations such as General Data Protection Regulation (GDPR) and Health Insurance Portability and Accountability Act (HIPAA) come into play.

3.3 Ethical Concerns

Generally, the debate for use of technology in healthcare settings focuses on the design and usage of technical systems. However, it is important not to ignore the human element [19]. It is crucial for the workforce using the interconnected and technologically advanced healthcare systems to follow ethical principles/guidelines. Here, it is important to note that the technical expertise of the medical professionals relying on CPS can largely affect the ethical usage of these systems. Even, the best design CPS in terms of data confidentiality, integrity, authenticity may fail if the user does not possess acceptable level of technology skillset.

3.4 *Interoperability*

Since the applications of smart healthcare are growing at a tremendous rate, the operating devices and protocols are increasing day by day. Mostly, the smart hospital operates with devices that are designed by diverse manufacturers and work on varying standards and protocols [20]. Although it seems quite simple to standardize the data and protocol formats for healthcare equipment, however, the healthcare data are often configured to follow pre-defined standards such as HL7 and DICOM. As a result, it becomes a challenge to ensure interoperability between all the CPS devices for ensuring communication and sharing of data. Moreover, since introduction of CPS and other technical systems in the healthcare sector is relatively a new concept, the integration of legacy systems is critical [21]. The technology standards and operating principles of legacy systems (such as older EHRs) and modern HIS are very different, which further adds to complexity of interoperability. The hospitals may even face challenges of Vendor lock-in, where it may not be possible to integrate components from different vendors; also, it is often not possible to upgrade or transition between the vendors without disrupting the operations.

It is also a challenge to ensure communication of data between devices/system operating at different levels. For example, the data from wearables of patient admitted in a critical care unit must be transmitted seamlessly to the immediate information systems and various other HISs without disrupting the workflow and routine operations; it becomes a challenge to ensure timely data delivery. Also, medical devices are subject to compliance with strict regulations; both software and hardware must be tested and verified through the established standard procedures.

Due to the integration of multiple devices and information systems together, the security and confidentiality of patients' data become more challenging to maintain. We need to ensure that the data is securely stored at diverse components of CPS. Higher level of connectivity means more possible entries for intrusions and attacks.

3.5 *Scalability*

Managing scalability is a key challenge for smart hospitals deploying CPS because there is a need to extend operations while still maintaining reliability, accuracy, and efficiency. All the resources in terms of hardware, software, networking infrastructure, computation capabilities as well as smart medical equipment need to be enhanced for efficient resource allocation. The first challenge in this context is to deal with increasing amount of data, that too coming from heterogenous devices and information systems. Secondly, the hospital must have access to enhanced cyber and physical infrastructure to collect, process, store and analyze the vast amount of data.

As previously discussed, maintaining interoperability between diverse equipment is a significant challenge for enabling efficient operation of CPS at a smart hospital. Clearly, with the increased operations, the integration of equipment and information systems seamlessly, even becomes a challenging situation. Moreover, conducting the routine maintenance operations also requires expansion, without causing disruption to any part of the interconnected system. In this context, the systems need to be made adaptable to expansion and technology changes. In today's environment, technology rapidly changes, be it wireless communication protocols, machine learning algorithms, big data analytics techniques, etc. Thus, the CPS systems need to be designed adaptable and scalable.

3.6 Communication Infrastructure

It is to be noted that there are serious challenges for the implementation of communication facilities for the smart hospitals due to their high demands of massive capacity, high spectrum access, high throughput and low Peak to Average Power (PAPR) [22]. The hospital networks need to operate at maximum speeds for transmitting data from wearables as well as medical images, which drastically increases the bandwidth requirements.

4 Opportunities

4.1 Improving Connectivity: 5G

As previously discussed, there are numerous limitations related to existing communication infrastructures which limit the possibilities for enhancing functionalities of smart hospitals. 5G systems have started to be regularized globally, which promise to reduce communication issues and meet the demands of smart hospitals. Use of 5G for smart hospitals is expected to significantly improve the challenges related to bandwidth by reducing the PAPR, guard band, spectrum leakage and detection delay. Novel waveforms such as Non-orthogonal multiple access (NOMA), Universal filter multi-carrier (UFMC), and filter bank multi-carrier (FBMC) system have been proposed [22] specifically for improving the bandwidth efficiency of smart hospitals.

4.2 Enhancing Security Through Anomaly Detection Systems (ADS)

Advances in technologies such as ADS can reduce the security risks for smart hospital networks. ADS in the smart hospital's environment is configured for detecting the events related to patient/environment or intrusion. A centralized ADS can offer benefit of network infrastructure monitoring, through optimizing the resources consumed in the monitoring activities [23]. Moreover, it also becomes easier to maintain the log of all the false alerts and intrusions, which subsequently leads to a quick identification of threat. Similarly, distributed processing approach can also be applied here; for example, ADS may be implemented at the edge devices to ensure low latency, leading to quick and accurate decisions.

4.3 Integration with Blockchains

To protect the confidential patient information, blockchains are proposed. The decentralized structure of blockchains eliminates the reliance on a single point, which significantly reduces the chances of unauthorized access [24]. Any update in the health records would require consensus from the participants, which improves the validation as it comes from multiple nodes. Also, the records are immutable and cannot be changed. All the audit trails are available showing the records of access, changes and interactions performed with the data; thus, the trends cannot be altered leading to more accurate analysis about the patient health. In addition to ensuring security for patient records, the blockchains also serve as a promising technology for smart hospitals as they would aid in complying with the regulations related to data privacy such as HIPAA or GDPR.

4.4 Managing Interoperability

Since interoperability is one of the major challenges for smart healthcare sector, several strategies have been adopted. First of all, as previously mentioned, adoption of standards such as HL7 and FHIR help to facilitate the data exchange. For the cases, where adoption of standard might not be possible, middleware solutions might be used which could translate data format to be used by end devices [20]. Thirdly, API based implementation has also been proposed as an interoperability management solution for smart hospitals working with rapidly changing technology. Finally, collaboration between the hospitals, healthcare and computing researchers and standards-setting organizations is the key for successful and sustainable interoperable solutions.

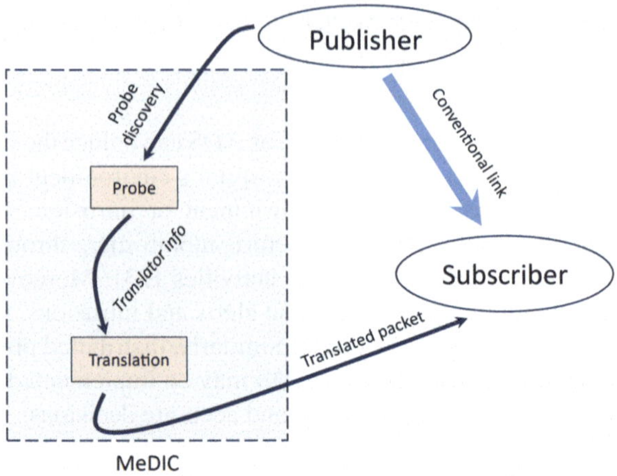

Fig. 5 Comparison of conventional publication/subscription framework and medic framework

Moreover, some frameworks have also been proposed to resolve the protocol and data format conflicts between the devices in the smart hospital environment. For example, a framework known as Medical Data Interoperability through Collaboration (MeDIC) has been proposed [20]. This framework involves using Probe and Translation interfaces on the top of conventional authentication, publish and subscribe interfaces of IoT devices, to facilitate resource sharing as shown in Fig. 5: Conventionally, the subscriber devices are expected to receive the data in whatever form as published. However, to counter heterogeneity, the module probes, and translations, translate the data in the format, interpretable by the subscriber. Therefore, these software interfaces offer an opportunity to heterogenous medical devices to collaborate.

Moreover, there has been an increasing interest in employing the adoption of interoperability standards such as HL7 FHIR (Fast Healthcare Interoperability Resources) by vendors looking for potential technology enabled future of healthcare industry. Due to the inherent interoperability characteristic, the CPS components from different vendors using HL7 FHIR may be easily integrated.

4.5 Gamification and Reward Systems

Gamification in the realm of smart hospitals has the potential to bring a revolution both for the patient and physicians. Using CPS and smart interfaces, gamification can encourage patients to engage in routine fitness activities in exchange for rewards. On the one hand, this approach shall improve the health state of patients and on the other hand, these practices shall also keep the physicians engaged and motivated. IoT based serious games are often encouraged in the smart hospitals, where wearable sensors and actuators are used to offer a pervasive and ubiquitous gaming experience to the players [25].

There could be various scenarios in which a reward system and gaming approach can be applied for the patients. For example, patients may be offered reward points or discount vouchers for achieving their fitness goals, adhering to medication schedules, participating in community activities etc. Similarly, gamification and simulations have long been used for training medical practitioners. The physicians' learning experience may improve through dynamic learning exercises developed with the help of virtual reality and simulated situations. The working experience at the medical facilities may also improve as the practitioners may learn team building, communication and collaboration while participating in the gaming exercises.

4.6 Trainings of Medical Professionals

In smart hospital settings, Entrustable Professional Activities (EPAs) have increasingly been adopted; this framework of activities defines the technical competencies medical professionals must possess to enable them to use advanced healthcare systems, while maintaining minimum required ethical standards [26]. For example, for medical imaging, the professional must have sufficient competence to deal with complex AI technologies often integrated with MRI equipment. Similarly, competencies are being defined for various CPS in the healthcare settings to ensure that the quality, privacy, and security of these systems are not compromised due to the ignorance/lack of skill among the workforces.

5 Conclusions

This chapter shed light on some of the ways in which the CPS enabled smart hospitals to demonstrate commitment towards providing patient centric care, while also maintaining sustainable practices. The advanced sensors, communication technologies and their integration with the physical systems promise to revolutionize the healthcare service delivery through generating enormous real-time data, which increase automation and improves the resource optimization. At the same time, smart hospitals offer enhanced patient centric care. Although there are current challenges in the implementation of CPS at the smart hospitals, including security, privacy, ethical concerns, interoperability, scalability and limitation of communication infrastructures, novel hardware and software technologies have been developed to cater to them. Therefore, CPS are expected to revolutionize the future of healthcare sector in the near future.

References

1. M. H. Kashani, M. Madanipour, M. Nikravan, P. Asghari and E. Mahdipour, "A systematic review of IoT in healthcare: Applications, techniques, and trends," *Journal of Network and Computer Applications*, vol. 192, no. 2021, 2021.
2. A. A. Khan, S. Siddiqui and S. Ghani, "FROG-MAC: A Fragmentation Based MAC Scheme for Prioritized Heterogeneous Traffic in Wireless Sensor Networks," *Wireless Personal Communications*, vol. 114, no. 2020, pp. 2327–2361, 2020.
3. S. Siddiqui, F. Nait-Abdesselam, A. A. Khan and I. Dey, "Enabling Real-Time Dashboards for Anxiety Risk Classification Using the Internet of Things," in *IEEE Global Communications Conference*, 2021.
4. M. El Khatib, S. Hamidi, I. A. Ameeri, H. A. Zaabi and R. A. Marqab, "Digital disruption and big data in healthcare-opportunities and challenges," *ClinicoEconomics and Outcomes Research*, pp. 563–574, 2022.
5. N. T. Le, M. M. T. Chit, T. L. Truong, A. Siritantikorn, N. Kongruttanachok, W. Asdornwised, S. Chaitusaney and W. Benjapolakul, "Deployment of Smart Specimen Transport System Using RFID and NB-IoT Technologies for Hospital Laboratory," *Sensors*, vol. 23, no. 1, 2023.
6. S. J. Trenfield, A. Awad, L. E. McCoubrey, M. Elbadawi, A. Goyanes, S. Gaisford and A. W. Basit, "Advancing pharmacy and healthcare with virtual digital technologies," *Advanced Drug Delivery Reviews*, vol. 182, no. 2022, 2022.
7. A. Fotaki, E. Puyol-Antón, A. Chiribiri, R. Botnar, K. Pushparajah and C. Prieto, "Artificial intelligence in cardiac MRI: is clinical adoption forthcoming?," *Frontiers in Cardiovascular Medicine*, 2022.
8. T. A. Shaikh, T. Rasool and P. Verma, "Machine intelligence and medical cyber-physical system architectures for smart healthcare: Taxonomy, challenges, opportunities, and possible solutions," *Artificial Intelligence in Medicine*, 2023.
9. R. Leon Sanz and P. Leon-Sanz, "Modeling Health Data Using Machine Learning Techniques Applied to Financial Management Predictions," *Applied Sciences*, vol. 12, no. 23, 2022.
10. D. V. Gunasekeran, A. Chew, E. K. Chandrasekar, P. Rajendram, V. Kandarpa, M. Rajendram, A. Chia, H. Smith and C. K. Leong, "The impact and applications of social media platforms for public health responses before and during the COVID-19 pandemic: systematic literature review," *Journal of Medical Internet Research*, vol. 24, no. 4, 2022.
11. T. Li, Z. Zeng, J. Sun and S. Sun, "Using data mining technology to analyse the spatiotemporal public opinion of COVID-19 vaccine on social media," *The Electronic Library*, vol. 40, no. 4, pp. 435–452, 2022.
12. N. Kumar, R. K. Kaushal, S. N. Panda and S. Bhardwaj, "Impact of the Internet of Things and Clinical Decision Support System in Healthcare," in *oT and WSN based Smart Cities: A Machine Learning Perspective*, Cham: Springer International Publishing, 2022.
13. R. Aluvalu, S. Mudrakola, A. C. Kaladevi, M. V. S. Sandhya and C. R. Bhat, "The novel emergency hospital services for patients using digital twins," *Microprocessors and Microsystems*, vol. 98, no. 2023, 2023.
14. A. Ugajin, "Automation in Hospitals and Health Care," in *Springer Handbook of Automation*, Springer International Publishing, 2023, pp. 1209–1233.
15. M. Doctorarastoo, K. Flanigan, M. Bergés and C. McComb, "Exploring the potentials and challenges of cyber-physical-social infrastructure systems for achieving human-centered objectives," in *Proceedings of the 10th ACM International Conference on Systems for Energy-Efficient Buildings, Cities, and Transportation*, 2023.
16. A. H. Issa, S. A. Gitaffa and Y. S. Al-Saffar, "Developing the Health Care System for Smart Drugstore Based on the IoT and the Embedded System," *Iraqi Journal of Industrial Research*, vol. 9, no. 1, pp. 12–30, 2021.
17. W. Triplett, "Ransomware attacks on the healthcare industry.," *Journal of Business, Technology and Leadership*, vol. 4, no. 1, pp. 1–3, 2022.

18. K. Kioskli, T. Fotis and H. Mouratidis, "The landscape of cybersecurity vulnerabilities and challenges in healthcare: Security standards and paradigm shift recommendations," in *Proceedings of the 16th International Conference on Availability, Reliability and Security*, 2021.
19. S. Nasir, R. A. Khan and S. Bai, "Ethical Framework for Harnessing the Power of AI in Healthcare and Beyond," *IEEE Access*, vol. 12, no. 2024, pp. 31014–31035, 2024.
20. A. Jaleel, T. Mahmood, M. A. Hassan, G. Bano and S. K. Khurshid, "Towards medical data interoperability through collaboration of healthcare devices," *IEEE Access*, pp. 132302–132319, 2020.
21. S. Renukappa, P. Mudiyi, S. Suresh, W. Abdalla and C. Subbarao, "Evaluation of challenges for adoption of smart healthcare strategies," *Smart health*, 2022.
22. A. Kumar, R. Dhanagopal, M. A. Albreem and D.-N. Le, "A comprehensive study on the role of advanced technologies in 5G based smart hospital," *Alexandria Engineering Journal*, vol. 60, no. 6, pp. 5527–5536, 2021.
23. A. M. Said, A. Yahyaoui and T. Abdellatif, "Efficient anomaly detection for smart hospital IoT systems," *Sensors*, vol. 2021, 2021.
24. G. Hameed, Y. Singh, S. Haq and B. Rana, "Blockchain-based model for secure IoT communication in smart healthcare," in *Emerging Technologies for Computing, Communication and Smart Cities: Proceedings of ETCCS*, Singapore, 2022.
25. S. Ahmad, F. Mehmood, F. Khan and T. K. Whangbo, "Architecting intelligent smart serious games for healthcare applications: a technical perspective," *Sensors*, vol. 3, no. 22, 2022.
26. M. Sand, J. M. Durán and K. R. Jongsma, "Responsibility beyond design: Physicians' requirements for ethical medical AI," *Bioethics*, vol. 36, no. 2, pp. 162–169, 2022.

Enhanced Cyber-Physical System in Health Care Using LSTM and Bi-LSTM

G. Maria Jones, S. Godfrey Winster, M. Maheswari, R. Sundar, A. Kalaivani, D. Menaka, and Sathyaprasad

Abstract Complex systems that are developed by integrating communication, computation, and control are known as cyber-physical systems (CPS). Compiling vast amounts of data from various sources worldwide, CPS is a significant player in the healthcare industry. In the healthcare industry, where personal health information is susceptible to data theft and cyberattacks, CPS is essential. This paper presents a comprehensive analysis of cyber-physical systems in healthcare through the use of machine learning models to analyze Enhanced Cyber-Physical Systems in healthcare (ECPS-HC). It shows that the healthcare data are acquired by IOT sensors, stored in the cloud, and analyzed through Machine Learning (ML) and Deep Learning (DL) models. Machine learning models predict the cyber-attacks which helps in decision-making. In order to better understand the design and modeling of CPS in the healthcare industry, this paper will concentrate on how the system architecture integrates LSTM, Bi-LSTM, and the Adam optimizer.

Keywords Cyber-physical system · ECPS-HC · Vulnerable · Machine learning (ML) · Deep learning (DL) · Cyber-attacks

1 Introduction

As the number of cyberattacks targeting cyber–physical systems (CPS) have increased, it is getting harder to protect CPS from these attacks [15]. Machine learning has become a popular technology in fields such as data analysis and classification in recent years. Furthermore, as CPS architecture advances. As the world grows more complex and data is produced at an exponential rate, applying machine learning

G. Maria Jones (✉) · M. Maheswari · R. Sundar · A. Kalaivani · D. Menaka · Sathyaprasad
Department of Computer Science and Engineering, Sathyabama Institute of Science and Technology, Chennai 600119, India
e-mail: Joneofarc26@gmail.com

S. Godfrey Winster
Department of Computer Science and Engineering, School of Computing, SRM Institute of Science and Technology, Chengalpattu 603203, India

M. Mittal and J. Narayan (eds.), *Intelligent Cyber-Physical Systems for Healthcare Solutions*, https://doi.org/10.1007/978-981-97-8983-2_17

(ML) techniques, Deep Learning (DL) techniques is becoming necessary to gain a competitive edge. As a result, both technologies can be used to both identify and counteract attacks on CPS through data-driven control mechanisms. Because of the profound effects that cyber-physical systems (CPSs) have on society, the economy, and the environment, academics, corporations, and the government have all expressed interest in CPSs. Interest in CPSs has increased recently due to the field's potential to benefit the environment, the economy, society, and the people themselves. More significantly, dominance and innovation in information transmission systems have resulted from the quick advances in computer, communication, and storage systems.

The next generation of integrated communications, computing, and management systems is referred to as cyber-physical systems, though a precise term is lacking. These systems strive to achieve strength, efficiency, and dependability when it comes to biological data. Simultaneously, research endeavors undertaken to accomplish these goals primarily concentrate on attaining security within the CPS. Advances in Cyber-Physical Systems (CPS) have yielded notable breakthroughs in a range of industries, including intelligent manufacturing, healthcare, and transportation, which have had a substantial impact on national economies in recent times [23]. Security concerns, however, continue to be the main obstacle to their widespread adoption despite these advancements. The reason for this is primarily the large number of internet-connected devices, which introduce vulnerabilities that conventional security solutions might not be able to handle, particularly in the face of sophisticated attacks catered to particular applications.

The healthcare delivery and management landscape are undergoing a paradigm shift due to the introduction of advanced deep learning architectures like Long Short-Term Memory (LSTM), Bidirectional LSTM (BiLSTM), and attention-based models, along with optimized algorithms like the Adaptive Moment Estimation (Adam) optimizer. In order to address the critical issues facing healthcare systems around the globe, this paper explores the complex fusion of CPS and AI methodologies. Healthcare professionals can analyze sequential data, such as patient records and physiological signals, with previously unheard-of accuracy and efficiency by utilizing LSTM and BiLSTM networks. By adding attention mechanisms, the models are even better able to concentrate on pertinent data, which makes diagnosis and treatment planning more accurate. Additionally, these intricate models' training is optimized by using the Adam optimizer, which speeds up convergence and improves generalization performance. This optimization makes sure that even in the face of dynamic and diverse data streams, the deployed CPS in healthcare settings functions flawlessly. The ECPS-HC facilitating more precise forecasts, individualized treatment plans, and efficient resource allocation, the integration of LSTM and Bi-LSTM models into healthcare CPS has the potential to completely transform patient care. These cutting-edge machine learning methods have the power to completely change a number of facets of healthcare delivery, which would ultimately improve patient outcomes and streamline healthcare systems.

This paper aims to investigate the intricate design Enhanced CPS in the healthcare domain, emphasizing the complementary functions of LSTM, BiLSTM, attention-based models, and the Adam optimizer. We hope to shed light on the revolutionary potential of these technologies in transforming patient care, clinical decision-making, and healthcare delivery by clarifying the underlying concepts and methods.

This article is structured as follows: Sect. 2 describes the crucial study about the cyber physical system in which only few papers have given the in-depth analysis of cyber-attack in cps. The proposed architecture of the system is described in Sect. 3. Section 4 gives the model development of the proposed system. The experimental analysis is presented in Sect. 5, and the conclusion and future work are covered in Sect. 6.

2 Literature Survey

In recent years, the integration of Cyber-Physical Systems (CPS) with cutting-edge AI technologies has revolutionized various industries, and healthcare stands at the forefront of this transformation. Kivrak et al. [13] introduced a cyber physical architecture for multi-robot ecosystem to ensure accurate and the experimental analysis was carried out using simulation. The proposed system used robots and voxel-grid map to generate for evaluating and managing bandwidth requirements. Lu et al. [15] suggested algorithm expands the models' capacity for robust generalization and increases the detection accuracy of the models by combining several carefully chosen classifiers that function on two distinct feature subsets. According to experimental results, the proposed algorithm performs better than both state-of-the-art and existing machine learning algorithms. It can also identify coordinated and single attacks with high accuracy, and our DCPIDS satisfies the real-time requirements for practical online applications. Shukla et al. [21] investigated and proposed encryption algorithm for blockchain application to secure the sharing the decryption keys. The authors have tested the proposed method using simulation platform called RTDS and stated that the proposed method has the efficiency. Garcia-Perez et al. [7] has investigated three fundamental concepts that support the transformative, adaptive, and absorptive abilities needed for healthcare systems to be cyber- and digitally resilient. These are Supply Chain and Partnerships, Risk Awareness, and Knowledge and Resources.

Özdemir Sönmez et al. [17] presented a case study based on two IT setup configurations that have been assessed by both IT and medical experts, as well as a healthcare cost optimization system. These setups would help illustrate how CySecTool addresses this challenge and communicate the intricacy of the decision parameters. Seventy vulnerabilities that could arise at any level of a hospital system dealing with both internal and external attacks/risks were linked to 64 different security controls in the study. Fei and Shen [6] developed a network control architecture in which the cyber-attack is introduced such as Dos attack, Replay attack and FDI attack. The authors have analyzed the attack using machine learning models and implemented security control of CPS. Jeffrey et al. [11] proposed a hybrid method to detect the anomaly threats to cyber physical system by using signature and threshold based IDS in the network. The authors mentioned that the proposed method provides more accurate in detecting the threats. Tartarisco et al. [22] presented a MCPS (medical cyber physical system) for classification of heart valve disease in automatic manner at timely. The authors used neural network model which was trained on new Italian dataset and the experiment was reached up to 98% accuracy with more feasible. Piardi et al. [18] examined the ways in which new digital technologies can help industrial CPS integrate people more harmoniously, providing insights into a range of factors and concerns that must be taken into consideration to properly enable the HitL and HitM integration levels. Four experimental case studies covering the HitL and HitM levels are presented to demonstrate that it is possible to use digital technologies to enhance the human-CPS integration.

Haque and Aziz [8] proposed a detection of false alarm in cyber physical system in healthcare. Since the Numerous medical sensors are employed in CPS healthcare applications, but they frequently cause false alarms. The overall efficiency of the healthcare system is decreased and confusion is increased by these false alarms. Despite the fact that some CPS healthcare architectures have been put forth for use in healthcare settings, none of them have effective false alarm detection. Blanco et al. [4] developed a semantic approach called Onto-CARMEN which allows security requirements to be automatically verified and diagnosed in accordance with OWASP and ENISA guidelines. This method offers a mechanism that uses semantic axioms and SPARQL rules to automatically diagnose problems and specify security requirements on top of ontologies. The method has been verified with security specifications taken from an actual case study. Alguliyev et al. [2] aimed to combine various malware visual representations and detection models using transfer learning. It uses pre-trained deep neural network models (AlexNet and MobileNet) and Radon transform to classify malware families using grayscale images. The model outperforms other methods in efficiency.

Tyagi and Sreenath [23] provided a risk assessment, a breakdown of the security vulnerabilities at each tier of the CPS architecture, and security measures. Ultimately, issues, directions for additional study, and potential fixes are highlighted and talked about. Kumar et al. [14] suggested a secure data exchange architecture for the cyber-physical healthcare industry 4.0 that is modeled after the blockchain. To enhance healthcare, the system makes use of BigchainDB, Tendermint, IPFS, MongoDB, and AES encryption algorithms. The patient-centric model ensures data control, security, and privacy. Experimental results show robustness against security attacks and data recovery in case of failure. Baranitharan et al. [3] examined the role of IoT in healthcare networks, focusing on the creation and dissemination of IoT-based software. It discusses current challenges and unanswered concerns, focusing on the IoT's constituent parts for secure mobile applications. Hossain et al. [10] presented a machine learning-based system for identifying the health risks that pregnant women in developing nations face. The system applies machine learning (ML) to temperature, blood pressure, glucose, and heart rate sensors in order to forecast health risks. Patients can input their risk factors and consult doctors through the program. The system's efficacy is evaluated using a pregnant woman dataset.

Admass et al. [1] examined the future of cyber security, stressing the need for continued adoption and cooperation among stakeholders while highlighting tactics and approaches to tackle growing threats, new trends, and innovations like AI and ML. Shishvan et al. [20] explored machine intelligence algorithms in healthcare applications, including their use in data acquisition, feature extraction, modeling, training, and execution. It provides detailed case studies and metrics for evaluating performance. One emerging application case study that is highlighted is medical cyber-physical systems. Along with providing a list of resources and databases for researchers, the paper also addresses the advantages and disadvantages of implementing machine intelligence in the healthcare industry. Johnphill et al. [12] explored the potential of machine learning for self-healing in cyber-physical systems, focusing on anomaly detection, fault alert, and fault auto-remediation. It highlights the importance of understanding these theories for practical implementation. The paper suggests that self-healing in cyber-physical systems holds great promise for future computing technology, offering seamless self-organization and self-restoration, increased security, and improved user experience. It critically analyzes existing vulnerabilities, threats, and challenges in machine learning self-healing for cyber-physical systems. Horvath [9] discussed the shift in CPS paradigms and uncertainty related to NG-CPSs, focusing on their intellectualization, adaptation, evolution, and automation. It emphasizes multi-dimensional interaction, socialization, and the need for aggregation, management, and utilizing the knowledge of synthetic systems generated by intelligent CPSs.

Priyadarshini et al. [19] examined the state-of-the-art of MCPS and proposes a new framework for MPCS, considering security/privacy. The framework is useful in healthcare industries, IoT environments, and efficient workflow operations for patients. It also establishes the framework for integrating cybersecurity systems into a range of medical applications. Dey et al. [5] reviewed and discussed the infrastructure of cyber-physical systems (CPS) in networked Medical Device systems, enhancing healthcare efficiency and safety. It addresses social networking, security, and wireless sensor networks, and concentrates on the big data framework of CPSs and healthcare based on CPSs. Verma [24] explored the growth and challenges of healthcare cyber physical systems, highlighting the role of various technologies and the challenges in successful implementation. Madani et al. [16] explored current solutions for semantic interoperability in CPS, integrating semantic models, ML, or both technologies in a reference architecture for visionary interoperable CPSs.

3 Proposed Architecture

Using the discussion from Sect. 2 as a foundation, the innovative ECPS-HC methodology finds and identifies suspicious activity in the health care monitoring system. This mechanism is incorporated with attention mechanism and deep learning models like LSTM and BiLSTM with attention-based model and added with Adam optimizer. The architecture of ECPS-HC is presented in Fig. 1.

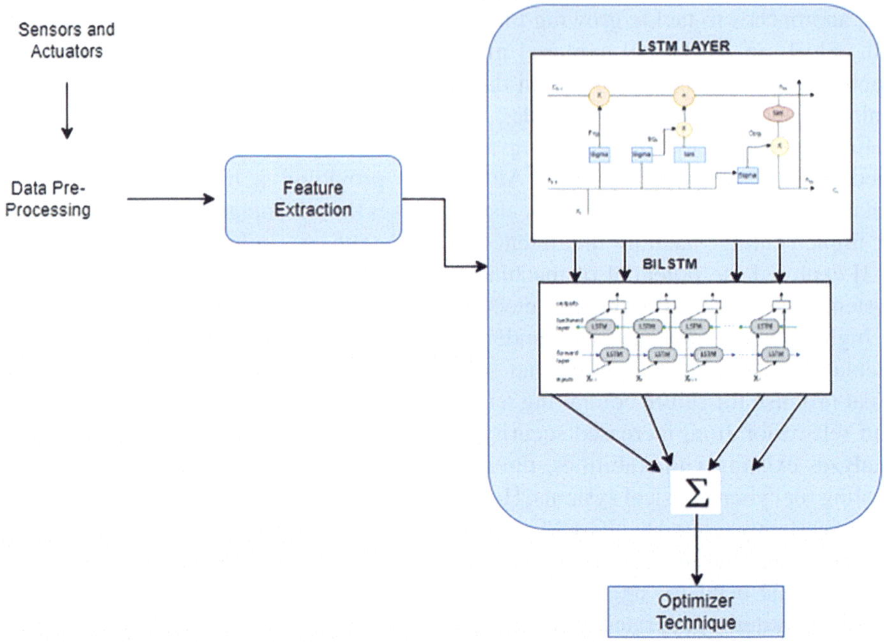

Fig. 1 Architecture of ECPS-HC system

3.1 Dataset and Pre-processing

The data is collected from sensors and actuators. All the healthcare data is collected and it is processed. Text preprocessing, a crucial step in natural language processing (NLP), comprises sanitizing and formatting raw text data so that it can be used for analysis or machine learning. The goals of text preprocessing are to enhance the data's quality and increase its susceptibility to further processing as shown in Fig. 2. Typical steps in text preprocessing include the following: 1. Making every word lowercase. This promotes uniformity and treats words in various contexts fairly. 2. The process of tokenization, which divides the text into. 3. Dropping All Punctuation. 4. Eliminating stop words. 5. Lemmatization and stemming, wherein words are reduced to their most basic or root form. Prefixes and suffixes are eliminated during the stemming process, which reduces words to their dictionary or base form lemmatization. 6. Handling HTML and URLs; 7. Eliminating special characters and numbers from the dataset.

3.2 Feature Extraction

The goal of feature extraction is to extract as much pertinent information as possible while reducing the complexity of the data (also referred to as "data dimensionality").

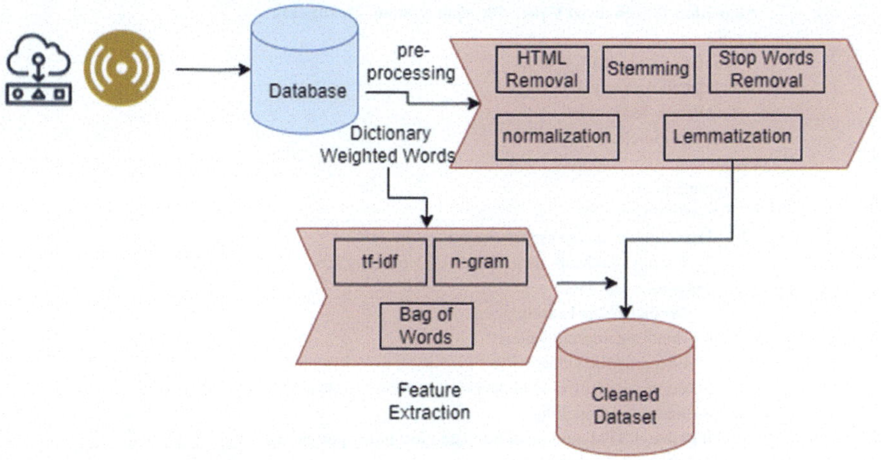

Fig. 2 Data pre-processing process

This facilitates the process of analysis and enhances the effectiveness and efficiency of machine learning algorithms. In order to distinguish and make it easier to use relevant features from irrelevant ones, feature extraction may entail the creation of new features (a process known as "feature engineering") and data manipulation. There could be a lot of redundant or unnecessary features in the raw data. This complicates the process of accurately processing the data by algorithms. The relevant features are "extracted" from the irrelevant ones through the process of feature extraction. The dataset gets simpler and the analysis's accuracy and efficiency rise when there are fewer features to process.

3.3 *Enhanced Cyber-Physical System-Healthcare*

This Algorithm 1 outlines the steps involved in designing and modeling Cyber-Physical Systems in Healthcare using LSTM and BiLSTM with attention mechanism and Adam optimizer, including data preprocessing, model architecture design, training, evaluation, optimization, deployment, and maintenance.

Algorithm 1: Enhanced Cyber-Physical System- Healthcare

Inputs:
  Training data x_data, y_data
  Validation data x_val, y_val
  Test data x_test, y_test
  Hyperparameters
Outputs:
  Training model
  Evaluation measures

1. Data Collection and preprocessing
   Collecting healthcare data X and corresponding labels Y.
   Preprocess the data
      Normalize the Feature
      Handling missing values
      Encoding the values
   Splitting the preprocessed data into training, validation and testing.
2. Structure the modelling
   Initialize LSTM parameter and attention-based parameters
   For each time step t
     Compute LSTM hidden state: h_t = LSTM (x_t, h_{t-1})
     Compute attention weights: α_t = softmax (W*tani(v*h_t))
     Compute Context vector: c_t = sum (α_t * h_t)
     Combine Context vector with LSTM output: h_t = tanh (w_c * [c_t, h_t)]
   BiLSTM with attention

3. Model training
   Initialize model parameter
   Define the loss function, such as cross-entropy
   Initialize Adam optimizer with β1, β2 and ε
   For each epoch
     Shuffle training data
     For each mini batch in training data:
       Forward pass
       Compute loss function
       Update the model using Adam optimizer

4. Model Evaluation
   Evaluate the trained model on validation dataset
      Forward pass validation dataset through the model.
      Compute the evaluation measure

5. Fine tuning and Optimization
   Adjust the parameters if necessary
   Repeat the steps 3 and 4untill the validation metrices reaches in good level

6. Model Testing
   Evaluate the trained model on the test dataset
    Forward pass test data through the model
    Compute evaluation measures

7. Output
   Trained model parameters
   Evaluation metrices

   End

4 Model Development

4.1 Long Short Term Memory and Bi-directional LSTM

As the Long Short Term Memory, or LSTM for short, is a kind of recurrent neural network that is also a conventional RNN. It can preserve information through deep learning. This kind of recurrent neural network is special because it can resolve the vanishing gradient problem with RNNs. Recalling past information and applying it to the current input is the role of RNNs. One disadvantage of RNNs is that they cannot remember long-term dependencies due to their vanishing gradient. LSTMs are specifically designed to avoid long-term dependency problems. Long-term information storage units, or memory cells, are introduced by LSTMs to address this problem. LSTM networks are a good fit for applications such as speech recognition, time series forecasting, and other applications where long-term dependencies need to be learned from sequential data.

The input gate (Ipgt), the forget gate (Frgt), and the output gate (Opgt), which manages the memory cell, are the three gates that make up long short term memory. These gates control the data that is input into, removed from, and added back to the memory cell. The input gate controls what data is added to the memory cell. The forget gate controls what information is removed from the memory cell. The data that the memory cell outputs is also controlled by the output gate. As a result, by enabling LSTM networks to selectively retain or discard information as it flows through the network, long-term dependencies can be learned.

As shown in Fig. 3, the LSTM architecture's chain structure is composed of four neural networks and different cells, or memory building blocks. Data that is no longer relevant in the cell state is removed using the forget gate. Prior to bias being added and fed into the gate, weight matrices are multiplied by two inputs: X_t (the input at that particular time) and h_{t-1} (the output of the preceding cell). The resultant is run through an activation function to produce a binary output. If the output for a particular cell state is 1, the information is lost for future use; otherwise, it is saved for future use. The equation for the forget gate is mentioned in (1)

$$Frg_t = \sigma\left(W_t \cdot (h_{t-1}, X_t) + b_f\right) \tag{1}$$

The input gate adds relevant information to change the state of the cell. Prior to filtering the values to be remembered like a forget gate, the information is first regulated using the sigmoid function and inputs h_{t-1} and X_t. Next, the Tani function—which yields an output ranging from -1 to $+1$—is used to create a vector containing all possible values from h_{t-1} and X_t. Ultimately, the vector values are multiplied by the regulated values to obtain the relevant information. The equation for the input gate in (2) is as follows:

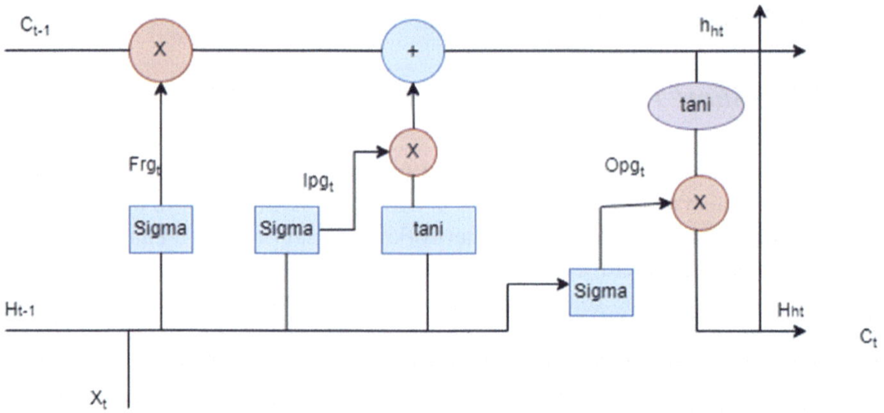

Fig. 3 Structure of LSTM

$$
\begin{aligned}
Ipg_t &= \sigma(W_i \cdot (h_{t-1}, X_t) + b_i) \\
C'_{cct} &= \tan_i(W_c \cdot (h_{t-1}, X_t) + b_c) \\
C_{cct} &= Fg_t \cdot C_{cct-1} + ig_t . C'_{cct}
\end{aligned}
\tag{2}
$$

The output gate's responsibility is to take important information out of the current cell state so that it can be shown as output. To create a vector, the cell is first subjected to the Tani function. The sigmoid function is then used to control the data after it has been filtered by the values that must be remembered using inputs h_{t-1} and X_t. Finally, they are multiplied in order to send the vector and regulated values as an output and an input to the next cell. Equation (3) gives the output gate's equation:

$$Opg_t = \sigma\left(W_t \cdot (h_{t-1}, X_t) + b_{op}\right) \tag{3}$$

As seen in Fig. 4, the two LSTM layers that comprise the bidirectional LSTM process the input sequence in both forward and backward directions. The network can now access data from both past and future time steps simultaneously thanks to this. Bidirectional LSTMs (Long Short-Term Memory) are recurrent neural network (RNN) architectures that process input data both forward and backward. A conventional LSTM only analyses data in a forward-looking way, basing its predictions on the prior context. Conversely, because bidirectional LSTMs also account for future context, the network can capture dependencies in both directions. In complex sequential data, bidirectional LSTMs enhance the model's ability to identify long-term dependencies and generate more accurate predictions by integrating data from both directions, as indicated in Eq. (4), in complex sequential data.

$$BiLSTM = \left[\overrightarrow{h_{t-1}}, \overleftarrow{h_{t-1}}\right] \tag{4}$$

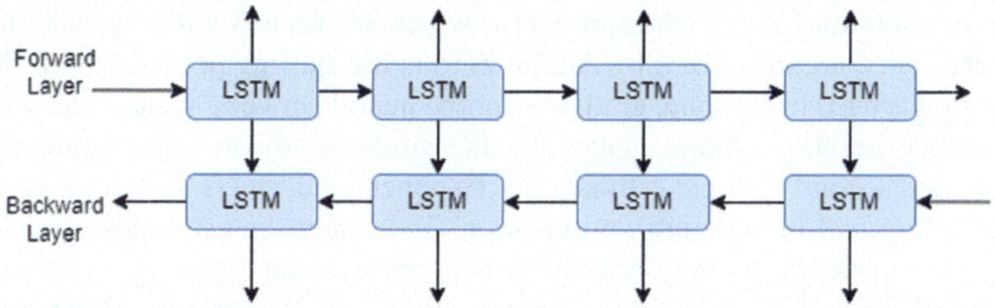

Fig. 4 Structure of BiLSTM

When neural networks are making predictions or decisions, an attention mechanism enables them to concentrate on particular portions of the input data. It imitates the mechanism of selective attention found in human cognition, which gives some information more weight or attention than other information. By allowing the model to dynamically balance the significance of various input features, attention mechanisms improve performance in the context of neural networks, particularly in tasks like speech recognition, image captioning, and machine translation. Attention mechanisms suppress noisy or irrelevant data and devote more resources to pertinent information, rather than evaluating all input equally.

Usually, the mechanism consists of three primary parts: To calculate the attention scores, three vectors—Query, Key, and Value—are extracted from the input data. While keys and values are representations of the input data, the query itself represents the state of the model at that moment. The similarity between the query and the keys is measured to determine the Attention Scores. Dot product, additive attention, and scaled dot-product attention are examples of common techniques. Attention Weights: A softmax function is used to normalize the attention scores so that they add up to one and then converts them into weights. The model's emphasis on each value when calculating the output is determined by these weights. Overall, by emphasizing significant portions of the input during the prediction process, attention mechanisms help neural networks handle variable-length inputs more skillfully, capture long-range dependencies, and enhance interpretability.

4.2 Adam Optimizer

As the number Adaptive Moment Estimation, or Adam optimizer, is an adaptive learning algorithm that deep learning models use to speed up dataset training. Algorithm 2 provides specifics about the Adam optimizer algorithm. It makes an analysis and adjusts the learning rate based on the standard gradient descent history. It incorporates Momentum and Root Mean Square Propagation, two optimization techniques. The gradient is accelerated by the momentum technique using an exponentially weighted average.

Two momentum-like variables, m and v, which are vectors with the same length as the gradients, are initialized by Adam. Zero is the starting point for both. Backpropagation is used to compute gradients for the neural network's parameters during each training iteration. Adam makes updates to the gradients' first moment estimate (m) and second moment estimate (v). Exponential decay is used for this, much like RMSProp and momentum optimization. To correct the estimates of m and v to take into consideration their initialization at zero, Adam applies bias correction. This lessens the early training stages' bias toward zero. Adam uses a learning rate, usually represented by α, to calculate the update values for each parameter based on the corrected momentum estimates. The gradients are scaled by a factor determined by the root mean square of the previous gradients. Adam then uses the computed update values to update the neural network's parameters, thereby minimizing the loss function.

Algorithm 2. Adam Optimizer

```
Initialization
   Initialize parameter θ
   Initialize first and second moment vector with zeros: m=0; v=0
   Initialize t=0
   Set decay rates as β1, β2 ε 0,1
   Set ε

While not converged do:
   t = t + 1
 Compute gradient gt for parameters θ
  Update First moment
    m = β1 * m + (1 - β1) * gt
Update Second Moment
    v = β2 * v + (1 - β2) * (gt^2)
correct bias in first moment
  m_hat = m / (1 - β1^t)
Correct bias in second moment
  V_hat = v / (1-β2 ^ t)
Compute the parameter update
  ~θ = - α * m_hat / (sqrt (V_hat) + ε)
Update Parameters
  θ = θ + ~θ
```

Because of its ability to handle noisy gradients, variable learning rates for various parameters, and automatic learning rate adaptation during training, Adam has gained popularity in the deep learning community. It is renowned for being reliable and effective in a variety of optimization scenarios.

5 Experimental Analysis

This section describes the experimental analysis of the proposed system. This article collected data from around 2000 from actuators and sensors related to healthcare data. After the pre-processed stage is completed, the entire dataset is divided into an 80:20 ratio, with 80% of the data going toward training and the remaining 20% going toward testing. One way to assess the model's performance is through the confusion matrix, which is made up of the True Positive, True Negative, False Positive, and False Negative values listed in Table 1. In order to determine the effectiveness of the ECPS-HC with Attention mechanism, accuracy and precision are computed as evaluation metrics. F1*score and recall. The following represents the evaluation equation for these parameters:

$$\mathrm{Acc}_{\mathrm{hc}} = \frac{TP_{hc} + TN_{hc}}{TP_{hc} + FP_{hc} + TN_{hc} + FN_{hc}}$$

$$\mathrm{Pre}_{\mathrm{hc}} = \frac{TP_{hc}}{TP_{hc} + FN_{hc}}$$

$$\mathrm{RC}_{\mathrm{hc}} = \frac{TP_{hc}}{TP_{hc} + FN_{hc}}$$

$$\mathrm{F1} * \mathrm{score}_{\mathrm{hc}} = \frac{2pre_{hc}RC_{hc}}{Pre_{hc} + RC_{hc}}$$

An appropriate quantitative measurement criterion is proposed to evaluate the effectiveness of detection techniques. The detection method divides the examined network data into normal and suspicious groups. The performance metrics are computed using True Positive (Trp), True Negative (Trn), False Positive (Frp), and False Negative (Frn) in terms of Accuracy (Acc), Precision (Pre), Recall (Rc), and F1*Score. The confusion matrix, as displayed in Table 1, is the basis for the computation of the evaluation measures.

Where Trn is the number that the algorithm correctly detects, Frn is the number that is incorrectly reported as a normal domain name, and Frp is the number that is incorrectly reported as suspicious. Moreover, Trp is the number that the algorithm recognizes accurately.

The suggested model's inputs for the network training phases are a 200-dimensional glove and an embedding initialization made by combining n-gram weighting with extra parameters. We applied the Attention mechanism after receiving

Table 1 Confusion matrix

		Actual data	
		Positive	Negative
Predicted data	Positive	True positive (Trp)	False positive (Frp)
	Negative	False negative (Frn)	True negative (Trn)

Table 2 Performance comparison of proposed system with four algorithms

Models	Accuracy (Acc)	Precision (Pre)	Recall (RC)	F1*score
RNN	82	80	79	80
CNN	84	83	85	84
LSTM	86	84	83	82
BiLSTM	87	85	84	83
ECPS-HC	90	92	95	93

Table 3 Evaluation measures of HybridCPS-health

Training loss	0.319	Training accuracy	0.935
Validation loss	0.291	Validation accuracy	0.940

the feature from the concatenation layer, which came from the feature extraction output that was fed to the BiLSTM layer. The dense size, batch size, and kernel regularization rate of the BiLSTM are 128 and 0.001, respectively. Following the dense layer, the binary classifier employs a sigmoid function. Finally, we trained the model using binary cross-entropy and the Adam optimizer to ascertain its learning rate. The authors have used an Intel Core i7 processor with 3.00 GHz and 16 GB of RAM to carry out the experiment.

As shown in Table 2, the suggested model was contrasted with four deep learning algorithms: RNN, CNN, LSTM, and BiLSTM. The Recurrent neural network has achieved 82% of accuracy whereas Convolutional Neural network, LSTM and BiLSTM has reached 84%, 86%, and 87% of accuracy respectively. The CNN model was unable to identify characteristics over time steps, which is required to detect ASD. To improve the sentence's context, the LSTM model could only store data about its prior status; it was unable to retain information about its subsequent status. Whereas, the BiLSTM model enhanced the performance of memory cell and also has the ability to process the data in the forward and backward direction. So, the accuracy improved than CNN and LSTM. The proposed algorithm without attention-based model has reached the accuracy of 90%.

The model with ECPS-HC with attention-based has improved the accuracy from 90 to 94% whereas other models also increased the accuracy, precision, recall and F1Score. Tables 3 and 4 provides good performance measures of the proposed model with attention based and Adam optimizer.

Table 4 Comparison of others modes with ECPS-HC

Models	Accuracy	Precision	Recall	F1*Score
CNN-Adam optimizer	86	85	84	84
LSTM-Adam optimizer	86	85	85	86
BiLSTM-Adam optimizer	91	90	89	89
ECPS-HC-Attention-Adam optimizer	94	96	97	97

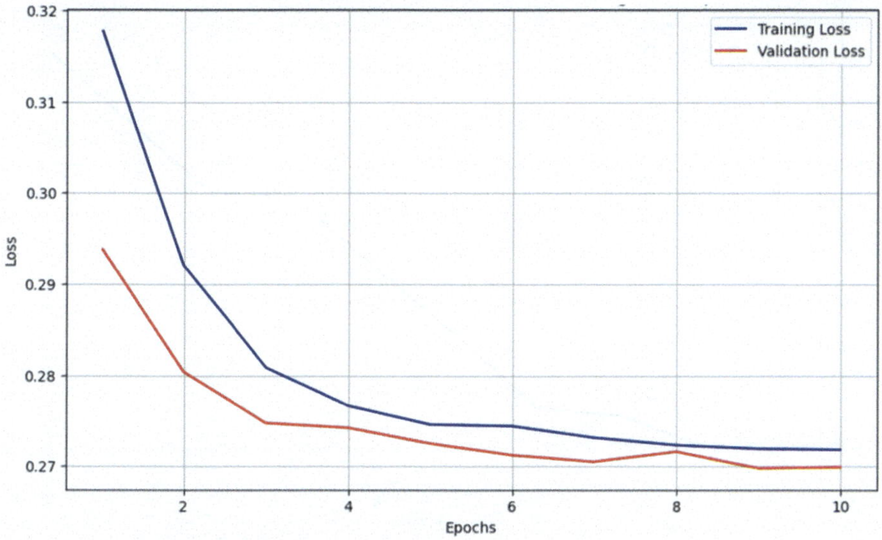

Fig. 5 Training and validation loss of ECPS-HC

In the training stage of deep learning, the model is trained on a training dataset by minimizing a predetermined loss function by modifying its parameters (weights and biases) in response to the observed input–output pairs (features and labels). At each iteration or training epoch, the training loss is a measure of how well the model performs on the training set. It calculates the difference between the model's predictions and the target values for the training cases.

Figure 5 represents the loss of training and validation loss for ECPS-HC in which it is calculated the error rate of actual and predicted values. The training loss is reached about 0.31 whereas the validation loss is reached about 0.29 with the epoch of 100.

In deep learning, two performance metrics—training accuracy and validation accuracy are used to evaluate a model's effectiveness during training. These metrics evaluate the model's predictive or classification accuracy across a range of datasets. The training and validation accuracy of ECPS-HC are shown in Fig. 6. The training accuracy of the suggested model is 93%, and the validation accuracy is 94%.

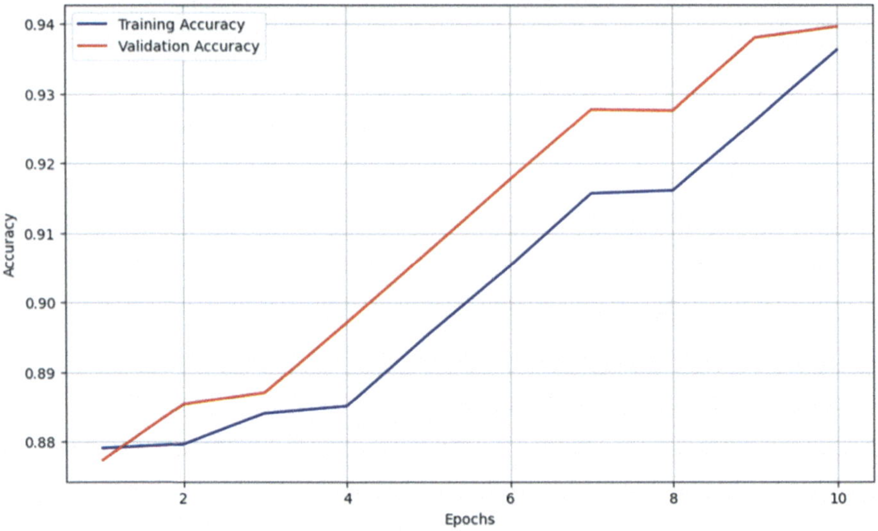

Fig. 6 ECPS-HC training and validation accuracy

6 Conclusion

Advanced computational methods, real-time data processing, and physically connected components are all used by CPS in the healthcare industry to monitor, evaluate, and improve a range of patient care, treatment procedures, and infrastructure. Among the many methods utilized in CPS are Long Short-Term Memory (LSTM) networks, Bidirectional LSTM (Bi-LSTM) architectures, Attention-based systems, and the Adam optimizer. The application of optimization algorithms, such as the Adam optimizer, improves deep learning model convergence and training efficiency, which raises prediction accuracy and generalization capacity. The Adam optimizer facilitates the efficient training of complex. CPS models on large-scale healthcare datasets by dynamically adjusting learning rates and adapting model parameters based on gradient descent optimization. This helps to develop scalable and reliable solutions for real-world healthcare applications. Design and modeling that have proven to be invaluable in managing the complexity of healthcare data and promoting thoughtful decision-making. The proposed system achieved 93% of training accuracy and 94% of validation accuracy in which it allows complex CPS models to be effectively trained on large-scale healthcare datasets, which in turn makes it easier to develop scalable and reliable solutions for real-world healthcare applications.

References

1. Admass, W. S., Munaye, Y. Y., & Diro, A. A. (2024). Cyber security: State of the art, challenges and future directions. *Cyber Security and Applications, 2*, 100031. https://doi.org/10.1016/j.csa.2023.100031
2. Alguliyev, R., Aliguliyev, R., & Sukhostat, L. (2024). Radon transform based malware classification in cyber-physical system using deep learning. *Results in Control and Optimization, 14*, 100382. https://doi.org/10.1016/j.rico.2024.100382
3. Baranitharan, K., Dineshbabu, V., Concepción-Lázaro, R., Balamanigandan, R., Selvakumarasamy, K., Mahaveerakannan, R., & Bhatt, M. W. (2023). A collaborative and adaptive cyber défense strategic assessment for healthcare networks using edge computing. *Healthcare Analytics, 3*. https://doi.org/10.1016/j.health.2023.100184
4. Blanco, C., Rosado, D. G., Varela-Vaca, Á. J., Gómez-López, M. T., & Fernández-Medina, E. (2023). Onto-CARMEN: Ontology-driven approach for Cyber–Physical System Security Requirements meta-modelling and reasoning. *Internet of Things (Netherlands), 24*. https://doi.org/10.1016/j.iot.2023.100989
5. Dey, N., Ashour, A. S., Shi, F., Fong, S. J., & Tavares, J. M. R. S. (2018). Medical cyber-physical systems: A survey. In *Journal of Medical Systems* (Vol. 42, Issue 4). Springer New York LLC. https://doi.org/10.1007/s10916-018-0921-x
6. Fei, C., & Shen, J. (2023). Machine learning for securing Cyber–Physical Systems under cyber attacks: A survey. *Franklin Open, 4*, 100041. https://doi.org/10.1016/j.fraope.2023.100041
7. Garcia-Perez, A., Cegarra-Navarro, J. G., Sallos, M. P., Martinez-Caro, E., & Chinnaswamy, A. (2023). Resilience in healthcare systems: Cyber security and digital transformation. *Technovation, 121*. https://doi.org/10.1016/j.technovation.2022.102583
8. Haque, S. A., & Aziz, S. M. (2013). False Alarm Detection in Cyber-physical Systems for Healthcare Applications. *AASRI Procedia, 5*, 54–61. https://doi.org/10.1016/j.aasri.2013.10.058
9. Horvath, I. (2023). Designing next-generation cyber-physical systems: Why is it an issue? *Journal of Integrated Design and Process Science, 26*(3–4), 317–349. https://doi.org/10.3233/JID-220008
10. Hossain, M. M., Kashem, M. A., Nayan, N. M., & Chowdhury, M. A. (2024). A Medical Cyber-physical system for predicting maternal health in developing countries using machine learning. *Healthcare Analytics, 5*. https://doi.org/10.1016/j.health.2023.100285
11. Jeffrey, N., Tan, Q., & Villar, J. R. (2024). A hybrid methodology for anomaly detection in Cyber–Physical Systems. *Neurocomputing, 568*. https://doi.org/10.1016/j.neucom.2023.127068
12. Johnphill, O., Sadiq, A. S., Al-Obeidat, F., Al-Khateeb, H., Taheir, M. A., Kaiwartya, O., & Ali, M. (2023). Self-Healing in Cyber–Physical Systems Using Machine Learning: A Critical Analysis of Theories and Tools. In *Future Internet* (Vol. 15, Issue 7). Multidisciplinary Digital Publishing Institute (MDPI). https://doi.org/10.3390/fi15070244
13. Kivrak, H., Karakusak, M. Z., Watson, S., & Lennox, B. (2024). Cyber–physical system architecture of autonomous robot ecosystem for industrial asset monitoring. *Computer Communications, 218*, 72–84. https://doi.org/10.1016/j.comcom.2024.02.013
14. Kumar, M., Raj, H., Chaurasia, N., & Gill, S. S. (2023). Blockchain inspired secure and reliable data exchange architecture for cyber-physical healthcare system 4.0. *Internet of Things and Cyber-Physical Systems, 3*, 309–322. https://doi.org/10.1016/j.iotcps.2023.05.006
15. Lu, Q., Gao, Q., Li, J., Xie, X. X., Guo, W., & Wang, J. (2024). Distributed cyber-physical intrusion detection using stacking learning for wide-area protection system. *Computer Communications, 215*, 91–102. https://doi.org/10.1016/j.comcom.2023.12.008
16. Madani, H. M., Djezzar, M., Mounir, H., Zianou, A. S., & Maimour, M. (n.d.). *Co-located with the KGSWC-2022*. http://ceur-ws.org
17. Özdemir Sönmez, F., Hankin, C., & Malacaria, P. (2022). Decision support for healthcare cyber security. *Computers and Security, 122*. https://doi.org/10.1016/j.cose.2022.102865

18. Piardi, L., Queiroz, J., Pontes, J., & Leitão, P. (2023). Digital Technologies to Empower Human Activities in Cyber-Physical Systems. *IFAC-PapersOnLine*, *56*(2), 8203–8208. https://doi.org/10.1016/j.ifacol.2023.10.1001
19. Priyadarshini, I., Kumar, R., Tuan, L. M., Son, L. H., Long, H. V., Sharma, R., & Rai, S. (2021). A new enhanced cyber security framework for medical cyber physical systems. *Software-Intensive Cyber-Physical Systems*, *35*(3–4), 159–183. https://doi.org/10.1007/s00450-021-00427-3
20. Shishvan, O. R., Zois, D. S., & Soyata, T. (2018). Machine Intelligence in Healthcare and Medical Cyber Physical Systems: A Survey. In *IEEE Access* (Vol. 6, pp. 46419–46494). Institute of Electrical and Electronics Engineers Inc. https://doi.org/10.1109/ACCESS.2018.2866049
21. Shukla, D., Chakrabarti, S., & Sharma, A. (2024). Blockchain-based cyber-security enhancement of cyber–physical power system through symmetric encryption mechanism. *International Journal of Electrical Power and Energy Systems*, *155*. https://doi.org/10.1016/j.ijepes.2023.109631
22. Tartarisco, G., Cicceri, G., Bruschetta, R., Tonacci, A., Campisi, S., Vitabile, S., Cerasa, A., Distefano, S., Pellegrino, A., Modesti, P. A., & Pioggia, G. (2024). An intelligent Medical Cyber–Physical System to support heart valve disease screening and diagnosis. *Expert Systems with Applications*, *238*. https://doi.org/10.1016/j.eswa.2023.121772
23. Tyagi, A. K., & Sreenath, N. (2021). Cyber Physical Systems: Analyses, challenges and possible solutions. *Internet of Things and Cyber-Physical Systems*, *1*, 22–33. https://doi.org/10.1016/j.iotcps.2021.12.002
24. Verma, R. (2022). Smart City Healthcare Cyber Physical System: Characteristics, Technologies and Challenges. *Wireless Personal Communications*, *122*(2), 1413–1433. https://doi.org/10.1007/s11277-021-08955-6

Harnessing Intelligent Cyber-Physical Systems for Advanced Healthcare Delivery: A Scoping Review and Future Directions

Obiora Reginald Ejinaka and Uchejeso Mark Obeta

Abstract Intelligent cyber-physical systems in healthcare are used to describe an intense integration networking of medical equipment and devices in virtual and physical forms. The systems are used with an emerging technological advanced technique, for health issues and parameters that are acquired and processed via advanced machine intelligence algorithms which can be taking place in the cloud thereby improving quality healthcare. In other words, the intelligent cyber-physical systems in healthcare can refer to any computer-controlled equipment used for the medical and health arena. The goal of this Chapter is to demonstrate the importance and benefits of intelligent cyber-physical systems in healthcare service for a very high-quality delivery to the patients and care givers. The Chapter employed a scoping review on the meaning, use, importance and benefits intelligent cyber-physical systems in healthcare for possible knowledge and applications across the globe. The chapter have identified importance, use and benefits of ICPS to include accountability of healthcare service, adequate and monitored coordination of healthcare, aiding remote patient monitoring, comprehensive healthcare packages, continuity in healthcare provision, disease Surveillance and outbreak prediction, efficient dimension in healthcare service delivery, enhancement of vaccination programs, persons and patients-centered services, quality improvement approach to healthcare, Security detection on healthcare cyber-attacks, universal accessibility of care including remote areas, wide coverage in healthcare. Despite the fact that this study has produced, identified and categorized numerous importance, use and benefits of intelligent cyber-physical systems in healthcare, global pandemic emphasizes the need for global healthcare reform to face the rising problems of modern-day ailments.

O. R. Ejinaka
Office of the Deputy Provost, Federal College of Medical Laboratory Science and Technology, Jos, Nigeria

U. M. Obeta (✉)
Department of Medical Laboratory Management, Federal College of Medical Laboratory Science and Technology, Jos, Nigeria
e-mail: uchejesoobeta@fcmlst.edu.ng

M. Mittal and J. Narayan (eds.), *Intelligent Cyber-Physical Systems for Healthcare Solutions*, https://doi.org/10.1007/978-981-97-8983-2_18

Keywords Intelligent cyber-physical systems in healthcare · Real-world computing · Artificial intelligence · MCPS · IoMLTs · IoTs · Healthcare · Internet-transmitted results

1 Introduction

Intelligent Cyber-physical systems in Healthcare entails new class of devices with integrated physical and computational capabilities that can communicate with people using a wide range of novel modalities. The current and near future technological advancements will be significantly aided by our ability to communicate with, manipulate, and interact with the physical environment in new ways that enhance its potential and this is gradually taking place in healthcare environments [1, 2].

Opportunities and research challenges include the creation of next-generation aircraft and spacecraft, hybrid gas-electric cars, completely autonomous city driving, and prosthetics that use brain impulses to operate actual items. Examples of CPS include industrial control systems, smart grids, and autonomous vehicles. It can be complex systems that integrate multiple technologies and components and require effective design and management. Observability is an essential aspect of it, as it allows organizations to monitor and understand the behaviour of these systems and identify any issues or bottlenecks that may arise. By implementing monitoring and analysis tools, organizations can gain insight into the performance and behaviour of it and take action to optimize or improve them [2].

Time and frequency domain methods, state space analysis, system identification, filtering, prediction, optimization, robust control, and stochastic control have all been pioneered by systems and control researchers over the years. Simultaneously, computer scientists have made significant advances in new programming languages, real-time computing techniques, visualization methods, compiler designs, embedded systems architectures and systems software, and novel approaches to ensuring computer system reliability, cyber security, and fault tolerance. Researchers in computer science have also created a number of powerful modelling formalisms and verification tools. Cyber-physical systems research, on the other hand, seeks to integrate knowledge and engineering principles from various computational and engineering disciplines (networking, control, software, human interaction, learning theory, as well as electrical, mechanical, chemical, biomedical, material science, and other engineering disciplines) in order to develop new CPS science and supporting technology [3].

1.1 Characteristic Features of CPS and Their Contribution to Improving Healthcare

The characters of CPS capable of improving healthcare such as: Observability, system identification, filtering, optimization, and robust control as highlighted by some authors [1–3] are presented with their contributions in healthcare improvement in Table 1.

1.1.1 Observability

In healthcare, observability is the ability to accurately measure and monitor clients' or patients' data and health information no matter how close or distant they could be. This observability character is essential for healthcare professionals including Doctors, Nurses, Medical Laboratory Scientists, Pharmacists etc. to make informed decisions and provide effective treatment plans. Take for example, in a CPS-enabled hospital, biosensors and wearable sensors can be used to continuously monitor a patient's vital signs, such as heart rate, blood pressure, and oxygen levels. This CPS components makes data readily integrated into a central system, and hence could provide real-time visibility of the patient's health status to the medical team.

1.1.2 System Identification

CPS technology can be used in healthcare to identify patterns and trends in patient data to better understand their health conditions. This identification capacity can aid in early diagnosis and proactive treatment planning. For instance, CPS-enabled wearable devices can continuously collect data on a patient's sleep patterns, daily activities, and vital signs. This data can be analyzed to identify any potential health issues and provide insights into the patient's overall health.

Table 1 Characters of CPS and their contribution to improving healthcare

Sn	Characters of CPS	Contribution to improving healthcare
1	Observability	Encouraging real-time healthcare
2	System identification	Aids in past healthcare challenge recall
3	Filtering	Discouraging double counting and work with irrelevant data in healthcare
4	Optimization	Encouraging e-healthcare and patient cases streamlining and real-time case study
5	Robust control	Ensures continuous monitoring and healthcare attention

1.1.3 Filtering

With a very large amount of data generated, analysed and distributed in various healthcare organizations, filtering techniques found in CPS are required in healthcare to extract relevant information and eliminate unwanted or irrelevant data. CPS-based systems can use filtering algorithms to identify and analyze critical patients' data, such as signs and symptoms, medical history, and medical laboratory results, drug prescriptions etc. to aid in providing accurate treatment plans. This helps healthcare professionals make timely and informed decisions for their patients and clients without mixing with other irrelevant data.

1.1.4 Optimization

CPS technology in healthcare cannot be ignored towards optimizing various processes and in turn increase efficiency of the system. For instance, CPS-enabled hospital equipment can communicate with each other to optimize resource usage and streamline patient care. As an example in Medical Laboratory, Equipment carrying out Glucose assay can be linked with others like Cholesterol, renal function tests and liver function tests and all linked to a central system where results are collated and possibly aiding the care and management of a diabetic patient. This optimization approach can help in reducing turn-around or wait times of patients, minimize errors, and improve overall patient outcomes.

1.1.5 Robust Control

In healthcare, robust control refers to the ability to maintain stable and effective performance despite changes or disturbances in the system. This kind of control in CPS is crucial in critical care situations, where patients' conditions can quickly deteriorate. CPS technology can help in maintaining robust control by continuously monitoring patients and instantly alerting healthcare professionals to any critical changes in their condition. This enables early intervention and can potentially save lives.

CPS is attracting a lot of attention in recent years and is being considered as an emerging technology. It combines computation and communication capabilities with the physical world. CPS was identified as a key research area in 2008 by the US National Science Foundation (NSF) and was listed as the number one research priority by the US President's Council of Advisors on Science and Technology [1].

2 Healthcare System

The healthcare certains be it tertiary, secondary, or primary levels have various components (Fig. 1) not minding the size and management of such institution. The figure rightly depicts that patient/client is the centre of healthcare as the picture is boldly seen. The constituents of healthcare in the said figure are key components in healthcare and none should be taken as a support system unless it falls under others like cleaning and food services which has been referred as support services [4].

The healthcare system maybe Tertiary like Teaching Hospitals and Federal Medical Centers; Secondary like Specialist Hospitals, State owned General Hospitals; and Primary which includes Cottage Hospitals, Primary healthcare centers and several private healthcare facilities. The healthcare system may differ from country to country, however, the essence of existence is to provide quality healthcare service towards saving lives.

The healthcare is composed of various professionals, and ideally it should be partners in progress where no one professional claims to be more important than the other. The patient is the center of every healthcare system professional. The rivalry in health sector is mostly precipitated by superiority complex of one professional over other(s). The global and national healthcare system not withstanding, the components are not far from the Fig. 1 where the patients are at the center of practice of various professionals.

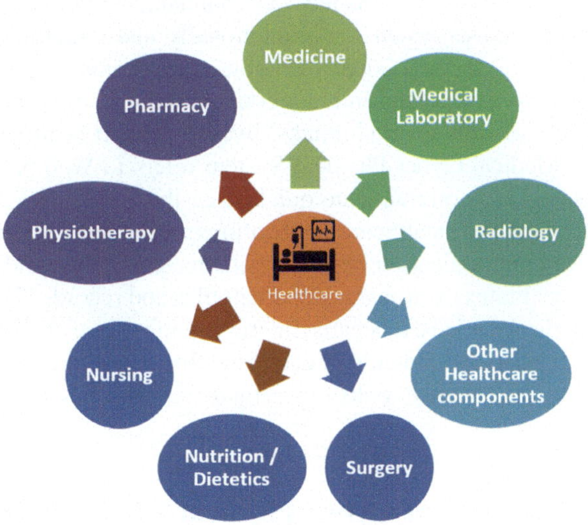

Fig. 1 Components of healthcare with intelligent cyber-physical system (ICPS)

3 General Overview of Cyber-Physical System in Healthcare

CPS connects the virtual world with the physical world. It can add more intelligence to social life. It integrates physical devices, such as sensors and cameras, with cyber components to form an analytical system that responds intelligently to dynamic changes in the real-world scenarios. CPS can have wide ranging applications, such as smart medical technology, assisted living, environmental control, and traffic management [3]. An important part of CPS is the integration of wireless sensor network (WSN) and Cloud Computing. CPS relies on sensing, processing, and networking. The recent advances in wireless sensor networks (WSN), medical sensors, and Cloud Computing are making CPS a powerful candidate for healthcare applications including in-hospital and in-home patient care [5].

In general, CPS and Medical Cyber-Physical System (MCPS) are physical, engineered systems whose processes are monitored, controlled, coordinated, and securely integrated at all levels and scales by a communication and computing core. It is divided into two sub-systems [6]:

i. The cyber sub-system—This is an event-oriented, logic-based, and discrete system responsible for communication, computation, and control.
ii. The physical sub-system—This operates continuously and integrates human-designed and natural components that adhere to physics laws.

As a result, MCPSs have a dynamism, evolutionary, and decentralization nature, in that these systems are functionally and structurally open, intelligent, context-sensitive, and self-adaptive engineered systems in which the physical and cyber sub-systems evolve and interact cooperatively to increasingly penetrate into the social space as well as into humans' lives to support healthcare.

Medical Cyber-Physical System refers to Web-based facilities/tools that enable persons to communicate quickly, easily, and widely. It has a significant impact in medical and healthcare applications, and it swiftly provides a platform for interactive communication between patients, clinicians, and health-organization workers. It facilitates the transfer of patient files and records [7]. With the advancement in the medical devices, it became interesting to replace the devices that designed to treat the patients independently of each other by integrating devices using distributed systems that concurrently control/investigate the patient's different physiological aspects [8].

4 Intelligent Cyber-Physical Systems in Healthcare

Intelligent Cyber-physical systems in Healthcare entails systems working like humans and humans using the systems to provided necessary result with an integration of computation (computers) including Cyber world and the physical processes

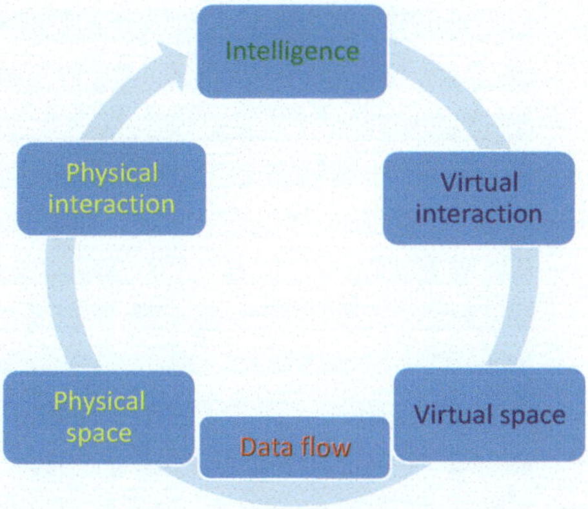

Fig. 2 Interactions existing in intelligent cyber-physical system in healthcare

that has to do with prognosis, diagnosis and treatment through computer networks [6–8].

Based on the principles of "garbage-in-garbage-out" computation, humans otherwise the healthcare professionals use the intelligence generated as a result of embedded computers and networks with various medical equipment as controlled by the physical processes through feedback loops amidst exchange of data [9]. Figure 2 illustrate the interactions existing among the virtual, physical and intelligence formations of healthcare especially in Intelligent cyber-physical system in healthcare.

Notably, intelligent cyber-physical system in healthcare can only exist and do well in the presence of digital twin, internet of health things (IoHTs) and other related IoTs like IoMLTs, IoMTs etc., big data, cloud computing, blockchain, artificial intelligence, machine learning and robotics. When all these components are in action, the field of healthcare under improved technologies such as Intelligent cyber-physical system in healthcare is fully assured.

The social media and emergence of light medical devices amidst networking and storage abilities and complex physical dynamics has contributed to transformation of the healthcare and no wonder the Intelligent cyber-physical system in healthcare [10]. Generally, Intelligent cyber-physical system in healthcare can be used for improvement networking abilities between patients, care givers and some medical devices; discovery of new software-empowered embedded systems; creation of need for automatic monitor for the patient's status; new inventions in the health care industry such as bio-sensors and other improved computing technologies and development of computer technology and wireless communication in healthcare.

Intelligent cyber-physical system in healthcare is creating an opportunity for rapid progress in diagnosis and treatment especially with the use of implantable and biocompatible devices, automation, electro-anatomical mapping, point of care testing, robotic prosthetics and invasive embedded devices.

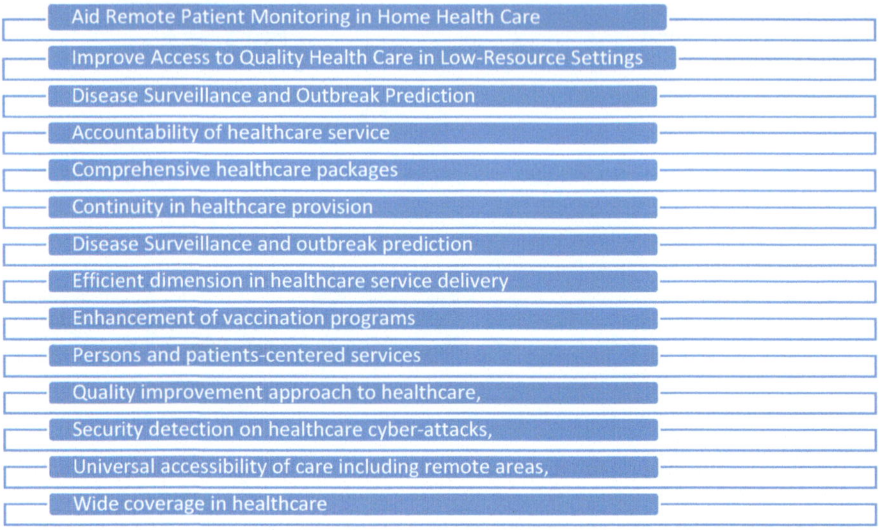

Fig. 3 Importance and potential benefits of intelligent cyber-physical system in healthcare

Intelligent cyber-physical system in healthcare can lead to computerization of different healthcare areas and equipment including training of various professionals to the latest technologies towards real-time computation of entire healthcare. Intelligent cyber-physical system in healthcare importance and potential benefits summarily put in Fig. 3 and explained to add value to the works of earlier writers [3, 7, 8, 11].

4.1 Intelligent Cyber-Physical System in Healthcare Aid in Remote Patient Monitoring and Home Health Care

The healthcare id advancing to home care and remote monitoring for security, economic and convenience reasons. Intelligent Cyber-Physical Systems in healthcare provides an important role in this procedure, allowing medical practitioners and other healthcare providers to remotely observe the health of their patients.

Furthermore, Intelligent cyber-physical system in healthcare are comprised of physical and software components that work in conjunction to provide real-time information regarding a patient's health. Using sensors and other wearable devices for monitoring, these systems collect and analyse vital information such as heart rate, temperature, blood sugar, cholesterol, bilirubin and blood pressure. This data is then used to detect changes in the patient's condition, allowing medical workers to provide prompt care if necessary.

Importantly, the application of Intelligent cyber-physical system in healthcare in home health care benefits both patients and medical professionals. Knowing that their wellness is being monitored at all times provides patients with an overwhelming feeling of assurance and tranquility of mind. It also eliminates the need for routine doctor visits, saving time and money. It makes it possible for medical professionals to provide better therapy remotely and respond to changes in condition promptly.

COVID-19 pandemic provided intelligent algorithms platform that made Intelligent cyber-physical system in healthcare a widely accepted package to monitor patients by healthcare providers' especially in serious illness and is compatible with the remote monitoring in healthcare [12].

4.2 Intelligent Cyber-Physical System in Healthcare Improves Access to Quality Health Care in Low-Resource Settings

As the globe becomes more digitally integrated and nearer to all with the aid of internet, cyber-physical systems will play an increasingly essential role in providing access to quality health care in low-resource situations. Cyber-physical systems have the potential to bridge the access gap between high-resource and low-resource environments.

These systems can give real-time data and feedback to health care providers, as well as enhanced access to care for patients in rural or difficult-to-reach places, by leveraging technology. For instance, Cyber-physical systems can be used to monitor vital signs and provide real-time input to doctors, allowing them to diagnose and treat patients more quickly.

These technologies can also be used to track and monitor illnesses, outbreaks COVID-19 as an instance, allowing health care providers to respond swiftly and effectively. This is especially useful in low-resource situations since it can help reduce disease transmission and give earlier access to treatment. Moreover, cyber-physical systems can be leveraged to improve access to health care services. These technologies can ensure that the proper care is administered at the right time by delivering real-time data and feedback to health care workers. This is particularly pertinent in low-resource situations where access to adequate health care is limited. Additionally, cyber-physical systems can enable remote access to health care services, making it easier for patients to get care no matter where they are in the world [13].

4.3 Intelligent Cyber-Physical System in Healthcare Used to Enhance Vaccination Programs

These technologies can be used in vaccination programs to check vaccine effectiveness, track rates of immunization, as well as make vaccine administration faster. The World Health Organization's (WHO) Smart Vaccination Program is one example of this technology in action. The effort uses an amalgam of cyber-physical systems, big data, and computational intelligence (AI) to assess vaccination effectiveness and track rates of immunization [14, 15]. The Yellow fever immunization program is globally monitored with aid of Intelligent cyber-physical system in healthcare.

The modern technology also allows health care workers to provide immunizations to patients quickly and easily, saving time and effort. The Intelligent cyber-physical system in healthcare has reduced the physical tracking and enumerations of houses and persons vaccinated at a given time as a press of one button would give the accurate value and spread.

4.4 Intelligent Cyber-Physical System in Healthcare in Disease Surveillance and Outbreak Prediction

The COVID-19 experience revealed to what extent Intelligent cyber-physical system in healthcare and other associated technologies could go during disease outbreaks and predictions. The pandemic was globally monitored for a real time service delivery from certain control rooms. The disease surveillance and predictions with aid of Intelligent cyber-physical system in healthcare can take care of all diseases of interest in a global stage. Data mining [16] aids disease surveillance and outbreaks that cannot be ignored in Intelligent cyber-physical system in healthcare.

4.5 Intelligent Cyber-Physical System in Healthcare for Accountability of Healthcare Service

Intelligent cyber-physical system in healthcare provides adequate accountability with regards to "who does what?" in the system. All the professional contributions to healthcare within the system is noted and archived. Also, all data inputs in the system are recorded with correct identifiers of those that have access and are responsible to one service or the other.

4.6 Intelligent Cyber-Physical System in Healthcare for Adequate and Monitored Coordination of Healthcare

The Intelligent cyber-physical system in healthcare improves information interchange between healthcare professionals and patients/clients in a well-controlled and coordinated unit. This monitored coordination checkmates all professional practice and their relevant data inputs for the patient thereby increasing the efficiency of integrated care while using eHealth.

With this coordination of professionals, the patient is equally empowered to have access thereby enhancing the effectiveness and efficiency of the healthcare Industry [17].

4.7 Intelligent Cyber-Physical System in Healthcare Provides Comprehensive Healthcare Packages

The Intelligent cyber-physical system in healthcare improves the comprehensive dimension of health service delivery in the aspect of preventative, diagnostic, curative, palliative and rehabilitation service dimensions. The target population for health in terms of equity and "right to healthcare" is managed by Intelligent cyber-physical system in healthcare.

Wearable devices, automated machines, point of care testing devices, robots and other complex Intelligent cyber-physical system in healthcare gadgets can be used for the elderly and sick patients without physical activity monitoring and tracking Robots and Intelligent cyber-physical system in healthcare compatible machines can aid in curative care, diagnostics, drug delivery, sample collections and delivery.

With Intelligent cyber-physical system in healthcare, there is no condition or practice that could be excluded making the healthcare comprehensive and all encompassing.

4.8 Intelligent Cyber-Physical System in Healthcare for Continuity in Healthcare Provision

Intelligent cyber-physical system in healthcare provides continuity of care across the network of services, health conditions especially in chronic ill health, other levels of care and over the lifecycle. The Intelligent cyber-physical system in healthcare in the continuity of care varies and can be infusion pumps or implant/wearable sensor devices [11] that can work over a lifetime in some patients.

Queenan et al. [10] opined that in chronic illness, counselling of patient coupled with technology enabled improved continuity of care especially when the patient has the skills, knowledge and motivation to manage chronic illness.

4.9 Intelligent Cyber-Physical System in Healthcare in Efficient Dimension in Healthcare Service Delivery

Intelligent cyber-physical system in healthcare gives a very good impression on the dimensions of services provided within the system. In cases where some professionals overlap in their services, the security and accessibility of the systems shows dimensions and services provided.

4.10 Intelligent Cyber-Physical System in Healthcare for Persons and Patients-Centered Services

Intelligent cyber-physical system in healthcare gives both the professionals and the patients/clients in healthcare [18] the satisfaction desired as the system is open to all stakeholders for ease of assessment and improvement. Ordinarily, the patients are the center of healthcare and their satisfaction indicates good and improved healthcare service in the healthcare system.

4.11 Intelligent Cyber-Physical System in Healthcare Towards Quality Improvement Approach to Healthcare

The Intelligent cyber-physical system in healthcare should positively improve the efficiency of the healthcare system based on value added, cost-efficient, good quality, reliable, and timely healthcare service delivery as Intelligent cyber-physical system in healthcare rightfully follows and improves the quality essentials.

With the availability of big data Intelligent cyber-physical system in healthcare promotes transparency in the healthcare system and could be further be used to design patient targeted applications, applications supporting healthcare professionals, human and capital resources management applications, and high-level healthcare systems management applications.

The patient is at the center and all healthcare professionals would be answerable to the patient without any rivalry and superiority complexes until the patient is satisfied.

4.12 Intelligent Cyber-Physical System in Healthcare for Security Detection on Healthcare Cyber-Attacks

There are numerous data generated in healthcare, Medical Laboratory Service not excluded [16]. These data needs security and privacy. The accountability aspect of

Intelligent cyber-physical system in healthcare helps to track who comes in contact with the data and as well monitor various hacking attempts within the system.

4.13 *Intelligent Cyber-Physical System in Healthcare for Wide Coverage in Healthcare*

The Intelligent cyber-physical system in healthcare provides coverage dimension to such targeted population whether old, young, sick, healthy, poor, rich and many more.

Health coverage for all can only be achieved with full implementation of Intelligent cyber-physical system in healthcare. Nigeria for example, healthcare tourism has been on the boom [19], but if the Intelligent cyber-physical system in healthcare is fully implemented, there is need for capital flight as one can remain in the comfort of the house and access quality care across the globe. There is an increase in complexity of diseases without consideration of various ages of the target population. Intelligent cyber-physical system in healthcare always creates an opportunity for data analysis in terms of various dimensions to enable appropriate decision-making process in healthcare coverage.

Without mincing words, Intelligent cyber-physical system in healthcare can provide several benefits to public health initiatives. One such advantage is the capacity to track and diagnose disease spread in real time. This has been demonstrated during the COVID-19 pandemic and should be made to stand for all disease conditions. This would indeed present the world as a global village with the agreement and collaboration of the WHO. The authors are of the opinion that no disease should be treated as more important than others basing our argument that COVID-19 has not killed people more than Malaria.

Intelligent cyber-physical system in healthcare can detect and respond to changes in the environment that might point to the spread of disease by using sensors, cameras, and other sensing devices. Sensors, for example, can be used to monitor temperature and humidity in an environment, while cameras can detect movement or changes in an area's population. This information can then be utilized to detect early warning signals of a disease an epidemic, allowing for a rapid response.

Intelligent cyber-physical system in healthcare can give useful analytical skills in addition to real-time monitoring in many cases of disease conditions including their diagnosis. Intelligent cyber-physical system in healthcare can provide accurate information into the distribution and danger indicators of a disease epidemic by merging data from tangible gadgets and computer systems.

Intelligent cyber-physical system in healthcare can be used to identify areas of high risk and predict disease trajectories. This information can be used to inform public health actions and also to assist mitigate the effects of an outbreak.

Intelligent cyber-physical system in healthcare has the potential to be more accurate and reliable than previous techniques. Intelligent cyber-physical system in healthcare can limit the possibility of human mistake as well as offer an additional reliable source of information by relying on physical instruments to collect data. This increased precision may result in more informed choices and more successful public health activities.

5 Challenges and Way Forward with Intelligent Cyber-Physical Systems in Healthcare

A wonderful innovation in health like Intelligent cyber-physical system in healthcare cannot be said to be free from challenges. Some of the challenges and possible examples are highlighted in Table 2 as mentioned among other authors [6, 10, 11, 15].

A good knowledge about the challenges provides a better way to tackling them for better use, applications and healthcare improvement in the aspect of Intelligent cyber-physical system in healthcare. The challenges creates opportunity to improve the loopholes associated with such technologies and for better applications.

5.1 Security

Security associated matter in Intelligent cyber-physical system in healthcare could be in form of the attacks in various domains or sub domains like "fault signal injection and hardware tampering of sensors", "packet replay attack and information theft in communication channels of closed loop with sensors", "controllers and actuators; equipment failure and software malfunctioning in computing resources". There could be "denial of service, replay, false data injection and deception attacks" [6, 20].

Table 2 Some challenges of intelligent cyber-physical systems in healthcare

SN	Challenges of intelligent cyber-physical system in healthcare	Possible examples
1	Security	Denial of service, replay, false data injection, deception attacks
2	Delay/Latency	Delays in threshold
3	Energy flow in cyber physical components	Inadequate power supply
4	Integration of heterogeneous devices/level	Old systems failure, non-synchronization
5	Human and technological issues	Less technical know how
6	Opposition to change	

Artificial intelligence, computing intelligence or machine intelligence have immense role towards the security of Intelligent cyber-physical system in healthcare and autonomous systems in aspect of abnormal behaviour detection due to faults or cyber-attacks. Importantly, malware detection systems would improve intelligent cyber physical systems in healthcare. Machine learning approaches while using system calls, energy consumption patterns, and operation codes can assist in the malwares regards. In consideration of the fact that many professionals are involved in healthcare, there should be approved and designated professionals that should have access to data at various levels and stages for smooth Intelligent cyber-physical system in healthcare and the Fig. 4 better illustrates accessibility of various professionals.

ROLES								DISABLE ☐	CHANGE ☐
Aps:	DR	ADMIN	PHARM	MLS	RN	RAD	PHYST	E.HTO	OTHERS
GENERAL SETTINGS									
ALL ABILITIES	☑	☑	☐	☑	☐	☐	☐	☑	☑
ACCOUNT ENTRY SETTINGS									
FULL ACCESS	☑	☑	☑	☑	☑	☑	☐	☑	☑
LIST	☑	☑	☑	☑	☑	☑	☑	☑	☑
VIEW	☑	☑	☑	☑	☑	☑	☑	☑	☑
CREATE	☑	☑	☑	☑	☐	☐	☑	☑	☑
EDIT	☑	☑	☐	☑	☐	☐	☐	☑	☑
DELETE	☑	☑	☐	☑	☐	☐	☐	☑	☐
SEND FOR REVIEW	☑	☑	☑	☑	☑	☐	☑	☑	☑
FINALIZE	☑	☑	☑	☑	☐	☐	☐	☑	☐
SENT TO TT	☑	☑	☑	☑	☑	☐	☐	☑	☑
SEND FOR COMPLIANCE	☑	☑	☑	☑	☐	☐	☐	☑	☐
SEND TO CLIENT	☑	☑	☐	☑	☐	☐	☑	☑	☐
PUBLISH	☑	☑	☐	☑	☐	☐	☐	☑	☐

Aps-Approved Professionals, DR-Doctor, ADMIN-Administrator, PHARM-Pharmacist, MLS-Medical Laboratory Scientist. RN Registered Nurse, PHYST-Physiotherapist, RAD-Radiologist/Radiographer, E.HTO-Electronic Health Technical Officer, ICTO-Information Communication Technology Officer, TT-Track & Trace

Ejinaka & Obeta

Fig. 4 Professionals access to security settings and e-health platforms in intelligent cyber-physical system in healthcare

5.2 *Delay/Latency*

In real time applications which is most likely in Intelligent cyber-physical system in healthcare is low latency. This is a critical requirement of real time and therefore delays the threshold value in transmission of patient data. This delay should not be accepted as it can lead to disrupting the telemonitoring cycle of cyber physical systems and may in turn affect timely medication and care to the patients under Intelligent cyber-physical system in healthcare. Further research should be in place to reduce the delay orchestrated by real time computing especially in healthcare.

5.3 *Energy Flow in Intelligent Cyber-Physical System in Healthcare Components*

Intelligent cyber-physical system in healthcare requires a continuous flow of energy. Such flow could either be from high-powered batteries or from direct power supply. However, the energy requirements are not usually met especially in resource limited certain. Such certain lacks adequate power supply, solar installations or sufficient rechargeable batteries.

For a successful implementation of Intelligent cyber-physical system in healthcare, there is a need for regular power supply, standby batteries or solar installations. This is basically an advice for underdeveloped and developing countries like Nigeria where power is lacking to sustain companies and new technologies.

5.4 *Integration of Heterogeneous Devices/Levels*

All kinds of computerization and linkages associated with Intelligent cyber-physical system in healthcare in a heterogeneous environment needs ways of interfaces to communicating devices with different technology level in terms of hardware and software resources. Such integrations involves data sharing and collaborative functionality and must be sorted out from the strategic planning of systems, design and prototype testing for better function.

Myriads of challenges affecting new technologies now in various societies and professions also affects Intelligent cyber-physical system in healthcare to mention but a few: integration with old systems, synchronization of various systems, professionals apathy to change, communication gaps, incompatibility of new applications with existing systems, lack of regulation of new applications and packages, incompatible old structures and high cost of updating or acquiring new applications and systems cannot be wished away from the challenges associated with Intelligent cyber-physical system in healthcare [2, 21, 22]. These challenges news a firm governance and quality improvement driven chief executives to drive the process to success for the benefit and satisfaction of clients in healthcare sector.

There is no doubt that integration of heterogeneous devices encompassing the Intelligent cyber-physical system in healthcare shall in so small measure improve healthcare services in various professional lines and areas viz-a-viz.

5.4.1 Medical Imaging Technologies (MIT)

CPS technologies in healthcare such as magnetic resonance imaging (MRI) and computed tomography (CT) scans tends to provide a high-resolution images of internal body structures, allowing for more accurate and precise diagnosis of conditions such as tumors, fractures, and organ damage. This helps Doctors and other healthcare givers to accurately pinpoint the location and severity of the condition, leading to more targeted and effective treatment options.

5.4.2 Artificial Intelligence (AI) Assisted Diagnosis (AIAD)

AI algorithms integrated into CPS technologies in healthcare aids to analyze medical data and images towards assisting Doctors and other healthcare givers in making medical decisions because of accurate and precise diagnoses. Take for instance, AI-powered diagnostic tools can help detect abnormalities in medical images that may be overlooked by human clinicians, leading to early detection and treatment of diseases rather than late diagnosis that may pose serious threat to manage.

5.4.3 Robotic Surgery (RS)

Robotics and CPS technologies have revolutionized surgical procedures by providing surgeons with enhanced precision, dexterity, and control. The use of surgical robots allows for minimally invasive procedures, which reduce the risk of complications and result in faster recovery times for patients.

5.4.4 Personalized Treatment Plans (PTPs)

CPS technologies in healthcare goes out of its way to collect and analyze large amounts of patients' data, including medical history, medical laboratory results, genetic information, and lifestyle factors for the purpose of current health status. This information can be used to develop personalized treatment plans for patients, taking into account their individual needs and characteristics. This leads to more accurate and effective treatment options that are tailored to the specific needs of the patient at a given time.

5.4.5 Virtual and Augmented Reality (VAR)

CPS technologies such as virtual and augmented reality are preferably being used in medical education and training to simulate real-life scenarios and allow Doctors, Nurses, Pharmacists, Medical Laboratory Scientists, Imaging Scientists and others to practice complex procedures in a safe and controlled environment. This enhances their skills and precision, leading to better outcomes for patients during actual treatments.

5.4.6 Precision Medicine (PM)

CPS technologies are playing a crucial role in the development of precision medicine, which involves tailoring treatments based on a person's genetic makeup, lifestyle factors, and environmental influences. This approach allows for more accurate diagnosis and targeted treatments, resulting in improved outcomes and reduced side effects for patients.

5.4.7 Remote Patient Monitoring (RPM)

CPS technologies in healthcare when used as wearable devices, biosensors and mobile health apps allow for remote monitoring of patients' health status including; vital signs, some laboratory parameters like Glucose, Cholesterol, Bilirubin, Uric Acid etc. and medication adherence pattern for the patients. This enables Doctors and other healthcare professionals to obtain real-time data and results and adjust treatment plans accordingly, leading to more accurate and precise management of acute or chronic conditions and improves patient outcomes in general.

6 Conclusion

Intelligent Cyber-Physical System in Health is very important and can provide numerous benefits to the healthcare system, such as greater efficiency and reliability, better safety, increased flexibility, and improved monitoring and control.

Not minding the militating challenges such as Security, Delay/Latency, Energy Flow in Cyber Physical Components, Integration of Heterogeneous Devices/Levels, Human and Technological issues and Opposition to change especially among professionals; the potential important beneficial factors from Intelligent cyber-physical system in healthcare including Remote Patient Monitoring in Home Health Care, Improve Access to Quality Health Care in Low-Resource Settings, Disease Surveillance and Outbreak Prediction, Accountability of healthcare service, Comprehensive healthcare packages, Continuity in healthcare provision, Disease Surveillance and outbreak prediction, Efficient dimension in healthcare service delivery, Enhancement of vaccination programs, Persons and patients-centered services, Quality improvement approach to healthcare, Security detection on healthcare cyber-attacks, Universal accessibility of care including remote areas, and Wide coverage in healthcare are more encouraging towards having Intelligent cyber-physical system in healthcare worldwide.

The authors call for use of Intelligent cyber-physical system in healthcare to strengthen the relationship among the Federal Ministries of Health of the WHO member countries towards a unified standardized Global Healthcare to reduce the differences existing between the developed and developing countries thereby reducing capital flight and medical tourism. Finally, the Intelligent cyber-physical system in healthcare presents a better opportunity for formation of global health regulatory agency or body as one and united Regulatory Agency under WHO.

References

1. Wang, J., Abid, H., Lee, S., Shu, L., & Xia, F. (2020). A secured health care application architecture for cyber-physical systems. Journal of Control Engineering and Applied Informatics, 13(3), 101–108.
2. Sony M, Antony J, McDermott O. (2022). The impact of medical cyber– physical systems on healthcare service delivery. The TQM Journal 34(7), 73–93. https://doi.org/10.1108/TQM-01-2022-0005.
3. Frąckiewicz, M. (2023, APRIL 27). The Role of Cyber-Physical Systems in Public Health and Epidemiology.
4. Siganporial P, Astrakianakis G, Alamgir H, Ostry A, Nicol AM, Koehoorn M. (2016). Hospital support services and the impacts of outsourcing on occupational health and safety. International Journal of Occupational and Environmental Health; 22(4), 274–282.
5. Milenkovic, A., Otto, C., & Jovanov, E. (2019). Wireless sensor networks for personal health monitoring: issues and an implementation. Journal of Computer Communications, 29(3), 2521–2533.
6. Dey N, Ashour AS, Shi F, Fong SJ, Tavares JMRS. (2018). Medical cyber-physical systems: A survey. Journal of Medical Systems. 42: 74. https://doi.org/10.1007/s10916-018-0921-x.
7. Ackerman, M. J., Filart, R., Burgess, L. P., I., L., & Poropatich, R. K. (2010). Developing next-generation telehealth tools and technologies. Journal of patients, systems, and data perspectives, 93–95.
8. Arney D, Pajic M, Goldman JM, Lee I, Mangharam R, Sokolsky O. Toward patient safety in closed-loop medical device systems. In Proceedings of the 1st ACM/IEEE International Conference on Cyber-Physical Systems. ACM. 139–148, 2010.
9. Shishvan OR, Zois DS, Soyata T. (2020). Incorporating Artificial Intelligence into Medical Cyber Physical Systems: A Survey. In El Saddik et al. (eds.), Connected Health in Smart Cities. https://doi.org/10.1007/978-3-030-27844-1_8.
10. Queenan, C., Cameron, K., Snell, A., Smalley, J. and Joglekar, N. (2019), "Patient heal thyself: reducing hospital readmissions with technology-enabled continuity of care and patient activation", Production and Operations Management, Vol. 28, No. 11, pp. 2841–2853. https://doi.org/10.1111/poms.13080.
11. Rahaman, M.O., Shuvo, A. and Abul, K. (2018), "Cyber physical systems for health care", International Journal of Advanced Research (IJAR), Vol. 6 No. 1, pp. 36–46. https://doi.org/10.21474/IJAR01/7968.

12. Loria, K. (2021), "Pandemic opens minds, loosens providers' purse strings for remote patient monitoring", Managed Healthcare Executive, Vol. 31 No. 3, pp. 28–30.
13. Panda, A. and Mohapatra, S. (2021), "Online healthcare practices and associated stakeholders: review of literature for future research agenda", Vikalpa, Vol. 46 No. 2, pp. 71–85. https://doi.org/10.1177/02560909211025361.
14. Alzahrani, A.; Alshehri, M.; AlGhamdi, R.; Sharma, S.K. Improved Wireless Medical Cyber-Physical System (IWMCPS) Based on Machine Learning. Healthcare 2023, 11, 384. https://doi.org/10.3390/healthcare11030384.
15. Haque SA, Aziz SM, Rahman M. (2014). Review of Cyber-Physical System in Healthcare. International Journal of Distributed Sensor Networks. https://doi.org/10.1155/2014/217415.
16. Obeta UM, Ejinaka OR, Etukudoh NS. (2022). Data Mining in Medical Laboratory Service Improves Disease Surveillance and Quality Healthcare; Chapter 17 In T. Saba et al. (eds.), Prognostic Models in Healthcare: AI and Statistical Approaches, Studies in Big Data 109. https://doi.org/10.1007/978-981-19-2057-8_17.
17. Al-Jaroodi, J., Mohamed, N. and Abukhousa, E. (2020), "Health 4.0: on the way to realizing the healthcare of the future", IEEE Access, Vol. 8 No. 1, pp. 211189–211210. https://doi.org/10.1109/ACCESS.2020.3038858.
18. Etukudoh NS & Obeta MU. (2021). Patients' (Clients) Satisfaction with Medical Laboratory Services Contributes to Health and Quality Improvement, A Chapter in Healthcare Access (Ed.) Prof. Amit Agrawal IntechOpen. https://doi.org/10.5772/intechopen.99290.
19. Folinas S, Obeta MU, Etim GU, Etukudoh NS. (2021). COVID-19 Pandemic: The Medical Tourism and its Attendant Outcome for Nigeria. IOSR Journal of Business and Management 23(7).VI, pp. 26–35.
20. Verma R. (2022). Smart City Healthcare Cyber Physical System: Characteristics, Technologies and Challenges. Wireless Personal Communications. 122:1413–1433. https://doi.org/10.1007/s11277-021-08955-613.
21. Hovorushchenko T, Hryshchuk I, Hovorushchenko O, Rei K, Boyarchuk A. (2023). Mobile Cyber-Physical System for Monitoring the Health of Patients with Cardiovascular Diseases. CITRisk'2022: 3rd International Workshop on Computational & Information Technologies for Risk-Informed Systems, January 12, 2023, Neubiberg, Germany. CEUR Workshop Proceedings (CEUR-WS.org) Vo1-3422/Paper 8.
22. Obeta UM, Njar VE, Etukudoh NS, Obiora OR. (2023). Applications of Information Management Systems (IMSML) in Medical Laboratories. Chapter 26 in Alex Khang (Eds.) AI and IoT-Based Technologies for Precision Medicine, pp. 447–463. https://doi.org/10.4018/979-8-3693-0876-9.ch026.

Transformative Impact of Modern Technology on Healthcare: Advancements, Challenges, and Opportunities

Nkereuwem Sunday Etukudoh, Obiora Reginald Ejinaka, Uchejeso Mark Obeta, and Iye Wariso Kalu

Abstract Technological advancement has been tremendous in recent years and cuts across every aspect of human activities, and it has changed the way we do certain things in everyday life and industrial activities including healthcare. Hospitals and healthcare facilities have introduced the use of technology to make their systems easier to access and provide more diagnosis and accurate results thereby making treatment options for patients more precise based on the individuality of their health challenges. Use of modern technologies in healthcare encouraged virtual consultation with healthcare professionals while the availability of smart mobile devices and applications have gained grounds as standards for ease of access to quality healthcare services irrespective of location or social status. Most medical laboratory and diagnostic equipment are technologically improved for global sharing such as microscopes, various analysers, MRI, X-Ray, CT scans, ECMO, PET, dialysis machines, heart–lung machines, among others. The chapter reviewed various literatures in relation to technology as currently applied in healthcare with its associated challenges. The challenges includes but not limited to: cybersecurity challenges, ownership and sharing of data, data breaches, cyber-attacks, data security and privacy, outdated technologies and equipment, poor messaging systems and communication among professionals, poor knowledge of ICT and emerging technologies by health professionals,

N. S. Etukudoh
Office of the Provost/CEO, Federal College of Medical Laboratory Science and Technology, Jos, Nigeria

O. R. Ejinaka
Office of the Provost Academics, Federal College of Medical Laboratory Science and Technology, Jos, Nigeria

U. M. Obeta (✉)
Department of Medical Laboratory Management, Federal College of Medical Laboratory Science and Technology, Jos, Nigeria
e-mail: uchejesoobeta@fcmlst.edu.ng

I. W. Kalu
Department of Information and Communication Technology (ICT), Federal College of Medical Laboratory Science and Technology, Jos, Nigeria

M. Mittal and J. Narayan (eds.), *Intelligent Cyber-Physical Systems for Healthcare Solutions*, https://doi.org/10.1007/978-981-97-8983-2_19

inefficiency of healthcare systems, poor structures to install new technologies, cost and accessibility, interoperability and standardisation, technology integration and usability, and ethical considerations. This paper provides and encouragement that though, the challenges are noted, the same technology can be applied to solve the lingering challenges for better healthcare improvement at the resource limited certain. The application of ICT has improved healthcare delivery in the twenty-first century better than it was in the past. Modern technologies have made it possible for health-care professionals to perform tests and or monitor patients and equally generate data that play an important role in identifying and treating illnesses and diseases and as well aids disease surveillance. Remote monitoring systems give rooms for patients to track and monitor their medical conditions without regular visit to doctors as noted in the case of diabetic and cardiac patients.

Keywords ICT challenges · Healthcare · Real-world computing · Artificial intelligence · IoTs · Cloud computing · Cyber security

1 Introduction

Technology can be defined as the use of improved seamless scientific cognition and skills to solve practical daily needs of humans. It affects every aspect of our everyday life, from increased communication, office productivity, education, commerce, information security, healthcare amongst others.

The main aim of technology is to solve problems and meet needs of man with less human efforts or involvement. Human beings always look for better and easier ways to solve problems and the use of technology can be definite in getting it done. Technology could be said to be as old as the existence of the human race and the first technological invention by man was stone tools originated about 2 millenium ago, used for blowing metals and other uses. In modern days, technologies are applied in every aspect of human life, with healthcare as an instance.

The advancement in technology developed the aspect of information communication technology (ICT) to be applied in healthcare much more than expected leading to healthcare intelligence, data mining, machine learning, automation and robotics, cyber system computing, internet of healthcare things (IoHTs) and very many of them to mention in healthcare [1]. Khosla et al. [2] expatiated that COVID-9 multiplied the use of technology in healthcare especially with tele-healthcare.

2 Technological Developments in Our Modern World

The technological developments in agreement with other authors [3, 4] spread across the following areas.

2.1 Communication

Information and communication technology comprises different means and techniques adopted by people to transmit and receive information among one another. Among the early models of the communication technology were the Telegraph and Morse Code while the modern days' examples include Television (TV), Internet and Cell phones.

2.2 Electricals

Various modern technology are in the form of electricity to an extent, among which are Artificial Intelligence (AI), Computers and Software, Circuitry, Audio and visual technology (like projectors, cameras, microphones).

2.3 Medicals

Application of technology in medical practice assists people to live better in various ways, among of which include the following:

Diagnostics where the medical professionals can access more patient's details with ease such as medical history, allergies and other information by use of microscopes, thermometers, X-ray and MRI machines, electrocardiographs, Point of care testing devices, stethoscopes, wearable and biosensors. These tools help medical professionals make a more informed judgement of patient's case with better therapeutic choices and can access and assess some body parts that ordinarily wouldn't be possible to analyze.

2.4 Pharmaceuticals

The evolution and transformation of medical practices have led to better technological advancement in the pharmaceuticals as well. Various technologies like synthetic organs, nanotechnology, and microchips are employed by researchers and practitioners to understand better how different chemicals and pharmaceutic products affect humans. They use the knowledge to develop divers prescription medicines cure or significantly reduce cases of unsafe drugs.

2.5 Surgicals

Surgical technology is applicable in any aspect of surgery, including simple procedures like appendectomy to complex ones like brain or spinal surgery. The use of technology has assisted surgeons in performing complicated operations. They now employ smart glasses that can reveal essential details directly in the surgeon's glasses and distant robotics enable the surgeons conduct surgeries virtually with maximum precision.

2.6 Health Monitoring

Monitoring patient's health status by healthcare professionals rely tremendously on the use of technology, and examples abound such as smart watches, that have the capacities to monitor biometric data (like quality of sleep and heart rates, and implant devices placed directly in a patient's body and are capable of providing more innovative monitoring efficiencies to healthcare professionals.

3 Advantages and Benefits of Technology in Healthcare

The advent and adoption of modern technology in the healthcare industry has changed the many ways that things were done. The impacts of leveraging technology in healthcare that are revolutionizing the industry are summarized in agreement with other positions [3–5].

3.1 Electronic Medical Record

The collection of patient's data is among the most important duties in healthcare. Patient's data are very important for analysis of the patient's medical conditions and possibly find a solution for it by the physicians and other healthcare professionals. To document and access patient's records in the past was very cumbersome and tedious because of the large volumes of paperwork to record everything using paper and pen. With digitisation, the medical records of patients can be easily inputted into a cloud based, digitalised system, known as Electronic Health Records (EHRs) or Electronic Medical Records (EMRs), which comprises patient and population health information stored electronically. EMRs make it easier for physicians to obtain patients' medical records and histories, including previous diagnoses, laboratory reports, surgeries, prescriptions and even details of hospital admissions to make informed decisions faster. This can be accessed by anyone involved on the patient management with just a click of a button from anywhere at any time [6, 7].

3.2 Reduction in Medical Errors

Medical errors are inevitable as is obtained in every human performance and are on the increase thereby raising public concerns due to repeated occurrence consistently. This accounts for the 3rd leading cause of death worldwide [1].

Technology has however facilitated systems development that help to reduce medical errors significantly and saving more lives. The Clinical Decision Support (CDS) system provides the healthcare professionals with patient specific information and medical records that are filtered and made available to the healthcare providers at when the need arises to enhance their decision making. This can provide evidence-based standards and guide, protocols, rules and advice for better care.

3.3 Improved Patient Care

The availability of advanced technological tools has provided the healthcare community with improved patient care. The tools has increased patient engagement, and provide insights to assist create reference point, wellness and personalized health plans. These tools are in the form of Health Apps, Devices and Gadgets [7].

With the Health Apps, patients can quickly access accurate medical information with their smart phones and use the Apps to track their appointments with healthcare providers, reminders, and access test results with ease. Physicians also use the Apps to access information about drug and use by patient to avoid debilitating side effects, resolve any issues and improved diagnosis. Smart watches, wearable devices such as fitness bands, and other wireless devices are capable to monitor patient's blood glucose, pressure, Uric acid, hemoglobin, cholesterol, and Electrocardiograph (ECG), and give patients and specialist ease of access to personalized information. The devices also depict calorie levels, exercise checks, and blood pressure variations. Such new technological diagnostic materials aiding healthcare improvement are highlighted in Fig. 1. Virtual Reality (VR) devices and apps help to reduce signs of anxiety and depression in older individuals and psychiatric patients. Radio-frequency identification (RFID) technology has improved patient care by providing information about a patient's vital signs and temperature.

Specialists can also track patients' health information more efficiently such as adherence to their treatment plans, diets, and life style changes. This is more pertinent for elderly people and people living alone, to promptly alert family members or healthcare providers of any abnormality emergency observed. The technology ensures that patients enjoy greatest care, deepening the healthcare experience and quality for the populace [7, 8].

Fig. 1 Some new technological approach that tends to improve healthcare

3.4 Improved Communication

Emergent technologies have expedited improved communication among the healthcare communitiess, between care providers and patients. More healthcare professionals now leverage on technology to communicate and spread knowledge among themselves via real-time meeting capacities, video conferencing, AR/VR, and other online platforms.

Patient education and counseling are essential in medical practice and specialists are adopting divers' technologies to help inform and engage patients better. There are software and applications that used to provide customized health education to specific patients according to their specific needs and conditions.

As an instance, Patient Electronic Portal, a secure online application, provides patients access to their personal health information and a 2-way electronic information system with the Healthcare provider by use of a computer or mobile device. Past studies reported that the application increases patient's compliance to medical advice, self-awareness and management of their illnesses [9].

3.5 *Big Data Management*

Big data are large magnitudes of complex or rapid data that can't be processed easily with conventional methods. Health technology lets accountants in medical facilities gather large data within a space of time. Data collection assists healthcare professionals learn and infer forefront techniques and trends. The data are applicable for predictions and analysis about possible disease outbreak and identifying risk factors. Access to big data also allows clinicians to recommend suitable preventive measures more effectively and reducing death rates. In addition, cloud storage of data guarantees higher efficiency and accessibility with less wastage. This is very important in medical research and development of new treatments and lifesaving drug formulations [10].

Cloud storage is a cost-effective and secure method that has recovery and back-up features, and are maintained/managed without the need for additional server hardware. This is an invaluable benefit for medical research and analysis for efficient health information transmission and exchange.

4 Technology and Applications Employed in Healthcare

Several technologies and applications have been employed in healthcare with numerous benefits and improvement in the medical services. Information communication technology is a major component of such technologies. The use of information technology has contributed significantly and will continue to enhance healthcare delivery towards improving the quality of healthcare for better life [7]. Ngafeeson [8] did not mince words in showing that some medical errors are reduced and overall quality of care improved with better patients' outcome including: accurate, complete, and structured medical data documentation; "automatic sorting and summarization of data", direct access to patient records and real time updates on patients' condition, reduced data entry mistakes, increased medical decision support, appropriate data mining, rapid dissemination of health information like medical laboratory results and quicker nursing care with good monitoring of care.

In a single parameter monitoring system like only glucose of a patient, only one healthcare technological application or instrument like a glucose sensor patch may be sufficient, but in the case of monitoring a detailed status of any patient, it may require many parameters and permits many wearable devices and wireless sensors to monitor the patients' heart rate with less stress, blood pressure, oxygen level, blood circulation, haemoglobin, breathing rate, muscle activities, uric acid, movement patterns, ECG, body inclination, and oxygen uptake as a multi-parameter system. Such multi-parameter system may involve using wearable and biosensors in form of bracelet, rings, eye glass, watches, rings belts, pants, socks, shirts, shoes meant for parameters of interest with necessary connections and links to healthcare providers no matter the locale of the patient.

With the advent of improved technologies, several applications in healthcare can be in virtual or biophysical form (Fig. 2) and many of them are evident as seen in Fig. 3. A lot of healthcare success stories in remote monitoring of patients are emerging after COVID-19 pandemic. Though we are yet to record rampart availability of wearable and biosensors in Nigeria, we encountered a patient that spends over Four Thousand Naira daily to visit the clinic because of his non communicable health status. The patient was diagnosed with Hypertension and Diabetes. After explaining his challenges especially as it affects time, travels, and financial expenditure. Our health Team advised the patient to buy Glucometer and Digital BP Monitor of which he gladly did and the Medical Laboratory Scientist and Nurse among our team were assigned to teach him the usage of the bought monitors. He was introduced to the use of his Android Phone to make WhatsApp video calls. The patient had a video call with the Nurse after checking the BP and as well had a video call with the Medical laboratory Scientist after the result of sugar is displayed for confirming the results. He then finally had a video call with the Doctor for medical advice and possible prescription. This client stayed for 6 months without visiting any clinic and was full of appreciation for helping his life and saving a lot of money for him. With the use of improved technologies, this patient may be at home for 2 years without visiting clinic physically. There is no doubt that many patients are taking queue in such online and monitoring services. Nigeria is the next market for new healthcare technological monitoring gadgets as many are demanding for remote monitoring packages.

Some of the improved technologies and numerous applications in healthcare [11] can be inform of the following:

- **Symptom checking and triage:** This is a kind of information to automatically assess disease progress/diagnosis, disease prediction, prevention, and outbreaks.

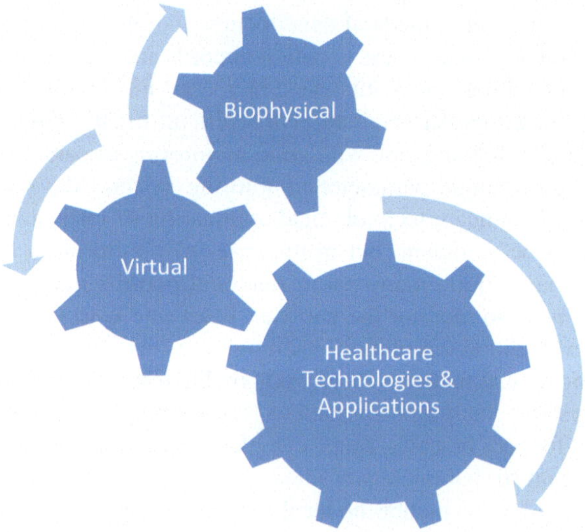

Fig. 2 Nature of healthcare technologies and applications

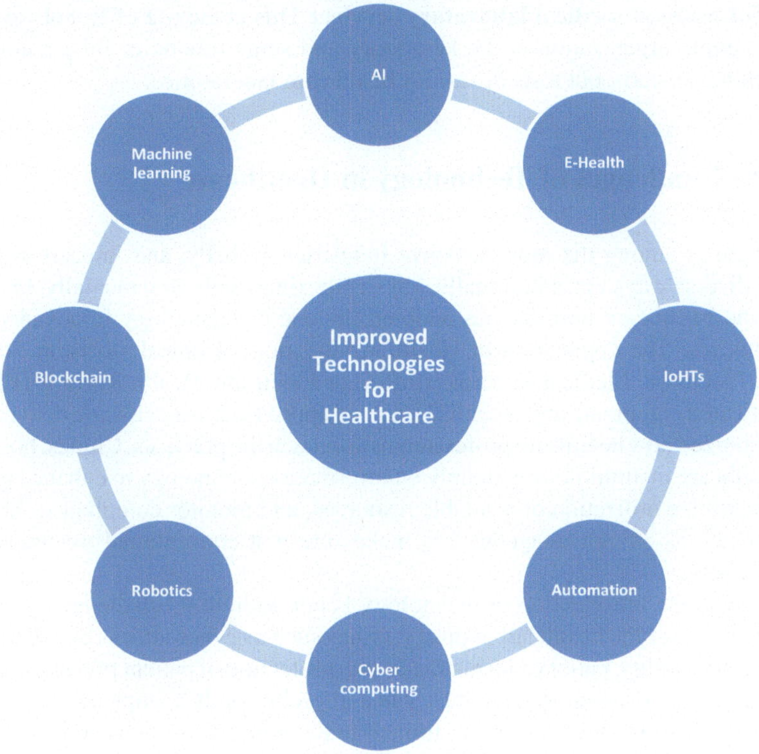

Fig. 3 Some technologies employed in healthcare

- **Robot-assisted surgery:** This is the use of Robots to carry out surgery.
- **Virtual nurses:** This is where a nursing care is provided from a very far place with use of technology and in some cases medical gadgets such as heartbeat trackers, Oximeters, and pulse rate checking.
- **Planning treatment and management of medication:** This employs real-time availability of patients' data and medical history to consult, treat and manage the patient.
- **Precision medicine:** This employs individual variability in genes, environment and lifestyle to manage and prevent an emerging disease.
- **Health monitoring:** This entails the use of biosensors and wearables to track patients' patient health towards making a medical predictions and decisions after a precise measurement of health data variables and its analysis.
- **Health-care system analysis:** This system uses industrial engineering tools and human factors analysis to contribute in treatment of patients safely. The Chief Executives and administrators use this system to assess performance of their healthcare facilities.

- **Robot-assisted medical laboratory service:** This is the use of Robots to carry out sample organization in the laboratory and some robotic or fully automated machines to carry out tests in various healthcare laboratories.

5 The Challenges of Technology in Healthcare

Healthcare is among the most sensitive industries globally, and impacts people's lives in diverse ways viz; emotionally, physically, financially, and mentally. In recent times, the healthcare industry has adopted the use of technology in advancement of healthcare. The application of Health Applications, Clinical Decision Support (CDS), Electronic Medical Records (EMRs) or Electronic Health Records (EHRs), Sophisticated equipment and other ICT enabled approaches in healthcare delivery has revolutionized how healthcare professionals approach the practices. Clinics, hospitals and healthcare institutions rely mainly on information technology to enhance patient care, maximize utilization of available resources, and monitor compliance. Most of the innovations are advantageous and make sure that conventional treatments are very effective.

However, the introduction of technology is not without its challenges. With the growing needs of the healthcare industry, issues such as cyber-attacks and data security, interoperability, patient data management, protection of patient privacy, communication etc., have arisen as the industry heavily relies on ICT implementation. The challenges [7, 8] include but are not limited to the points (Fig. 1) listed below.

5.1 Cybersecurity Challenges

Healthcare organisations have access to extremely sensitive and valuable data such as patient health records and large financial data. They are over reliant on internet of healthcare things (IoHTs), internet of Medical Laboratory things (IoMLTs) or Internet of Medical Things (IoMT) or devices to provide medical care. Hacking or attacks on these networked devices can result in data breeches and disruption to adequate care [12]. The healthcare industry is a target for cybercriminals globally, and therefore needs a strong cybersecurity to identify, protect and prevent common attack vectors.

Cybersecurity challenges especially in IoT related issues, depending on the specific layer of concern should be noted that confidentiality is rooted from all-embracing security and that security originates from the need to maintain strict privacy. The protection of patients' confidential information or data from illegitimate access and right to control access to such data is best described as security and privacy [13].

5.1.1 The Security at Perception Layer of IoHTs

This layer consists of radio frequency identification (RFID), sensors, devices, and actuators with the following security risks in line with [12–14]:

i. **Denial of Service (DoS)**—DoS attack by intruders disrupts service because of limited capacity of computation around the detectors and other appliances within the sensing layer.
ii. **Brute force**—This employs an exhaustive search for possible combinations username and passwords to access a network, device or account.
iii. **Malicious node insertion**—This involves the insertion of a malicious, fake node together with real nodes to access and control the IoT network of the healthcare.
iv. **Hardware jamming**—This occurs when an attacker physically changes a node's element or any of the components to damage and disrupt services.
v. **Embedded passwords**—This is where the hackers gain control using embedded passwords that were stored to help technicians without encryption for the purpose of remote troubleshooting or installing updates.
vi. **Default credentials**—This is credentials expected to be changed after installation and training of which in most cases, the healthcare users continue to use them without change. Examples are the use of Admin as username and password and is continued to be used.

5.1.2 The Security at Gateway Layer of IoHTs

This is the middle layer in IoHTs and are associated with security risks such as:

i. **DoS**—As in the perception layer, attacks on DoS impede connection between devices and servers in the lower and higher strata.
ii. **Man-in-the-middle**—An attacker while monitoring a non-encrypted communication can take hold of and take the health data being transmitted.
iii. **Session hijacking**—Here, an attacker gets a session token or identification, to be able to take control of a session thereby having a good network access.

5.1.3 The Security at Cloud Layer of IoHTs

Cloud layer is the top layer of IoHT where controlling and monitoring of IoT devices can be possible. The security concerns are:

i. **Data breach**—This occurs when an unauthorized or external person to the system penetrates, infiltrates, transmits or have access to confidential data. Data breach is an intentional and malicious attack on healthcare data, and such must be guided.
ii. **Data leak**—This is possibly unintentional but not malicious as a result of human error. This can be in the form of information transmission to external, unauthorized entities, like other employees or patients in the form of unexpectedly attaching delicate text file to an email of such a legitimate individual.

iii. **Insider threat**—This is a malicious intention for a worker or former worker, employees, contractors and partners to have access to the cloud thereby stealing confidential information or altering same while remaining unnoticed.

iv. **Application vulnerability**—This is a situation where applications are saved on the cloud level for user interface purposes which can increase cyber security risks. Hackers and Attackers can gain access to the cloud network using some methods like backdoors, address resolution protocol (ARP) poisoning or cross-site scripting (XSS).

v. **Malware**—This can increase cyber vulnerability.

5.2 Cyber Attacks, Data Security and Privacy

Data Security is among the most serious challenges that the healthcare industry face today. It is plagued by a myriad of cyber security related issues and vast amount of patient data held by medical organisations make them prime targets. With the increasing use of Electronic Health Records (EHRs) and interconnected systems, protecting patient data from breeches and unauthorized access becomes crucial [8].

Data security and privacy would require that new technologies use large volumes of data to train and evaluate healthcare staff. Inappropriate use or unauthorized access to healthcare data needs to be handled with caution and right data security protocols should be taught and provided. Security of data should be of optimum importance to avoid data breaches and vulnerabilities in data management, transmission and sharing at various areas [4] (Fig. 4).

Fig. 4 Challenges associated with technologies in healthcare

5.3 Ownership and Sharing of Data

The ownership and data sharing of healthcare data has challenged technologies applied in healthcare for improvement. Such could also affect healthcare research, individual freedoms, and professional usage. Ownership of data is determined by the one's legal right or actual ability to prevent others from using the same data especially in healthcare [14]. In healthcare where one particular profession claims ownership of patients, the other professional ease of assessing patients data and information using same portal creates a big challenge. The healthcare leadership and healthcare system improvement Engineers have to create opportunities for accessing information within one system for various professionals without rancor and interference so as to equilibrate the involvements of different stakeholders (society, Doctors, Pharmacists, Medical laboratory Scientists, Nurses, researchers, and patients) and also overcome economic, technological, ethical and legal challenges.

5.4 Data Breaches

Healthcare organizations use and store large amounts of data and the advent of Electronic Health Records (EHR's) means that this data must be available to patients. Data breaches occur when there is a serious need for proper device management and encryption of sensitive data related to patients. Data breach simply implies that unauthorized person in the healthcare system gains access no matter the means.

5.5 Outdated Technologies and Equipment

There has been existing equipment with their level of technology before arrival of new technologies. For example, some 2G network structures may not be compatible with 4G network structures and technology. This implies that such outdated technology and equipment must be replaced for the needed new technology to be in place. The difficulty and cost of such changes is also a challenge in healthcare.

5.6 Poor Messaging Systems and Communication Among Professionals

When a new technology is introduced in a healthcare system, poor messaging and communication issues are a human challenge as it involves many different stakeholders that needs a very good communication for the success. This entails communication between healthcare professionals and patients, software developers, interaction designers, and their clients. There is a need for a common comprehensible language for procurement, installation, training and streamlines for collaboration in the future [15].

5.7 Poor Knowledge of ICT and Emerging Technologies by Health Professionals

In the first place, new technology introduced to healthcare should be accompanied by enough training for all medical and health professionals expected to use such technology e.g., automated tools and software. There is supposed to be updated training once in a while, but in most cases, there is apathy to change an improvement among professionals. The professionals are expected to grow with the growth in technology. In some cases, it is slow to adapt due to low enthusiasm to adopt the new technologies maybe because of lack of confidence and knowledge about the technology or slow to change [16].

5.8 Inefficiency of Healthcare Systems

Epileptic power supply especially in healthcare sectors as seen in Nigeria [17] contributes to the inefficiency of healthcare that needs latest technologies. The inefficiency cuts across all areas ranging from professional approach to regulatory authorities. Nigerian healthcare is politicized to the extent that if you are not in tune with the ruling Party, your government and private approach to healthcare would be suppressed. Government Agencies suppress others without recourse to patients or the system improvement.

5.9 Poor Structures to Install New Technologies

This poor structure is mostly experienced in developing countries where dilapidated structures and poorly planned buildings and structures are used for healthcare services. New technological fittings are nearly impossible to install except when the structures are renovated or rebuilt to suit the purpose for installing new technologies.

5.10 Cost and Accessibility

In the first instance, the cost and access to new technology vendors is usually seen as herculean task but this cost and accessibility is not indefinite. Cost for example in Nigerian Healthcare, most technologically improved equipment is procured with the help of international partners or donations. Some private healthcare organizations get the equipment as Loans with understanding to procure the reagents and consumables from the manufacturers or distributors. All the equipment are in hard currencies to the extent that Naira equivalent is discouraging to use for the procurement.

This chapter shall not be complete without elaborating on the measures to mitigate and address cost barriers in resource limited certain taking Nigeria and Africa in general as an example. The healthcare provision is one of the key roles of government, and these measures may be referring to government, however, the private healthcare organizations need such measures. The following are helpful in ensuring adoption of modern healthcare technologies not minding the cost related implication:

i. **Government subsidies:** Governments of low-resource countries, Nigeria for instance, can provide subsidized rates for internet, medical technologies, applications and equipment to reduce the cost burden on individuals and healthcare facilities.
ii. **Funding for research and development:** Governments and organizations can fund medical research and development of new technologies in healthcare, which can ultimately lead to lowering the costs of the technologies in the future because of the local content.
iii. **Donor support:** International donor organizations and agencies, manufacturers and distributors can provide financial support for the procurement and distribution of medical technologies in low-resource countries. Alternatively, the needed new technologies can be enlisted by the requiring organization and the donors provide them without giving the financial value. This would reduce corruption associated with leaders in developing countries.
iv. **Local production support:** Governments can encourage and support local production of medical and health technologies from available local materials, which can reduce the cost of importing them from other countries.
v. **Public–private partnerships:** This entails government collaboration with private companies to develop and distribute medical and health technologies at affordable prices. Such partnership should thoroughly identify healthcare issues and solutions to ensure best outcome in health indices
vi. **Price negotiations:** It is better for Governments to negotiate with medical and health technology manufacturers to lower the cost of their products and services for her citizen than individual approach. Such bilateral relationship

and discussion will attract more healthcare technologies to be used in such a low-resource country.

vii. **Bulk purchasing:** Governments and healthcare facilities can leverage their collective purchasing power to negotiate bulk discounts for medical technologies. This shall be the case in procuring Medical laboratory equipment, BP monitors, wearable gadgets, batches, biosensors, and so on.

viii. **Technology sharing:** Developed countries can share their medical technology knowledge and expertise with low-resource countries, allowing for more affordable production and distribution of these technologies at realistic affordable prizes.

ix. **Health insurance coverage:** Governments can establish health insurance schemes to cover the cost of medical and health technologies for low-income individuals and organizations especially government owned healthcare facilities.

x. **Transparency in pricing:** Governments can enforce regulations that require the medical and health technology manufacturers to be transparent about their pricing and ensure that it is fair and affordable for organizations and individuals from her countries.

xi. **Education and training:** Investment in education and training programs by governments for ICT experts, healthcare professionals and researchers in low-resource countries to increase their proficiency in production, using and maintaining medical and health technologies, thereby reducing the need for costly external technical support.

xii. **Recycling and reuse:** Governments and healthcare facilities can promote the recycling and reuse of medical and health technologies to reduce the need for frequent replacement, purchase and maintenance thereby reducing costs on healthcare facilities.

xiii. **Sustainable procurement policies:** Governments can adopt sustainable procurement policies that prioritize the purchase of cost-effective medical and health technologies, encouraging manufacturers to produce and sell at lower prices.

xiv. **Tele-healthcare:** The government should make Tele-health policies functional and healthcare professionals should be ready to use of tele-healthcare which can help to reduce the cost of medical and health technologies, as it enables remote consultations and diagnoses. Invariably, tele-healthcare leads to reducing the need for expensive equipment.

xv. **Awareness and demand generation:** Governments and healthcare institutions can raise awareness about the availability and benefits of new medical and healthcare technologies in low-resource countries to increase demand and potentially drive down costs. For instance, the awareness on Blood Pressure, and Glucose Monitor wearable and biosensors for all patients suffering Hypertension and Diabetes respectively on knowing that they must not be in the healthcare facility for their parameters to be monitored would be glad to get the technological instrument for use.

5.11 Interoperability and Standardization

Interpretability especially in technologies involving deep learning models are difficult to interpret thereby making the understanding of the result difficult especially as the size of network increases. The standard of practice should in no way be compromised by new technologies in healthcare. This is achieved when the responsible technology user is well trained to diagnose and interpret the findings.

5.12 Technology Integration, Synchronization and Usability

The healthcare system is made up of numerous subsystems. Such technology to work should be well made to be used is supposed to be integrated and synchronized to solve all healthcare processes and stakeholders with contrasting needs and concerns. It is a major challenge to make complex systems and the technology that have a clear perspective on how the various systems are related and where they are dependent on one another.

It is necessary to define uniform communicating protocols so that different products from different developers can work together.

5.13 Ethical Considerations

The ethical considerations of technology in healthcare cannot be in isolation with the four basic principles of non-maleficence, autonomy, beneficence and justice. There maybe risks from device information leakage and social networking when technology is employed between healthcare giver and patients [18].

Though there are ethical challenges, unclearness in the laws governing technologies are still germane issues. Although some laws may be available to secure information, many laws and ethical regulations may be very ambiguous as there seems to be no clear denotation on the issue of responsibility and the limit of information [19].

Data breach contributes to ethical issues in technology aided healthcare patient's rights on privacy and confidentiality may be affected. However, the source of information or leakage could lead to ethical discussion. There could be a case of a healthcare professional liability for failure of technological equipment or gadgets [17].

6 Way Forward with Technology in Healthcare in the Midst of Challenges

New technologies are very much welcomed in healthcare industry across the globe. The new technologies shall soon bridge the gap of medical tourism and associated capital flight especially from Africa [20]. The COVID-19 experience expanded the use of healthcare technologies [21–23] and should not be discontinued or discouraged.

Addressing the challenges possibly with the new technologies remains germane in the innovations. All hands must be on deck to protect consumer rights, and the associated privacy [17, 19].

The policy makers should ensure adequate security and privacy protection laws while the technical authorities and technology vendors should find technological means to prevent technicians from leaking information. In healthcare, ICT officers should detect and determine related devices that can cause information leakage and ensure their protection. Such devices should include but not limited to "unauthorized link to medical machines, sensors, entryways, fog nodes, and mobile devices that acquire, combine, process, and transfer medical data to the cloud" [24].

All associated interference must be noted and adequately monitored to disallow any form of threat. It is recommended that strong validation algorithms and befitting management systems for each technology are used to dismiss and stop unauthenticated requests [25]. All healthcare technologies and wireless sensor networks should ensure identity verification, tracking capabilities, network authorization and network firewalls that provides adequate network security and possibly with a two-factor authentication and authorization methods.

All cyber-attacks should be well understood and ICT officers well trained to prevent such possibly through the use of trusted routing mechanism, message integrity verification techniques and peer-to-peer encryption algorithms. There is a need to have an adequate checklist for all security concerns. Such checklist [26] should be dedicated to a well-trained officer for the sake of security quality control.

For Domain-specific Security Concerns

Are the patients' vital details like blood glucose concentrations, and results transmission through the oral pills well-encrypted and conserved?

Are virtual meter devices in insulin pumps protected from modification?

Is "Movement disorder API" in Apple smart watch checked regularly for updates?

Are human errors preventable during configurations or operations of devices?

Are System failures well-managed, despite the increased complexities and dynamics of the systems?

Are the data quality obtained by combing the medical data with some sensed data such as body motion, location or temperature well verified and immediately informed to the healthcare provider in case of emergencies?

For the Exclusive Subdomain Vulnerabilities

Is the wireless sensor network (WSN) using encryption and protection mechanisms against attacks.

Is Zigbee protocol used to communicate between sensors well-protected against detection of Zigbee networks, recordings and displaying information about the found devices?

Are the Actuators that work alongside the sensors checked for maintenance on a regular basis?

Are the Cloud systems keeping data secret by restricting it only to authorized entities and not to unauthorized access?

Are the Cloud systems keeping data not modified by any means while it is stored or transmitted through the network?

Is Classified traffic based on authorization and blocks traffic that is identified as unauthorized and allows traffic that is identified as authorized?

Are the patients and physicians and other healthcare providers well-trained to use the technology?

For the Past Vulnerability Mistakes

Is Public key encryption used instead of symmetric encryption?

Is any incoming traffic well-filtered for safety?

Is physically plugged malware prevented and instead wireless router like firewall used?

Is the Wi-Fi network is well-secured with non-default passwords?

Are the responsible teams for implementing the devices aware of installation specifications?

For the Design Concerns

Are Machine and trust boundaries identified and protected based on each boundary?

Is the patient comfortable using/wearing the remote monitoring device?

Are healthcare organizations' gadgets protected from using antivirus software?

Is the network we secured by firewalls and proxies?

Is the rapid accessibility of patient's data possible?

Are appropriate communication protocols between components used?

Do the remote devices achieve usability concern and do not require heavy training/ instruction for use?

For the Availability Concerns

Does Cloud service ensure that data and services are always available for legitimate users anytime and anywhere needed?

Are only authorized persons accessible to patient healthcare records within the organization possible?

Are prevention techniques against denial-of-service attacks used?

Is there a backup plan maintained and used when necessary?

Is there an alternative power supply for the healthcare organization resources available once needed?

From the check list questions when well handled by the responsible officer and answered in affirmation, the challenges of technologies in healthcare especially in the areas of security shall be totally overcome.

7 The Future of Healthcare Technology Evolution

The future of healthcare and medical practice globally will be greatly shaped by the continuous development and evolution of new healthcare technologies. Advances in technology have already revolutionized the healthcare industry, making treatments more effective, efficient, and accessible. As we move into the future, we can expect even more groundbreaking innovations to transform the way we approach healthcare and medical practice.

One major trend that is likely to continue is the rise of telemedicine and remote patient monitoring. Though it seems to be difficult when you mention medical laboratory science practice that needs sample to carry out diagnosis but be assured that telemedicine and monitoring gadgets would make the difference. With the integration of virtual platforms and devices, patients will be able to receive medical consultations, diagnosis and testing, monitoring, and treatment from the comfort of their own homes. This will not only improve convenience for patients but also reduce the strain on healthcare facilities and providers, particularly in rural and underserved areas of low income countries of the world.

Machine learning (ML) and artificial intelligence (AI) will play important roles in the future of healthcare. These technologies can analyze large volumes of data, like patient information, medical records, and scientific research, to denote forms and make predictions. This can aid in diagnosis and treatment planning, as well as predicting potential health risks and improving overall population health management.

In addition to telemedicine and AI, the use of 3D printing is also set to accelerate in the health care settings. This technology has the possibility to revolutionize the production of medical devices, prosthetics, and even organs. With 3D printing, medical professionals can customize treatments and devices for each patient, leading to better outcomes and potentially reducing healthcare costs.

The Internet of Medical Things (IoMT), Internet of Medical Laboratory Things (IoMLTs), Internet of Healthcare Things (IoHTs) and no matter how it is coined in relation to medical and health is also expected to have a profound impact on the future of healthcare. This refers to the interconnectedness of medical devices and systems, allowing for real-time data sharing and remote monitoring. This can improve patient care by providing healthcare professionals with up-to-date and accurate information, leading to more personalized and effective treatments.

Another major technological advancement that will shape the future of healthcare is precision medicine. This approach involves tailoring treatments based on a patient's genetic makeup and other individual characteristics such as lifestyle, environment, and medical history. With the help of genetics and molecular biology, Psychonanomedicine, precision medicine aims to deliver more targeted and effective treatments, resulting in better patient outcomes.

Furthermore, the use of virtual and augmented reality in healthcare is likely to increase. These technologies can aid in medical training, patient education, and even pain management. Essential and increased reality can also ameliorate the accuracy and efficiency of surgeries, reducing complications and recovery time.

Lastly, the evolution of blockchain technology has the likelyhood to transmute the healthcare industry by raising data security and interoperability. By securely storing and sharing patient data, blockchain can facilitate more efficient healthcare processes and improve patient outcomes.

The future of medical practice will be driven by advanced technologies that will improve patient care, increase efficiency, and reduce costs. With the continued development and integration of these technologies, we can expect significant advancements in the healthcare industry in the years to come. However, it's crucial to ensure that these technologies are ethically and equitably used to benefit all individuals and communities. It is the authors' opinion that all the associated healthcare technologies and improvements recorded via Artificial intelligence, data mining and healthcare information analytics, wearables, biosensors, automation, robotics, and so on; should not be ignored but improved for the next decade challenges [26–33].

8 Conclusion

The chapter has given an overview of technologies as currently associated in healthcare. Such technologies includes but not limited to Artificial intelligence, Electronic healthcare records, Internet of health things, Automation, Cyber computing, Robotics, Blockchain, Machine learning, fuzzy logic and so on. The challenges of technologies associated with healthcare are well enumerated and expatiated They includes: cybersecurity challenges, ownership and sharing of data, data breaches, cyber-attacks, data security and privacy, outdated technologies and equipment, poor messaging systems and communication among professionals, poor knowledge of

ICT and emerging technologies by health professionals, inefficiency of healthcare systems, poor structures to install new technologies, cost and accessibility, interoperability and standardisation, technology integration and usability, and ethical considerations. These challenges are caused by technologies and mostly handled by technologies in addition to political wills of government and Chief Executives of different healthcare institutions [34].

References

1. Lee, D.H., Yoon, S.N. Application of Artificial Intelligence-Based Technologies in the Healthcare Industry: Opportunities and Challenges. *Int. J. Environ. Res. Public Health*(2021), 18, 271.
2. Khosla PK, Mittal M, Goyal LM, Chachra K. Mitigate the Impact of Covid-19: Telehealth. In P. K. Khosla et al. (eds.), Predictive and Preventive Measures for Covid-19 Pandemic, Algorithms for Intelligent Systems, 2021. https://doi.org/10.1007/978-981-33-4236-1_1.
3. Liu, P., Lu, L., Zhang, J., Huo, T., Liu, S., Ye, Z. Application of Artificial Intelligence in Medicine: An Overview. *Current Medical Science.* (2021).
4. Iqbal S, Tariq M, Ayesha H, Ayesha N. AI Technologies in Health-care Applications. In Goyal LM, Saba T, Rehman A, and Larabi S (Eds), Artificial Intelligence and Internet of Things Applications in Smart Healthcare, 2021. CRC Press.
5. Etukudoh NS, Njar VE, Obeta UM, Ejinaka OR, Khang A. Automations and Robotics Improves Quality Healthcare in the Era of Digital Medical Laboratory. Chapter 24 In Alex Khang, Abdullayev V, Hybluk O, Shukla AK (Eds) Computer Vision and AI-Integrated IoT Technologies in Medical Ecosystem, 2024. CRC Press.
6. Qidwai W. Advances in Information and Communication Technology (ICT): Issues, Challenges and Opportunities for Health Care Professionals Journal of the College of Physicians and Surgeons Pakistan 2011, Vol. 21(11): 651–653.
7. Lamo Y, Rabbi F, Barendregt R. Challenges for technology innovation in health care. 2016 International Conference on Advances in Electrical, Electronic and System Engineering, 14–16th Nov 2016, Putrajaya, Malaysia, pp. 48–55.
8. Ngafeeson NN. Healthcare Information Systems Opporunities and Challenges (Ed) Meliki KP. Encyclopedia of Information Science and Technology 3rd Edition. IGI Global Press.
9. Graham S, Estrin D, Horvitz E, Kohane I, Mynatt E, Ida Sim I. Information Technology Research Challenges for Healthcare: From Discovery to Delivery. SIGHIT Record 2011. 1(1) 4–9.
10. Piasecki J and Cheah PY. Ownership of individual-level health data, data sharing, and data governance BMC Medical Ethics (2022) 23:104. https://doi.org/10.1186/s12910-022-00848-y.
11. Saba, T., Bokhari, S. T. F., Sharif, M., Yasmin, M., & Raza, M. (2018). Fundus image classification methods for the detection of glaucoma: a review. Microscopy Research and Technique, https://doi.org/10.1002/jemt.23094.
12. Patra SS, Harshvardhan GM, Gourisaria MK, Mohanty JR, Choudhury S. Emerging Healthcare Problems in High-Dimensional Data and Dimension Reduction. In Roy S, Goyal LM, Mittal M. (Eds.) Advanced Prognostic Predictive Modelling in Healthcare Data Analytics, 2021. Springer.
13. Gervais, J. (2020). Privacy vs. Security: What's the Difference? Accessed from https://us.norton.com/internetsecurity-privacy-privacy-vs-security-whats-thedifference.html.
14. Thilakarathne, N. N. (2020). Security and privacy issues in IOT environment. International Journal of Engineering and Management Research, 10(01), 26–29. https://doi.org/10.31033/ijemr.10.1.5.

15. Peterssonl L, Larsson I, Nygren JM, Nilsen P, Neher M, Reed JE, Tyskbo D, Svedberg P. Challenges to implementing artificial intelligence in healthcare: a qualitative interview study with healthcare leaders in Sweden. BMC Health Services Research (2022) 22:850. https://doi.org/10.1186/s12913-022-08215-8.
16. Lippi, G., Rin, G.D. (2019). Advantages and limitations of total laboratory automation: a personal overview. Clinical Chemistry and Laboratory Medicine 57(6): 802–811.
17. Adesoji KA, Bankole FA, Adebayo JA. The impact and challenges of information and communication technology on health care delivery in Nigeria. Munfolli Journal (1) 2021.
18. Sony M, Antony J, McDermott O. (2022). The impact of medical cyber– physical systems on healthcare service delivery. The TQM Journal 34(7), 73–93. https://doi.org/10.1108/TQM-01-2022-0005.
19. Chung, J., Demiris, G., & Thompson, H. J. (2016). Ethical Considerations Regarding the Use of Smart Home Technologies for Older Adults: An Integrative Review. Annual Review of Nursing Research, 34(1), 155–181.
20. Folinas S, Obeta MU, Etim GU, Etukudoh NS. (2021). COVID-19 Pandemic: The Medical Tourism and its Attendant Outcome for Nigeria. IOSR Journal of Business and Management 23(7).VI, pp 26–35. www.iosrjournals.org.
21. Kannan, S., Subbaram, K., Ali, S., Kannan, H. (2020). A systematic Review with narrative synthesis on medical robotics and laboratory automation in the control of SARS-CoV-2, Ebola and H1N1 (Swine Flu) viruses Journal of Health and Social Sciences; 5(2):193–208.
22. Sisman, A.R., Basok, B. I. Digitalization and Artificial Intelligence in Laboratory Medicine. *Int J Med Biochem* (2020); 3(2): 106–110.
23. Almogbil A. IoT Security and Privacy Issues A Game of Catch-Up. In Goyal LM, Saba T, Rehman A, and Larabi S. (Eds), Artificial Intelligence and Internet of Things Applications in Smart Healthcare, 2021. CRC Press.
24. Farahani, B., Firouzi, F., Chang, V., Badaroglu, M., Constant, N., & Mankodiya, K. (2018). Towards fogdriven IoT eHealth: Promises and challenges of IoT in medicine and healthcare. Future Generation Computer Systems, 78, 659–676.
25. Gayathri, P., Gopichand, G., Amali, G.B., Santhi, H.A. Case Study on Artificial Intelligence Application in Medical Diagnostics. *World Wide Journal of Multidisciplinary Research and Development*. (2018).
26. Ali A, Sina M. Recent Advances in Biosensor Technology. 2021, 3(6) https://doi.org/10.38125/OAJBS.000361.
27. Milenkovic, A., Otto, C., & Jovanov, E. (2019). Wireless sensor networks for personal health monitoring: issues and an implementation. Journal of Computer Communications,, 29(3), 2521–2533.
28. Obeta UM, Njar VE, Etukudoh NS, Obiora OR. (2023). Applications of Information Management Systems (IMSML) in Medical Laboratories. Chapter 26 in Alex Khang (Eds.) AI and IoT-Based Technologies for Precision Medicine, pp. 447–463. https://doi.org/10.4018/979-8-3693-0876-9.ch026.
29. Etukudoh NS, Obeta UM, Ejinaka OR, Etim UG. An Innovative Cloud Computing in Medical Laboratory Data Storage and Analytics. Chapter 23 In Alex Khang (Ed) Medical Robotics and AI-Assisted Diagnostics for a High–Tech Healthcare Industry 2024 IGI Global Press.
30. Verma R. (2022). Smart City Healthcare Cyber Physical System: Characteristics, Technologies and Challenges. Wireless Personal Communications. 122:1413–1433 https://doi.org/10.1007/s11277-021-08955-613.
31. Al-katrangi A, Al-kharsa S, Kharsah E, Ara A. An Empirical Study of Domain, Design and Security of Remote Health Monitoring Cyber-Physical Systems. (Eds) Goyal LM, Saba T, Rehman A, and Larabi S. 2021. CRC Press.
32. Obeta UM, Ejinaka OR, Etukudoh NS. (2022). Data Mining in Medical Laboratory Service Improves Disease Surveillance and Quality Healthcare; Chapter 17 In T. Saba et al. (eds.), Prognostic Models in Healthcare: AI and Statistical Approaches, Studies in Big Data 109, https://doi.org/10.1007/978-981-19-2057-8_17.

33. Obeta UM, Lawrence A, Etukudoh NS, Ejinaka OR, Ibanga I. Internet of Medical Laboratory Things (IoMLTs) in the High-Tech Healthcare Industry. Chapter 14 In Alex Khang (Ed) Driving Medical Diagnostics through AI-Powered Technologies and Applications 2024 IGI Global Press.
34. Obeta MU, Etukudoh NS, Okoli CC. (2021). Nigerian Medical Laboratory Diagnosis of COVID-19; from Grass to Grace as Chapter 5 of Intelligent Computing Applications for COVID-19: Predictions, Diagnosis, and Prevention (Ed.) Tanzila Saba and Amjad Rehman Khan, CRC Press Tailor and Francis Group. 84–93. https://doi.org/10.1201/9781003141105-5.

Unleashing the Power of Intelligent Cyber Physical Systems in Healthcare: A Paradigm Shift for the Workforce

Amandeep Kaur, Aaditya Sharma, Manish Kumar, and Rajesh Kumar Bhatia

Abstract The realm of healthcare is experiencing a remarkable transformation, propelled by the rise of Intelligent Cyber Physical Systems (ICPS). These groundbreaking systems possess the remarkable ability to automate numerous tasks previously undertaken by healthcare professionals. However, this progress raises concerns regarding the displacement and replacement of jobs. Delving into this pivotal issue, this chapter explores the potential impact of ICPS on the healthcare workforce, shedding light on both the challenges and opportunities that lie ahead. Additionally, it investigates the factors that will shape the future landscape of work within the healthcare industry, encompassing the vital skills and competencies required for success in this evolving paradigm. By unveiling a nuanced perspective, this chapter asserts that ICPS will undoubtedly have a profound influence on the healthcare workforce, yielding a complex blend of outcomes. While certain job roles may be displaced, the advent of ICPS simultaneously generates fresh employment prospects. Consequently, proactive measures are necessary to prepare healthcare organizations for this paradigm shift. Recommendations include strategic investment in workforce development initiatives and fostering a culture of perpetual learning.

Keywords Intelligent cyber physical systems · Healthcare workforce · Job displacement · Job replacement · Future of work

1 Introduction

Cyber physical systems integrate computational elements like software and hardware with physical devices to control, monitor and automate processes. When computational, communication and physical systems combine to generate intelligence; the resulting systems are termed as intelligent Cyber Physical Systems (ICPS). Healthcare domain has seen a rise in medical devices and medical internet of things. Wireless

A. Kaur (✉) · A. Sharma · M. Kumar · R. K. Bhatia
Department of Computer Science and Engineering, Punjab Engineering College (Deemed to Be University), Chandigarh, India
e-mail: amandeepkaur@pec.edu.in

M. Mittal and J. Narayan (eds.), *Intelligent Cyber-Physical Systems for Healthcare Solutions*, https://doi.org/10.1007/978-981-97-8983-2_20

sensor networks play an important role in extending the services of ICPS towards healthcare. ICPS in amalgamation with wireless sensor networks helps in providing high quality healthcare [1]. Internet of medical things (IoMT) interconnects and integrates the devices into health networks in order to improve the health of patients and cyber physical systems provide formal methodologies to improve IoMT [2]. Medical Cyber Physical systems are said to be the intelligent cyber physical systems applied in medical domain. Recently, various technologies such as artificial intelligence, wearable computing, cloud computing, big data analytics, blockchain, data mining etc. are being used to provide smart healthcare (Fig. 1). However, the integration of these technologies has posed new challenges for the construction of reliable, efficient and secure intelligent cyber physical systems. The authentication, access control and integration frameworks are highly researched to realize the true potential of intelligent cyber physical systems in healthcare. The integrity, availability and confidentiality needs to be ensured while sharing medical data and information over heterogeneous networks [3].

Various machine intelligence algorithms are used in conjunction with other techniques in medical cyber physical systems. The processing of data takes place using data pre-processing, feature extraction and feature aggregation techniques and decision making processes are automatized by using artificial intelligence and machine learning models. The machine learning algorithms work at the core of the medical cyber physical system, making them to be the "intelligent" aspect of such systems. The decision support system component of the medical cyber physical systems

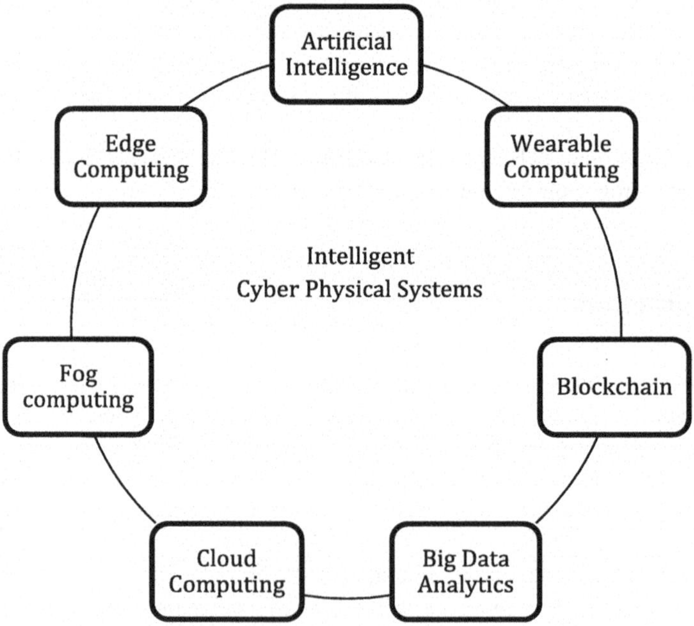

Fig. 1 Integration of technologies in intelligent CPS

consists of visualization engine, analytics engine, inference engine and training engine. These engines interact with the real time data, social network data, historical data and medical databases in order to generate the required output [4].

The medical cyber physical systems are being deployed in various hospitals to provide high quality care and continuous monitoring of patient health. There are a variety of challenges that needs to be tackled in order to develop secure and efficient medical cyber physical systems. These challenges comprise of software quality assurance, rigorous testing and interoperability, autonomous and certifiable nature of devices, context awareness and machine intelligence [5]. There are four levels of medical cyber physical systems general architecture, which are data collection, data aggregation, cloud computing and action. In order to ensure data privacy and security, different encryption techniques must be employed. However, the development of encryption approaches increases the computational cost and storage overheads. Due to differences in communication and hardware capabilities of each layer, various encryption schemes must be used to guarantee data privacy and security within those layers [6, 7]. The integration of medical cyber physical systems, health cloud, big data analytics, health fog, artificial intelligence, blockchain and Internet of health things (IoHT) have given rise to the paradigm of Health 4.0. But in order to realize its true potential, extremely strong authentication mechanisms and access control policies need to be developed [8].

Recently, a medical cyber physical system has been proposed to predict maternal healthcare risks using machine learning algorithms and Internet of things. It aims to collect metrics like blood pressure, temperature, glucose levels and heart rate. These metrics are then used to predict the health risks [9]. Another intelligent medical cyber physical system has been developed to support the diagnosis and screening of heart valve disease. This system can be installed in mobile phones for easier accessibility and efficiency of use [10].

Intelligent cyber physical systems in healthcare are bound to affect the workforce, but ideal scenario is not just the displacement of jobs. Human machine collaborations through human computer interfaces and embracing the technological advancements in the area of healthcare may lead to a positive shift in the evolving healthcare landscape. The next sections discuss the overall architecture of the intelligent cyber physical systems, impact on healthcare workforce, opportunities and challenges in the way forward towards the realization of such systems.

2 Components of ICPS in Healthcare

The layered architecture of ICPS in healthcare comprises of physical layer, cyber layer and intelligence layer (Fig. 2). It also consists of a feedback loop. There are various components of ICPS in Healthcare which are categorized under the physical, cyber and intelligence layers.

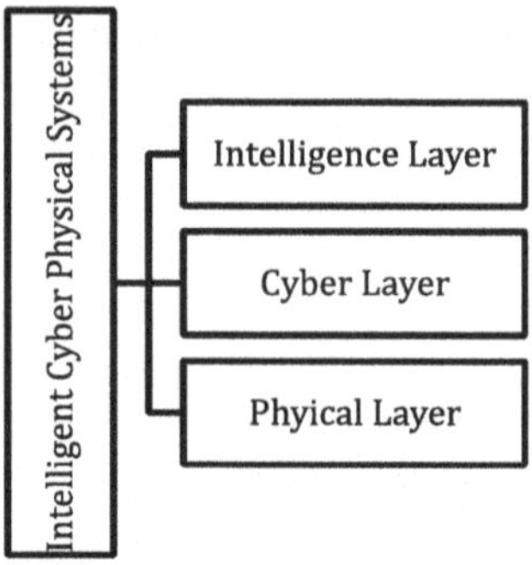

Fig. 2 Layered architecture of ICPS

(i) Physical layer:

- This acts as a low level layer which comprises of sensing nodes or devices which collect real time physiological data such as Electrocardiogram (ECG), Electroencephalogram (EEG); environmental information such as air quality, temperature, weather; user interactions such as button presses, voice recordings; and other parameters such as heart rate variability, pulse rate etc.
- Physical layer also contains actuators which are the workhorses of the machine world like drug delivery pumps, smart home appliances, blood pressure monitors, robotic surgical tools etc.
- The backbone of the physical layer is the communication network which allows all devices to connect with each other through the wireless sensor networks and internet of things. The communication network could have any topology depending upon the scenario where it is being used.
- There are a variety of other devices like wearables, fitness trackers, insulin pumps, pacemakers, implantable medical devices which are termed as Internet of Medical Things. These computing devices are embedded with low-power and real-time electronics which manages data processing, control mechanisms and various communication protocols.

(ii) Cyber layer:

- Cyber layer is the middle level layer, which consists of data acquisition and pre-processing techniques and cryptographic technologies.
- The raw sensor data acquired at physical layer is prone to noise and contain non uniform data. This is pre-processed using various kinds of noise removal, feature extraction and data augmentation techniques.
- Edge computing is one of the important technologies that are used at cyber layer to perform local level analysis and take decisions on critical data in real time.
- Machine learning and artificial intelligence helps in analysing the data for detection, prediction and monitoring of health outcomes. It also helps to generate recommendations and train supervised and unsupervised machine

learning models. The amount of data generated through physical layer devices needs to be processed using big data analytics [11].
- Cloud computing is used to store and analyse large datasets and process complex computations. Cloud based platforms perform data analysis by providing the required storage space and power. They also ensure scalability, coverage, quality, efficiency and accessibility [12].
- The cryptographic techniques ensure security and privacy of the data, data integrity, confidentiality and availability. Sensitive data of patients over the cloud must be protected and this can be managed through strong encryption, access control, intrusion detection and secure communications.

(iii) Intelligence layer:

- Intelligence layer consists of various components like decision support system, adaptive control system and human machine interface.
- Decision support systems perform data analysis using artificial intelligence and machine learning techniques and provide suitable recommendations to healthcare professionals.
- Adaptive control systems ensure the adaptability of the system in real time environments and changing conditions.
- Human machine interface provides an interconnection between users of the system and computer through interactive graphical user interfaces. Today's graphical user interfaces are equipped with augmented reality and virtual reality for better user experiences.
- There can be remote monitoring tools and telemedicine to equip the medical professionals with keeping a check on the health status of patients from a remote location [11].

(iv) Feedback loop:

- Feedback loops are closed loop control systems where data from physical world is used to adjust the behaviour of cyber world and vice versa. This continuous monitoring, analysis and control makes the intelligent cyber physical systems more effective and adaptive.
- There is a continuous feedback loop that connects all the layers together. It ensures that information exchange occurs proactively in unison considering user inputs and feedbacks.
- The interoperability between various devices and systems can be managed by incorporating feedback loop frameworks and collaborative efforts.

(v) Networking Infrastructure:

- High speed networking infrastructure is essential part of intelligence CPS in healthcare in order to provide reliable and real-time communication and data transmission between various components of the layered structure of ICPS.
- Wireless, wired and hybrid networks can be used to ensure heterogeneity, reliability and secure communications.

- Fog computing is used to bring the computations closer to the edge devices in order to reduce network traffic and ensure faster decision making.
- The ethical considerations and regulations must be taken into account while designing the network structure and deciding on the software solutions to be used in various components.

Overall, the three layers work in close coordination to realise the intelligent cyber physical systems in the healthcare domain. The general architecture of healthcare ICPS is displayed in Fig. 3.

3 What Makes ICPS Intelligent in Healthcare?

Healthcare ICPS is a combination of various technologies that aspire to achieve intelligence and impact the diagnosis, treatment, detection and overall patient monitoring and care. Following are some of the key points which make ICPS "intelligent" in Healthcare (Fig. 4).

3.1 Data-driven Intelligence

- Real-time data acquisition: Sensors are used to collect physiological, psychological, environmental, and user interaction. This helps to provide a comprehensive picture of patient healthcare.
- Advanced data processing: Techniques like edge computing, cloud computing and big data analytics combine to draw meaningful insights from raw data and identifies trends and patterns [14].
- Artificial Intelligence and Machine learning: Machine learning models learn from vast datasets and enable accurate predictions of disease progression, personalized treatment interventions and risk analysis.

3.2 Adaptive and Responsive Systems

- Edge computing: It helps in local analysis and decision making at the end system level and allows for faster response time and improvement in performance in critical and real time circumstances.
- Closed loop control: ICPS is able to adapt to real time situations and adjust the systems as per real time data. Such as adjusting the dose of medication as per patient need, activating the robotic tools for surgery on conditional basis, generating alerts during complicated situations.

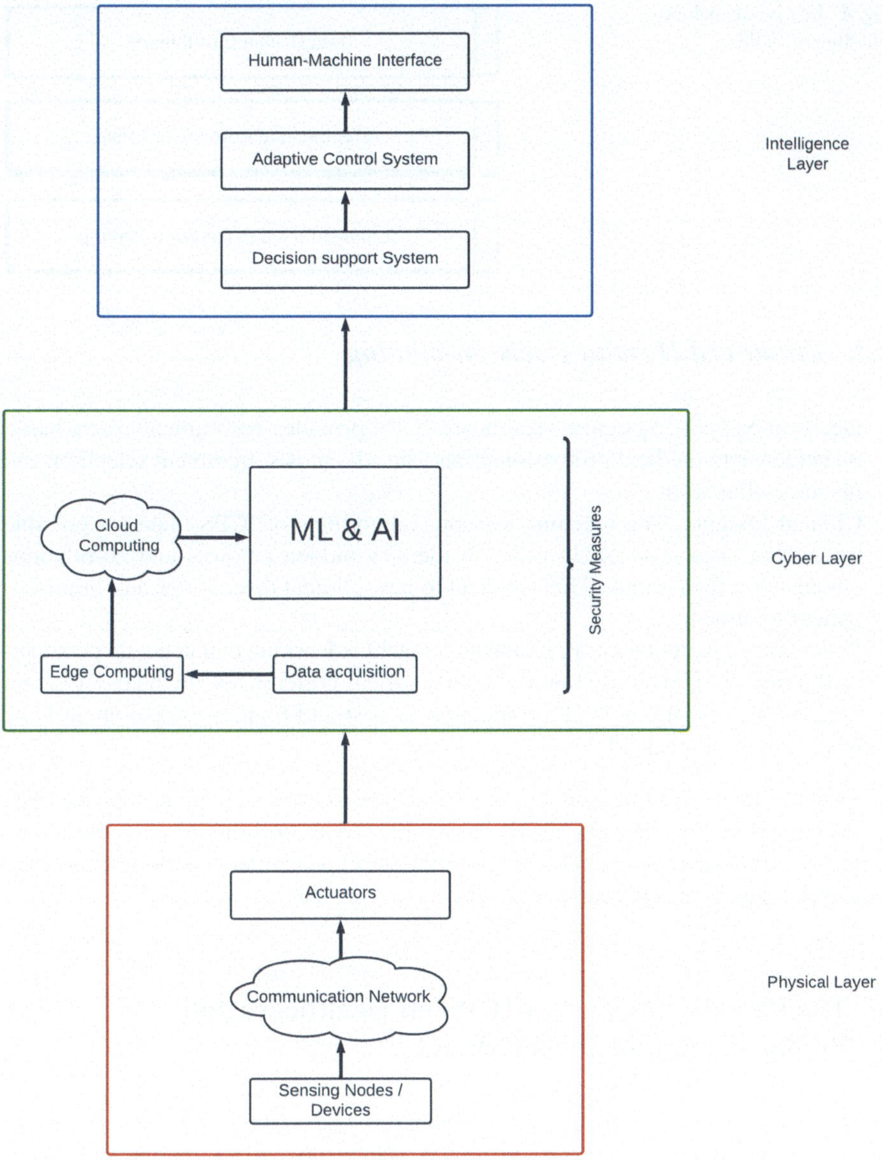

Fig. 3 General architecture of healthcare ICPS system [13]

- Adaptive Algorithms: machine learning models are trained in such a manner that they can adapt to new data and improve their accuracy over time. The effectiveness of these models is depicted from the fact that they can continuously learn from the data.

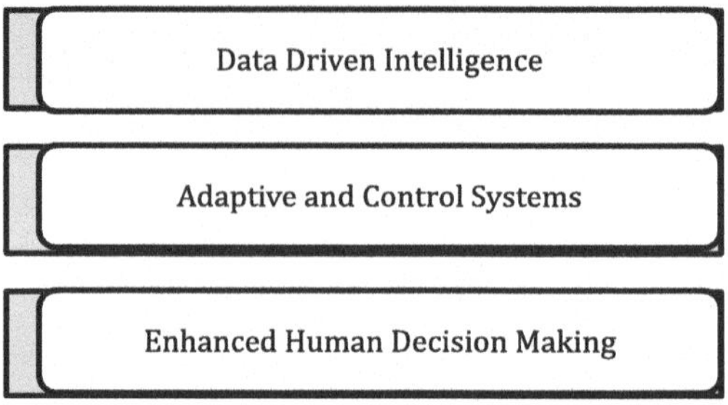

Fig. 4 Key points behind "intelligent" CPS

3.3 Enhanced Human Decision-making

- Decision Support Systems: Healthcare ICPS provides recommendations based on evidence to medical professionals and aids diagnosis, treatment selection, and resource allocation.
- Clinical Insights: The machine learning capabilities of ICPS makes it possible to analyze large datasets in order to identify hidden patterns and correlations amongst the data points. This can lead to new clinical discoveries and improved patient treatment.
- Personalized patient care: ICPS through machine learning can generate personalized treatment plans based on individual patient preferences, characteristics and medical history. It can lead to reduction of cost and higher utilizations in large healthcare systems [15].

The intelligence abilities, on the other hand, lead to several challenges such as data privacy and security, ethical considerations, bias in algorithms, responsible usage, regulatory compliances; and interoperability issues for seamless communication and data exchanges between various systems.

4 The Potential Impact of ICPS on Healthcare Job Replacement and Displacement

The introduction of ICPS in healthcare domain raises several concerns about potential job displacement, however it is multifaceted. While some jobs might be replaced or transformed, the integration of ICPS could also lead to the creation of a number of new opportunities. Following is the breakdown of the potential effects.

4.1 Jobs at Risk of Replacement: The Jobs at Risk of Replacement Can Be Divided into Three Categories as Follows

- Routine tasks: These jobs face the highest risk of replacement and can already be seen in today's market. Automation done by ICPS can computerize routine and repetitive tasks like data entry, scheduling appointments, and basic patient monitoring.
- Low skilled manual tasks: Robots and other automated systems might take over tasks like medication dispensing, basic lab tests, or patient transport, affecting some technician and support staff roles.
- Diagnostic tasks: Neural networks and machine learning models which are becoming increasingly accurate could be used to analyze medical images and data to provide a preliminary diagnosis, potentially impacting some radiologists and other diagnostic specialists.

4.2 Jobs Less Likely to Be Replaced

- Complex clinical decision-making: In order to take real time decisions, doctors and healthcare personnel cannot completely rely on ICPS. Human judgement and control during critical decision making needs to be there while providing personalized care to patients.
- Mental and emotional care: Extending necessary emotional and mental support to the patients is an integral part of providing high quality healthcare. ICPS lack the human touch and emotional intelligence needed for patient interaction support. Jobs of nurses, therapists and other care providers will definitely remain crucial in the future.
- Creative and problem-solving skills: ICPS excel at repetitive tasks and data analysis, but they lack the ability to think creatively and solve unforeseen problems. These skills will remain essential for various healthcare roles.

4.3 New Job Opportunities

As ICPS is becoming more prevalent, new job opportunities are emerging for those with the right skills and knowledge. This section discusses these new career paths that promise to revolutionize patient care, improve efficiency, and unlock new possibilities.

- Data analysts and AI specialists: Integration of ICPS systems would lead to a large inflow of complex healthcare data which would need to be analysed and processed. This will create new roles in data science and machine learning specializations.

- ICPS developers and engineers: Designing, maintaining, and integrating ICPS into healthcare systems will require specialized skills in engineering and technology.
- Human–computer interaction specialists: Designing intuitive interfaces and ensuring ethical and responsible use of ICPS will require experts in human–computer interaction.
- Healthcare educators and trainers: Preparing healthcare professionals to work effectively with ICPS will require educators and trainers specializing in technology integration.
- Cyber Security specialists: ICPS need to ensure a level of safety and privacy so that the identity of the patients as well as their personal data is not compromised. This would require a healthy investment into cyber security roles.

As per the above observations, ICPS are unlikely to cause widespread job displacement in healthcare. Instead, they will transform existing roles and create new opportunities requiring different skill sets. The key idea is to adapt and up-skill the workforce to meet the changing demands of the healthcare landscape. Additionally, the speed and extent of the displacement of jobs will heavily depend upon factors like the speed of technological advancements, healthcare system adaptations, workforce trainings and educational programmes. Continuous investment in training and education will pave the way for a smooth transition. By understanding the impact of healthcare ICPS, one can ensure that it contributes to a more effective and efficient healthcare system while minimizing the job displacement and leading to the creation of new job opportunities.

5 Impact of ICPS on Healthcare Workforce

Healthcare ICPS may revolutionize the delivery of quality healthcare and impact healthcare workforce in many ways as listed below:

- Job displacement: There can be a possible effect on routine jobs such as data entry, monitoring, nursing and scheduling. And this affects the people in administration and technical roles.
- Job transformation: There would be rising need for healthcare professionals to transform and adapt according to the challenges posed by ICPS. This change will be required to facilitate complex decision making, human interaction and adopt critical thinking.
- Rise of new job opportunities: Due to generation of huge amount of wearable sensor data, there would be a need of data analysts, human computer interaction experts and artificial intelligence specialists who can design, process, analyse, manage the data in accordance with the complexities of ICPS.
- Impact on roles and responsibilities: Healthcare ICPS automates routine workflows and allows healthcare professionals to focus on complex activities like patient care coordination, data processing and interpretation, decision making

etc. This shift in responsibilities required re-evaluation of the job profiles and skill sets in the healthcare domain.

- Training and Education Requirements: Healthcare professionals need to have new skills and competencies in order to effectively engage with ICPS. The skill set required is of data analysis, artificial intelligence, cyber security and advanced medical technologies.
- Workforce shortage and redistribution: With the streamlining of healthcare workflows by ICPS, some redistribution of workforce needs to be done. Certain tasks which were previously performed by workforce can be automated and this leads to creating demand of skilled workers in some other areas.
- Ethical and legal considerations: The integration of artificial intelligence and machine learning in healthcare domain raises concerns related to data privacy, informed consent, bias in algorithms and other errors. Healthcare workforce needs to pass through these complex challenges to ensure patient safety and meeting all compliances.
- Collaboration with technologists: Technology specialists such as data scientists and engineers develop, implement and optimize the healthcare ICPS solutions. This requires interdisciplinary collaboration for successful integration and operation of these systems.

However, the above mentioned changes bring up a significant number of challenges too. These challenges are listed as follows:

- Reskilling and up-skilling of workforce needs to be done in accordance with healthcare ICPS. The workforce needs to be equipped with the required skills to work effectively with ICPS. This needs significant investment in their training and education.
- Ethical considerations are also crucial to ensure patient privacy and security of data. Fair access of healthcare by all stakeholders needs to be ensured in this exceedingly data driven environment.
- Due to job displacements and automation, the mental health status of healthcare workers is also a point of concern leading towards stress, anxiety and resistance. The emotional well-being and empathy needs to be restored even with technological advancements, thereby maintaining the core human element.
- Resistance towards change: Some healthcare professionals who have been working with traditional methods find it difficult to adapt to the changing paradigm and are reluctant to embrace ICPS.
- Investment costs: Significant initial investment is required to implement ICPS. The investments in infrastructure, trainings, system integration etc. are required and may pose financial challenges to the healthcare organizations.
- Data integration and interoperability: For seamless integration and interoperability of healthcare ICPS solutions, systems might use disparate software and inconsistent data formats. This causes several challenges during integration.
- Security issues: Cyber security vulnerabilities, data breaches, malware attacks, unauthorized access etc. may lead to compromise of sensitive patient information and requires robust security protocols.

In order to address above mentioned challenges, continuous education and training of healthcare professionals needs to be carried out to develop relevant skills and competencies. Regulatory frameworks and standards must be followed to ensure patient safety, data privacy and regulatory compliance. Collaboration and engagement with stakeholders is also essential for addressing the challenges and driving innovation in ICPS. Apart from challenges, there lies a world full of opportunities such as the following:

- ICPS can help to streamline the healthcare workflows leading to improved patient care and better healthcare delivery.
- AI-powered systems can provide personalized treatment plans and lead to better patient experience and satisfaction. For instance, diet and exercise recommendation via mobile application could help monitoring and tracking the health status of patients of various diseases which can be controlled via dietary interventions.
- Data Analysis and Artificial Intelligence can drive new discoveries and advancements in healthcare leading to improvements in diagnosis, detection, monitoring and treatments of the patients. Data driven insights can help healthcare professionals to take complex decisions with good level of accuracy.

In order to turn these opportunities into strengths; Data literacy, digital literacy, *critical* thinking and problem solving skills are required to be developed so as to enable the healthcare workforce to make informed decisions. Interdisciplinary collaboration and effective communication between stakeholders can further lead to successful integration and operation of healthcare ICPS. Following are some more ways to address the challenges associated with the paradigm shift caused by healthcare ICPS.

- Collaborative efforts between governments, healthcare institutions and educators can help in comprehensive developments of up-skilling and reskilling programmes.
- Open communication amongst all these stakeholders will help to address concerns and anxiety related to displacement and replacement of jobs.
- The development and deployment of ICPS needs to be done in a way that follows ethical guidelines and ensures responsible usage and trust.
- Although, technology plays an important role, human skills can never be overshadowed. Communication, clear and critical thinking and collaboration plays a vital role.
- In addition, technological literacy through training programmes may help in understanding the basics of ICPS and its application in healthcare.
- Data analysis and interpretation skills can help to draw meaningful information from the raw data acquired via sensors.
- Critical thinking and problem solving skills can help with better evaluation of information and designing solutions of complex problems in dynamic environment. Adaptability and lifelong learning skills may help the workers to learn continuously and adapt to the challenging and changing healthcare practices due to introduction of dynamic digital systems like ICPS. Effective communication

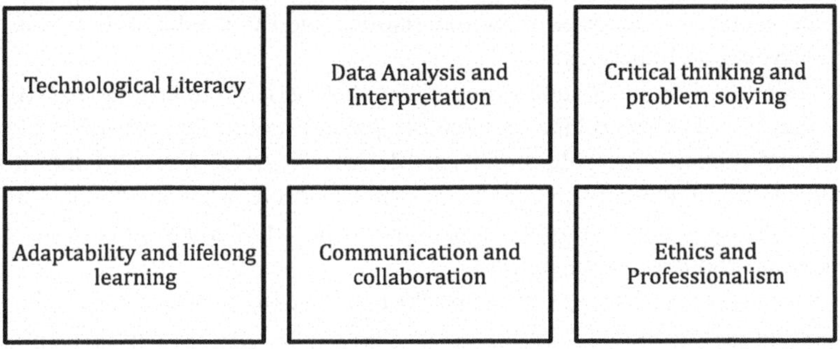

Fig. 5 Human skills and core competencies for better realization of healthcare ICPS

skills help the professionals to interact with patients and make them understand the intricacies of digital systems and technology use. These skills and core competencies may help healthcare workforce to remain the driving forces behind the ICPS and bridge the digital divide (Fig. 5).

6 The Paradigm Shift and New Opportunities

With the rise of intelligent cyber physical healthcare systems there has been a paradigm shift that leads to transformation of existing jobs and also generates fresh opportunities. Following are some key points related to this paradigm shift.

- Development and Implementation of Technology: The design, development, and implementation of healthcare ICPS solutions requires the professionals to have a variety of skills which includes software and hardware development, big data analytics, cyber-security and systems integration. This also creates opportunities for healthcare professionals who have specializations in these areas to work for various hospitals, research institutions, organizations etc.
- Data Science and Analytics: Healthcare ICPS at physical layer generate vast amounts of healthcare data through sensors and digital devices that need thorough analysis in order to extract actionable insights and information. This can lead to improvement of patient care, efficiency of operations and better clinical outcomes. There is an increasing demand of data scientists, statisticians, developers and analysts, who can collect, store, process, analyse, and interpret healthcare data. This leads to the development of personalized recommendations of medicine, predictive analytics and population health monitoring and management solutions.
- Artificial Intelligence and Machine Learning: These technologies play an important role in powering the intelligent decision support systems, predictive modelling and diagnosis in healthcare workflows. Professionals who have expertise in these technologies are required to develop and optimize these systems, in order to

provide accurate diagnosis, recommendations and other interventions based on deep learning architectures.

- Telemedicine, Tele-health and Remote Monitoring: ICPS in healthcare will facilitate the rise of telemedicine and remote patient monitoring services. This can enable the healthcare professionals to deliver care remotely and monitor the health status of patients in real time. This also creates opportunities for the medical professionals to provide consultations in virtual mode and extend remote monitoring and tele-health support.
- Cyber-security and Privacy Concerns: With the rise of connected medical devices and digital platforms, the security and privacy of the sensitive patient information becomes vital. There is a high demand of cyber-security professionals who have specialization in healthcare information systems security, encryption technique, network security etc. Secure healthcare systems are the need of the hour to protect systems from cyber threats and terrorism.
- Clinical informatics and health information management: In order to integrate ICPS, expertise is required in the areas of clinical informatics, health information management and electronic health record systems. Healthcare organizations need professionals who have deep knowledge of healthcare workflows and can understand the optimization strategies to implement and manage the ICPS solutions effectively.
- Improved patient outcomes: Healthcare ICPS enable more personalized recommendations, efficient and timely healthcare delivery leading to improvements in patient satisfaction and outcomes.
- Training and Education to strengthen healthcare workforce: Along with the adoption of ICPS solutions, there is a rising demand of professionals who can manage these solutions effectively. There is a need of training programmes, educational materials and curricula for the healthcare professionals so that they can enhance their proficiency for using the ICPS tools and technologies and increase their productivity.
- Policy development, ethics and regulatory compliance: The integration of ICPS systems in healthcare domain requires strict adherence to the ethical norms and regulatory standards governed by law. There is a need to follow the privacy laws and ethical guidelines religiously in order to avoid the misuse of sensitive information. Compliance officers and policy analysts are required to design and develop regulatory frameworks ensuring compliance with the legal requirements.
- Enhanced efficiency and productiveness: Automation of routine activities and streamlining of workflows can help to achieve operational efficiency and productiveness in the healthcare organizations.
- Expanded Access to Healthcare: Healthcare access can be expanded through telemedicine and remote monitoring. This paves the way for remote consultations, care at home based setup, and outreach to underprivileged sections of the society.
- Blockchain based ICPS: Blockchain is the latest technology to offer an optimal solutions for healthcare ICPS applications. Blockchain is vulnerable to cyberattacks, there lies opportunities for cyber security professionals [16].

The impact of healthcare ICPS may lead to creation of a number of new employment opportunities and widen the scope of healthcare towards interdisciplinary jobs across various sectors like information technology, data science and analytics, telemedicine, cybersecurity, clinical informatics and regulatory compliance. The skill and innovation required to embrace this digital transformation leads to the demand of experts in the diverse areas who can make a positive impact on the delivery of quality and effective healthcare to the patients.

7 Workforce Development Recommendations and Initiatives

For the development of workforce, there are several recommendations and initiatives that can be taken into consideration in order to address the evolving requirement of healthcare workforce to adapt with the intelligent cyber physical systems.

- Comprehensive Training Programmes on ICPS integration: In order to educate the healthcare professionals on integration, operation, management and use of ICPS in healthcare settings, comprehensive training programmes should be developed. These programmes should cover topics such as data analytics, big data, artificial intelligence applications, cyber-security, human machine intelligence, computer vision etc. The training programmes must be developed in collaborations with healthcare professionals, engineers, data scientists, developers and managers, so as to cover all the possible aspects of the subjects. This will help in building strength of the workforce to tackle new challenges and leverage opportunities.
- Continuing Education and Professional development: Healthcare professionals should be offered with continuous education and professional development opportunities in order to keep themselves updated about latest advancements, techniques and technologies related to ICPS. This may include workshops, seminars, webinar, online courses and other programmes targeted for various people in various healthcare roles and responsibilities.
- Simulation and hands on trainings: Simulation exercises may be useful to familiarize healthcare professionals with ICPS enabled solutions, virtual care platforms and decision support systems. This practical exposure will lead to increase in confidence and proficiency in using these technologies in real world scenarios.
- Industry-Academia Collaborations: Collaborations between industry and academics may be promoted in order to develop tailored curricula, training materials and certifications to enhance the knowledge exchange.
- Apprenticeship Programs: These programs help in allowing healthcare professionals to gain practical exposure working with ICPS under the mentorship of technology experts. These provide valuable hands-on-training experience to individuals who are interested in pursuing their careers in the healthcare domain.

- Diversity and Inclusiveness: The inclusiveness in workforce development supports underprivileged people, women, minorities and people with disabilities. This enriches the talent pool and fosters innovations in healthcare technologies.
- Research funding and grants: Government funding and grants may encourage budding researchers to contribute for the development of efficient healthcare ICPS. This will generate evidence based best practices and innovative approaches for training to enhance the readiness of workforce to acceptance of ICPS.
- Clinical mentorship programmes: These programmes may provide guidance to navigate through the complexities of adopting ICPS in healthcare workflows.
- Evaluation and Quality Assurance: The effectiveness of all these workforce development initiatives related to ICPS need to be evaluated and quality improvement should be ensured. Regular feedbacks should be taken from the participants and learning outcomes may be assessed. The impact of ICPS in healthcare can be maximised if these programmes are benchmarked against industry standards and refined accordingly.

In addition to above points, several research studies have also been conducted to study the barriers in realization of healthcare ICPS and digital health technologies. Table 1 describes the types of barriers in the effective realization of digital health technologies and their possible solutions with respect to healthcare ICPS systems based on literature.

Apart from above barriers and proposed solutions; another research study [18] was recently conducted to explore the barriers and facilitators for the use of digital health technology for management of chronic obstructive pulmonary disease. In this study, participants engaged in a discussion regarding the potential obstacle of data quality in the utilization of digital health technology (DHT). Their perception was that consumer devices often fail to meet the expected clinical standards, such as lacking validation and calibration. Consequently, there may be doubts regarding the accuracy of the generated data, which could give rise to patient safety concerns if inaccurate readings cause undue health anxieties. Following were some of the key findings of this study.

- If patients are expected to collect objective data at home, it is imperative that the data is usable; otherwise, it would be wastage of resources and, more worryingly, could pose serious safety concerns.
- The participants expressed doubts about the diligence of their patients in generating complete datasets and deliberated on how this could impact the reliability of the data captured by DHT. They also discussed the necessity of a robust evidence base before adopting DHT in clinical practice. They believed that the absence of evidence not only affected their ability to prescribe these technologies safely but also influenced their willingness to promote or recommend DHT as a treatment option.
- The lack of clinical guidelines outlining the use of DHT in COPD posed a significant barrier to adoption.
- Healthcare professionals mainly emphasized the need for guidelines to define the recommended actions patients should take based on the data observed from their

Table 1 Types of barriers and possible solutions (from [17], licensed under CC-BY 4.0)

S. no	Type of barrier	Description	Possible solutions
1	Infrastructure and technical	These barriers relate to issues with limited networks, lack of existing technology, lack of devices, connectivity speed, healthcare capacity of technology integration, interconnectedness, absence of standardized/harmonized systems at different facilities, limited access to electricity, and requirement of a functional database system or large disk space	(A) Ensuring availability (especially in rural areas) and affordability, guaranteeing high-speed fiber connectivity (B) Involvement of healthcare professionals in developing and implementing any health technology tool
2	Personal and psychological	They include complex thematic components including the healthcare professionals' resistance to change, difficulty understanding the technology, perception of less human interaction, technophobia, ages, education levels, professional experience, low literacy, poor writing skills, linguistic features, adherence behavior, and fear of using particular health technology. Unwillingness, low expectations and skepticism from healthcare providers are also factors	(A) Using and adopting training programs suited to healthcare professionals' needs (B) High-quality, real-time technical support and coaching to professionals (C) User-friendly design, intuitive system navigation, and easy-to-use interfaces are critical to improving overall product performance
3	Time and workload-related	Concerns about increased workload and altered workflow, along with requiring additional purchase time and increased set-up, implementation, training, access, adaptation, and establishment stages	(A) Useful written guidelines, instructions, and handouts (B) Incentives from government agencies and multisectoral organizations were shown to significantly improve digital health technologies' effectiveness and chances of success in large-scale healthcare systems

(continued)

Table 1 (continued)

S. no	Type of barrier	Description	Possible solutions
4	Training and educational	Deficit or inadequate training impact the success and effectiveness of digital technologies Without training, healthcare providers tend to feel low self-efficacy when utilizing any digital health technologies, resulting in negative attitudes toward these technologies	(A) Training could be provided through certain digital health technologies itself as well as mobile phones and computers
5	Legal and ethical related factors	Legal- and ethical-related barriers were shown to be a relevant factor for healthcare providers, as privacy and security concerns, national legislation, jurisdiction, and the existence of unclear legal liability regarding response protocols would directly affect healthcare professionals	(A) Development of safer storage systems (B) Establishment of requirements on safety and security in cooperation with healthcare professionals and patients (C) The creation of an international legal framework and legislative norm, which would clarify security regulation policies that could help ensure patients' privacy and confidentiality, as well as define healthcare professionals' liabilities

DHT, as the absence of such guidelines could confuse patients regarding their treatment.

- The participants addressed the challenges encountered by their clinical setting if the data obtained from DHT becomes part of the routine care.
- They expressed concerns that the necessary level of resources might not be available to oversee the management or utilization of the data generated by DHT, while others worried about ethical concerns arising from the inability to appropriately act upon the data due to limited resources [18].

One more recent research was conducted about implementation of telehealth for remote surveillance of patient health and following were the key findings.

- The involved nurses considered the experience with telehealth positive and raised issues about lack of resources, patient selection criteria, technical support, education and organizational support.
- The nurses highlighted that these issues can become barriers in the successful implementation of tele-health services.
- They also suggested an increase in the team size, expanded patient selection criteria and widespread training in order to enhance and ensure the successful implementation of tele-health [19].

8 Conclusion and Open Problems

The integration of intelligent cyber physical systems in healthcare domain presents a transformative paradigm shift. This has profound implications for the healthcare professionals and workforce. As the healthcare ICPS continues to evolve and revolutionize the healthcare delivery, it is quite imperative to prioritize the workforce development initiatives that can equip the healthcare workforce with the requisite knowledge, skills and competencies required in order to leverage the benefits of these technologies in effective manner.

This chapter presents several challenges and opportunities associated with this paradigm shift and also provide key recommendations for the workforce development in context of healthcare ICPS. The recommendations include:

- Comprehensive training programmes by developing effective curricula inclusive of technologies like Artificial intelligence and machine learning
- Training on ICPS integration, development and implementation and interdisciplinary industry-academia collaborations,
- Hands-on simulation training, apprenticeship programmes, diversity and inclusiveness, research fundings.
- Clinical mentorship programmes and quality assurance evaluation can further strengthen the healthcare workforce.

It is important to realise the barriers and facilitators while implementing digital technological solutions and take stakeholders inputs while designing such solutions so as to meet the ultimate objectives with better efficiency. By implementing these recommendations, healthcare organizations may empower their workforce and help them navigate through the complexities of ICPS integration, improve patient care outcomes and promote innovation. Investing in the workforce is essential to realize the full potential of healthcare ICPS and ensure the readiness of workforce to meet the evolving needs of patients and society at large. The paradigm shift is here to stay and evolve further, therefore the risk of job displacement and replacement is there, but there lies a world of opportunities which can lead to creation of new employment opportunities and strengthening the current workforce may help with the better and fruitful implementation and realization of ICPS healthcare.

References

1. Haque SA, Aziz SM, Rahman M. Review of Cyber-Physical System in Healthcare. International Journal of Distributed Sensor Networks. 2014; 10(4). https://doi.org/10.1155/2014/217415.
2. A. Gatouillat, Y. Badr, B. Massot and E. Sejdić, "Internet of Medical Things: A Review of Recent Contributions Dealing With Cyber-Physical Systems in Medicine," in IEEE Internet of Things Journal, vol. 5, no. 5, pp. 3810–3822, Oct. 2018.
3. Chen, F., Tang, Y., Wang, C., Huang, J., Huang, C., Xie, D., ... & Zhao, C. (2021). Medical cyber–physical systems: A solution to smart health and the state of the art. IEEE Transactions on Computational Social Systems, 9(5), 1359–1386.
4. O. Rajabi Shishvan, D. -S. Zois and T. Soyata, "Machine Intelligence in Healthcare and Medical Cyber Physical Systems: A Survey," in IEEE Access, vol. 6, pp. 46419–46494, 2018.
5. Lee, I., Sokolsky, O., Chen, S., Hatcliff, J., Jee, E., Kim, B., & Venkatasubramanian, K. K. (2011). Challenges and research directions in medical cyber–physical systems. Proceedings of the IEEE, 100(1), 75–90.
6. Shaikh, T. A., Rasool, T., & Verma, P. (2023). Machine intelligence and medical cyber-physical system architectures for smart healthcare: Taxonomy, challenges, opportunities, and possible solutions. Artificial Intelligence in Medicine, 102692.
7. Kocabas, O., Soyata, T., & Aktas, M. K. (2016). Emerging security mechanisms for medical cyber physical systems. IEEE/ACM transactions on computational biology and bioinformatics, 13(3), 401–416.
8. Al-Jaroodi, J., Mohamed, N., & Abukhousa, E. (2020). Health 4.0: on the way to realizing the healthcare of the future. Ieee Access, 8, 211189–211210.
9. Hossain, M. M., Kashem, M. A., Nayan, N. M., & Chowdhury, M. A. (2024). A Medical Cyber-physical system for predicting maternal health in developing countries using machine learning. Healthcare Analytics, 5, 100285.
10. Tartarisco, G., Cicceri, G., Bruschetta, R., Tonacci, A., Campisi, S., Vitabile, S., ... & Pioggia, G. (2024). An intelligent Medical Cyber–Physical System to support heart valve disease screening and diagnosis. Expert Systems with Applications, 238, 121772.
11. Dey, N., Ashour, A. S., Shi, F., Fong, S. J., & Tavares, J. M. R. (2018). Medical cyber-physical systems: A survey. Journal of medical systems, 42, 1–13.
12. Sony, M., Antony, J., & McDermott, O. (2022). The impact of medical cyber–physical systems on healthcare service delivery. The TQM Journal, 34(7), 73–93.
13. Zhang, Y., Qiu, M., Tsai, C. W., Hassan, M. M., & Alamri, A. (2015). Health-CPS: Healthcare cyber-physical system assisted by cloud and big data. IEEE Systems Journal, 11(1), 88–95.
14. Sultanovs, E., Skorobogatjko, A., & Romanovs, A. (2016, October). Centralized healthcare cyber-physical system's architecture development. In 2016 57th International scientific Conference on power and electrical Engineering of Riga Technical University (RTUCON) (pp. 1–6). IEEE.
15. Fertel, B. S., Podolsky, S. R., Mark, J., Muir, M. R., Ladd, M. E., & Smalley, C. M. (2019). Impact of an individual plan of care for frequent and high utilizers in a large healthcare system. The American Journal of Emergency Medicine, 37(11), 2039–2042.
16. Mohammed, M. A., Lakhan, A., Zebari, D. A., Abd Ghani, M. K., Marhoon, H. A., Abdulkareem, K. H., ... & Martinek, R. (2024). Securing healthcare data in industrial cyber-physical systems using combining deep learning and blockchain technology. Engineering Applications of Artificial Intelligence, 129, 107612.

17. Borges do Nascimento, I. J., Abdulazeem, H., Vasanthan, L. T., Martinez, E. Z., Zucoloto, M. L., Østengaard, L., ... & Novillo-Ortiz, D. (2023). Barriers and facilitators to utilizing digital health technologies by healthcare professionals. NPJ digital medicine, 6(1), 161.
18. Slevin, P., Kessie, T., Cullen, J., Butler, M. W., Donnelly, S. C., & Caulfield, B. (2020). Exploring the barriers and facilitators for the use of digital health technologies for the management of COPD: a qualitative study of clinician perceptions. QJM: An International Journal of Medicine, 113(3), 163–172.
19. Odeh, B., Kayyali, R., Nabhani-Gebara, S., & Philip, N. (2014). Implementing a telehealth service: nurses' perceptions and experiences. British Journal of Nursing, 23(21), 1133–1137.

SPRINGER NATURE

GPSR Compliance

The European Union's (EU) General Product Safety Regulation (GPSR) is a set of rules that requires consumer products to be safe and our obligations to ensure this.

If you have any concerns about our products, you can contact us on ProductSafety@springernature.com

In case Publisher is established outside the EU, the EU authorized representative is:

Springer Nature Customer Service Center GmbH
Europaplatz 3
69115 Heidelberg, Germany

The manufacturer's authorised representative in the EU is Springer Nature Customer Service Centre GmbH, Europaplatz 3, 69115 Heidelberg, Germany. If you have any concerns regarding our products, please contact ProductSafety@springernature.com

Printed and bound by CPI Group (UK) Ltd, Croydon, CR0 4YY
01/10/2026
02225858-0019